CADOGAN
guides

Dana Facaros & Michael Pauls

ITALY:
W9-CFI-360

TUSCANY

Cadogan Books plc
London House, Parkgate Road, London SW11 4NQ

Distributed in North America by
The Globe Pequot Press
6 Business Park Road, PO Box 833, Old Saybrook,
Connecticut 06475–0833

Copyright © Dana Facaros and Michael Pauls 1989, 1990,
    1992, 1994, 1996
Illustrations © Horatio Monteverde 1996

Updating: Alice Keown

Book and cover design by Animage
Cover illustration by Povl Webb
Maps © Cadogan Guides, drawn by Map Creation Ltd

Series Editors: Rachel Fielding and Vicki Ingle
Proofreading: Lorna Horsefield
Indexing: Dorothy Frame and Fiona Clarkson Webb
Production: Rupert Wheeler Book Production Services
DTP: Kicca Tommasi

A catalogue record for this book is available from the British Library
ISBN 1-86011-081-9

The author and publishers have made every effort to ensure the accuracy of the information in this book
at the time of going to press. However they cannot accept any responsibility for any loss, injury or
inconvenience resulting from the use of information contained in this guide.

Printed and bound in Great Britain by Redwood Books Ltd.

About the Authors

Dana Facaros and Michael Pauls have now written over 20 Cadogan Guides. For three years they and their two children lived in a tiny Umbrian hilltop village. Now they have moved to an equally remote French village in the Lot.

Acknowledgements

Our thanks and appreciation to everyone who has contributed to this and all earlier editions, especially Michael and Brian, Fred Rainer and the 49 residents of Rosciano. Finally, and especially, we would like to thank Alice, for her professionalism and sheer hard work in updating the practical information in the guide.

About the Updater

Alice Keown studied History of Art and Italian at Glasgow University and the university of Viterbo, specialising in 14th-century Italian art. She was introduced to Tuscany by childhood holidays to the Casetta in Cortona and her love for the region has grown ever since.

Updater's Acknowledgements

I would like to thank Lyndal Passerini and Massimiliano Rossi for their part in the research for the new edition.

Please help us to keep this guide up to date

We have done our best to ensure that the information in this guide is correct at the time of going to press. But places and facilities are constantly changing, and standards and prices in hotels and restaurants fluctuate. We would be delighted to receive any comments concerning existing entries or omissions, as well as suggestions for new features. All contributors will be acknowledged in the next edition, and will receive a copy of the Cadogan Guide of their choice.

Contents

Travel   1–16

Practical A–Z   17–42

Maps and Plans

A glass of wine before dinner on the garden terrace, the olives glinting in the last flash of the setting sun as the curling geometric vineyards lose their rigid order in the melting darkness, and only the black daggers of the cypresses on the hills stand out—where could you be but Tuscany? It needs no introduction, this famous twilit land, where Titans of art five hundred years ago copied, and then outdid nature, and where nature gets her gentle revenge by rivalling art.

Introduction

Travellers have been coming to this region ever since the Middle Ages, to learn, to see and to understand. Most have come with their Baedekers or Ruskins or Berensons in hand, and even today it is often hard to escape the weight of generations of Tuscan opinions or to avoid treading on those same old grapes of purple prose. After all, most of what we call

Western civilization and culture was either rediscovered or invented here; at times it seems as if the artists of the early 1400s descended from outer space with their secret messages for the imagination. Anyway, to the mass of opinion we've added ours, for better or worse, but mostly in the hope of provoking some of your own.

But at the end of the day—or, as we are, at the twilight of the 20th century, when times seem to be changing faster than we can or care to— the enduring charm of Tuscany is in that dreamy glass of wine, in those hills that look exactly as they did when Piero painted them, in the bartender who's a dead ringer for Lorenzo de' Medici, in those bewitching Etruscan smiles that seem to have been smiled only yesterday. Things have stayed the same way for centuries not by any accident, or economic reason, or by divine decree of some Tuscan National Trust, but because that's the way people like them. Tuscans make as few concessions to the 20th century as possible, and their Brigadoon may not be for everyone. They're not catching up with the world; the world's catching up with them.

The Best of Tuscany

Antiquities

Etruscan sites and museums in Chiusi, Volterra, Cortona, Florence and Fiesole; **prehistoric menhirs** of Pontrémoli; Tempietto del Clitunno.

Beaches

Island of **Capraia**, several on **Elba**.

Best-kept Secrets

Italy's **Sword in the Stone**, San Galgano; Niki de Saint-Phalle's **Giardino dei Tarocchi**, Capalbio; the exquisite tiny city of **Massa Marittima**; ceramic chapels of the monastery of **San Vivaldo**; 18th-century spa of **Bagni di Lucca**.

Castles

Castiglion Fiorentino, Prato, Fosdinovo.

Ceramic Town

Montelupo.

Festivals

Renaissance theatre and barrel-rolling in **Montepulciano**; **Siena**'s Palio; carnival in **Viareggio**.

Hotels

Villa Scacciapensieri, **Siena**; Torre di Bellosguardo, **Florence**; Villa le Barone, **Greve**; Locanda dell'Amorosa, **Sinalunga**; Principessa Elisa, **Lucca**; Excelsior, **Viareggio**; Castello dei Gargonza, **Monte San Savino**; Relais Vignale, **Radda**.

Landscapes

Classic Tuscan in **Chianti**, and almost as immaculately elegant in the **Casentino** and **Pratomagno**; the hills **south of Siena**.

Coastal Scenery

The **Maremma**, **Elba**, **Monte Argentario**. Also the marbly **Apuan Alps**.

Medieval Art and Architecture

Pisa, Siena, Florence, Lucca.

Renaissance Art and Architecture

Besides **Florence**, of course, **Siena**, **San Gimignano**, **Arezzo**, **Pienza**, **Montepulciano**.

Restaurants

Enoteca Pinchiorri, **Florence**

Sergio, **Pisa**

Enoteca Ombrone, **Grosseto**

Solferino, **Lucca**

L'Oca Bianca, **Viareggio**

La Chiusa, **Montefollonico**

Gambero Rosso, **San Vincenzo**

Symposium, **Cartoceto**

How this Guide is Organized

The **Introduction** contains an unashamedly subjective selection of the highlights of the region, in **The Best of Tuscany**. Then, there is a comprehensive **Travel** section which includes themed Itineraries and details of Special-interest Holidays. **Practical A–Z** covers everything you are likely to need, on subjects ranging from Climate to Insurance and Health and Tourist Offices. A chapter on **History and Art** provides a detailed background to the development and culture of the region, one of the most artistically rich in the world. **Topics**, a series of short essays, gives more insights into the people and customs.

The book starts in the treasure-house of **Florence**, and then moves out to the delights of the surrounding countryside with its villages and hill towns, and other major art centres including **Pisa**, **Siena** and **Arezzo**.

The gazetteer is divided into sections which focus on a key city or town and the area around it, or on a journey between two featured places. Each section begins and ends with practical information: **Getting Around** and **Tourist Offices** at the beginning and **Where to Stay** and **Eating Out** at the end, with recommended hotels and restaurants in all price ranges. Where appropriate, details are given of Sports and Activities, Entertainment and Nightlife.

The book concludes with a glossary of **Architectural, Artistic and Historical Terms**. A chapter on **Language** supplies essential vocabulary for travelling around, booking hotels and, of course, eating out! To enrich your appreciation of the area, there are suggestions for **Further Reading**. Finally, the comprehensive **Index** lists every location of any significance featured in the guide, together with the more prominent artists and personalities.

Travel

By Air

Alitalia and British Airways offer direct flights from London to the main international airports at Pisa and Rome, as well as to Genoa (near the Lunigiana) and Bologna (just over the Apennines from the Mugello or Casentino). There are also direct flights from Manchester to Rome. The real challenge is finding a bargain, especially in the high season (mid-May–mid-September); start hunting around a few months in advance, or if you're a gambler, at the last minute. Most of the cheap flights from London are on long distance flights bound for Africa with stopovers in Rome.

From North America the major carriers are TWA and Air Canada, with flights to Rome or Milan, though British Airways does a New York–London–Pisa service called the Manhattan Express that departs at 9pm and has you in Florence by 4pm the next day. Fares from Canada are often much higher than they are from the States. Also, it's worthwhile checking into budget fares to London (especially if Virgin Atlantic stays around), Brussels, Paris, Frankfurt or Amsterdam; these routes are more competitive than the Italian ones, and you may save money by either flying or riding the rails to Italy from there.

There are advantages in paying an airline's normal fare, mainly that it does not impose any restrictions on when you go or return; most are valid for a year. To sweeten the deal, Alitalia in particular often has promotional perks like rental cars (Jetdrive), or discounts on domestic flights within Italy, on hotels, or on tours. Ask your travel agent. Children under the age of two usually travel for free and both British Airways and Alitalia offer cheaper tickets on some flights for students and the under 26s.

The same carriers listed above have a variety of discounts for those who book in advance or are able to decide their departure and return dates in advance. If you're travelling from Europe, you can save quite a tidy sum by paying for your ticket when you make your reservations (Eurobudget); an extra advantage is that the return date is left open. Travellers from anywhere can save money by swallowing a little alphabet soup—PEX, APEX and SUPERPEX, which like Eurobudget require reservations and payment at the same time on return-only flights. APEX fares, like PEX fares, have fixed arrival and departure dates, and the stay in Italy must include at least one Saturday night; from North America the restrictions are at least a week's stay but not more than 90 days, but need an advance booking. SUPERPEX, the cheapest normal fares available, have the same requirements as PEX. Disadvantages of PEXing are that there are penalty fees if you change your flight dates. At the time of writing, the lowest SUPERPEX return fare between London and Pisa in the off-season is £228 midweek, £243 weekend; the lowest mid-week SUPERPEX between New York and Rome in the off-season is $696 midweek, $756 weekend.

Other advantages of taking a regular flight over a charter are an increase in reliability in dates and in punctuality, and you're not out of a wad of cash if you miss your flight. Also, if you live in neither London nor New York, they will often offer big discounts to get you from your home airport to the international one. If you live in the US boondocks, you can dial some '800' numbers to check out prices on your own: Alitalia's number is 800 223 5730.

Both Pisa's Galileo airport and Rome's international airport, Leonardo da Vinci/ Fiumicino, are now linked to their respective central rail stations by train and bus.

To confirm your return flight home when in Italy go to any travel agent, for example CTS in Via del Ginori 25r, Florence, ✆ (055) 289721. Alternatively you can call BA direct on ✆ 167 289 289 and Alitalia, Lungoarno Acciaioli 10–12r, Florence, ✆ (055) 27889.

charter flights

These aren't as much of a bargain to Italy as they are to other Mediterranean destinations, though they're certainly worth looking into—check ads in the travel section of your newspaper (in Britain *The Sunday Times* and *Time Out* are especially good, in the US try the *Sunday New York Times*) and your travel agent. From London, TransEuropean (227 Shepherds Bush Rd, London W6 7AS, ✆ (0181) 748 1333) has regularly scheduled charters to Milan; from the US, Delta Airlines has regular charters from New York, Chicago and Los Angeles to Rome and Milan (✆ 800 241 4141). Other charter flights are usually booked by the big holiday companies. To find out about extra seats on these and on commercial flights, visit your local bucket shop (in the US, call Access (✆ 800 333 7280) or Air Hitch for similar services—check listings in the *Sunday New York Times*). Pickings are fairly easy in the off-season, and tight in the summer months, but not impossible. You take your chances, but you can save some of your hard-earned dough. The cheapest fare from London to Rome at the time of writing is £139, from New York $610.

The problems with charters are that they are delayed more often than not, you have to accept the given dates, and if you miss your flight (bus and train strikes in Italy do make this a distinct possibility) there's no refund. Most travel agencies, however, offer traveller's insurance that includes at least a partial refund of your charter fare if strikes and illness keep you from the airport.

flights for students

Besides saving 25 per cent on regular flights, students under 26 have the choice of flying on special discount charters. From the US, STA Travel is a good place to start looking: 10 Downing St, New York NY 10003, ✆ (212) 627 3111 and 166 Geary Street, Suite 702, San Francisco, CA 94108, ✆ (415) 391 8407. From Canada, contact Travel Cuts (Canadian Universities Travel Services), 187 College St, Toronto, Ontario M5T 1P7, ✆ (416) 979 2406, ✆ 979 8167. From London, check out STA Travel, 117 Euston Road, NW1 or 86 Old Brompton Rd, SW7; ring (0171) 937 9921, ✆ 937 9570 with enquiries on European destinations; CTS Travel, 44 Goodge Street, London W1, ✆ (0171) 937 3366, ✆ 937 9027 or Campus Travel, 52 Grosvenor Gardens, SW1, ✆ (0171) 730 3402, ✆ 730 6893.

By Train

From London's Charing Cross Station to Florence it's about 23 hours, and will set you back around £98 one-way second class, £191 first class. These trains require reservations and a couchette and on the whole are a fairly painless way of getting there. Discounts are available for families travelling together, for children—free under age four and 50 per cent discount between the ages of four and eight. Tickets for the passenger train of the Channel Tunnel range from £76 to £155 return; for information call Eurostar, ✆ (01233) 617 575, ✉ 617 998. Under 26-ers, students or not, can purchase the BIJ ticket offering discounts on tickets from London to any Italian city. They are valid for two months and you can make as many stopovers as you wish. BIJ tickets are available from Eurotrain (call Campus Travel above for details), and throughout Europe at student travel offices (CTS in Italy) in main railway stations. Rail travel to Italy becomes an even more attractive option if you intend to purchase an Inter-Rail pass (in Europe), or a EurRail pass (from North America). Inter-Rail cards (about £250) are sold by British Rail to people under 26 and offer discounts of over 30 per cent in Britain and 30 or 50 per cent on some Channel ferries (although it is still cheaper to catch a bus to Calais and start from there, single £18, return £25), and unlimited rail passage on the Continent, and are valid for a month. Inter-Rail Senior cards offer similar discounts to people over 60. EurRail passes must be purchased before leaving for Europe, and are valid for anywhere from 15 days to three months of unlimited first-class travel for the over 26s. The EurRail Youth Pass gives unlimited travel in 17 different countries for one or two months. These passes are a good deal if you plan to do lots and lots of rail travel and can't be bothered to buy tickets, etc. They seem rather less rosy if your travelling is limited to Italy, where domestic rail tickets are one of the few bargains available. Within Italy itself there are several discount tickets available (*see* below, 'Getting Around'), which you can inquire about at CIT (Italian state railways) offices before you leave home:

CIT Offices

UK

Marco Polo House, 3-5 Landsdowne Rd, Croydon, Surrey, ✆ (0181) 686 0677; or Wastels, Adj Platform 2, Victoria Station, SW1 V1JT, ✆ (0171) 834 7066, and any branch of Thomas Cook Ltd.

USA

342 Madison Ave, Suite 207, New York, NY 10173,
✆ (212) 697 2100, ✉ 697 1394.

There's also an 800 number you can call from anywhere: (800) 223 7987.

Canada

1450 City Counsellors, Suite 750, Montreal, Quebec H3A 2E6,
✆ (514) 845 9101, ✉ 854 9137.

By Coach

This is the cheapest way (but just barely, compared with the trains) to get to Italy from London and not too much torture if you get off at Milan, a little worse if you go on to Florence. There are, again, discounts for students, senior citizens and children. Contact **National Express**, Victoria Coach Station, London SW1, ✆ (0990) 808080, for times and bookings.

Driving to Italy from the UK is a rather lengthy and expensive proposition, and if you're only staying for a short period figure your costs against Alitalia's or other airlines' fly-drive schemes. No matter how you cross the Channel, it is a good two-day drive—about 1600km from Calais to Rome. Le Shuttle does a standard return for £260 but it is possible to find a cheaper deal. Ask at your travel agent or the Customer Services at P.O. Box 300, Dept. 302, Cheriton Park, Folkstone, CT19 4QD, ✆ (0990) 353 535. Ferry information is available at any travel agent or direct from the ferry companies. You can cut many of the costly motorway tolls by going from Dover to Calais, through France, to Basle, Switzerland, and then through the Gotthard Tunnel over the Alps; in the summer you can save the steep tunnel tolls by taking one of the passes. You can avoid some of the driving by putting your car on the train (although again balance the sizeable expense against the price of hiring a car for the period of your stay): Express Sleeper Cars run to Milan from Paris or Boulogne, and to Bologna from Boulogne. Services are drastically cut outside the summer months, however. For more information, contact the CIT offices listed above.

To bring your car into Italy, you need your car registration (log book), valid driving licence and valid insurance (a Green Card is not necessary, but you'll need one if you go through Switzerland). Make sure everything is in excellent working order or your slightly bald tyre may enrich the coffers of the Swiss or Italian police—it's not uncommon to be stopped for no reason and have your car searched until the police find something to stick a fine on. Also beware that spare parts for some non-Italian cars are difficult to come by, almost impossible for pre-1988 Japanese models. If you're coming to live in Italy, remember that cars with foreign plates are obliged to leave the country every six months for a hazily defined period of time.

At the time of writing the motorway tunnel tolls are:

Mont Blanc Tunnel, from Chamonix (France) to Courmayeur: small car or motorcycle L29,000 single, L37,000 return. Medium-sized car (axle distance 2.31–2.63m) L44,000 single, L55,000 return. Large cars (axle distance 2.64–3.30m) L58,000 single or L73,000 return and cars with caravans, L145,000 single and L233,000 return.

Fréjus Tunnel, from Modane (France) to Bardonécchia: prices range from L29,000 to L56,000

Gran San Bernardo, from Bourg St Pierre (Switzerland) to Aosta: small and medium cars or motorcycle L28,000 single, L40,000 return. Large car or car with caravan L59,000 single, L95,000 return.

Passports and Customs Formalities

To get into Italy you need a valid passport or a British Visitor's Card. EC citizens do not need visas to get into Italy. USA, Canada and Australia nationals do not need visas for stays up to three months. (However, if you're not an EC national and mean to reach Italy through France, see if you need to pick up a French transit visa.) If you mean to stay longer than three months in Italy you will have to get a *permesso di soggiorno*. For this you will need to state your reason for staying, be able to prove a source of income and have medical insurance. After a couple of exasperating days at some provincial Questura office filling out forms, you should walk out with your permit.

According to Italian law, you must register with the police within eight days of your arrival. If you check into a hotel this is done automatically. If you come to grief in the mesh of rules and forms, you can at least get someone to explain it to you in English by calling the Rome police office for visitors, © (06) 4686, ext. 2987.

EC nationals over the age of 17 can now import a limitless amount of goods for their personal use. Non-EC nationals have to pass through the Italian customs which are usually benign. Nevertheless how the frontier police manage to recruit such ugly, mean-looking characters to hold the submachine guns and drug-sniffing dogs from such a good-looking population is a mystery, but they'll let you be if you don't look suspicious and haven't brought along more than 150 cigarettes or 75 cigars, or not more than a litre of hard drink or three bottles of wine, a couple of cameras, a movie camera, 10 rolls of film for each, a tape-recorder, radio, record-player, one canoe less than 5.5m, sports equipment for personal use, and one TV (though you'll have to pay for a licence for it at Customs). Pets must be accompanied by a bilingual Certificate of Health from your local veterinary inspector. You can take the same items listed above home with you without hassle— except of course your British pet. US citizens may return with $400 worth of merchandise—keep your receipts.

There are no limits to how much money you bring into Italy: legally you may not export more than L400,000 in Italian banknotes, though they rarely check.

Courses for Foreigners and Specialist Holidays

The Italian Institute, 39 Belgrave Square, London SW1X 8NX, © (0171) 235 1461 or 686 Park Avenue, New York, NY 10021, © (212) 397 9300, is the main source of information on courses for foreigners in Italy; visit between 10 and 1 or send an SAE. Graduate students should also contact their nearest Italian consulate to find out about scholarships—apparently many go unused each year because no one knows about them.

One obvious course to take, especially in this linguistically pure land of Dante, is **Italian language and culture**: there are special summer classes offered by the Scuola Lingua e Cultura per Stranieri of the University of Siena. Similar courses are held in Cortona, Viareggio (run by the University of Pisa), and, not surprisingly, Florence—sometimes there seem to be more American students than Florentines in the city. The following have courses all year round: the British Institute in Florence, Via Tornabuoni 2, © 284031, organizes language and cultural courses; the Centro Fiorenza, Via di Santo Spirito 14, © 2398274, ● 287148, offers language, history, literature and art at both basic and advanced levels; the Scuola Lorenzo de' Medici, Via dell'Alloro, ● 289514, has classes in language and art; the Centro Linguistico Italiano Dante Alighieri, Via de' Bardi 12, © 2342984, ● 2342766, specializes in language courses.

Music courses complement the regions' numerous music festivals: in the summer Florence's Villa Schifanoia holds master classes for instrumentalists and singers; Certaldo's medieval music society, Ars Nova, sponsors a seminar in July. Siena's Accademia Musicale Chigiana, Via di Città, offers master classes for instrumentalists and conductors; in July and August Barga holds an international opera workshop.

Art lovers can take a course on medieval art in the Palazzo Ancaiani. Florence's Università Internazionale dell'Arte, in the Villa Tornabuoni, Via Incontri 3, offers courses October–April in history of art, restoration and design, while the Istituto per l'Arte e il Restauro, in Palazzo Spinelli, Borgo Santa Croce 10, holds workshops in art restoration.

Specialist Tour Operators in the UK

Abercrombie and Kent (tailor-made travel for individuals), Sloane Sq. House, Holbein Place, London, SW1W 8NS, ✆ (0171) 730 9600, ✆ 730 9376

Art History Abroad (group tours to the major art centres with knowledgable guides), Priory Field House, 20 Canon St, Taunton, Somerset, TA1 1SW, ✆ (01823) 323 363, ✆ 271 072.

Alternative Travel Group (walking holidays and wine tours in Tuscany), 69–71 Banbury Rd, Oxford OX2 6PE, ✆ (01865) 310 399, ✆ 310 299.

The British Institute (courses based in Florence, on Florentine art and history), Palazzo Lanfredini, Lungarno Giucciardini 9, Firenze, ✆ (055) 284 033, ✆ 289 557.

Citalia (tailor-made tours for individuals and groups; regular cookery courses in Tuscany), Marco Polo House, 3–5 Lansdowne Rd, Croydon, Surrey, ✆ (0181) 686 5533.

Inter-Church (Florence and Siena), Saga Building, Middelburg Square, Folkestone, Kent CT20 1AZ, ✆ (0800) 300 444.

Italiatour (city breaks), 205 Holland Park Ave, London W11 4 XV, ✆ (0171) 371 1114.

Kirker Europe, (city-based excursions), 3 New Concordia Wharf, Mill St., London, SE1 2BB, ✆ (0171) 231 3333, ✆ 231 4771..

Magnum (senior citizens in Florence), 7 Westleigh Park, Blaby, Leicester, ✆ (01162) 777 123.

Nadfas (National Association of Decorative and Fine Arts Societies; art tours of Florence and Tuscany), Hermes House, 80–89 Beckenham Rd, Beckenham, Kent, ✆ (0181) 658 2308, for members only.

Plantagenet Tours, 85 The Grove, Moordown, Bournemouth BH9 2TY, ✆ (01202) 521 895. Medici tours to Florence and Tuscany.

Prospect Art Tours (art and music tours in Florence; specialist holidays devoted to figures such as Dante and Piero della Francesca), 454–458 Chiswick High Rd, London W4 5TT, ✆ (0181) 995 2151.

Ramblers (walking and sightseeing tours in Siena), Box 43, Welwyn Garden City, Herts AL8 6PQ, ✆ (01707) 331 133.

Serenissima Travel (exclusive art and architecture tours), 21 Dorset Square, London NW1 6QG, ✆ (0171) 723 5066/730 9841.

SJA (art in Florence, Pisa, and Siena), 48 Cavendish Rd, London SW12 0DG, ✆ (0181) 673 4849, 🖹 673 8763.

Sovereign Small World (singles holidays), First Choice House, Peel Cross Road, Solford, Manchester, M5 2AN, ✆ (0161) 742 2266, 🖹 745 4542.

Specialtours (cultural tours of Tuscany), 81a Elizabeth St, London SW1W 9PG, ✆ (0171) 730 2297.

Swan Hellenic (art and architecture tours), 77 New Oxford Street, London WC1A 1PP, ✆ (0171) 800 2200.

Voyages Jules Verne (everything from painting holidays to National Trust Discovery Holidays such as 'Villas and Gardens of Northern Italy'), 21 Dorset Square, London NW1 6QG, ✆ (0171) 723 5066/730 9841.

Waymark (walking tours of San Gimignano and southern Tuscany), 44 Windsor Road, Slough, ✆ (01753) 516 477.

Specialist Tour Operators in the US

Archaeological Tours, Inc. (occasional tours of Etruscan sites in Tuscany), 271 Madison Ave, Suite 904, NY 10016, ✆ (212) 986 3054.

The Bombard Society (organizes balloon flights that take in Florence, Siena, San Gimignano and Monte Oliveto Maggiore), 6727 Curran St, McLean, VA, 22101, ✆ (703) 448 9407.

NRCSA (arranges language courses in Florence and Siena), 823 North 2nd St, Milwaukee, WI, 53203, ✆ (414) 278 0631 🖹 271 8884 and internet http://ww.worldwide.edu.

University Vacations (offers a cultural programme for adult Americans in Cambridge and Florence), 10461 NW 26th St, Miami, FL, 33172, ✆ (305) 591 1736, 🖹 591 9102.

Getting Around

The republic has an excellent network of airports, railways, highways and byways, and you'll find getting around fairly easy—unless one union or another takes it into its head to go on strike (to be fair, this rarely happens during the main holiday season). There's plenty of talk about passing a law to regulate strikes, but don't count on it happening soon. Instead learn how to recognize the word in Italian: *sciopero* (SHO-PER-O) and be prepared to do as the Romans do when you hear it—quiver with resignation. There's always a day or two's notice in advance, and usually strikes last only 12 or 24 hours—but long enough to throw a spanner in the works if you have to catch a plane. Keep your ears open.

Italy's national railway, the FS (*Ferrovie dello Stato*) is well run, inexpensive (though prices have recently risen, it is still cheap by British standards) and often a pleasure to ride. There are also several private rail lines around cities and in country districts. We have tried to list them all in this book. Some, you may find, won't accept Inter-Rail or EurRail passes. On the FS, some of the trains are sleek and high-tech, but much of the rolling stock hasn't been changed for fifty years. Possible FS unpleasantnesses you may encounter, besides a strike, are delays, crowding (especially at weekends and in the summer), and crime on overnight trains, where someone rifles your bags while you sleep. The crowding, at least, becomes much less of a problem if you reserve a seat in advance (*fare una prenotazione*). The fee is small and on the Intercity trains it is free and it can save you hours standing in some train corridor. On the upper echelon trains, reservations are mandatory. Do check when you purchase your ticket in advance that the date is correct; unlike in some countries, tickets are only valid the day they're purchased unless you specify otherwise. A number on your reservation slip will indicate in which car your seat is—find it before you board rather than after. The same goes for sleepers and couchettes on overnight trains, which must also be reserved in advance.

Tickets may be purchased not only in the stations, but at many travel agents in the city centres. The system is computerized and runs smoothly, at least until you try to get a reimbursement for an unused ticket (usually not worth the trouble). Be sure you ask which platform (*binario*) your train arrives at; the big permanent boards posted in the stations are not always correct. If you get on a train without a ticket you can buy one from the conductor, with an added 20 per cent penalty. You can also pay a conductor to move up to first class or get a couchette, if there are places available.

There is a fairly straightforward hierarchy of trains. At the bottom of the pyramid is the humble *Locale* (euphemistically known sometimes as an *Accelerato*), which often stops even where there's no station in sight; it can be excruciatingly slow. When you're checking the timetables, beware of what may look like the first train to your destination—if it's a *Locale*, it will be the last to arrive. A *Diretto* stops far less, an *Espresso* just at the main towns. *Intercity* trains whoosh between the major cities and rarely deign to stop and the *Eurocity* trains link Italian cities with major European ones. Both of these services require a supplement—some 30 per cent more than a regular fare and on some there are only first-class coaches. Reservations are free but must be made at least five hours before the trip. Trains serving the most important routes have names such as the *Vesuvio* (Milan, Bologna, Florence, Rome, Naples), the *Adriatico* (Milan, Rimini, Pesaro, Ancona, Pescara, Foggia, Bari), the *Colosseo/Ambrosiano* (Milan, Bologna, Florence, Rome) and the *Napoli Express* (Paris, Genoa, Pisa, Rome, Naples). The real lords of the rails are the *ETR 450 Pendolino* trains, kilometre-eaters that will speed you to your destination as fast as trains can go. For these there is a more costly supplement and on some only first-class luxury cars.

The FS offers several passes. One which you should ideally arrange at a CIT office before arriving in Italy, is the 'Travel-at-Will' ticket (*Biglietto Turistico Libera Circolazione*), available only to foreigners. This is a good deal only if you mean to do some very serious train riding on consecutive days; it does, however, allow you to ride the *Inter/Eurocity* without paying the supplement. Tickets are sold for 8- , 15- , 21- or 30-day periods, first or second class, with 50 per cent reduction for children under 12. At the time of writing an 8-day second-class ticket is around £102 and the 30-day ticket is £176. Another ticket, the *Kilometrico* gives you 3000 kilometres of travel, made on a maximum of 20 journeys and is valid for two months; one advantage is that it can be used by up to five people at the same time. However, supplements are payable on Intercity trains. Second-class tickets are currently £90, first-class £152. Other discounts, available only once you're in Italy, are 15 per cent on same-day return tickets and three-day returns (depending on the distance involved), and discounts for families of at least four travelling together.

Refreshments on routes of any great distance are provided by bar cars or trolleys; you can usually get sandwiches and coffee from vendors along the tracks at intermediary stops. Station bars often have a good variety of take-away travellers' fare; consider at least investing in a plastic bottle of mineral water, since there's no drinking water on the trains.

Besides trains and bars, Italy's stations offer other facilities. All have a *Deposito*, where you can leave your bags for hours or days for a small fee. The larger ones have porters (who charge L1000–1500 per piece) and some even have luggage trolleys; major stations have an *Albergo Diurno* ('Day Hotel', where you can take a shower, get a shave and haircut, etc.), information offices, currency exchanges open at weekends (not at the most advantageous rates, however), hotel-finding and reservation services, kiosks with foreign papers, restaurants, etc. You can also arrange to have a rental car awaiting you at your destination—Avis, Hertz, Eurotrans and Maggiore are the firms that provide this service.

Beyond that, some words need to be said about riding the rails on the most serendipitous national line in Europe. The FS may have its strikes and delays, its petty crime and bureaucratic inconveniences, but when you catch it on its better side it will treat you to a dose of the real Italy before you even reach your destination. If there's a choice, try for one of the older cars, depressingly grey outside but fitted with comfortably upholstered seats, Art Deco lamps, and old pictures of the towns and villages of the country. The washrooms are invariably clean and pleasant. Best of all, the FS is relatively reliable, and even if there has been some delay, you'll have an amenable station full of clocks to wait in; some of the station bars have astonishingly good food (some do not), but at any of them you may accept a well-brewed *cappuccino* and look blasé until the train comes in. Try to avoid travel on Friday evenings, when the major lines out of the big cities are packed. The FS is an honest crap shoot; you may have a train uncomfortably full of Italians (in which case stand by the doors, or impose on the salesmen in first class, where the conductor will be happy to change your ticket). Now and then, you and your beloved will have a beautiful 1920s compartment all to yourselves for the night.

By Coach and Bus

Intercity coach travel is often quicker than train travel, but also a bit more expensive. The Italians aren't dumb; you will find regular coach connections only where there is no train to offer competition. Coaches almost always depart from the vicinity of the train station, and tickets usually need to be purchased before you get on. In many regions they are the only means of public transport and are well used, with frequent schedules. If you can't get a ticket before the coach leaves, get on anyway and pretend you can't speak a word of Italian; the worst that can happen is that someone will make you pay for a ticket. Understand clearly that the base for all country bus lines will be the provincial capitals; we've done our best to explain the connections even for the most out-of-the-way routes.

City buses are the traveller's friend. Most cities label routes well; all charge flat fees for rides within the city limits and immediate suburbs, at the time of writing around L1200. Bus tickets must be purchased before you get on, either at a tobacconist's, a newspaper kiosk, in many bars, or from ticket machines near the main stops. Once you get on, you must 'obliterate' your ticket in the machines in the front or back of the bus; controllers stage random checks to make sure you've punched your ticket. Fines for cheaters are between L50,000 and L100,000, and the odds are about 12 to 1 against a check, so you may take your chances against how lucky you feel. If you're good-hearted, you'll buy a ticket and help some overburdened municipal transit line meet its annual deficit.

By Taxi

Taxis are about the same price as in London. The average meter starts at L6400, and adds L300 per kilometre. There's an extra charge for luggage and for trips to the airport; and rates go up after 10pm and on Sundays and holidays.

By Car

The advantages of driving in Tuscany generally outweigh the disadvantages. Before you bring your own car or hire one, consider the kind of holiday you're planning. If it's a tour of art cities, you'd be best off not driving at all: parking is impossible, traffic impossible, deciphering one-way streets, signals and signs impossible. In nearly every other case, however, a car gives you the freedom and possibility of making your way through Italy's lovely countryside.

Be prepared, however, to encounter the highest fuel costs in Europe (when everyone else lowered theirs with slumping international prices, Italy raised them) and the Italians themselves behind the wheel, many of whom, from 21-year-old madcaps to elderly nuns, drive like idiots, taking particular delight in overtaking at blind curves on mountainous roads. No matter how fast you're going on the *autostrade* (Italy's toll motorways, official speed limit **130km** per hour), someone will pass you going twice as fast. Americans in particular should be wary about driving in Italy. If you're accustomed to the generally civilized rules of motoring that North Americans adhere to, Italy will be a big surprise. Italians, and their northern visitors, do not seem to care if someone kills them or not. Especially in the cities, rules do not seem to exist, and if you expect them to stop riding your tail you'll have a long time to wait. Even the most cultured Italians become aggressive, murderous humanoids behind the wheel, and if you value your peace of mind you'll stick with public transport.

If you aren't intimidated, buy a good road map of Italy or a detailed one of the region you're travelling in (the Italian Touring Club produces excellent ones). Many petrol stations close for lunch in the afternoon, and few stay open late at night, though you may find a 'self-service' where you feed a machine nice smooth L10,000 notes. Autostrada tolls are high—to drive on the A1 from Milan to Rome will cost you around L60,000 at the time of writing. The rest stops and petrol stations along the motorways are open 24 hours. Other roads—*superstrade* on down through the Italian grading system—are free of charge. The Italians are very good about signposting, and roads are almost all excellently maintained—some highways seem to be built of sheer bravura, suspended on cliffs, crossing valleys on enormous piers—feats of engineering that will remind you, more than almost anything else, that this is the land of the ancient Romans. Beware that you may be fined on the spot for speeding, a burnt-out headlamp, etc.; if you're especially unlucky you may be slapped with a *super multa*, a superfine, of L150,000 or more. You may even be fined for not having a portable triangle danger signal (pick one up at the frontier or from an ACI office for L2500).

The **Automobile Club of Italy** (ACI) is a good friend to the foreign motorist. Besides having bushels of useful information and tips, they offer a free breakdown service, and can be reached from anywhere by dialling 116—also use this number if you have an accident, need an ambulance, or simply have to find the nearest service station. If you need major repairs, the ACI can make sure the prices charged are according to their guidelines.

Automobile Club of Italy (ACI)

Arezzo	Viale Luca Signorelli 24/a, ✆ (0575) 350060 /30350
Florence	Viale Amendola 36, ✆ (055) 24861, 🖷 2343257
Grosseto	Via Mazzini 105, ✆ (0564) 415777, 🖷 415449
Livorno	Via G. Verdi 32, ✆ (0586) 829090, 🖷 898387
Lucca	Via Catalani 59, ✆ (0583) 582627, 🖷 418058
Massa Carrara	Via Aurelia Ovest 193, ✆ (0585) 831941, 🖷 831944
Pisa	Via Cisanello 168, ✆ (050) 950111, 🖷 950399
Pistoia	Via Racciardetto 2, ✆ (0573) 976019
Siena	Viale Vittorio Veneto 47, ✆ (0577) 49001, 🖷 47003

Hiring a car is fairly simple if not particularly cheap. Italian car rental firms are called *Autonoleggi*. There are both large international firms through which you can reserve a car in advance, and local agencies, which often have lower prices. Air or train travellers should check out possible discount packages.

Most companies will require a deposit amounting to the estimated cost of the hire, and there is 19 per cent VAT added to the final cost. At the time of writing, a 5-seat Fiat Panda costs around L70,000 a day. Petrol is 50 per cent more expensive than in the UK. Rates become more advantageous if you take the car for a week with unlimited mileage. If you need a car for more than three weeks, leasing is a more economic alternative. The National Tourist Office has a list of firms in Italy that hire caravans (trailers) and campers.

By Motorbike or Bicycle

The means of transport of choice for many Italians, motorbikes, mopeds and Vespas can be a delightful way to see the country. You should only consider it, however, if you've ridden them before—Italy's hills and aggravating traffic make it no place to learn. Italians are keen cyclists as well, racing drivers up the steepest hills; if you're not training for the Tour de France, consider the region's mountains and hills well before planning a bicycling tour—especially in the hot summer months. Bikes can be transported by train in Italy, either with you or within a couple of days—apply at the baggage office (*ufficio bagagli*). Depending on how long you're staying, you may find it sensible (especially if you're coming from North America) to buy a second-hand bike in Italy when you arrive, either in a bike shop or through the classified ad papers put out in nearly every city and region. Alternatively, if you bring your own bike, do check the airlines to see what their policies are on transporting them.

Disabled Travellers

Facilities aren't great for the disabled anywhere in Italy. If you're in Britain it's worth obtaining a copy of *Holidays and Travel Abroad: a guide for disabled people* (£5) from the Royal Association for Disability and Rehabilitation (RADAR), 12 City Forum, 250 City Road, London, EC1V 8AF, ✆ (0171) 250 3222, 🖷 250 0212. It lists hotels with facilities for the disabled plus specialist tour operators, self-catering apartments and more. Americans should contact SATH (Society for the Advancement of Travel for the Handicapped), 347 5th Ave, Suite 610, NY 10016, ✆ and 🖷 (212) 447 7284.

The Italian Tourist Office will offer advice on hill towns that are particularly difficult to get around. Some will tire out the fittest tourist. Italian churches are a problem unto themselves. Long flights of steps in front were designed to impress on the would-be worshipper the feeling of going upwards to God—another raw deal for the disabled. The best thing you can do once you're in Italy is contact the local tourist offices; they're generally very helpful, and have even been known to find pushers on the spot.

Itineraries

One Week of Roman and Etruscan Sites

1 **Florence** (Archaeology Museum; Etruscan tombs at Sesto Fiorentino) and **Fiesole** (Etruscan Walls, Roman theatre, and museum).

2 **Volterra** (museum, Etruscan arch and Roman theatre).

3–4 The Etruscan cities of the coast: **Populonia, Vetulonia, Roselle** and **Ansedonia**, with stops at the Archaeology Museum in **Grosseto** and 'Frontone' (temple pediment) in **Orbetello**.

    5 **Chiusi** (fine museum and only painted Etruscan tombs in Tuscany).

    6 **Arezzo** (Roman amphitheatre and museum).

    7 **Cortona** (Etruscan walls, gate, tombs and museum).

Early Medieval Art and Architecture, in 10 Days

The best in Tuscany before 1200:

    1 **Florence** (Baptistry, San Miniato).

    2 **Pistoia** (Sant'Andrea, San Giovanni Fuoricivitas).

    3 The bizarre **Pieve di Castelvecchio**, near **Pescia,** and **Barga** cathedral.

    4 **Lucca** (Cathedral and San Michele).

    5 **Pisa** (Piazza of Miracles, Museums and San Piero a Grado).

    6 **Rosia, Sovicille** and the other churches just west of **Siena**.

    7 **Sant'Antimo,** outside **Montalcino** and **Abbadia San Salvatore** (town and abbey).

    8 The well-preserved medieval town of **Sovana**, near **Pitigliano**.

    9 **Gròpina**, near Loro Ciuffenna in the Valdarno, and **Poppi** (Castle).

    10 **Stia** (San Pietro and Castello di Romena).

8-Day Tour of High Medieval Art and Architecture

    1–2 **Florence:** Orsanmichele, Bargello, Cathedral, Palazzo Vecchio, Palazzo Davanzati.

    2 **Empoli** (Collegiata and museum) and **Certaldo** (Boccaccio's well-preserved home town).

    3 **San Gimignano:** Collegiata frescoes and the city itself—a genuine medieval monument.

    4 **Volterra:** civic buildings and art in Cathedral, San Francesco.

    5 **Massa Marittima** and **San Galgano**.

    6–8 **Siena:** Palazzo Pubblico, Cathedral—and nearly everything else!

11 Days Shooting a Renaissance Loop Outside Florence

Renaissance art somehow seems especially rarefied out in the provinces. Once you've paid your respects to Great Aunt Florence, visit

    1 **Impruneta** (Collegiata), **Certosa del Galluzzo, Lastra a Signa** (Alberti's church) and **Poggio a Caiano**, the archetypal Renaissance villa.

    2 **Prato** (Santa Maria delle Carceri, Filippo Lippi's fresco cycle in the Cathedral, Donatello and Michelozzo's pulpit).

    3 **Lucca,** for the sculpture of Matteo Civitali and Jacopo della Quercia.

    4 **San Gimignano,** which has much of the best painting outside Florence, by Gozzoli, Ghirlandaio, Sodoma, and more.

    5 **Siena,** for the Sienese side of the Renaissance (Cathedral, especially pavements, tombs, and Piccolomini Library, and the Pinacoteca).

    6–7 The exquisite monastic complex and frescoes at **Monte Oliveto Maggiore**, on the way to Pius II's planned city of **Pienza**; nearby **Montepulciano** for the best of classic Renaissance temples, Sangallo's San Biagio, as well as other churches and palaces.

8   **Cortona** (two Renaissance temples, Signorelli and Fra Angelico) and **Monte San Savino**.

9   **Arezzo** (Piero della Francesco's frescoes and S. Maria delle Grazie).

10   More Pieros in **Monterchi** and **Sansepolcro**.

11   **La Verna** (Andrea della Robbia) and over the Passo di Consuma to Florence.

Villas and Gardens, in a week or so

A 'Two-Centre Holiday' as all are located near Florence and Lucca. Do check the opening hours and do the necessary telephoning before setting out. In **Florence** itself there are beautiful walks around the Boboli Gardens, the villas and gardens of **Arcetri**, the **Villa Stibbert and Garden**, and the villas and gardens in and around **Fiesole**.

1   Medici villas and gardens of **La Petraia**, **Castello** and **Careggi**.

2   Into the Mugello: Gardens of **Pratolino**, and Medici Villas at **Cafaggiolo** and **Trebbio**.

3   More Medici villas and gardens: **Poggio a Caiano**, **Villa Artimino** and **Cerreto Guidi**.

4–5   Villas in Chianti: although only the **Castello di Brolio** and **Badia a Coltibuono** are open to the public, other striking estates include: Villa Tattali, Palazzo al Bosco, Villa Le Corti, Poggio Torselli, Vignamaggio, and several around Castellina.

6–7   From **Lucca, Castello Garzoni**, with fabulous gardens, near Collodi, and the three villas northeast of Lucca itself: **Villa Mansi**, **Villa Torrigiani**, and **Villa Pecci-Blunt**. Other possibilities: the Medici **Villa della Magia** in Quarrata, southeast of Pistoia, and **Fosdinovo** castle up in the Lunigiana.

Nature and Scenery

For Tuscany at its least civilized, starting with southern Tuscany's **Monte Amiata**, an isolated patch of lovely mountain forests. **Mediterranean Coastal Scenery**: maquis and pine forests, on **Monte Argentario**, with side trips to **Giglio** and the surrounding marshlands with wildlife reserves and exotic birds, like the **Monti dell'Uccellina**. Further north, there are ancient coastal forests around **Pietrasanta** and **San Rossore**. **Coastal Mountains**: the **Apuan Alps**, lush, streaked with marble, are located along the coast from Carrara down, while a bit further inland are the dense oak and chestnut forests of the **Garfagnana**. **Serious Apennines**: the entire ridge between Tuscany and Emilia-Romagna, around **Abetone**, **Firenzuola**, **Camaldoli** (with its ancient forest), **Pratomagno** (Monte Secchieta, and its panoramic roads), and the enchanting **Casentino**.

Two Weeks of Wine

For the best of Tuscan DOC wines, and the most ravishing scenery the region can offer:

1   **Florence** to **Carmignano**, **Cerreto Guidi** and **Vinci** (wines: Carmignano and Chianti).

2   **Montecatini Alta**, **Collodi** and **Montecarlo** (wines: Bianco della Valdinievole and Montecarlo).

3   South of the Arno to **San Miniato** and environs, and **Certaldo** (wines: Bianco Pisano di S. Torpè and Chianti).

4   **San Gimignano** and **Colle di Val d'Elsa** (wines: Vernaccia di San Gimignano and Chianti Colli Senesi).

5   **Barberino Val d'Elsa** and **San Casciano** to the Florence–Siena wine route, the Chiantigiana and **Greve in Chianti** (wines: Chianti, Chianti Colli Fiorentini and Chianti Classico).

6   **Panzano** and **Radda in Chianti** (wine: Chianti Classico).

7   **Gaiole in Chianti**, **Castello di Brolio** and **Siena**, with a stop at the Enoteca Nazionale (wines: Chianti Classico and Chianti Colli Senesi).

8   **Montalcino** (wine: Brunello).

9   **Montepulciano** (wine: Vino Nobile).

10   **Cortona** (wine: Bianco Vergine della Valdichiana).

11   **Sovana**, **Pitigliano**, **Saturnia** (wines: Morellino di Scansano and Bianco di Pitigliano).

12   Check in at the spa at **Chianciano Terme** for liver repairs!

One Week of Curiosities

The unexpected, unique side of Tuscany doesn't jump out at you; you'll have to look for it. In **Florence** you spend

1–3   seeing **Galileo's Forefinger** at the Museum of the History of Science; gruesomely realistic **wax anatomical models** at La Specola museum; a **151-kilo topaz** at the Museum of Mineralogy; a **16th-century Mexican Bishop's mitre** made out of feathers, in the Museo degli Argenti; **Islamic and Japanese armour** in the Villa Stibbert; or an ornate **Mozarabic Synagogue** or onion-domed **Russian Orthodox Church**. From there, head to Tuscany's northernmost town, **Pontrémoli**...

4   to see the mysterious **Neolithic statue-steles**, and then down to **Carrara** for the eerie, almost black whiteness of the **marble quarries**.

5   **Pisa—the Leaning Tower** is only one of a score of oddities in the Piazza of Miracles; also take a look at the **Turkish war pennants** in Santo Stefano.

6   **Volterra**, to see the *balze* and the unusual **Etruscan sculpture** in the Guarnacci Museum, on your way to the geothermal carnival of the **Metal Hills—geysers and sulphur lakes** around Larderello and Monterotondo.

7   Detour to Elba for **Napoleon's Death Mask**, or even better, inland to **San Galgano**, with its ruined Gothic abbey and genuine **Sword-in-the-stone**.

8   If it's Saturday or Sunday, try the **Giardino dei Tarocchi** (at Capalbio, east of Orbetello), a bizarre collection of colossal modern sculptures, covered in bright ceramics and mirrors, dedicated to the 22 major arcana of the Tarot deck.

Practical A–Z

Even though a declining birthrate and the legalization of abortion may hint otherwise, children are still the royalty of Italy, and are pampered, often obscenely spoiled, probably more fashionably dressed than you are, and never allowed to get dirty. Yet most of them somehow manage to be well-mannered little charmers. If you're bringing your own *bambini* to Italy, they'll receive a warm welcome everywhere. Many hotels offer advantageous rates for children and have play areas, and most of the larger cities have permanent **Luna Parks**, or fun fairs. Other activities young children enjoy (besides the endless quantities of pizza, spaghetti and ice cream) are the **Pinocchio Park** in Collodi, near Pisa and the **Nature Park** in Cavriglia in the Valdarno. If a **circus** visits town, you're in for a treat; it will either be a sparkling showcase of daredevil skill or a poignant, family-run, modern version of Fellini's *La Strada*.

Climate and When to Go

The climate in Tuscany is temperate along the coasts and in the valleys, and considerably cooler up in the mountains; the higher Apennines and Monte Amiata have enough snow to support skis until April. Summers are hot and humid; in August the Florentines, Sienese and Pisans hand their cities over to the tourist (even the good restaurants tend to close) and seek relief by the sea or in the mountains. Spring days, especially in the month of May, when it rains less, are pleasantly and not insufferably warm, and the fields and gardens are brimming with flowers. Autumn, too, is a classic time to visit, in October and November; before the winter rains begin, the air is clear and the colours of the countryside are brilliant and rare. The hills of Tuscany are always beautiful, but in October, they're extraordinary.

Winter can be an agreeable time to visit the indoor attractions of the cities and avoid crowds, particularly in Florence, where it seldom snows but may rain for several days at a time. The mountains, especially the Apuan Alps along the coast, also get a considerable amount of rain, with 80–120mm in a year.

Average Temperatures in °C (°F)

	January	April	July	October
Florence	6 (42)	13 (55)	25 (77)	16 (60)
Livorno	9 (47)	15 (59)	24 (75)	15 (59)
Siena	5 (40)	12 (54)	25 (77)	15 (59)

Average monthly rainfall in millimetres (inches)

	January	April	July	October
Florence	61 (3)	74 (3)	23 (1)	96 (4)
Livorno	71 (3)	62 (3)	7 (0)	110 (4)
Siena	70 (3)	61 (3)	21 (1)	112 (4)

In Italy, the three Ms (the Madonna, Mamma and *Mangiare*) are still a force to be reckoned with, and in a country where millions of otherwise sane people spend much of their waking hours worrying about their digestion, standards both at home and in the restaurants are understandably high. Everybody is a gourmet, or at least thinks they are, and food is not only something to eat, but a subject approaching the heights of philosophy—two Tuscan businessmen once overheard on a train heatedly discussed mushrooms for over four hours. Although ready-made pasta, tinned minestrone and frozen pizza in the *supermercato* tempt the virtue of the Italian cook, few give in (although many a working mother wishes she could at times).

Regional traditions are strong in Italy, not only in dialect but in the kitchen. Tuscany is no exception and firmly maintains its distinctive cuisine even when you wish it wouldn't. Although Tuscany does not rank among the great culinary regions of Italy, it offers good, honest, traditional dishes, often humble, rarely elaborate. The Medici may have put on some magnificent feeds, but the modern Tuscan is known by his fellow Italians as a *mangiafagioli*, or bean-eater. Some observers hold it as part of the austere Tuscan character, others as another sign of their famous alleged miserliness.

The truth is, that although beans and tripe often appear on the menu, most people when dining out want to try something different, from other regions, perhaps, or the recent concoctions of Italian *nouvelle cuisine*, or *cucina nuova*, or perhaps a recipe from the Middle Ages or Renaissance. Some of the country's finest restaurants are in Tuscany, including two generally ranked among the top five in all Italy; in practice, the diversity of dishes in Tuscany, from traditional to bizarre, is almost endless. First, though, a few general comments on eating in Italy.

Eating Out

In Italy the various types of restaurants—*ristorante, trattoria* or *osteria*—have been confused. A *trattoria* or *osteria* can be just as elaborate as a restaurant, though rarely is a *ristorante* as informal as a traditional *trattoria*. Unfortunately the old habit of posting menus and prices in the windows has fallen from fashion, so it's often difficult to judge variety or prices. Invariably the least expensive restaurant-type place is the increasingly rare *vino e cucina*, simple places serving simple cuisine for simple everyday prices. It is essential to remember that the fancier the fittings, the fancier the bill, though neither of these points has anything at all to do with the quality of the food. If you're uncertain, do as you would at home—look for lots of locals.

Prices

When you eat out, mentally add to the bill (*conto*) the bread and cover charge (*pane e coperto*, between L1500–3000) and a 10 per cent service charge. This is often included in the bill (*servizio compreso*); if not, it will say *servizio non compreso*, and you'll have to do your own arithmetic. Additional tipping is at your own discretion, but never do it in family-owned and -run places. Prices quoted for meals in this book are for an average complete meal, Italian-style with wine, for one person.

We have divided restaurants into the following price categories:

very expensive	over L85,000
expensive	L55,000—85,000
moderate	L35,000—55,000
inexpensive	below L35,000

People who haven't visited Italy for years and have fond memories of eating full meals for under a pound will be amazed at how much prices have risen, though in some respects eating out in Italy is still a bargain, especially when you figure out how much all that wine would have cost you at home. In many places you'll often find restaurants offering a *menu turistico*—full, set meals of usually meagre inspiration for L20–25,000. Good, imaginative chefs often offer a *menu degustazione*—a set-price gourmet meal that allows you to taste their daily specialities and seasonal dishes. Both of these are cheaper than if you had ordered the same food à la carte. When you leave a restaurant you will be given a receipt (*ricevuta fiscale*) which according to Italian law you must take with you out of the door and carry for at least 300 metres. If you aren't given one, it means the restaurant is probably fudging on its taxes and thus offering you lower prices. There is a slim chance the tax police may have their eye on you and the restaurant, and if you don't have a receipt they could slap you with a heavy fine.

Eating on the Hoof

There are several alternatives to sit-down meals. The 'hot table' (*tavola calda*) is a buffet selling hot and cold foods, where you can choose a simple prepared dish or a whole meal, depending on your appetite. The food in these can be truly impressive, though many offer only a few hot dishes, pizza and sandwiches. Little shops that sell pizza by the slice are common in city centres; some, called *gastronomie*, offer other take-out delicacies as well. At any delicatessen (*pizzicheria*), or grocer's (*alimentari*) or market (*mercato*) you can buy the materials for countryside or hotel-room picnics; some places in the smaller towns will make the sandwiches for you. For really elegant picnics, have a *tavola calda* pack up something nice for you. And if everywhere else is closed, there've always the railway station bars—these will at least have sandwiches and drinks, and perhaps some surprisingly good snacks you've never heard of before. Some of the station bars also prepare *cestini da viaggio*, full-course meals in a basket to help you through long train trips. Common snacks you'll encounter include *panini* of prosciutto, cheese and tomatoes, or other meats; *tramezzini*, little sandwiches on plain, square white bread that are always much better than they look; pizza, of course, or the traditional sandwich of Tuscany, a hard roll filled with warm *porchetta* (roast whole pig stuffed with fennel and garlic).

the meals

Breakfast (*prima colazione*) in Italy is no lingering affair, but an early morning wake-up shot to the brain: a *cappuccino*, a *caffè latte* (white coffee), or a *caffè lungo* (a generous portion of espresso), accompanied by a croissant-type roll, called a *cornetto* or *briosce*. This can be consumed in nearly any bar, and repeated during the morning as often as necessary, which is why breakfast in most Italian hotels is no big deal and seldom worth the price charged.

Lunch or *pranzo*, generally served around 1pm, is the most important meal of the day for the Italians, with a minimum of a first course (*primo*—any kind of pasta dish, broth or soup, or rice dish or pizza), a second course (*secondo*—a meat or fish dish, accompanied by a *contorno* or side dish—a vegetable, salad or potatoes usually), followed by fruit or dessert and coffee. You can, however, begin with a platter of *antipasti*—the appetizers Italians do so brilliantly, ranging from warm seafood delicacies, to raw ham (*prosciutto crudo*), salami in a hundred varieties, lovely vegetables, savoury toasts, olives, pâté, and many, many more. There are restaurants that specialize in antipasti, and they usually don't take it amiss if you decide to forget the pasta and meat and just nibble on these scrumptious hors d'oeuvres (though in the end it will probably cost as much as a full meal). Most Italians accompany their meal with wine and mineral water (*acqua minerale*, with or without bubbles, *con* or *senza gas*, which supposedly aids digestion), concluding their meals with a *digestivo* (liqueur).

Cena, the evening meal, is usually eaten at around 8pm. This is much the same as *pranzo* although lighter, without the pasta; a pizza and beer, eggs, or a fish dish. In restaurants, however, Italians often order all the courses, so if you have only a sandwich for lunch you have a full meal in the evening.

Some Regional Specialities

The Tuscans will tell you the basic simplicity of their kitchen is calculated to bring out the glories of their wine, which may well be true, as it tends to be the perfect complement to a glass of Chianti or Vino Nobile. Nearly all are born of thrift, like *bruschetta*, a Tuscan favourite that takes sliced stale bread, roasted over the fire, covered with olive oil and rubbed with garlic. *Acqua cotta*, popular in southern Tuscany, is *bruschetta* with an egg; another version adds mashed tomatoes. The other traditional Tuscan antipasto is *crostini*, thin slices of toast with a piquant pâté spread of chicken livers, anchovies, capers and lemons, or other variations.

For *primo*, the traditional Tuscan relies mostly on soups. Perhaps most traditional is *ribollita* ('reboiled'), a hearty mushy vegetable soup with beans, cabbage, carrots and chunks of boiled bread. Another is *pappa col pomodoro*, which is basically *ribollita* with fresh tomatoes. *Panzanella*, or Tuscan *gazpacho* (a cold soup of tomatoes, cucumbers, onions, basil, olive oil and bread) can be a godsend on a hot summer's day. The prince of Tuscan soups is Livorno's *cacciucco*, a heavenly fish soup that you have to go to Livorno to try. Other first courses you'll find are *fagioli al fiasco* (beans with oil and black pepper simmered in an earthenware pot) or *fagioli all' uccelletto* (beans with garlic and tomatoes); the most Tuscan of pasta dishes is *pappardelle alla lepre* (wide noodles with a sauce of stewed hare); others are the simple but delicious *spaghetti con briciolata* (with olive oil, breadcrumbs and parsley); *nastri alla Borracina* (ribbons of pasta served with a 'moss' of freshly chopped spinach and marjoram, basil, rosemary, mint and sage); and most splendid of all *turtui cu la cua* (*tortellini* with tails), filled with mascarpone, ricotta and spinach, with a butter and basil sauce.

Tuscany does not offer exceptional *secondi*. The region has its famous steak, *bistecca alla fiorentina* (cooked over coals, charred on the outside and pink in the middle, and seasoned with salt and pepper); otherwise, Tuscans are content with grilled chops—lamb, pork or veal. *Fritto misto* is an interesting alternative, where lamb chops, liver, sweet-breads, artichokes and courgettes (*zucchine*) are dipped in batter and deep fried. Otherwise look for *arista di maiale* (pork loin with rosemary and garlic), *francesina* (meat, onion and tomato stew in Vernaccia di San Gimignano wine), *anatra* (duck, often served with truffles), *piccione* (stuffed wild pigeon), *cinghiale* (boar), either roasted or in sausages or *stufato* (stewed). Tuscans are rather too fond of their *girarrosto*, a great spit of tiny birds and pork livers. It's fairly easy to find seafood as far inland as Florence—one traditional dish is *seppie in zimino*, or cuttlefish simmered with beets. Hardy souls in Florence can try *cibreo* (cockscombs with chicken livers, beans and egg yolks).

Tuscany's tastiest cheese is tangy *pecorino* made from ewe's milk; the best is made around Pienza. When it's aged it becomes quite sharp and is grated over pasta dishes. Typical desserts, to be washed down with a glass of Vinsanto, include Siena's *panforte* (a rich, spicy dense cake full of nuts and candied fruit), *cenci,* a carnival sweet (deep-fried strips of dough), *castagnaccio* (chestnut cake, with pine nuts, raisins and rosemary), Florentine *zuccotto* (a cake of chocolate, nuts and candied fruits), *biscottini di* Prato (almond biscuits softened in wine), or *crostate* (fruit tarts).

wine

Quaffing glass after glass of Chianti inspired Elizabeth Barrett Browning to write her best poetry, and the wines of Tuscany may bring out the best in you as well. The first really to celebrate Tuscan wines was a naturalist by the name of Francesco Redi in the 1600s, who, like many of us today, made a wine tour of the region, then composed a dithyrambic eulogy called 'Bacchus in Tuscany'. Modern Bacchuses in Tuscany will find quite a few treats, some famous and some less well known, and plenty of cellars and *enoteche* (wine bars) where you can do your own survey—there's a famous one in Siena with every wine produced in Tuscany and the rest of Italy as well.

Most Italian wines are named after the grape and the district they come from. If the label says DOC (*Denominazione di Origine Controllata*) it means that the wine comes from a specially defined area and was produced according to a certain traditional method; DOCG (the G stands for *Garantita*) means that a high quality is also guaranteed, a badge worn only by the noblest wines. *Classico* means that a wine comes from the oldest part of the zone of production; *Riserva*, or *Superiore*, means a wine has been aged longer. Most Tuscan farmers also make a cask of *Vinsanto*, a dessert wine that can be sweet or almost dry, and which according to tradition is holy only because priests are so fond of it.

Tuscany produces 19 DOC and DOCG wines, including some of Italy's noblest reds: the dry, ruby red **Brunello di Montalcino** and the garnet **Vino Nobile di Montepulciano**, deep red with the fragrance of violets. Chianti may be drunk young or as a *Riserva*, especially the higher octane Chianti Classico. There are seven other DOC Chianti wines (Montalbano, Rufina, Colli Fiorentini, Colli Senesi, Colli Aretini, Colline Pisa and simple Chianti). Sangiovese is the chief grape of all Chianti as well as all the classified red wines of Tuscany. Lesser known DOC reds include dry, bright red **Rosso delle Colline Lucchesi**, from the hills north of Lucca; hearty **Pomino Rosso**, from a small area east of Rufina in the Mugello; **Carmignano**, a consistently fine ruby red that can take considerable ageing, produced just west of Florence; and **Morellino di Scansano**, from the hills south of Grosseto, a dry red to be drunk young or old. The three other DOC reds from the coast are **Parrina Rosso**, from Parrina near Orbetello, **Montescudaio Rosso**, and **Elba Rosso**, a happy island wine, little of which makes it to the mainland. All three have good white versions as well.

Of the Tuscan whites, the most notable is **Vernaccia di San Gimignano** (also a *Riserva*), dry and golden in colour, the perfect complement to seafood; delicious, but more difficult to find are dry, straw-coloured **Montecarlo** from the hills east of Lucca and **Candia dei Colli Apuani**, a light wine from mountains of marble near Carrara. From the coast comes **Bolgheri**, white or rosé, both fairly dry. Cortona and its valley produce **Bianco Vergine Valdichiana**, a fresh and lively wine; from the hills around Montecatini comes the golden, dry **Bianco della Valdinievole**. **Bianco di Pitigliano**, of a yellow straw colour, is a celebrated accompaniment to lobster.

Embassies and Consulates

UK

Florence: Lungarno Corsini 2, ✆ (055) 284 133.

Ireland

Rome: Largo Nazareno 3, ✆ (06) 678 2541.

USA

Florence: Lungarno Amerigo Vespucci 38, ✆ (055) 239 8276.

Canada

Rome: Via Zara 30, ✆ (06) 445 891.

Festivals

Although festivals in Tuscany are often more show than spirit (though there are several exceptions to the rule), they can add a note of pageantry or culture to your holiday. Some are great costume affairs, with roots dating back to the Middle Ages, and there are quite a few music festivals, antique fairs, and most of all, festivals devoted to food and drink. The following is a calendar of the major events.

January

1   Feast of the Gift, the mayor's donation of gold, frankincense and myrrh at **Castiglione di Garfagnana**

February

Carnival is celebrated in private parties nearly everywhere, and in **Viareggio** there's an enormous public one, with huge satirical floats, music and parades. In **Bibbiena**, last day of Carnival is celebrated with a grand dance called the *Bello Ballo* and a huge bonfire, the *Bello Pomo*

March

19	**Greve in Chianti** pancake festival
	San Giuseppe, **Siena** (with rice fritters) and **Torrita di Siena**, with a donkey race and tournament

April

Good Friday	Way of the Cross candlelight procession, **Grássina**, near Florence
Easter	Easter morning, *Scoppio del Carro*, expulsion of the cart in **Florence**
	Exposition of Mary's girdle from Donatello's pulpit, **Prato**
10	Liberty Festival, **Lucca**, honouring the former Republic of Lucca with a special mass, costumes, etc
1st Sunday after Easter	National Kite Festival, **San Miniato**
2nd Sunday after Easter	Donkey Palio, in **Querceta** (Lucca)
April–June	Music festival, **Lucca**

May

All month	Iris Festivals, Florence, San Polo Robbiana (Chianti)
Third week	Historical parade and crossbow tournament, Massa Marittima
Ascension Day	Cricket Festival, with floats, and crickets sold in little cages, Florence
May and June	Maggio Musicale Fiorentino, in Florence

June

Early June	Procession on sawdust designs in the streets at **Camaiore** (Lucca); *Palio dei micci*, donkey race and historical re-enactments at **Querceta** (Lucca)
First Sunday	**Montecatini Terme**, garlic toast (*bruschetta*) festival
Mid-June–August	*Estate Fiesolana*—music, cinema, ballet and theatre, in **Fiesole**
16–17	*Festa di San Ranieri*—lights festival and historic regatta in **Pisa**
18	*Festa del Barbarossa*, celebrating the meeting of the pope and emperor, with ballet, archery, snails, beans and *pici* at **San Quirico d'Orcia**
3 weekends	*Calcio in Costume*, Renaissance football game, in **Florence**
24	St John the Baptist's Day, with fireworks, in **Florence**
25	*Giocco del Ponte*, a traditional bridge tug-of-war game with a cart in the middle, **Pisa**

| Last Sunday | **San Donato in Poggio** (Florence province), *La Bruscellata*, a week of dancing, old love songs around a flowering tree |

July

All month	**Cortona,** Umbria Jazz Festival
1	Versilian Historical Trophy, with a flag-throwing contest, **Querceta** (Lucca)
1–15	**Camaiore** (Lucca), lyric season
2	*Palio,* in **Siena**
2nd Sunday	16th-century archery contest in **Fivizzano** (Massa) between court and country archers
3rd Sunday	Feast of San Paolino, **Lucca**, torchlight parade and crossbow contest
25	Joust of the Bear, a tournament dating back to the 1300s, **Pistoia**
Last week	Elban Wine Festival, **Le Ghiaie**
July–August	**San Gimignano** concert and theatre festival

August

All month	Outdoor opera festival, **Torre del Lago Puccini**
August– September	Chamber music festival, **Città di Castello**
First weekend	Traditional thanksgiving festival in honour of San Sisto, **Pisa**
2nd Sunday	Regatta, **Porto Santo Stefano**; *Bruscello* stories, food and wine, in **Montepulciano** Crossbow tournament, **Massa Marittima**
15	Beefsteak Festival, **Cortona**
16	*Palio,* dating from 1147, in **Siena**
17	*Palio Marinaro*, neighbourhood boat races, in **Livorno**
15–30	International choir contest, **Arezzo**

September

First Sunday	**Arezzo**, Joust of the Saracen; **Cerreto Guidi**, *Palio dei Cerri* competition between neighbourhood groups and Renaissance processions; **Florence**, lantern festival
2nd Sunday	Eating and dancing in **Greve in Chianti**
13	Holy Procession in honour of the *Volto Santo* by torchlight in **Lucca**
3rd Sunday	**Impruneta** wine festival

October

| 3–4 | Wine festivals |

November

| 22 | Santa Cecilia, patroness of music, celebrated with concerts in **Siena** |

December

8	Fair of the Immaculate Conception, **Bagni di Lucca**
13	Santa Lucia, celebrated with a pottery fair in **Siena**
24	Evergreen bonfire at **Camporgiano** (Lucca)
25–26	Display of the holy girdle and St Stephen's feast, **Prato**

Insurance and Health

You can insure yourself for almost any possible mishap—cancelled flights, stolen or lost baggage, and health. While national health coverage in the UK and Canada takes care of their citizens while travelling, the US doesn't. Check your current policies to see if they cover you while abroad, and under what circumstances, and judge whether you need a special traveller's insurance policy. Travel agencies sell them, as well as insurance companies; they are not cheap.

Minor illnesses and problems that crop up in Italy can usually be handled free of charge in a public hospital clinic or *ambulatorio*. If you need minor aid, Italian pharmacists are highly trained and can probably diagnose your problem; look for a *Farmacia* (they all have a list in the window with details of which ones are open during the night and on holidays). Extreme cases should head for the *Pronto Soccorso* (First Aid services). The emergency number from anywhere in Italy is 113.

Few Italian doctors speak even rudimentary English, so if you can't find one, contact your embassy or consulate for a list of English-speaking doctors.

Lavatories

Frequent travellers have noted a steady improvement over the years in the cleanliness of Italy's public conveniences, although as ever you will only find them in places like train and bus stations and bars. Ask for the *bagno*, *toilette*, or *gabinetto*; in stations and the smarter bars and cafés, there are washroom attendants who expect a few hundred lire for keeping the place decent. You'll probably have to ask them for paper (*carta*). Don't confuse the Italian plurals: *Signori* (gents), *Signore* (ladies).

Maps

For a wide range of maps, try Stanford's, 12–14 Long Acre, London WC2 9LP, © (0171) 836 1321, ✆ 836 0189; in the US try The Complete Traveller, 199 Madison

Ave, New York, NY 10016, ✆ (212) 685 9007, ✉ 481 3253: the green Touring Club Italiano map of Tuscany is the most detailed.

It's a good idea to bring some Italian lire with you; unforeseen delays and unexpected public holidays may foul up your plans to change at a bank when you arrive. Traveller's cheques or Eurocheques remain the most secure way of financing your holiday in Italy; they are easy to change and an insurance against unpleasant surprises. Credit cards (American Express, Diner's Club, Mastercard, Access, Eurocard, Barclaycard, Visa) are accepted in most hotels, restaurants and shops (but rarely at any petrol stations). If you have a PIN number you can use the many cashpoint machines. Do not be surprised if you are asked to show an identification document when paying with a credit card.

There's been a lot of loose talk about knocking three noughts off the Italian lira, but it never seems to happen; as it is, everybody can be a 'millionaire'. It is also confusing to the visitor unaccustomed to dealing with rows of zeros, and more than once you'll think you're getting a great deal until you realize you've simply miscounted the zeros on the price tag. Some unscrupulous operators may try to take advantage of the confusion when you're changing money, so do be careful. Notes come in denominations of L100,000, L50,000, L10,000, L5,000, L2000 and L1000; coins are in L500, L200, L100, L50, all the way down to the now rare, ridiculous and practically worthless aluminium coinage of L20 and L10. Telephone tokens (*gettoni*) may be used as coins as well and are worth L200.

The easiest way to have money sent to you in Italy is for someone from home to get a bank to telex the amount to an Italian bank, and for you to go and pick it up. Technically, it shouldn't take more than a couple of days to arrive, but make sure the telex includes the number of your passport, ID card, or driver's licence, or the Italians may not give you your money. Save all the receipts of your currency exchanges. Money can also be sent through Thomas Cook travel agents, Western Union and American Express.

Banking hours

In Italy banks are usually open 8.30am–1.20pm, and for one hour in the afternoon (3–4 or 4–5pm). They are closed on Saturdays, Sundays and national holidays. Some banks are worth visiting for their space-capsule doors alone!

The Italians have cut down somewhat on their official national holidays, but note that every town has one or two local holidays of its own—usually the feast day of its patron saint. Official holidays, shown on transport timetables and museum opening hours etc., are treated the same as Sundays.

1 January   New Year's Day—*Capodanno.*

6 January   Epiphany, better known to Italians as the day of *La Befana*— a kindly witch who brings the *bambini* the toys Santa Claus or *Babbo Natale* somehow forgot.

Easter Monday	usually pretty dull.
25 April	Liberation Day—even duller.
1 May	Labour Day—lots of parades, speeches, picnics, music and drinking.
15 August	Assumption, or *Ferragosto*—the biggest of them all—woe to the innocent traveller on the road or train!
1 November	All Saints, or *Ognissanti*—liveliest at the cemeteries.
8 December	Immaculate Conception of the Virgin Mary—a dull one.
25 December	Christmas Day.
Boxing Day	*Santo Stefano.*

Opening Hours and Museums

Although it's beginning to change in the cities, most of Tuscany closes down at 1pm until 3 or 4pm to eat and properly digest the main meal of the day. Afternoon hours are 4–7, often 5–8 in the hot summer months. Many of the **museums** are now open all day from 9am to 7pm and tend to close on a Monday. **Food shops** shut on Thursday afternoons in the winter and Saturday afternoons in the summer. Other shops often shut on Monday mornings or all day Saturday and on a Sunday you'll be lucky to find anything open. Bars are often the only places open during the early afternoon and sometimes on a Sunday. (For **bank** opening hours *see* p.27.)

Churches have always been a prime target for art thieves and as a consequence are usually locked when there isn't a sacristan or caretaker to keep an eye on things. All churches, except for the really important cathedrals and basilicas, close in the afternoon for the same hours as the shops, and the little ones tend to stay closed. Always have a pocketful of L100, L200 and L500 coins to batten the light machines in churches, or what you came to see is bound to be hidden in ecclesiastical shadows. Some churches in Tuscany now have light machines that accept only L1000 notes, but the light-up time rarely lasts more than a minute. Don't do your visiting during services, and don't come to see paintings and statues in churches the week preceding Easter—you will probably find them covered with mourning shrouds.

Many of Italy's museums are magnificent, many are run with shameful neglect, and many have been closed for years for 'restoration' with slim prospects of reopening in the near future. With an estimated one work of art per inhabitant, Italy has a hard time financing the preservation of its national heritage; in the big cities you would do well to enquire at the tourist office to find out exactly what is open and what is 'temporarily' closed before setting out on a wild goose chase across town.

We have listed the hours of the important sights and museums. In general, Monday and Sunday afternoons are dead periods for the sightseer—you may want to make these your travelling days. Places with no hours listed usually open on request—but it is best to go before 1pm. We have also specified which attractions charge admission; unless labelled 'adm exp' you'll have to pay between L500 and L5000 to get in. Expensive ones are more—up to L12,000 for the Uffizi and other purveyors of big league culture. Citizens of EC countries under 18 and over 60 get in free.

Packing

You simply cannot overdress in Italy; whatever grand strides Italian designers have made on the international fashion merry-go-round, most of their clothes are purchased domestically, prices be damned. Now whether or not you want to try to keep up with the natives is your own affair and your own heavy suitcase—you may do well to compromise and just bring a couple of smart outfits for big nights out. It's not that the Italians are very formal; they simply like to dress up with a gorgeousness that adorns their cities just as much as those old Renaissance churches and palaces. The few places with dress codes are the major churches and basilicas (no shorts or sleeveless shirts), and the smarter restaurants.

After agonizing over fashion, remember to pack small and light: transatlantic airlines limit baggage by size (two pieces are free, up to 1.5m, in height and width; in second class you're allowed one of 1.5m and another up to 110cm). Within Europe limits are by weight: 20 kilos (44lb) in second class, 30 kilos (66lb) in first. You may well be penalized for anything bigger. If you're travelling mainly by train, you'll especially want to keep bags to a minimum: jamming big suitcases in overhead racks in a crowded compartment isn't much fun for anyone. Never take more than you can carry, but do bring the following: any prescription medicine you need, an extra pair of glasses or contact lenses, a pocket knife and corkscrew (for picnics), a torch (for dark frescoed churches and hotel corridors), a travel alarm (for those early trains) and a pocket Italian-English dictionary (for flirting and other emergencies; outside the main tourist centres you may well have trouble finding someone who speaks English). If you're a light sleeper, you may want to invest in ear plugs. Your electric appliances will work in Italy, just change your plug to the two-prong variety or buy a travel plug. Of course, what you bring depends on when and where you go (*see* 'Climate', p.18).

Photography

Film and developing are much more expensive than they are in the US or UK. You are not allowed to take pictures in most museums or in some churches. Most cities now offer one-hour processing if you need your pics in a hurry.

Police Business

Police: ✆ 113

There is a fair amount of petty crime in the cities—purse snatchings, pickpocketing, minor thievery of the white-collar kind (always check your change) and car break-ins and theft— but violent crime is rare. Nearly all mishaps can be avoided with adequate precautions. Scooter-borne purse-snatchers can be foiled if you stay on the inside of the pavement and keep a firm hold on your property; pickpockets most often strike in crowded buses and gatherings; don't carry too much cash or keep some of it in another place. Be extra careful in train stations, don't leave valuables in hotel rooms, and always park your car in garages, guarded car parks, or on well-lit streets, with temptations like radios, cassettes, etc., out of sight. Purchasing small quantities of reefer, hashish, cocaine and LSD is legal although what a small quantity might be exactly is unspecified, so if the police don't like you to begin with, it will probably be enough to get you into big trouble.

Once the scourge of Italy, political terrorism has declined drastically in recent years, mainly thanks to special squads of the *Carabinieri*, the black-uniformed national police, technically part of the Italian army. Local matters are usually in the hands of the *Polizia Urbana*; the nattily dressed *Vigili Urbani* concern themselves with directing traffic and handing out parking fines. You probably will not have anything to do with the *Guardia di Finanza*, the financial police, who spend their time chasing corrupt politicians and their friends. If you need to summon any of them, dial 113.

Post Offices

The postal service in Italy is both the least efficient and the most expensive in Europe, and disgracefully slow; if you're sending postcards back home you often arrive there before they do. If it's important that it arrive in less than a week send your letter *Espresso* (Swift Air Mail) or *Raccomandata* (registered delivery), for a L2000 supplement fee. Stamps (*francobolli*) may also be purchased at tobacconists (look for a big black T on the sign), but you're bound to get differing opinions on your exact postage. Mail to the UK goes at the same rate as domestic Italian mail, but it's still twice as much to send a letter from Italy to Britain as vice versa. Airmail letters to and from North America can quite often take up to two weeks. This can be a nightmare if you're making hotel reservations and are sending a deposit—telex or telephoning ahead is far more secure if time is short. Most hotels now have a fax machine.

Ask for mail to be sent to you in Italy either care of your hotel or addressed *Fermo Posta* (poste restante: general delivery) to a post office, or, if you're a card-holder, to an American Express Office. When you pick up your mail at the *Fermo Posta* window, bring your passport for identification. Make sure, in large cities, that your mail is sent to the proper post office; the **Posta Centrale** is often the easiest option.

The Italian postal code is most inscrutable in dealing with packages sent overseas. Packages have to be of a certain size, under a certain weight to be sent in certain ways, and must have a flap open for inspection or be sealed with string and lead. You're best off taking it to a stationer's shop (*cartoleria*) and paying L800 for them to wrap it—they usually know what the postal people are going to require.

Telegrams (sent from post offices) are expensive but the surest way to get your message out of Italy. You can save money by sending it as a night letter (22 words or less).

Purchasing a House

Of all the regions in Italy Tuscany has the most foreigners with homes, so many, in fact, that prices have shot into the stratosphere in the most popular areas (especially around Florence and Siena, and in the Chianti). The more obscure areas of Tuscany, on the other hand, still have a number of abandoned farmhouses just waiting for someone to renovate them. Rural real estate is one of Italy's great buys, and the recommended way to do it is to buy a run-down property and restore it to your own needs and taste. But beware the pitfalls.

One agent we know is amazed that all English clients invariably express two major concerns about a property: drainage and the presence of a bidet in the bathroom, as if it were a tool of the devil! What they should be asking are questions about water supply (a major problem in Tuscany), electricity and road access—often big problems for that isolated, romantic farmhouse that has caught your eye. Another thing to remember before purchasing a home or land is that you need permission from the local *comune* to make any changes or improvements, and it's no good buying anything unless you're pretty sure the *comune* will consent (for a sizeable fee, of course) to let you convert the old cellar or stable into a spare bedroom. A further point to remember is that though there are no annual rates (property tax) to pay, there is a 10 per cent IVA tax (VAT) to be paid on the purchase price for a house and 19 per cent on land, as well as hefty Capital Gains Tax on selling price and profit to be paid by the seller. Italians tend to get around this by selling at one price and writing down another on the contract. But remember if you sell you'll be in the same bind.

Once you've agreed to buy, you pay a deposit (usually 25–30 per cent) and sign a *compromesso*, a document that states that if you back out, you lose your deposit, and if the seller changes his mind, he forfeits double the deposit to you (be sure your *compromesso* includes this feature, called *caparra confermatoria*). Always transfer payment from home through a bank, taking care to get and save a certificate of the transaction so you can take the sum back out of Italy when you sell. After the *compromesso*, your affairs will be handled by a *notaio*, the public servant in charge of registering documents and taxes who works for both buyer and seller. If you want to make sure your interests are not over-looked, you can hire a *commercialista* (lawyer-accountant) who will handle your affairs with the *notaio*, including the final transfer deed (*rogito*), which completes the purchase at the local Land Registry. Upon signing, the balance of the purchase price generally becomes payable within a year.

The next stage for most buyers, restoration, can be a nightmare if you aren't careful. Make sure the crew you hire is experienced and that you're pleased with their work else-where—don't hesitate to ask as many other people in your area as possible for advice. Keep all receipts, and beware when builders and agents give you receipts for far less than their charges (or no receipts at all) to avoid taxes; you'll pay the difference in sales tax when you sell. Also expect to pay a lofty surcharge on electricity, water and telephone bills unless you become an Italian resident and your Italian house is your primary residence. One book that offers some clues on the ins and outs of taxes, inheritance law, residency, gardening etc., is *Living in Italy*, published by Robert Hale, London 1991.

Shopping

'Made in Italy' has long been a byword for style and quality, especially in fashion and leather, but also in home design, ceramics, kitchenware, jewellery, lace and linens, glassware and crystal, chocolates, hats, straw-work, art books, engravings, handmade stationery, gold and silverware, a hundred kinds of liqueurs, wine, aperitifs, coffee machines, gastronomic specialities, antique reproductions, as well as the antiques themselves. If you are looking for the latter and are spending a lot of money, be sure to demand a certificate of authenticity—reproductions can be very, very good. To get your antique or modern art purchases home, you will have to apply to the Export Department of the Italian Ministry of Education—a possible hassle. You will have to pay an export tax as well; your seller should know the details.

Florence, which increasingly resembles a glittering medieval shopping mall, has the best variety of goods in the region. There are major monthly antique fairs in Arezzo (first Sunday), Pistoia (second Sunday), Lucca (third Sunday), and Florence (last Sunday). Ceramics are an old tradition in Montelupo; porcelain in Sesto Fiorentino; glassware in Empoli. Volterra is famous for its alabaster and alabaster art; in Elba you can buy semi-precious stones and minerals, in the Mugello and Casentino wrought iron and copperware, straw goods in the lower Valdarno, and marble in Carrara, though

taking it home may pose a bit of a problem.
Wine and olive oil, bags of *porcini* mushrooms, jars of truffles and other 'gastronomic' specialities are available everywhere.

Italians don't like department stores, but there are a few chains—*COIN* stores often have good buys on almost the latest fashions. *Standa* and *UPIM* are more like Woolworth's; they have a reasonable selection of clothes, houseware, etc., and often supermarkets in their basements. Most stay open throughout the day, but some take the same break as other Italian shops—from 1pm to 3 or 4pm. Non-EC nationals should make sure to save their receipts for customs on the way home. Shipping goods is a risky business unless you do it through a very reputable shop. Note well that the attraction of shopping in Italy is strictly limited to luxury items; for less expensive clothes and household items you'll always, always do better in Britain or America. Prices for clothes, even in street markets, are often ridiculously high. Bargains of any kind are rare, and the cheaper goods are often very poor quality.

Italian clothes are lovely, but if you have a large-boned Anglo-American build, you may find it hard to get a good fit, especially on trousers or skirts (Italians are a long-waisted, slim-hipped bunch). Shoes are often narrower than the sizes at home.

Women's Shirts/Dresses

UK	10	12	14	16	18
US	8	10	12	14	16
Italy	40	42	44	46	48

Sweaters

10	12	14	16
8	10	12	14
46	48	50	52

Women's Shoes

3	4	5	6	7	8
4	5	6	7	8	9
36	37	38	39	40	41

Men's Shirts

UK/US	14	14½	15	15 ½	16	16 ½	17	17½
Italy	36	37	38	39	40	41	42	43

Men's Suits

UK/US	36	38	40	42	44	46
Italy	46	48	50	52	54	56

Men's Shoes

UK	2	3	4	5	6	7	8	9	10	11	12
US	5	6	7	7 ½	8	9	10	10½	11	12	13
Italy	34	36	37	38	39	40	41	42	43	44	45

weights and measures

1 kilogramme (1000 g)—2.2 lb
1 etto (100 g)— 1/4 lb (approx)
1 litre—1.76 pints

1 lb—0.45 kg

1 pint—0.568 litres
1 quart—1.136 litres
1 Imperial gallon—4.546 litres
1 US gallon—3.785 litres

1 metre—39.37 inches
1 kilometre—0.621 miles

1 foot—0.3048 metres
1 mile—1.61 kilometres

✆ (0564–)

Sports and Activities

birdwatching

Giglio and the other small islands, and the coastal parks near Argentario, are great places to go bird-watching; ecologically hyper-aware Giglio offers **nature appreciation** and **sketching** classes for those who speak Italian, ✆ 809034. The bird park at Lago Burano near Capalbio run by the WWF is another place for bird-watching, ✆ 898829.

boats and sailing

The **sailing** is beautiful among the coves of the Tuscan archipelago and around the Argentario; if you want to learn how, there's a good sailing school in Torre del Lago Puccini, ✆ 342084. You can bring your boat to Italy for six months without any paperwork if you bring it by car; if you arrive by sea you must report to the Port Authority of your first port to show passports and receive your 'Constituto' which identifies you and allows you to purchase fuel tax free. Boats with engines require a number plate, and if they're over 3 horsepower you need insurance. If you want to leave your boat in Italy for an extended period, you must have a Navigation Licence; after a year you have to start paying taxes on it. All yachts must pay a daily berthing fee in Italian ports. The National Tourist office has a list of ports that charter yachts in Tuscan ports.

clubs

Sporting clubs are usually privately owned and open only to members who pay on a yearly basis. Do not expect to be able to use a gym or sailing club paying a daily rate. The best (cleanest) **swimming** is to be found on the islands, especially on the beaches that look away from the mainland.

fishing

Fishing in the sea is possible from the shore, boats, or under water (but not with an aqualung) without a permit, though it may not be especially fruitful; the Tyrhennian has been so thoroughly fished commercially that the government has begun to declare two- and three-month moratoriums on all fishing to give the fish a break. Man-made lakes and streams are well stocked, however, and if you're more interested in the fresh fish than the sport, there are trout farms where you can almost pick the fish out of the water with your hands. To fish in fresh water you need to purchase a year's membership card and you must be resident in Italy. The licence costs L189,000 for a year and is available from the Federazione Italiana della Pesca Sportiva which has an office in every province and can inform you about local conditions and restrictions. Bait and equipment are readily available.

golf

There are golf courses in Florence, Montecatini Terme, Punta Ala, Tirrenia, Orbetello, Lucca, Poppi, Prato, Pietrasanta and on Elba at Portoferraio.

hunting

The most controversial sport in Italy is hunting, pitting avid enthusiasts against a burgeoning number of environmentalists who stage protests. The Apennines are boar territory, and in autumn the woods are full of hunters. Pathetically tiny birds, as well as ducks and pigeons, are the other principal game.

medieval sports

Some **ancient sports** like the annual horse races, or *palios* (two in Siena) are still popular, and not entirely as a tourist attraction; the rivalries between neighbourhoods and cities are intense. The Florentines play three games of Renaissance football a year (*calcio in costume*); Sansepolcro and Gubbio stage two crossbow matches a year against each other, while in Lucca the archers compete from different city quarters. Arezzo and Pistoia have annual jousts; in Pisa it's medieval tug-of-war.

potholing

Spelunkers can find Tuscan caves to explore around Montecatini Alta, Monsummano and Sarteano.

riding

Horse riding is increasingly popular, and AGRITURIST (*see* 'Where to Stay', p. 41) has a number of villa and riding holidays on offer in Tuscany. The National Association of Equestrian Tourism (ANTE) is probably more active here than anywhere in Italy. For more information, write directly to the local Agriturist office. There are **race and trotting courses** in Florence and Montecatini Terme.

rowing

When there's enough water, you can try your skills in the Arno (*see* **Florence**, p. 180). There is also the annual rowing race between the four old maritime republics of Venice, Amalfi, Genoa and Pisa, which alternates between the cities.

skiing

Tuscany has major ski resorts at Abetone, north of Pistoia, and at Monte Amiata; many people also head south of the border into Lazio to the big ski complex at Terminillo, east of Rieti.

tennis

Tennis-courts are nearly everywhere; each *comune* has at least one or two that you can hire by the hour.

walking

Hiking and signed trails are well developed in Tuscany; April–October is the best and safest time to go.

There are several scenic routes through the mountains: the four-day High Trail of the Apuan Alps, beginning from the Rifugio Carrara, above Carrara (for information call (0585) 841972, or the Italian Alpine Club (CAI) in Carrara, Via Giorgio, © (0585) 776782). A second trail, the Grand Apennine Excursion from Lake Scaffaiolo, goes along the mountain ridge that separates Tuscany from Emilia-Romagna, departing from Pracchia, © (0573) 630790 for information. There's a circular trail through the Garfagnana, starting from Castelnuovo di Garfagnana; contact the Comunità Montana Garfagnana, © (0583) 658990. In southern Tuscany, trails cover Monte Amiata from Abbadia San Salvatore (Comunità Montana dell'Amiata, © (0564) 967064). Other fine day trails are in the Casentino, from Badia Prataglia or Stia, or in the Nature Parks of Monti dell'Uccellina from Alberese or the Maremma. **Maremmagica** organizes trekking and walking tours with guides, © (0564) 496670 for information. In Florence, you can get information from CAI, Via dello Studio 5, © (055) 211731.

Direct-dial codes: USA and Canada ℂ 001

UK: ℂ 0044 (omitting the first '0' of the British area code)

If you're calling Italy from abroad, the country code is 39, followed by the area prefix—omitting the first '0'.

Like many things in Italy, telephoning can be unduly complicated and usually costs over the odds to boot. Only a few places still have the old token (*gettoni*) telephones, in which you must insert a token (or better yet, several) before dialling. *Gettoni* cost L200 and are often available in machines next to the telephones, or from bars, news-stands, or *tabacchi*. Other public phones will accept regular coinage, as well as *gettoni* and telephone cards. A digital display will indicate the money you have put in or how much credit is left on your card. When you hear the beep it is usually too late to put any more money in, so keep an eye on the display. If your credit on the phone card runs out, insert another one when you hear a beep.The cards are the best option for long-distance phoning and are available from tobacconist shops for L5,000 and L10,000.

Alternatively, head either for a telephone office with booths (usually only in the larger cities and major train stations, operated by either SIP or ASST) or a bar with a telephone meter. If you want to reverse charges (call collect) you can call from a phone box; dial 172 followed by the country code and you will be connected to an international operator.

Rates are lower if you call on Sunday or after 10pm at night until 8am in the morning — unfortunately just when many provincial telephone offices are closed. Phoning long-distance from your hotel can mean big surcharges.

Tourist Offices

UK

1 Princes Street, London W1R 8AY, ℂ (0171) 408 1254; ✉ 493 6695

USA

630 Fifth Avenue, Suite 1565, New York, NY 10111, ℂ (212) 245 4822; ✉ 586 9249

401 N. Michigan Avenue, Suite 3030, Chicago, Ill. 60611, ℂ (312) 644 0990/1; ✉ 644 3019

12400 Wilshire Boulevard, Suite 550 Los Angeles, 90025, ℂ (310) 820 0098; ✉ 820 6357

Canada

1 Place Ville Marie, Suite 1914, Montreal, Quebec, H3B 2C3, ℂ (514) 866 7667; ✉ 392 1429

You can pick up more detailed information by writing directly to any of the city or provincial tourist offices. These are usually very helpful in sending out lists of flats, villas or farmhouses to hire, or at least lists of agents who handle the properties.

Tuscany is endowed with hotels (*alberghi*) of every description, from the spectacular to the humble. These are rated by the government's tourism bureaucracy, from five stars at the luxurious top to one star at the bottom. The ratings take into account such things as a restaurant on the premises, plumbing, air-conditioning, etc., but not character, style or charm. Use the stars, which we include in this book, as a quick reference for prices and general amenities only. Another thing to remember about government ratings is that a hotel can stay at a lower rating than it has earned, so you may find a three-star hotel as comfortable as a four.

There's no inflation in Italy, if you believe the government; the prices just go up by themselves. With the holiday business booming, this curious paradox is well expressed in hotel prices; every year costs rise by 6–8 per cent across the board, and are often more expensive then hotels in northern Europe. The prices listed in this book are for double rooms only. For a single, count on paying two-thirds of a double; to add an extra bed in a double will add 35 per cent to the bill. Taxes and service charges are included in the given rate. Some establishments charge L10–25,000 for air-conditioning. Also note that if rooms are listed without bath, it simply means the shower and lavatory are in the corridor. Prices are by law listed on the door of each room and will be printed in the hotel lists available from the local tourist office; any discrepancies should be reported to the tourist office. Most rooms have two or three different rates, depending on the season. Costs are sometimes a third less if you travel in the district's low season. Some hotels, especially in resorts, close down altogether for several months of the year.

Breakfast is optional only in some hotels, and in pensions it is mandatory. And you may as well expect to face half- (breakfast and lunch or dinner) or full-board requirements in the hotels that can get away with it—seaside, lake or mountain resorts in season, spas and country villa hotels. Otherwise, meal arrangements are optional. Although eating in the hotel restaurant can be a genuine gourmet experience, in the majority of cases hotel food is bland, just as it is anywhere else.

Each province or region sets its own price guidelines for accommodation: a three-star hotel in Florence, for instance, will cost much more than a three-star hotel in southern Tuscany. In general, the further south you go, the cheaper the rates.

Throughout this book, prices listed are for a double room in high season; unless otherwise stated, a private bath is included. Here is the range of prices you are likely to encounter for hotels in the various classifications in 1996:

Category	Double with Bath
luxury (★★★★★)	L450–800,000
very expensive, Class I (★★★★)	L250–450,000
expensive, Class II (★★★)	L160–250,000
moderate, Class III (★★)	L85–160,000
inexpensive, Class IV (★)	up to 85,000

For rooms without bath, subtract 20–30 per cent. Many resort hotels in particular offer discounts for children and children's meals. A *camera matrimoniale* is a room with a double bed, a *camera doppia* has twin beds, a single is a *camera singola*. There are several hotel chains in Italy. CIGA (*Compagnia Grandi Alberghi*) has many of the most luxurious, many of them grand, turn-of-the-century establishments that have been exquisitely restored. Another plush chain, *Châteaux et Relais* specializes in equally comfortable, but more intimate accommodation, often in historical buildings. Both chains pride themselves on their gourmet restaurants. Even the once fairly standard *Jolly Hotels*, Italy's oldest chain, are quickly up-grading. The petrol company AGIP operates most of the motels along the major motorways, and usually makes a decent effort to give them good restaurants. The National Tourist Office has a complete list of these and booking information for both motels and five- and four-star hotels and chains. If you want to stay in a different kind of accommodation, you'll have to book ahead on your own. Outside the high season this is generally unnecessary; otherwise, and especially if you have a certain place in mind, it is essential to book several months in advance or even earlier if possible, considering the sorry state of the Italian post. (While you're at it, remember to request a room with a view, in places where that is the hotel's chief attraction.) If your Italian is non-existent, the National Tourist Office's *Travellers' Handbook* has a sample letter and list of useful terms. Under Italian law, a booking is valid once a deposit has been paid. If you have to cancel your reservation, the hotel will keep the deposit unless another agreement has been reached. If you're coming in the summer without reservations, start calling around for a place in the morning.

One Italian institution, the *albergo diurno* (Day Hotel), may prove handy, though there seem to be fewer of them all the time. Located in the centre of the largest cities and at the railway stations, these are places where you can take a shower, a shave, have your hair done, etc. They are open 6 am–midnight.

inexpensive accommodation

Bargains are few and far between in Italy. The cheapest kind of hotel is called an inn, or *locanda* ; some provinces treat these as one-star hotels or list them separately (or not at all). The majority of inexpensive places will always be around the railway station, though in the large cities you'll often find it worth your while to seek out some more pleasant location in the historic centre. You're likely to find anything in a one-star Italian hotel. Often they will be practically perfect, sometimes almost luxurious; memorably bad experiences will be few, and largely limited to the major cities. In rural areas and islands that see some tourists, ask around for rooms in private homes.

Besides the youth hostels (*see* below), there are several city-run hostels, with dormitory-style rooms open to all. In cities like Florence religious institutions often rent out rooms. Monasteries and convents in the country sometimes take guests as well; if you seek that kind of quiet experience, bring a letter of introduction from your local priest, pastor, etc.

youth and student hostels

You'll find youth hostels in Florence, Lucca, in Chianti, Abetone, Cortona, San Gimignano, Marina di Massa e Carrara. The head organization in Italy is the Associazione

Alberghi per la Gioventù, Via Cavour 44 (terzo piano), Roma, ✆ (06) 487 1152. They can send you a list and map of all the hostels in Italy, which officially require an IYHF card. There are no age limits, and senior citizens are often given added discounts. Many youth hostels sell cards or you can pick up one in advance from:

UK

Youth Hostels Association, 14 Southampton St, London WC2E 7HY, ✆ (0171) 836 1036, ▤ 836 6372.

US

American Youth Hostels, PO Box 37613, Washington, DC 20005, ✆ (202) 783 6161, ▤ 783 6171.

Canada

Canadian Hostelling Association, 400–205 Catherine St, Otawa, Ontario, K2P 1C3, ✆ (613) 237 7884, ▤ 237 7868.

Accommodation— a bunk bed in a single-sex room and breakfast—costs around L16,000 per day. There is often a curfew, and you usually can't check in before 5 or 6pm. You can book in advance by sending your arrival and departure dates along with the number of guests (by sex) to the individual hostel, including international postal coupons for the return reply. The worst time to use the hostels is the spring, when noisy Italian school groups use them for field trips.

There is one other organization to help students find lodgings in Italy—the Centro Turistico Studentesco e Giovanile (CTS), which has offices in every Italian city of any size (and one in London, 44 Goodge St, WP1 1FH, ✆ (0171) 436 4878) and can book cheap accommodation for you, in their own town or at your next stop.

self-catering holidays: villas, farmhouses and flats

Renting a villa, farmhouse, cottage or flat has always been the choice way to visit Tuscany. If you're travelling with a family it is the most economic alternative—there are simple, inexpensive cottages as well as the fabulous Renaissance villas furnished with antiques, gourmet meals and swimming-pools. One place to look for holiday villas is in the Sunday paper; or, if you have your heart set on a particular area, write to its tourist office for a list of local rental agencies. These ought to provide photos of the accommodation to give you an idea of what to expect, and make sure all pertinent details are written down in your rental agreement to avoid misunderstandings later. In general minimum lets are for two weeks; rental prices usually include insurance, water and electricity, and sometimes linen and maid service. Don't be surprised if upon arrival the owner 'denounces' (*denunciare*) you to the police; according to Italian law, all visitors must be registered upon arrival. Common problems are water shortages, unruly insects (*see* **Topics**, 'Flora and Fauna', p. 65), and low kilowatts (often you can't have your hot-water heater and oven on at the same time). Many of the companies listed below offer in addition to homes, savings on charter flights, ferry crossings or fly-drive schemes to sweeten the deal. Try to book as far in advance as possible for the summer season.

In the UK

International Chapters, 102 St John's Wood Terrace, London NW8 6PL, ✆ (0171) 722 9560, ✉ 722 9140, has the listings and handles bookings for the major Italian holiday home companies, the largest of which is **Cuendet** which publishes an extensive illustrated catalogue of holiday villas, flats and farmhouses in Tuscany; their headquarters are at Il Cerreto, 53030 Strove, Siena; they also have the listings of **Tuscan Enterprises**, a company with headquarters in Castellina in Chianti, and their own listings called **Italian Chapters**.

Other worthy firms specializing in holiday rentals in the region include:

Citalia, Marco Polo House, 3–5 Lansdowne Road, Croydon CR9 1LL, ✆ (0181) 686 0677

Interhome, 383 Richmond Rd, Twickenham TW1 2EF, ✆ (0181) 8911294, ✉ 891 5331

Invitation to Tuscany, 18 Sinclair Gardens, London, W14 0AT, ✆ (0171) 603 7111, ✉ 610 4175

Hello Italy, Woodstock, Forest Road, East Horsley, Surrey, KT24 5ES, ✆ (01483) 284 011, ✉ 285 264, for brochures

Magic of Italy, 227 Shepherds Bush Rd, London W6 7AS, ✆ (0181) 748 4999

David Newman's European Collection, PO Box 733, 40 Upperton Rd, Eastbourne, ✆ (01323) 410 347

Perrymead Properties Overseas, 55 Perrymead St, London SW6, ✆ (0181) 878 5788

Sovereign Villas, First Choice House, Peel Cross Road, Solford, Manchester, M5 2AN, ✆ (0161) 745 7000, ✉ 745 4545

In the USA

At Home Abroad, 405 East 56th St, New York, NY 10022, ✆ (212) 4219165, ✉ 752 1591

CUENDET: Posarelli Vacations, Suzanne T. Pidduck, 1742 Calle Corva, Camarillo, CA, 93010, ✆ (805) 987 5278, ✉ 482 7976

Hideaways International, 767 Islington St, Portsmouth, New Hampshire, 03801, ✆ (603) 430 4433, ✉ 430 4444

Homeowners International, 1133 Broadway, New York, NY 10010, ✆ (800) 367 4668

Italian Villa Rentals, 550 Kirkland Way, Suite 100, Kirkland, Washington DC, 98033, ✆ (206) 827 3694

Overseas Connection, 70 West 71st St, Suite 1C, New York, NY, 10023, ✆ (212) 769 1170

RAVE (Rent-a-Vacation-Everywhere),135 Meigs St, Rochester, NY 14607, ✆ (716) 256 0760, ✉ 256 2676

Italian Rentals, Elaine Muoio, 3801 Ingomar St N.W., Washington DC, 20015, ✆ (202) 244 5345, ✉ (202) 362 0520; specialist in Italian villa rentals

In Italy

The Best in Italy, Via Ugo Foscolo 72, Firenze, ✆ (055) 223 064, ✉ 229 8912, which specializes in posh villas with domestic staff

Casaclub, Via Termini 83, Siena, ✆ (0577) 44 041, ✉ 247 053 (villas in Chianti)

Immobiliare Tirrenia, Via XXIV Maggio 63, Marina di Grosseto (GR), ✆ (0564) 34 672

Toscana Vacanze, Via XX Settembre 6, 52047 Marciano della Chiana, ✆ (0575) 845 348, ✉ 845 462 (villas in Valdichiana)

Toscanamare Villas, Via W della Gheradesca 5, Castagneto Carducci (LI), ✆ (0565) 744 012, ✉ 744 339 (villas on the Versilia coast)

Tuscan Enterprises, for houses in Chianti; write to PO Box 34, Via delle Mura 22/24, Castellina in Chianti, 53011 Siena, ✆ (0577) 740 623, ✉ 740 950

Vela, Via Colombo 16, Castiglione della Pescaia, ✆ and ✉ (0564) 933 495 (villas and flats on the seaside and panoramic locations)

farm holidays

Associazione Regionale Agriturist, Piazza S. Firenze 3, 50122 Firenze, ✆ (055) 287 838, ✉ 230 2285

Solemar, Via Cavour 80, Firenze, ✉ (055) 287 157

Turismo Verde, c/o Confcoltivatori, Piazza Indipendenza 10, 50129 Firenze, ✉ (055) 471 261

Or write directly to the provincial **Agriturist** office (UPA):

Via Guido Monaco, 52100 **Arezzo**, ✆ (0575) 300 751

Via della Chiesa 4, 58100 **Grosseto**, ✆ (0564) 21 010

Via G. Marradi 14, 57126 **Livorno**, ✆ (0586) 812 744

Viale. Barsanti e Matteucci, 55100 **Lucca**, ✆ (0583) 332 044

Via V.M. Giuliani 9, 54011 **Massa Carrara**, ✆ (0187) 421 028

Via B. Croce 62, 56100 **Pisa**, ✆ (050) 26 221

Via F. Pacini 45, 51100 **Pistoia**, ✆ (0573) 21 231

Via della Sapienza 39, 53100 **Siena**, ✆ (0577) 46 194

alpine refuges

The Club Alpino Italiano operates a large percentage of the *Rifugi Alpini*, or mountain huts in the Apennines. Facilities range from the basic to the grand; some are exclusively for hikers and mountain-climbers, while others may be reached by *funivie*, and are used by skiers in the winter and holiday-makers in the summer. Rates average L18-25,000 a night, but rise by 20 per cent between December and April. Write to the club at Via Fonseca Pimental 7, Milan, ✆ (02) 26141378, for a list of huts, their opening dates, and booking information.

camping

Most of the official camp-sites are near the sea, but there are also quite a few in the mountains and near the lakes, and usually one within commuting distance of major tourist centres. A complete list with full details for all of Italy is published annually in the Italian Touring Club's *Campeggi e Villaggi Turistici*, available in Italian bookshops for L29,500, or you can obtain an abbreviated list free from the Centro Internazionale Prenotazioni Federcampeggio, Casella Postale 23, 50042, Calenzano (Firenze); request their booking forms as well to reserve a place—essential in the summer months when the tents and caravans (campers) are packed cheek to cheek. Camping fees vary according to the camp ground's facilities, roughly L6-8000 per person (less for children); L8000–15,000 per tent or caravan; and L4000 per car. Camping outside official sites is kosher if you ask the landowner's permission first.

Caravans are expensive to hire and are available at: INNOCENTI NOLEGGIO, Piazza Italia 25, Montecatini Terme, ✆ (0572) 78873; ACI TOUR, Via Catalani 1, S. Lucia, Lucca, ✆ (0583) 582626; CAMPERTOUR, Via S. Pietro a Quaracchi, Florence, ✆ (055) 315336.

Women Travellers

Italian men, with the heritage of Casanova, Don Giovanni and Rudolph Valentino as their birthright, are very confident in their role as great Latin lovers, and local swains will invariably pick on any female under a certain age, Italian or foreign. Most of these are unlikely to give any trouble but obviously you should avoid lonely streets and train stations after dark. Travelling with a male companion practically cancels out any problems—you're instantly a man's property and as such inviolable—an aspect of Italian culture most women find extremely galling.

History and Art

At times, the history of Tuscany has been a small part of a bigger story—Rome's, or modern Italy's. However, the crucial eras of the Middle Ages and the Renaissance provided a tremendous chronicle of contending city states, each with a complex history of its own. For that reason, we have included detailed histories of the most important towns—Florence, Siena and Pisa, and covered the rest to a lesser extent. Here is a brief historical outline for the region as a whole.

The Etruscans

Neolithic cultures seem to have occupied this region of Italy since about 4500 BC without distinguishing themselves artistically or politically. The dawn of history in these parts comes with the arrival of the **Etruscans**, though where they came from and precisely when they arrived remains one of the major mysteries of early Mediterranean history. According to their traditions, the Etruscans migrated from western Anatolia, c. 900 BC. Classical authors were divided on this point; some believed the migration theory, while others saw the Etruscans as the indigenous inhabitants of west-central Italy. Their language remains murky to modern scholars, but the discovery of Etruscan inscriptions on the Greek island of Lemnos, along with other clues, tends to support the Etruscan story.

Whatever it was, they were a talented people, and the great wealth they derived from an intensive agriculture, manufacturing, and above all mining (Elba and the Metal Hills) allowed these talents to blossom into opulence by the 7th century BC. Though they gave their name to modern Tuscany, the real centre of Etruscan civilization lay to the south; roughly the coast from Orbetello to Cervéteri (Caere) in Lazio and around Lakes Bolsena and Trasimeno. Never a unified nation, the Etruscans preferred the general Mediterranean model of the independent city state; the 12 greatest dominated central Italy in a federation called the **Dodecapolis**. Which cities were members is uncertain, but the 14 possible cities include *Veii, Cervéteri, Tarquinia* and *Vulci* (in Lazio), *Roselle, Vetulonia* and *Populonia* (on or near the Tuscan coast), *Volterra, Fiesole, Arezzo, Chiusi, Orvieto, Cortona* and *Perugia.*

The Etruscans always maintained extremely close trade and cultural ties with classical Greece. They sold Elban iron and bought Greek culture wholesale; the artistic thieving magpies of antiquity, they adapted every style of Greek art, from the Minoan-style frescoes at Tarquinia to the classical bronzes now in the Florence Museum, and created something of their very own. In expressive portrait sculpture, though, they surpassed even the Greeks. A considerable mythology has grown up around the Etruscans. Some historians and poets celebrate them as a nation of free peoples, devoted to art, good food and easy living. A less sentimental views shows a slave society run for the benefit of a military, aristocratic elite. Whichever, the art they left behind gives them a place as the most enigmatic, vivid and fascinating people of early Italy. It isn't difficult to see echoes of their culture in everything that has happened in this part of Italy for the last 2000 years.

Romans

Etruscan kings once ruled in Rome, but after the establishment of the Republic, this precocious city was to prove the end of the Etruscan world. All of southern Etruria was swallowed up by 358 BC, and internal divisions between the Etruscan cities allowed the Romans to push their conquest inevitably northwards. After the conquest of an Etruscan city, Roman policy was often diabolically clever; by establishing veterans' colonies in new towns nearby to draw off trade, Rome was able to ensure the withering of Etruscan culture and the slow extinction of many of Etruria's greatest cities.

Most of the Etruscan cities joined with neighbouring peoples, the Umbrii of Umbria and the Piceni of the Marches, in the Social Wars of 92–89 BC, the last doomed attempt of the Italians to fight free of Roman imperialism. Two distinct cultures occupies the northern fringes. The wandering Celts, who occupied all northern Italy until the 3rd century BC, often made themselves at home in the Apennines and northern Etruria; their influence on the region's culture is slight. And there was the unnamed culture of the rugged **Lunigiana**, around Pontrémoli, a people who carried their neolithic customs and religion (see the statue-steles in the Pontrémoli museum) well into the modern era.

Under the empire, Etruria and Umbria was relatively quiet, though the region experienced a north–south economic split to mirror the bigger one beginning across Italy. Southern Etruria, the old Etruscan heartland, shrivelled and died under Roman misrule, never to recover. The north became more prosperous, and important new cities appeared: Lucca, Pisa, Florence, and to a lesser extent Assisi, Gubbio and Siena.

The Dark Ages

Later Italians' willingness to create fanciful stories about the 'barbarian invasions' makes it hard to define what did happen in this troubled time. The first (5th-century) campaigns of the **Goths** in Italy did not seem to cause too much damage, but the curtain finally came down on Roman civilization with the Greek-Gothic wars of 536–563, when Eastern Emperor Justinian and his generals Belisarius and Narsus attempted to recapture Italy for Byzantium. The chronicles of many cities record the devastation of the Gothic King, Totila (for example, the sack of Florence), though the imperial aggressors were undoubtedly just as bad. In any case, the damage to an already weakened society was fatal, and the wars opened the way for the conquest of much of Italy by the terrible **Lombards** (568), who established the Duchy of Spoleto, with loose control over much of central Italy. Lucca, the late Roman and Gothic capital of Etruria, alone managed to keep the Lombards out. By this time, low-lying cities like Florence had practically disappeared, while the remnants of the other towns survived under the control of local barons, or occasionally under their bishops. Feudal warfare and marauding became endemic. In the 800s even a band of Arabs came looting and pillaging up the Valnerina, almost in the centre of the peninsula.

By the 9th century, things were looking up. Florence had re-established itself, and built its famous baptistry. The old counts of Lucca extended their power to become counts of

Tuscany, under the Attoni family, lords of Canossa. As the leading power in the region, they made themselves a force in European affairs. In 1077, the great Countess Matilda, allied with the Pope, humbled Emperor Henry IV at Canossa—the famous 'penance in the snow' during the struggles over investiture. Perhaps most important of all was the growth of the maritime city of **Pisa** which gave Tuscany a new window on the world, building wealth through trade and inviting new cultural influences from France, Byzantium and the Muslim world.

Medieval Tuscany

By 1000, with the new millennium, all of northern Italy was poised to rebuild the civilization that had been lost centuries before. In Tuscany, as elsewhere, increasing trade had created a rebirth of towns, each doing its best to establish its independence from local nobles or bishops, and to increase its influence at the expense of its neighbours. Thus a thousand minor squabbles were played out against the background of the major issues of the day; first the conflict over investiture in the 11th century, evolving into the endless factional struggles of **Guelphs** and **Ghibellines** after 1215. Throughout, the cities were forced to choose sides between the partisans of the popes and those of the emperors. The Ghibellines' brightest hours came with the reigns of strong Hohenstaufen emperors **Frederick I Barbarossa** (1152–90) and his grandson **Frederick II** (1212–46), both of whom spent much time in Tuscany. An early Guelph wave came with the papacy of **Innocent III** (1198–1216), most powerful of the medieval pontiffs, and the Guelphs would come back to dominate Tuscany after the invasion of Charles of Anjou in 1261. Florence, Arezzo and Lucca were the mainstays of the Guelphs, while Pisa, Pistoia and Siena usually supported the Ghibellines.

In truth, it was every city for itself. By 1200, most towns had become free *comuni* ; their imposing public buildings can be seen in almost every corner of Tuscany. All the trouble they caused fighting each other (at first with citizen militias, later increasingly with the use of hired *condottieri*) never troubled the booming economy. Florence and Siena became bankers to all Europe, great building programmes went up, beginning with the Pisa cathedral complex in the 1100s, and the now tamed and urbanized nobles built fantastical skyscraper skylines of tower-fortresses in the towns. Above all, it was a great age for culture, the age of Dante (b. 1265) and Giotto (b. 1266). Another feature of the time was the 13th-century religious revival, dominated by the figure of **St Francis of Assisi**.

Background of the Renaissance

Florence, biggest and richest of the Tuscan cities, increased its influence all through the 1300s, gaining Prato and Pistoia, and finally winning a seaport with the capture of declining Pisa in 1406. This set the stage for the relative political equilibrium of Tuscany during the early Renaissance, the height of the region's wealth and artistic achievement.

The **Wars of Italy**, beginning in 1494, put an end to Renaissance tranquillity. Florence was once more lost in its internal convolutions, twice expelling the **Medici**, while French and Imperial armies marched over the two regions. When the dust had cleared, the last of the free cities (with the exception of Lucca) had been extinguished, and most of Tuscany came under the rule of the Grand Duke **Cosimo I** (1537–74), the Medici propped on a newly made throne by Emperor Charles V. Tuscany's economic and artistic decline was gentle until 1600. After that, it was precipitate; the old banking and textile businesses collapsed, and serious artistic production practically ceased.

The Modern Era

Though maintaining a relative independence, Tuscany had little to say in Italian affairs. After the Treaty of Câteau-Cambrésis in 1559, the Spaniards established a military enclave, called the Presidio, around Orbetello, precisely to keep an eye on central Italy. Cosimo I proved a vigorous ruler, though his successors gradually declined in ability. By 1600 it didn't matter. The total exhaustion of the Florentine economy kept pace with that of the Florentine imagination. By 1737, when the Medici dynasty became extinct, Tuscany was one of the torpid backwaters of Europe. It had no chance to decide its own destiny; the European powers agreed to bestow Tuscany on the House of Lorraine, cousins to the Austrian Habsburgs. Surprisingly enough, the Lorraines proved able and popular rulers, especially during the rule of the enlightened, progressive Peter Leopold (1765–90).

The languor of Lorraine and papal rule was interrupted by Napoleon, who invaded central Italy twice and established a Kingdom of Etruria from 1801 to 1807. Austrian rule returned after 1815, continuing the series of well-meaning, intelligent Grand Dukes. By now, however, the Tuscans and the rest of the Italians wanted something better. In the tumults of the Risorgimento, one of the greatest and kindest of the Lorraines, Leopold II, saw the writing on the wall and allowed himself to be overthrown in 1859. Tuscany was almost immediately annexed to the new Italian kingdom.

Since then, the two regions have followed the history of modern Italy. The head start Tuscany gained under the Lorraine dukes allowed it to keep up economically with northern Italy. Florence had a brief moment of glory (1865–70) as capital of Italy, awaiting the capture of Rome. Since then, the biggest affair was World War II, with a long, tortuous campaign dragging across Tuscany and the Marches. The Germans based their Gothic Line on the Arno, blowing up all but one of Florence's bridges.

Art and Architecture

Etruscans

Although we have no way of knowing what life was like for the average man in Camars or Velathrii, their tomb sculptures and paintings convince us that they were a talented, likeable people. Almost all their art derives from the Greek; the Etruscans built classical temples (unfortunately of wood, with terracotta embellishments, so little survives), carved themselves sarcophagi decorated with scenes from Homer, and painted their pottery in red and black after the latest styles from Athens or Corinth. They excelled at portrait sculpture, and had a remarkable gift for capturing personality, sometimes seriously, though never heroically, often with an entirely intentional humour, and usually the serene smiles of people who truly enjoyed life.

Etruscan art in museums is often maddening; some of the works are among the finest productions of antiquity, while others—from the same time and city—are awkward and childish. Their talent for portraiture, among much else, was carried on by the Romans, and they bequeathed their love of fresco painting to the artists of the Middle Ages and Renaissance, who of course weren't even aware of the debt. After introducing yourself to the art of the Etruscans, it will be interesting to reconsider all that came later—in Tuscany, and indeed all Italy, you will find subtle reminders of this enigmatic people.

Romans and Dark Ages

After destroying the Etruscan nation, the Romans also began the extinction of its artistic tradition; by the Empire, there was almost nothing left that could be called distinctively Etruscan. Tuscany contributed little under the Empire. In the chaos that followed, there was little room for art. What painting survived followed styles current in Byzantium.

Middle Ages

In both architecture and sculpture, the first influence came from the north. Lombard masons filled Tuscany with simple Romanesque churches; the first (Grópina, Abbadia S. Salvatore and several in the Garfagnana, to name a few) follow the northern style, although it wasn't long before two distinctive Tuscan forms emerged: the Pisan style, characterized by blind rows of colonnades, black and white zebra stripes, and lozenge-shaped designs; and the 'Tuscan Romanesque' which developed around Florence, notable for its use of dark and light marble patterns and simple geometric patterns, often with intricate mosaic floors to match (the Baptistry and San Miniato in Florence are the chief examples). In the cities in between—Lucca, Arezzo and Pistoia—there are variations on the two different styles, often carrying an element like stripes or arcades to remarkable extremes. The only real example of French Gothic in Tuscany is San Galgano, built by Cistercians in the 1200s, although the style never caught on here or anywhere else in Italy.

From the large pool of talent working on Pisa's great cathedral complex in the 13th century emerged Italy's first great sculptor, **Nicola Pisano**, whose Baptistry pulpit, with its realistic figures, derived from ancient reliefs. His even more remarkable son, **Giovanni Pisano**, prefigures Donatello in the expressiveness of his statues and the vigour of his pulpits; his façade of Siena cathedral, though altered, is a unique work of art. **Arnolfo di Cambio**, a student of Nicola Pisano, became chief sculptor-architect of Florence during its building boom in the 1290s, designing its cathedral and Palazzo Vecchio with a hitherto unheard-of scale and grandeur, before moving on to embellish Orvieto with statues and tombs. Painting at first lagged behind the new realism and more complex composition of sculpture. The first to depart from Byzantine stylization, at least according to the account in Vasari's *Lives of the Artists* (*see* **Topics**, p.65), was **Cimabue**, in the late 1200s, who forsook Greek forms for a more 'Latin' or 'natural' way of painting. Cimabue found his greatest pupil, **Giotto**, as a young shepherd, chalk-sketching sheep on a piece of slate. Brought to Florence, Giotto soon eclipsed his master's fame (artistic celebrity being a recent Florentine invention) and achieved the greatest advances on the road to the new painting with a plain, rather severe approach that shunned Gothic prettiness while exploring new ideas in composition and expressing psychological depth in his subjects. Even more importantly, Giotto through his intuitive grasp of perspective was able to go further than any previous artist in representing his subjects as actual figures in space. In a sense Giotto actually invented space; it was this, despite his often awkward and graceless draughtsmanship, that so astounded his contemporaries. His followers, **Taddeo and Agnolo Gaddi** (father and son), **Giovanni da Milano**, and **Maso di Banco** filled Florence's churches with their own interpretations of the master's style. In the latter half of the 1300s, however, there also appeared the key figure of **Andrea Orcagna**, the most important Florentine sculptor, painter and architect of his day. Inspired by the more elegant style of **Andrea Pisano's** Baptistry doors, Orcagna broke away from the simple Giottesque forms for a more elaborate, detailed style in his sculpture, while the fragments of his frescoes that survive have a vivid dramatic power which undoubtedly owes something to the time of the Black Death and social upheavals in which they were painted.

Siena never produced a Vasari to chronicle its accomplishments, though they were considerable; in the 13th and 14th centuries, Siena's Golden Age, the city's artists, like its soldiers, rivalled and often surpassed those of Florence. For whatever reason, it seemed purposefully to seek inspiration in different directions from Florence; at first from central Italian styles around Spoleto, then, with prosperity and the advent of **Guido da Siena** in the early 1200s to the more elegant line and colour of Byzantium. Guido's work paved the way for the pivotal figure of **Duccio di Buoninsegna**, the catalyst who founded the essentials of Sienese art by uniting the beauty of Byzantine line and colour with the sweet finesse of western Gothic art. With Duccio's great followers **Pietro and Ambrogio Lorenzetti** and **Simone Martini**, the Sienese produced an increasingly elegant and rarefied art, almost oriental in its refined stylization. They were less innovative than the Florentines, though they brought the 'International Gothic' style—flowery and ornate, with all the bright tones of May—to its highest form in Italy. Simone Martini introduced the Sienese manner to Florence in the early 1400s, where it influenced most notably the work of **Lorenzo Monaco, Masolino**, and the young goldsmith and sculptor, **Ghiberti**.

The Renaissance

Under the assaults of historians and critics over the last two centuries, the term 'Renaissance' has become a vague and controversial word. Nevertheless, however you choose to interpret this rebirth of the arts, and whatever dates you assign to it, Florence inescapably takes the credit for it. This is no small claim. Combining art, science and humanist scholarship into a visual revolution that often seemed pure sorcery to their contemporaries, a handful of Florentine geniuses taught the Western eye a new way of seeing. Perspective seems a simple enough trick to us now, but its discovery determined everything that followed, not only in art, but in science and philosophy as well.

Leading what scholars used self-assuredly to call the 'Early Renaissance' is a triumvirate of three geniuses: Brunelleschi, Donatello and Masaccio. **Brunelleschi**, neglecting his considerable talents in sculpture for architecture and science, not only built the majestic dome of Florence cathedral, but threw the Pandora's box of perspective wide open by mathematically codifying the principles of fore-shortening. His good friend **Donatello**, the greatest sculptor since the ancient Greeks, inspired a new generation of both sculptors and painters to explore new horizons in portraiture and three-dimensional representation. The first painter to incorporate Brunelleschi and Donatello's lessons of spatiality, perspective and expressiveness was the young prodigy **Masaccio**, who along with his master Masolino painted the famous Brancacci Chapel in the Carmine, studied by nearly every Florentine artist down to Michelangelo.

Brunelleschi's Cupola

The new science of architecture, sculpture and painting introduced by this triumvirate ignited an explosion of talent unequalled before or since—a score of masters, most of them Tuscan, each following the dictates of his own genius to create a remarkable range of themes and styles. To mention only the most prominent: **Lorenzo Ghiberti**, who followed Donatello's advice on his second set of Baptistry doors to cause a Renaissance revolution; **Leon Battista Alberti**, who took Brunelleschi's ideas to their most classical extreme in architecture, creating new forms in the process; **Paolo Uccello**, one of the most provocative of artists, who according to Vasari drove himself bats with the study of perspective and the possibilities of illusionism; **Piero della Francesca** of Sansepolcro, who explored the limits of perspective and geometrical forms to create the most compelling, haunting images of the quattrocento; **Fra Angelico**, who combined Masaccio's innovations and International Gothic colours and his own deep faith to create the most purely spiritual art of his time; **Andrea del Castagno**, who made use of perspective to create monumental, if often restless figures.

Some of Donatello's gifted followers were **Agostino di Duccio, Benedetto da Maiano, Desiderio da Settignano, Antonio and Bernardo Rossellino, Mino da Fiesole** and perhaps most famously, **Luca della Robbia**, who invented the coloured terracottas his family spread throughout Tuscany. And still more: **Benozzo Gozzoli**, whose enchanting springtime colours and delight in detail are a throwback to the International Gothic; **Antonio and Piero Pollaiuolo**, sons of a poultryman, whose new, dramatic use of line and form, often violent and writhing, would be echoed in Florentine Mannerism; **Fra Filippo Lippi**, a monk like Fra Angelico but far more earthly, the master of lovely Madonnas, teacher of his talented son **Filippino Lippi; Domenico Ghirlandaio**, whose gift of easy charm and flawless technique made him society's fresco painter; **Andrea del Verrocchio**, who could cast in bronze, paint, or carve with perfect detail; **Luca Signorelli**, who achieved apocalyptic grandeur in Orvieto Cathedral; **Perugino** (Pietro Vannucci) of Umbria, who painted the stillness of his native region into his landscapes and taught the young **Raphael** of Urbino; and finally **Sandro Botticelli**, whose highly intellectual but lovely and melancholy, mythological paintings are in a class of their own.

The 'Early Renaissance' came to a close near the end of the 1400s with the advent of **Leonardo da Vinci**, whose unique talent in painting, only one of his hundred interests, challenged the certainty of naturalism with a subtlety and chiaroscuro that approaches magic. One passion, however, obsessed the other great figure of the 'High Renaissance', **Michelangelo Buonarroti**: his consummate interest was the human body, at first graceful and serene as in most of his Florentine works, and later, contorted and anguished after he left for Rome.

Mannerism

Michelangelo left in Florence the seeds for the bold, neurotic avant-garde art that has come to be known as Mannerism. The first conscious 'movement' in Western art can be seen as a last fling amidst the growing intellectual and spiritual exhaustion of 1530s Florence, conquered once and for all by the Medici. The Mannerists' calculated exoticism and exaggerated, tortured poses, together with the brooding self-absorption of Michelangelo, are a prelude to Florentine art's remarkably abrupt turn into decadence and prophesy its final extinction. Foremost among the Mannerist painters are two surpassingly strange characters, **Jacopo Pontormo** and **Rosso Fiorentino**, who were not in such great demand as the coldly classical **Andrea del Sarto** and **Bronzino**, consummate perfectionists of the brush, both much less intense and demanding. There were also charming reactionaries working at the time, especially **Il Sodoma** and **Pinturicchio**, both of whom left their best works in Siena. In sculpture **Giambologna** and to a lesser extent **Bartolommeo Ammannati** specialized in virtuoso *contrapposto* figures, each one more impossible than the last. With their contemporary, **Giorgio Vasari**, Florentine art lost almost all imaginative and intellectual content, and became a virtuoso style of interior decoration perfectly adaptable to saccharine holy pictures, portraits of newly enthroned

dukes, or absurd mythological fountains and ballroom ceilings. In the cinquecento, with plenty of money to spend and
a long Medici tradition of patronage to uphold, this tendency
soon got out of hand. Under the reign of Cosimo I, indefatigable collector of *pietra dura* tables, silver and gold
gimcracks, and exotic stuffed animals, Florence gave birth to
the artistic phenomenon modern critics call kitsch.

The Rest Compressed

In the long, dark night of later Tuscan art a few artists stand out—the often whimsical
architect and engineer, **Buontalenti**; **Pietro Tacca**, Giambologna's pupil with a taste for
the grotesque; the charming Baroque fresco master **Pietro da Cortona**. Most of Tuscany,
and particularly Florence, chose to sit out the Baroque—almost by choice, it seems, and
we can race up to the 19th century for the often delightful 'Tuscan Impressionists' or
Macchiaioli ('Splatterers'; best collection in Modern Art section of Pitti Palace); and in the
20th century, **Modigliani** of the oval faces (from Livorno); the Futurist **Gino Severini**
(from Cortona); and **Ottone Rosai**, the master of the quiet Florentine countryside.

Artists' Directory

This includes the principal architects, painters and sculptors of Tuscany. The works listed
are far from exhaustive, bound to exasperate partisans of some artists and do scant justice
to the rest, but we have tried to include only the best and most representative works that
you'll find in our region.

Agostino di Duccio (Florence, 1418–81). A precocious and talented sculptor, his best
    work is in the Malatesta Temple at Rimini. Sometimes seems a precursor of Art
    Deco (**Florence**, Bargello; **Pontrémoli**, S. Francesco).

Alberti, Leon Battista (1404–72). Architect, theorist, and writer. His greatest contribu-
    tion was recycling the classical orders and the principles of Vitruvius into
    Renaissance architecture (**Florence**, Palazzo Rucellai, façade of S. Maria Novella,
    SS. Annunziata; **Lastra a Signa**, S. Martino).

Allori, Alessandro (1535–1607). Florentine Mannerist painter, prolific follower of
    Michelangelo and Bronzino (**Florence**, SS. Annunziata, S. Spirito, Spedale degli
    Innocenti).

Ammannati, Bartolommeo (1511–92). Florentine architect and sculptor. Restrained,
    elegant in building (**Florence**, S. Trínita bridge, courtyard of Pitti Palace);
    neurotic, twisted Mannerist sculpture (**Florence**, Fountain of Neptune, Villa di
    Castello).

Andrea del Castagno (*c.* 1423–57). Precise, dry Florentine painter, one of the first and
    greatest slaves of perspective (**Florence**, Uffizi, S. Apollonia, SS. Annunziata).

Angelico, Fra (or Beato) (Giovanni da Fiesole, *c.* 1387–1455). Monk first and painter second, but still one of the great visionary artists of the Renaissance (**Florence**, S. Marco—spectacular Annunciation and many more; **Cortona**, Cathedral Museum; **Fiesole**, S. Domenico).

Arnolfo di Cambio (born in Colle di Val d'Elsa; *c.* 1245–1302). Architect and sculptor, pupil of Nicola Pisano and a key figure in his own right. Much of his best sculpture is in Rome, but he changed the face of Florence as main architect to the city's greatest building programme of the 1290s (**Florence**, cathedral and Palazzo Vecchio).

Baldovinetti, Alesso (Florence, 1425–99). A delightful student of Fra Angelico who left few tracks; most famous for fresco work in **Florence** (SS. Annunziata, Uffizi, S. Niccolò sopr'Arno, S. Miniato).

Bandinelli, Baccio (1488–1559). Florence's comic relief of the late Renaissance; supremely serious, vain, and so awful it hurts—of course he was court sculptor to Cosimo I (**Florence**, Piazza della Signoria and SS. Annunziata).

Barna da Siena (active mid-1300s). One of the chief followers of Simone Martini, more dramatic and vigorous than the usual ethereal Sienese (**San Gimignano**, Collegiata).

Bartolo di Fredi (Siena, active *c.* 1353–1410). Student of Ambrogio Lorenzetti, a genuine pre-Raphaelite soul, entirely at home in the Sienese trecento; employs colours never before seen on this planet (**Montepulciano**, Duomo; **San Gimignano**, Collegiata).

Beccafumi, Domenico (*c.* 1486–1551). Sienese painter; odd mixture of Sienese conservatism and Florentine Mannerism (**Siena**, Pinacoteca).

Benedetto da Maiano (Florence, 1442–97). Sculptor, specialist in narrative reliefs (**Florence**, S. Croce, Strozzi Palace, Bargello; he also designed the brilliant loggia of S. Maria delle Grazie, **Arezzo**).

Bigarelli, Guido (13th century). Talented, travelling sculptor from Como, who excelled in elaborate and sometimes bizarre pulpits (**Barga**, **Pistoia**, S. Bartolomeo, and **Pisa** Baptistry).

Botticelli, Sandro (Florence, 1445–1510). Though technically excellent in every respect, and a master of both line and colour, there is more to Botticelli than this. Above every other quattrocento artist, his works reveal the imaginative soul of the Florentine Renaissance, particularly the great series of mythological paintings (**Florence**, Uffizi). Later, a little deranged and under the spell of Savonarola, he reverted to intense, though conventional religious paintings. Almost forgotten in the philistine 1500s and not rediscovered until the 19th century, many of his best works are probably lost (**Florence**, Accademia; **Montelupo**, S. Giovanni Evangelista).

Bronzino, Agnolo (1503–72). Virtuoso Florentine Mannerist with a cool, glossy hyper-elegant style, at his best in portraiture; a close friend of Pontormo (**Florence**, Palazzo Vecchio, Uffizi, S. Lorenzo, SS. Annunziata).

Brunelleschi, Filippo (1377–1446). Florentine architect of genius, credited in his own time with restoring the ancient Roman manner of building—but really deserves more credit for developing a brilliant new approach of his own (**Florence**, Duomo cupola, Spedale degli Innocenti, S. Spirito, S. Croce's Pazzi Chapel, S. Lorenzo). Also one of the first theorists on perspective.

Buontalenti, Bernardo (1536–1608). Late Florentine Mannerist architect and planner of the new city of **Livorno**, better known for his Medici villas (**Artimino**, also the fascinating grotto in **Florence's** Boboli Gardens, and Belvedere Fort, Uffizi Tribuna).

Cellini, Benvenuto (1500–71). Goldsmith and sculptor. Though a native of Florence, Cellini spent much of his time in Rome. In 1545 he came to work for Cosimo I and to torment Bandinelli (*Perseus*, Loggia dei Lanzi; also works in the Bargello). As famed for his catty *Autobiography* as for his sculpture.

Cimabue (*c.* 1240–1302). Florentine painter credited by Vasari with initiating the 'rebirth of the arts'; one of the first painters to depart from the stylization of the Byzantine style (**Florence**, mosaics in Baptistry, Crucifix in Santa Croce; **Pisa**, cathedral mosaic).

Civitali, Matteo (Lucca, *c.* 1435–1501). Sweet yet imaginative, apparently self-taught. He would be much better known if all of his works weren't in Lucca (**Lucca**, cathedral, Guinigi Museum).

Coppo di Marcovaldo (Florence, active *c.* 1261–75). Another very early painter, as good as Cimabue if not as well known (**San Gimignano**; **Pistoia**, cathedral).

Daddi, Bernardo (active 1290–*c.* 1349). Master of delicate altarpieces (**Florence**, Orsanmichele, S. Maria Novella's Spanish chapel).

Desiderio da Settignano (Florence, 1428/31–61). Sculptor, follower of Donatello (**Florence**, S. Croce, Bargello, S. Lorenzo).

Dolci, Carlo (1616–86). Unsurpassed Baroque master of the 'whites of their eyes' school of religious art (**Florence**, Palazzo Corsini; **Prato**, Museo del Duomo).

Domenico di Bartolo (*c.* 1400–46). An interesting painter, well out of the Sienese mainstream; the unique naturalism of his art is a Florentine influence. His best work (not on view at the time of writing) are the frescoes of 15th-century hospital life in the Spedale di Santa Maria della Scala in **Siena**.

Domenico Veneziano (Florence 1404–61). Painter, teacher of Piero della Francesca; master of perspective with few surviving works (**Florence**, Uffizi).

Donatello (Florence, 1386–1466). The greatest Renaissance sculptor appeared as suddenly as a comet at the beginning of Florence's quattrocento. Never equalled in technical ability, expressiveness, or imaginative content, his works influenced Renaissance painters as much as sculptors. A prolific worker, and a quiet fellow who lived with his mum, Donatello was the perfect model of the early Renaissance artist—passionate about art, self-effacing, and a little eccentric (**Florence**, Bargello—the greatest works including the original *St George* from Orsanmichele, *David* and *Cupid-Atys*, also at San Lorenzo, Palazzo Vecchio, and the Cathedral Museum; **Siena**, cathedral).

Duccio di Buoninsegna (d. 1319). One of the first and greatest Sienese painters, Duccio was to Sienese art what Giotto was to Florence; ignored by Vasari, though his contributions to the new visual language of the Renaissance are comparable to Giotto's (**Siena**, parts of the great Maestà in the Cathedral Museum, also Pinacoteca; **Florence**, altarpiece in the Uffizi; **Castelfiorentino**, Pinacoteca).

Francesco di Giorgio Martini (Siena, 1439–1502). Architect—mostly of fortresses—sculptor and painter, his works are scattered all over Italy (**Cortona**, S. Maria di Calcinaio).

Franciabigio (1482–1525). Most temperamental of Andrea del Sarto's pupils but only mildly Mannerist (**Florence**, Poggio a Caiano and SS. Annunziata).

Gaddi, Taddeo (*c.* 1300–*c.* 1366). Florentine; most important of the followers of Giotto. He and his son **Agnolo** (d. 1396) contributed some of the finest trecento fresco cycles (notably at S. Croce, and S. Ambrogio, **Florence**).

Gentile da Fabriano, Francesco di (*c.*1360–1427). Master nonpareil of the International Gothic style. Best works in the Uffizi, **Florence**.

Ghiberti, Lorenzo (1378–1455). The first artist to write a biography was naturally a Florentine. He would probably be better known had he not spent most of his career working on the two sets of doors for the Florence Baptistry after winning the famous competition of 1401 (also **Florence**, statues at Orsanmichele; **Pistoia**).

Ghirlandaio, Domenico (Florence, *c.* 1448–94). The painter of the quattrocento establishment, master of elegant fresco cycles in which he painted all the Medici and Florence's banking elite. A great portraitist with a distinctive, dry, restrained style (**Florence**, Ognissanti, S. Maria Novella, S. Trínita, Spedale degli Innocenti; **San Gimignano**, Collegiata).

Giambologna (1529–1608). A Fleming, born Jean Boulogne; court sculptor to the Medici after 1567 and one of the masters of Mannerist virtuosity—also a man with a taste for the outlandish (**Florence**, Loggia dei Lanzi, Bargello, Villa della Petraia; **Pratolino**, the *Appennino*).

Giotto (*c.* 1266–1337). Shepherd boy of the Mugello, discovered by Cimabue, who became the first great Florentine painter—recognized in his own time. Invented an essential and direct approach to portraying narrative fresco cycles, but is even more important for his revolutionary treatment of space and of the human figure (**Florence**, S. Croce, cathedral campanile, Horne Museum, S. Maria Novella).

Giovanni da Milano (14th century). An innovative Lombard inspired by Giotto (**Florence**, S. Croce; **Prato**, Cathedral Museum).

Giovanni di Paolo (d. 1483). One of the best of the quattrocento Sienese painters; like most of them, a colourful reactionary who continued the traditions of the Sienese trecento (**Siena**, Pinacoteca).

Giovanni di San Giovanni (1592–1633). One of Tuscany's more prolific, but winning Baroque fresco painters (**Florence**, Pitti Palace, Villa della Petraia).

Gozzoli, Benozzo (Florence, d. 1497). Learned his trade from Fra Angelico, but few artists could have less in common. The most light-hearted and colourful of quattrocento artists, Gozzoli created enchanting frescoes at **Florence**, Medici chapel; **San Gimignano**, S. Agostino; **Pisa**, Campo Santo.

Guido da Siena (active c. 1345–70). Interesting Sienese trecento painter; little is known about his life (**Grosseto** museum).

Leonardo da Vinci (1452–1519). We could grieve that Florence's 'universal genius' spent so much time on his scientific interests and building fortifications, and that his meagre artistic output was left unfinished or lost. All that is left in Tuscany is the *Annunciation* (**Florence**, Uffizi) and also models of all his gadgets at his birthplace, **Vinci**. As the pinnacle of the Renaissance marriage of science and art, Leonardo requires endless volumes of interpretation. As for his personal life, Vasari records him buying up caged birds in the market-place just to set them free.

Lippi, Filippino (Florence, 1457–1504). Son and artistic heir of Fra Filippo. Often seems a neurotic Gozzoli, or at least one of the most thoughtful and serious artists of the quattrocento (**Florence**, S. Maria Novella, S. Maria del Carmine, Badia, Uffizi).

Lippi, Fra Filippo (Florence, d. 1469). Never should have been a monk in the first place. A painter of exquisite, ethereal Madonnas, one of whom he ran off with (the model, at least, a brown-eyed nun named Lucrezia). The pope forgave them both. Lippi was a key figure in the increasingly complex, detailed painting of the middle 1400s (**Florence**, Uffizi; **Prato**, cathedral and Civic Museum).

Lorenzetti, Ambrogio (Siena, d. 1348). He could crank out golden Madonnas as well as any Sienese painter, but Lorenzetti was also a great innovator in subject matter and the treatment of landscapes. Created the first and greatest of secular frescoes, the *Allegories of Good and Bad Government* in **Siena's** Palazzo Pubblico, while his last known work, the 1344 *Annunciation* in Siena's Pinacoteca is one of the 14th century's most revolutionary treatments of perspective (also **Massa Marittima**, museum).

Lorenzetti, Pietro (Siena, d. 1348). Ambrogio's big brother, and also an innovator, standing square between Duccio di Buoninsegna and Giotto; one of the precursors of the Renaissance's new treatment of space (**Siena**, S. Spirito; **Arezzo**, Pieve di S. Maria; **Cortona**, Cathedral Museum). Both Lorenzettis seem to have died in Siena during the Black Death.

Lorenzo di Credi (1439–1537). One of the most important followers of Leonardo da Vinci, always technically perfect if occasionally vacuous (**Florence**, Uffizi).

Lorenzo Monaco (Siena, 1370–1425). A monk at S. Maria degli Angeli in Florence and a brilliant colourist, Lorenzo forms an uncommon connection between the Gothic style of Sienese painting and the new developments in early Renaissance Florence (**Florence**, Uffizi, S. Trínita).

Manetti, Rutilio (1571–1639). Quirky but somehow likeable Baroque painter, the last artist of any standing produced by Siena (**Massa Marittima**, cathedral).

Margarito d'Arezzo (13th century). A near contemporary of Giotto who stuck firmly to his Byzantine guns (**Arezzo**, museum).

Martini, Simone (Siena, d. 1344). Possibly a pupil of Giotto, Martini took the Sienese version of International Gothic to an almost metaphysical perfection, creating luminous, lyrical, and exquisitely drawn altarpieces and frescoes perhaps unsurpassed in the trecento (**Siena**, Palazzo Pubblico; **Pisa**, Museo S. Matteo).

Masaccio (Florence, 1401–*c.* 1428). Though he died young and left few works behind, this precocious 'shabby Tom' gets credit for inaugurating the Renaissance in painting by translating Donatello and Brunelleschi's perspective onto a flat surface. Also revolutionary in his use of light and shadow, and in expressing emotion in his subjects' faces (**Florence**, S. Maria del Carmine, S. Maria Novella; **Pisa**, Museo S. Matteo).

Maso di Banco (Florence, active 1340s). One of the more colourful and original followers of Giotto (**Florence**, S. Croce).

Masolino (Florence, d. 1447). Perhaps 'little Tom' also deserves much of the credit, along with Masaccio, for the new advances in art at the Carmine in **Florence**; art historians dispute endlessly how to attribute the frescoes. It's hard to tell, for this brilliant painter left little other work behind to prove his case (**Empoli**, civic museum; also attributed Tau chapel, **Pistoia**).

Matteo di Giovanni (Siena, 1435–95). One Sienese quattrocento painter who could keep up with the Florentines; a contemporary described him as 'Simone Martini come to life again' (**Siena**, Pinacoteca, S. Agostino, S. Maria di Nevi).

Memmi, Lippo (Siena, 1317–47). Brother-in-law and assistant of Simone Martini (**Siena**, S. Spirito; **San Gimignano**, museum).

Michelangelo Buonarroti (Florence, 1475–1564). Born in Caprese (now Caprese Michelangelo) into a Florentine family of the minor nobility come down in the world, Michelangelo's early years and artistic training are obscure; he was apprenticed to Ghirlandaio, but showing a preference for sculpture was sent to the court of Lorenzo de' Medici. Nicknamed Il Divino in his lifetime, he was a complex, difficult character, who seldom got along with mere mortals, popes, or patrons. What he couldn't express by means of the male nude in paint or marble, he did in his beautiful but difficult sonnets. In many ways he was the first modern artist, unsurpassed in technique but also the first genius to go over the top (**Florence**, Medici tombs and library in San Lorenzo, three works in the Bargello, the *Pietà* in the Museo del Duomo, the *David* in the Accademia, Casa Buonarroti, and his only oil painting, in the Uffizi).

Michelozzo di Bartolomeo (Florence, 1396–1472). Sculptor who worked with Donatello (**Prato**, pulpit of the Holy Girdle, and the tomb in **Florence's** Baptistry), he is better known as the classicizing architect favoured by the elder Cosimo de' Medici (**Florence**, Medici Palace, Chiostro of SS. Annunziata, convent of San Marco; Villas at **Trebbio** and **Cafaggiolo**, **Montepulciano**, S. Agostino; **Impruneta**, Tempietto).

Mino da Fiesole (Florence, 1429–84). Sculptor of portrait busts and tombs; like the della Robbias a representative of the Florentine 'sweet style' (**Fiesole**, cathedral; **Empoli**, museum; **Volterra**, cathedral; **Florence**, Badia, Sant'Ambrogio; **Prato**, cathedral).

Nanni di Banco (Florence, 1384–1421). Florentine sculptor influenced by the Gothic style (**Florence**, Orsanmichele, Porta della Mandorla).

Orcagna, Andrea (Florence, d. 1368). Sculptor, painter and architect who dominated the middle 1300s in Florence, though greatly disparaged by Vasari, who destroyed much of his work. Many believe he is the mysterious 'Master of the Triumph of Death' of Pisa's Campo Santo (**Florence**, Orsanmichele, S. Croce, S. Maria Novella, *Crucifixion* in refectory of S. Spirito, also often given credit for the Loggia dei Lanzi).

Perugino (Pietro Vannucci, Perugia, d. 1523). Perhaps the most distinctive of the Umbrian painters; created some works of genius, along with countless idyllic nativity scenes, each with its impeccably sweet Madonna and characteristic blue-green tinted background (**Florence**, Uffizi, S. Maddalena dei Pazzi, Cenacolo di Foligno).

Piero della Francesca (d. 1492). Painter, born at Sansepolcro, and one of the really unique quattrocento artists. Piero wrote two of the most important theoretical works on perspective, then illustrated them with a lifetime's work reducing painting to the bare essentials: geometry, light and colour. In his best work his reduction creates nothing dry or academic, but magic, almost eerie scenes similar to those of Uccello. And like Uccello or Botticelli, his subjects are often archetypes of immense psychological depth, not to be fully explained now or ever (**Arezzo**, S. Francesco and the cathedral; **Sansepolcro**, civic museum; **Monterchi**, cemetery church; **Florence**, Uffizi).

Piero di Cosimo (Florence, 1462–1521). Painter better known for his personal eccentricities than his art, which in itself is pretty odd (**Florence**, Uffizi; **Fiesole**, S. Francesco).

Pietro da Cortona (1596–1699). Perhaps the most charming of Tuscan Baroque painters; his best is in Rome, but there are some florid ceilings in the Pitti Palace (**Florence**; also works in **Cortona**).

Pinturicchio (Perugia, 1454–1513). This painter got his name for his use of gold and rich colours. Never an innovator, but as an absolute virtuoso in colour, style and grace no one could beat him. Another establishment artist, especially favoured by the popes, and like Perugino, he was slandered most vilely by Vasari (**Siena**, Piccolomini Library).

Pisano, **Andrea** (Pisa, d. 1348). Artistic heir of Giovanni and Nicola Pisano and teacher of Orcagna; probably a key figure in introducing new artistic ideas to **Florence** (Baptistry, south doors).

Pisano, **Nicola** (Pisa, active *c.* 1258–78). The first great medieval Tuscan sculptor created a little Renaissance all his own, when he adapted the figures and composition of ancient reliefs to make his wonderful pulpit reliefs in **Siena** and **Pisa Baptistry**. His son **Giovanni Pisano** (active *c.* 1265–1314) carried on the tradition, notably in the façade sculptures at **Siena** cathedral (also great relief pulpits in **Pisa** cathedral, Sant'Andrea, **Pistoia**).

Pollaiuolo, **Antonio** (Florence, d. 1498). A sculptor, painter and goldsmith whose fame rests on his brilliant, unmistakable line; he occasionally worked with his less gifted brother **Piero** (**Florence**, Uffizi and Bargello).

Pontormo, **Jacopo** (Florence, 1494–1556). You haven't seen pink and orange until you've seen the work of this determined Mannerist eccentric. After the initial shock, though, you'll meet an artist of real genius, one whose use of the human body as sole means for communicating ideas is equal to Michelangelo's (**Florence**, S. Felicità—his *Deposition*—and Uffizi; **Poggio a Caiano**; **Carmignano**).

Quercia, **Jacopo della** (Siena, 1374–1438). Sculptor who learned his style from Pisano's cathedral pulpit; one of the unsuccessful contestants for the Florence baptistry doors. Maybe Siena's greatest sculptor, though his most celebrated work, that city's Fonte Gaia, is now ruined (**Lucca**, cathedral *tomb of Ilaria del Carretto*; **San Gimignano**, Collegiata; **Siena**, Baptistry; **Volterra**, cathedral).

Raphael (1483–1520). Born in Urbino in the Marches, Raphael spent time in Città di Castello, Perugia, and Florence before establishing himself in Rome. Only a few of the best works of this High Renaissance master remain in our area; those are in the Pitti Palace and Uffizi, **Florence**.

Robbia, **Luca della** (Florence, 1400–82). Greatest of the famous family of sculptors; he invented the coloured glaze for terracottas that we associate with the della Robbias, but was also a first-rate relief sculptor (the *cantorie* in **Florence's** cathedral museum; **Impruneta**, Collegiata). His nephew Andrea (1435–1525) (best works in convent of **La Verna** and the Tempietto at **Montevarchi**) and Andrea's son Giovanni (1469–1529; best work, **Pistoia**, Ospedale del Ceppo) carried on the blue and white terracotta sweet style in innumerable buildings across Tuscany.

Rosselli, Cosimo (1434–1507). Competent middle of the road Renaissance painter who occasionally excelled (**Florence**, S. Ambrogio).

Rossellino, Bernardo (1409–64). Florentine architect and sculptor best known as the planner and architect of the new town of **Pienza**. Also a sculptor (**Florence**, S. Croce, S. Miniato; **Empoli**, Pinacoteca). His brother **Antonio Rossellino** (1427–79) was also a talented sculptor (**Florence**, S. Croce).

Rossi, Vicenzo de' (1525–87). Florentine Mannerist sculptor of chunky male nudes (**Florence**, Palazzo Vecchio).

Rosso Fiorentino (Giovanni Battista di Jacopo, 1494–1540). Florentine Mannerist painter, perhaps very much underrated. He makes a fitting complement to Pontormo, both for his tortured soul and for the exaggerations of form and colour he used to create gripping, dramatic effects. Fled Italy after the Sack of Rome and worked for Francis I at Fontainebleau. (**Volterra** Pinacoteca has his masterpiece, the *Deposition*; **Florence**, Uffizi and S. Lorenzo).

Salviati, Francesco (Florence, 1510–63). Friend of Vasari and a similar sort of painter—though much more talented. Odd perspectives and decoration, often bizarre imagery (**Florence**, Palazzo Vecchio and Uffizi).

Sangallo, Antonio da (brother of Giuliano, 1455–1537). Architect at his best in palaces and churches in the monumental style—notably at the great temple of S. Biagio, **Montepulciano**; the son, **Antonio da Sangallo the Younger**, also an architect, and the family's best, practised mainly in Rome.

Sangallo, Giuliano da (Florence, 1443–1516). Architect of humble origins who became the favourite of Lorenzo de' Medici. Often tripped up by an obsession, inherited from Alberti, with making architecture conform to philosophical principles (**Poggio a Caiano**; **Florence**, S. Maddalena dei Pazzi; **Prato**, S. Maria delle Carceri).

Il Sassetta (Stefano di Giovanni; active *c*. 1390–1450). One of the great Sienese quattrocento painters, though still working in a style the Florentines would have found hopelessly reactionary; an artist who studied Masaccio but preferred the Gothic elegance of Masolino. His masterpiece, the Borgo Sansepolcro polyptych, is dispersed through half the museums of Europe.

Signorelli, Luca (Cortona, d. 1523). A rarefied Umbrian painter and an important influence on Michelangelo. Imaginative, forceful compositions, combining geometrical rigour with a touch of unreality, much like his master Piero della Francesca (**Cortona**, civic and cathedral museums; **Monte Oliveto Maggiore**; **Sansepolcro**, museum).

Il Sodoma (Giovanni Antonio Bazzi, 1477–1549). Born in Piedmont, but a Sienese by choice, he was probably not the libertine his nickname, and Vasari's biography, suggest. An endearing, serene artist, who usually eschewed Mannerist distortion, he got rich through his work, then blew it all feeding his exotic menagerie and died in the poorhouse (**Monte Oliveto Maggiore**; **Siena**, Pinacoteca and S. Domenico).

Spinello Aretino (late 14th century–1410). A link between Giotto and the International Gothic style; imaginative and colourful in his compositions (**Florence**, S. Miniato; **Arezzo**, museum). His son **Parri di Spinello** did many fine works, all around **Arezzo** (S. Maria delle Grazie).

Tacca, Pietro (1580–1640). Born in Carrara, pupil of Giambologna and one of the best early Baroque sculptors (**Livorno**, *Quattro Mori*; **Florence**, Piazza SS. Annunziata fountain; **Prato**, Piazza del Comune).

Taddeo di Bartolo (1363–1422). The greatest Sienese painter of the late 1300s—also the least conventional; never a consummate stylist, he often shows a remarkable imagination in composition and treatment of subject matter (**Siena**, Palazzo Vecchio, S. Spirito; **Colle di Val d'Elsa** museum and Collegiata; **Volterra**, Pinacoteca).

Talenti, Francesco (early 14th century). Chief architect of **Florence** cathedral and campanile after Arnolfo di Cambio and Giotto; his son **Simone** made the beautiful windows in **Orsanmichele** (and perhaps the Loggia dei Lanzi) in **Florence**.

Torrigiano, Pietro (1472–1528). Florentine portrait sculptor, famous for his work in Westminster Abbey and for breaking Michelangelo's nose (**Siena**, cathedral).

Uccello, Paolo (1397–1475). No artist has ever been more obsessed with the possibilities of artificial perspective. Like Piero della Francesca, he used the new technique to create a magic world of his own; contemplation of it made him increasingly eccentric in his later years. Uccello's provocative, visionary subjects (*Noah* fresco in S. Maria Novella, and *Battle of San Romano* in the Uffizi, **Florence**) put him up with Piero della Francesca and Botticelli as the most intellectually stimulating of quattrocento artists (also attributed frescoes, **Prato** cathedral).

Vasari, Giorgio (Arezzo, 1511–74). Florentine sycophant, writer and artist; *see* p.67. Also a pretty fair architect (**Florence**, Uffizi, Corridoio, and Fish Loggia).

Il Vecchietta (Lorenzo di Pietro, 1412–80). Sienese painter and sculptor, dry and linear, part Sienese Pollaiuolo and part Donatello (**Siena**, Loggia della Mercanzia, Baptistry).

Verrocchio, Andrea del (1435–88). Florentine sculptor who worked in bronze; spent his life trying to outdo Donatello. Mystic alchemist in his spare time, and interestingly enough the master of both Botticelli and Leonardo (Uffizi, S. Lorenzo, Orsanmichele, Palazzo Vecchio, and Bargello, **Florence**).

Angel's head - Verrocchio

Topics

If there's a great sense of continuity in the land, it is the same with the rhythms of rural life in Tuscany. Old traditions and seasonal changes are still of primary importance—Italians, for the most part, won't buy imported fruit or vegetables; even in the cities it's difficult to find a decent tomato in January. Even the chocolates disappear off the counter in July. Tuscany, like most of Italy, chooses to follow the calendar as a sort of sentimental journey through the rise and fall of the Year.

The traditional Florentine New Year was Annunciation Day in March, the time when the countryside really did seem to awaken—until the Medici Grand Dukes finally aligned Tuscany to the papal calendar in the 1500s. **January** still hibernates; if the ground is soft farmers may put in peas and garlic; roast chestnuts, *polenta*, *bruschetta* and game dishes are the highlights of the table. **February** is the month of pruning and planting garden vegetables in frames. Sticky sweet carnival pastries are unavoidable.

In **March** new fruit trees are planted and the vines are pruned; potatoes, fennel, spinach, carrots, parsley and lettuce are planted directly in the garden. Blood oranges (from Sicily) and artichokes appear in the shops. The fruit trees burst into blossom, and continue through **April**, the time to plant sunflowers and corn, the other garden vegetables and most flowers. Lambs are slaughtered for Easter; young turkeys and pigs are purchased. The hunt for wild asparagus and salad greens is in full swing. Strawberries and medlars are the fruits of **May**, Tuscany's most glorious month, when the irises and roses bloom in profusion. *Fave* (broad beans) are the big treat, and in the mountains, in most years, you can stop lighting fires to stay warm in the evening. The first garlic, French beans and potatoes are harvested in **June**, which is also the time to plant cabbage and cauliflowers. Cherries, apricots, plums, the first watermelons and fresh tomatoes appear; everyone's eating melon and prosciutto antipasti and dishes with courgette flowers (*fiori di zucca*). **July** brings an avalanche of *zucchini* and peaches. Country folk begin staying up past 10pm, and scorpions come into your house to cool off.

In **August** an awful lot of chickens meet their maker, while the end of the month brings masses upon masses of tomatoes, which country families join together to conserve—a messy operation of steaming kettles and grinders that puts up a year's supply of tomato sauce. Apples, pears and fresh figs are harvested in **September**, a golden, placid month when the village stationery shops begin stocking the schoolbooks for the new year. **October** is the *vendemmia*, or grape harvest; to make *vinsanto* it's essential to pick out very mature bunches and hang them up to dry. The hunting season opens, and folks begin to poke around for wild mushrooms. **November** is a busy month, the time to hunt for truffles, harvest olives, pomegranates, chestnuts, and take care of wine business. In **December** the family pig is slaughtered for next year's prosciutto and sausages. Orange persimmons hang like ornaments on the trees and plague the table—no one likes them, but everyone has plenty to give away; if they are indeed the apples of the Hesperides, as some scholars suggest, the afterlife must be a major disappointment. Much more delightful are the tiny tangerines from the south that flood the market. Christmas turkeys realize their time has come; and cakes are everywhere: dense confections of walnuts, raisins and chocolate (*panforte* of Siena) or tall, airy *panettone* sold in cylindrical boxes.

The First Professional Philistine

Many who have seen Vasari's work in Florence will be wondering how such a mediocre painter should rate so much attention. Ingratiating companion of the rich and famous, workmanlike over-achiever and tireless self-promoter, Vasari was the perfect man for his time. Born in Arezzo, in 1511, a fortunate introduction to Cardinal Silvio Passerini gave him the chance of an education in Florence with the young Medici heirs, Ippolito and Alessandro. In his early years, he became a fast and reliable frescoist gaining a reputation for customer satisfaction—a real innovation in an age when artists were increasingly becoming eccentric prima donnas. In the 1530s, after travelling around Italy on various commissions, he returned to Florence just when Cosimo I was beginning his plans to remake the city in the image of the Medici. It was a marriage made in heaven. Vasari became Cosimo's court painter and architect, with a limitless budget and a large group of assistants, the most prolific fresco machine ever seen in Italy—painting over countless good frescoes of the 1300s along the way.

But more than for his paintings, Vasari lives on through his book, the *Lives of the Artists*, a series of exhaustive biographies of artists. Beginning with Cimabue, Vasari traces the rise of art out of Byzantine and Gothic barbarism, through Giotto and his followers, towards an ever-improving naturalism, finally culminating in the great age of Leonardo, Raphael, and the divine Michelangelo, who not only mastered nature but outdid her. Leon Battista Alberti gets the credit for drafting the first principles of artistic criticism, but it was Vasari who first applied such ideas on a grand scale. His book, being the first of its kind, and containing a mine of valuable information on dozens of Renaissance artists, naturally has had a tremendous influence on all subsequent criticism. Art critics have never really been able to break out of the Vasarian straitjacket.

Much of Vasari's world seems quaint to us now: the idea of the artist as a kind of knight of the brush, striving for Virtue and Glory, the slavish worship of anything that survived from ancient Rome, artistic 'progress' and the conviction that art's purpose was to imitate nature. But many of Vasari's opinions have had a long and mischievous career in the world of ideas. His blind disparagement of everything medieval—really the prejudice of his entire generation—lived on until the 1800s. His dismissal of Sienese, Umbrian and northern artists—of anyone who was not a Florentine—has not been entirely corrected even today. Vasari was the sort who founded academies, a cheerful conformist who believed in a nice, tidy art that went by the book. With his interior decorator's concept of Beauty, he created a style of criticism in which virtuosity, not imagination, became the standard by which art was to be judged; history offers few more instructive examples of the stamina and resilience of dubious ideas.

Flora and Fauna

No one would come to this part of Italy expecting to find an unspoiled wilderness. Most of Tuscany, in particular, has been cultivated so long and so intensively, that wildlife is completely pushed to the fringes. Nevertheless, there is a great variety of birds and beasts to complement the surprisingly wide range of landscapes. Cultivated Tuscany (*see*

'Landscapes', *below*) is another world, the land of vineyards and olive groves, cypresses, poplars and the occasional umbrella pine. The rest of the territory divides neatly into three parts: the coastal zone, with its beaches and wetlands, the central hills and the mountains.

For nature lovers, the coast will be by far the most interesting region; the malaria mosquito kept much of the southern Maremma undeveloped for centuries, leaving vast stretches of pine forest, along with cork oak and holm oak, a thriving wildlife (including even some wild horses) and marshlands that host a marvellous array of birds, from eagles to woodpeckers. Its protected nesting grounds (*see* 'the Monti dell'Uccellina' p.308, Orbetello lagoons p.309 and Lago di Burano p.316) are Italy's greatest stopover for migrating waterfowl—herons, cormorants, storks, kingfishers, osprey and the only cranes left on the mainland. Deforested land beyond the marshes is covered with the characteristic Mediterranean scrub, or maquis (*macchia*, in Italian); either *macchia alta* with shrub versions of pines (they harvest the pine nuts), oaks, beech, cypress and laurel; or the *macchia bassa* in drier regions, thick patches of broom, heather, lentisk and other fragrant plants.

As for the animals, there are pretty much the same characters throughout Tuscany, starting with those two regional totems, the viper and the boar. The bad old viper, the only really unpleasant thing you may meet out in the woods and fields, proliferates especially where farmlands have been abandoned; he's brownish-grey, about 60cm long (never more than 1m), and has a vaguely diamond-shaped head. Vipers are a nuisance only because there are so many of them, and because they object to being stepped on. If one bites you, you've got half an hour to find someone with the serum—or you can buy your own in any pharmacy. The boar, a shy, well-mannered creature, flourishes everywhere despite the Italians' best efforts to turn him into boar salami. In summer, you may hear them nosing around the villages at night looking for water.

Beyond these, there are plenty of hares and rabbits, foxes and weasels, also polecats, badgers and porcupine in the wilder areas. Wolves, lynx and deer are extinct in most of Tuscany, though a few of each survive in the higher reaches of the Apennines and deer have been reintroduced in the Maremma coastal parks. There is a little isolated region in Tuscany, the Val di Farma north of Roccastrada, where you can find all of these, and even wildcats. The only mountain goats are found on the island of Montecristo.

Many writers on this part of Italy comment on the absence of birdsong. They're exaggerating. Italian hunters do shoot anything that flies, but there are still quite a few thrushes, starlings, wrens, and such. Cuckoos unfailingly announce the spring, pheasants lay low during the hunting season, and an occasional owl can be heard in the country. Nightingales are rare, but there are supposed to be some around Lago di Massaciuccoli and the northern coasts—in the evening you're far more likely to see little bats.

The insect world is well represented, and if you spend time in the country, you'll meet many of them: lovely butterflies and moths and delicate white creatures, with wings apparently made of feathers; rather forbidding black bullet bees and wasps that resemble vintage fighter planes. Beetles especially reach disproportionate sizes—if you're lucky you may see a *diavolo*, a large black or red beetle with long, gracefully curving antlers that sing when you trap it; Leonardo drew one in his notebooks. There are enough mosquitoes, midges and little biting flies to be a nuisance in the summer, and perhaps most alarming at first sight, the shiny black scorpion, who may crawl inside through the window or up drains (you may want to keep the plugs in) or come in with the wood if you have a fire. Once inside they head for dark places like beds or shoes. One thwack with a shoe will do in even the largest scorpion (they're actually quite soft). If you happen to be stung, it may be painful but not deadly; the Italians recommend a trip to the doctor for treatment against an infection or allergic reaction.

As for the forests, oaks, chestnuts and beech predominate, along with tall, upright poplars ('Lombardy' type), pines, willows (not the weeping variety) and a few maples—with rounded leaves, not pointed as in northern Europe and America. Cypress trees are common. Incidentally the idea that there are erect, needle-like 'male' cypresses and blowsy 'female' ones is a misconception; the tidier ones have been planted, while shaggy cypresses are the wild variety. Umbrella pines (really the maritime pine), that most characteristic Italian tree, make a grand sight isolated on a hill crest, or in large groves along the Maremma coast. At higher altitudes, there are large beech forests, along with pines and firs—some beautiful groves of silver firs grow around Monte Amiata, while in the Casentino near Camaldoli is a vast stretch of old, protected beech and pine forest; another, primarily chestnut forest, is contained in the Garfagnana's *Parco Naturale dell'Orecchiella*.

Though at first they may seem unfamiliar, many of the most common Italian wild flowers are close cousins to those seen in northern Europe and America. There are a million varieties of buttercup, usually tiny ones like the *ranuncolo* and *bottoncini d'oro*, and of bluebell, often called *campanella* or *campanellina*. Many of the common five-petalled pink blossoms in spring fields are really small wild geraniums (*geranio*), with pointed leaves like the anemone, and you'll see quite a few varieties of violets (*violette*) with round or spade-shaped leaves (a few species are yellow). A daisy, in Italian, is a *margherita*, and they come in all sizes. Tiniest of all are the wild pink and blue forget-me-nots (*non ti scordar di me*); you'll have to look closely to see them in overgrown fields. Large swatches of lavender are one of the charms of the hills of Chianti.

The real star of Italian fields is the poppy, bright red and thriving everywhere. Dandelions and wild mustard are also plentiful, along with white, umbrella-like bunches of florets called *tragosellino* or *podragraria*, similar to what Americans call Queen Anne's Lace. More exotic flowers include wild orchids, some with small florets growing in spiky shoots, rhododendrons (in mountainous areas), five-petalled wild roses and water lilies in the coastal Maremma.

There are other plants to look for; a dozen different kinds of greens the Italians gather for salads, anise, fennel, wild hemp (only a fool would try to smoke it); mint, rosemary and sage are common, and Italians beat the bushes with fervour every spring looking for wild asparagus. Also wild strawberries (*fragole del bosco*), raspberries (*lamponi*) and blackberries (*more*).

Landscapes

Other regions in Italy are lusher, others have taller mountains and more fertile valleys, others support a far greater variety of flora and enjoy a more temperate climate. Yet when all is said and done, it is the landscapes of Tuscany that exert the most lasting charm. In the painting of the Renaissance, the background of rolling hills, cypresses, poplars and umbrella pines, the vineyards and winding lanes are often more beautiful than the nominally religious subject in the foreground. Very early on, beginning with Giotto, artists took care to relate the figures in their composition to the architecture and the landscape around them, epitomized in the paintings of Leonardo da Vinci, where each tree and rock takes on an almost mystic significance.

Every Italian is born with an obsessive instinct to put in order, or '*sistemare*' things; with a history of wars, earthquakes, foreign rulers, and an age-old tendency to extremes of all descriptions, the race has had a bellyful of disorder and unpredictability. The tidy, ordered geometry and clipped hedges of an Italian garden are a perfect example of the urge to *sistemare* nature, and you'll find good examples of these in the Boboli, the Medici villas at Castello and Collodi; the Tuscans, in the vanguard of Italy in so many ways, were the first to *sistemare* their entire territory. The vicious wars of the Middle Ages between cities and the Guelphs and Ghibellines devastated the countryside and much of the forests (as is visible in the harsh, barren brown and grey hills of trecento painting); the Black Death in the 1300s depopulated the cultivated areas, giving the Tuscans the unique opportunity to arrange things just so. Not entirely by coincidence, the late 14th century was the time when the elite, weary of the strife in the city, were discovering the joys of the country and building villas, playing the country squire and gentleman farmer whenever possible—already, in the *Decameron*, the nobles had estates in the environs of Florence. And they planted everything in its place according to elegance and discipline, each tree with its own purpose, a boundary marker, for shade, or to support a vine. Often cypresses and umbrella pines stand strikingly along the crest of hills, not for aesthetics or a study in perspective, but for a windbreak. Strongest of all is the feeling that nothing has changed for centuries, that in the quattrocento Gozzoli and Fra Angelico painted the same scene you see today. Few landscapes anywhere are more ancient, or civilized.

Tuscany on Wheels

Tuscans have always loved a parade, and to the casual reader of Renaissance history, it seems they're forever proceeding somewhere or another, even to their own detriment—during outbreaks of plague, holy companies would parade through an inflicted area, invoking divine mercy, while in effect aiding the spread of the pestilence. They also had a great weakness for allegorical parade floats. During the centuries of endless war each Tuscan city rolled out its war chariot or battle wagon, called the *Carroccio*, invented by a Milanese bishop in the 11th century. A *Carroccio*, drawn by six white oxen, was a kind of holy ship of state in a hay cart; a mast held up a crucifix while a battle standard flew from the yard-arm, there was an altar for priests to say mass during the battle and a large bell to send signals over the din to the armies. The worst possible outcome of a battle was to lose one's *Carroccio* to the enemy, as Fiesole did to Florence. One is still in operation, in Siena, rumbling out twice a year for the Palio.

Medieval clerical processions, by the time of Dante, became melded with the idea of the Roman 'triumph' (*trionfo*); in Purgatory, the poet finds Beatrice triumphing with a cast of characters from the Apocalypse. Savonarola wrote of a *Triumph of the Cross*; Petrarch and Boccaccio wrote allegorical triumphs of virtues, love and death. More interesting, however, are the secular Roman-style Triumphs staged by the Medici, especially at Carnival (the name of which, according to Burckhardt, comes from a cart, the pagan *carrus navalis*, the ship of Isis, launched every 5 March to symbolize the reopening of navigation). You can get a hint of their splendour from the frescoes at Poggio a Caiano; the best artists of the day would be commissioned to design the decorations—two particularly famous *trionfi* in Florence celebrated the election of the Medici Pope Leo X. The last relics of these parades are the huge satirical carnival floats at Viareggio.

Two lovely memories of Florence's processions remain. One is Gozzoli's fairy-tale frescoes in the chapel of the Medici palace, of the annual procession staged by the Compagnia de' Re Magi, the most splendid and aristocratic of pageants. The other comes from the Florentine Carnival, famous for its enormous floats, in which scenes from mythology were portrayed to songs and music. One year, for the masque of Bacchus and Ariadne, Lorenzo de' Medici composed the loveliest Italian poem to come out of the Renaissance, with the melancholy refrain:

> *Quanto è bella giovinezza,*
> *Che si fugge tuttavia!*
> *Chi vuol esser lieto, sia:*
> *Di doman non c'è certezza.*

Florentines 2, Giants 1

Sono vulgari, quei Fiorentini.... You won't spend much time in Italy (or especially in Tuscany) before you hear someone commenting on the vulgarity of the Florentines. Such a remark may be occasioned by a lad standing next to an Alfa with Florence number plates, leaning on the horn and waking up the babies, or by a couple with sunglasses in a dark restaurant who manage to get in three cigarettes after each course. As everyone knows, Florentines are also the most arrogant and conceited people in the universe, surpassing even the Romans and Milanese.

After some initial dismay, you may find it refreshing to encounter a people with so many peculiar facets to their personality. We know about the Florentines of old, their fascination with mathematics and technology, and their matchless talent for art, and we know about the foppish prancing Florentine courtiers of the decadent 1600s. But more up-to-date models are not entirely without interest. Florentines are famous for their dry wit, and their penny-pinching economy, a talent for making a little go a long way. Their tenaciously conservative *dov'era com'era* mentality towards their museum city-home is extreme even by Italian standards. And a redeeming share of their old Renaissance craftsmanship remains, an attention to detail that makes them skilled seamstresses and the best art restorers in the world.

The refinement, as well as the arrogance and conceit, are one side of the coin; on the other we find a surprising streak of down-to-earth hillbilly cussedness. Florentines and the rest of the Tuscans are after all dismissed as *mangiafagioli*, 'beaneaters', by other Italians. According to one perceptive observer, all the shortcomings of the Florentines are due to a diet of too much beans, tripe and cockscombs—the very mention of these conjures up the uneasy shade of the bloated, horrible Catherine de' Medici up in Paris, gorging herself on cockscombs and puking all over the Louvre.

For all these singular qualities, it is surprising that Florentines hardly ever make it into literature; it's hard to imagine a novel that could not be improved by giving a Florentine a small role. The only interesting one we have been able to find is the star of a fairy-tale heard in Pisa, one of those transcribed by Italo Calvino in his wonderful collection *Italian Folktales*. It seems there was this Florentine who had never in his entire life left Florence. Unable to talk knowledgeably about the comings and goings of the wide world, he felt at a loss in polite conversation, and finally he resolved to go out and do some travelling. He packed his bags and hit the road, in no particular direction, and along the way he met first a priest and then a farmer, both of whom felt the same way about their own lives and decided to join the Florentine as travelling companions. Eventually the three of them came to the house of a giant. The Florentine thought they should go and knock on the door, so that he could tell the folks back home about meeting a giant, and when they did they found the giant a rather courteous fellow who had need of a priest for his village church, and a farmer for his farm. He couldn't think of any particular use for a Florentine, but he took him in too.

Now, in fact this giant's courtesy was but a devious façade concealing a giant-size black-hearted stinker. He took the priest aside, supposedly to show him his duties, but once the door was closed he whacked off his head and kicked the corpse through a trap door. He did the same to the farmer—but the Florentine was watching through the keyhole this time, as Florentines will do, and while he was pretty excited about the story he would have to entertain folks back home, it dawned on him that he would most certainly be next. At this point the storyteller, for lack of something better, gives the tale a turn straight from Homer (remember Odysseus and the Cyclops?). The giant had a squinty eye, and the Florentine had the presence of mind to tell him that he could cure it with a decoction made from a certain herb, which he had noticed growing in those parts. The giant was delighted to let him try, and the Florentine tied him to a marble table and poured the boiling mess into both his eyes. Now comes the chase scene, but the blinded giant couldn't very well catch a Florentine with a marble table tied to his back, and he tried to trick him by offering him his gold ring to finish the cure for his eyes. This was a magic ring, unfortunately, and when the poor guy put it on, his finger became as heavy as stone and weighed him to the ground. The Florentine couldn't get it off again (because it was a magic ring, remember), but he saved himself by chopping off the finger with a penknife. He made it home to Florence, finally, but he never bothered to tell anyone about his wonderful adventures, and whenever anyone asked him about the finger he said he'd had an accident while cutting the grass.

The First Tuscans

Up in Rome's Capitoline Museum you can see the famous bronze statue of the she-wolf suckling Romulus and Remus, the symbol of Rome since ancient times. Not many people know that this was actually not the work of a Roman artist, but an Etruscan. There are plenty of other things they never taught you in school about the Romans. Specifically, nearly every art or talent we usually give them credit for was bought or more likely stolen from somebody else. Roman painting, sculpture and architecture were seldom more than a grandiose pastiche of the Greek, and plenty of the other Roman trademarks—religion and superstition, gladiators, rectilinear surveying and town planning, portrait sculpture, sewers, togas and even concrete—were simply taken over whole from Rome's nearest neighbours and favourite victims, the Etruscans.

We often forget that long before Brunelleschi and Donatello, Tuscany was home to another great civilization—Italy's first. But when Rome was still a collection of mud and timber huts among the miasmal swamps of the Tiber, the people of Etruria were collecting Greek urns, reclining on couches at their lavish banquets, and dressing up for the races. Etruscan culture blossomed in the 8th century for the usual reasons—most importantly, a nice surplus of ready cash. Just as classical Athens's rise to prominence was financed by the silver mines at nearby Laurion, Etruria exploited the mineral wealth of the Colline Metallifere and Elba; there was plenty of iron, especially, for weapons and for exports. Cities grew opulent as trade boomed, and to protect their trade routes the cities developed powerful navies that dominated the Etruscan *mare nostrum*, the Tyrrhenian (so named because the Greeks called this people *Tyrrhenoi*; to the Romans they were *Tuscii* or *Etruscii*, while in their own language they are properly called the *Rasena*).

The overwhelming impression given by painting and sculpture is of a people, whatever their flaws, who were wonderfully alive. Etruscan art is full of expressive faces that either wear a smile, or are blissfully caught on the verge of breaking into one. Some of the jolly sculptures in the museums of Volterra and Rome must rank among the first conscious caricatures in art. Everything about this art paints a picture, true or not, of a people cheerfully devoted to the joys of this world. Indeed, their contemporaries dropped plenty of gossip about Etruscan hedonism and licentiousness (much of this comes from the devoutly male-chauvinist Greeks and Romans, shocked at a society where women seem to have enjoyed considerable rights and respect).

In any case, it would be difficult to find anyone in antiquity more fashion-conscious. Elaborately carved mirrors and make-up cases constitute a large part of the Etruscan collection in any museum, and the evidence from tomb frescoes suggests the ladies also liked to dye their hair blonde. The jewellery is remarkable—as good as anything between the Minoans and Fabergé. Some of it goes completely over the top, filigree work and granulation so ornate and flashy it could be worn in Las Vegas. Or whatever was the Etrurian equivalent thereof—after considering the Etruscans closely you'll begin to suspect they must have had one somewhere (perhaps Tuscany's thermal spas; the Etruscans, celebrated for their medical skills, were the first to develop these, and passed the habit down to the Romans). Coiffures and clothes could be equally elaborate; in art you will hardly ever find two Etruscan ladies with the same hairdo. Then, as now, Tuscan shoemakers were famous around the known world; the fashions of the 5th century, as shown in frescoes, featured pointed, curling toes.

Another of their talents was music; Etruscans are often pictured dancing or playing the trumpet, the lyre, and, most commonly of all, a type of pan-pipes. According to a Hellenistic Greek account, they even used music in their hunting; pipers would play charmed melodies to draw the animals out of their lairs and towards the nets. Such a story is not surprising, considering another essential Etruscan trait, an attachment to magic and fortune telling unsurpassed in the ancient world. Etruscan augurs, or *haruspices*, scrutinized the livers of sacrificed animals and scanned the skies for birds to fortell the future. Their skill was so great that *haruspices* were still employed around the Roman Empire in the 4th-century AD, the last people on earth who understood the Etruscan language.

Nobody knows quite why, but after 500 BC everything started to fall apart for the Etruscans. Manufacture and art declined, slave revolts recame common, and the archaeologists report that everything from tombs to pottery were being made less skilfully, more cheaply. The once-formidable Etruscan navy was getting regularly whipped by the Greeks, while the Celts destroyed the colonies in the north that had been built up with so much painstaking effort for so long. Most dire of all were the Romans. Rome's closest Etruscan neighbours, Fidenae and Veii, were captured and wiped out in 425 and 396. Veii suffered an epic siege of ten years, and typically, during that time none of the other Etruscan cities did much to help. Chronic disunity among the members of the Dodecapolis allowed Rome to gobble up Etruria a bit at a time. The last important city, Volsinii, fell about 350, and from then on Etruria was nothing more than a Roman province—the first of many.

But the cultural heritage of these gifted people was too great to disappear completely. The Romans, as we have seen, swallowed Etruscan culture whole, and they passed quite a bit of it on to us. Hundreds of words in modern languages probably stem from the Etruscan, by way of Latin: *person*, for example, which originally meant an Etruscan theatre or ritual mask, or *temple* (this meant one of the 16 sections into which the Etruscan augurs divided the sky for divination by birdflight).

The Etruscan influence on the art of the Renaissance is a fascinating subject that has never been thoroughly explored. When medieval Tuscans revived the art of fresco painting, they probably had no idea they were simply following in the footsteps of their ancestors. Raymond Bloch, an authority on the Etruscans, noticed an eerily perfect resemblance between Donatello's famous *St George*, the very model of quattrocento *prontezza*, and an Etruscan head found long ago at Veii. In one of Michelangelo's sketchbooks we see an image of the Etruscan god Atia, undoubtedly copied from the frescoes in a tomb. And all those little faces we see staring out at us from Renaissance sculptural friezes, frescoes and book decorations are called 'grotesques', because Raphael found their originals in a painted 'grotto' in Rome. This was really a floor of buried rooms of Emperor Nero's palace, the famous Golden House, decorated in a style inherited from the Etruscans of old.

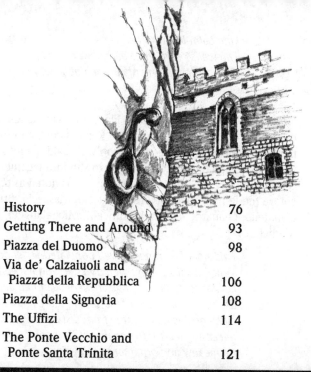

Florence

Fine balm let Arno be;
The walls of Florence all of silver rear'd,
And crystal pavements in the public way . . .

a 14th-century madrigal by Lapo Gianni

'Magari!'—If only!—the modern Florentine would add to this vision, to this city of art and birthplace of the Renaissance, built by bankers and merchants whose sole preoccupation was making more florins. The precocious capital of Tuscany began to slip into legend back in the 14th century, during the lifetime of Dante; it was noted as *different* even before the Renaissance, before Boccaccio, Masaccio, Brunelleschi, Donatello, Leonardo da Vinci, Botticelli, Michelangelo, Machiavelli, the Medici . . .

> *This city of Florence is well populated, its good air a healthy tonic; its citizens are well dressed, and its women lovely and fashionable, its buildings are very beautiful, and every sort of useful craft is carried on in them, more so than any other Italian city. For this many come from distant lands to see her, not out of necessity, but for the quality of its manufactures and arts, and for the beauty and ornament of the city.*

Dino Compagni in his Chronicle of 1312

According to the tourist office, in 1993, 81 years after Dino, a grand total of over 2,300,000 Americans, Germans, French, Britons (the top four groups) as well as Spanish, Brazilians, Egyptians, and some 800,000 Italians spent at least one night in a Florentine hotel. Some, perhaps, had orthodontist appointments. A large percentage of the others came to inhale the rarefied air of the cradle of Western civilization, to gaze at some of the loveliest things made by mortal hands and minds, to walk the streets of new Athens, the great humanist 'city built to the measure of man'. Calling Florence's visitors 'tourists', however, doesn't seem quite right; 'tourism' implies pleasure, a principle alien to this dour, intellectual, measured town; 'pilgrims' is perhaps the better word, cultural pilgrims who throng the Uffizi, the Accademia, the Bargello to gaze upon the holy mysteries of our secular society, to buy postcards and replicas, the holy cards of our day.

Someone wrote a warning on a wall near Brunelleschi's Santo Spirito, in the Oltrarno: *'Turista con mappa/alla caccia del tesoro/ per finire davanti ad un piatto/ di spaghetti al pomodoro'* (Tourist with a map, on a treasure hunt, only to end up in front of a plate of spaghetti with tomato sauce). Unless you come with the right attitude, Florence can be as disenchanting as cold spaghetti. It only blossoms if you apply your mind as well as your vision, if you go slowly and do not let the art bedazzle until your eyes glaze over in dizzy excess (a common complaint, known in medical circles as the Stendhal syndrome). Realize that loving and hating Florence at the same time may be the only rational response. It is the capital of contradiction; you begin to like it because it goes out of its way to annoy.

Florentine Schizophrenia

Dante's *Vita Nuova*, the autobiography of his young soul, was only the beginning of Florentine analysis; Petrarch, the introspective 'first modern man', was a Florentine born in exile; Ghiberti was the first artist to write an autobiography, Cellini wrote one of the most readable; Alberti invented art criticism; Vasari invented art history; Michelangelo's personality, in his letters and sonnets, looms as large as his art. In many ways Florence broke away from the medieval idea of community and invented the modern concept of the individual, most famously expressed by Lorenzo de' Medici's friend, Pico della Mirandola, whose *Oration on the Dignity of Man* tells us what the God on the Sistine Chapel ceiling was saying when he created Adam: '... And I have created you neither celestial nor terrestrial, neither mortal nor immortal, so that, like a free and able sculptor and painter of yourself, you may mould yourself entirely in the form of your choice.'

To attempt to understand Florence, remember one historical constant: no matter what the issue, the city always takes both sides, vehemently and often violently, especially in the Punch and Judy days of Guelphs and Ghibellines. In the 1300s this was explained by the fact that the city was founded under the sign of Mars, the war god; but in medieval astronomy Mars is also connected with Aries, another Florentine symbol and the time of spring blossoms. (The Annunciation, at the beginning of spring, was Florence's most important festival.) One of the city's oldest symbols is the lily (or iris), flying on its oldest gonfalons. Perhaps even older is its *marzocco*, originally an equestrian statue of Mars on the Ponte Vecchio, later replaced by Donatello's grim lion.

Whatever dispute rocked the streets, Great Aunt Florence often expressed her schizophrenia in art, floral Florence versus stone Florence, epitomized by the irreconcilable differences between the two most famous works of art in the city: Botticelli's graceful, enigmatic *Primavera* and Michelangelo's cold perfect *David*. The 'city of flowers' seems a joke; it has nary a real flower, nor even a tree, in its stone streets; indeed, all effort has gone into keeping nature at bay, surpassing it with geometry and art. And yet the Florentines were perhaps the first since the Romans to discover the joys of the country-side. The rough, rusticated stone palaces, like fortresses or prisons, hide charms as delightful as Gozzoli's frescoes in the Palazzo Medici. Luca della Robbia's dancing children and floral wreaths are contemporary with the naked, violent warriors of the Pollaiuolo brothers; the writhing, quarrelsome statuary in the Piazza della Signoria is sheltered by the most delicate and beautiful loggia imaginable.

After 1500, all of the good, bad and ugly symptoms of the Renaissance peaked in the mass fever of Mannerism. Then, drifting into a debilitating twilight of *pietra dura* tables, gold gimcracks, and interior decoration, Florence gave birth to the artistic phenomenon known as kitsch—the Medici Princes' chapel is an early kitsch classic, still one of the heaviest baubles in the solar system. Since then, worn out perhaps, or embarrassed, this city built by merchants has kept its own counsel, expressing its argumentative soul in overblown controversies about traffic, art restoration, and the undesirability of fast-food counters and cheap pensions. We who find her fascinating hope she some day comes to remember her proper role, bearing the torch of culture instead of merely collecting tickets for the culture torture.

History

The identity of Florence's first inhabitants is a matter of dispute. There seems to have been some kind of settlement along the Arno long before the Roman era, perhaps as early as 1000 BC; the original founders may have been either native Italics or Etruscans. Throughout the period of Etruscan dominance, the village on the river lived in the shadow of *Faesulae*—Florence's present-day suburb of Fiesole was then an important city, the northernmost member of the Etruscan Dodecapolis. The Arno river cuts across central Italy like a wall. This narrow stretch of it, close to the mountain pass over to Emilia, was always the most logical place for a bridge.

Roman Florence can claim no less a figure than **Julius Caesar** for its founder. Like so many other Italian cities, the city began as a planned urban enterprise in an under-developed province; Caesar started it as a colony for his army veterans in 59 BC. The origin of the name—so suggestive of springtime and flowers—is another mystery. First it was *Florentia*, then *Fiorenza* in the Middle Ages, and finally *Firenze*. One guess is that its foundation took place in April, when the Romans were celebrating the games of the Floralia.

The original street plan of *Florentia* can be seen today in the neat rectangle of blocks between Via Tornabuoni and Via del Proconsolo, between the Duomo and Piazza della Signoria. Its Forum occupied roughly the site of the modern Piazza della Repubblica, and the outline of its amphitheatre can be traced in the oval of streets just west of Piazza Santa Croce. Roman *Florentia* never really imposed itself on the historian. One writer mentions it as a *municipia splendidissima*, a major town and river crossing along the Via Cassia, connected to Rome and the thriving new cities of northern Italy, such as Bononia and Mediolanum (Bologna and Milan). At the height of Empire, the municipal boundaries had expanded out to Via de' Fossi, Via S. Egidio, and Via de' Benci. Nevertheless, Florentia did not play a significant role either in the Empire's heyday or in its decline.

After the fall of Rome, Florence weathered its troubles comparatively well. We hear of it withstanding sieges by the Goths around the year 400, when it was defended by the famous imperial general Stilicho, and again in 541, during the campaigns of Totila and Belisarius; all through the Greek–Gothic wars Florence seems to have taken the side of Constantinople. The Lombards arrived around 570; under their rule Florence was the seat of a duchy subject to the then Tuscan capital of Lucca. The next mention in the chronicles refers to Charlemagne spending Christmas with the Florentines in the year 786. Like the rest of Italy, Florence had undoubtedly declined; a new set of walls went up under Carolingian rule, about 800, enclosing an area scarcely larger than the original Roman settlement of 59 BC. In such times Florence was lucky to be around at all; most likely throughout the Dark Ages the city was gradually increasing its relative importance and strength at the expense of its neighbours. The famous Baptistry, erected some time between the 6th and 9th centuries, is the only important building from that troubled age in all Tuscany.

By the 1100s, Florence was the leading city of the County of Tuscany. **Countess Matilda**, ally of Pope Gregory VII against the emperors, oversaw the construction of a new set of walls in 1078, this time coinciding with the widest Roman-era boundaries. Already the city had recovered all the ground lost during the Dark Ages, and the momentum of growth did not abate. New walls were needed again in the 1170s, to enclose what was becoming one of the largest cities in Europe. In this period, Florence owed its growth and prosperity largely to the textile industry—weaving and 'finishing' cloth not only from Tuscany but wool shipped from as far afield as Spain and England. The capital gain from this trade, managed by the *Calimala* and the *Arte della Lana*, Florence's richest guilds, led naturally to an even more profitable business—banking and finance.

The Florentine Republic Battles with the Barons

In 1125, Florence once and for all conquered its ancient rival Fiesole. Wealth and influence brought with them increasing political responsibilities. Externally the city often found itself at war with one or other of its neighbours. Since Countess Matilda's death in 1115, Florence had become a self-governing *comune*, largely independent of the emperor and local barons. The new city republic's hardest problems, however, were closer to home. The nobles of the county, encouraged in their anachronistic feudal behaviour by the representatives of the imperial government, proved irreconcilable enemies to the new merchant republic, and Florence spent most of the 12th century trying to keep them in line. Often the city actually declared war on a noble clan, as with the Alberti, or the Counts of Guidi, and razed their castles whenever they captured one. To complicate the situation, nobles attracted by the stimulation of urban life—not to mention the opportunities for making money there—often moved their entire families into Florence itself. They brought their country habits with them, a boyish eagerness to brawl with their neighbours on the slightest pretext, and a complete disregard for the laws of the *comune*. Naturally, they couldn't feel secure without a little urban castle of their own, and before long Florence, like any prosperous Italian city of the Middle Ages, featured a remarkable skyline of hundreds of tower-fortresses, built as much for status as for defence. Many were over 60m in height. It wasn't uncommon for the honest citizen to come home from a hard day's work at the bank, hoping for a little peace and quiet, only to find siege engines parked in front of the house and a company of bowmen commandeering the children's bedroom.

But just as Florence was able to break the power of the rural nobles, those in the town also eventually had to succumb. The last tower-fortresses were chopped down to size in the early 1300s. But even without the nobles, the Florentines found new ways to keep the pot boiling. The rich merchants who dominated the government, familiarly known as the *popolari grossi*, resorted to every sort of murder and mayhem to beat down the demands of the lesser guilds, the *popolari minuti*, for a fair share of the wealth; the two only managed to settle their differences when confronted by murmurs of discontent from what was then one of Europe's largest urban proletariats. But even beyond simple class issues, the city born under the sign of Mars always found a way to make trouble for itself. Not only did Florentines pursue the Guelph–Ghibelline conflict with greater zest than almost any Tuscan city; according to the chronicles of the time, they actually started it. In 1215, men of the Amidei family murdered a prominent citizen named Buondelmonte de' Buondelmonti over a broken engagement, the spark that touched off the factionalist struggles first in Florence, then quickly throughout Italy.

Guelphs and Ghibellines

In 13th-century Florence, there was never a dull moment. Guelphs and Ghibellines, often more involved with some feud between noble families than with real political issues, cast each other into exile and confiscated each other's property with every change of the wind. Religious strife occasionally pushed politics off the front page. In the 1240s, a curious foreshadowing of the Reformation saw Florence wrapped up in the **Patarene heresy**. This sect, closely related to the Albigensians of southern France, was as obsessed with the presence of Evil in the world as John Calvin—or Florence's own future fire-and-brimstone preacher, Savonarola. Exploiting a streak of religious eccentricity that has always seemed to be present in the Florentine psyche, the Patarenes thrived in the city, even electing their own bishop. The established Church was up to the challenge; St Peter Martyr, a bloodthirsty Dominican, led his armies of axe-wielding monks to the assault in 1244, exterminating almost the entire Patarene community.

In 1248, with help from Emperor Frederick II, Florence's Ghibellines booted out the Guelphs—once and for all, they thought, but two years later the Guelphs were back, and it was the Ghibellines' turn to pack their grips. The new Guelph regime, called the *primo popolo*, was for the first time completely in the control of the bankers and merchants. It passed the first measures to control the privileges of the turbulent, largely Ghibelline nobles, and forced them all to chop the tops off their tower-fortresses. The next decades witnessed a series of wars with the Ghibelline cities of Tuscany—Siena, Pisa and Pistoia, not just by coincidence Florence's habitual enemies. Usually the Florentines were the aggressors, and more often than not fortune favoured them. In 1260, however, the Sienese, reinforced by Ghibelline exiles from Florence and a few imperial cavalry, destroyed an invading Florentine army at the **Battle of Monteaperti**. Florence was temporarily at the Ghibellines' mercy. Only the refusal of Farinata degli Uberti, leader of the exiles, to allow the city's destruction kept the Sienese from putting it to the torch—a famous episode recounted by Dante in the *Inferno*. (In a typical Florentine gesture of thanks, Dante found a home for Uberti in one of the lower circles of hell.)

In Florence, a Ghibelline regime under Count Guido Novello made life rough for the wealthy Guelph bourgeoisie. As luck would have it, though, only a few years later the Guelphs were back in power, and Florence was winning on the battlefield once again. The new Guelph government, the *secondo popolo*, earned a brief respite from factional strife. In 1289, Florence won a great victory over another old rival, Arezzo. This was the **Battle of Campaldino**, where the Florentine citizen army included young Dante Alighieri. In 1282, and again in 1293, Florence tried to clean up an increasingly corrupt government with a series of reforms. The 1293 *Ordinamenti della Giustizia* once and for all excluded the nobles from important political offices. By now, however, the real threat to the Guelph merchants' rule came not so much from the nobility, which had been steadily falling behind in wealth and power for two centuries, but from the lesser guilds, which had been completely excluded from a share of power, and from the growing working class employed in the textile mills and foundries.

Despite all the troubles, the city's wealth and population grew tremendously throughout the 1200s. Its trade contacts spread across Europe, and crowned heads from London to Constantinople found Florentine bankers ready to float them a loan. About 1235 Florence minted modern Europe's first gold coin, the *florin*, which soon became a standard currency across the continent. By 1300 Florence counted over 100,000 souls—a little cramped, even inside the vast new circuit of walls built by the *comune* in the 1280s. It was not only one of the largest cities in Europe, but certainly one of the richest. Besides banking, the wool trade was also booming: by 1300 the wool guild, the *Arte della Lana*, had over 200 large workshops in the city alone.

Naturally, this new opulence created new possibilities for culture and art. Florence's golden age began perhaps in the 1290s, when the *comune* started its tremendous programme of public buildings—including the Palazzo della Signoria and the cathedral; important religious structures, such as Santa Croce, were under way at the same time. Cimabue was the artist of the day; Giotto was just beginning, and his friend Dante was hard at work on the *Commedia*.

As in so many other Italian cities, Florence had been developing its republican institutions slowly and painfully. At the beginning of the *comune* in 1115, the leaders were a class called the *boni homines*, made up mostly of nobles. Only a few decades later, these were calling themselves *consules*, evoking a memory of the ancient Roman republic. When the Ghibellines took over, the leading official was a *podestà* appointed by the Emperor. Later, under the Guelphs, the *podestà* and a new officer called the *capitano del popolo* were both elected by the citizens. With the reforms of the 1290s Florence's republican constitution was perfected—if that is the proper word for an arrangement that satisfied few citizens and guaranteed lots of trouble for the future. Under the new dispensation, power was invested in the council of the richer guilds, the *Signoria*; the new

Palazzo della Signoria was designed expressly as a symbol of their authority, replacing the old Bargello, which had been the seat of the *podestà*. The most novel feature of the government, designed to overcome Florence's past incapacity to avoid violent factionalism, was the selection of officials by lot from among the guild members. In effect, politics was to be abolished.

Business as Usual: Riot, War, Plagues and Revolution

Despite the reforms of the *Ordinamenti*, Florence found little peace in the new century. As if following some strange and immutable law of city-state behaviour, no sooner had the Guelphs established total control than they themselves split into new factions. The radically anti-imperial **Blacks** and the more conciliatory **Whites** fought each other through the early 1300s with the same fervour they both had once exercised against the Ghibellines. The Whites, who included Dante among their partisans, came out losers when the Blacks conspired with the pope to bring Charles of Valois' French army into Florence; almost all of the losing faction were forced into exile in 1302. Some of them must have sneaked back, for the chronicles of 1304 record the Blacks trying to burn them out of their houses with incendiary bombs, resulting in a fire that consumed a quarter of the city.

Beginning in 1313, Florence was involved in an almost constant series of inconclusive wars with Pisa, Lucca and Arezzo, among others. In 1325, the city was defeated and nearly destroyed by the great Lucchese general **Castruccio Castracani Lucca** p. 245). Castruccio died of a common cold while the siege was already under way, another example of Florence's famous good luck, but unfortunately one of the last. The factions may have been suppressed, but fate had found some more novel disasters for the city. One far-off monarch did more damage to Florence than its Italian enemies had ever managed— King Edward III of England, who in 1339 found it expedient to repudiate his foreign debts. Florence's two biggest banks, the Bardi and the Peruzzi, immediately went bust, and the city's standing as the centre of international finance was gravely damaged.

If anything was constant throughout the history of the republic, it was the oppression of the poor. The ruling bankers and merchants exploited their labour and gave only the bare minimum in return. In the 14th century, overcrowding, undernourishment and plenty of rats made Florence's poorer neighbourhoods a perfect breeding ground for epidemics. Famine, plagues and riots became common in the 1340s, causing a severe political crisis. At one point, in 1342, the Florentines gave over their government to a foreign dictator, Walter de Brienne, the French–Greek 'Duke of Athens'. He lasted only a year before a popular revolt ended the experiment. The **Black Death** of 1348, the background for Boccaccio's *Decameron*, carried off perhaps one half of the population. Coming on the heels of a serious depression, it was a blow from which Florence would never really recover.

In the coming two centuries, when the city was to be the great innovator in western culture, it was already in relative decline, a politically decadent republic with a stagnant economy, barely holding its own among the turbulent changes in trade and diplomacy. For the time being, though, things didn't look too bad. Florence found enough ready cash to buy control of Prato, in 1350, and was successful in a defensive war against expansionist Milan in 1351. Warfare was almost continuous for the last half of the century, a strain on the exchequer but not usually a threat to the city's survival; this was the heyday of the mercenary companies, led by famous *condottieri* like **Sir John Hawkwood** (Giovanni Acuto), immortalized by the equestrian 'statue' in Florence's cathedral. Before the Florentines made him a better offer, Hawkwood was often in the employ of their enemies.

Throughout the century, the Guelph party had been steadily tightening its grip over the republic's affairs. Despite the selection of officials by lot, by the 1370s the party organization bore an uncanny resemblance to some of the big-city political machines common not so long ago in America. The merchants and the bankers who ran the party used it to turn the Florentine Republic into a profit-making business. With the increasingly limited opportunities for making money in trade and finance, the Guelph ruling class tried to make up the difference by soaking the poor. Wars and taxes stretched Florentine tolerance to breaking point, and finally, in 1378, came revolution. The **Ciompi Revolt** (*ciompi*— wage labourers in the textile industries) began in July, when a mob of workers seized the Bargello. Under the leadership of a wool-carder named Michele di Lando, they executed a few of the Guelph bosses and announced a new, reformed constitution. They were also foolish enough to believe the Guelph magnates when they promised to abide by the new arrangement if only the *ciompi* would go home. Before long di Lando was in exile, and the ruling class firmly back in the seat of power, more than ever determined to eliminate the last vestiges of democracy from the republic.

The Rise of the Medici

Medici - coat of arms

In 1393, Florentines celebrated the 100th anniversary of the great reform of the *Ordinamenti*, while watching their republic descend irresistibly into oligarchy. In that year **Maso degli Albizzi** became *gonfaloniere* (the head of the *Signoria*) and served as virtual dictator for many years afterwards. The ruling class of merchants, more than a bit paranoid after the Ciompi revolt, were generally relieved to see power concentrated in strong hands; the ascendancy of the Albizzi family was to set the pattern for the rest of the republic's existence. In a poisoned atmosphere of repression and conspiracy, the spies of the Signoria's new secret police hunted down malcontents while whole legions of Florentine exiles plotted against the republic in foreign courts. Florence was almost constantly at war. In 1398 she defeated an attempt at conquest by Giangaleazzo Visconti of Milan. The imperialist policy of the Albizzi and their allies resulted in important territorial gains, including the conquest of Pisa in 1406, and the purchase of Livorno from the Genoese in 1421. Unsuccessful wars against Lucca finally disenchanted the Florentines with Albizzi rule. An emergency *parlamento* (the infrequent popular assembly usually called when a coming change of rulers was obvious) in 1434 decreed the recall from exile of the head of the popular opposition, **Cosimo de' Medici**. Perhaps it was something that could only have happened in Florence—the darling of the plebeians, the great hope for reform, happened to be the head of Florence's biggest bank. The Medici family had their roots in the Mugello region north of Florence. Their name seems to suggest they once were pharmacists (later enemies would jibe at the balls on the family arms as 'the pills'). For two centuries they had been active in Florentine politics; many had acquired reputations as troublemakers; their names turned up often in the lists of exiles and records of lawsuits. None of the Medici had ever been particularly rich until **Giovanni di Bicci de' Medici** (1360–1429) parlayed his wife's dowry into the founding of a bank. Good fortune—and a temporary monopoly on the handling of the pope's finances—made the Medici Bank Florence's biggest.

Giovanni had been content to stay on the fringe of politics; his son, Cosimo (known in Florentine history as 'il Vecchio', the 'old man') took good care of the bank's affairs but aimed his sights much higher. His strategy was as old as Julius Caesar—the patrician reformer, cultivating the best men, winning the favour of the poor with largesse and gradually, carefully forming a party under a system specifically designed to prevent such things. In 1433 Rinaldo degli Albizzi had him exiled, but too late; continuing discontent forced his return only a year later, and for the next 35 years Cosimo would be the unchallenged ruler of Florence. Throughout this period, Cosimo occasionally held public office—this was done by lottery, with the electoral lists manipulated to ensure a majority of Medici supporters at all times. Nevertheless, he received ambassadors at the new family palace (built in 1444), entertained visiting popes and emperors, and made all the important decisions. A canny political godfather and usually a gentleman, Cosimo also proved a useful patron to the great figures of the early Renaissance—Donatello and Brunelleschi, among others. His father had served as one of the judges in the famous competition for the baptistry doors, and Cosimo was a member of the commission that picked Brunelleschi to design the cathedral dome.

Cosimo did oversee some genuine reforms; under his leadership Florence began Europe's first progressive income tax, and a few years later the state invented the modern concept of the national debt—endlessly rolling over bonds to keep the republic afloat and the creditors happy. The poor, with fewer taxes to pay, were also happy, and the ruling classes, after some initial distaste, were positively delighted; never in Florence's history had any government so successfully muted class conflict and the desire for a genuine democracy. Wars were few, and the internal friction negligible. Cosimo died in August 1464; his tomb in San Lorenzo bears the inscription *Pater patriae,* and no dissent was registered when his 40-year-old son **Piero** took up the boss's role.

Lorenzo the Magnificent

Piero didn't quite have the touch of his masterful father, but he survived a stiff political crisis in 1466, outmanoeuvring a new faction led by wealthy banker Luca Pitti. In 1469 he succumbed to the Medici family disease, the gout, and his 20-year-old son **Lorenzo** succeeded him in an equally smooth transition. He was to last for 23 years. Not necessarily more 'magnificent' than other contemporary princes, or other Medici, Lorenzo's honorific reveals something of the myth that was to grow up around him in later centuries. His long reign corresponded to the height of the Florentine Renaissance. It was a relatively peaceful time, and in the light of the disasters that were to follow, Florentines could not help looking back on it as a golden age.

As a ruler, Lorenzo showed many virtues. Still keeping up the pretence of living as a private citizen, he lived relatively simply, always accessible to the voices and concerns of his fellow citizens, who would often see him walking the city streets. In the field of foreign policy he was indispensable to Florence and indeed all Italy; he did more than anyone to keep the precarious peninsular balance of power from disintegrating. The most dramatic affair of his reign was the **Pazzi conspiracy**, an attempt to assassinate Lorenzo plotted by Pope Sixtus IV and the wealthy Pazzi family, the pope's bankers and ancient rivals of the Medici. In 1478, two of the younger Pazzi attacked Lorenzo and his brother Giuliano during mass at the cathedral. Giuliano was killed, but Lorenzo managed to escape into the sacristy. The botched murder aborted the planned revolt; Florentines showed little interest in the Pazzis' call to arms, and before nightfall most of the conspirators were dangling from the cornice of the Palazzo Vecchio.

Lorenzo de' Medici (dalla Primavera di Botticelli)

Apparently, Lorenzo had angered the pope by starting a syndicate to mine for alum in Volterra, threatening the papal monopoly. Since Sixtus failed to murder Lorenzo, he had to settle for excommunicating him, and declaring war in alliance with King Ferrante of Naples. The war went badly for Florence and, in the most memorable act of his career, Lorenzo walked into the lion's cage, travelling to negotiate with the terrible Neapolitan, who had already murdered more than one important guest. As it turned out, Ferrante was only too happy to dump his papal entanglements; Florence found itself at peace once more, and Lorenzo returned home to a hero's welcome.

In other affairs, both foreign and domestic, Lorenzo was more a lucky ruler than a skilled one. Florence's economy was entering a long, slow decline, but for the moment the banks and mills were churning out just enough profit to keep up the accustomed level of opulence. The Medici Bank, unfortunately, was on the ropes. Partly because of Lorenzo's neglect, the bank came close to collapsing on several occasions—it seems Lorenzo made up the losses with public funds. Culturally, he was fortunate to be nabob of Florence at its most artistically creative period; future historians and Medici propagandists gave him a reputation as an art patron that is entirely undeserved. His own tastes tended towards bric-a-brac, jewellery, antique statues and vases; there is little evidence that he really understood or appreciated the scores of great artists around him. Perhaps because he was too nearsighted to see anything clearly, he never commissioned an important canvas or fresco in Florence (except for Luca Signorelli's mysterious *Pan*, lost in Berlin during the last war). His favourite architect was the hack Giuliano da Sangallo.

The Medici had taken great care with Lorenzo's education; he was brought up with some of the leading humanist scholars of Tuscany for tutors and his real interests were literary. His well-formed lyrics and winsome pastorals have earned him a place among Italy's greatest 15th-century poets; they neatly reflect the private side of Lorenzo, the retiring, scholarly family man who enjoyed life better on one of the many rural Medici estates than in the busy city. In this, he was perfectly in tune with his class and his age. Plenty of Florentine bankers were learning the joys of country life, reading Horace or Catullus in their geometrical gardens and pestering their tenant farmers with well-meant advice.

Back in town, they had thick new walls of rusticated sandstone between them and the bustle of the streets. The late 15th century was the great age of palace building in Florence. Following the example of Cosimo de' Medici, the bankers and merchants erected dozens of palaces (some of the best can be seen around Via Tornabuoni). Each one turns blank walls and iron-barred windows to the street. Historians always note one very pronounced phenomenon of this period—a turning inward, a 'privatization' of Florentine life. In a city that had become a republic only in name, civic interest and public life ceased to matter so much. The very rich began to assume the airs of an aristocracy, and did everything they could to distance themselves from their fellow citizens. Ironically, just at the time when Florence's artists were creating their greatest achievements, the republican ethos, the civic soul that had made Florence great, began to disintegrate.

Savonarola

Lorenzo's death, in 1492, was followed by another apparently smooth transition of power to his son Piero. But after 58 years of Medicean quiet and stability, the city was ready for a change. The opportunity for the malcontents came soon enough, when the timid and inept Piero allowed the invading King of France, **Charles VIII**, to occupy Pisa and the Tuscan coast. A spontaneous revolt chased Piero and the rest of the Medici into exile, while a mob sacked the family's palace. A new regime, hastily put together under Piero Capponi, dealt more sternly with the French (*see* p. 110) and tried to pump some new life into the long-dormant republican constitution.

The Florence that threw out the Medici was a city in the mood for some radical reform. Already, the dominating figure on the political stage was an intense Dominican friar from Ferrara named **Girolamo Savonarola**. Perhaps not surprisingly, this oversophisticated and overstimulated city was also in the mood to be told how wicked and decadent it was, and Savonarola was happy to oblige. A spellbinding revival preacher with a touch of erudition, Savonarola packed as many as 10,000 into the Duomo to hear his weekly sermons, laced with political sarcasm and social criticism. Though an insufferable prig, he was also a sincere democrat. There is a story that the dying Lorenzo called Savonarola to his bedside for the last rites, and that the friar refused him absolution unless he 'restored the liberty of the Florentines', a proposal that only made the dying despot sneer with contempt.

Savonarola also talked Charles VIII into leaving Florence in peace. Pisa, however, took advantage of the confusion to revolt, and the restored republic's attempts to recapture it were in vain. Things were going badly. Piero Capponi's death in 1496 left Florence without a really able leader, and Savonarolan extremists became ever more influential. The French invasion and the incessant wars that followed cost the city dearly in trade, while the Medici, now in Rome, intrigued endlessly to destroy the republic. Worst of all,

Savonarola's attacks on clerical corruption made him another bitter enemy in Rome—none other than Pope Alexander VI himself, the most corrupt cleric who ever lived. The Borgia Pope scraped together a league of allies to make war on Florence in 1497.

This war proceeded without serious reverses for either side, but Savonarola was able to exploit it brilliantly, convincing the Florentines that they were on a moral crusade against the hated and dissolute Borgias, Medici, French, Venetians and Milanese. 1497 was undoubtedly the high point of Savonarola's career. The good friar's spies—mostly children—kept a close eye on any Florentines suspected of enjoying themselves, and collected books, fancy clothes and works of art for the famous **Bonfire of Vanities**. It was a climactic moment in the history of Florence's delicate psyche. Somehow the spell had been broken; like the deranged old Michelangelo, taking a hammer to his own work, the Florentines gathered the objects that had once been their greatest pride and put them to the torch. The bonfire was held in the centre of the Piazza della Signoria; a visiting Venetian offered to buy the whole lot, but the Florentines had someone hastily sketch his portrait and threw that on the flames, too.

One vanity the Florentines could not quite bring themselves to part with was their violent factionalism. On one side were the *Piagnoni* ('weepers') of Savonarola's party, on the other the party of the *Arrabbiati* ('the angry'), including the gangs of young delinquents who would demonstrate their opposition to piety and holiness by sneaking into the cathedral and filling Savonarola's pulpit with cow dung. A Medicean party was also gathering strength, a sort of fifth column sowing discontent within the city and undermining the war effort. Three times, unsuccessfully, the exiled Medici attempted to seize the city with bands of mercenaries. The Pisan revolt continued, and Pope Alexander had excommunicated Savonarola and was threatening to place all Florence under an interdict. In the long hangover after the Bonfire of Vanities, the Florentines were growing weary of their preacher. When the *Arrabbiati* won the elections of 1498, his doom was sealed. A kangaroo court found the new scapegoat guilty of heresy and treason. After some gratuitous torture and public mockery, the very spot where the Bonfire of Vanities had been held now witnessed a bonfire of Savonarola.

Pope Alexander still wasn't happy. He sent an army under his son, Cesare Borgia, to menace the city. Florence weathered this threat, and the relatively democratic 'Savonarolan' constitution of 1494 seemed to be working out well. Under an innovative idea, borrowed from Venice and designed to circumvent party strife, a public-spirited gentleman named **Piero Soderini** was elected *gonfaloniere* for life in 1502. With the help of his friend and adviser, **Niccolò Machiavelli**, Soderini kept the ship of state on an even keel. Pisa finally surrendered in 1509. Serious trouble returned in 1512, and once more the popes were behind it. As France's only ally in Italy, Florence ran foul of Julius II. Papal and Spanish armies invaded Florentine territory, and after their gruesome sack of Prato, designed specifically to overawe Florence, the frightened and politically apathetic city was ready to submit to the pope's conditions—the expulsion of Soderini, a change of alliance, and the return of the Medici.

The End of the Republic

At first, the understanding was that the Medici would live in Florence strictly as private citizens. But **Giuliano de' Medici**, son of Lorenzo and current leader of the clan, soon united the upper classes for a rolling back of Savonarolan democracy. With plenty of hired soldiers to intimidate the populace, a rigged *parlamento* on September 1512 restored Medici control. The democratic Grand Council was soon abolished; its new meeting hall in the Palazzo Vecchio (where Leonardo and Michelangelo were to have their 'Battle of the Frescoes') was broken up into apartments for soldiers. Soldiers were everywhere, and the Medicean restoration immediately took on the aspect of a police state. Hundreds of political prisoners spent time undergoing torture in the Palazzo Vecchio's dungeons, among them Machiavelli.

Giuliano died in 1516, succeeded by his nephew **Lorenzo, Duke of Urbino**, a snotty young sport with a tyrant's bad manners. Nobody mourned much when syphilis carried him off in 1519, but the family paid Michelangelo to give both Lorenzo and Giuliano fancy tombs. Ever since Giuliano's death, however, the real Medici boss had been not Lorenzo, but his uncle Giovanni, who in that year became **Pope Leo X**. The Medici, original masters of nepotism, had been planning this for years. Back in the 1470s, Lorenzo il Magnifico realized that the surest way of maintaining the family fortunes would be to get a Medici on the papal throne. He had little Giovanni ordained at the age of eight, purchased him a cardinal's hat at 13, and used bribery and diplomacy to help him accumulate dozens of benefices all over France and Italy.

For his easy-going civility (as exemplified in his famous quote: 'God has given us the papacy so let us enjoy it'), and his patronage of scholars and artists, Leo became one of the best-remembered Renaissance popes. On the other side of the coin was his criminal mismanagement of the Church; having learned the advantages of parasitism, the Medici were eager to pass it on to their friends. Upper-class Florentines descended on Rome like a plague of locusts, occupying all the important sinecures and rapidly emptying the papal treasury. Their rapacity, plus the tremendous expenses involved in building the new St Peter's, caused Leo to step up the sale of indulgences all over Europe—disgusting reformers like Luther and greatly hastening the onset of the Reformation.

Back in Florence, Lorenzo Duke of Urbino and his successor Giulio, bastard son of Lorenzo's brother the murdered Giuliano, were little more than puppets; Leo always found enough time between banquets to manage the city's affairs. Giulio himself became pope in 1523, as **Clement VII**, thanks largely to the new financial interdependence between Florence and Rome, and now the Medici presence in their home city was reduced to two more unattractive young bastards, Ippolito and Alessandro, under the guardianship of Cardinal Silvio Passerini. As Leo had done, Clement attempted to run the city from Rome, but high taxes and the lack of a strong hand made the new Medici regime increasingly precarious; its end followed almost immediately upon the sack of Rome in 1527. With Clement a prisoner in the Vatican and unable to intervene, a delegation of Florentine notables discreetly informed Passerini and the Medicis that it was time to go.

Know your Medici

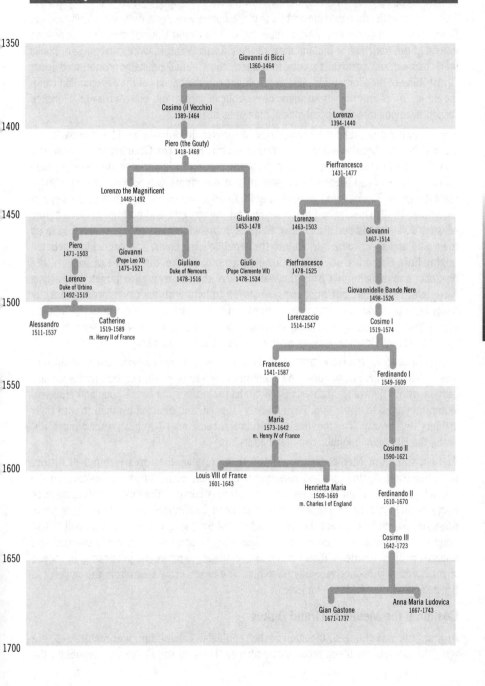

1350

1400

1450

1500

1550

1600

1650

1700

Giovanni di Bicci
1360-1464

Cosimo (il Vecchio)
1389-1464

Lorenzo
1394-1440

Piero (the Gouty)
1418-1469

Pierfrancesco
1431-1477

Lorenzo the Magnificent
1449-1492

Giuliano
1453-1478

Lorenzo
1463-1503

Giovanni
1467-1514

Piero
1471-1503

Giovanni
(Pope Leo XI)
1475-1521

Giuliano
Duke of Nemours
1478-1516

Giulio
(Pope Clemente VII)
1478-1534

Pierfrancesco
1478-1525

Lorenzo
Duke of Urbino
1492-1519

Giovannidelle Bande Nere
1498-1526

Alessandro
1511-1537

Catherine
1519-1589
m. Henry II of France

Lorenzaccio
1514-1547

Cosimo I
1519-1574

Francesco
1541-1587

Ferdinando I
1549-1609

Maria
1573-1642
m. Henry IV of France

Cosimo II
1590-1621

Louis VIII of France
1601-1643

Henrietta Maria
1509-1669
m. Charles I of England

Ferdinando II
1610-1670

Cosimo III
1642-1723

Gian Gastone
1671-1737

Anna Maria Ludovica
1667-1743

87

They took the hint, and for the third time in less than a century Florence had succeeded in getting rid of the Medici.

The new republic, though initiated by the disillusioned wealthy classes, soon found radical Savonarolan democrats gaining the upper hand. The Grand Council met once more, and extended the franchise to include most of the citizens. Vanities were cursed again, books were banned and carnival parades forbidden; the Council officially pronounced Jesus Christ 'King of the Florentines', just as it had done in the heyday of the Savonarolan camp meetings. In an intense atmosphere of republican virtue and pious crusade, Florence rushed headlong into the apocalyptic climax of its history.

This time, it did not take the Medici long to recover. In order to get Florence back, the witless Clement became allied to his former enemy, **Emperor Charles V**, a sordid deal that would eventually betray all Italy to Spanish control. Imperial troops were to help subdue Florence, and Clement's illegitimate son Alessandro was to wed Charles' illegitimate daughter. The bastards were closing in. Charles' troops put Florence under siege in December 1529. The city had few resources for the struggle, and no friends, but a heroic resistance kept the imperialists at bay all through the winter and spring. Citizens gave up their gold and silver to be minted into the republic's last coins. The councillors debated seizing little Catherine de' Medici, future Queen of France, but then a prisoner of the republic, and dangling her from the walls to give the enemy a good target. Few artists were left in Florence, but Michelangelo stayed to help with his city's fortifications (by night he was working on the Medici tombs in San Lorenzo, surely one of the all-time astounding feats of fence-straddling in history; both sides gave him safe passage when he wanted to leave Florence, and again when he decided to come back).

In August of 1530, the Florentines' skilful commander, Francesco Ferruccio, was killed in a skirmish near Pistoia; at about the same time the republic realized that its mercenary captain within the walls, Malatesta Baglioni, had sold them out to the pope and emperor. When they tried to arrest him, Baglioni only laughed, and directed his men to turn their artillery on the city. The inevitable capitulation came on 12 August; after almost 400 years, the Florentine republic had breathed its last.

At first, this third Medici return seemed to be just another dreary round of history repeating itself. Again, a packed *parlamento* gutted the constitution and legitimized the Medici takeover. Again the family and its minions combed the city, confiscating back every penny's worth of property that had been confiscated from them. This time, however, was to be different. Florence had gone from being a large fish in a small Italian pond to a miniscule but hindersome nuisance in the pan-European world of papal and imperial politics. Charles V didn't much like republics, or disorderly politicking, or indeed anyone who might conceivably say no to him. The orders came down from the emperor in Brussels; it was to be Medici for ever.

Cosimo I: the Medici as Grand Dukes

At first little was changed, the shell of the republican constitution was maintained, but with the 20-year-old illegitimate Alessandro as 'Duke of the Florentine Republic'; the harsh reality was under construction on the height above the city's west end—the Fortezza da Basso, with its Spanish garrison, demanded by Charles V as insurance that Florence would never again be able to assert its independence. If any further symbolism was necessary, Alessandro ordered the great bell to be removed from the tower of the Palazzo Vecchio, the bell that had always summoned the citizens to political assemblies and the mustering of the army.

In 1537, Alessandro was treacherously murdered by his jealous cousin Lorenzino de' Medici. With no legitimate heirs in the direct line Florence was in danger of falling under direct imperial rule, as had happened to Milan two years earlier, upon the extinction of the Sforza dukes. The assassination was kept secret while the Medici and the diplomats angled for a solution. The only reasonable choice turned out to be 18-year-old **Cosimo de' Medici**, heir of the family's cadet branch. This son of a famous mercenary commander, Giovanni of the Black Bands, had grown up on a farm and had never been involved with Florentine affairs; both the elder statesmen of the family and the imperial representatives thought they would easily be able to manipulate him.

It soon became clear that they had picked the wrong boy. Right from the start, young Cosimo had a surprisingly complete idea of how he meant to rule Florence, and also the will and strength of personality to see his commands carried out. No one ever admitted liking him; his puritanical court dismayed even the old partisans of Savonarola, and Florentines always enjoyed grumbling over his high taxes, going to support 'colonels, spies, Spaniards, and women to serve Madame' (his Spanish consort Eleanor of Toledo).

More surprising still, in this pathetic age when bowing and scraping Italians were everywhere else losing both their liberty and their dignity, Cosimo held his own against both pope and Spaniard. To back up his growing independence, Cosimo put his domains on an almost permanent war footing. New fortresses were built, a big fleet begun, and a paid standing army took the place of mercenaries and citizen levies. The skeleton of the old republic was revamped into a modern, bureaucratic state, governed as scientifically and rationally as any in Europe. The new regime, well prepared as it was, never had a severe test. Early in his reign Cosimo defeated the last-ditch effort of the republican exiles, unreconstructed oligarchs led by the banker Filippo Strozzi, at the Battle of Montemurlo, the last threat ever to Medici rule. Cosimo's masterstroke came in 1557, when with the help of an imperial army he was able to gobble up the entire Republic of Siena. Now the Medici rule extended over roughly the boundaries of modern Tuscany; Cosimo was able to cap off his reign in 1569 by purchasing from the Pope the title of Grand Duke of Tuscany.

Knick-knacks and Tedium: the Later Medici

For all Cosimo's efforts, Florence was a city entering a very evident decline. Banking and trade did well throughout the late 16th century, a prosperous time for almost all of Italy, but there were few opportunities for growth, and few Florentines interested in looking for it. More than ever, wealth was going into land, palaces and government bonds; the old tradition of mercantile venture among the Florentine elite was rapidly becoming a thing of the past. For culture and art, Cosimo's reign turned out to be a disaster. It wasn't what he intended; indeed the Duke brought to the field his accustomed energy and compulsion to improve and organize. Academies were founded, and research underwritten. Cosimo's big purse and his very modern concept of art as political propaganda helped change the Florentine artist from a slightly eccentric guild artisan to a flouncing courtier, ready to roll over at his master's command.

Michelangelo, despite frequent entreaties, always refused to work for Cosimo. Most of the other talented Florentines eventually found one excuse or another to bolt for Rome or even further afield, leaving lapdogs like **Giorgio Vasari** to carry on the grand traditions of Florentine art. Vasari, with help from such artists as Ammannati and Bandinelli, transformed much of the city—especially the interiors of its churches and public buildings. Florence began to fill up with equestrian statues of Medici, pageants and plaster triumphal arches displaying the triumphs of the Medici, sculptural allegories (like Cellini's *Perseus*) reminding us of the inevitability of the Medici, and best of all portraits of semi-divine Medici floating up in the clouds with little Cupids and Virtues.

It was all the same to Cosimo and his successors, whose personal tastes tended more to engraved jewels, exotic taxidermy and sculptures made of seashells. But it helped hasten the extinction of Florentine culture and the quiet transformation of the city into just another Mediterranean backwater. Cosimo himself grew ill in his later years, abdicating most responsibility to his son **Francesco** from 1564 to his death ten years later. Francesco, the genuine oddball among the Medici, was a moody, melancholic sort who cared little for government, preferring to lock himself up in the family palaces to pursue his passion for alchemy, as well as occasional researches into such subjects as perpetual motion and poisons—his agents around the Mediterranean had to ship him crates of scorpions every now and then. Despite his lack of interest, Francesco was a capable ruler, best known for his founding of the port city of Livorno.

Later Medici followed the general course established by other great families, such as the Habsburgs and Bourbons—each one was worse than the last. Francesco's death in 1587 gave the throne to his brother, **Ferdinando I**, founder of the Medici Chapels at San Lorenzo and another indefatigable collector of bric-a-brac. Next came **Cosimo II** (1609–21), a sickly nonentity who eventually succumbed to tuberculosis, and **Ferdinando II** (1621–70), whose long and uneventful reign oversaw the impoverishment of Florence and most of Tuscany. For this the Medici do not deserve much blame. A long string of bad harvests, beginning in the 1590s, plagues that recurred with terrible frequency as late as the 1630s, and general trade patterns that redistributed wealth and power from the Mediterranean to northern Europe, all set the stage for the collapse of the Florentine economy. The fatal blow came in the 1630s, when the long-deteriorating wool trade collapsed with sudden finality. Banking was going too, partly a victim of the age's continuing inflation, partly of high taxes and lack of worthwhile investments. Florence, by mid-century, found itself with no prospects at all, a pensioner city drawing a barely respectable income from its glorious past.

With **Cosimo III** (1670–1723), the line of the Medici crossed over into the realm of the ridiculous. A religious crank and anti-Semite, this Cosimo temporarily wiped out free thought in the universities, allowed Tuscany to fill up with nuns and Jesuits, and decreed fantastical laws like the one that forbade any man to enter a house where an unmarried woman lived. To support his lavish court and pay the big tributes demanded by Spain and Austria (something earlier Medici would have scorned) Cosimo taxed what was left of the Florentine economy into an early grave. His heir was the incredible **Gian Gastone** (1723–37). This last Medici, an obese drunkard, senile and slobbering at the age of fifty, has been immortalized by the equally incredible bust in the Pitti Palace. Gian Gastone had to be carried up and down stairs on the rare occasions when he ever got out of bed (mainly to disprove rumours that he was dead); on the one occasion he appeared in public, the chronicles report him vomiting repeatedly out of the carriage window.

As a footnote on the Medici there is Gian Gastone's perfectly sensible sister, **Anna Maria Ludovica**. As the very last surviving Medici, it fell to her to dispose of the family's vast wealth and hoards of art. When she died, in 1743, her will revealed that the whole bundle was to become the property of the future rulers of Tuscany—whoever they should be—with the provision that not one bit of it should ever, ever be moved outside Florence. Without her, the great collections of the Uffizi and the Bargello might long ago have been packed away to Vienna or Paris.

Post-Medici Florence

When Gian Gastone died in 1737, Tuscany's fate had already been decided by the great powers of Europe. The Grand Duchy would fall to **Francis Stephen**, Duke of Lorraine and husband-to-be of the Austrian Empress Maria Theresa; the new duke's troops were already installed in the Fortezza da Basso a year before Gian Gastone died. For most of the next century, Florence slumbered peacefully under a benign Austrian rule. Already the first Grand Tourists were arriving on their way to Rome and Naples, sons of the Enlightenment like Goethe, who never imagined anything in Florence could possibly interest him and didn't stop, or relics like the Pretender Charles Edward Stuart, 'Bonnie Prince Charlie', Duke of Albany, who stayed two years. Napoleon's men occupied the city for most of two decades, without making much of an impression.

After the Napoleonic Wars, the Habsburg restoration brought back the Lorraine dynasty. From 1824 to 1859, Florence and Tuscany were ruled by Leopold II, that most useful and likeable of all Grand Dukes. This was the age when Florence first became popular among the northern Europeans—the time when the Brownings, Dostoevsky, Leigh Hunt and dozens of other artists and writers took up residence, rediscovering the glories of the city and of the early Renaissance. Grand Duke Leopold was decent enough to let himself be overthrown in 1859, during the tumults of the Risorgimento. In 1865, when only the Papal State remained to be incorporated into the Kingdom of Italy, Florence briefly became the new nation's capital. King Vittorio Emanuele moved into the Pitti Palace, and the Italian Parliament met in the great hall of the Palazzo Vecchio.

It was not meant to last. When the Italian troops entered Rome in 1870, Florence's brief hour as a major capital was at an end. Not, however, without giving the staid old city a memorable jolt towards the modern world. In an unusual flurry of exertion, Florence finally threw up a façade for its cathedral, and levelled the picturesque though squalid market area and Jewish ghetto to build the dolorous Piazza della Repubblica. Fortunately, the city regained its senses before too much damage was done. Throughout this century, Florence's role as a museum city has been confirmed with each passing year. The hiatus provided by World War II allowed the city to resume briefly its ancient delight in black-and-white political epic. In 1944–5, Florence offered some of the most outrageous spectacles of Fascist fanaticism, and also some of the most courageous stories of the Resistance—including that of the German consul Gerhard Wolf, who used his position to protect Florentines from the Nazi terror, often at great personal risk.

In August 1944, the Allied armies were poised to advance through northern Tuscany. For the Germans, the Arno made a convenient defensive line, requiring that all the bridges of Florence be demolished. All were, except for the Ponte Vecchio, saved in a last-minute deal, though the buildings on either side of it were destroyed to provide piles of rubble around the bridge approaches. After the war, all were repaired; the city had the Ponte della Trínita rebuilt stone by stone exactly as it was. No sooner was the war damage redeemed, however, than an even greater disaster attacked the Florentine past. The flood of 1966, when water reached as high as 6.5m, did more damage than Nazis or Napoleons; an international effort was raised to preserve and restore the city's monuments.

Careful planning has saved the best of the immediate countryside from a different sort of flood—post-war suburbanization—but much of the territory around the city has become covered by an atrocity of suburban sprawl, some of the most degraded landscapes in all of Italy. Today, Florentines worry most about creeping obsolescence and a lack of initiative. Business is slipping. Recently it was announced that the new high-speed Milan–Rome train will not even stop here. Increasingly, Florence is left with its memories and its tourists. In May 1993 a bomb attack destoyed the Gregoriophilus library opposite the Uffizi galleries, damaging also the Vasari Corridor.

Highlights of Florence

Florence's museums, palaces and churches contain more good art than perhaps any city in Europe, and to see it all without hardship to your eyes, feet and sensibilities would take at least three weeks and some L100,000 in admissions. If you have only a few days to spend, and if you might never come back again, the highlights will easily take up all of your time—the **Cathedral** and **Baptistry**, the paintings in the **Uffizi** (preferably not all in the same day) and the sculptures in the **Bargello**, which is more worthy of your brief time than the **Accademia**, where the rubbernecks pile in to see Michelangelo's *David*. Stop in for a look at the eccentric **Orsanmichele**, and see the Arno from the **Ponte Vecchio**, taking in some of the oldest streets in the city. If your heart leans towards the graceful lyri-cism of the 1400s, don't miss the **Cathedral Museum** and the Fra Angelicos in **San Marco**; if the lush virtuosity of the 1500s is your cup of tea, visit the **Pitti Palace**'s Galleria Palatina. Two churches on the edges of the centre, **Santa Maria Novella** and **Santa Croce** are galleries in themselves, containing some of the greatest Florentine art;

Santa Maria del Carmine has the restored frescoes of Masaccio and company. Devotees of the Michelangelo cult won't want to miss the Medici Chapels and library at **San Lorenzo**. When the stones begin to weary you, head for the green oasis of the **Boboli Gardens**. Finally, climb up to **San Miniato**, for the beautiful medieval church and the enchanting view over the city.

Florence's 'secondary' sights are just as interesting. You could spend a day walking around old **Fiesole**, or 15 minutes looking at Gozzoli's charming fresco in the **Palazzo Medici-Riccardi**. The **Palazzo Vecchio** has more, but less charming, Medici frescoes. You can see how a wealthy medieval Tuscan merchant lived at the **Palazzo Davanzati**, while the **Museum of the History of Science** will tell you about the scientific side of the Florentine Renaissance; **Santa Trínita, Santo Spirito, Ognissanti**, and the **Annunziata** all contain famous works from the Renaissance. The **Casa Buonarroti** has some early sculptures of Michelangelo; the **Archaeology Museum** has even earlier ones by the Etruscans, Greeks and Egyptians; the Pitti Palace's **Museo degli Argenti** overflows with Medicean jewellery and trinkets. Take a bus or car out to Lorenzo il Magnifico's villa at **Poggio a Caiano,** or to the Medicis' other garden villas: **La Petraia** and **Castello,** or **Pratolino**.

There are three museums with 19th- and 20th-century collections to bring you back to the present: the **Galleria d'Arte Moderna** in the Pitti Palace, the **Collezione della Ragione** and the **Photography Museum** in the Palazzo Rucellai. There are two museums founded by Englishmen: the **Horne Museum** with Renaissance art, and the eccentric **Stibbert Museum** with everything but the kitchen sink. Strangest of all are the museums in **La Specola**, featuring stuffed animals and anatomical wax figures.

© (055–)   *Getting There*

by air

Florence is the central transport node for Tuscany and harder to avoid than to reach. It has only a dinky **civil airport,** A. Vespucci, Peretola, at Via del Termine 11, © 373498, with flight connections to Milan, Naples, Lugano, Rome, Nice, Munich, London and Paris. Special train connections, however, link the city to the much larger international airport in Pisa (1hr, L8000 one way, daily every 1–2hrs). For flight information, ring © 2788.

Airline offices in Florence are: Alitalia, Lungarno Acciaioli 10/12r, © 27881; British Airways, Via Vigna Nuova 36r, © 21655; TWA, Via dei Vecchietti 4, © 2396856; Meridiana (for London) © 308711.

by train

Florence's central station is **Santa Maria Novella**, © 288785; there is another, **Campo di Marte**, located at the east end of town, mainly used for local lines and some trains to Rome. Bus 19 connects the two stations.

Florence

Cenacolo di Sant' Apollonia

VIA SAN ZANOBI

VIA SAN GALLO

VIA GUELFA

Lazzi Buses

VIA NAZIONALE

VIA PANICALE

VIA TADDEA

Piazza del Mercato Centrale

VIA DE' GINORI

VIA CAVOUR

RICASOLI

Stazione Centrale

Piazza della Stazione

VIA SANT' ANTONINO

BORGO LA NOCE

Sita Buses

VIA DELLA SCALA

VIA D'AMELIO

VIA DEI PANZANI

Santa Maria Novella

Piazza dell' Unità Italiana

V.D. MELARANCIO

Piazza Madonna

Palazzo Medici-Riccardi

VIA DE' PUCCI

VIA DE' MARTELLI

VIA DELLA VIGNA NUOVA

San Lorenzo and Medici Chapels

BORGO SAN LORENZO

VIA PALAZZUOLO

VIA MASO FINIGUERRA DELL'ALBERO

Piazza Santa Maria Novella

VIA DEI BANCHI

VIA DELLE BELLE DONNE

VIA DEI CERRETANI

Duomo

Museo dell'Opera del Duomo

BORGO OGNISSANTI

VIA HELENONI

Ognissanti

VIA DEL PORCELLANA

VIA DEI FOSSI

VIA DEL MORO

Piazza di San Giovanni

Baptistry

Piazza del Duomo

VIA DELLO STUDIO

VIA DEGLI AGLI

VIA DE' PECORI

VIA ROMA

VIA DELLE OCHE

Museo Nazionale di Antropologia ed Etnologia

LUNGARNO AMERIGO VESPUCCI

San Pancrazio

Palazzo Antinari

VIA D. CAMPIDOGLIO

Piazza della Repubblica

VIA DEL CORSO

VIA DE' CALZAIUOLI

Dante's House

VIA DANTE ALIGHIERI

Palazzo Pazzi Quar

Piazza di Cestello

LUNGARNO SODERINI

Palazzo Rucellai

Piazza Goldoni

VIA D. VIGNA NUOVA

VIA DEL PARIONE

VIA STROZZI

Piazza d. Strozzi

VIA

Piazza della Strozzi

Post Office & Telephones

VIA SPEZIALI

Arte della Lana

Orsanmichele

Badia

BORGO SAN FREDIANO

LUNGARNO CORSINI

Santa Trinita

Piazza S. Trinita

Palazzo Davanzati

VIA PORTA ROSSA

Mercato Nuovo

VIA CONDOTTA

Bargello

Piazza del Carmine

PONTE ALLA CARRAIA

LUNGARNO GUICCIARDINI

Ponte Santa Trinita

BORGO SS. APOSTOLI

SS. Apostoli

LUNG. ACCIAIOLI

VIA POR S. MARIA

Palazzo di Parte Guelfa

Piazza della Signoria

Palazzo Goudi

Piazza San Firenze

VIA S. MONACA

Santa Maria del Carmine

VIA DI S. SPIRITO

Loggia dei Lanzi

Uffizi

Palazzo Vecchio

VIA DEI N

VIA DEL SERRAGLI

Santo Spirito

VIA DEL PRESTO DI SAN MARTINO

BORGO SAN JACOPO

Ponte Vecchio

VIA DE CASTELLANI

VIA SANT' AGOSTINO

Piazza San Spirito

VIA MAGGIO

Mueseum of the History of Science

LUNG. DIAZ

VIA DI GUICCIARDINI

Fiume

BORGO TEGOLAIO

Santa Felicità

COSTA DI SAN GIORGIO

LUNGARNO TORRIGIANI

VIA DE' BARDI

Piazza dei Pitti

Grotta Buontalenti

Museo Bardini

VIA ROMANA

Piazza San Felice

Pitti Palace

Piazza dei Mozzi

La Specola Museum

Boboli Gardens

Belvedere Fort

N

250 metres
250 yards

San Marco

Piazza San Marco

Accademia

Santissima Annunziata

Giardino dei Semplici

Giardino della Gherardesca

Piazzale Donatello

English Cemetery

Piazza SS. Annunziata

Opificio delle Pietre Dure

Archaeology Museum

Spedale degli Innocenti

Rotonda di Santa Maria degli Angeli

Santa Maria Nuova Hospital

Santa Maria Maddalena dei Pazzi

Piazza M. D'Azeglio

Piazza di Santa Maria Nuova

Museo Firenze Com'era

Synagogue

BORGO DEGLI ALBIZI

Piazza G. Salvemini

VIA PIETRAPIANA

Sant'Ambrogio

Piazza S. Ambrogio

BORGO LA CROCE

Piazza Beccaria

VIA VINCENZO

VIA DE' PANDOLFINI

Piazza dei Ciompi

VIA GHIBELLINA

Piazza L. Ghiberti

D. VIGNA VECCHIA

A DELL'ANGUILLARA

Casa Buonarroti

GO DEI GRECI

Piazza Santa Croce

Santa Croce

Horne Museum

LUNG. DELLE GRAZIE

VIA TRIPOLI

LUGARNO DELLA ZECCA VECCHIA

LUNG. PECORI GIRALDI

LUNG. DEL TEMPIO

Arno

LUNGARNO SERRISTORI

LUNG. B. CELLINI

VIA DI SAN NICCOLO

San Miniato

DI BELVEDERE

VIA C. BATTISTI

VIA GINO CAPPONI

VIA GIUSEPPE GIUSTI

BORGO PINTI

VIA GIUSEPPE GIUSTI

VIA V. ALFIERI

VIALE ANTONIO GRAMSCI

VIA LAURA

VIA DELLA COLONNA

VIA C. FARINI

VIA DELLA PERGOLA

VIA DEGLI ALFANI

DEI SERVI

VIA BUFALINI

VIA SAN EGIDIO

VIA DELL'ORIUOLO

BORGO PINTI

VIA DEI PILASTRI

VIA DEL MEZZO

VIA G. CARDUCCI

VIA DELLA MATTONAIA

VIA MANZONI

VIA DE' PEPI

MACCI

VIA DELL' AGNOLO

BORGO ALLEGRI

VIA DE' MACCI

VIA DE' GHIBELLINA

VIALE GIOVINE ITALIA

VIA GIUSEPPE VERDI

VIA DE' PEPI

VIA DE' BENCI

BORGO S. CROCE

VIA MAGLIABECHI

VIA SAN GIUSEPPE

VIA DELLE CASINE

VIA DE' MALCONTENTI

VIALE GIOVANNI AMENDOLA

CORSO DEI TINTORI

PONTE S. NICCOLO

95

It's possible to reach nearly every city, town and village in Tuscany from Florence, which is wonderfully convenient—once you know which of several bus companies to patronize. The tourist office has a complete list of destinations, but here are some of the most popular:

SITA (near the station, Via S. Caterina da Siena 15, © 483651 Mon–Fri, 211487 weekends): towns in the Val d'Elsa, Chianti, Val di Pesa, Mugello and Casentino; Arezzo, Bibbiena, Castelfiorentino, Certaldo, Consuma, Figline Valdarno, Firenzuola, Marina di Grosseto, Montevarchi, Poggibonsi (for S. Gimignano and Volterra), Pontassieve, Poppi, Pratovecchio, Scarperia, Siena, Stia, Vallombrosa.

LAZZI (Piazza Stazione 4, © 298840): along the Arno to the coast, including Calenzano, Cerreto Guidi, Empoli, Forte dei Marmi, Livorno, Lucca, Marina di Carrara, Marina di Massa, Montecatini Terme, Montelupo, Montevarchi, Pescia, Pisa, Pistoia, Pontedera, Prato, Signa, Tirrenia, Torre del Lago, and Viareggio.

CLAP (Piazza Stazione 15r, © 283734): Lucca.

CAT (Via Fiume 2r, © 283400): Anghiari, Arezzo, Caprese, Città di Castello, Incisa Valdarno, Sansepolcro.

CAP (Via Nazionale 13, © 214637): Borgo S. Lorenzo, Impruneta, Incisa Valdarno, Montepiano, Prato.

COPIT (Piazza S. Maria Novella 22, © 215451): Abetone, Cerreto Guidi, Pistoia, Poggio a Caiano, Vinci.

RAMA (Lazzi Station, © 298840): Grosseto.

© *(055–)*   **Getting Around**

Florence is now one of the best Italian cities to get around; best, because nearly everything you'll want to see is within easy walking distance and large areas in the centre are pedestrian zones; there are no hills to climb, and it's hard to lose your way for very long.

Just a few years ago the traffic problem in Florence was one of the grimmest and most carcinogenic in Italy; a walk along the Lungarno or the remaining streets where the traffic is now chanelled will demonstrate that Dante didn't have to go far to find Purgatorio. But in 1988, with great fanfare and howls of protest, Florence attempted to do something about the cars that were choking it to death by greatly enlarging the limited access zone, the *zona a traffico limitato*, which the Florentines, with clenched teeth, somehow pronounce as ZTL. Within ZTL only buses, taxis, and cars belonging to residents are permitted; otherwise, you may pay to park in one of the city's car parks (the Fortezza da Basso is biggest and perhaps most convenient) or take your chances on a side street. This new regulation was then followed by whole areas especially around Piazza della Signoria and the

Duomo becoming totally traffic-free zones. The only danger in these areas is the odd ambulance or police car, the speeding mopeds (all of which you can usually hear) and the deadly silent bicycle.

Just to make life difficult, Florence has two sets of address numbers on every street—red ones for business, blue for residences; your hotel might be either one.

by bus

City buses (ATAF) can whizz or inch you across Florence, and are an excellent means of reaching sights on the periphery. Most lines begin at Santa Maria Novella station, and pass by Piazza del Duomo or Piazza San Marco. There's an information/ticket booth in the station, and at ATAF's central office in Piazza della Stazione, ✆ 5650222. Tickets are good for 60 or 120 minutes after validation on the bus; 24-hour passes are available as well. The most useful buses for visitors are:

6: Via Rondinella–Piazza Unità–Duomo–Piazza San Marco–Soffiano

7: Station–Duomo–San Domenico–Fiesole

10: Station–Duomo–S. Marco–Ponte a Mensola–Settignano

11: Viale Calatafimi–Duomo–Porta Romana–Poggio Imperiale

13: Station–Duomo–Piazzale Michelangelo–Porta Romana

14: Rovezzano–Duomo–Station–Careggi

17: Cascine–Station–Duomo–Via Lamarmora–Salviatino (for the youth hostel)

25: Station–S. Marco–Piazza Libertà–Via Bologna–Pratolino

28: Station–Via R. Giuliani–Castello–Sesto Fiorentino

37: Station–Ponte alla Carraia–Porta Romana–Certosa del Galluzzo

38: Porta Romana–Pian del Giullari

62: Station–Peretola Airport

by taxi

Taxis in Florence don't cruise; you'll find them in ranks at the station and in the major *piazze*, or else ring for a radio taxi: ✆ 4798 or 4390.

bicycle, scooter and car hire

Hiring a bike can save you tramping time and angst, but watch out for cars and pedestrians. If you park your car at the car park at the Fortezza da Basso, you can have two bikes for two hours for free, between the hours of 8am and 8pm, on the presentation of your SCAF parking coupon at the Bici-Città booth, on the north side near the tour bus parking area. You can also hire a bike at **Ciao & Basta**, ✆ 2342726, located in Lungarno Pecori Girardi 1, down the steps from the station or at Costa dei Magnoli 24, or in spring and summer in Piazza Libertà.

Vesparent,Via Pisana, 103r, ✆ 715691, hires out bikes and motorbikes and scooters; motorbikes are also available from **Alinari**, Via Guelfa 85r, ✆ 280500; **Motorent**, Via S. Zanobi 9r, ✆ 490113.

When you can't take any more art, hire a car and escape into the ravishing coun-tryside. Most firms are in easy walking distance from the station: Avis, Borgo Ognissanti 128r, ✆ 213629, ✉ 2382697; Europcar, Borgo Ognissanti 53r, ✆ 2360072; Hertz, Via M. Finiguerra 33r, ✆ 2398205; Maggiore, Via M. Finiguerra 31, ✆ 294578; Program, Borgo Ognissanti 135r, ✆ 282916; Italy by Car, Borgo Ognissanti 134r, ✆ and ✉ 293021.

✆ *(055–)*   ***Tourist Information***

The head office is a bit out of the way, near Piazza Beccaria on Via Manzoni 16, ✆ 290832, open 8.30–1.30 Mon–Sat. There's also a booth outside the station, at the end of the bus ranks, that is open daily until 9pm in summer and very genial, ✆ 212245. There's an office in Fiesole at Piazza Mino 37, ✆ 598720, ✉ 598822, open 9–1 and 3–6.

There are no end of places to help you find a hotel (*see* 'Where to Stay' p. 182) but these tourist offices usually cannot help.

Piazza del Duomo

Tour groups circle around the three great spiritual monuments of medieval Florence like sharks around their prey. Saxophone players by the cathedral croon to a human carnival from a hundred nations that mills about good-naturedly while ambulances of a medieval brotherhood dedicated to first aid stand at the ready in case anyone swoons from ecstasy or art-glut. As bewildering as it often is, however, the Piazza del Duomo and the adjacent Piazza San Giovanni are the best introduction to this often bewildering city, beginning with the Baptistry.

The Baptistry

To begin to understand what magic made the Renaissance first bloom by the Arno, look here; this ancient, mysterious building is the egg from which Florence's golden age was hatched. By the quattrocento Florentines firmly believed their baptistry was originally a Roman temple to Mars, a touchstone linking them to a legendary past. Scholarship sets its date of construction between the 6th and 9th centuries, in the darkest Dark Ages, which makes it even more remarkable; it may as well have dropped from heaven. Its distinctive dark green and white marble facing, the tidily classical pattern of arches and rectangles that deceived Brunelleschi and Alberti, was probably added around the 11th century. The masters who built it remain unknown, but their strikingly original exercise in geometry provided the model for all of Florence's great church façades. When it was new, there was nothing remotely like it in Europe; to visitors from outside the city it must have seemed almost miraculous.

Every 21 March, New Year's Day on the old Florentine calendar, all the children born over the last 12 months would be brought here for a great communal baptism, a habit that helped make the baptistry not merely a religious monument but a civic symbol, in fact the oldest and fondest symbol of the republic. As such the Florentines never tired of embellishing it. Under the octagonal cupola, the glittering 13th- and 14th-century gold-ground mosaics show a strong Byzantine influence, perhaps laid by mosaicists from Venice. The decoration is divided into concentric strips: over the apse, dominated by a 8.5m figure of Christ, is a *Last Judgement*, while the other bands, from the inside out, portray the *Hierarchy of Heaven*, *Story of Genesis*, *Life of Joseph*, *Life of Christ* and the *Life of St John the Baptist*, the last band believed to be the work of Cimabue. The equally beautiful mosaics over the altar and in the vault are the earliest, signed by a monk named Iacopo in the first decades of the 1200s.

To match the mosaics, there is an intricate tessellated marble floor, decorated with signs of the Zodiac; the blank, octagonal space in the centre was formerly occupied by the huge font. The green and white patterned walls of the interior, even more than the exterior, are remarkable, combining influences from the ancient world and modern inspiration for something entirely new, the perfect source that architects of the Middle Ages and Renaissance would ever strive to match. Much of the best design work is up in the **galleries**, not accessible, but partially visible from the floor.

The baptistry is hardly cluttered; besides a 13th-century Pisan style baptismal font, only the **Tomb of Anti-Pope John XXIII** by Donatello and Michelozzo stands out. This funerary monument, with scenographic marble draperies softening its classical lines, is one of the great prototypes of the early Renaissance. But how did this Anti-Pope John, deposed by the Council of Constance in 1415, earn the unique privilege of a fancy tomb in the baptistry? Why, it was thanks to him that Giovanni di Bicci de' Medici made the family fortune as head banker to the Curia.

The Gates of Paradise

Historians used to pinpoint the beginning of the 'Renaissance' as the year 1401, when the merchants' guild, the Arte di Calimala, sponsored a competition for the baptistry's north doors. The **South Doors** (the main entrance into the baptistry) had already been completed by Andrea Pisano in 1330, and they give an excellent lesson on the style of the day. The doors are divided into 28 panels in quatrefoil frames with scenes from the life of St John the Baptist and the eight Cardinal and Theological Virtues—formal and elegant works in the best Gothic manner.

The celebrated competition of 1401—perhaps the first ever held in the annals of art—pitted the seven greatest sculptors of the day against one another. Judgement was based on trial panels on the subject of the *Sacrifice of Isaac*, and in a dead heat at the end of the day were the two by Brunelleschi and Lorenzo Ghiberti, now displayed in the Bargello. Ghiberti's more classical-style figures were eventually judged the better, and it was a serendipitous choice; he devoted nearly the rest of his life to creating the most beautiful bronze doors in the world while Brunelleschi, disgusted by his defeat, went on to build the most perfect dome. Ghiberti's first efforts, the **North Doors** (1403–24), are contained, like Pisano's, in 28 quatrefoil frames. In their scenes on the Life of Christ, the Evangelists, and the Doctors of the Church, you can trace Ghiberti's progress over the 20 years he worked in the increased depth of his compositions, not only visually but dramatically; classical backgrounds begin to fill up the frames, ready to break out of their Gothic confines. Ghiberti also designed the lovely floral frame of the doors; the three statues, of John the Baptist, the Levite and the Pharisee, by Francesco Rustici, were based on a design by Leonardo da Vinci and added in 1511.

Ghiberti's work pleased the Arte di Calimala, and they set him loose on another pair of portals, the **East Doors** (1425–52), his masterpiece and one of the most awesome achievements of the age. Here Ghiberti (perhaps under the guidance of Donatello) dispensed with the small Gothic frames and instead cast 10 large panels that depict the Old Testament in Renaissance high gear, reinterpreting the forms of antiquity with a depth and drama that have never been surpassed. Michelangelo declared them 'worthy to be the Gates of Paradise', and indeed it's hard to believe these are people, buildings and trees of bronze and not creatures frozen in time by some celestial alchemy.

Ghiberti wasn't exactly slow to toot his own horn; according to himself, he personally planned and designed the Renaissance on his own. His unabashedly conceited *Commentarii* were the first attempt at art history and autobiography by an artist, and a work as revolutionary as his doors in its presentation of the creative God-like powers of the artist. It is also a typical exhibition of Florentine pride that he should put busts of his friends among the prophets and sibyls that adorn the frames of the East Doors. Near the centre, the balding figure with arched eyebrows and a little smile is Ghiberti himself.

The Duomo

For all its importance and prosperity, Florence was one of the last cities to plan a great cathedral. Work began in the 1290s, with the sculptor Arnolfo di Cambio in charge, and from the beginning the Florentines attempted to make up for their delay with sheer audacity. 'It will be so magnificent in size and beauty,' according to a decree of 1296, 'as to surpass anything built by the Greeks and Romans.' In response Arnolfo planned what in its day was the largest church in Catholicism; he confidently laid the foundations for an enormous octagonal crossing 44.5m in diameter, then died before working out a way to cover it, leaving future architects the job of designing the biggest dome in the world.

Beyond its presumptuous size, the cathedral of Santa Maria del Fiore shows little interest in contemporary innovations and styles; a visitor from France or England in the 1400s would certainly have found it somewhat drab and architecturally primitive. Visitors today often don't know what to make of it; they circle confusedly around its grimy, ponderous bulk (this is one of the very few cathedrals in Italy that you can walk completely around). Instead of the striped bravura of Siena or the elegant colonnades of Pisa, they behold an astonishingly eccentric green, white and red pattern of marble rectangles and flowers—like Victorian wallpaper, or as one critic better expressed it, 'a cathedral wearing pyjamas'. On a sunny day, the cathedral under its sublime dome seems to sport festively above the dullish dun and ochre sea of Florence; in dismal weather it sprawls morosely across its piazza like a beached whale tarted up with a lace doily front.

The fondly foolish **façade** cannot be blamed on Arnolfo. His original design, only one-quarter completed, was taken down in a late 16th-century Medici rebuilding programme that never got off the ground. The Duomo turned a blank face to the world until the present neogothic extravaganza was added in 1888. Walk around to the north side to see what many consider a more fitting door, the **Porta della Mandorla** crowned with an Assumption of the Virgin in an almond-shaped frame (hence 'Mandorla') made by Nanni di Banco in 1420.

Brunelleschi's Dome

Yet if this behemoth of a cathedral, this St Mary of the Floral Wallpaper, was created for no other reason than to serve as a base for its dome, it would be more than enough. Brunelleschi's dome, more than any landmark, makes Florence Florence. Many have noted how the dome repeats the rhythm of the surrounding hills, echoing them with its height and beauty; from those city streets fortunate enough to have a clear view, it rises among the clouds with all the confident mastery, proportions, and perfect form that characterize the highest aspirations of the Renaissance. But if it seems miraculous, it certainly isn't divine; unlike the dome of the Hagia Sophia, suspended from heaven by a golden chain, Florence's was made by man—one man, to be precise.

Losing the competition for the baptistry doors was a bitter disappointment to Filippo Brunelleschi. His reaction was typically Florentine; not content with being the second-best sculptor, he turned his talents to a field where he thought no one could beat him, launching himself into an intense study of architecture and engineering, visiting Rome and probably Ravenna to snatch secrets from the ancients. When proposals were solicited for the cathedral's dome in 1418, he was ready with a brilliant *tour de force*. Not only would he build the biggest dome of the time, and the most beautiful, but he would do it without any need for expensive supports while work was in progress, making use of a cantilevered system of bricks that could support itself while it ascended.

Brunelleschi studied, then surpassed the technique of the ancients with a system more simple than that of the Pantheon or Hagia Sophia. To the Florentines, a people who could have invented the slogan 'form follows function' for their own tastes in building, it must have come as a revelation; the most logical way of covering the space turned out to be a work of perfect beauty. Brunelleschi, in building this dome, put a crown on the achievements of Florence. After 500 years it is still the city's pride and symbol.

The best way to appreciate Brunelleschi's genius is by touring inside the two concentric shells of the dome (*see* below), but before entering, note the eight marble ribs that define its octagonal shape; hidden inside are the three huge stone chains that bind them together. Work on the balcony around the base of the dome, designed by Giuliano da Sangallo, was halted in 1515 after Michelangelo commented that it resembled a cricket's cage. As for the **lantern**, the Florentines were famous for their fondness and admiration for Doubting Thomas, and here they showed why. Even though they marvelled at the dome, they still doubted that Brunelleschi could construct a proper lantern, and forced him to submit to yet another competition. He died before it was begun, and it was completed to his design by Michelozzo.

The Interior

After the façade, the austerity of the duomo interior is almost startling. There is plenty of room; contemporary writers mention 10,000 souls packed inside to hear the brimstone and hell-fire sermons of Savonarola. Even with that in mind, the duomo hardly seems a religious building—more a *Florentine* building, with simple arches and counterpoint of grey stone and white plaster, full of old familiar Florentine things. Near the entrance, on the right-hand side, are busts of Brunelleschi and Giotto. On the left wall, posed inconspicuously, are the two most conspicuous monuments to private individuals ever erected by the Florentine Republic. The older one, on the right, is to **Sir John Hawkwood**, the famous English *condottiere* whose name the Italians mangled to Giovanni Acuto, a legendary commander who served Florence for many years and is perhaps best known to English speakers as the hero of *The White Company* by Arthur Conan Doyle. All along, Hawkwood had the promise of the Florentines to build him an equestrian statue after his death; it was a typical Florentine trick to pinch pennies and cheat a dead man—but they hired the greatest master of perspective, Paolo Uccello, to make a fresco that looked like a statue (1436). Twenty years later, they pulled the same trick again, commissioning another great illusionist, Andrea del Castagno, to paint the non-existent equestrian statue of another *condottiere*, Niccolò da Tolentino. A little further down, Florence commemorates its own secular scripture with Michelino's well-known fresco of Dante, a vision of the poet and his *Paradiso* outside the walls of Florence. Two singular icons of Florence's fascination with science stand at opposite ends of the building: behind the west front, a bizarre clock painted by Uccello, and in the pavement of the left apse, a gnomon fixed by the astronomer Toscanelli in 1475. A beam of sunlight strikes it every year on the day of the summer solstice.

For building the great dome, Brunelleschi was accorded a special honour—he is one of the few Florentines to be buried in the cathedral. His tomb may be seen in the **Excavations of Santa Reparata** (*the stairway descending on the right of the naval*; *open 9.30–5.30, closed Sun; adm*). Arnolfo di Cambio's cathedral was constructed on the ruins of the ancient church of Santa Reparata, which lay forgotten until 1965. Excavations have revealed not only the palaeo-Christian church and its several reconstructions, but also the remains of its Roman predecessor—a rather confusing muddle of walls that have been tidied up in an ambience that resembles an archaeological shopping centre. A coloured model helps explain what is what, and glass cases display items found in the dig, including the spurs of Giovanni de' Medici, who was buried here in 1351. In the ancient crypt of Santa Reparata are 13th-century tomb slabs, and in another section there's a fine pre-Romanesque mosaic pavement.

There is surprisingly little religious art—the Florentines for reasons of their own have carted most of it off into the Cathedral Museum (*see* below). Under the dome are the entrances to the two sacristies, with terracotta lunettes over the doors by Luca della Robbia; the scene of the *Resurrection* over the north sacristy is one of his earliest and best works. He also did the bronze doors beneath it, with tiny portraits on the handles of Lorenzo il Magnifico and his brother Giuliano de' Medici, targets of the Pazzi conspiracy in 1478. In the middle apse, there is a beautiful bronze urn by Ghiberti containing relics of the Florentine St Zenobius. The only really conventional religious decorations are the hack but scarcely visible frescoes high in the dome (some 90m up, and recently restored), mostly the work of Vasari. As you stand there squinting at them, try not to think that the cupola weighs an estimated 25,000 tons.

A door on the left aisle near the Dante fresco leads up into the **dome** (*open daily 9.30–5.30, closed Sun; adm*). The complicated network of stairs and walks between the inner and outer domes (not too difficult, if occasionally claustrophobic and vertiginous) was designed by Brunelleschi, and offers an insight on how thoroughly the architect thought out the problems of the dome's construction, even inserting hooks to hold up scaffolding for future cleaning or repairs; Brunelleschi installed restaurants to save workers the trouble of descending for meals. There is also no better place to get an idea of the dome's scale; the walls of the inner dome are 4m thick, and those of the outer dome 2m. These give the dome enough strength and support to preclude the need for further buttressing.

From the gallery of the dome you can get a good look at the lovely **stained glass** by Uccello, Donatello, Ghiberti and Castagno, in the seven circular windows, or *occhi*, made during the construction of the dome. Further up, the views through the small windows offer tantalizing hints of the breathtaking panorama of the city from the marble lantern at the top. The bronze ball at the very top was added by Verrocchio, and can hold almost a dozen people when it's open.

Giotto's Campanile

There's no doubt about it; the dome steals the show on Piazza del Duomo, putting one of Italy's most beautiful bell towers in the shade both figuratively and literally. The dome's great size—111.6m to the bronze ball—makes the campanile look small, though 85.4m is not exactly tiny. Giotto was made director of the cathedral works in 1334, and his basic design was completed after his death (1337) by Andrea Pisano and Francesco Talenti. It is difficult to say whether they were entirely faithful to the plan. Giotto was an artist, not an engineer. After he died, his successors realized the thing, then only 12m high, was about to tumble over, a problem they overcame by doubling the thickness of the walls.

Besides its lovely form, the green, pink and white campanile's major fame rests with Pisano and Talenti's **sculptural reliefs**— a veritable encyclopaedia of the medieval world view with prophets, saints and sibyls, allegories of the planets, virtues and sacraments, the liberal arts and industries (the artist's craft is fittingly symbolized by a winged figure of Daedalus). All of these are copies of the originals now in the Cathedral Museum. If you can take another 400 steps or so, the terrace on top offers a slightly different view of Florence and of the cathedral itself (*open summer, daily 8.30–7, winter 9–4.30; adm*).

Giotto's campanile

Loggia del Bigallo

The most striking secular building on the Piazza del Duomo is the Loggia del Bigallo, south of the baptistry near the beginning of Via de' Calzaiuoli. This 14th-century porch was built for one of Florence's great charitable confraternities, the Misericordia, which still has its headquarters across the street and operates the ambulances parked in front; in the 13th and 14th centuries members courageously nursed and buried victims of the plague. The Loggia itself originally served as a lost and found office, although instead of umbrellas it dealt in children; if unclaimed after three days they were sent to foster homes. In the 15th century the Misericordia merged with a similar charitable confraternity called the Bigallo, and works of art accumulated by both organizations over centuries are displayed in the diminutive but choice **Museo del Bigallo**, located next to the loggia at Piazza San Giovanni 1 (*only open 2 months of the year during the summer, at other times ring © (055) 215440*). The most famous picture here is the fresco of *Madonna della Misericordia*, featuring the earliest known view of Florence (1342); other 14th-century works (by Bernardo Daddi, Niccolò di Pietro Gerini, and sculptor Alberto Arnoldi) portray the activities of the brotherhood, members of which may still be seen wearing the traditional black hoods that preserve their anonymity.

East of the Loggia del Bigallo is a stone bench labelled the 'Sasso di Dante'—**Dante's Seat**—where the poet would sit and take the air, observing his fellow citizens and watching the construction of the cathedral.

The Museo dell'Opera del Duomo

Open 9–7.30 summer, 9–6 winter, closed Sun; adm.

The Cathedral Museum (Piazza del Duomo 9, near the central apse) is one of Florence's finest, and houses both relics from the actual construction of the cathedral and the masterpieces that once adorned it. The first hall is devoted to the cathedral's sculptor-architect Arnolfo di Cambio and contains a drawing of his ornate, sculpture-filled façade that was but a quarter completed when the Medici had it removed in 1587. Here, too, are the statues he made to adorn it: the unusual Madonna with the glass eyes, Florence's old patron saints, Reparata and Zenobius, and nasty old Boniface VIII, who sits stiffly on his throne like an Egyptian god. There are the four Evangelists, including a St John by Donatello, and a small collection of ancient works—Roman sarcophagi and an Etruscan cippus carved with dancers. Two small rooms nearby contain materials from the construction of the dome—wooden models, tools, brick moulds and instruments—as well as Brunelleschi's death mask. Also on the ground floor are several hack Mannerist models (one by dilettante Giovanni de' Medici) proposed in the 1580s for the cathedral, reminders that the façade could have been much, much worse. The Florentines were never enthusiastic about the worship of relics, and long ago they shipped San Girolamo's jaw-bone, John the Baptist's index finger and St Philip's arm across the street to this museum; note the 16th-century 'Libretto', a fold-out display case of saintly odds and ends, all neatly labelled.

On the landing of the stairs stands the *Pietà* that Michelangelo intended for his own tomb. The artist, increasingly cantankerous and full of *terribilità* in his old age, became exasperated with this complex work and took a hammer to the arm of the Christ—the first known instance of an artist vandalizing his own creation. His assistant repaired the damage and finished part of the figures of Mary Magdalene and Christ. According to Vasari, the hooded figure of Nicodemus is Michelangelo's self-portrait.

Upstairs, the first room is dominated by the two **Cantorie**, two marble choir balconies with exquisite bas-reliefs, made in the 1430s by Luca della Robbia and Donatello. Both works rank among the Renaissance's greatest productions. Della Robbia's delightful horde of laughing children dancing, singing and playing instruments is a truly angelic choir, Apollonian in its calm and beauty, perhaps the most charming work ever to have been inspired by the forms of antiquity. Donatello's *putti*, by contrast, dance, or rather race, through their quattrocento decorative motifs with fiendish Dionysian frenzy. Even less serene is his statue of *Mary Magdalene*, surely one of the most jarring figures ever sculpted, ravaged by her own piety and penance, her sunken eyes fixed on a point beyond this vale of tears. Grey and weathered prophets by Donatello and others stand along the white walls. These originally adorned the façade of the campanile. According to Vasari, while carving the most famous bald one, *Habbakuk* (better known as '*lo zuccone*'), Donatello would mutter 'Speak, damn you. Speak!' The next room contains the original panels on the *Spiritual Progress of Man* from Giotto's campanile, made by Andrea Pisano.

The last room is dedicated to works removed from the baptistry, especially the lavish silver altar (14th–15th-century), made by Florentine goldsmiths, portraying scenes from the life of the Baptist. Antonio Pollaiuolo used the same subject to design the 27 needlework panels that once were part of the priest's vestments. There are two 12th-century Byzantine mosaic miniatures, masterpieces of the intricate, and a *St Sebastian* triptych by Giovanni del Biondo that may well be the record for arrows; the poor saint looks like a hedgehog. This room also contains four panels from Ghiberti's 'Gates of Paradise', which make fascinating viewing close up.

Via de' Calzaiuoli and Piazza della Repubblica

Of all the streets that radiate from the Piazza del Duomo, most people almost intuitively turn down the straight, pedestrian-only Via de' Calzaiuoli, the Roman street that became the main thoroughfare of medieval Florence, linking the city's religious centre with the Piazza della Signoria. Widening of this 'Street of the Shoemakers' in the 1840s has destroyed much of its medieval character, and the only shoe shops to be seen are designer-label. Its fate seems benign, though, compared with what happened to the Mercato Vecchio, in the fit of post-Risorgimento 'progress' that converted it into the **Piazza della Repubblica**, a block to the right along Via Speziali.

On the map, it's easy to pick out the small rectangle of narrow, straight streets around Piazza della Repubblica; these remain unchanged from the little *castrum* of Roman days. At its centre, the old forum deteriorated through the Dark Ages into a shabby market square and the Jewish ghetto, a piquant, densely populated quarter known as the Mercato Vecchio, the epitome of the picturesque for 19th-century tourists but an eyesore for the movers and shakers of the new Italy, who tore down its alleys and miniature *piazze* to create a fit symbol of Florence's reawakening. They erected a triumphal arch to themselves and proudly blazoned it with the inscription: 'THE ANCIENT CITY CENTRE RESTORED TO NEW LIFE FROM THE SQUALOR OF CENTURIES'. The sad result of this well-intentioned urban renewal, the Piazza della Repubblica, is one of the most ghastly squares in Italy, a brash intrusion of ponderous 19th-century buildings and parked cars. Just the same it is popular with locals and tourists alike, full of outdoor cafés, something of an oasis among the narrow, stern streets of medieval Florence.

Mercato Nuovo

From Piazza della Repubblica the natural flow of street life will sweep you down to the **Mercato Nuovo**, the old Straw Market, bustling under a beautiful loggia built by Grand Duke Cosimo in the 1500s. Although you won't see more than a wisp of straw these days, vendors hawk purses, stationery, toys, clothes, umbrellas and knick-knacks. In medieval times this was the merchants' exchange, where any merchant who committed the crime of bankruptcy was publicly spanked before being carted off to prison; in times of peace it sheltered Florence's battle-stained *carroccio*. Florentines often call the market the 'Porcellino' (piglet) after the large bronze boar erected in 1612, a copy of the ancient statue in the Uffizi. The drool spilling from the side of its mouth reminds us that unlike Rome, Florence is no splashy city of springs and fountains. Rub the piglet's shiny snout, and supposedly destiny will one day bring you back to Florence. The pungent aroma of the tripe sandwiches sold nearby may give you second thoughts.

Orsanmichele

Open 8–12 and 3–6.30.

There is a wonderfully eccentric church on Via Calzaiuoli that looks like no other church in the world; Orsanmichele rises up in a tall, neat three-storey rectangle. It was built on the site of ancient San Michele ad Hortum (popularly reduced to 'Orsanmichele'), a 9th-century church located near a vegetable garden, which the *comune* destroyed in 1240 to erect a grain market; after a fire in 1337 the current market building (by Francesco Talenti and others) was erected, with a loggia on the ground floor and emergency storehouses on top where grain was kept against a siege.

The original market had a pilaster with a painting of the Virgin that became increasingly celebrated for performing miracles. The area around the Virgin became known as the Oratory, and when Talenti reconstructed the market, his intention was to combine both its secular and religious functions; each pilaster of the loggia was assigned to a guild to adorn with an image of its patron saint. In 1380, when the market was relocated, the entire ground floor was given over to the functions of the church, and Francesco Talenti's talented son Simone was given the task of closing in the arcades with lovely Gothic windows, later bricked in.

The church, however, is most famous as a showcase of 15th-century Florentine sculpture; there is no better place to get an idea of the stylistic innovations that succeeded one another throughout the decades. Each guild sought to outdo the others by commissioning the finest artists of the day to carve their patron saints and create elaborate canopied niches to hold them. The first statue to the left of the door is one of the oldest; Ghiberti's bronze *St John the Baptist*, erected in 1416 for the Arte di Calimala, was the first life-sized Renaissance statue cast in bronze. Continuing to the left on Via de' Lamberti you can compare it with Donatello's *St Mark*, patron of the linen dealers and used-cloth merchants. Finished in 1411, it is considered the first free-standing marble statue of the Renaissance.

The niches continue around Via dell'Arte della Lana, named after the Wool Merchants' Guild, the richest after that of the Bankers. Their headquarters, the **Palazzo dell'Arte**

della Lana is linked by an overhead arch with Orsanmichele; built in 1308, it was restored in 1905 in a delightful William Morris style of medieval picturesque. The first statue on this façade of Orsanmichele is *St Eligio*, patron of smiths, by Nanni di Banco (1415), with a niche embellished with the guild's emblem (black pincers) and a bas-relief below showing one of this rather obscure saint's miracles—apparently he shod a horse the hard way, by cutting off its hoof, shoeing it, then sticking it back on the leg. The other two statues on this street are bronzes by Ghiberti, the Wool Guild's *St Stephen* (1426) and the Exchange Guild's *St Matthew* (1422), the latter an especially fine work in a classical niche. On the Via Orsanmichele façade stands a copy of Donatello's famous *St George* (the original now in the Bargello) done in 1417 for the Armourers' Guild, with a dramatic predella of the saint slaying the dragon, also by Donatello, that is one of the first-known works making use of perspective; next are the Stonecutters' and Carpenters' Guild's *Four Crowned Saints* (1415, by Nanni di Banco), inspired by Roman statues. Nanni also contributed the Shoemakers' *St Philip* (1415), while the next figure, *St Peter* is commonly attributed to Donatello (1413). Around the corner on Via Calzaiuoli stands the bronze *St Luke*, patron of the Judges and Notaries, by Giambologna, a work of 1602 in a 15th-century niche, and the *Doubting of St Thomas* by Andrea del Verrocchio (1484), made not for a guild but the Tribunal of Merchandise, who like St Thomas wanted to be certain before making a judgement. In the rondels above some of the niches are terracottas of the guilds' symbols by Luca della Robbia. (*At the time of writing some statues were under restoration.*)

Orsanmichele's dark **interior** (*under restoration at time of writing*) is ornate and cosy, with more of the air of a guildhall than a church. It makes a picturebook medieval setting for one of the masterpieces of the trecento: Andrea Orcagna's beautiful Gothic **Tabernacle** (*open 8–12 and 15–18.30*), a large, exquisite work in marble, bronze and coloured glass framing a contemporary painting of the Madonna (either by Bernardo Daddi or Orcagna himself), replacing the miraculous one, lost in a fire. The Tabernacle was commissioned by survivors of the 1348 Black Death. On the walls and pilasters are faded 14th-century frescoes of saints, placed as if members of the congregation; if you look at the pilasters on the left as you enter and along the right wall you can see the old chutes used to transfer grain.

Piazza della Signoria

Italian city builders are renowned for effortlessly creating beautiful squares, but it's an art where the Florentines are generally all thumbs. Only here, in the city's civic stage do they achieve a grand, meaningful space, a much needed antidote to the stone gullies of the ancient centre, dominated by the sombre fortress and tower of the Palazzo Vecchio and a lively gathering of some of the best and worst of Florentine sculpture.

Although the Piazza della Signoria currently serves as Great Aunt Florence's drawing-room-cum-tourist-overflow-tank, in the old days it saw the public assemblies of the republic, which in Florence meant that the square often degenerated into a battleground for impossibly inscrutable internecine quarrels. These could be stirred up to mythic levels of violence; in the 14th century a man was eaten by a crowd maddened by a political speech. Such speeches were given from the *arringhiera*, or oration terrace in front of the

Palazzo Vecchio, a word which gave us 'harangue'. It was in the Piazza della Signoria that Savonarola ignited his notorious Bonfire of Vanities in 1497, and here, too, the following year, the disillusioned Florentines ignited Savonarola himself. A small plaque in the pavement marks the exact spot, not far from Ammanati's fountain.

If, on the other hand, trouble came from without, the Florentines would toll the famous bell in the tower of the Palazzo Vecchio, and the square would rapidly fill with the gonfalons of the citizens' militia and the guilds. 'We will sound our trumpets!' threatened the French king Charles VIII, when the Florentines refused to shell out enough florins to make him and his army leave town. 'And we will ring our bell!' countered the courageous republican Piero Capponi—a threat that worked; Charles had to settle for a smaller sum. When Alessandro de' Medici was restored as duke of Tuscany three years later, one of his first acts was to smash the bell as a symbol of Florence's lost liberty.

Having a citizen's militia, as opposed to depending on foreign mercenaries, answered one of Machiavelli's requirements for a well-governed state. Training was taken fairly seriously; to build up their endurance, the republic's citizens played a ball game similar to rugby, believed to be descended from a Roman sport. Known these days as *Calcio in Costume*, it is played every June on a special ground of sand in the Piazza della Signoria, and it's good fun to watch the usually immaculate Florentines in their Renaissance duds mixing it up in the dirt (fighting is more than permitted, as long as it's one to one).

Since the 1970s and 80s a different kind of battle has been waged in this piazza, spiced with good old-fashioned Florentine factionalism. At stake is the future of the Piazza della Signoria itself. In 1974, while searching for signs of the original paving stones, the Soprintendenza ai Beni Archeologici found, much to their surprise, an underground medieval kasbah of narrow lanes, houses and wells—the ruins of 12th-century Ghibelline Florence, built over the baths and other portions of Roman and Etruscan *Florentia*. The *comune* ordered the excavations filled in; from the city's point of view, the piazza, essential to the essential tourist trade, was untouchable. In the 80s, the communal government fell, and the excavations were reopened on the portion of the piazza near the loggia. There are proposals to excavate the rest of the square, much to the horror of the *comune*, and to create eventually an underground museum similar to the one in Assisi. Until the issue is decided, don't be surprised to find the piazza full of gaping holes.

The Loggia dei Lanzi

Generally of a lower key than a political harangue was the *parlamento*, a meeting of eligible male citizens to vote on an important issue (usually already decided by the bosses). On these occasions, the Florentines heard speeches from the platform of the graceful three-arched Loggia dei Lanzi, also known as the Loggia della Signoria or the Loggia dell'Orcagna, after Andrea Orcagna, the probable architect. Completed in 1382, when pointed Gothic was still the rage, the Loggia with its lofty round arches looks back to classical antiquity and looks forward to the Renaissance; it is the germ of Brunelleschi's revolutionary architecture. If the impenetrable, stone Palazzo Vecchio is a symbol of the republic's strength and authority, the Loggia dei Lanzi is a symbol of its capacity for beauty, a vote for the gentle, floral side of its personality.

The loggia received its name 'of the lances' after the Swiss lancers, the private bodyguard of Cosimo I, and it was the Grand Duke who in 1560 commissioned the most famous sculpture sheltered in the arcade, Cellini's bronze *Perseus*, a *tour de force* with its attention to detail and expressive composition, graceful and poised atop the gruesome bleeding trunk, eyes averted from the horrible head capable of turning the onlookers into stone. The subject was a hint to the Florentines, to inspire their gratitude for Grand Ducal rule which spared them from the monstrosity of their own unworkable republic (*covered for restoration at the time of writing*). Nearby Giambologna's *Rape of the Sabines* (1583) is an essay in three-dimensional Mannerism. Its three figures of an old man, a young man and a woman spiral upwards in a fluid *contrapposto* convulsion, one of the first sculptures designed to be seen from all sides. The loggia also shelters Giambologna's less successful *Hercules and Nessus*, a chorus line of six Roman vestal wallflowers, and several other works that contribute to the rather curious effect, especially at night, of people at a wild party frozen into stone by Medusa's magical gaze.

The first two statues placed in the square were carried there by republican enthusiasm. Donatello's *Judith and Holofernes* was hauled from the Medici palace and placed here in 1494 as a symbol of the defeat of tyranny. Michelangelo's *David* was equally seen as the embodiment of republican triumph (when it was finished in 1504, the Medici were in exile), though it is doubtful whether Michelangelo himself had such symbolism in mind, as the statue was intended to stand next to the cathedral, only to be shanghaied to the Piazza della Signoria by eager republican partisans. It was replaced by a copy in 1873 when the original was relocated with much pomp on a specially built train to the Accademia. Later Florentine sculptors attempted to rival the *David*, especially the awful Baccio Bandinelli, who managed to get the commission to create a pendant to the statue and boasted that he could surpass Il Divino himself. The pathetic result, *Hercules and Cacus*, was completed in 1534; as a reward for his efforts, Bandinelli had to listen to his arch-enemy Cellini insult the statue in front of their patron, Cosimo I. An 'old sack full of melons' he called it, bestowing what has since become, for all practical purposes, the sculpture's alternative title.

Another overgrown victim of the chisel stands at the corner of the Palazzo Vecchio. Ammanati's **Neptune Fountain** (1575) was dubbed *Il Biancone* ('Big Whitey') almost as soon as it was unveiled; Michelangelo felt sorry for the huge block of marble Ammannati 'ruined' to produce Neptune, a lumpy, bloated symbol of Cosimo I's naval victories, who stands arrogantly over a low basin and a few half-hearted spurts of water, pulled along by four struggling sea steeds, mere hobby-horses compared with Big Whitey himself.

The last colossus in the Piazza della Signoria is the *Equestrian Monument to Cosimo I* by Giambologna (1595), the only large-scale equestrian bronze of the Late Renaissance. The scheme on the panels below the statue depicts scenes of Cosimo's brutal conquest of Siena, and of the 'Florentine Senate' and the Pope conferring the Grand Dukedom on Cosimo.

Directly behind Cosimo stands the **Tribunale di Mercanzia**, built in the 14th century as a commercial court for merchants of the guilds and adorned with heraldic arms. To the left of this (No. 7) is a fine, 16th-century contribution, the **Palazzo Uguccioni**, very much in the spirit of High Renaissance in Rome, and sometimes attributed to a design by Raphael.

Palazzo Vecchio

When Goethe made his blitz-tour of Florence, the Palazzo Vecchio (also called the Palazzo della Signoria) helped pull the wool over his eyes. 'Obviously,' thought the great poet, 'the people . . . enjoyed a lucky succession of good governments'—a remark which, as Mary McCarthy wrote, could make the angels in heaven weep. But none of Florence's chronic factionalism mars Arnolfo di Cambio's temple of civic aspirations, part council hall and part fortress. In many ways, the Palazzo Vecchio is the ideal of stone Florence: rugged and imposing, with a rusticated façade that was to inspire so many of the city's private palaces, yet designed according to the proportions of the Golden Section of the ancient Greeks. Its dominant feature, the 94m tower, is a typical piece of Florentine bravado, for long the highest point in the city.

The Palazzo Vecchio occupies the site of the old Roman theatre and the medieval Palazzo dei Priori. In the 13th century this earlier palace was flattened along with the Ghibelline quarter interred under the piazza, and in 1299, the now ascendant Guelphs called upon Arnolfo di Cambio, master builder of the cathedral, to design the most impressive 'Palazzo del Popolo' (as the building was originally called) possible, with an eye to upstaging rival cities. The palace's unusual trapezoidal shape is often, but rather dubiously, explained as Guelph care not to have any of the building touch land once owned by Ghibellines. One doubts that even in the 13th century real estate realities allowed such delicacy of sentiments; nor does the theory explain why the tower has swallowtail Ghibelline crenellations, as opposed to the square Guelph ones on the palace itself. Later additions to the rear of the palace have obscured its shape even more, though the façade is essentially as Arnolfo built it, except for the bet-hedging monogram over the door hailing Christ the king of Florence, put up in the nervous days of 1529, when the imperial army of Charles V was on its way to destroy the last Florentine republic; the inscription replaces an earlier one left by Savonarola. The room at the top of the tower was used as prison for celebrities and dubbed the *alberghetto* ('the little hotel'); inmates included Cosimo il Vecchio before his brief exile, and Savonarola, who spent his last months, between torture sessions, enjoying a superb view of the city before his execution in the piazza below.

Inside the Palazzo Vecchio

Open 9–7; holidays 8–1; closed Thurs; adm.

Today the Palazzo Vecchio serves as Florence's city hall, but nearly all of its historical rooms are open to the public. With few exceptions, the interior decorations date from the time of Cosimo I, when he moved his Grand Ducal self from the Medici palace in 1540. To politically 'correct' its acres of walls and ceilings in the shortest amount of time, he turned to his court artist Giorgio Vasari, famed more for the speed at which he could execute a commission than for its quality. On the ground floor of the palazzo, before you buy your ticket, you can take a gander at some of Vasari's more elaborate handiwork in the **Courtyard**, redone for the occasion of Francesco I's unhappy marriage to the plain and stupid Habsburg Joanna of Austria in 1565.

Vasari's suitably grand staircase ascends to the largest room in the palace, the vast **Salone dei Cinquecento**. The *salone* was added at the insistence of Savonarola for meetings of the 500-strong Consiglio Maggiore, the reformed republic's democratic assembly. Art's two reigning divinities, Leonardo da Vinci and Michelangelo, were commissioned in 1503 to paint the two long walls of the *salone* in a kind of Battle of the Brushes to which the city eagerly looked forward. Unfortunately, neither of the artists came near to completing the project; Leonardo managed to fresco a section of the wall, using the experimental techniques that were to prove the undoing of his *Last Supper* in Milan, while Michelangelo only completed the cartoons before being summoned to Rome by Julius II, who required the sculptor of the *David* to pander to his own personal megalomania.

In the 1560s Vasari removed what was left of Leonardo's efforts and refrescoed the entire room as a celebration of Cosimo's military triumphs over Pisa and Siena, complete with an apotheosis of the Grand Duke on the ceiling. These wall scenes are inane, big and busy, crowded with men and horses who appear to have all the substance of overcooked pasta. The sculptural groups lining the walls of this almost uncomfortably large room (the Italian parliament sat here from 1865 to 1870 when Florence was the capital) are only slightly more stimulating; even Michelangelo's *Victory*, on the wall opposite the entrance, is more virtuosity than vision: a vacuous young idiot posing with one knee atop a defeated old man still half-submerged in stone, said to be a self-portrait of the sculptor, which lends the work a certain bitter poignancy. The neighbouring work, a muscle-bound *Hercules and Diomedes* by Vicenzo de' Rossi, probably was inevitable in this city obsessed by the possibilities of the male nude.

Beyond the *salone*, behind a modern glass door, is a much smaller and much more intriguing room the size of a closet. This is the **Studiolo of Francesco I**, designed by Vasari in 1572 for Cosimo's melancholic and reclusive son, where he would escape to brood over his real interests in natural curiosities and alchemy. The little study, windowless and more than a little claustrophobic, has been restored to its original appearance, lined with allegorical paintings by Vasari, Bronzino and Allori, and bronze statuettes by Giambologna and Ammanati, their refined, polished, and erotic mythological subjects part of a carefully thought-out 16th-century programme on Man and Nature. The lower row of paintings conceals Francesco's secret cupboards where he kept his most precious belongings, his pearls and crystals and gold.

After the *salone* a certain fuzziness begins to set in. Cosimo I's propaganda machine in league with Vasari's fresco factory produced room after room of self-glorifying Medicean poofery. The first series of rooms, known as the **Quartiere di Leone X**, carry ancestor worship to extremes, each chamber dedicated to a different Medici: in the first Cosimo il Vecchio returns from exile amid tumultuous acclaim; in the second Lorenzo il Magnifico receives the ambassadors in the company of a dignified giraffe; the third and fourth are dedicated to the Medici popes, while the fifth, naturally, is for Cosimo I, who gets the most elaborate treatment of all.

Upstairs the next series of rooms is known as the **Quartiere degli Elementi**, with more works of Vasari and his studio, depicting allegories of the elements. In a small room, called **Terrazzo di Giunone**, is the original of Verrocchio's boy with the dolphin, from the courtyard fountain.

A balcony across the Salone dei Cinquecento leads to the **Quartiere di Eleonora di Toledo**, Mrs Cosimo I's private apartments. Of special note here is her chapel, one of the masterpieces of Bronzino, who seemed to relish the opportunity to paint something besides Medici portraits. The **Sala dell'Udienza**, beyond the second chapel, has a magnificent quattrocento coffered ceiling by Benedetto and Giuliano da Maiano, and walls painted with a rather fine romp by Mannerist Francesco Salviati (1550–60).

The last room, the **Sala dei Gigli** ('of the lilies') boasts another fine ceiling by the da Maiano brothers; it contains Donatello's restored bronze *Judith and Holofernes*, a late and rather gruesome work of 1455; the warning to tyrants inscribed on its base was added when the statue was abducted from the Medici palace and placed in the Piazza della Signoria. Off the Sala dei Gigli are two small rooms of interest: the **Guardaroba**, or unique 'wardrobe' adorned with 57 maps painted by Fra Egnazio Danti in 1563, depicting all the world known at the time. The **Cancelleria** was Machiavelli's office from 1498 to 1512, when he served the republic as a secretary and diplomat. He is commemorated with a bust and a portrait. Poor Machiavelli died bitter and unaware of the notoriety that his works would one day bring him, and he would probably be amazed to learn that his very name had become synonymous with cunning, amoral intrigue. After losing his job upon the return of the Medici, and at one point tortured and imprisoned on a false suspicion of conspiracy, Machiavelli was forced into idleness in the country, where he wrote his political works and two fine plays, feverishly trying to return to favour, even dedicating his most famous book, *The Prince*, to the incompetent Lorenzo, Duke of Urbino (further glorified by Michelangelo's Medici tombs); his concern throughout was to advise realistically, without mincing words, the fractious and increasingly weak Italians on how to create a strong state. His evil reputation came from openly stating what rulers do, rather than what they would like other people to think they do.

Two collections long housed in the Palazzo Vecchio, the excellent **Collection of Old Musical Instruments**, and the **Collezione Loeser**, a fine assortment of Renaissance art left to the city in 1928 by Charles Loeser, the Macy's department-store heir, have at the time of writing tumbled into Italian museum limbo. The violins and cellos (several by Cremona greats like Stradivarius and Guarneri) have been earmarked for a new destination; in summer they are on show every Mon, Wed, Fri and Sat 8–11pm.

Collezione della Ragione

Open 9–2, closed Tues; information ℂ (055) 217305.

After the pomposity of the Palazzo Vecchio and a Campari cure at the Piazza della Signoria's landmark **Café Rivoire**, you may be in the mood to reconsider the 20th century. The best place to do this in Florence is at its only museum of modern art, the Collezione della Ragione, located on the Piazza della Signoria, above the Cassa di Risparmio bank. There are typical still lifes by De Pisis; equally still landscapes by Carlo Carra; mysterious baths by De Chirico; Tuscan landscapes by Mario Mafai, Antonio Donghi and Ottone Rosai; a speedy Futurist horse by Fortunato Depero and a window with doves by Gino Severini; a number of richly coloured canvases by Renato Guttuso and paintings after Tintoretto by Emilio Vedova, and many others, surprises, perhaps, for those unfamiliar with living Italians as opposed to dead ones.

The Uffizi

Queues in the summer are very common; try to arrive early. Open daily exc Mon 9–7, and 9–2 Sun; adm exp.

Florence has the most fabulous art museum in Italy, and as usual we have the Medici to thank; for the building that holds these treasures, however, credit goes to Grand Duke Cosimo's much maligned court painter. Poor Giorgio Vasari! His roosterish boastfulness and the conviction that his was the best of all possible artistic worlds, set next to his very modest talents, have made him a comic figure in most art criticism. Even the Florentines don't like him. On one of the rare occasions when he tried his hand as an architect, though, he gave Florence something to be proud of. The Uffizi ('offices') were built as Cosimo's secretariat, incorporating the old mint (producer of the first gold florins in 1252), the archives, and the large church of San Pier Scheraggio, with plenty of room for the bureaucrats needed to run Cosimo's efficient, modern state. The matched pair of arcaded buildings have coldly elegant façades that conceal Vasari's surprising innovation: iron reinforcements that make the huge amount of window area possible and keep the building stable on the soft sandy ground. It was a trick that would be almost forgotten until the Crystal Palace and the first American skyscrapers.

Almost from the start the Medici began to store some of their huge art collection in parts of the building. There are galleries in the world with more works of art—the Uffizi counts some 1800—but the Uffizi overwhelms by the fact that every one of its paintings is worth looking at.

Near the ticket counter you can see what remains of the church of San Pier Scheraggio, now decorated with Andrea del Castagno's stately **Frescoes of Illustrious Men** (1450), including the Cumaean Sibyl(!) as well as Dante and Boccaccio, both of whom attended political debates in this very church. From here you can take the lift or sweeping grand stair up to the second floor, where the Medici once had a huge theatre, now home to the **Cabinet of Drawings and Prints**. Although the bulk of this extensive and renowned collection is only open to scholars with special permission, a roomful of tempting samples gives a hint at what they have a chance to see.

Nowadays one thinks of the Uffizi as primarily a gallery of paintings, but for some hundred years after its opening, visitors came almost exclusively for the fine collection of Hellenistic and Roman marbles. Most of these were collected in Rome by Medici cardinals, and not a few were sources of Renaissance inspiration. The **Vestibule** at the top of the stair contains some of the best, together with Flemish and Tuscan tapestries made for Cosimo I and his successors. **Room 1**, usually shut, contains excellent early Roman sculpture.

Rooms 2–6: 13th and 14th centuries

The Uffizi's paintings are arranged in chronological order, the better to educate its visitors on trends in Italian art. The roots of the Early Renaissance are most strikingly revealed in **Room 2**, dedicated to the three great **Maestà** altarpieces by the masters of the 13th century. All portray the same subject of the Madonna and Child enthroned with angels. The one on the right, by Cimabue, was painted around the year 1285 and represents a breaking away from the flat, stylized Byzantine tradition. To the left is the so-called *Rucellai Madonna*, painted around the same period by the Sienese Duccio di Buoninsegna for Santa Maria Novella. It resembles Cimabue's in many ways, but with a more advanced technique for creating depth, and the bright colouring that characterizes the Sienese school. Giotto's altarpiece, painted some 25 years later, takes a great leap forward, not only in his use of perspective, but in the arrangement of the angels, standing naturally, and in the portrayal of the Virgin, gently smiling, with real fingers and breasts.

To the left, **Room 3** contains representative Sienese works of the 14th century, with a beautiful Gothic *Annunciation* (1333) by Simone Martini and the brothers Pietro and Ambrogio Lorenzetti. **Room 4** is dedicated to 14th-century Florentines: Bernardo Daddi, Nardo di Cione, and the delicately coloured *San Remigio Pietà* by Giottino. **Rooms 5 and 6** portray Italian contributions to the International Gothic school, most dazzlingly Gentile da Fabriano's *Adoration of the Magi* (1423), two good works by Lorenzo Monaco, and the *Thebaid* of Gherardo Starnina, depicting the rather unusual activities of the 4th-century monks of St Pancratius of Thebes, in Egypt; a composition strikingly like Chinese scroll scenes of hermits.

Rooms 7–9: Early Renaissance

In the Uffizi, at least, it's but a few short steps from the superbly decorative International Gothic to the masters of the Early Renaissance. **Room 7** contains minor works by Fra Angelico, Masaccio and Masolino, and three masterpieces: Domenico Veneziano's pastel *Madonna and Child with Saints* (1448), one of the rare pictures by this Venetian master who died a pauper in Florence. It is a new departure not only for its soft colours but for the subject matter, unifying the enthroned Virgin and saints in one panel, in what is known as a *Sacra Conversazione*. Piero della Francesca's famous *Double Portrait of the Duke Federigo da Montefeltro and his Duchess Battista Sforza of Urbino* (1465) depicts one of Italy's noblest Renaissance princes—and surely the one with the most distinctive nose. Piero's ability to create perfectly still, timeless worlds is even more evident in the allegorical 'Triumphs' of the Duke and Duchess painted on the back of their portraits. A similar stillness and fascination floats over into the surreal in Uccello's *Rout of San Romano* (1456), or at least the third of it still present (the other two panels are in the Louvre and London's National Gallery; all three once decorated the bedroom of Lorenzo il Magnifico in the Medici palace). Both Piero and Uccello were deep students of perspective, but Uccello went half-crazy; applying his principles to a violent battle scene has left us one of the most provocative works of all time—a vision of warfare in suspended animation, with pink, white and blue toy horses, robot-like knights, and rabbits bouncing in the background.

Room 8 is devoted to the works of the rascally romantic Fra Filippo Lippi, whose ethereally lovely Madonnas were modelled after his brown-eyed nun. In his *Coronation of the Virgin* (1447) she kneels in the foreground with two children, while the artist, dressed in a brown habit, looks dreamily towards her; in his celebrated *Madonna and Child with Two Angels* (1445) she plays the lead before the kind of mysterious landscape Leonardo would later perfect. Lippi taught the art of enchanting Madonnas to his student Botticelli, who has some lovely works in this room and the next; Alesso Baldovinetti, a pupil of the far more holy Fra Angelico, painted the room's beautiful *Annunciation* (1447). **Room 9** has two small scenes from the *Labours of Hercules* (1470) by Antonio Pollaiuolo, whose interest in anatomy, muscular expressiveness and violence presages a strain in Florentine art that would culminate in the great Mannerists. He worked with his younger brother Piero on the refined, elegant *SS. Vincent, James and Eustace*, transferred here from San Miniato. This room also contains the Uffizi's best-known forgery: *The Young Man in a Red Hat* or self-portrait of Filippino Lippi, believed to have been the work of a clever 18th-century English art dealer who palmed it off on the Grand Dukes.

Botticelli: Rooms 10–14

To accommodate the bewitching art of 'Little Barrels' and his throngs of 20th-century admirers, the Uffizi converted four small rooms into one great Botticellian shrine. Although his masterpieces displayed here have become almost synonymous with the Florentine Renaissance at its most spring-like and charming, they were not publicly displayed until the beginning of the 19th century, nor given much consideration outside Florence until the turn of the century.

Botticelli's best works date from the days when he was a darling of the Medici—family members crop up most noticeably in the *Adoration of the Magi* (1476), where you can pick out Cosimo il Vecchio, Lorenzo il Magnifico and Botticelli himself (in the right foreground, in a yellow robe, gazing at the spectator). His *Annunciation* is a graceful, cosmic dance between the Virgin and the Angel Gabriel. In the *Tondo of the Virgin of the Pomegranate* the lovely melancholy goddess who was to become his Venus makes her first appearance.

Botticelli is best known for his sublime mythological allegories, nearly all painted for the Medici and inspired by the Neoplatonic, humanistic and hermetic currents that pervaded the intelligentsia of the late 15th century. Perhaps no painting has been debated so fervently as *La Primavera* (1478). This hung for years in the Medici Villa at Castello, and it is believed that the subject of the Allegory of Spring was suggested by Marsilio Ficino, one of the great natural magicians of the Renaissance, and that the figures represent the 'beneficial' planets able to dispel sadness. *Pallas and the Centaur* has been called another subtle allegory of Medici triumph—the rings of Athena's gown are supposedly a family symbol. Other interpretations see the taming of the sorrowful centaur as a melancholy comment on reason and civilization. Botticelli's last great mythological painting, *The Birth of Venus*, was commissioned by Lorenzo di Pierfrancesco and inspired by a poem by Poliziano, Lorenzo il Magnifico's Latin and Greek scholar, who described how Zephyr and Chloris blew the newborn goddess to shore on a scallop shell, while Hora hastened to robe her, a scene Botticelli portrays once again with dance-like rhythm and delicacy of line. Yet the goddess of love floats towards the spectator with an expression of wistfulness—perhaps reflecting the artist's own feelings of regret. For artistically, the poetic, decorative style he perfected in this painting would be disdained and forgotten in his own lifetime. Spiritually, Botticelli also turned a corner after creating this haunting, uncanny beauty—his, and Florence's farewell to a lovely road not taken. Although Vasari's biography of Botticelli portrays a prankster rather than a sensitive soul, the painter absorbed more than any other artist the *fin-de-siècle* neuroticism that beset the city with the rise of Savonarola. So thoroughly did he reject his Neoplatonism that he would only accept commissions of sacred subjects or supposedly edifying allegories like his *Calumny*, a small but disturbing work, and a fitting introduction to the dark side of the quattrocento psyche.

This large room also contains works by Botticelli's contemporaries. Two paintings of the *Adoration of the Magi*, one by Ghirlandaio and one by Filippino Lippi, show the influence of Leonardo's unfinished but radical work in pyramidal composition (in the next room); Leonardo himself got the idea from the large *Portinari Altarpiece* (1471) by Hugo Van der Goes in the middle of the room, a work brought back from Bruges by Medici agent Tommaso Portinari. Behind it hangs Lorenzo di Credi's *Venus*, a charmer inspired by Botticelli.

Rooms 15–24: More Renaissance

Room 15 is dedicated to the Florentine works of Leonardo da Vinci's early career. Here are works by his master Andrea Verrocchio, including the *Baptism of Christ*, in which the young Leonardo painted the angel on the left. Modern art critics believe the large *Annunciation* (1475) is almost entirely by Leonardo's hand—the soft faces, the botanical details, the misty, watery background would become the trademarks of his magical brush. Most influential, however, was his unfinished *Adoration of the Magi* (1481), a highly unconventional composition that Leonardo abandoned when he left Florence for Milan. Although at first glance it's hard to make out much more than a mass of reddish chiaroscuro, the longer you stare, the better you'll see the serene Madonna and Child surrounded by a crowd of anxious, troubled humanity, with an exotic background of ruins, trees and horsemen, all charged with expressive energy. Other artists in Room 15 include Leonardo's peers: Lorenzo di Credi, whose religious works have eerie garden-like backgrounds, and the nutty Piero di Cosimo, whose dreamy *Perseus Liberating Andromeda* includes an endearing mongrel of a dragon that gives even the most reserved Japanese tourist fits of giggles. Tuscan maps adorn **Room 16**, as well as scenes by Hans Memling.

The octagonal **Tribuna** (Room 18) with its mother-of-pearl dome and *pietra dura* floor and table was built by Buontalenti in 1584 for Francesco I, and like the Studiolo in the Palazzo Vecchio, was designed to hold Medici treasures. For centuries the best-known of these was the *Venus de' Medici*, a 2nd-century BC Greek sculpture, farcically claimed as a copy of Praxiteles' celebrated Aphrodite of Cnidos, the most erotic statue in antiquity. In the 18th century, amazingly, this rather ordinary girl was considered the greatest sculpture in Florence; today most visitors walk right by without a second glance. Other antique works include the *Wrestlers* and the *Knife Grinder*, both copies of Pergamese originals, the *Dancing Faun*, the *Young Apollo*, and the *Sleeping Hermaphrodite* in the adjacent room, which sounds fascinating but is usually curtained off.

The real stars of the Tribuna are the Medici court portraits, many by Bronzino, who could not only catch the likeness of Cosimo I, Eleanor of Toledo and their children, but aptly portrayed the spirit of the day—these are people who took themselves very seriously indeed. They have for company Vasari's posthumous portrait of *Lorenzo il Magnifico* and Pontormo's *Cosimo il Vecchio*, Andrea del Sarto's *Girl with a Book by Petrarch*, and Rosso Fiorentino's *Angel Musician*, an enchanting work entirely out of place in this stodgy temple.

Two followers of Piero della Francesca, Perugino and Luca Signorelli, hold pride of place in **Room 19**; Perugino's *Portrait of a Young Man* is believed to be modelled on his pupil Raphael. Signorelli's *Tondo of the Holy Family* was to become the inspiration for Michelangelo's (*see* below). The Germans appear in **Room 20**, led by Dürer and his earliest known work, the *Portrait of his Father* (1490), done at age 19, and *The Adoration of the Magi* (1504), painted after his first trip to Italy. Also here are Lucas Cranach's Teutonic *Adam and Eve* and *Portrait of Martin Luther* (1543), not someone you'd expect to see in Florence. **Room 21** is dedicated to the great Venetians, most famously Bellini and his uncanny *Sacred Allegory* (1490s), the meaning of which has never been satisfactorily explained. There are two minor works by the elusive Giorgione, and a typically weird *St Dominic* by Cosmè Tura. Later Flemish and German artists appear in **Room 22**, works by Gerard David and proto-Romantic Albrecht Altdorfer, and a portrait attributed to Hans Holbein of *Sir Thomas More*. **Room 23** is dedicated to non-Tuscans Correggio of Parma and Mantegna of the Veneto, as well as Boltraffio's strange *Narcissus* with an eerie background reminiscent of Leonardo.

Rooms 25–27: Mannerism

The window-filled South Corridor, with its views over the city and its fine display of antique sculpture, marks only the halfway point in the Uffizi but nearly the end of Florence's contribution. In the first three rooms, however, local talent rallies to produce a brilliantly coloured twilight in Florentine Mannerism. By most accounts, Michelangelo's only completed oil painting, the *Tondo Doni* (1506), was the spark that ignited Mannerism's flaming orange and turquoise hues. Michelangelo was 30 when he painted this unconventional work, in a medium he disliked (sculpture and fresco being the only fit occupations for a man, he believed). It's a typical Michelangelo story that when the purchaser complained the artist was asking too much for it, Michelangelo promptly doubled the price. As shocking as the colours are the spiralling poses of the Holy Family, sharply delineated against a background of five nude, slightly out-of-focus young men of uncertain purpose (are they pagans? angels? boyfriends? or just filler?)—an ambiguity that was to become a hallmark of Mannerism. In itself, the *Tondo Doni* is more provocative than immediately appealing; the violent canvas in Room 27, Rosso Fiorentino's *Moses Defending the Children of Jethro*, was painted some 20 years later and at least in its intention to shock the viewer puts a cap on what Michelangelo began.

Room 26 is dedicated mainly to Raphael, who was in and out of Florence 1504–8. Never temperamental or eccentric like his contemporaries, Raphael was the sweetheart of the High Renaissance. His Madonnas, like *The Madonna of the Goldfinch*, a luminous work painted in Florence, have a tenderness that was soon to be over-popularized by others and turned into holy cards, a cloying sentimentality added like layers of varnish over the centuries. It's easier, perhaps, to see Raphael's genius in non-sacred subjects, like *Leo X with Two Cardinals*, a perceptive portrait study of the first Medici pope with his nephew Giulio de' Medici, later Clement VII. The same room contains Andrea del Sarto's most original work, the fluorescent *Madonna of the Harpies* (1517), named after the figures on the Virgin's pedestal. Of the works by Pontormo, the best is in **Room 27**, *Supper at Emmaus* (1525), a strange canvas with peasant-faced monks emerging out of the darkness, brightly clad diners with dirty feet, and the Masonic symbol of the Eye of God hovering over Christ's head.

Rooms 28–45

Although we now bid a fond farewell to the Florentines, the Uffizi fairly bristles with masterpieces from other parts of Italy and abroad. Titian's delicious nudes, especially the incomparably voluptuous *Venus of Urbino*, raise the temperature in **Room 28**; Parmigianino's hyper-elegant *Madonna with the Long Neck* (1536) in **Room 30** is a fascinating Mannerist evolutionary dead-end, possessing all the weird beauty of a foot-long dragonfly. Sebastiano del Piombo's recently restored *Death of Adonis*, in **Room 32**, is notable for its melancholy, lagoony, autumn atmosphere and the annoyed look on Venus' face. **Room 34** holds Paolo Veronese's *Holy Family with St Barbara*, a late work bathed in a golden Venetian light, with a gorgeously opulent Barbara gazing on. In **Room 35** his contemporary Tintoretto is represented by a shadowy *Leda* languidly pretending to restrain the lusty swan; the Uffizi's El Greco is here as well, reminding us that this most Mannerist of Mannerists learned how to do it in Venice.

Room 41 is Flemish domain, with brand-name art by Rubens and Van Dyck; the former's *Baccanale* may be the most grotesque canvas in Florence. Struggle on gamely to **Room**

43 to see three striking Caravaggios. His *Bacchus* and *The Head of Medusa* are believed to be self-portraits; in its day the fleshy, heavy-eyed Bacchus, half portrait and half still life, but lacking the usual mythological appurtenances, was considered highly iconoclastic. There are three portraits by Rembrandt in **Room 44**, including two of himself, young and old, and landscapes by Ruysdael. **Room 45** is given over to some fine 18th-century works, including two charming portraits of children by Chardin, and others by Goya and Longhi, and Venetian landscapes by Guardi and Canaletto. Even more welcome by this time is the bar at the end of the corridor, with a lovely summer terrace.

Corridoio Vasariano

In 1565, when Francesco I married Joanna of Austria, the Medici commissioned Vasari to link their new digs in the Pitti Palace with the Uffizi and the Palazzo Vecchio in such a manner that the Archdukes could make their rounds without rubbing elbows with their subjects. With a patina of 400 years, it seems that Florence wouldn't look quite right without this covered catwalk, leapfrogging on rounded arches from the back of the Uffizi, over the Ponte Vecchio, daintily skirting a medieval tower, and darting past the façade of Santa Felicità to the Pitti Palace.

The Corridoio not only offers interesting views of Florence, but has been hung with a celebrated collection of artists' self-portraits, beginning with Vasari himself before continuing in chronological order, past the Gaddis and Raphael to Rembrandt, Van Dyck, Velazquez, Hogarth, Reynolds, Delacroix, Corot and scores in between. To visit make an appointment with the Uffizi secretary, although the bomb of May 1993 damaged parts of the Vasari Corridor and it is currently closed for restoration. Other parts of the gallery are also temporarily closed to repair bomb damage, but all the major works displayed in these areas have been moved and are visible.

The Museum of the History of Science

Open 9.30–1 Mon–Sat, 2–5 also Mon, Wed and Fri, closed Sun; adm exp.

For all that Florence and Tuscany contributed to the birth of science, it is only fitting to have this museum in the centre of the city, behind the Uffizi in Piazza Giudici. Much of the ground floor is devoted to instruments measuring time and distance that are often works of art in themselves: Arabian astrolabes and pocket sundials, Tuscan sundials in the shape of Platonic solids, enormous elaborate armillary spheres and a small reliquary holding the bone of Galileo's finger, erect, like a final gesture to the city that until 1737 denied him a Christian burial. Here, too, are two of his original telescopes and the lens with which he discovered the four moons of Jupiter. Other scientific instruments come from the Accademia del Cimento (of 'trial', or 'experiment'), founded in 1657 by Cardinal Leopoldo de' Medici, the world's first scientific organization, dedicated to Galileo's principle of inquiry and proof by experimentation. 'Try and try again' was its motto.

Upstairs, there's a large room filled with machines used to demonstrate principles of physics, which the ladies who run the museum will operate if you ask. Two unusual ones are the 18th-century automatic writer and the instrument of perpetual motion. The rooms devoted to medicine contain a collection of 18th-century wax anatomical models, designed to teach budding obstetricians about unfortunate foetal positions, as well as a fine display of surgical instruments from the period.

The Ponte Vecchio and Ponte Santa Trínita

Bent bridges seeming to strain like bows
And tremble with arrowy undertide . . .

Elizabeth Barrett Browning, 'Casa Guidi Windows'

Often at sunset the Arno becomes a stream of molten gold, confined in its walls of stone and laced into its bed with the curving arches of its spans. That is, during those months when it has a respectable flow of water. But even in the torrid days of August, when the Arno shrivels into muck and spittle, its two famous bridges retain their distinctive beauty. The most famous of these, the Ponte Vecchio, the 'Old Bridge', crosses the Arno at its narrowest point; the present bridge, with its three stone arches, was built in 1345, and replaces a wooden construction from the 970s, which in turn was the successor to a span that may well have dated back to the Romans.

On this bridge, at the foot of the Marzocco, or statue of Mars, Buondelmonte dei Buondelmonti was murdered in 1215, setting off the wars of the Guelphs and Ghibellines. The original Marzocco was washed away in a 14th-century flood, and Donatello's later version has been carted off to the Bargello.

Like old London Bridge, the Ponte Vecchio is covered with shops and houses. By the 1500s, for hygienic reasons, it had become the street of hog butchers, though after Vasari built Cosimo's secret passage on top, the Grand Duke, for personal hygienic reasons, evicted the butchers and replaced them with goldsmiths. They have been there ever since, and shoppers from around the world descend on it each year to scrutinize the traditional Florentine talent for jewellery—not a few of the city's great artists began their careers as goldsmiths, beginning with Ghiberti and Donatello, and ending with Cellini, who never gave up the craft, and whose bust adorns the middle of the bridge. In the 1966 flood the shops did not prove as resilient as the Ponte Vecchio itself, and a fortune of gold was washed down the Arno. All has since been excellently restored.

In the summer of 1944, the river briefly became a German defensive line during the slow painful retreat across Italy. Before leaving Florence, the Nazis blew up every one of the city's bridges, saving only, on Hitler's special orders, the Ponte Vecchio, though they blasted a large number of ancient buildings on each side of the span to create piles of rubble to block the approaches. Florence's most beautiful span, the **Ponte Santa Trínita** was the most tragic victim. Immediately after the war the Florentines set about replacing the bridges exactly as they were: for Santa Trínita, old quarries had to be reopened to duplicate the stone, and old methods revived to cut it (modern power saws would have done it too cleanly). The graceful curve of the three arches was a problem; they could not

Ponte Vecchio

be constructed geometrically, and considerable speculation went on over how the architect (Ammanati, in 1567) did it.

Finally, recalling that Michelangelo had advised Ammanati on the project, someone noticed that the same form of arch could be seen on the decoration of the tombs in Michelangelo's Medici Chapel, constructed most likely by pure artistic imagination. Fortune lent a hand in the reconstruction; of the original statues of the 'Four Seasons', almost all the pieces were fished out of the Arno and rebuilt. 'Spring's head was eventually found by divers completely by accident in 1961.

Dante's Florence

In 1265 Dante Alighieri was born in the quarter just to the north of the Piazza della Signoria; he was nine, attending a May Feast, 'when first the glorious Lady of my mind was made manifest to mine eyes; even she who was called Beatrice by many who know not wherefore'. Beatrice went on to wed another, and died suddenly in 1290; Dante tried to forget his disappointment and grief in battle, fighting in the wars against Arezzo and Pisa, then in writing his 'autopsychology' *La Vita Nuova*. In 1302, as a White Guelph, he was sent into exile. A friend just managed to rescue the manuscript of the *Inferno* from the crowds who came to sack and pillage his home. Dante died in Ravenna in 1321, and although he was never allowed to return home, the Florentines have belatedly tried to make amends to their poet. Yet the memorials fall curiously flat. His grand tomb in Santa Croce is empty and his huge statue in front of the church a glowering failure.

The best place to summon the shade of Italy's greatest poet is in the narrow medieval lanes of Florence, especially in his old haunts just to the north of Piazza della Signoria. Most scholars believe Dante was born on what is now Via Dante Alighieri. A modern bas-relief on one of the buildings shows the sights that would have been familiar to Dante, one of which would have been the sturdy well-preserved **Torre del Castagno** on Piazza San Martino, used as the residence of the *priori* before the construction of the Palazzo Vecchio. Here, too, is the tiny **San Martino del Vescovo**, Dante's parish church (*open 10–12 and 3–5, closed Sun*), founded in 986 but rebuilt in 1479 when it became the headquarters of the charitable Compagnia dei Buonuomini. The Compagnia commissioned a follower of Ghirlandaio to paint a series of colourful frescoes on the Life of St Martin and the Works of Charity, scenes acted out by quattrocento Florentines, in their own fashions on their own streets. The church also has a fine Byzantine Madonna, and one by Perugino.

Opposite the Piazza San Martino, an alley leads back to the **Casa di Dante**, traditionally considered the poet's birthplace. Now a museum dedicated to Dante (*open 10–6, Sun 10–2, closed Tues; adm*), it makes a game attempt to evoke Dante's life and times, in spite of neglect and stingy Florentine low-watt light bulbs. Near the entrance is an edition of *The Divine Comedy*, printed in tiny letters on a poster by a mad Milanese; of the manuscript reproductions, the most interesting is an illumination of the infamous murder of Buondelmonte dei Buondelmonti, with the Ponte Vecchio and a statue of Mars, the original *Marzocco* in place. Upstairs there are copies of Botticelli's beautiful line illustrations for the *Commedia*.

From the house, Via S. Margherita continues to **Santa Margherita de' Cerchi**, where Dante married his second choice, Gemma Donati, whose family arms are among those adorning the 13th-century porch.

The Badia

Entrance on Via Dante Alighieri, open Mon–Sat 5–7, Sun 7.30–11.30.

Dante would also recognize the two great towers in Piazza San Firenze, the looming Bargello and the beautiful Romanesque campanile of the ancient Benedictine abbey, or Badia, which he cited in the *Paradiso*. The abbey was founded at the end of the 10th century by the widow of Umberto, the Margrave of Tuscany, and further endowed by their son Ugo, 'the Good Margrave'. Dante would come here to gaze upon his Beatrice, and some 50 years after the poet's death, Dante's first biographer, Boccaccio, used the Badia as his forum for innovative public lectures on the text of *The Divine Comedy*. Curiously, Boccaccio's (and later, the Renaissance's) principal criticism of the work is that Dante chose to write about lofty, sacred things in the vulgar tongue of Tuscany.

Except for the campanile (*at the time of writing, under restoration*), the Badia has become a hotchpotch from too many remodellings. Inside, however, are two beautiful things from the Renaissance: the *Tomb of Count Ugo* (1481) by Mino da Fiesole and the *Madonna Appearing to St Bernard* (1485), a large painting by Filippino Lippi. Through an unmarked door to the right of the choir, you can reach the upper loggia of the **Chiostro degli Aranci**, where the Benedictines grew oranges. Built in the 1430s, it is embellished with a fine contemporary series of frescoes on the life of St Bernard, painted by an unknown artist.

Museo Nazionale del Bargello

Open 9–2, closed Mon; adm.

Across from the Badia looms the Bargello, a battlemented urban fortress, well proportioned yet of forbidding grace; for centuries it saw duty as Florence's prison. Today its only inmates are men of marble, gathered together to form Italy's finest collection of sculpture, a fitting complement to the paintings in the Uffizi. The Bargello is 'stone Florence' squared to the sixth degree, rugged and austere *pietra forte*, the model for the even grander Palazzo Vecchio. Even the treasures it houses are hard, definite, certain—and almost unremittingly masculine. The Bargello offers the best insight available into Florence's golden age, and it was a man's world indeed.

Completed in 1255, the Bargello was originally intended as Florence's Palazzo del Popolo, though by 1271 it served instead as the residence of the foreign *podestà*, or chief magistrate, installed by Guelph leader Charles of Anjou. The Medici made it the headquarters of the captain of police (the *Bargello*), the city jail and torture chamber, a function it served until 1859. In the Renaissance it was the peculiar custom to paint portraits of the condemned on the exterior walls of the fortress; Andrea del Castagno was so good at it that he was nicknamed Andrea of the Hanged Men. All of these ghoulish souvenirs have long since disappeared, as have the torture instruments—burned in 1786, when the death sentence was abolished. Today the **Gothic courtyard**, former site of the gallows and chopping block, is a delightful place, owing much to an imaginative restoration in the 1860s. The encrustation of centuries of *podestà* armorial devices and plaques in a wild vocabulary of symbols, the shadowy arcades and stately stairs combine to create one of Florence's most romantic corners.

The Michelangelo Room

The main ground-floor gallery is dedicated to Michelangelo and his century, although it must be said that the Michelangelo of the Bargello somewhat lacks the accustomed angst and ecstasy. Especially irritating is his *Bacchus* (1496), a youthful work inspired by bad Roman sculpture, with all the personality of a cocktail party bore. Better to invite his noble *Brutus* (1540), even if he's just a bust—the only one the sculptor ever made, in a fit of republican fervour after the assassination of Duke Alessandro de' Medici. Also by Michelangelo is the lovely *Pitti Tondo* and the unfinished *Apollo/David*. From Michelangelo's followers there's another tippling *Bacchus* by Sansovino, and Ammannati's *Leda and the Swan* (a work inspired by a famous but lost erotic drawing by Michelangelo).

The real star of the room is Benvenuto Cellini, who was, besides many other things, an exquisite craftsman and daring innovator. His large bust of *Cosimo I* (1548), with its fabulously detailed armour, was his first work cast in bronze; the unidealized features did not curry favour with the boss that poor Cellini worked so avidly to please. Here, too, are two preliminary models of the *Perseus*, as well as four small statuettes and the relief panel from the original in the Loggia dei Lanzi.

The last great work in the room is by Medici court sculptor Giambologna, now again enjoying a measure of the fashionableness he possessed during his lifetime; art historians consider him the key Mannerist figure between Michelangelo and Bernini. Giambologna's most famous work, the bronze *Mercury* (1564), has certainly seeped into popular consciousness as the representation of the way the god should look. The stairway from the courtyard leads up to the shady **Loggia**, now converted into an aviary for Giambologna's charming bronze birds, made for the animal grotto at the Medici's Villa di Castello.

Donatello: the Salone del Consiglio Generale

This magnificent hall, formerly the courtroom of the *podestà*, contains the greatest masterpieces of Early Renaissance sculpture. And when Michelangelo's maudlin self-absorption and the Mannerists' empty virtuosity begin to seem tiresome, a visit to this room, to the profound clarity of the greatest of Renaissance sculptors, will prove a welcome antidote. Donatello's originality and vision are strikingly modern—and mysterious. Unlike Michelangelo, who went so far as to commission his own biography when Vasari's didn't please him, Donatello left few traces, not only of his long life, but of what may have been the sources of inspiration behind his three celebrated works displayed here. The chivalric young *St George* (1416), from the façade of Orsanmichele, has an alert watchfulness, or *prontezza*, which created new possibilities in expressing movement, emotion and depth of character in stone. Note the accompanying bas-relief of the gallant saint slaying the dragon, a masterful work in perspective. Donatello's fascinatingly androgynous *David*, obviously from a different planet to Michelangelo's David, is cool and suave, and conquers his Goliath more by his charming enigmatic smile than muscles and virile arrogance. This was the first free-standing nude figure since antiquity, and one of the most erotic, exploring depths of the Florentine psyche that the Florentines probably didn't know they had. No one knows for whom Donatello cast it, or exactly when—around 1440, give or take 10 years.

The same erotic energy and mystery surrounds the laughing, dangerous-looking, precocious boy Cupid, or *Atys Amor*; with its poppies, serpents and winged sandals, it could easily be the ancient idol people mistook it for in the 1700s. Like Botticelli's mythological paintings, Cupid is part of the artistic and intellectual undercurrents of the period, full of pagan philosophy, a possibility rooted out in the terror of the Counter-Reformation and quite forgotten soon after.

Other Donatellos in the *salone* further display the sculptor's amazing diversity. The small marble *David* (1408) was his earliest important work. In the centre of the hall, his *Marzocco*, the symbol of Florence, long stood on the Ponte Vecchio. Although the two versions of Florence's patron saint, John the Baptist, are no longer attributed to Donatello, they show his influence in that they strive to express the saint's spiritual character physically rather than by merely adding his usual holy accessories. The *Dancing Putto* and two busts are Donatello's; his workshop produced the gilded bas-relief of the Crucifixion.

On the wall hang the two famous trial reliefs for the second set of baptistry doors, by Ghiberti and Brunelleschi, both depicting the Sacrifice of Isaac. Between the panels, the vigorous relief of a tumultuous *Battle Scene* is by the little-known Bertoldo di Giovanni, Donatello's pupil and Michelangelo's teacher. There are a number of other excellent reliefs and busts along the walls, by Agostino di Duccio, Desiderio da Settignano, and some of Luca della Robbia's sweet Madonnas.

Decorative Arts

The remainder of the first floor houses fascinating collections of decorative arts donated to the Bargello in the last century. The **Sala della Torre** is devoted to Islamic art. The **Sala Carrand**, named after the French donator of works in this room, contains splendiferous Byzantine and Renaissance jewellery, watches and clocks, and a Venetian astrolabe. Off this room is the **Cappella del Podestà** with its frescoes once attributed to Giotto.

Some of the most interesting items are in the next rooms, especially the works in the **ivory collection**—Carolingian and Byzantine diptychs, an 8th-century whalebone coffer from Northumbria adorned with runes, medieval French miniatures chronicling 'The Assault on the Castle of Love', 11th-century chess pieces, and more.

David del Verrocch

A stairway from the ivory collection leads up to the **Second Floor**. It houses some of the finest enamelled terracottas of the della Robbia family workshop, a room of portrait busts, beautiful works by Antonio Pollaiuolo and Verrocchio, including his *David* and lovely *Young Lady with a Nosegay*, with her hint of a smile and long, sensitive fingers. There is also a collection of armour, and the most important collection of small Renaissance bronzes in Italy.

Piazza San Firenze to the Duomo

The strangely shaped square that both the Badia and the Bargello call home is named after the large church of **San Firenze**, an imposing ensemble, now partially used as Florence's law courts. At the corner of the square and Via Gondi, the **Palazzo Gondi** is a fine Renaissance palace built for a merchant by Giuliano da Sangallo in 1489 but completed only in 1884; it's not easy to pick out the discreet 19th-century additions. A block from the square on Via Ghibellina, the **Palazzo Borghese** (No.110) is one of the finest neoclassical buildings in the city, erected in 1822—for a party in honour of Habsburg Grand Duke Ferdinand III. The host of this famous affair was one of the wealthiest men of his day, the Roman prince Camillo Borghese, husband of the fascinating Pauline Bonaparte and the man responsible for shipping many of Italy's artistic treasures off to the Louvre.

From Piazza San Firenze, Via del Proconsolo leads straight to the Piazza del Duomo, passing by way of the **Palazzo Pazzi-Quaratesi** (No.10), the 15th-century headquarters of the banking family that organized the conspiracy against Lorenzo and Giuliano de' Medici. No. 12, the Palazzo Nonfinito—begun in 1593 but, as its name suggests, never completed—is now the home of the **Museo Nazionale di Antropologia ed Etnologia** (*open Thurs, Fri and Sat and third Sun of the month 9–1,* *except July, Aug and Sept*), founded in 1869, the first ethnological museum in Italy, with an interesting collection of Peruvian mummies, musical instruments collected by Galileo Chini (who decorated the Liberty-style extravaganzas at Viareggio), some lovely and unusual items of Japan's Ainu and Pakistan's Kafiri, and a large number of skulls from all over the world.

Florence As It Was

Borgo degli Albizi, the fine old street passing in front of the Palazzo Nonfinito, was in ancient times the Via Cassia, linking Rome with Bologna, and it deserves a leisurely stroll for its palaces. If it, too, fails to answer to the Florence you've been seeking, take Via dell'Oriuolo (just to the left at Piazza G. Salvemini) for the **Museo di Firenze Com'Era** (Museum of Florence as It Was), located at No. 4 (*open 9–2, closed Thurs; adm*). The jewel of this museum is right out in front, the nearly room-sized *Pianta della Catena*, most beautiful of the early views of Florence. It is a copy as the original made in 1490 by an unknown artist—that handsome fellow pictured in the lower right-hand corner—was lost during the last war in a Berlin museum. This fascinating painting captures Florence at the height of the Renaissance, a city of buildings in bright white, pink and tan; the great churches are without their façades, the Uffizi and Medici chapels have not yet appeared, and the Medici and Pitti palaces are without their later extensions.

The museum is not large. At present it contains only a number of plans and maps, as well as a collection of amateurish watercolours of Florence's sights from the last century, and paintings of Florence's surroundings by Ottone Rosai, a local favourite who died in 1957. Today's Florentines seem much less interested in the Renaissance than in the city of their grandparents. For some further evidence, look around the corner of Via S. Egidio, where some recent remodelling has uncovered posters over the street from 1925, announcing plans for paying the war debt and a coming visit of the *Folies Bergère*. The Florentines have restored them and put them under glass.

From Via dell'Oriuolo, Via Folco Portinari will take you to Florence's main hospital, **Santa Maria Nuova**, founded in 1286 by the father of Dante's Beatrice, Folco Portinari. A tomb in the hospital's church, Sant'Egidio, is all that remains of the Portinari family. Readers of Iris Origo's *The Merchant of Prato* will recognize it as the work-place of the good notary, Ser Lapo Mazzei. The portico of the hospital, by Buontalenti, was finished in 1612.

Medieval Streets North of the Arno

Just west of Via Por S. Maria, the main street leading down to the Ponte Vecchio, you'll find some of the oldest and best-preserved lanes in Florence. Near the Mercato Nuovo at the top of the street (*see* p.106) stands the **Palazzo di Parte Guelfa**, the 13th-century headquarters of the Guelph party, and often the real seat of power in the city, paid for by property confiscated from the Ghibellines; in the 15th century Brunelleschi added a hall on the top floor and an extension. Next door is the guildhall of the silk makers, the 14th-century **Palazzo dell'Arte della Seta** still bearing its bas-relief emblem, or 'stemma', of a closed door, the age-old guild symbol. It's worth continuing around the Guelph Palace to Via Pellicceria to see the fine ensemble of medieval buildings on the tiny square near Via delle Terme, named after the old Roman baths.

Palazzo Davanzati

Open 9–2, Sun 9–12.45, closed Mon; adm; closed for restoration at the time of writing.

To get an idea of what life was like inside these sombre palaces some 600 years ago, stroll over to nearby Via Porta Rossa, site of the elegant Palazzo Davanzati, now arranged as the **Museo della Casa Fiorentina Antica**, one of the city's most delightful museums, offering a chance to step back into domestic life of yore. Originally built in the mid-14th century for the Davizzi family, the house was purchased by merchant Bernardo Davanzati in 1578 and stayed in the family until the 1900s. Restored by an antique collector in 1904, it is the best-preserved medieval-Renaissance house in Florence and has been furnished with period trappings and art.

The façade is basically as it was, except for a 16th-century addition of a fifth-floor loggia, replacing the battlements—in the rough-and-tumble urban 14th century, a man's home literally had to be a castle. But it was also a showroom for his prosperity, and by the standards of the day, the dwellers of this huge palace were multi-millionaires. From the grand loggia, used for sumptuous public entertainment, you enter the palace by way of a strikingly vertical **Courtyard**, which could be quickly cut off from the street in times of danger, as evidenced by the stout, iron-bolted door. Nor would any family feel safe without a year's store of grain and oil—against famine, siege, plagues or inflation. One storeroom is now used for an audio-visual history of the house. The well in the corner served all the floors of the house, and there is a kind of medieval dumb waiter to transport the shopping up to the kitchen on the top floor.

Upstairs, past a 14th-century fresco of St Christopher on the landing, you arrive at the elegant **Sala Grande** used for formal gatherings, and again, for defence, when boiling oil and such could be dropped through the four hatches in the floor. The room contains a beautiful 16th-century table and cupboard, and luxuries like an automatic bellows and flues at the fireplace, glass windows, and a prettily painted ceiling. The bright and cosy dining room next door, the **Sala dei Pappagalli**, was named after the parrots that adorn the frescoes, cleverly painted with pretend hooks to resemble far more costly tapestries. Off the **Sala Piccola**, a child's bedroom, is one of the palace's bathrooms, which must have seemed almost decadently luxurious in the medieval city, where one of the laws declared that one had to shout three loud warnings before emptying a chamber pot into the street. The last room on the floor is an elegant bedroom called the **Sala dei Pavoni**, with an almost Moorish-style pattern painted on the walls with coats-of-arms, topped by a frieze of peacocks and other exotic birds flitting among the trees. The bedspread is a rare 14th-century example from Sicily, portraying the story of Tristan and King Mark.

The pattern of rooms is repeated on the next floor. The **Salone** is adorned with 15th-century Flemish tapestries and a portrait of Giovanni di Bicci de' Medici. The dining room contains outlandish salt cellars (17–18th centuries) and games chests. The **Sala Piccola** houses a fine collection of 15th-century *cassoni*, the elaborate wedding chests in which a bride stored her dowry of household linens, one of the main housewifely obsessions. They are especially interesting for the secular subjects chosen to adorn them, often depicted in contemporary dress. The bedroom, the **Camera della Castellana di Vergi**, is decorated with a lovely if slightly faded fresco from a medieval French romance. The 14th-century shoes displayed here were discovered in Boccaccio's house.

The **kitchen**, as is usual in a medieval house, is located on the top floor in the hope that in case of fire, only that part would burn. Women would spend most of their day here, supervising the servants, sewing and gossiping; as no servants' quarters existed in the palace, it is believed that the help sacked out on the floor.

Piazza Santa Trínita

Three old Roman roads—Via Porta Rossa, Via delle Terme and Borgo SS. Apostoli—lead into the irregularly shaped Piazza Santa Trínita. Borgo SS. Apostoli is named after one of Florence's oldest churches, the little Romanesque **Santi Apostoli** (11th-century), located in the sunken Piazzetta del Limbo, former cemetery of unbaptized babies.

Piazza Santa Trínita itself boasts an exceptionally fine architectural ensemble, grouped around the 'Column of Justice' from the Roman Baths of Caracalla, given by Pius IV to Cosimo I, and later topped with a statue of Justice by Francesco del Tadda. Its pale granite is set off by the palaces of the piazza: the High Renaissance-Roman **Palazzo Bartolini-Salimbeni** by Baccio d'Agnolo (1520) on the corner of Via Porta Rossa, formerly the fashionable Hôtel du Nord where Herman Melville stayed, and now the French Consulate; the medieval **Palazzo Buondelmonti**, with a 1530 façade by Baccio d'Agnolo, once home to the reading room and favourite haunt of such literati in Florence in the 19th century as Dumas, Browning, Manzoni and Stendhal; and the magnificent curving **Palazzo Spini-Ferroni**, to the right of Borgo SS. Apostoli, built in 1289 and still retaining its original battlements. Directly across Via de' Tornabuoni, the British Consulate occupies the **Palazzo Masetti**, ironically once home to the flamboyant Countess of Albany, wife of Bonnie Prince Charlie, who found happiness by leaving the Pretender for Italian dramatist Vittorio Alfieri, but insisted to the end that she was England's rightful Queen Louise.

Santa Trínita

The **Church of Santa Trínita** has stood here, in one form or another, since the 12th century; its unusual accent on the first syllable (from the Latin *Trinitas*) is considered proof of its ancient foundation. Although the pedestrian façade added by Buontalenti in 1593 isn't especially welcoming, step into its shadowy 14th-century interior for several artistic treats, beginning with the **Bartolini-Salimbeni Chapel** (fourth on the right), frescoed in 1422 by the Sienese Lorenzo Monaco; his marriage of the Virgin takes place in a Tuscan fantasy backdrop of pink towers. He also painted the chapel's graceful, ethereally coloured altarpiece of the *Annunciation*.

In the choir, the **Sassetti Chapel** is one of the masterpieces of Domenico Ghirlandaio, completed in 1495 for wealthy merchant Francesco Sassetti and dedicated to the *Life of St Francis*, but also to the life of Francesco Sassetti, the city and his Medici circle: the scene above the altar, of Francis receiving the Rule of the Order, is transferred to the Piazza della Signoria, watched by Sassetti (to the right, with the fat purse) and Lorenzo il Magnifico; on the steps stands the great Latinist Poliziano with Lorenzo's three sons. The *Death of St Francis* pays homage to Giotto's similar composition in Santa Croce. The altarpiece, the *Adoration of the Shepherds* (1485), is one of Ghirlandaio's best-known works, often described as the archetypal Renaissance painting, a contrived but charming classical treatment; the Magi arrive through a triumphal arch, a Roman sarcophagus is used as manger and a ruined temple for a stable—all matched by the sibyls on the vault; the sibyl on the outer arch is the one who supposedly announced the birth of Christ to Augustus.

Santa Trínita is a Vallombrosan church and the first chapel to the right of the altar holds the Order's holy of holies, a painted crucifix formerly located up in San Miniato. The story goes that on a Good Friday, a young noble named Giovanni Gualberto was on his way to Mass when he happened upon the man who had recently murdered his brother. But rather than take his revenge, Gualberto pardoned the assassin in honour of the holy day. When he arrived at church to pray, this crucifix nodded in approval of his mercy. Giovanni was so impressed that he went on to found the Vallombrosan order in the Casentino.

The **Sanctuary** was frescoed by Alesso Baldovinetti, though only four Old Testament figures survive. In the second chapel to the left the marble *Tomb of Bishop Benozzo Federighi* (1454) is by Luca, the first and greatest of the della Robbias, and features his trademark enamelled terracotta in a gold-ground mosaic. In the north side of the nave, in the fourth chapel, a detached fresco by Neri di Bicci portrays San Giovanni Gualberto and his fellow Vallombrosan saints; over the arch you can see him forgiving the murderer of his brother.

West of Piazza della Repubblica

The streets west of Piazza della Repubblica have always been the choicest district of Florence, and **Via de' Tornabuoni** the city's smartest shopping street. These days you won't find many innovations—Milan's current status as headquarters of Italy's fashion industry is a sore point with Florence, which used to be top dog and lost its position in the 1970s for lack of a large international airport.

In the bright and ambitious 1400s, however, when Florence was the centre of European high finance, Via de' Tornabuoni and its environs was the area the new merchant elite chose for their palaces. Today's bankers build great skyscrapers for the firm and settle for modest mansions for themselves; in Florence's heyday, things were reversed. Bankers and wool tycoons really owned their businesses. While their places of work were quite simple, their homes were imposing city palaces, all built in the same conservative style and competing with each other in size like some Millionaires' Row in 19th-century America.

The champion was the **Palazzo Strozzi**, a long block up Via de' Tornabuoni from Piazza Trínita. This rusticated stone cube of fearful dimensions squats in its piazza like the inscrutable monolith in *2001: A Space Odyssey*, radiating almost visible waves of megalomania. The palazzo was begun by Benedetto da Maiano in 1489 for the extraordinarily wealthy Filippo Strozzi, head of one of Florence's greatest banking clans and adviser to Lorenzo il Magnifico. When he died in 1491, the façade facing Piazza Strozzi was almost complete; future generations had neither the money nor the interest to finish the job. And one wonders whether his son, also called Filippo, ever took much pleasure in it; though at first a Medici ally like his father and wed to Piero de' Medici's daughter, Filippo attempted to lead a band of anti-Medici exiles against Florence; captured and imprisoned in the Fortezza da Basso, he stabbed himself, while many other Strozzi went to Paris to become bankers and advisers to the king of France.

There are few architectural innovations in the Palazzo Strozzi, but here the typical Florentine palace is blown up to the level of the absurd: although three storeys like other palaces, each floor is as tall as three or four normal ones. Like Michelangelo's *David*, Florence's other beautiful monster, it emits the unpleasant sensation of what Mary McCarthy called the 'giganticism of the human ego', the will to surpass not only antiquity but nature herself. Nowadays, at least, the Strozzi palace is moderately useful as a space to hold temporary exhibitions.

Palazzo Rucellai

There are two other exceptional palaces in the quarter. At the north end of Via de' Tornabuoni stands the beautiful golden **Palazzo Antinori** (1465, architect unknown), which has Florence's grandest Baroque temple, **San Gaetano** (1648, by Gherardo Silvani) as its equally golden companion. The second palace, Florence's most celebrated example of domestic architecture, is the **Palazzo Rucellai**, in Via della Vigna Nuova. Its original owner, Giovanni Rucellai, was a quattrocento tycoon like Filippo Strozzi, but an intellectual as well, whose *Zibaldone*, or 'commonplace book' is one of the best sources available on the life and tastes of the educated Renaissance merchant. In 1446 Rucellai chose his favourite architect, Leon Battista Alberti, to design his palace. Actually built by Bernardo Rossellino, it follows Alberti's precepts and theories in its use of the three classical orders; instead of the usual rusticated stone, the façade has a far more delicate decoration of incised irregular blocks and a frieze, elements influential in subsequent Italian architecture—though far more noticeably in Rome than Florence itself. Originally the palace was only five bays wide, and when another two bays were added later the edge was left ragged, unfinished, a nice touch, as if the builders could return at any moment and pick up where they left off. The frieze, like that on Santa Maria Novella, portrays the devices of the Medici and Rucellai families (Giovanni's son married another daughter of Piero de' Medici), a wedding believed to have been fêted in the **Loggia dei Rucellai** across the street, also designed by Alberti.

Since 1987, the Palazzo Rucellai has housed the **Museo di Storia della Fotografia Fratelli Alinari** (*open 10–7.30, Fri and Sat 10–11.30, closed Wed; adm*) devoted to the history of photography. Exhibits come from the fascinating archives of the Alinari brothers, who founded the world's first photography society in 1852. Keep an eye out for posters concerning special shows.

Behind the Rucellai palace (on Via della Spada) stands the ancient church of **San Pancrazio**, with an antique-style porch by Alberti; at one point in its up-and-down career the church served as a tobacco factory. The reason for visiting, however, is the **Rucellai Chapel,** designed in 1467 by Alberti (*entrance at No. 18, open erratic hours*), built to house the unique model of the Sanctuary of the Holy Sepulchre in Jerusalem that is Giovanni Rucellai's funerary monument.

Piazza Goldoni and Ognissanti

Before taking leave of old Florence's west end, head back to the Arno and **Piazza Goldoni,** named after the great comic playwright from Venice. The bridge here, the **Ponte alla Carraia,** is new and nondescript, but its 1304 version played a leading role in that year's most memorable disaster: a company staging a water pageant of the *Inferno,* complete with monsters, devils and tortured souls, attracted such a large crowd that the bridge collapsed under the weight, and all were drowned. Later it was drily commented that all the Florentines who went to see Hell that day found what they were looking for.

The most important building on the piazza, the **Palazzo Ricasoli,** was built in the 15th century but bears the name of one of unified Italy's first Prime Ministers, Bettino 'Iron Baron' Ricasoli. Just to the west on Lungarno Corsini looms the enormous **Palazzo Corsini,** the city's most prominent piece of Roman Baroque extravagance, begun in 1650 and crowned with a bevy of statues. The Corsini, the most prominent family of 17th- and 18th-century Florence, were reputedly so wealthy that they could ride from Florence to Rome entirely on their own property. The **Galleria Corsini** (*adm by appointment only, © 283 044; enter from Via Parione*) is considered the finest private gallery in the city, with paintings by Giovanni Bellini, Signorelli, Filippino Lippi and Pontormo, and *Muses* from the ducal palace of Urbino, painted by Raphael's first master, Timoteo Viti. Further east on Lungarno Corsini stood the Libreria Orioli, which published the first edition of *Lady Chatterley's Lover* in 1927.

To the west of Piazza Goldoni lies the old neighbourhood of the only Florentine to have a continent named after him. Amerigo Vespucci (1451–1512) was a Medici agent in Seville, and made two voyages from there to America on the heels of Columbus. His parish church, **Ognissanti** (All Saints)(*open 8–12 and 4–7*), is set back from the river behind a

Baroque façade, on property donated in 1256 by the Umiliati, a religious order that specialized in wool-working. The Vespucci family tomb is below the second altar to the right, and little Amerigo himself is said to be pictured next to the Madonna in the fresco of the Madonna della Misericordia—probably another Florentine tall story. Also buried in Ognissanti was the Filipepi family, one of whom was Botticelli.

The best art is in the **Convent**, just to the left of the church at No. 42 (*open 9–12 Sat, Mon and Tues; you may have to ring*). Frescoed in the refectory is the great Last Supper, or *Cenacolo*, painted by Domenico Ghirlandaio in 1480. It's hard to think of a more serene and elegant Last Supper, almost like a garden party with its background of fruit trees and exotic birds; a peacock sits in the window, cherries and peaches litter the lovely tablecloth. On either side of the fresco are two scholarly saints moved here from the church itself: Ghirlandaio's *St Jerome* and on the right, young Botticelli's *St Augustine*.

Santa Maria Novella

As in Venice and so many other Italian cities, the two churches of the preaching orders—the Dominicans' Santa Maria Novella and the Franciscans' Santa Croce—became the largest and most prestigious in the city, where wealthy families vied to create the most beautiful chapels and tombs. In Florence, by some twitch of city planning, both of these sacred art galleries dominate broad, stale squares that do not invite you to linger; in the irregular **Piazza Santa Maria** you may find yourself looking over your shoulder for the ghosts of the carriages that once raced madly around the two stout obelisks set on turtles, just as in a Roman circus, in the fashionable carriage races of the 1700s. The arcade on the south side, the **Loggia di San Paolo**, is very much like Brunelleschi's Spedale degli Innocenti, although it suffers somewhat from its use as a busy bus shelter; the lunette over the door, by Andrea della Robbia, shows the *Meeting of SS. Francis and Dominic.*

Santa Maria Novella redeems the anomie of its square with its stupendous black and white marble **façade**, the finest in Florence. The lower part, with its looping arcades, is Romanesque work in the typical Tuscan mode, finished before 1360. In 1456 Giovanni Rucellai commissioned Alberti to complete it, a remarkably fortunate choice. Alberti's half not only perfectly harmonizes with the original, but perfects it with geometrical harmonies to create what appears to be a kind of Renaissance Sun Temple. The original builders started it off by orienting the church to the south instead of west, so that at noon the sun streams through the 14th-century rose window. The only symbol Alberti put on the façade is a blazing sun; the unusual sundials, over the arches on the extreme right and left, were added by Cosimo I's court astronomer Egnazio Danti. Note how the base of the façade is also the base of an equilateral triangle, with Alberti's sun at the apex.

The beautiful frieze depicts the Rucellai emblem (a billowing sail), as on the Palazzo Rucellai. The wall of Gothic recesses to the right, enclosing the old cemetery, are *avelli*, or family tombs.

The **interior** is vast, lofty and more 'Gothic' in feel than any other church in Florence—no thanks to Vasari, who was set loose to remodel the church to 16th-century taste, painting over the original frescoes, removing the rood screen and Dominicans' choir from the nave, and remodelling the altars; in the 1800s restorers did their best to de-Vasari Santa Maria with neogothic details. Neither party, however, could touch two of the interior's most distinctive features—the striking stone vaulting of the nave and the perspective created by the columns marching down the aisles, each pair placed a little closer together as they approach the altar.

Over the portal at the entrance is a fresco lunette by Botticelli that has recently been restored. One of Santa Maria Novella's best-known pictures is at the second altar on the left: Masaccio's *Trinity*, painted around 1425, and one of the revolutionary works of the Renaissance. Masaccio's use of architectural elements and perspective gives his composition both physical and intellectual depth. The flat wall becomes a deeply recessed Brunelleschian chapel, calm and classical, enclosed in a coffered barrel vault; at the foot of the fresco a bleak skeleton decays in its tomb, bearing a favourite Tuscan reminder: 'I was that which you are, you will be that which I am.' Above this morbid suggestion of physical death kneel the two donors; within the celestially rational inner sanctum the Virgin and St John stand at the foot of the Cross, humanity's link with the mystery of the Trinity. In the nearby Brunelleschi-designed pulpit Galileo was first denounced by the Inquisition for presuming to believe that the earth went around the sun.

There is little else to detain you in the aisles, but the first chapel in the left transept, the **Cappella Strozzi**, is one of the most evocative corners of 14th-century Florence, frescoed entirely by Nardo di Cione and his brother, Andrea Orcagna; on the vault pictures of St Thomas Aquinas and the Virtues are echoed in Andrea's lovely altarpiece of *The Redeemer Donating the Keys to St Peter and the Book of Wisdom to St Thomas Aquinas*; on the left wall there's a crowded scene of Paradise, with the righteous lined up in a medieval school class photograph. On the right, Nardo painted a striking view of Dante's Inferno, with all of a Tuscan's special attention to precise map-like detail.

In the richly decorated **Sacristy** hangs Giotto's *Crucifix* (*c.* 1300) (*under restoration*), one of the artist's first works. In the **Gondi Chapel** hangs another famous Crucifix, carved in wood by Brunelleschi, which, according to Vasari, so astonished his friend Donatello that he dropped the eggs he was carrying in his apron when he first saw it.

The charming fresco cycle in the **Sanctuary** (1485–90), painted by Domenico Ghirlandaio, portrays the *Lives of the Virgin, St John the Baptist and the Dominican Saints* in magnificent architectural settings; little Michelangelo was among the students who helped him complete it. Nearly all of the bystanders are portraits of Florentine quattrocento VIPs, including the artist himself (in the red hat, in the scene of the *Expulsion of St Joachim from the Temple*), but most prominent are the ladies and gents of the Tornabuoni house. More excellent frescoes adorn the **Filippo Strozzi Chapel**, the finest work ever to come from the brush of Filippino Lippi, painted in 1502 near the end of his life; the exaggerated, dark and violent scenes portray the lives of St Philip (his crucifixion and his subduing of the dragon before the Temple of Mars, which creates such a stench it kills the heathen prince) and of St John the Evangelist (raising Drusiana from the dead and being martyred in boiling oil). The chapel's beautifully carved tomb of Filippo Strozzi is by Benedetto da Maiano. The **Rucellai Chapel** contains a marble statue of the Madonna and Bambino by Nino Pisano and a fine bronze tomb by Ghiberti, which makes an interesting comparison with the three Gothic tombs nearby in the right transept. One of these contains the remains of the Patriarch of Constantinople, who died in here after the failure of the Council of Florence in 1439 to reunite the Western and Eastern Churches.

Santa Maria Novella

1   Masaccio' s 'Trinity'
2   Brunelleschi's Pulpit
3   Cappella Strozzi
4   Sacristy
5   Cappella Gondi
6   Sanctuary
7   Filippo Strozzi Chapel
8   Ruccellai Chapel
9   Gothic Tombs
10   Universal Deluge
11   Spanish Chapel
12   Chiostrino dei Morti
13   Refectory

The Green Cloister and Spanish Chapel

More great frescoes await in Santa Maria Novella's Cloisters, all recently restored and open as a city museum (*entrance just to the left of the church; open 9–2, closed Fri; weekends 8–1; adm; free Sun*). The first cloister, the so-called Green Cloister, one of the masterpieces of Paolo Uccello and his assistants, is so named after the *terraverde* or green earth pigment used by the artist, which lends the scenes from Genesis their eerie, ghostly quality. Much damaged by time and neglect, they are nevertheless striking for their two Uccellian obsessions—perspective and animals, the latter especially on display in the scene of the Creation. Best known, and in better condition than the others, is Uccello's surreal *Universal Deluge*, a composition framed by the steep walls of two arks, before and after views, which have the uncanny effect of making the scene seem to come racing out of its own vanishing point, a vanishing point touched by divine wrath in a searing bolt of lightning. In between the claustrophobic walls the flood rises, tossing up a desperate ensemble of humanity, waterlogged bodies, naked men bearing clubs, crowded in a jam of flotsam and jetsam and islets rapidly receding in the dark waters. In the right foreground, amidst the panic, stands a tall robed man, seemingly a visionary, perhaps even Noah himself, looking heavenward while a flood victim seizes him by the ankles. Some of Uccello's favourite perspective studies were of headgear, especially the wooden hoops called *mazzocchi* which he puts around the necks and on the heads of his figures.

The **Spanish Chapel** opens up at the far end of the cloisters, taking its name from the Spanish court followers of Eleonora di Toledo who worshipped here; the Inquisition had earlier made the chapel its headquarters in Florence. The chapel is, again, famous for its frescoes, the masterpiece of a little-known 14th-century artist named Andrea di Buonaiuto, whose subject was the Dominican cosmology, perhaps not something we have much empathy for these days, but here beautifully portrayed so that even the 'Hounds of the Lord' (a pun on the Order's name, the 'Domini canes') on the right wall seem more like pets than militant bloodhounds sniffing out unorthodox beliefs. The church behind the scene with the hounds is a fairy pink confection of what Buonaiuto imagined the Duomo would look like when finished; it may well be Arnolfo di Cambio's original conception. Famous Florentines, including Giotto, Dante, Boccaccio and Petrarch, stand to the right of the dais supporting the pope, emperor and various sour-faced hierophants. Off to the right the artist has portrayed four rather urbane Vices with dancing girls, while the Dominicans lead stray sheep back to the fold. On the left wall, St Thomas Aquinas dominates the portrayal of the Contemplative Life, surrounded by Virtues and Doctors of the Church. (*Restoration began in 1995. Only one part will be covered at a time so that you can still visit.*)

The oldest part of the monastery, the **Chiostrino dei Morti** (1270s), contains some 14th-century frescoes, while the **Great Cloister** beyond is now off limits, the property of the Carabinieri, the new men in black charged with keeping the Italians orthodox. Off the Green Cloister, the **Refectory** is a striking hall with cross vaulting and frescoes by Alessandro Allori, now serving as a museum.

Around Santa Maria Novella

Just behind, but a world apart from Santa Maria Novella, another large, amorphous square detracts from one of Italy's finest modern buildings—Florence's **Stazione Centrale**, designed by the architect Michelucci in 1935. Adorned by only a glass block canopy at the entrance (and an early model of that great Italian invention, the digital clock), the station is nevertheless remarkable for its clean lines and impeccable practicality; form following function in a way that even Brunelleschi would have appreciated.

One of the medieval lanes leading south from Piazza Santa Maria Novella, Via delle Belle Donne was once known for its excellent brothels. Today it is worth a short stroll to see one of the very few crossroads in Italy marked by a cross, a Celtic custom that never really caught on here—Italians are far more fond of corner shrines to the Madonna or some lucky saint. According to legend, **Croce del Trebbio** (from a corruption of 'trivium') marks the spot of a massacre of Patarene heretics in the 1240s, after the masses had been excited by a sermon given by the fire-eating Inquisitor St Peter Martyr from the pulpit of Santa Maria Novella.

San Lorenzo

The lively quarter just east of Santa Maria Novella has been associated with the Medici ever since Giovanni di Bicci de' Medici commissioned Brunelleschi to rebuild the ancient church of San Lorenzo in 1420; subsequent members of the dynasty lavished bushels of florins on its decoration and Medici pantheon, and on several projects commissioned from Michelangelo. The mixed result of all their efforts could be held up as an archetype of the Renaissance, and one which Walter Pater described as 'great rather by what it designed or aspired to do, than by what it actually achieved'. One can begin with San Lorenzo's façade of corrugated brick, the most *nonfinito* of all of Michelangelo's unfinished projects; commissioned by Medici Pope Leo X in 1516, the project never got further than Michelangelo's scale model, which may be seen in the Casa Buonarroti. To complete the church's dingy aspect, the piazza in front contains a universally detested 19th-century statue of Cosimo I's dashing father, Giovanni delle Bande Nere, who died at the age of 28 of wounds received fighting against Emperor Charles V.

The **interior**, although completed after Brunelleschi's death is true to his design, classically calm in good grey *pietra serena* (*under restoration at the time of writing*). The artistic treasures it contains are few but choice, beginning with the second chapel on the right housing *The Marriage of the Virgin*, a 1523 work by the Mannerist Rosso Fiorentino. Joseph, usually portrayed as an old man, according to Rosso is a Greek god with golden curls in a flowing scene of hot reds and oranges—a powerful contrast to the chapel's haunting, hollow-eyed tomb slab of the Ray Charles of the Renaissance, Francesco Landini (d. 1397), the blind organist whose madrigals were immensely popular and influential in Italian music. At the end of the right aisle, there's a lovely delicately worked tabernacle by Desiderio da Settignano.

San lorenzo

Most riveting of all, however, are **Donatello's pulpits**, the sculptor's last works, completed by his pupils after his death in 1466. Cast in bronze, the pulpits were commissioned by Donatello's friend and patron Cosimo il Vecchio, some think to keep the sculptor busy in his old age. Little in Donatello's previous work prepares the viewer for these scenes of Christ's passion and Resurrection with their rough and impressionistic details, their unbalanced and overcrowded compositions, more reminiscent of Rodin than anything Florentine. Unfortunately they were set up on columns in the 17th century, just above eye level, like so many things in Florence, a fault somewhat redeemed by a new lighting system. Nearby, directly beneath the dome, lies buried Donatello's patron and Florence's original godfather, Cosimo il Vecchio; the grille over his grave bears the Medici arms and the simple inscription, *Pater Patriae*.

It was the godfather's father, Giovanni di Bicci de' Medici, who in 1420 commissioned Brunelleschi to build the **Old Sacristy** off the left transept (*erratic opening hours*). Often cited as one of the first and finest works of the early Renaissance, Brunelleschi designed this cube of a sacristy according to carefully calculated mathematical proportions, emphasized with a colour scheme of white walls, articulated in soft grey *pietra serena* pilasters and cornices; a dignified decoration that would become his trademark, something Florentine architects would borrow for centuries. Donatello contributed the terracotta tondi and lunettes, as well as the bronze doors, embellished with lively Apostles. The Sacristy was built to hold the sarcophagi of Giovanni di Bicci de' Medici and his wife; in 1472 Lorenzo il Magnifico and his brother Giuliano had Verrocchio design the beautiful bronze and red porphyry wall tomb for their father Piero the Gouty and their uncle Giovanni. Unfortunately Verrocchio saw fit to place this in front of Brunelleschi's original door, upsetting the careful balance.

The chapel across the transept from the entrance to the Old Sacristy houses a 19th-century monument to Donatello, who is buried here at his request near Cosimo il Vecchio. The lovely *Annunciation* is by Filippo Lippi; the large, colourful fresco of the *Martyrdom of St Lawrence* around the corner in the aisle is by Bronzino and has just been restored.

Just beyond the Bronzino a door leads into the 15th-century **Cloister**, and from there a stair leads up to Michelangelo's celebrated **Biblioteca Laurenziana** (*open Mon–Sat 9–1*).

If Brunelleschi's Old Sacristy heralded the Renaissance, Michelangelo's library is Mannerism's prototype, or Brunelleschi gone haywire, no longer serene and mathematically perfect, but complicated and restless, the architectural elements stuck on with an eye for effect rather than for any structural purpose. The vestibule barely contains the remarkable stair, flowing down from the library like a stone cascade, built by Vasari after a drawing by Michelangelo. This grand entrance leads into a collection that ranges from a very rare 5th-century Virgil and other Greek and Latin codices, to beautifully illuminated manuscripts, and the original manuscript of Cellini's autobiography; ask for a look around.

The Medici Chapels

San Lorenzo is most famous, however, for the Medici Chapels, which lie outside and behind the church (*open 9–2, closed Mon; adm exp*). The entrance leads through the crypt, a dark and austere place where many of the Medici are actually buried. Their main monument, the family obsession, is just up the steps, and has long been known as the **Chapel of the Princes**, a stupefying, fabulously costly octagon of death that, as much as the Grand Dukes fussed over it, lends their memory an unpleasant aftertaste of cancerous bric-a-brac that grew and grew. Perhaps only a genuine Medici could love its insane, trashy opulence; all of Grand Duke Cosimo's descendants, down to the last, Anna Maria Ludovica, worked like beavers to finish it according to the plans left by Cosimo's illegitimate son, dilettante architect Giovanni de' Medici. Yet even today it is only partially completed, the *pietre dure* extending only part of the way up the walls. The 19th-century frescoes in the cupola are a poor substitute for the originally planned 'Apotheosis of the Medici' in lapis lazuli, and the two statues in gilded bronze in the niches over the sarcophagi (each niche large enough to hold a hippopotamus) are nothing like the intended figures to be carved in semi-precious stone. The most interesting feature is the inlaid *pietra dura* arms of Tuscan towns and the large Medici arms above, with their familiar six red boluses blown up as big as beachballs.

A passageway leads to Michelangelo's **New Sacristy**, commissioned by Leo X to occupy an unfinished room originally built to balance Brunelleschi's Old Sacristy. Michelangelo's first idea was to turn it into a new version of his unfinished, overly ambitious Pope Julius Tomb, an idea quickly quashed by his Medici patrons, who requested instead four wall tombs. Michelangelo only worked on two of the monuments, but managed to finish the New Sacristy itself, creating a silent and gloomy mausoleum, closed in and grey, a chilly introspective cocoon calculated to depress even the most chatty tour groups.

Nor are the famous tombs guaranteed to cheer. Both honour nonentities: that of *Night and Day* belongs to Lorenzo il Magnifico's son, the Duke of Nemours, and symbolizes the Active Life, while the *Dawn and Dusk* is of Guiliano's nephew, Lorenzo, Duke of Urbino (and dedicatee of *The Prince*), who symbolizes the Contemplative Life (true to life in one respect—Lorenzo was a disappointment to Machiavelli and everyone else, passively obeying the dictates of his uncle Pope Leo X). Idealized statues of the two men, in Roman patrician gear, represent these states of mind, while draped on their sarcophagi are

Michelangelo's four allegorical figures of the Times of Day, so heavy with weariness and grief they seem ready to slide off on to the floor. The most finished figure, *Night*, has always impressed the critics; she is almost a personification of despair, the mouthpiece of Michelangelo's most bitter verse:

> *Sweet to me is sleep, and even more to be like stone*
> *While wrong and shame endure;*
> *Not to see, nor to feel, is my good fortune.*
> *Therefore, do not wake me; speak softly here.*

Both statues of the dukes look towards the back wall, where a large double tomb for Lorenzo il Magnifico and his brother Giuliano was originally planned, to be decorated with river gods. The only part of this tomb ever completed is the statue of the *Madonna and Child* now in place, accompanied by the Medici patron saints, *Cosmas and Damian*.

In 1975, charcoal drawings were discovered on the walls of the little room off the altar. They were attributed to Michelangelo, who may have hidden here in 1530, when the Medici had regained Florence and apparently would only forgive the artist for aiding the republican defence if he would finish their tombs. But Michelangelo had had enough of their ducal pretences and went off to Rome, never to return to Florence. (*Ask at the cash desk for a permit to see the drawings, as only 12 people can enter at one time*).

Mercato Centrale and Perugino

What makes the neighbourhood around San Lorenzo so lively is its street market, which the Florentines run with an almost Neapolitan flamboyance every day except Sunday and Monday. Stalls selling clothes and leather extend from the square up Via dell'Ariento and vicinity (nicknamed 'Shanghai') towards the **Mercato Centrale**, Florence's main food market (*open Mon–Sat 7–1.30, also Sat 4.30–7.30*), a cast-iron and glass confection of the 1870s, brimful of fresh fruit and vegetables, leering boars' heads and mounds of tripe.

Beyond the market, at Via Faenza 42, is the entrance to Perugino's **Cenacolo di Foligno** fresco, housed in the ex-convent of the Tertiary Franciscans of Foligno (*visit by appointment only, © (055) 284272*). This 1490s Umbrian version of the Last Supper was discovered in the 1850s and has recently been restored.

Palazzo Medici-Riccardi

A block from San Lorenzo and the Piazza del Duomo stands the palace that once held Florence's unofficial court, where ambassadors would call, kings would lodge, and important decisions would be made. Built in 1444 by Michelozzo for Cosimo il Vecchio, it was the principal address of the Medici for a hundred years, until Cosimo I abandoned it for larger quarters in the Palazzo Vecchio and the Pitti Palace. In 1659 the Riccardi purchased the palace, added to it and did everything to keep it glittering until Napoleon and his debts drove them to bankruptcy in 1809. The palace is now used as the city's prefecture.

In its day, though, it was the largest private address in the city, where the family lived with the likes of Donatello's *David* and *Judith and Holofernes*, Uccello's *Battle of San Romano* and other masterpieces now in the Uffizi and Bargello. Frescoes are much harder to move, however, and the Palazzo Medici is worth visiting to see the most charming one in Italy, Benozzo Gozzoli's 1459 *Procession of the Magi*, located in the **Medici Chapel** upstairs (*open 9–1 and 3–6; Sun 9–1, closed Wed; adm*).

Painting in a delightful, decorative manner more reminiscent of International Gothic than the awakening Renaissance style of his contemporaries, Gozzoli took a religious subject and turned it into a merry, brilliantly coloured pageant of beautifully dressed kings, knights and pages, accompanied by greyhounds and a giraffe, who travel through a springtime landscape of jewel-like trees and castles. This is a largely secular painting, representing less the original Three Kings than the annual pageant of the *Compagnia dei Magi*, Florence's richest confraternity. The scene is wrapped around three walls of the small chapel—you feel as if you had walked straight into a glowing fairytale world. Most of the faces are those of the Medici and other local celebrities; Gozzoli certainly had no qualms about putting himself among the crowd of figures on the right wall, with his name written on his red cap. In the foreground, note the black man carrying a bow. Blacks, as well as Turks, Circassians, Tartars and others, were common enough in Renaissance Florence, originally brought as slaves. By the 1400s, however, contemporary writers mention them as artisans, fencing masters, soldiers and one famous archery instructor, who may be the man pictured here.

The altarpiece is a copy of an ethereal *Madonna* by Filippo Lippi, the original being in Berlin. In the **Gallery**, up the second flight of stairs on the right, from the courtyard, is a different, but original Lippi *Madonna*. It's hard to imagine a more striking contrast than that between Gozzoli and the Neapolitan Luca Giordano (nicknamed 'Luca fa presto' or 'Luke Does-it-fast'), who painted this hilarious ceiling for the Riccardi in 1683, as a left-handed compliment to the Medici for selling them the palace. No longer mere players in a religious pageant, the Medici, or at least the overstuffed Grand Duke Cosimo III and his unspeakable heir Gian Gastone, take the leading roles, defying the laws of gravity and good taste in an apotheosis of marshmallow clouds.

San Marco

From the Medici palace, Via Cavour heads north for Piazza San Marco, a lively square full of art students from the nearby Accademia. The north side of the square is occupied by the **Church and Dominican Convent of San Marco** (*open 9–2, closed Mon; adm*). The Convent was Cosimo il Vecchio's favourite pious project; in 1437 he commissioned Michelozzo to enlarge and rebuild it, and to add to it Europe's first public library, where Florentine scholars and humanists rediscovered the ancient classics collected by Cosimo's agents (now in the Laurenziana Library). A later prior of San Marco, Savonarola, had little use for the Medici family, though he owed his position to the influence of Lorenzo il Magnifico in 1491.

San Marco is best known for the works of the other-worldly Fra Angelico, in residence here between 1436 and 1447, and in charge of decorating the new convent constructed by Cosimo. His paintings and frescoes in San Marco, itself unchanged from the 1400s, offer a unique opportunity to see his works in the peaceful, contemplative environment in which they were meant to be seen.

Every painter in the 15th century earned his living painting sacred subjects, but none painted them with the deep conviction and faith of the 'Blessed' Angelico, who communicated his biblical visions in soft angelic pastels, bright playroom colours and an ethereal blondness, so clear and limpid that they just had to be true. 'Immured in his quiet convent', wrote Henry James, 'he apparently never received an intelligible impression of evil; and his conception of human life was a perpetual sense of sacredly loving and being loved.' Yet the gentle friar was certainly not artistically naive, and adopted many of his contemporaries' innovations, especially artificial perspective, in his technique.

A visit to San Marco begins with Michelozzo's harmonious **Cloister of Sant' Antonio** in which Fra Angelico painted the frescoes in the corners. Just off the cloister, the **Pilgrims' Hospice**, also by Michelozzo, has been arranged as a gallery of Fra Angelico's paintings, gathered from all over Florence. Here you'll find his great *Last Judgement* altarpiece (1430), a serenely confident work in which all the saved are well-dressed Italians holding hands, led by an angel in a celestial dance. They are allowed to keep their beautiful clothes in heaven, while the bad (mostly princes and prelates) are stripped to receive their interesting tortures.

One of the most charming works is the *Thirty-five Scenes from the Life of Christ*, acted out before strikingly bare, brown Tuscan backgrounds, painted as cupboard doors for Santissima Annunziata. Three of the scenes are by Fra Angelico's talented apprentice, Alesso Baldovinetti. The noble, gracefully lamenting figures in the magnificent *Deposition* altarpiece from Santa Trínita stand before an elegant townscape dominated by Fra Angelico's ziggurat-style concept of the Temple in Jerusalem. Other masterpieces include the *Tabernacle of the Linaioli* (the flax-workers), with a beautiful predella. The same holds true for the *Pala di San Marco*, the predella picturing SS. Cosmas and Damian, patrons of medicine and the Medici, in the act of performing history's first leg transplant.

Other rooms off the cloister contain works by Fra Bartolomeo, another resident of the convent, whose portraits capture some of the most sincere

San Marco

spirituality of the late 15th century. The **Chapter House** contains Fra Angelico's over-restored fresco of *Crucifixion and Saints*, a painting that lacks his accustomed grace; in the smaller **Refectory** there's a more pleasing *Last Supper* by the down-to-earth Domenico Ghirlandaio.

Stairs lead up to Michelozzo's beautiful **Convent**, where at the top your eyes meet the Angelic Friar's masterpiece, a miraculous *Annunciation* that must have earned him his beatification. The subject was a favourite with Florentine artists, not only because it was a severe test—expressing a divine revelation with a composition of strict economy—but because the Annunciation, falling near the spring equinox, was New Year's Day for Florence until the Medici adopted the pope's calendar in the 1600s.

The monks of San Marco each had a small white cell with a window and a fresco to serve as a focal point for their meditations. Fra Angelico and his assistants painted 44 of these; those believed to have been done by the master are along the outer wall (cells 1–9, the *Noli me Tangere*, another *Annunciation*, a *Transfiguration*, a *Harrowing of Hell*, a *Coronation of the Virgin*, and others). He also painted the scene in the large cell used occasionally by Cosimo il Vecchio and other visiting celebrities. One corridor is entirely painted with scenes of the Crucifixion, all the same but for some slight difference in the pose of the Dominican monk at the foot of the Cross; walking past and glancing in the cells successively gives the impression of an animated cartoon. In 1993, during restoration on the structure of the convent, fragments of paintings were found under the cells' floor. They are the incomplete 14th-century remains of the wall decoration in the original building and are only made visible by a series of mirrors in holes in the floor. Although it is hard to imagine the frescoes in their original glory, a comparison between them and the work of Beato Lippi underlines the artistic developments that occured in Florence during the 14th and early 15th centurys. The **Prior's cell** at the end belonged to Savonarola; it has simple furniture of the period and a portrait of Savonarola in the guise of St Peter Martyr (with an axe in his brain) by his friend Fra Bartolomeo. A copy of the anonymous painting in the Corsini Gallery, of Savonarola and two of his followers being burned at the stake in the Piazza della Signoria, also hangs here. The **Library**, entered off the corridor, is as light and airy as the cloisters below, and contains a collection of beautiful choir books. Architecturally the library was one of Michelozzo's greatest works, radiating a wonderful spirit of serenity, church-like with its vaulted nave and aisles.

The **church of San Marco** was rebuilt, along with the convent, in the 15th century, though the interior was rearranged by Giambologna and the Baroque façade added in 1780. The right aisle has an altar topped by an 8th-century mosaic from Constantinople, reminiscent of works from Ravenna. There's a painting by Fra Bartolomeo nearby of a *Madonna and Six Saints*.

University Museums and the Botanical Garden

Near San Marco, at Via G. La Pira 4, the University of Florence runs several small museums; nearly all the collections were begun by the indefatigable Medici. The **Geology** and **Palaeontology Museum** (*open Mon 2–6; Tues, Wed, Thurs and Sat 9–1; first Sun of the month 9.30–12.30*) has one of Italy's best collections of fossils, many uncovered in Tuscany, including antiquated elephants from the Valdarno. The **Mineralogy and Lithology Museum** (*open weekdays 9–1; adm*) houses strange and beautiful rocks, especially from Elba, the treasure island of minerals; there's a topaz weighing in at 151kg, meteorites, and a bright collection of Medici trinkets, worked from stones in rainbow hues. The **Botanical Museum** (*open Mon, Wed and Fri 9–12*) is of less interest to the casual visitor, though it houses one of the most extensive herbariums in the world; most impressive here are the exquisite wax models of plants made in the early 1800s. Also on Via La Pira is the entrance to the University's **Giardino dei Semplici**, the botanical garden created for Cosimo I (*open Mon, Wed, Fri and Sat 9–12; also 9–1 Suns in April and first Sun in May*). The garden maintains its original layout, with medicinal herbs, Tuscan plants, flowers and tropical plants in its greenhouses.

Sant'Apollonia and the Scalzo

Cenacoli, or frescoes of the Last Supper, became almost *de rigueur* in monastic refectories; in several of these the Last Supper is all that remains of a convent.

Until 1860, the Renaissance convent of **Sant'Apollonia**, off Piazza S. Marco at Via XXVII Aprile 1 (*open 9–2, closed Mon*); was the abode of cloistered nuns, and the fresco of the Last Supper in their refectory was a secret. When the convent was suppressed, and the painting discovered under the whitewash, the critics believed it to be the work of Paolo Uccello, but lately have unanimously attributed it to Andrea del Castagno, painted 1445–50. The other walls have sinopie of the Crucifixion, Entombment and Resurrection by Castagno; in the vestibule there are good works by Neri di Bicci and Paolo Schiavo.

Not far away you can enter a radically different artistic world in the **Chiostro dello Scalzo**, again off Piazza S. Marco at Via Cavour 69 (*open Mon and Thurs 9–1, ring the bell*). Formerly part of the Confraternity of San Giovanni Battista, all that has survived is this cloister, frescoed (1514–24) with scenes of the life of St John the Baptist by Andrea del Sarto and his pupil Franciabigio. Del Sarto, Browning's 'perfect painter', painted these in monochrome grisaille, and while the scene of the *Baptism of Christ* is a beautiful work, some of the other panels are the most unintentionally funny things in Florence—the scene of Herod's banquet is reduced to a meagre breakfast where the king and queen look up indignantly at the man bringing in the platter of the Baptist's head as if he were a waiter who had made a mistake with their order.

The Galleria dell'Accademia

Open Tues–Sat 9–7,Sun 9–2, closed Mon; adm exp.

From Piazza San Marco, Via Ricasoli makes a beeline for the Duomo, but on most days the view is obstructed by the crowds milling around No. 60; in the summer the queues are as long as those at the Uffizi, everyone anxious to get a look at Michelangelo's *David*. Just over a hundred years ago Florence decided to take this precocious symbol of republican liberty out of the rain and install it, with much pomp, in a specially `built classical exedra in this gallery.

Michelangelo completed the *David* for the city in 1504, when he was 29, and it was the work that established the overwhelming reputation he had in his own time. The monstrous block of marble—5m high but unusually shallow—had been quarried 40 years earlier by the Cathedral Works and spoiled by other hands. The block was offered around to other artists, including Leonardo da Vinci, before young Michelangelo decided to take up the challenge of carving the largest statue since Roman times. And it is the dimensions of the *David* that remain the biggest surprise in these days of endless reproductions. Certainly as a political symbol of the Republic, he is excessive—the irony of a David the size of a Goliath is disconcerting—but as a symbol of the artistic and intellectual aspirations of the Renaissance he is unsurpassed.

And it's hard to deny, after gazing at this enormous nude, that these same Renaissance aspirations by the 1500s began snuggling uncomfortably close to the frontiers of kitsch. Disproportionate size is one symptom; the calculated intention to excite a strong emotional response is another. In the *David*, virtuosity eclipses vision, and commits the even deadlier kitsch sin of seeking the sterile empyrean of perfect beauty—most would argue that Michelangelo here achieves it, perhaps capturing his own feelings about the work in the *David*'s chillingly vain, self-satisfied expression. This is also one of the few statues to have actually injured someone. During a political disturbance in the Piazza della Signoria, its arm broke off and fell on a farmer's toe. In 1991 it was David's toe which fell victim when a madman chopped it off. Since then, the rest of his anatomy has been shielded by glass.

In the Galleria next to the *David* are Michelangelo's famous *nonfiniti*, the four *Prisoners* or Slaves, worked on between 1519 and 1536, sculpted for Pope Julius' tomb and left in various stages of completion, although it is endlessly argued whether this is by design or through lack of time. Whatever the case, they illustrate Michelangelo's view of sculpture as a prisoner in stone just as the soul is a prisoner of the body.

The Gallery was founded by Grand Duke Pietro Leopold in 1784 to provide students with examples of art from every period. The big busy Mannerist paintings around the *David* are by Michelangelo's contemporaries, among them Pontormo's *Venus and Cupid*, with a Michelangelesque Venus among theatre masks. Other rooms contain a good selection of quattrocento painting, including the *Madonna del Mare* by Botticelli, a damaged Baldovinetti, the *Thebaid* by a follower of Uccello, and Perugino's *Deposition*. The painted frontal of the **Adimari chest** shows a delightful wedding scene of the 1450s with the Baptistry in the background that has been reproduced in half the books ever written about the Renaissance.

The hall off to the left of the *David* was formerly the women's ward of a hospital, depicted in a greenish painting by Pontormo. Now it is used as a gallery of plaster models by 19th-century members of the Accademia, a surreal, bright white neoclassical crowd.

Opificio delle Pietre Dure

Open 9–6.30, Sun 9–1, closed Tues adm.

Around the corner from the Accademia, in Via degli Alfani 78, is the workshop of *pietre dure*, inlaid 'hard stones' or semi-precious stones. Cosimo I was the first to actively promote what was to become Florence's special craft, and it was Ferdinando I who founded the Opificio in 1588 as a centre for craftsmen.

Still on Via degli Alfani, across Via dei Servi, stands the **Rotonda di Santa Maria degli Angeli**, an octagonal building begun by Brunelleschi in 1434, one of his last works and one of the first centralized buildings of the Renaissance.

Piazza Santissima Annunziata

This lovely square, really the only Renaissance attempt at a unified ensemble in Florence, is surrounded on three sides by arcades. In its centre, gazing down the splendid vista of Via dei Servi towards the Duomo, stands the equestrian statue of Ferdinand I (1607) by Giambologna and his pupil Pietro Tacca, made of bronze from Turkish cannons captured during the Battle of Lepanto. More fascinating than Ferdinand are the pair of bizarre Baroque fountains, also by Tacca, that share the square. Though possessed of a nominally marine theme, they resemble tureens of bouillabaisse that any ogre would be proud to serve.

In the 1420s Filippo Brunelleschi struck the first blow for classical calm in this piazza when he built the celebrated **Spedale degli Innocenti** and its famous portico—an architectural landmark, but also a monument to Renaissance Italy's long, hard and ultimately unsuccessful struggle towards some kind of social consciousness. Even in the best of times, Florence's poor were treated like dirt; if any enlightened soul had been so bold as to propose even a modern conservative 'trickle down' theory to the Medici and the banking elite, their first thought would have been how to stop the leaks. Babies,

at least, were treated a little better. The Spedale degli Innocenti was the first hospital for foundlings in Italy and the world, and still serves as an orphanage today, as well as the local nursery school.

The Spedale was Brunelleschi's first completed work and demonstrates his use of geometrical proportions adapted to traditional Tuscan Romanesque architecture. His lovely portico is adorned with the famous blue and white tondi of infants in swaddling clothes by Andrea della Robbia, added

fontana di Piazza SS. Annunziata

as an appeal to charity in the 1480s after several children died of malnutrition. Brunelleschi also designed the two beautiful cloisters of the convent; the **Chiostro delle Donne**, reserved for the hospital's nurses (located up the ramp on the right at No. 13), is especially fine. Upstairs, the **Museo dello Spedale** (*open 8.30–1.30, closed Wed; adm*) contains a number of detached frescoes from Ognissanti and other churches, among them an unusual series of red and orange prophets by Alessandro Allori; other works include a *Madonna and Saints* by Piero di Cosimo, a *Madonna and Child* by Luca della Robbia, and the brilliant *Adoration of the Magi* (1488) painted by Domenico Ghirlandaio for the hospital's church, a crowded, colourful composition featuring portraits of members of the Arte della Lana, who funded the Spedale.

Santissima Annunziata

The second portico on the piazza was built in 1600 in front of Florence's high society church, Santissima Annunziata. Founded in 1250, the church was rebuilt by Michelozzo beginning in 1444 and funded by the Medici, who saw the need for a grander edifice to contain the pilgrims attracted by a miraculous image of the Virgin. As a shelter for the crowds, Michelozzo designed the **Chiostrino dei Voti**, an atrium in front of the church. Most of the Chiostrino's frescoes are by Andrea del Sarto and his students but the most enchanting work is Alesso Baldovinetti's *Nativity* (1462)—unfortunately faded, though you can make out the ghost of a transcendent landscape. Also present are two youthful works: Pontormo's *Visitation* and Rosso Fiorentino's more Mannerist *Assumption.*

The interior is the most gaudy, lush Baroque creation in the city, the only one the Florentines ever spent much money on during the Counter-Reformation. Michelozzo's design includes an unusual polygonal Tribune around the sanctuary, derived from antique buildings and entered by way of a triumphal arch designed by Alberti. Directly to the left as you enter is Michelozzo's marble **Tempietto**, hung with lamps and candles, built to house the miraculous *Annunciation*, painted by a monk with the help of an angel who painted the Virgin's face. Its construction was funded by the Medici, who couldn't resist adding an inscription on the floor that 'The marble alone cost 4000 florins'! The ornate canopy over the *tempietto* was added in the 17th century.

The next two chapels on the left side (*the first under restoration*) contain frescoes by Andrea del Castagno, painted in the 1450s but whitewashed over by the Church when it read Vasari's phoney story that Castagno murdered his fellow painter Domenico Veneziano—a difficult feat, since Veneziano outlived his supposed murderer by several years. Rediscovered in 1864, Castagno's fresco of *St Julian and the Saviour* in the first chapel has some strange Baroque bedfellows by Giambattista Foggini; the next chapel contains his highly unusual *Holy Trinity with St Jerome.* The right aisle's fifth chapel contains a fine example of an early Renaissance tomb, that of the obscure Orlando de' Medici by Bernardo Rossellino. The neighbouring chapel in the transept contains a painted crucifix by Baldovinetti, while the next one has a *Pietà,* the funerary monument of Cosimo I's court sculptor and Cellini's arch-rival Baccio Bandinelli; in this *Pietà* he put his own features on Nicodemus, as Michelangelo did in the *Pietà* in the Museo del Duomo.

Bandinelli's most lasting contribution (or piece of mischief) was his establishment of the first 'Accademia' of art in 1531, which eventually did away with the old artist-pupil relationship in favour of the more impersonal approach of the art school.

Nine semicircular chapels radiate from the Tribune. The one at the rear contains the sarcophagus of Giambologna, a far more successful follower of Michelangelo; his pupil Pietro Tacca is buried with him, in this chapel designed by Giambologna before his death. The next chapel to the left contains a *Resurrection* by Bronzino, one of his finest religious paintings. On the left side of Alberti's triumphal arch, under a statue of St Peter, is the grave of Andrea del Sarto; next to it is the tomb of bishop Angelo Marzi Medici (1546), one of Florence's loudest Counter-Reformation blasts.

A door from the left transept leads into the **Chiostro dei Morti**, most notable for Andrea del Sarto's highly original fresco, the *Madonna del Sacco* (1525), named after the sacks of grain on which St Joseph leans. The **Cappella di San Luca**, located off the cloister (*but rarely open; ask the priest*) belongs to Florence's Academy of Design and contains the graves of Cellini, Pontormo, Franciabigio and other artists.

Archaeology Museum

Open 9–2, Sun 9–1, closed Mon; adm.

From Piazza SS. Annunziata, Via della Colonna leads to Florence's **Museo Archeologico**, housed in the 17th-century Palazzo della Crocetta, originally built for Grand Duchess Maria Maddalena of Austria. Like nearly every other museum in Florence, this impressive collection was begun by the Medici, beginning with Cosimo il Vecchio and accelerating with the insatiable Cosimo I and his heirs. The Medici were especially fond of Etruscan things, while the impressive Egyptian collection was begun by Leopold II in the 1830s. At the time of writing the museum is undergoing rearrangement, but with a little luck you'll be able to find your way around.

The ground floor is devoted to Greek and Etruscan art, including the famous bronze *Chimera*, a remarkable beast with the three heads of a lion, goat and snake. This Etruscan work of the 5th century BC, dug up near Arezzo in 1555 and immediately snatched by Cosimo I, had a great influence on Mannerist artists. There is no Mannerist fancy about its origins, though; like all such composite monsters, it is a religious icon, a calendar beast symbolizing the three seasons of the ancient Mediterranean agricultural year. In the same hall stands the *Arringatore*, or Orator, a monumental bronze of the Hellenistic period, a civic-minded and civilized-looking gentleman, dedicated to Aulus Metellus.

Among the beautiful, often strange Etruscan urns and alabaster sarcophagi, mirrors and small bronzes, there is plenty of Greek art; Etruscan noble families were wont to buy up all they could afford. The beautiful Hellenistic horse's head once adorned the Palazzo Medici-Riccardi. The *Idolino*, a bronze of a young athlete, is believed to be a Roman copy of a 5th-century BC Greek original. There is an excellent *Kouros*, a young man in the archaic style from 6th-century BC Sicily, and some beautiful vases. An unusual, recent find, the silver *Baratti Amphora*, was made in the 4th century BC in Antioch and covered with scores of small medallions showing mythological figures. Scholars believe that the images and their arrangement may encode an entire system of belief, the secret teaching of one of the mystic-philosophical cults common in Hellenistic times, and they hope some day to decipher it.

The Egyptian collection has recently been modernized; there are some interesting small statuettes, mummies, canopic vases, and a unique wood-and-bone chariot, nearly completely preserved, found in a 14th-century BC tomb in Thebes. Out in the garden are several reconstructed Etruscan tombs (*usually closed*). A magnificent collection of precious stones and cameos, coins, and sculpture is kept under wraps and may only be visited by scholars with special permission.

Santa Maria Maddalena dei Pazzi and the Synagogue

East of the Archaeological Museum, Via della Colonna becomes one of Florence's typical straight, boring Renaissance streets. It's worth detouring down Borgo Pinti, to No. 58, to visit one of the city's least known but most intriguing churches, **Santa Maria Maddalena dei Pazzi**, a fine example of architectural syncretism (*open 9–12 and 5–7*). The church itself was founded in the 13th century, rebuilt in classically Renaissance style by Giuliano da Sangallo, then given a full dose of Baroque when the church was rededicated to the Counter-Reformation saint of the Pazzi family. Inside it's all high theatre, with a gaudy *trompe-l'oeil* ceiling, paintings by Luca Giordano, florid chapels, and a wild marble chancel. From the Sacristy a door leads down into a crypt full of mouldering ecclesiastics to the Chapter House, which contains a fresco of the *Crucifixion* (1496), one of Perugino's masterpieces. Despite the symmetry and quiet, contemplative grief of the five figures at the foot of the Cross and the magic stillness of the luminous Tuscan-Umbrian landscape, the fresco has a powerful impact, giving the viewer the uncanny sensation of being able to walk right into the scene.

Florence's Jewish community, although today only 1200 strong, has long been one of the most important in Italy, invited to Florence by the Republic in 1430, but repeatedly exiled and readmitted until Cosimo I founded Florence's Ghetto in 1551. When the Ghetto was opened up in 1848 and demolished soon after, a new **Synagogue** (1874–82) was built in Via L.C. Farini: a tall, charming Mozarabic Pre-Raphaelite hybrid inspired by the Hagia Sophia and the Transito Synagogue of Toledo (*security is tight, but the synagogue may be toured April–Sept, Sun–Thurs ,10– 1 and 2–5; men must cover their heads*). Although seriously damaged by the Nazis in August 1944—and later by the Arno in 1966—it has been lovingly restored. There's a small **Jewish Museum** upstairs (*open same hours as synagogue; © (055) 245252/3 for information*), with a documentary history of Florentine Jews as well as ritual and ceremonial items from the synagogue's treasure.

From the synagogue it's a long two blocks north to Piazzale Donatello. Donatello's name deserves better than this traffic conundrum, a swollen artery in Florence's busy system of *viali* that take traffic around the centre. Pity Elizabeth Barrett Browning (1809–61) and the other expatriates buried in the piazza's **English Cemetery**; they deserve better than to spend eternity in a traffic island.

Sant'Ambrogio and the Flea Market

South of the synagogue the streets of Sant'Ambrogio are among the most dusty and piquant in the city centre, a neighbourhood where tourists seldom tread. Life revolves around **Sant'Ambrogio** and its neighbouring food market made of cast iron in 1873; the church (rebuilt in the 13th century, 19th-century façade) is of interest for its artwork: the second chapel on the right has a lovely fresco of the *Madonna Enthroned with Saints* by Orcagna (or his school) and the **Cappella del Miracolo**, just left of the high altar, contains Mino da Fiesole's celebrated marble *Tabernacle* (1481) and his own tomb. The chapel has a fresco of a procession by Cosimo Rosselli, especially interesting for its depiction of 15th-century costume and its contemporary portraits. Andrea Verrocchio is buried in the fourth chapel on the left; on the wall by the second altar, there's a *Nativity* by Baldovinetti. The fresco of an atypical *St Sebastian* in the first chapel of the left is by Agnolo Gaddi.

From Sant'Ambrogio take Via Pietrapiana to the bustling **Piazza dei Ciompi**, named after the wool-workers' revolt of 1378. In the morning, Florence's flea market or **Mercatino** takes place here, the best place in town to buy that 1940s radio or outdated ball gown you've always wanted. One side of the square is graced with the **Loggia del Pesce**, built by Vasari in 1568 for the fishmongers of the Mercato Vecchio; when that was demolished the loggia was salvaged and re-erected here.

Casa Buonarroti

Open 9.30–1.30, closed Tues; adm; look out for their summer exhibitions.

Michelangelo never lived in this house at Via Ghibellina 70, although he purchased it in 1508. That wasn't the point, especially to an artist who had no thought for his own personal comfort, or anyone else's—he never washed, and never took off his boots, even in bed. Real estate was an obsession of his, as he struggled to restore the status of the semi-noble but impoverished Buonarroti family. His nephew Leonardo inherited the house and several works of art in 1564; later he bought the two houses next door to create a memorial to his uncle, hiring artists to paint scenes from Michelangelo's life. In the mid-19th century, the house was opened to the public as a Michelangelo museum.

The ground floor is dedicated to mostly imaginary portraits of the artist, and works of art collected by his nephew's descendants, including an eclectic Etruscan and Roman collection. The main attractions, however, are upstairs, beginning with Michelangelo's earliest known work, the beautiful bas-relief of *The Madonna of the Steps* (1490–1), the precocious work of a 16-year-old influenced by Donatello and studying in the household of

Lorenzo il Magnifico; the relief of a *Battle Scene*, inspired by classical models, dates from the same period. Small models and drawings of potential projects line the walls; there's the wooden model for the façade of San Lorenzo, with designs for some of the statuary Michelangelo intended to fill in its austere blank spaces—as was often the case, his ideas were far too grand for his patron's purse and patience.

The next four rooms were painted in the 17th century to illustrate Michelangelo's life, virtues and apotheosis, depicting a polite, deferential and pleasant Michelangelo hob-nobbing with popes. Those who know the artist best from *The Agony and the Ecstasy* may think they painted the wrong man by mistake. One of the best sections is a frieze of famous Florentines in the library. Other exhibits include a painted wooden *Crucifix* discovered in Santo Spirito in 1963 and believed by most scholars to be a documented one by Michelangelo, long thought to be lost; the contrapposto position of the slender body, and the fact that only Michelangelo would carve a nude Christ weigh in favour of the attribution. There is also a predella of the *Life of St Nicolas of Bari* by Giovanni di Francesco.

Santa Croce

No place in Florence so feeds the urge to dispute as the church of Santa Croce, Tuscany's 'Westminster Abbey', the largest Franciscan basilica in Italy, a must-see for every tour group. It was here that Stendhal gushed: 'I had attained to that supreme degree of sensibility where the divine intimations of art merge with the impassioned sensuality of emotion. As I emerged from the port of Santa Croce, I was seized with a fierce palpitation of the heart; I walked in constant fear of falling to the ground.' But don't be put off; most people manage to emerge from a visit without tripping over themselves.

The contradictions begin in the **Piazza Santa Croce**, which has its interesting points—the row of medieval houses with projecting upper storeys, supported by stone brackets; the faded bloom of dancing nymphs on the **Palazzo dell'Antella**; the curious 14th-century **Palazzo Serristori-Cocchi**, opposite the church; a grim 19th-century statue of Dante (if Dante really looked like that, it's no wonder Beatrice married someone else). Because this piazza is the lowest-lying in the city, it suffered the worst in the 1966 flood, when 5.5m of oily water poured in.

Dominant over all is Santa Croce's neogothic façade, built in 1857–63 and financed by Sir Francis Sloane, whose Sloane Square in London has more admirers than this black and white design, derived from Orcagna's Tabernacle in Orsanmichele. Yet of all the modern façades built on Italy's churches to atone for the chronic Renaissance inability to finish anything, this is one of the least offensive.

The Interior

Santa Croce was reputedly founded by St Francis himself; during repairs after the flood, vestiges of a small early 13th-century church were discovered under the present structure. It went by the board in Florence's colossal building programme of the 1290s. The great size of the new church speaks for the immense popularity of Franciscan preaching. Arnolfo di Cambio planned it, and it was largely completed by the 1450s, but as in Santa Maria

Novella, Giorgio Vasari and the blinding forces of High Renaissance mediocrity were unleashed upon the interior. Vasari never had much use for the art of Andrea Orcagna— he not only left him out of his influential *Lives of the Artists* but in Santa Croce he destroyed Orcagna's great fresco cycle that once covered the nave, replacing it with uninspired side altars.

For centuries it was the custom to install monuments to illustrious men in Santa Croce, and as you enter, you can see them lining the long aisles. Like many Franciscan churches, Santa Croce's large size, its architectural austerity and open timber roof resemble a barn, but at the end there's a lovely polygonal sanctuary, which shimmers with light and colour streaming through 14th-century stained glass.

Perversely, the greater the person buried in Santa Croce, the uglier their memorial. A member of the Pazzi conspiracy, Francesco Nori, is buried by the first pillar in the right aisle, and graced by one of the loveliest works of art, the *Madonna del Latte* (1478), a bas-relief by Antonio Rossellino, while the **Tomb of Michelangelo** (1570, the first in the right aisle) by Vasari is one of the least attractive. Michelangelo died in Rome in 1564, refusing for 35 years to return to Florence while alive, but agreeing to give the city his corpse. Dante has fared even worse, with an 1829 neoclassical monument that's as disappointing as the fact (to the Florentines) that Dante is buried in Ravenna, where he died in exile in 1321.

Facing the nave, Benedetto da Maiano's **marble pulpit** (1476) is one of the most beautiful the Renaissance ever produced. Behind it, the **Vittorio Alfieri Monument** (1809) was sculpted by neoclassical master Antonio Canova and paid for by his lover, the Countess of Albany. Next is the nondescript 18th-century **Monument of Niccolò Machiavelli**, and then Donatello's **Annunciation** (1430s?), a tabernacle in gilded limestone, the angel wearing a remarkably sweet expression as he gently breaks the news to a grave, thoughtful Madonna. Bernardo Rossellino's **Tomb of Leonardo Bruni** (1447), another masterpiece of the Renaissance, is perhaps the one monument that best fits the man it honours. Bruni was a Greek scholar, a humanist, and the author of the first major historical work of the period, *The History of Florence*, a copy of which his tranquil effigy holds. The tomb, with its Brunelleschian architectural setting, proved a great inspiration to other artists, most obviously Desiderio da Settignano and his equally beautiful **Tomb of Carlo Marsuppini** (1453) directly across the nave, and the less inspired, more imitative **Monument to Rossini** crowded in to the left. The last tomb in the aisle belongs to poet and patriot Ugo Foscolo.

Santa Croce is especially rich in trecento frescoes, providing a unique opportunity to compare the work of Giotto with his followers. The south transept's **Castellani Chapel** has some of the later, more decorative compositions by Agnolo Gaddi (*Scenes from the Lives of Saints*, 1380s). The beautiful **Baroncelli Chapel** was painted with *Scenes from the Life of the Virgin* by Agnolo's father Taddeo, Giotto's assistant in the 1330s and includes a bright gilded altarpiece, the *Coronation of the Virgin* by Giotto and his workshop. The *Annunciation to the Shepherds* by Taddeo, seen to the left of the window, is important as it is thought to be the first nocturnal scene in the history of western art.

1	Madonna del Latte	15	Rinnuccini Chapel
2	Tomb of Michelangelo	16	Peruzzi Chapel
3	Monument to Dante	17	Bardi Chapel
4	Benedetto da Maiano's Pulpit	18	Sanctuary
5	Vittorio Alfieri's Tomb	19	Bardi di Libertà Chapel
6	Tomb of Machiavelli	20	Bardi di Vernio Chapel
7	Donatello's 'Annunciation'	21	Niccolini Chapel
8	Tomb of Leonardo Bruni	22	Bardi Chapel
9	Tomb of Carlo Malaspini	23	Salviati Chapel
10	Tomb of Rossini	24	Monument to Alberti
11	Castellani Chapel	25	Tomb of Lorenzo Ghiberti
12	Baroncelli Chapel	26	Galileo's Tomb
13	Medici Chapel	27	Museo dell'Opera di S. Croce
14	Sacristy		

The next portal gives on to a **Corridor** and the **Medici Chapel** (*open only for Mass*), both designed by Michelozzo, containing one of Andrea della Robbia's finest altarpieces and a 19th-century fake Donatello, a relief of the *Madonna and Child* that fooled the experts for decades. From the corridor a door leads to the **Sacristy**, its walls frescoed by Taddeo Gaddi (*The Crucifixion*), Spinello Aretino and Niccolò di Pietro Gerini. Behind the 14th-century grille, the **Rinuccini Chapel** was frescoed by one of Giotto's most talented followers, the Lombard Giovanni da Milano, in the 1360s.

Giotto's Chapels

The frescoes in the two chapels to the right of the sanctuary, the **Peruzzi Chapel** and the **Bardi Chapel**, were painted by the legendary Giotto in the 1330s, towards the end of his life when the artist returned from Padua and his work in the Arena chapel. The frescoes have not fared well during the subsequent 660 years. Firstly Giotto painted large parts of the walls *a secco* (on dry plaster) instead of *affresco* (on wet plaster), presenting the same kind of preservation problems that bedevil Leonardo's *Last Supper;* secondly, the 18th century thought so little of the frescoes that they were whitewashed over as eyesores. Rediscovered some 150 years later and finally restored in 1959, the frescoes now, even though fragmentary, may be seen more or less as Giotto painted them. The Peruzzi Chapel contains scenes from the *Lives of St John the Evangelist and the Baptist.* In the Bardi Chapel the subject is the *Life of St Francis*, which makes an interesting comparison with the frescoes in Assisi. The contrast between Giotto's frescoes and the chapel's 13th-century altarpiece, also showing scenes of the *Life of St Francis*, is a fair yardstick for measuring the breadth of the Giottesque revolution.

Agnolo Gaddi designed the stained glass around the **Sanctuary**, as well as the fascinating series of frescoes on the *Legend of the True Cross.*

The Legend of the True Cross

This popular medieval story begins with Noah's son, Seth, as an old man, asking for the essence of mercy. The Angel Gabriel replies by giving Seth a branch, saying that 5000 years must pass before mankind may know true redemption. Seth plants the branch over Adam's grave on Mount Sinai, and it grows into a magnificent tree. King Solomon orders the tree cut, but as it is too large to move, the trunk stays where it is and is used as the main beam of a bridge. The Queen of Sheba is about to cross the bridge when she has a vision that the saviour of the world will be suspended from its wood, and that his death will mark the end of the Kingdom of the Jews. She refuses to cross the bridge, and writes of her dream to Solomon, who has the beam buried deep underground. Nevertheless, it is dug up and used to make the cross of Christ.

The cross next appears in the dream of Emperor Constantine before the Battle of Milvan Bridge, when he hears a voice saying that under this sign he will conquer. When it proves true, he sends his mother Helen to find the cross in Jerusalem.

There she meets Judas Cyriacus, a pious Jew who knows where Golgotha is, but won't tell until Helen has him thrown in a well and nearly starved to death. When at last he agrees to dig, a sweet scent fills the air, and Judas Cyriacus is immediately converted. To discover which of the three crosses they find is Christ's, each is held over the coffin of a youth; the True Cross brings him back to life. After all this trouble in finding it, Helen leaves the cross in Jerusalem, where it is stolen by the Persians. Their King Chosroes thinks its power will bring him a great victory, but instead he loses the battle, and Persia, to Emperor Heraclius, who decides to return the holy relic to Jerusalem. But the gate is blocked by the Angel Gabriel, who reminds the proud Heraclius that Jesus entered the city humbly, on the back of an ass. And so, in a similar manner, the emperor returns the cross to Jerusalem.

Further to the left are two more chapels frescoed by followers of Giotto: the fourth, the **Bardi di Libertà Chapel**, by Bernardo Daddi and the last, the **Bardi di Vernio Chapel** (*under restoration*), by Maso di Banco, one of the most innovative and mysterious artists of the trecento. The frescoes illustrate the little-known *Life of St Sylvester*—his baptism of Emperor Constantine, the resurrection of the bull, the closing of the dragon's mouth and resurrection of two sorcerers; on the other wall of the chapel are a *Dream of Constantine* and *Vision of SS. Peter and Paul*. In the corner of the transept, the richly marbled **Niccolini Chapel** offers a Mannerist-Baroque change of pace, built by Antonio Dossi in 1584 and decorated with paintings by Allori (*under restoration*). Next, the second **Bardi Chapel** houses the famous Crucifix by Donatello that Brunelleschi called 'a peasant on the Cross'. The last of the funeral monuments, near the door, are those of Lorenzo Ghiberti and Galileo, the latter an 18th-century work. For running afoul of the Inquisition, Galileo was not permitted a Christian burial until 1737.

The Pazzi Chapel

Open 10–12.30, 3–5, until 6.30 in summer, closed Wed; adm.

This chapel carries an entrance fee, but it's well worth it. Brunelleschi, who could excel on the monumental scale of the cathedral dome, saved some of his best work for small places. Without knowing the architect, and something about the austere religious tendencies of the Florentines, the Pazzi Chapel is inexplicable, a Protestant reformation in architecture unlike anything ever built before. The 'vocabulary' is essential Brunelleschi, the geometric forms emphasized by the simplicity of the decoration: *pietra serena* pilasters and rosettes on white walls, arches, 12 terracotta tondi of the Apostles by Luca della Robbia, coloured rondels of the Evangelists in the pendentives by Donatello, and a small stained-glass window by Baldovinetti. Even so, that is enough. The contemplative repetition of elements makes for an aesthetic that posed a direct challenge to the International Gothic of the time.

Leaving the Pazzi Chapel (notice Luca della Robbia's terracotta decorations on the portico), a doorway on the left of the cloister leads to another work of Brunelleschi, the **Second Cloister**, designed with the same subtlety and one of the quietest spots in Florence.

The old monastic buildings off the first cloister now house the **Museo dell'Opera di Santa Croce** (*open 10–12.30 and 2.30–6.30 summer; 10–12.30 and 3–5 winter; adm*), where you can see Cimabue's celebrated *Crucifix*, devastated by the flood, and partly restored after one of Florence's perennial restoration controversies. The refectory wall has another fine fresco by Taddeo Gaddi, of the *Tree of the Cross and the Last Supper*; fragments of Orcagna's frescoes salvaged from Vasari's obliteration squads offer powerful, nightmarish vignettes of *The Triumph of Death and Hell*. Donatello's huge gilded bronze statue of *St Louis of Toulouse* (1423)—a flawed work representing a flawed character, according to Donatello—was made for the façade of Orsanmichele. The museum also contains works by Andrea della Robbia, and a painting of Mayor Bargellini with a melancholy Santa Croce submerged in the 1966 flood for a backdrop; under the colonnade there's a statue of Florence Nightingale, born in and named after the city in 1820.

Around Santa Croce: the Horne Museum

The east end of Florence, a rambling district packed with artisans and small manufacturers, traditionally served as the artists' quarter in Renaissance times. Still one of the livelier neighbourhoods, with a few lingering artists lodged in the upper storeys, hoping to breathe inspiration from the very stones where Michelangelo walked, it is a good place to observe the workaday Florence behind the glossy façade. Just west of Piazza Santa Croce is a series of streets—Via Bentaccordi, Via Torta and Piazza dei Peruzzi—which makes an almost complete ellipse. These mark the course of the inner arcade of the Roman amphitheatre, some stones of which can still be seen among the foundations of the old palaces.

From Santa Croce, the pretty Borgo Santa Croce leads towards the Arno and the delightful **Horne Museum**, housed in a Renaissance palace, Via de' Benci 6 (*open 9–1, closed Sun and holidays; adm*); Herbert Percy Horne (1844–1916) was an English art historian, biographer of Botticelli, and Florentinophile, who bequeathed his collection to the nation. A large *Deposition*, the last work of Gozzoli, sadly darkened with age, a painting by the great Sienese Pietro Lorenzetti, and a tondo by Piero di Cosimo hang on the first floor. The next room contains Horne's prize, Giotto's golden painting of young *St Stephen*, also Signorelli's *Redeemer*, a beardless, girlish youth, Beccafumi's *Decalione e Pirra*, and a saccharine *St Sebastian* by Carlo Dolci. Room 3 has a rousing quattrocento battle scene, taken from a marriage chest, good 15th-century wood inlays, and a relief of the head of *St John the Baptist* by Desiderio da Settignano. Upstairs a diptych attributed to Barna da Siena holds pride of place, together with an impressive array of Renaissance furniture and household objects.

North Bank Peripheral Attractions

The Cascine

The newer sections of the city are irredeemably dull. Much of Florence's traffic problem is channelled through its ring of avenues, or *viali*, laid out in the 1860s by Giuseppe Poggi to replace the demolished walls. On and along them are scattered points of interest, including some of the old city gates; the distances involved and danger of carbon monoxide poisoning on the *viali* make the idea of walking insane.

Bus 17C from the station or Duomo will take you through the congestion to the **Cascine**, the long (3.5km), narrow public park lining this bank of the Arno, originally used as the Medici's dairy farm, or *cascina*, and later as a Grand Ducal hunting park and theatre for public spectacles. A windy autumn day here in 1819 inspired Shelley to compose the 'Ode to the West Wind'. Three years later Shelley's drowned body was burnt on a pyre in Viareggio, by his friend Trelawny; curiously, a similar incineration took place in the Cascine in 1870 when the Maharaja of Kohlapur died in Florence. According to ritual his body had to be burned near the confluence of two rivers, in this case, the Arno and Mugnone at the far end of the park, on a spot now marked by the Maharaja's equestrian statue. Florentines come to the Cascine to play; it contains a riding school, race tracks, a small amusement park and zoo for the children, tennis courts, and a swimming-pool.

Beyond the train station, cars and buses hurtle around and around the **Fortezza da Basso**, an enormous bulk built by Antonio da Sangallo on orders from Alessandro de' Medici in 1534. It immediately became the most hated symbol of Medici tyranny. Ironically, the duke who built the Fortezza da Basso was one of very few to meet his end within its ramparts—stabbed by his relative and bosom companion 'Lorenzaccio' de' Medici. As a fortress, the place never saw any action as thrilling or vicious as the Pitti fashion shows that take place behind the walls in its 1978 aluminium exhibition hall.

Just east of the Fortezza, at the corner of Via Leone X and Viale Milton, there's an unexpected sight rising above the sleepy residential neighbourhood—the five graceful onion domes of the **Russian Church**, made even more exotic by the palm tree tickling its side. In the 19th century, Florence was a popular winter retreat for Russians who could afford it, among them Dostoevsky and Maxim Gorky. Completed by Russian architects in 1904, it is a pretty jewel box of brick and majolica decoration, open on the third Sunday of the month, when morning services are held in Russian.

The Stibbert Museum

Open for tours on the hour, 9–1, when you may wander at will; closed Thurs; adm, free Sun 9–12.30.

From Piazza della Libertà, dull Via Vittorio Emanuele heads a kilometre north to Via Stibbert and the Stibbert Museum (alternatively, take bus 4 from the station). Those who make the journey to see the lifetime's accumulations of Frederick Stibbert (1838–1906), who fought with Garibaldi and hobnobbed with Queen Victoria, can savour Florence's most bizarre museum, and one of the city's most pleasant small parks, laid out by Stibbert with a mouldering Egyptian temple sinking in a pond; and just try to obey the sign on the door: 'Comply with the Forbidden Admittances!').

Stibbert's Italian mother left him a 14th-century house, which he enlarged, joining it to another house to create a sumptuous Victorian's version of what a medieval Florentine house should have looked like—64 rooms to contain a pack-rat's treasure hoard of all things brilliant and useless, from an attributed Botticelli to snuff boxes, to what a local guide intriguingly describes as 'brass and silver basins, used daily by Stibbert'. Stibbert's serious passion, however, was armour, and he amassed a magnificent collection from all times and places. The best pieces are not arranged in dusty cases, but with a touch of Hollywood, on grim knightly mannequins ranked ready for battle.

The Oltrarno

Once over the Ponte Vecchio, a different Florence reveals itself: greener, quieter, and less burdened with traffic. The Oltrarno is not a large district. A chain of hills squeezes it against the river, and their summits afford some of the best views over the city. Once across the Arno, the Medici's catwalk becomes part of the upper façade of **Santa Felicità**, one of Florence's most ancient churches, believed to have been founded by the Syrian Greek traders who introduced Christianity to the city, and established the first Christian cemetery in the small square in front of the church. Rebuilt in the 18th century, there is one compelling reason to enter, for here, in the first chapel on the right, is the *ne plus ultra* of Mannerism: Pontormo's weirdly luminous *Deposition* (1528), painted in jarring pinks, oranges and blues that cut through the darkness of the little chapel. The composition itself is highly unconventional, with an effect that derives entirely from the use of figures in unusual, exaggerated poses; there is no sign of a cross, the only background is a single cloud. Sharing the chapel is Pontormo's *Annunciation* fresco, a less idiosyncratic work, as well as four tondi of the Evangelists in the cupola, partly the work of Pontormo's pupil and adopted son, Bronzino.

The Pitti Palace

As the Medici consolidated their power in Florence, they made a point of buying up the most important properties of their former rivals, especially their proud family palaces. The most spectacular example of this was Cosimo I's acquisition of the Pitti Palace, built in 1457 by a powerful banker named Luca Pitti who seems to have had vague ambitions of toppling the Medici and becoming the big boss himself. The palace, with its extensive grounds, now the Boboli Gardens, was much more pleasant than the medieval Palazzo Vecchio, and in the 1540s Cosimo I and his wife Eleanor of Toledo moved in for good. The palace remained the residence of the Medici, and later the House of Lorraine, until 1868. The original building, said to have been designed by Brunelleschi, was only as wide as the seven central windows of the façade. Succeeding generations found it too small for their burgeoning hoards of bric-a-brac, and added several stages of symmetrical additions, resulting in a long bulky profile, resembling a rusticated Stalinist ministry on its bleak asphalt piazza.

There are eight separate museums in the Pitti, including collections dedicated to clothes, ceraĩmics and carriages—a tribute to Medici acquisitiveness in the centuries of decadence, a period from which, in the words of Mary McCarthy, 'flowed a torrent of bad taste that has not yet dried up . . . if there had been Toby jugs and Swiss weather clocks available, the Grand Dukes would certainly have collected them.' For the diligent visitor who wants to see everything, the Pitti is pitiless; it is impossible to see all in one day.

Galleria Palatina

Open 9–7, closed Mon; adm exp; during the week expect some rooms to be closed, but on Sundays the whole gallery is open.

The Pitti museum most people see is the Galleria Palatina, containing the Grand Dukes' famous collection of 16th–18th-century paintings, stacked on the walls in enormous gilt frames under the berserk opulence of frescoed ceilings celebrating planets, mythology, and of course, the Medici. The gallery is on the first floor of the right half of the palace; the ticket office is on the ground floor, off Ammanati's exaggerated rustic courtyard, a Mannerist masterpiece.

After the entrance to the Galleria is the neoclassical **Sala Castagnoli**, with the *Tavola delle Muse* in its centre, itself an excellent introduction to the Florentine 'decorative arts'; the table, a paragon of the intricate art of *pietra dura*, was made in the 1870s. The Galleria's best paintings are in the five former reception rooms off to the left, with colourful ceilings painted in the 1640s by Pietro da Cortona, one of the most interesting Italian Baroque artists. The first is the **Sala di Venere**, with several works by Titian, including his early *Concert*, believed to have been partly painted by Giorgione and a powerful *Portrait of Pietro Aretino*, Titian's close and caustic friend, who complained to the artist that it was all too accurate and gave it to Cosimo I. There are two beautiful, optimistic landscapes by Rubens, painted at the end of his life, and an uncanny self-portrait, *La Menzogna* (the Falsehood) by Neapolitan Salvator Rosa. The centrepiece statue, the *Venus Italica*, was commissioned by Napoleon from neoclassical master Antonio Canova in 1812 to replace the Venus de' Medici which he 'centralized' off to Paris—a rare case of the itchy-fingered Corsican trying to pay for something he took.

In the **Sala di Apollo** there's more Titian—his *Portrait of a Grey-eyed Gentleman*, evoking the perfect 16th-century English gentleman, a romantic character with an intense gaze, and his more sensuous than penitent *Mary Magdalene*—as well as works by Andrea del Sarto and Van Dyck.

The **Sala di Marte** has two works by Rubens, *The Four Philosophers* and the *Consequences of War*, as well as some excellent portraits by Tintoretto and Van Dyck (*Cardinal Bentivoglio*), and Titian's rather dashing *Cardinal Ippolito de' Medici* in Hungarian costume. Ippolito, despite being destined for the Church, was one of the more high-spirited Medici, and helped defend Vienna from the Ottomans before being poisoned at the age of 24.

The **Sala di Giove**, used as the Medici throne room, contains one of Raphael's best-known portraits, the lovely and serene *Donna Velata* (1516). The small painting of *The Three Ages of Man* is usually attributed to Giorgione. Salviati, Perugino, Fra Bartolomeo and Andrea del Sarto are also represented; in the **Sala di Saturno** Raphael dominates, with several paintings from his Florence days: *Maddalena and Agnolo Doni* (1506) and the *Madonna 'del Granduca'*, influenced by the paintings of Leonardo. Some 10 years later, Raphael had found his own style, beautifully evident in his famous *Madonna della Seggiola* ('of the chair'), perhaps the most popular work he ever painted, and one that is far more complex and subtle than it appears. The rounded, intertwining figures of the Madonna and Child are seen as if through a slightly convex mirror, bulging out—one of the first examples of conscious illusionism in the Renaissance.

The last of the reception rooms, the **Sala dell'Iliade** (frescoed in the 19th century), has some fine portraits by the Medici court painter and Rubens' friend, Justus Sustermans. Two *Assumptions* by Andrea del Sarto, *Philip II* by Titian, and a Velazquez equestrian portrait of Philip IV share the room with one of the most unusual residents of the gallery, *Queen Elizabeth*, who seems uncomfortable in such company. Just off this room lies the pretty **Sala della Stufa**, frescoed with the *Four Ages of the World* by Pietro da Cortona. Caravaggio's *Sleeping Cupid* is in the next room, the **Sala dell'Educazione di Giove**. A couple of rooms down you can peek into the Empire bathroom of Elisa Baciocchi, Napoleon's sister, who ruled the Département de l'Arno between 1809 and 1814, and seemingly spent much of those years redecorating the Pitti.

Some of the more interesting paintings to ferret out in the remainder of the gallery include Filippino Lippi's *Death of Lucrezia* and Raphael's *Madonna dell'Impannata*, both in the **Sala di Ulisse**. In the adjacent **Sala di Prometeo** don't miss Filippo Lippi's lovely *Tondo of the Madonna and Child*, and Baldassare Peruzzi's unusual *Dance of Apollo*.

The State Apartments

The right half of the Pitti also contains the State Apartments (*open 9–7 Sun only; winter apartments by appointment only, © (055) 287096*). These were last redone in the 19th century by the Dukes of Lorraine, with touches by the Kings of Savoy, who occupied them during Florence's interlude as national capital. Among the garish furnishings, there is a fine series of Gobelin tapestries ordered from Paris by Elisa Baciocchi.

Galleria d'Arte Moderna

On the second floor above the Galleria Palatina has been installed Florence's modern—read late 18th- and 19th-century—art museum (*tickets on second floor; same hours as the Galleria Palatina; adm*). Though the monumental stair may leave you breathless (the Medici negotiated it with sedan chairs and strong-shouldered servants), consider a visit for some sunny painting of the Italy of your great-grandparents and some amazing, kitsch statuary, obsessed with death and beauty. The underrated 'Splatterers' or *Macchiaioli* (Tuscan Impressionists) illuminate Room 16 and the rest of the museum, forming an excellent introduction to the works by Silvestro Lega, Giovanni Fattori, Nicolo Cannicci, Francesco Gioli, Federigo Zandomeneghi and Telemaco Signorini, with an interval dedicated to the Risorgimento battle scenes. While the canvases radiate light, the morbid statues become more frequent and stupefying: don't miss the *Pregnant Nun* and the *Suicide*, by Antonio Ciseri in Room 19.

Museo degli Argenti

The ground floor on the left side of the Pitti was used as the Medici summer apartments and now contains the family's remarkable collection of jewellery, vases, trinkets and pricey curiosities (*open 9–2, closed Mon; adm valid for Costume Museum*). The Grand Duke's guests would be received in four of the most delightfully frescoed rooms in Florence, beginning with the **Sala di Giovanni di San Giovanni,** named after the artist who painted it in the 1630s. The theme is the usual Medicean self-glorification—but nowhere does such dubious material achieve such flamboyant treatment. Here the Muses, chased from Paradise, find refuge with Lorenzo il Magnifico; Lorenzo smiles as he studies a bust of Pan by Michelangelo. His real passion, a collection of antique vases carved of semi-precious stones or crystal, is displayed in a room off to the left; the vases were dispersed with the rise of Savonarola, but Lorenzo's nephew Cardinal Giulio had no trouble in relocating them, as Lorenzo had his initials LAUR.MED. deeply incised into each. The three **Reception rooms** were painted in shadowy blue *trompe l'oeil* by two masterful Bolognese illusionists, Agostino Michele and Angelo Colonna.

The Grand Dukes' treasure hoard is up on the mezzanine. These golden toys are only a fraction of what the Medici had accumulated; despite the terms of Anna Maria's will, leaving everything to Florence, the Lorraines sold off the most valuable pieces and jewels to finance Austria's wars. Among the leftovers here, however, is a veritable apoplexy of fantastical bric-a-brac: jewelled bugs, cameos, sea monster pendants, interlaced ivory cubes, carved cherry pits, gilt nautilus shells, chalices made of ostrich eggs, enough ceramic plates to serve an army, a Mexican mitre made of feathers, intricate paper cut-outs, cups carved from buffalo horns, and 17th-century busts and figurines made of seashells that would not shame the souvenir stand of any seaside resort.

More Pitti Museums

The **Museum of Costumes** (*same hours as the Argenti*) is housed in the Meridiana pavilion, the south extension of the Pitti, a dull addition added by the Lorraines; its prize exhibit is the reconstructed dress that Eleanor of Toledo was buried in—the same one that she wears in Bronzino's famous portrait. The **Porcelain Museum** (*open same hours as gardens, museum is included in the garden ticket*) is housed in the airy casino of Cosimo III, out in the Giardino del Cavaliere in the Boboli Gardens (*follow the signs*). The **Museo delle Carrozze**, with a collection of Medici and Lorraine carriages and sedan chairs, has been closed for years.

Finally, the hardest part of the Pitti to get into may be worth the trouble if you're fond of Spanish painting. Until it finds a permanent home, the **Contini Bonacossi Collection** resides in the Meridiana pavilion (*open for tours Tues, Thurs and Sat at 10am—you must make an appointment with the secretary of the Uffizi Gallery*). This recent bequest includes works of Cimabue, Duccio and Giovanni Bellini, some sculpture and china, and also paintings by El Greco, Goya and Velazquez—the last represented by an exceptional work, *The Water Carrier of Seville.*

Boboli Gardens

Open 9am until one hour before sunset; closed first and last Mon of each month; adm.

Stretching back invitingly from the Pitti, the shady green of the Boboli Gardens, Florence's largest (and only) central public garden, is an irresistible oasis in the middle of a stone-hard city. Originally laid out by Buontalenti, the Boboli reigns as queen of all formal Tuscan gardens, the most elaborate and theatrical, a Mannerist–Baroque co-production of Nature and Artifice laid out over a steep hill, full of shady nooks and pretty walks and beautifully kept. The park is guarded by a platoon of statuary, many of them Roman works, while others are absurd Mannerist pieces like Cosimo I's court dwarf posing as a chubby Bacchus astride a turtle (near the left-hand entrance, next to Vasari's Corridor).

Just beyond this lies the remarkable **Grotta di Buontalenti**, one of the architect's most imaginative works, anticipating Gaudì with his dripping, stalactite-like stone, from which fantastic limestone animals struggle to emerge. Casts of Michelangelo's *nonfiniti* slaves stand in the corners, replacing the originals put there by the Medici, while back in the shadowy depths stands a luscious statue of Venus coming from her bath by Giambologna. For all that, the grotto is not a favourite with the Florentines and is usually locked up.

The **Amphitheatre**, ascending in regular tiers from the palace, was designed like a small Roman circus to hold Medici court spectacles. It has a genuine obelisk, of Rameses II from Heliopolis, snatched by the ancient Romans and shipped here by the Medici branch in Rome. The granite basin, large enough to submerge an elephant, came from the Roman Baths of Caracalla. Straight up the terrace is the **Neptune Fountain**; a signposted path leads from there to the pretty **Kaffeehaus**, a boat-like pavilion with a prow and deck offering a fine view of Florence and drinks in the summer. From here the path continues up to the **Belvedere Fort** (*see* p.167). Other signs from the Neptune Fountain point the way up to the secluded **Giardino del Cavaliere**, located on a bastion on Michelangelo's fortifications (*open same hours as the Porcelain Museum*). Cosimo III built the casino here to escape the heat in the Pitti Palace; the view over the ancient villas, vineyards and olives is pure Tuscan enchantment.

Casa Guidi

In the old days the neighbourhood around the Pitti was a fashionable address, but in the 19th century rents for a furnished palace were incredibly low. Shortly after their secret marriage, the Brownings found one of these, the **Casa Guidi** at Piazza San Felice 8, the perfect place to settle; during their 13 years here they wrote their most famous poetry. Now owned by the Browning Institute, you can visit it weekdays (*open Easter–Nov, Mon, Wed and Fri 3–6; donation*). Dostoevsky wrote *The Idiot* while living nearby, at No. 21 Piazza Pitti.

Stuffed Animals and Wax Cadavers

Past the Pitti on Via Romana 17, are two of Florence's great oddball attractions, both part of the **La Specola** museum. The Zoological Section (*open 9–12 and 9–1 Sun, closed Wed*) has a charmingly old-fashioned collection of nearly everything that walks, flies or swims, from the humble sea worm to the rare Madagascar Aye-Aye or the swordfish, with an accessory case of different blades. Some trophies bagged by the hunt-crazy House of Savoy are displayed, and near the end come small wax models of human and animal anatomy, wax eggs, a wax peeled chicken and wax skinned cat. The real horror show stuff, however, is kept hidden away in the **Museum of Waxes** (*open same hours as La Specola*). Dotty, prudish old Cosimo III was a hypochondriac and morbidly obsessed with diseases, which his favourite artist, a Sicilian priest named Gaetano Zumbo, was able to portray with revolting realism. His macabre anatomical models were one of the main sights for Grand Tourists in the 18th century.

Santo Spirito

Piazza Santo Spirito, the centre of the Oltrarno, usually has a few market stalls in the morning under the plane trees as well as a quiet café or two. In the evening it changes face and the bars fill with people, who meet and chat in the piazza and on the church steps until the early hours. On one side, a plain 18th-century façade hides Brunelleschi's last, and perhaps greatest church (*open 8–12, closed Mon; adm*). He designed Santo Spirito in 1440 and lived to see only one column erected, but subsequent architects were faithful to his elegant plan for the interior. This is done in the architect's favourite pale grey and *pietra serena* articulation, a rhythmic forest of columns with semicircular chapels is gracefully recessed into the transepts and the three arms of the crossing. The effect is somewhat spoiled by the ornate 17th-century *baldacchino*, which sits in this enchanted garden of architecture like a 19th-century bandstand.

The art in the chapels is meagre, as most of the good paintings were sold off over the years. The best include Filippino Lippi's beautiful *Madonna and Saints* in the right transept and Verrocchio's jewel-like *St Monica and Nuns* in the opposite transept, an unusual composition and certainly one of the blackest paintings of the Renaissance, pervaded with a dusky, mysterious quality; Verrocchio, who taught both Leonardo and Botticelli, was a Hermetic alchemist on the side. The fine marble altarpiece and decoration in a nearby chapel is by Sansovino; the elaborate barrel-vaulted **Vestibule** and octagonal **Sacristy**, entered from the left aisle, are by Giuliano da Sangallo, inspired by Brunelleschi.

To the left of the church, in the refectory of the vanished 14th-century convent are the scanty remains of a *Last Supper* and a well-preserved, highly dramatic *Crucifixion* by Andrea Orcagna, in which Christ is seen alone against an enormous dark sky, with humanity ranged below and angels like white swallows swirling around in a cosmic whirlwind. The refectory also contains an interesting collection of Romanesque odds and ends, including 13th-century stone sea-lions from Naples.

Santa Maria del Carmine

Open 10–4.30 and 1–4.30
Sun, closed Tues; adm.

There is little to say about the surroundings, the piazza, the rough stone façade, or the interior of the Oltrarno's other great church, Santa Maria del Carmine, which burned in 1771 and was reconstructed shortly after. Miraculously, the **Brancacci Chapel**, one of the landmarks in Florentine art, survived both the flames and attempts by the authorities to replace it with something more fashionable. Three artists worked on the Brancacci's frescoes: Masolino, who began them in 1425, and who designed the cycle, his pupil Masaccio, who worked on them alone for a year before following his master to Rome, where he died at the age of 27, and Filippino Lippi, who finished them 50 years later. Filippino took care to imitate Masaccio as closely as possible, and the frescoes have an appearance of stylistic unity. Between 1981 and 1988 they were subject to one of Italy's most publicized restorations, cleansed of 550 years of dirt and overpainting, enabling us to see what so thrilled the painters of the Renaissance.

Masaccio in his day was a revolution and a revelation in his solid, convincing naturalism; his figures stand in space, without any fussy ornamentation or Gothic grace, very much inspired by Donatello's sculptures. Masaccio conveyed emotion with broad, quick brush strokes and with his

use of light, most obvious in his almost Impressionistic scene of the *Expulsion of Adam and Eve*, one of the most memorable and harrowing images created in the Renaissance. In the *Tribute Money*, the young artist displays his mastery of Brunelleschian artificial perspective and light effects. The three episodes in the fresco show an official demanding tribute from the city, St Peter fetching it, on Christ's direction, from the mouth of a fish, and lastly, his handing over of the money to the official. Other works by 'Shabby Tom' include *St Peter Baptizing* on the upper register, and *St Peter Healing with his Shadow* and *St Peter Enthroned and Resurrecting the Son of the King of Antioch*, the right half of which was finished by Filippino Lippi. The more elegant and unearthly Masolino is responsible for the remainder, except for the lower register's *Release of St Peter from Prison*, *St Peter Crucified* and *St Paul Visiting St Peter in Prison*, all by Filippino Lippi, based on Masaccio's sketches.

Among the detached frescoes displayed in the cloister and refectory is a good one by Filippino's dad, Fra Filippo Lippi, who was born nearby in Via dell'Ardiglione.

Around the Oltrarno

Those with the time or inclination to stroll the streets of the Oltrarno can discover one of the city's last real residential neighbourhoods, the streets lined with bakeries and barber-shops instead of boutiques and restaurants. The westernmost quarter within the medieval walls, Borgo San Frediano, is known for its workshops and unpretentious antique dealers. The **Porta San Frediano**, its tall tower guarding the Pisa road, has its old wooden door and locks still in place. The domed 17th-century church of **San Frediano in Cestello**, with its blank poker face, is the landmark along this stretch of the Arno.

The neighbourhoods get trendier as you head east, especially along busy Via di Santo Spirito, its extension Borgo San Jacopo, and wide Via Maggio, leading inland from the Ponte Santa Trínita. All have fine palaces and medieval towers pruned by the Republic. Many great medieval bankers also erected their palaces in the Oltrarno. Several may still be seen along Via de' Bardi, east of the Ponte Vecchio, especially the 13th–14th-century **Palazzo dei Mozzi** in the piazza of the same name. Across the piazza is the **Museo Bardini/Galleria Corsi** (*open 9–2, 8–1 Sun, closed Wed; adm*), an eclectic collection of art and architectural fragments left to the city in 1922 by art dealer Stefano Bardini. Bardini built this rather lugubrious palace to incorporate the doorways, ceilings and stairs that he salvaged from the demolition of the Mercato Vecchio and other buildings in central Florence; he even installed a mock crypt to display his tombs and funereal altar-pieces (there's an especially fine one by Andrea della Robbia). Also outstanding are Tino da Camaino's trecento *Charity*, a *Madonna* attributed to Donatello, a panel painting of *St Michael* by Antonio Pollaiuolo, and a magnificent set of Persian carpets, old musical instruments, furniture and armour. Near the museum, the nondescript postwar **Ponte alle Grazie** replaced a famous medieval bridge with seven chapels on it, home to seven nuns, who one imagines spent much of their time praying that the Arno wouldn't flood.

Further east, narrow Via di San Niccolò leads to **San Niccolò sopr'Arno**, a church rebuilt in the 14th century, with a lovely fresco in the sacristy of the *Madonna della*

Cintola ('of the girdle') by Baldovinetti. The street ends with a bang at **Porta San Niccolò**, an impressively looming gate of 1340 that has recently been restored. A smaller gate just to the south, the **Porta San Miniato**, stands near the walkway up to San Miniato (*see* below).

A City with a View

Great Aunt Florence, with her dour complexion and severe, lined face, never was much of a looker from street level, but improves with a bit of distance, either mental or from one of her hilltop balconies: the Belvedere Fort, San Miniato, Piazzale Michelangelo, Bellosguardo, Fiesole or Settignano. Few cities are so endowed with stunning vistas; and when you look down upon Florence's palaces and towers, her loping bridges and red tile roofs and famous churches, Brunelleschi's incomparable dome seems even more remarkable, hovering like a benediction over the city.

Belvedere Fort and Arcetri

One of Florence's best and closest balconies is the **Belvedere Fort**, a graceful six-point star designed by Buontalenti and built 1590–5, not so much for the sake of defence but to remind any remaining Florentine republicans who was boss. Since 1958, it has been used for special exhibitions, but you can always enjoy the unforgettable views of Florence and countryside from its ramparts, daily between 8am and 8pm. It can be reached by ascending one of Florence's prettiest streets, **Costa San Giorgio**, which begins in Piazza Santa Felicità, just beyond the Ponte Vecchio. Costa San Giorgio winds up the hill, lined with old villas and walled gardens. The villa at No. 19 was, from 1610 to 1631, the home of Galileo. At the top of the street stands the arch of the **Porta San Giorgio**, guarded by a 13th-century relief of St George and the dragon.

In this part of Florence, the countryside begins right at the city wall, a rolling landscape of villas and gardens. Via San Leonardo winds its way out towards Arcetri; a 10-minute walk will take you to the 11th-century **San Leonardo in Arcetri** (*usually open Sunday mornings*). There is a wonderful 13th-century pulpit, originally built for San Pier Scheraggio, and a small rose window, made according to legend from a wheel of Fiesole's *carroccio*, captured by Florence in 1125. A half kilometre further on, past the Viale Galileo crossroads, Via San Leonardo changes its name to Via Viviani, where it passes the **Astrophysical Observatory** and the **Torre del Gallo**, a reconstruction of a 14th-century tower by art dealer Stefano Bardini. Another kilometre further on Via Viviani reaches the settlement of Pian de' Giullari, where Galileo spent the last years of his life, in the 16th-century **Villa il Gioiello**, virtually under house arrest after his encounter with the Inquisition in 1631, and where Milton is believed to have visited him.

San Miniato

From Porta San Miniato you can walk up to San Miniato church on the stepped Via di San Salvatore al Monte, complete with the Stations of the Cross, or take the less pious bus 13 up the scenic Viale dei Colli from the station or Via de Benci, near Ponte alle Grazie. High atop its monumental steps, San Miniato's distinctive and beautiful façade can be seen from almost anywhere in the city, although relatively few visitors take the time to visit one of the finest Romanesque churches in Italy.

San Miniato was built in 1015, over an even earlier church. According to legend, the head of 3rd-century martyr St Minias bounced up here when the Romans knocked it off down below in Florence. Despite its distance from the centre San Miniato has always been one of the churches dearest to the Florentines' hearts. The remarkable geometric pattern of green, black and white marble that adorns its façade was begun in 1090, though funds only permitted the embellishment of the lower, simpler half of the front; the upper half was added in the 12th century, paid for by the Arte di Calimala, the medieval cloth merchants' guild, whose gold eagle stands at the top of the roof. The glittering mosaic of Christ, the Virgin and St Minias, came slightly later.

The Calimala was also responsible for decorating the interior, an unusual design with a raised choir built over the crypt. As the Calimala became richer, so did the fittings; the delicate intarsia **marble floor** of animals and zodiac symbols dates from 1207. The lower walls were frescoed in the 14th and 15th centuries, including an enormous St Christopher. At the end of the nave stands Michelozzo's unique, free-standing **Cappella del Crocifisso**, built in 1448 to hold the crucifix that spoke to St John Gualberto (now in Santa Trínita); it is magnificently carved and adorned with terracottas by Luca della Robbia.

Off the left nave is one of Florence's Renaissance showcases, the **Chapel of the Cardinal of Portugal** (1461–6). The 25-year-old Cardinal, a member of the Portuguese royal family, happened to die in Florence at an auspicious moment, when the Medici couldn't spend enough money on publicly prominent art, and when some of the greatest artists of the quattrocento were at the height of their careers. The chapel was designed by Manetti, Brunelleschi's pupil; the ceiling exquisitely decorated with enamelled terracotta and medallions by Luca della Robbia; the Cardinal's tomb beautifully carved by Antonio Rossellino; the fresco of the *Annunciation* charmingly painted by Alesso Baldovinetti; the altarpiece of *Three Saints* is a copy of the original by Piero Pollaiuolo.

San Miniato

Up the steps of the choir more treasures await. The marble transenna and pulpit were carved in 1207, with art and a touch of medieval humour. Playful geometric patterns frame the mosaic in the apse, *Christ between the Virgin and St Minias,* made in 1297 by artists imported from Ravenna, and later restored by Baldovinetti. The colourful **Sacristy** on the right was entirely frescoed by Spinello Aretino in 1387, but made rather flat by subsequent restoration. In the **Crypt** an 11th-century altar holds the relics of St Minias; the columns are topped by ancient capitals.

The panorama of Florence from San Miniato is lovely to behold, but such thoughts were hardly foremost in Michelangelo's mind during the Siege of Florence. The hill was vulnerable, and to defend it he hastily erected the fortress (now surrounding the cemetery to the left of the church), placed cannons in the unfinished 16th-century campanile (built to replace an original which fell over), and shielded the tower from artillery with mattresses. He grew fond of the small church below San Miniato, **San Salvatore al Monte**, built by Cronaca in the late 1400s, which he called his 'pretty country lass'.

With these associations in mind, perhaps, the city named the vast, square terrace car park below, **Piazzale Michelangelo**, the most popular viewpoint only because it is the only one capable of accommodating an unlimited number of tour buses. Besides another copy of the *David* and a fun, tacky carnival atmosphere rampant with souvenirs, balloons and ice cream, the Piazzale offers views that can reach as far as Pistoia on a clear day.

Bellosguardo

Many would argue that the finest of all views over Florence is to be had from Bellosguardo, located almost straight up from Porta Romana at the end of the Boboli Gardens or Piazza Torquato Tasso. Non-mountaineers may want to take a taxi; the famous viewpoint, from where you can see every church façade in the city, is just before Piazza Bellosguardo.

Fiesole

Florence liked to look at itself as the daughter of Rome, and in its fractious heyday explained its quarrelsome nature by the fact that its population from the beginning was of mixed race, of Romans and 'that ungrateful and malignant people who of old came down from Fiesole', according to Dante. First settled in the 2nd millennium BC, it became the most important Etruscan city in the region. Yet from the start Etruscan *Faesulae*'s relationship with Rome was rocky, especially after sheltering Catiline and his conspirators in 65 BC. Because of its lofty position, Fiesole was too difficult to capture, so the Romans built a camp below on the Arno to cut off its supplies. Eventually Fiesole was taken, and it dwindled as the Roman camp below grew into the city of Florence, growth the Romans encouraged to spite the old Etruscans on their hill. This easily defended hill, however, ensured Fiesole's survival in the Dark Ages. When times became safer, families began to move back down to the Arno to rebuild Florence. They returned to smash up most of Fiesole after defeating it in 1125; since then the little town has remained aloof, letting Florence dominate and choke in its own juices far, far below.

But ever since the days of the *Decameron*, whose storytellers retreated to its garden villas to escape the plague, Fiesole has played the role of Florence's aristocratic suburb; its cool breezes, beautiful landscapes and belvedere views make it the perfect refuge from the torrid Florentine summers. There's no escaping the tourists, however; we foreigners have been tramping up and down Fiesole's hill since the days of Shelley. A day trip has become an obligatory part of a stay in Florence, and although Fiesole has proudly retained its status as an independent *comune*, you can make the 20-minute trip up on Florence city bus 7 from the station or Piazza San Marco. If you have the time, walk up (or perhaps better, down) the old lanes bordered with villas and gardens to absorb some of the world's most civilized scenery.

Around Piazza Mino

The long sloping stage of Piazza Mino is Fiesole's centre, with the bus stop, the local tourist office, the cafés, and the **Palazzo Pretorio**, its loggia and façade emblazoned with coats of arms. The square is named after a favourite son, the quattrocento sculptor Mino da Fiesole, whom Ruskin preferred to all others. An example of his work may be seen in the **Duomo**, whose plain façade dominates the north side of the piazza. Built in 1028, it was the only building spared by the vindictive Florentines in 1125. It was subsequently enlarged and given a scouring 19th-century restoration, leaving the tall, crenellated campanile as its sole distinguishing feature. Still, the interior has an austere charm, with a raised choir over the crypt similar to San Miniato. Up the steps to the right are two beautiful works by Mino da Fiesole: the *Tomb of Bishop Leonardo Salutati* and an altar front. The main altarpiece in the choir, of the Madonna and saints, is by Lorenzo di Bicci, from 1440. Note the two saints frescoed on the columns; it was a north Italian custom to paint holy people as if they were members of the congregation. The crypt, holding the remains of Fiesole's patron, St Romulus, is supported by ancient columns bearing doves, spirals and other early Christian symbols.

Behind the Cathedral, on Via Dupré, the **Bandini Museum** (*open 10–7, exc Tues; in winter 10–6; adm*) contains sacred works, including numerous della Robbia terracottas and some good trecento paintings by Lorenzo Monaco, Neri di Bicci and Taddeo Gaddi.

Archaeological Zone

Behind the cathedral and museum is the entrance to what remains of *Faesulae*. Because Fiesole avoided trouble in the Dark Ages, its Roman monuments have survived in much better shape than those of Florence; although hardly spectacular the ruins are charmingly set amid olive groves and cypresses. The small **Roman Theatre** has survived well enough to host plays and concerts in the summer; Fiesole would like to remind you that in the ancient times it had the theatre and plays while Florence had the amphitheatre and wild beast shows. Close by are the rather confusing remains of two superimposed temples, the baths, and an impressive stretch of Etruscan walls (best seen from Via delle Mure Etrusche, below) that proved their worth against Hannibal's siege. The **Archaeology Museum** (*open 9–7 summer; 9–6 winter, closed Tues; adm*) is housed in a small 20th-century Ionic temple, displaying some very early small bronze figurines with flapper wing arms, Etruscan funerary urns and stelae, including the interesting 'stele Fiesolana' with a banquet scene.

Walking Around Fiesole

From Piazza Mino, Via S. Francesco ascends steeply (at first) to the hill that served as the Etruscan and Roman acropolis. Halfway up is a terrace with extraordinary views of Florence and the Arno sprawl, with a monument to the three *carabinieri* who gave themselves up to be shot by the Nazis in 1944 to prevent them from taking civilian reprisals. The church nearby, the **Basilica di Sant'Alessandro**, was constructed over an Etruscan/Roman temple in the 6th century, reusing its lovely *cipollino* (onion marble) columns and Ionic capitals, one still inscribed with an invocation to Venus. At the top of the hill, square on the ancient acropolis, stands the monastery of **San Francesco**, its church containing a famous early cinquecento *Annunciation* by Raffaellino del Garbo and an *Immaculate Conception* by Piero di Cosimo. A grab-bag of odds and ends collected from the four corners of the world, especially Egypt and China, is displayed in the quaint **Franciscan Missionary Museum** in the cloister (*open 10–12 and 3–6 summer; 10–12 and 3–5 winter*); it also has an Etruscan collection.

There are much longer walks along the hill behind the Palazzo Pretorio. The panoramic Via Belvedere leads back to Via Adriano Mari, and in a couple of kilometres to the bucolic **Montecéceri**, a wooded park where Leonardo da Vinci performed his flight experiments, and where Florentine architects once quarried their dark *pietra serena* from quarries now abandoned but open for exploration. In Borgunto, as this part of Fiesole is called, there are two 3rd-century BC **Etruscan tombs** on Via Bargellino; east of Borgunto scenic Via Francesco Ferrucci and Via di Vincigliata pass by Fiesole's castles, the **Castel di Poggio**, site of summer concerts, and the **Castel di Vincigliata**, dating back to 1031, while further down is American critic Bernard Berenson's famous **Villa I Tatti**, which he left, along with a distinguished collection of Florentine art, to Harvard University as the Centre of Italian Renaissance Studies. The road continues down towards Ponte a Mensola (6km from Fiesole; *see* below) and Settignano, with buses back to Florence.

San Domenico di Fiesole

Located between Fiesole and Florence, San Domenico is a pleasant walk down from Fiesole by way of Via Vecchia Fiesolana, the steep and narrow old road that passes, on the left, the **Villa Medici** (*no adm*), built by Michelozzo for Cosimo il Vecchio; in its lovely garden on the hillside, Lorenzo and his friends of the Platonic Academy would come to get away from the world; it was also the lucky Iris Origo's childhood home. San Domenico, at the bottom of the lane, is the church and convent where Fra Angelico first entered his monkish world. The 15th-century church of **San Domenico** contains his lovely *Madonna with Angels and Saints*, in the first chapel on the left, as well as a photograph of his *Coronation of the Virgin*, which the French snapped up in 1809 and sent to the Louvre. Across the nave there's a *Crucifixion* by the school of Botticelli, an unusual composition of verticals highlighted by the cypresses in the background. In the chapterhouse of the monastery (*ring the bell at No. 4*) Fra Angelico left a fine fresco of the *Crucifixion* and a *Madonna and Child*, which is shown with its sinopia, before moving down to Florence and San Marco.

Badia Fiesolana

Open only on Sunday mornings.

The lane in front of San Domenico leads down in five minutes to the Badia Fiesolana, the ancient cathedral of Fiesole, built in the 9th century by Fiesole's bishop, an Irishman named Donatus, with a fine view over the rolling countryside and Florence in the background. Though later enlarged, perhaps by Brunelleschi, it has preserved the elegant façade of the older church, a charming example of the geometric black and white marble inlay decoration that characterizes Tuscan Romanesque churches. The interior, is adorned with *pietra serena* very much in the style of Brunelleschi. The convent buildings next door are now the home of the European University Institute.

Settignano

The least touristic hill above Florence sits under the village of Settignano (bus 10 from the station or Piazza San Marco). The road passes by way of **Ponte a Mensola**, where Boccaccio spent his childhood, and where it is believed he set the first scenes of the *Decameron*, at the Villa Poggio Gherardo. A Scottish Benedictine named Andrew founded its church of **San Martino a Mensola** in the 9th century and was later canonized. Rebuilt in the 1400s, it has three good trecento works: Taddeo Gaddi's *Triptych*, his son Agnolo's panel paintings on St Andrew's casket, and on the high altar another triptych by the school of Orcagna. From the quattrocento there's a *Madonna and Saints* by Neri di Bicci and an *Annunciation* by a follower of Fra Angelico.

Settignano is one of Tuscany's great cradles of sculptors, producing Desiderio da Settignano and brothers Antonio and Bernardo Rossellino; Michelangelo spent his childhood here as well, in the Villa Buonarroti. Strangely enough, not one of them left any work as a reminder here; the good art in the central church of **Santa Maria** is by Andrea della Robbia (an enamelled terracotta of the Madonna and Child) and Buontalenti (the pulpit). There are, however, more splendid views of Florence from Piazza Desiderio, and a couple of places to quaff a leisurely glass of Chianti.

Medici Villas

Like their Bourbon cousins in France, the Medici dukes liked to pass the time acquiring new palaces for themselves. In their case, however, the reason was less self-exaltation than simple property speculation; the Medici always thought several generations ahead. As a result the countryside is littered with Medici villas, most of them now privately owned, though some are at least partly open to the public.

Villa Careggi

Open 9–1, 3–6, closed Sat and Sun afternoon; for information © (055) 4277329. You can stroll through the gardens and woods for free.

Perhaps the best-known of all is Careggi (Viale Pieraccini 17, bus 14 from the station), a villa that began as a fortified farmhouse and was enlarged for Cosimo il Vecchio by Michelozzo in 1434. In the 1460s the villa at Careggi became synonymous with the birth of humanism. The greatest Latin and Greek scholars of the day, Ficino, Poliziano, Pico della Mirandola and Argyropoulos, would meet here with Lorenzo il Magnifico and hold philosophical discussions in imitation of a Platonic symposium, calling their informal society the Platonic Academy. It fizzled out when Lorenzo died. Cosimo il Vecchio and Piero had both died at Careggi, and when he felt the end was near, Lorenzo had himself carried out to the villa, with Poliziano and Pico della Mirandola to bear him company. After Lorenzo died, the villa was burned by Florentine republicans, though Cosimo I later had it rebuilt, and Francis Sloane had it restored.

Villa la Petraia

Open 9–6.30; 9–5.30 winter; closed Mon; adm.

Further east, amid the almost continuous conurbation of power lines and industrial land-scapes that blight the Prato road, the Villa la Petraia manages to remain Arcadian on its steeply sloping hill. It's very hard to reach on your own. If you don't have a car, take a taxi or, if you are adventurous, bus 28 from the station, and get off after the wastelands, by Via Reginaldo Giuliano. La Petraia was purchased by Grand Duke Ferdinando I in 1557 and rebuilt by Buontalenti, keeping the tower of the original country castle intact. Unfortunately Vittorio Emanuele II liked it as much as the Medici, and redesigned it to suit his relentlessly bad taste. Still, a tour of the villa's interior is worthwhile for the ornate Baroque court, frescoed with a pastel history of the Medici by 17th-century masters Volterrano and Giovanni di San Giovanni; Vittorio Emanuele II added the glass roof so that he could use the space as a ballroom. Of the remainder of the palace, you're likely to remember best the Chinese painting of Canton and the games room, with billiard tables as large as football fields and perhaps the world's first pinball machine, made of wood. A small room contains one of Giambologna's most endearing statues, *Venus Wringing Water from Her Hair*. La Petraia's beautiful garden and park, shaded by ancient cypresses, are open throughout the afternoon.

Villa di Castello

Adm. Garden open 9–6.30 in the summer, until 5.30 in winter, closed Mon.

One of Tuscany's most famous gardens is just down the hill from La Petraia, at Villa di Castello (turn right at Via di Castello and walk 450 metres). The villa was bought in 1477 by Lorenzo di Pierfrancesco and Giovanni de' Medici, cousins of Lorenzo il Magnifico who were Botticelli's best patrons, and they hung the walls of this villa with his great mytho-logical paintings now in the Uffizi. The villa was sacked in the 1530 siege, restored by Cosimo I, and today is the headquarters of the Accademia della Crusca, founded in 1582 and dedicated to the study of the Italian language. The garden was laid out for Cosimo I by Tribolo, who also designed the fountain in the centre, with a statue of *Hercules and Antenaeus* by Ammannati. Directly behind the fountain is the garden's main attraction, a fascinating example of the Medici penchant for the offbeat and excessive, an artificial cavern known as the **Grotto degli Animali**, filled by Ammanati and Giambologna with marvellous, true-to-life statues of every animal, fish and bird known to man (some of them are copies of Giambologna's originals in the Bargello), and lined with mosaics of pebbles and seashells. The shady terrace above offers the best view over the geometric patterns of the garden below; a large statue by Ammanati of January, or *Gennaio*, emerges shivering from a pool of water among the trees.

A 20-minute walk north from Villa di Castello to Quinto will take you to two unusual 7th-century BC **Etruscan Tombs: La Montagnola**, Via Filli Rosselli 95 (*open Tues, Thurs, Sat and Sun 9–12, 2–5, also in winter 9–12, 2–4*); **La Mula**, Via della Mula 2 (*open Sat 10–12, also in summer Tues 10–12 and Sat 3–6.30*). Neither has any art, but the chambers under their 8-metre artificial hills bear an odd relationship to ancient cultures elsewhere in the Mediterranean—domed tholos tombs as in Mycenaean Greece, corbelled passages like the *navetas* of Majorca, and entrances that look like the sacred wells of Sardinia.

Sesto Fiorentino

You can change gears again by heading out a little further in the sprawl to Sesto Fiorentino, a suburb that since 1954 has been home to the famous Richard-Ginori china and porcelain firm. Founded in Doccia in 1735, the firm has opened the **Doccia Museum** on Via Pratese 31 (*signposted; open Tues, Thurs and Sat, 9.30–1 and 3.30–6.30; closed Aug; adm*) to display a neat chronology of its production of Doccia ware, including many Medici commissions (a ceramic Venus de' Medici), fine painted porcelain, and some pretty Art Nouveau works.

Villa Demidoff at Pratolino

Open May–Sept, Thurs, Fri, Sat and Sun, 10–8; adm.

The village of Pratolino lies 12km north of Florence along Via Bolognese and was the site of Duke Francesco I's favourite villa in the 1570s, later demolished. Its enormous park, however, has survived and has recently been opened to the public. For its design, Francesco commissioned Buontalenti—artist, architect, and hydraulics engineer, nicknamed 'delle Girandole' for the wind-up toys he made—and he made Pratolino the marvel of its day, full of water tricks, ingenious automata and a famous menagerie. Sadly, none of Buontalenti's tricks has survived, but the largest ever example of this play between art and the environment has (perhaps because it is impossible to move)—Giambologna's massive *Appennino*, a giant rising from stone, part stalactite, part fountain himself. The rest of the park is an invitingly cool refuge from a Florentine summer afternoon.

Poggio a Caiano

Open 9–12.30, 3–4.30, Sun 9–2.30, closed Mon; adm; © (055) 877012.

Of all the Medici villas, Poggio a Caiano, is the most evocative of the country idylls so delightfully described in the verses of Lorenzo il Magnifico; this was his favourite retreat. COPIT buses go past every half-hour, departing from the loggia in Piazza Santa Maria Novella.

Originally a farmhouse purchased by Lorenzo in 1480, he had it rebuilt by Giuliano da Sangallo in a classical style that presages Palladio. It was Lorenzo's sole architectural commission, and its classicism matched the mythological nature poems he composed here, most famously *L'Ambra*, inspired by the stream Ombrone that flows nearby.

Sangallo designed the villa according to Alberti's description of the perfect country house, and added a classical frieze on the façade, sculpted with the assistance of Andrea Sansovino (now replaced with a copy). Some of the other features—the clock, the curved stair and central loggia—were later additions. In the **interior** Sangallo designed an airy, two-storey **Salone**, which the two Medici popes had frescoed by 16th-century masters Pontormo, Andrea del Sarto, Franciabigio and Allori. The subject, as usual, is Medici self-glorification, and depicts family members dressed as Romans in historical scenes that parallel events in their lives. In the right lunette, around a large circular window, Pontormo painted the lovely *Vertumnus and Pomona* (1521), a languid summer scene under a willow tree, beautifully coloured. The pleasant **grounds** contain many fine old trees and a 19th-century statue celebrating Lorenzo's *L'Ambra*.

Carmignano and Villa Artimino

A local bus continues 5km southwest of Poggia a Caiano to the village of **Carmignano**, which possesses in its church of San Michele, Pontormo's uncanny painting of *The Visitation* (1530s), one of the masterpieces of Florentine Mannerism. There are no concessions to naturalism here—the four soulful, ethereal women, draped in Pontormo's accustomed startling colours, barely touch the ground, standing before a scene as substantial as a stage backdrop. The result is one of the most unforgettable images produced in the 16th century.

Also south of Poggio a Caiano, at **Comeana** (*3km, signposted*) is the well-preserved Etruscan **Tomba di Montefortini**, a 7th-century BC burial mound, 11m high and 80m in diameter, covering two burial chambers. A long hall leads down to the vestibule and rectangular tomb chamber, both carefully covered with false vaulting, the latter preserving a wide shelf, believed to have been used for gifts for the afterlife. An equally impressive tomb nearby, the **Tomba dei Boschetti**, was seriously damaged over the centuries by local farmers (*Montefortini and Boschetti open 9–12, closed Wed*).

The Etruscan city of Artimino, 4km west, was destroyed by the Romans and is now occupied by a small town and another Medici property, the **Villa Artimino** ('La Ferdinanda'), built as hunting lodge for Ferdinando I by Buontalenti. Buontalenti gave it a semi-fortified air with buttresses to fit its sporting purpose, but the total effect is simple and charming, the long roofline punctuated by innumerable chimneys; the graceful stair was added in the last century from a drawing by the architect in the Uffizi. An **Etruscan Archaeological Museum** has been installed in the basement, containing items found in the tombs; among them a unique censer with two basins and a boat, bronze vases, and a red figured krater painted with initiation scenes, found in a 3rd-century tomb (*villa open only by appointment, © 8792030; museum open Mon–Sun 9–12.30, closed Wed; adm*). There's a convenient place for lunch in the grounds. Also in Artimino is an attractive Romanesque church, **San Leonardo**, built of stones salvaged from earlier buildings.

Poggio Imperiale and the Certosa del Galluzzo

One last villa open for visits, the **Villa di Poggio Imperiale** (*open by request, © (055) 220151*), lies south of Florence, at the summit of Viale del Poggio Imperiale, which leaves Porta Romana with a stately escort of cypress sentinels. Cosimo I grabbed this huge villa from the Salviati family in 1565, and it remained a ducal property until there were no longer any dukes to duke. Its neoclassical façade was added in 1808, and the audience chamber was decorated in the 17th century by Rutilio Manetti and others. Much of the villa is now used as a girls' school .

The **Certosa del Galluzzo** (also known as the Certosa di Firenze) lies further south, scenically located on a hill off the Siena road (*take bus 36 or 37 from the station*). Founded as a Carthusian monastery by 14th-century tycoon Niccolò Acciaiuoli, the monastery has been inhabited since 1958 by Cistercians, one of whom takes visitors around (*open 9–12 and 3–6, 3–5 in winter, closed Mon*). The Certosa has a fine 16th-century courtyard and an uninteresting church, though the crypt-chapel of the lay choir contains some impressive tombs. The **Chiostro Grande**, surrounded by the monks' cells, is decorated with 66 majolica tondi of prophets and saints by Giovanni della Robbia and assistants; one cell is opened for visits, and it seems almost cosy. The Gothic **Palazzo degli Studi**, intended by the founder as a school, contains five lunettes by Pontormo, painted while he and his pupil Bronzino hid out here from the plague in 1522.

American Express: Via Dante Alghieri 22r, ✆ 217241, just off Piazza della Repubblica.

Central Post Office: Via Pellicceria 8, near Piazza della Repubblica, open 8–6, Sat 8.15–12.30, ✆ 214145; telegram and telephone office open 8–11.30pm, or ✆ 184.

Consulates: **UK**, Lungarno Corsini 2, ✆ 284133. **US**, Lungarno Vespucci 38, ✆ 2398276.

Libraries: British Institute Library, Lungarno Guicciardini 9, ✆ 284031, open 9.45–1 and 3.15–6.30, closed Sat and Sun. American Library, Via S. Gallo 10, open 9–12.30, closed Sat and Sun. There are so many other libraries in Florence that one, the Biblioteca del Servizio Beni Librari, Via G. Modena 13, ✆ 4382266, does nothing but dispense information on all the others.

Lost Property: in Italian is *Oggetti smarriti* or *Oggetti ritrovati*. Office is in Via Circondaria 19, ✆ 367943. For **towed-away cars** it is in Via Circondaria 16, ✆ 351562. Open 9–12, closed Thurs and Sun.

Medical: for an ambulance or first aid, Misericordia, Piazza del Duomo 20, ✆ 287 788. Doctor's night service, ✆ 477891. General Hospital Santa Maria Nuova, in Piazza S. M. Nuova, ✆ 27581, is the most convenient hospital. Tourist Medical Service, 24 hours a day, staffed by English- and French-speaking physicians at Via Lorenzo il Magnifico 59, ring first ✆ 475411.

Pharmacies: open 24 hours every day in S. Maria Novella station, also Molteni, Via Calzaiuoli 7r and Taverna, Piazza S. Giovanni 20r, by the Baptistry.

Police: emergency ✆ 113. The Ufficio Stranieri, in the Questura, Via Zara 2, ✆ 49771, handles most foreigners' problems, and usually has someone around who speaks English. Go here for residents' permits, etc.

Telephones: open 24 hours in the Central Post Office, and in Via della Pelliceria.

Festivals and Annual Events

Traditional festivals in Florence date back centuries. Easter Sunday's *Scioppio del Carro*, or 'Explosion of the Cart', commemorates Florentine participation in the First Crusade in 1096. The Florentines were led by Pazzino de' Pazzi, who upon returning home, received the special custody of the flame of Holy Saturday, with which the Florentines traditionally relit their family hearths. To make the event more colourful, the Pazzi constructed a decorated wooden ox cart to carry the flame. They lost the job after the Pazzi conspiracy in 1478, and since then the city has taken over the responsibility. In the morning, a fireworks-filled wooden float is pulled by white oxen from the Porta a Prato to the Cathedral, where, at noon, during the singing of the Gloria, it is ignited by a 'dove' that descends on a wire from the high altar.

On Ascension Day (in May), there's the *Festa del Grillo* (cricket festival) in the Cascine; Michelangelo was thinking of its little wooden cricket cages when he mocked Ammanati's gallery on the cathedral dome. June is the time of the three matches of *Calcio Storico in Costume* (historical football in 16th-century costume) in the Piazza della Signoria, played by 27-men teams from Florence's four quarters, in memory of a defiant football match played in Piazza Santa Croce in 1530, during the siege by Charles V. Flag throwing and a parade in historical costume are part of the pre-game ceremonies. The *Festa delle Rificolone* on 7 September is one of Florence's more lively festivals, with a parade of floats followed by a party in the streets. The best fireworks are reserved for the day of Florence's patron, St John (24 June).

Florentines adore cultural events. The big summer festival is the *Estate Fiesolana*: from late June to August the old Roman theatre is the site of concerts, ballet, theatre and films, for reasonable prices. The *Maggio Musicale Fiorentino*, the city's big music festival, spans from late April to the beginning of July and brings in big-name concert stars. Events take place in the Teatro Comunale, Corso Italia 12 (just off Lungarno Vespucci, © *211158 for ticket information*). There's usually some kind of music in the Piazza della Signoria on Thursday nights during the summer, and the summer season of the **Teatro Comunale** (opera, concerts and ballet) takes place in the Boboli Gardens, the Teatro Comunale and the Teatro della Pergola (Via della Pergola 10a, © 242361). From April to June you can see the offerings of independent film makers at the **Florence Festival** in the Palazzo dei Congressi, © 2382241. In May, don't miss the **Iris Festival** up at Piazzale Michelangelo.

Florence © (055–)   ***Shopping***

Although central Florence sometimes seems like one solid boutique, the city is no longer the queen of Italian fashion—the lack of an airport, more than anything else, has sent most of the big designers to Milan. Many of the big **fashion** names of the 1960s and 70s, the international chain stores of the 1980s, are represented in smart Via Tornabuoni, Via Calzaiuoli and in the streets around the Duomo. **Leather** is something Florence is still known for, and you'll see plenty of it in the centre, around Via della Vigna Nuova and Via del Parione, and less expensively at an unusual institution called the **Leather School**, which occupies part of Santa Croce's cloister (entrance at Piazza Santa Croce 16 or Via S. Giuseppe 5r). Florence is also famous for its **jewellery**: the shops on and around the Ponte Vecchio are forced by the nature of their location into wide-open competition, and good prices for Florentine brushed gold (although much of it is made in Arezzo these days) and antique jewellery are more common than you may think.

Florence is also one of the few places in the world to make **marbled paper**, an art brought over from the Orient by Venice in the 12th century. Each sheet is hand dipped in a bath of colours to create a delicate, lightly coloured clouded design; no two sheets are alike. Marbled-paper-covered stationery items or just sheets of marbled paper are available at **Giulio Giannini e Figlio**, Piazza Pitti 37r, the oldest manufacturer; at **Il Papiro**, with three shops (Via Cavour 55r, Piazza del Duomo 24r, and Lungarno Acciaiuoli 42r); **La Bottega Artigiana del Libro**, Lungarno Corsini 40r; and **Il Torchio**, Via de' Bardi 17. These shops (and many others) also carry Florentine paper with its colourful Gothic patterns.

Bookworms do better in Florence than most Italian cities, although the prices of **books** in English will make you weep. The **Paperback Exchange**, Via Fiesolana 31r or **Seeber**, Via Tornabuoni 70r, have the widest selections in English, with many books about Florence. **Feltrinelli**, Via Cavour 12–20r, has books in English and an excellent selection of art books; ditto for the **BM Bookshop** at Borgo Ognissanti 4r. **Franco Maria Ricci**, Via delle Belle Donne 41r, has a fabulous collection of art books.

Borgo Ognissanti and the various Lungarni are the place to look for **antiques** and **art galleries** like **P. Bazzanti e Figli**, Lungarno Corsini 44, where you can pick up an exact replica of the bronze pig in the Mercato Nuovo. An Italian carnival mask is much easier to carry and can be found at **Atelier Alice**, Via Faenza 72r, and for those who are keen to learn more about the art of the mask, the shop runs 5 lesson courses. Ring Prof. A. Dessi on ℂ 215961 for details. If you are looking for an antique shop with a difference, go to the retro heaven of **Exnovo**, Via delle Belle Donne 32r (just off the south side of Piazza Sta Maria Novella). Here you will find all the gaudy colours and kitsch objects that symbolise the economic boom of the 1950s. They have a large collection of original 50s sunglasses too. The **Casa dei Tessuti**, Via de' Pecori 20–24r, keeps Florence's ancient **cloth** trade alive with lovely linens, silks and woollens. During the lunch break, you might catch a lecture on the history of Florence with special reference to the textile industry. Ring Sig. Romoli on ℂ 215 961. For **silver**, **crystal** and **porcelain** (including Florence's own Richard-Ginori), **A. Poggi**, Via Calzaiuoli 105r and 116r, has one of the city's widest selections. **Città del Sole**, on Borgo Ognissanti 37, is the best **toy** shop in Florence, and if you happen to have or know the kind of little girls who can wear white, **Cirris**, Via Por S. Maria 38–40r, has a fairytale selection of **dresses**.

Serious collectors may want to check Florence's busy **auction houses**: **Sotheby's Italia**, Via G. Capponi 26, ℂ 2479021; **Casa d'Aste Pitti**, Via Maggio 15, ℂ 2396382; and **Casa d'Aste Pandolfini**, Borgo degli Albizi 26, ℂ 2340888.

There are a number of speciality **food** shops around the Mercato Centrale, or you can pick up items like truffle cream at **Gastronomia Tassini**, in Borgo SS. Apostoli 24r; for **wines** and **spirits** try **Biagini**, Via dei Banchi 57, off Piazza S. Maria Novella; **De Rhan International**, Via del Campofiore 112, has a wide range of Tuscan and Italian **wines** and **olive oil** products. **Medieval cures** and **Dominican remedies** are still sold in the **Farmaceutica di Santa Maria Novella**, Via della Scala 16n, which hasn't changed much since 1612.

Florence's lively **street markets** offer good bargains, fake designer clothing and even some authentic labels. The huge **San Lorenzo market** is the largest and most boisterous, where many Florentines buy their clothes; the **Mercato Nuovo** or Straw Market is the most touristic, but not flagrantly so. There's an extensive clothes and shoes market every Tuesday morning in the Cascine, but perhaps the most fun is the **Flea Market** in Piazza dei Ciompi, offering all kinds of desirable junk.

Florence ✆ (055–)   ***Sports***

The one activity many summertime visitors begin to crave after tramping through the sights is a dip in a **pool**. The prettiest one is the Piscina le Pavoniere, Viale degli Olmi, in the Cascine, *open June–Sept 10–6*, ✆ 367506, bus 17C; others are Bellariva, up the Arno at Lungarno Colombo 6, *open June–Sept 10–6*, ✆ 677521, bus 14. There are two covered, year-round pools: Amici del Nuoto, Via del Romito 38, ✆ 483951, and Costoli, Via Paoli, near Campo di Marte, (*open 10–6, Mon 2–6*) , ✆ 678012, bus 10 or 17. If there's enough water in the Arno, you can try **rowing** or canoeing; contact the Società Canottieri Comunali, Lungarno Ferrucci 6, ✆ 6812151, or the Società Canottieri Firenze, Lungarno dei Medici 8, ✆ 282130 (membership only). The Cascine has Florence's **race course** (Ippodromo Le Cascine, ✆ 360598) and **trotting course** (Ippodromo della Mulina, ✆ 411107); the nearest place to go riding in the Tuscan hills is the Country Riding Club, Via di Grioli, at Badia a Settimo in Scandicci, 6km southwest of Florence, ✆ 790277. The nearest **golf course**, the 18-hole Golf Club Ugolino, is in Gràssina, 7km southeast of Florence, on the Chiantigiana–Impruneta, ✆ 2301096, a lovely course laid out among olives and cypresses. For **tennis**, try the Circolo Tennis alle Cascine, ✆ 356651.

Florence ✆ (055–)   ***Entertainment***

Nightlife with Great Aunt Florence is still awaiting its Renaissance; according to the Florentines themselves she's conservative, somewhat deaf and retires early—1am is very, very late in this city. However, there are plenty of people who wish it weren't so, and slowly, slowly, Florence by night is beginning to mean more than the old *passeggiata* over the Ponte Vecchio and an ice cream, and perhaps a late trip up to Fiesole to contemplate the lights. Look for listings of concerts and events in Florence's daily, *La Nazione* ; the tourist office's free *Florence Today* contains bilingual monthly information and calendar, as does a booklet called *Florence Concierge Information*, available in hotels and tourist offices; the monthly *Firenze Spettacolo*, sold in news-stands, is published only in Italian but fills you in on ecology and trekking activities, film societies, bar music and the latest New Age mumbo jumbo to rock Florence. For a listing of all current films being shown in Florence (Italian and dubbed in Italian), ✆ 198.

The opera and concert season runs Nov–April at the **Teatro Comunale**. Big-name jazz performers, classical artists and others are brought to Florence by **Musicus Concentus**, Piazza del Carmine 14, ✆ 287347, while rock and jazz tours that stop in Florence happen in the big Palasport, at Campo di Marte, in Viale Paoli. Films in English are shown daily at the **Cinema Astro**, Piazza San Simone near Santa Croce (*no tel; closed Mon and July*). **Spazio Uno** in Via del Sole 10, occasionally has films in their original language.

If you want to join Florence's swells, put on the dog and head out to elegant **Caffedecò**, Piazza della Libertà 45–46r, done up in tasteful art deco, with live jazz (*closed Mon*); **Dolce Vita**, Piazza del Carmine, is one of the most popular places in the Oltrarno, a bar to see and be seen in; the older pub/wine bar **Rifrullo**, Via S. Niccolò 55r, is probably the most popular of all and one of the first to attract people to the Oltrarno; there's no word for 'cosy' in Italian, but the Rifrullo does the best it can (*closed Wed*). For the past 10 years alternative-minded Florentines have frequented the **Caffè Voltaire**, Via della Scala 9r (Piazza S. Maria Novella), where on any given evening you may find a poetry reading, salsa, reggae, jazz, samba, blues, or *cucina nuova*; if you're going to live in Florence for a while, consider becoming a member of its club (*closed Sun*). Italian craziness and banana splits are on tap at the **Drunk's Ladder**, Piazza IV Novembre, Sesto Fiorentino, a video-pub with the occasional live band (*closed Wed*); **Saxbar**, Viale dei Mille 83/84r, has one of the city's widest selections of foreign beers to wash down its fancy cold or hot sandwiches and jazz on Thurs and Sun (*closed Wed*). One that stays open later than the average club (i.e. after 1am) is **Stonehenge**, Via dell'Amorino 16r, near S. Lorenzo, with rock and cocktails from 10pm on. There's live music and dancing at **Caffé Latino**, Via Faenza 27 and **Caffé Caruso**, Via Lambertesca 16r. Caribbean music and exotic cocktails are on offer at **Puerto Rico**, Viale Redi 29b. Jazz and rock music plays at **Amadeus**, Via Alfani 26r. **Du Monde** cocktail bar, Via San Niccolò 103r, offers food, drink and music for the elegant Florentine and stays open to 5 in the morning. A more relaxed place is **Mago Merlino,** Via dei Pilastri 31r, a tea-room/bar with live music, theatre, shows and games.

Among the discos **Tenax**, out near the airport in Via Pratese 47, is always busy; **Jackie 'O**, an old favourite in Via Erta Canina 24, attracts a friendly group in their early 30s. The current hotspot however is **Rockafe**, Borgo Albize 66r, which has a different theme every night. **Andromeda**, Via dei Climatori 13, is particularly popular with young foreigners (*open Thurs–Sun*). Another club in the centre of town that opens later than most is **Dolce Zucchero**, Via Pandolfini 36–38r, attracting people not only with the promise of live music and a second dance floor downstairs, but also with all kinds of tempting sweet things. Two old standbys see most of the Florentine/foreigners disco action, with the provocative names of **Space Electronic Disco**, Via Palazzuolo 37, a high-tech noise box and **Yab Yum**, Via dei Sassetti 5r (*closed Mon*); check in the papers as here there could be anything from Acid Jazz to Italian Folk music. **055** in Via Verdi 57r, is open only at weekends and organizes different themed evenings. The younger crowd get their kicks at **Meccanó**, Piazzale delle Cascine (*closed Mon and Wed*), and **Happyland** where the music pounds and the atmosphere is feverish. There are three gay clubs in Florence; the best is **Flamingo**, Via Pandolfi 26.

Cafés and Gelaterie

Many of Florence's grand old cafés were born in the last century, although the oldest, **Gilli**, Piazza della Repubblica 13–14r, dates back to 1733, when the Mercato Vecchio still occupied this area; its two panelled back rooms are especially pleasant in the winter. Another famous café in Piazza della Repubblica is the **Giubbe Rosse**, rendezvous of Florence's literati at the turn of the century; the chandelier-lit interior has changed little since. Florence's most elegant and classy watering hole, however, is **Rivoire**, in the Piazza della Signoria 5r, with a marble detailed interior as lovely as the piazza itself. **Giacosa**, Via Tornabuoni 83, has a certain sparkle, good sandwiches and ice cream, and a reputation for having invented the Negroni (gin, Campari and vermouth).

Florence lays some claim to being the ice-cream capital of the world, a reputation that owes much to the decadently delicious confections and rich *semifreddi* served at **Vivoli**, Via Isola delle Stinche 7r (between the Bargello and S. Croce; *closed Mon*). It has plenty of challengers for the *gelato* throne; try **Festival del Gelato**, Via del Corso 75r, with over 100 variations, and **Perché no?**, Via Tavolini 19r, near Via Calzaiuoli.

Where to Stay

Florence has some exceptionally lovely hotels, and not all of them at Grand Ducal prices, although base rates here are the highest in Tuscany. In this town historic old palace-hotels are the rule rather than the exception; those listed below are some of the more atmospheric and charming, but to be honest, few are secrets, so reserve as far in advance as possible. There are almost 400 hotels in Florence but not enough for anyone who arrives in July and August without a reservation. But don't despair; there are several hotel consortia that can help you find a room in nearly any price range for a small commission. If you're arriving by car or train, the most useful will be ITA:

ITA: in Santa Maria Novella station, © 282 893, open 9–8.30; in the AGIP service station at Peretola, to the west of Florence on A11, © 4211800. Between March and November there's an office in the Chianti-Est service plaza on the A1, © 621349 and another in the Fortezza da Basso, © 471960. No bookings can be made over the telephone.

Florence Promhotels: Viale A. Volta 72, © 570481, @ 587189

Toscana Hotels 80: Viale Gramsci 9, © 2478543.

These last two take bookings by phone or mail.

Nearly every hotel in Florence with a restaurant will require half-board, and many will try to lay down a heavy breakfast charge as well that is supposed to be optional.

luxury

In the city the luxury leader is ★★★★★**Excelsior**, Piazza Ognissanti 3, ✆ 264201, ✆ 210278, former Florentine address of Napoleon's sister Caroline. Lots of marble, neoclassically plush, lush and green with plants, immaculately staffed, with a smart roof garden with views down the Arno, and decadently luxurious bedrooms; not even Gian Gastone de' Medici had heated towel rails. The bar and restaurant are added amenities. In a more tranquil spot, on Florence's plane-tree shaded 'London Square', there's ★★★★★**Regency**, Piazza d'Azeglio 3, ✆ 245247, ✆ 2342937, charming and intimate with only 33 air-conditioned rooms; between the two wings there's an elegant town garden. The public rooms are beautifully panelled, and the fare in the dining room superb; there's a private garage for your car.

very expensive

A Renaissance palace now owned by the descendants of sculptor Giovanni Dupre, ★★★★**Mona Lisa**, Borgo Pinti 27, ✆ 2479751, ✆ 2479755, is one of the most charming small hotels in Florence, hiding behind its stern façade. The palazzo is well preserved, the furnishings are family heirlooms, as are the many works of art. Try to reserve one of the tranquil rooms that overlook the garden; all are air-conditioned and have frigo-bars. The Mona Lisa has no restaurant, though breakfast is available; it also has private parking. The Tuscan-Edwardian ★★★★**Villa Carlotta**, Via Michele di Lando 3, ✆ 2336134, ✆ 2336147, is in a quiet residential district in the upper Oltrarno, close to the Porta Romana. The 27 sophisticated rooms have recently been tastefully refurnished and have every luxury; there's a garden and glassed-in veranda, where the large breakfasts are served; a private garage offers safe parking.

Among the many hotels along the Arno, one of the most pleasant is ★★★★**Principe**, Lungarno Vespucci 34, ✆ 284848, ✆ 283458, a small comfortable hotel, centrally air-conditioned and sound-proofed, with a little garden at the back; the nicer rooms have terraces over the Arno. Near the train station one of the most attractive hotels is ★★★★**Atlantic Palace**, Via Nazionale 12, ✆ 294234, ✆ 268353, with large, striking bedrooms built in the framework of a 17th-century convent, luxuriously furnished and air-conditioned. A large, but attractive hotel in an older palace, ★★★★**Anglo-American**, near the Cascine on Via Garibaldi 9, ✆ 282114, ✆ 268513, is decorated in a light, airy, garden style that makes a pleasant retreat after pounding the pavements; the rooms are air-conditioned and there's parking nearby.

expensive

The most delightful choice in this category was designed for the Servite fathers by Antonio da Sangallo the Elder, who added a loggia to match Brunelleschi's Spedale degli Innocenti across the square. The ★★★**Loggiato dei Serviti**, Piazza SS. Annunziata 3, ✆ 289592, ✉ 289595, has since been redone with the best of Florentine taste and refinement, with Italian and English antiques; all rooms have mini-bars, and air conditioning and colour TVs are available as well; parking is possible in a nearby garage. Another excellent small hotel, ★★★**Beacci Tornabuoni**, Via Tornabuoni 3, ✆ 212645, ✉ 283594, puts you in the centre of fashionable Florence, on the top three floors of an elegant Renaissance palace. The rooms are comfortable, air-conditioned and equipped with mini-bars, though it's more fun to sit over your drink on the panoramic roof terrace. One of the best places to stay in the very heart of Florence is the popular ★★★**Hermitage**, very near the Ponte Vecchio in Vicolo Marzio 1, ✆ 287216, ✉ 212208. Reserve well in advance to get one of its 16 cosy old rooms, even further in advance to get one overlooking the Arno; the views from the roof garden while sipping your morning coffee make it worth the trouble.

A 15th-century palace in the Oltrarno, ★★★**Annalena**, Via Romana 34, ✆ 222402, ✉ 222403, is a grand and famous old *pensione*, with high ceilings, antiques and art, its rooms large and comfortable, all with private baths, and a friendly atmosphere. The large garden at the back is a boon.

moderate

★★★**Aprile**, Via della Scala 6, ✆ 216237, ✉ 280947, is near the station but miles away in atmosphere. Housed in a 15th-century Medici palace, it is still decorated with frescoes and paintings, and there's a small courtyard for sitting outside. ★★★**La Residenza**, on top of a Renaissance palace at Via Tornabuoni 8, ✆ 218684, ✉ 284197, has the overgrown Palazzo Strozzi for a neighbour, and you can gaze down Florence's version of Fifth Avenue from the roof garden. The decor is pretty and welcoming, the elevator a well-maintained antique. Right in the middle of Florence, on a narrow lane off Piazza della Signoria, there's the noisy, ageing, dimly lit ★★★**Porta Rossa** at Via Porta Rossa 19, ✆ 287551, ✉ 282179. It isn't for everyone, but there are plenty of visitors to Florence who swear they wouldn't stay anywhere else. The Porta Rossa, which traces its origins back to the Middle Ages, has character, with its frayed 19th-century grandeur and a difficult, classically Florentine staff, who have plenty of tales to tell from the hotel's long history. A good choice if you want to stay over in the less frenetic Oltrarno is ★★**La Scaletta**, Via Guicciardini 13, ✆ 283028 ✉ 214255, near the Ponte Vecchio, offering good rooms and a great roof terrace. Also in the Oltrarno, ★**Bandini**, Piazza S. Spirito 9, ✆ 215308, ✉ 282761, is located on a busy, noisy square far from tourist Florence. Recently endowed with a lift, it rewards its guests with a beautiful Tuscan loggia; it was one of the first buildings to have this delightful architectural feature. However, the rooms themselves are uncomfortable and expensive.

inexpensive

The obvious place to look is the seedy, crowded, tourist-student inferno that surrounds the central station, especially in Via Nazionale, Via Fiume, Via Guelfa and Via Faenza down to Piazza Indipendenza. Many of the cheapest places post minions in the station to snatch up weary back-packers. Although convenient if you arrive by train, few of these hotels will brighten your stay in Florence; grouchy owners who lock the door at midnight seem to be the rule. There are a couple of noteworthy exceptions: ★★★**Splendor**, Via San Gallo 30 (off Via Guelfa), ✆ 483427, ✉ 461276, is on the fringe of the zone, near Piazza S. Marco; its old frescoes and antiques hint of past splendour, and some of the bedrooms are almost palatial; others aren't, but there's an attractive terrace. Another solid recommendation in the area, ★**Tony's Inn**, Via Faenza 77, ✆ 217975, ✉ 210101, is run by a friendly Italian-Canadian couple; rooms are pleasant, most have private baths. Near S. Maria Novella, also in spitting distance of the station, ★**La Mia Casa**, Piazza S. Maria Novella 23, ✆ 213061, offers simple rooms, inexpensive breakfasts, free showers and a free film in English every night. Alternatively, try ★**Desirée**, Via Fiume 20, ✆ and ✉ 2382382.

The old town has a number of inexpensive hotels, less touristic than those by the station. Just off Via Calzaiuoli, ★**Maxim**, Via de' Medici 4, ✆ 217474, ✉ 283729, has nice, quiet rooms. ★**Bavaria**, Borgo Albizi 26, ✆ 2340313, ✉ 2340313, has only eight rooms in a 16th-century palace, L55,000 without bath, L65,000 with. You can sleep in the palace of Dante's in-laws at ★**Orchidea**, Borgo degli Albizi 11, ✆ 2480346, a charming old place, but with no private baths or breakfast. In the same vicinity, ★**Brunori**, Via del Proconsolo 5, ✆ 289648, is a small friendly place. Right in the centre, near the Duomo, is the cheap and pleasant ★**Firenze**, Piazza dei Donati 4, ✆ 214203, ✉ 212370, the classiest inexpensive hotel in Florence; ask for one of the newer rooms and book in advance.

Besides hotels, a number of institutions and private homes let rooms—there's a complete list in the back of the annual provincial hotel book. Many take women only, and fill up with students in the spring when Italian schools make their annual field trips. There are three youth hostels to choose from in Florence: **Ostello Europa Villa Camerata**, Viale A. Righe 2/4 (bus 17B from the station), ✆ 601451, ✉ 610300, has 322 beds for people with IYHF cards. Located in an old palazzo with gardens, it is a popular place, and you'd be wise to show up at 2pm to get a spot in the summer; maximum stay three days. **Ostello Santa Monaca**, Via Santa Monaca 6, ✆ 268338, has 111 beds near the Carmine church; sign up for a place in the morning. The third is **Ostello Archi Rossi**, Via Faenza 94r, ✆ 290804, privately run, clean and friendly. It is very popular as it is the closest to the station, but is rather small with capacity for just 60 guests. Istituto Gould, Via dei Serragli 44, is so popular that you must book well in advance, ✆ 212576.

Fiesole ✆ (055–)

Many frequent visitors to Florence wouldn't stay anywhere else: it's cooler, quieter, and at night the city far below twinkles as if made of fairy lights. If money is no object, the superb choice is ★★★★**Villa San Michele** (*very expensive*), in a breathtaking location just below Fiesole on Via Doccia 4, ✆ 59451, ✉ 598734, with a façade and loggia reputedly designed by Michelangelo himself. Originally a monastery in the 14th century, it has been carefully reconstructed after bomb damage in World War II to create one of the most beautiful hotels in Italy, set in a lovely Tuscan garden, complete with a pool. Each of its 29 rooms is richly and elegantly furnished and air-conditioned; the more plush suites have jacuzzis. The food is delicious, and the reasons to go down to Florence begin to seem insignificant; a stay here is complete in itself. Paradise, however, comes at a price: L450–750,000 per person on half-board terms. *Closed mid-Nov–mid-March.*

Even if you aren't driving, you can reach ★★★**Pensione Bencista**, Via B. da Maiano 4, in S. Domenico di Fiesole, ✆ and @ 59163 (*expensive*), by bus 7. The *pensione* is located in a sprawling villa dating back to the 14th century, added to over the centuries. Many of the rooms are furnished with antiques and there's a garden and view. The hotel has recently been revamped to push it up a category. Right in the centre of Fiesole, on Piazza Mino, the ★★★★**Villa Aurora**, ✆ 59100, @ 59587 (*expensive*), has air-conditioned rooms in a totally modernized, very elegant 19th-century building.

Villa Hotels in the Florentine Hills ✆ (055–)

If you're driving, you may be inspired to lodge outside central Florence, where you can park without hassles or paying a fortune for the privilege. A luxurious choice near Piazzale Michelangelo is the opulent ★★★★★**Grand Hotel Villa Cora**, Viale Machiavelli 18–20, ✆ 2298451, @ 229086 (*luxury*), a 19th-century mansion set in a beautiful formal garden overlooking the Oltrarno. Built by the Baron Oppenheim, it later served as the residence of the wife of Napoleon III, Empress Eugénie. Its conversion to a hotel has dimmed little of its splendour; some of the bedrooms have frescoed ceilings and lavish 19th-century furnishings—all are air-conditioned and have frigo-bars, and there's a pretty pool. In the summer meals are served in the garden, and there's a fine view of Florence from the roof terrace. In the same area there's the far less pretentious ★★★**Villa Liberty**, a 17-room charmer, with a garden and air-conditioned rooms on Viale Michelangelo 40, ✆ 6810581, @ 6812595 (*expensive*).

In the 12th century a tower was built at Bellosguardo, enjoying one of the most breathtaking views over the city. It was later purchased by the Cavalcanti, friends of Dante, and a villa was added below the tower; Cosimo I confiscated it; the Michelozzi purchased it from the Medici; Elizabeth Barrett Browning wrote about it. In 1988 it opened its doors as a small hotel, ★★★★**Torre di Bellosguardo**, Via Roti Michelozzi 2, ✆ 2298145, @ 229008 (*very expensive*). Frescoes by Baroque master Poccetti adorn the entrance hall, fine antiques adorn the rooms, each unique, and fitted out with modern baths. The large and beautiful terraced garden has a pool; for a splurge reserve the two-level tower suite, with fabulous views in four directions. Another lovely choice, ★★★★★**Villa La Massa**, Via La Massa 6, ✆ 6510101, @ 6510109 (*very expensive to luxury*), is located up the Arno, some 6km from Florence at Candeli. The former 15th-century villa of Count Giraldi, the hotel retains the old dungeon (now one of two restaurants), the family chapel (now a bar), and other early Renaissance amenities, combined with 20th-century features like tennis-courts, a pool and air-conditioning. The furnishings are fit for a Renaissance princeling, there's dining and dancing on the Arno in the summer, a shady garden, and a hotel bus to whizz you into the city.

In the other direction, at Colonnata di Sesto Fiorentino, ★★★★**Villa Villoresi**, Via Ciampi 2, © 443692, 🖃 442063 (*very expensive*), is a lovely oasis on a hill above one of Florence's more unbecoming tentacles. One of its charms is that it hasn't been too pristinely restored, and has kept much of its slightly faded appeal as well as its frescoed ceilings, antiques, chandeliers and hospitable Contessa. There's a garden and pool—a great place to bring the children. There are two former residences north of the centre: ★★★**Villa le Rondini**, Via Bolognese Vecchia 224, © 400081 (*expensive*), with a number of separate villas in a large park, a heated pool and tennis, and the far simpler ★★**Villa Natalia**, Via Bolognese 106, © 490773, 🖃 470773 (*moderate*), with a garden and quiet rooms.

Further afield, near Poggio a Caiano, ★★★**Hermitage**, Via Gineparia 12 at Bonistallo, © 877040 (*moderate*), is a fine affordable choice for families; there's a pool in the grounds, air-conditioned rooms, not to mention gallons of fresh air and quiet. Near Carmignano you can play the Medici in the refurbished outbuildings of Grand Duke Ferdinand's Villa at Artimino in ★★★★**Paggeria Medicea**, Viale Papa Giovanni XXIII 3, © 8718081, 🖃 8718080 (*expensive*). It has some unusual amenities—a hunting reserve and a lake stocked with fish, also a pool and tennis court, and pleasant modern rooms, many with balconies, all air-conditioned.

Florence © (055–)   **Eating Out**

Like any sophisticated city with lots of visitors, Florence has plenty of fine restaurants; even in the cheaper places standards are high, and if you don't care for anything fancier, there will be lots of good red Chianti to wash down your meal. Please note that many of the best places are likely to close for all of August; you would also be wise to call ahead and reserve, even a day or two in advance.

Florence's Most Ephemeral Art

Florence in its loftier moods likes to call itself the 'birthplace of international haute cuisine', a claim that has very much to do with Catherine de' Medici, a renowned trencherwoman, who brought a brigade of Florentine chefs with her to Paris and taught the Frenchies how to eat artichokes, but has little to do with the city's contribution to the Italian kitchen. Florentine food is on the whole extremely simple with the emphasis on the individual flavours and fresh ingredients. A typical *primo* could be *pappardelle*, a type of wide tagliatelle egg-pasta, served usually with a meat sauce, or game such as wild boar, rabbit and duck. Soups are also popular: try the *minestrone toscano* with a base of cauliflower, *borlotti* beans and potatoes. The most famous main course in Florence is the *bistecca alla fiorentina*, a large steak on the bone, two inches thick, cut from loin of beef, cooked on charcoal and simply seasoned with salt and pepper. As for the vegetables, you could try *piselli alla fiorentina*, peas cooked with oil, parsley and diced bacon, or *tortino di carciofi*, a delicious omelette with fried artichokes. Florentine desserts tend to be sweet and fattening: *bomboloni alla crema* are vanilla-filled doughnuts and *le fritelle di San Giuseppe* are bits of deep-fried batter covered in sugar. If you prefer cheese try the sturdy *pecorino toscano*. For better or worse, the real Florentine specialities rarely turn up on many restaurant menus, and you'll probably never learn what a Florentine cook can do with cocks' combs, calves' feet and tripe.

very expensive

Florence is blessed with one of the finest gourmet restaurants in Italy, the **Enoteca Pinchiorri**, Via Ghibellina 87, near the Casa Buonarroti, © 242777. The owners inherited the building, a wine shop, some 10 years ago, and have converted it into a beautifully appointed restaurant, with meals served in a garden court in the summer; they've also increased what was already in the cellars to an astonishing collection of some 80,000 bottles of the best Italy and France have to offer. The cooking, a mixture of *nouvelle cuisine* and traditional Tuscan recipes, wins prizes every year. You may leave behind as much as L150,000 here—much more if you order a prestigious wine or champagne. *Closed Sun and Mon lunch, and Aug.* **Relais le Jardin**, the restaurant in the Regency Umbria hotel in Piazza d'Azeglio 3, © 245247, is rapidly establishing itself as one of Florence's best; the setting is lovely and refined, and dishes like delicate crêpes filled with zucchini blossoms, artichoke hearts, or asparagus and medallions of veal with rhubarb are bringing Florentines and visitors back for more. *Closed Sun.* For top quality cooking and elegant surroundings try **The Bristol**, Via dei Pescioni 2, © 287814, where you can eat well-prepared Italian food, as well as local specialities.

expensive

One of the most Florentine of Florentine restaurants, **Cibreo**, overlooks the market of Sant'Ambrogio on Via dei Macci 118r, © 2341100. The decor is simple—food is the main concern here, and all of it is market fresh. You can go native and order tripe antipasto, pumpkin soup, and cocks' combs and kidneys, or play it safe with *prosciutto* from the Casentino, a fragrant soup (no pasta here) of tomatoes, mussels, or bell pepper, leg of lamb stuffed with artichokes or duck stuffed with sultanas and pine nuts. Top it off with a delicious lemon *crostata* or cheese-cake; accompany it with an excellent choice of Italian or French wines, or a prized bottle of Armagnac. *Closed Sun and Mon, end of July–Sept.* **Buca Lapi**, Via del Trebbio 1r, © 213768, is another traditional Florentine restaurant, located since 1800 in the old wine cellar of the lovely Palazzo Antinori. Experiment with *pappardelle al cinghiale* (wide pasta with boar), which tastes better than it sounds; the *bistecca fiorentina con fagioli* here is hard to beat, downed with many different Tuscan wines. *Closed Mon lunch.*

In the Oltrarno, **Pierot**, Piazza Taddeo Gaddi, ✆ 702100, near Ponte Vittoria, is an old-style place with good food, wine and prices; try the fresh salmon with red pepper. *Closed Sun.* **Sabatini**, Via Panzani 9a, behind S. Maria Novella, ✆ 282802, the only Florentine restaurant with a branch in Tokyo, has been a favourite with tourists and locals for decades. It's a little old-fashioned, but you may find the sober elegance the perfect setting for enjoying their big Florentine steaks, the flamboyant *spaghetti alla lampada* and *pappardelle con lepre*, herb-strewn leg of lamb, and a decadent *semifreddo al croccantino* with hot chocolate sauce. *Closed Mon.* **Le Fonticine**, Via Nazionale 79r, ✆ 282106, in the tourist madness near the railway station, has not let its considerable success ruin it; fine homemade pasta cooked in the style of Italy's culinary capital, Bologna, the thickest *bistecca* in Florence, and lots of truffles, served in a cosy atmosphere with beamed ceiling and walls covered with Tuscan paintings. *Closed Mon, Aug.* Near the Piazza dei Ciompi, **La Vie en Rose**, Borgo Allegri 68r, ✆ 245860, is a popular place serving delights like fresh green pasta with clams and saffron, and duck with prunes. *Closed Tues.* **Taverna del Bronzino** in Via delle Ruote 25r, ✆ 495220, has a spacious atmosphere and is a good place to try the *ossobuco alla fiorentina*. *Closed Sun and Aug.*

moderate

If *cucina nuova fiorentina* sounds intriguing, try the fare at **Caffè Concerto**, Lungarno C.Colombo 7, ✆ 677377, served on a fine veranda overlooking the Arno; it stays open late for light midnight suppers. *Closed Sun and three weeks in Aug.*

Housed in a subterranean wine cellar, **Il Cantinone**, Via S. Spirito 6r, ✆ 218898, specializes in Chianti Classico and country cooking—*pappa al pomodoro* (thick tomato soup), polenta with boar, beans and sausage; one room is devoted to wine tasting and antipasti. **Angiolino**, Via Santo Spirito 36r, ✆ 2398976, is perhaps the most characteristic place this side of the river, with a stove in the centre of the room and the kitchen in full view; the food is typical and of good quality (their vegetable antipasti are especially tasty). *Closed Sun evening and Mon.*

inexpensive

For a change of pace, **Il Cuscussù**, Via Farini 2a, ✆ 241890, offers imaginative meals—couscous, goulash and near-eastern favourites, served with Chianti or Israeli wines. *Closed Sat.* **Il Latini**, near Santa Maria Novella, Via dei Palchetti 6r, ✆ 210916, is noisy, chaotic and great fun. Huge hams hang from the ceiling and you share the long tables with fellow eaters; the food is good local fare and the prices are modest. You cannot book so come early to avoid the queues *Closed Mon.* **Garga**, Via del Moro 48r, ✆ 2398898, is a charming if slightly cramped place run by a Florentine and his Canadian wife, serving mouthwatering home-made pasta, and delicately prepared meat and fish dishes. *Closed Mon.* On Via Ghibellina 51, **Ristorante Dino**, ✆ 241452, has excellent seasonal dishes and a famous *filettino di maiale al cartoccio* (pork fillets baked in paper) and a wide selection of wines. *Closed Sun evening and Mon.* **Pane e Vino** in Via San Nicolò

60–70r is simple and spartan with service to match, *2476956. *Closed Sun.* A cheap option is **La Casalinga** just by Piazza Santo Spirito, particularly popular with students and young tourists (Via Michelozzo 9r, *218624). And finally, for the cheapest meal in Florence, there's the lunch counter in the **Sant'Ambrogio Market**; no tables, no courtesies, and plenty of butchers and grocers to rub elbows with, but two courses of home cooking for L15,000. A good place for a sit-down snack or full meal is at **Benvenuto**, situated just behind the Uffizzi in Via della Mosca 16r. A cheap, charming recommendation for lunch is **La Mescita** (the bottle counter), a cold buffet in Via degli Alfani 70r. You can either sit at one of the few tables and eat a piece of delicious vegetable *frittata* with the local regulars, or order a huge sandwich to take away.

Central Florence, by popular demand, is full of *tavole calde*, pizzerias, cafeterias and snack bars, where you can grab a sandwich or a salad instead of a full sit-down meal (one of the best pizza-by-the-slice places is just across from the Medici Chapels). This may change. Lately the city has been trying to banish 'fast food' from the centre, in a bizarre attempt to upscale its tourism—they would prefer that we bought fewer hamburgers and more jewellery.

Around Florence *(055–)

In Fiesole there are plenty of mediocre overpriced restaurants and one where the food is excellent: **Cave di Maiano**, Via delle Cave 16, *59133 (*moderate*), at Maiano. On its beautiful garden terrace are served delights like green *tortellini* filled with veal and chicken, or an excellent risotto; roast pigeon, *involtini* of veal and mushrooms, followed by excellent desserts. *Closed Thurs and Sun evening.* **Il Trebbiolo**, *8300098, also has a picturesque terrace with views over the valley; the food is good and the atmosphere is relaxed. After the meal you can retire into the soggiorno to sip a liqueur and coffee. *Closed Sat evening and Mon.* In Artimino, near Carmignano, **Da Delfina**, Via della Chiesa 1, *8718074 (*moderate*), is worth the drive out for its enchanting surroundings, lovely views, the charming atmosphere and sublime cooking—homemade tagliatelle with a sauce made from greens, risotto with garden vegetables, wild asparagus, succulent kid and lamb dishes—at equally lovely prices. Near the Medici villa in Artimino **Biagio Pignatta**, *8718080 (*moderate*), has an excellent *ribollita*, *crêpes alla Catherine de' Medici* and more.

If you're on, or heading to or from the Florence–Siena Superstrada, a convenient lunch stop is at La Piazza, near Santi Donato e Sicelle, where the **Osteria alla Piazza**, *(0577) 733580 (*moderate*), will treat you to Tuscan classics in refined rustic surroundings.

Chianti and the Mugello

These two regions, Chianti to the south and the Mugello to the north of Florence, one world-famous and one obscure, are delightfully rural and endowed with every Tuscan charm. No Brunelleschi could have designed the grand stone farmhouses that crown every hill, built with an intuitive aesthetic that rarely fails, each different, offering endless variations of arches, loggias and towers, set in an equally endless variety of rolling hills, vineyards, olives and cypresses. Towns are few, monuments scattered and of minor interest, paintings and sculpture very rare. But you'll find few places more enchanting to explore—by car, by bicycle, by foot—in a day or a lifetime.

Chianti

From good Chianti, an aged wine, majestic and
imperious, that passes through my heart and chases
away without trouble every worry and grief...

Francesco Redi, *Bacchus in Tuscany*

In the 17th century, naturalist and poet Francesco Redi was the first to note the virtues of 'Florentine red' from Chianti, but since then the Italians have invested a lot of worry and grief into defining exactly what 'Chianti' means. The name apparently derives from an Etruscan family named Clanti; geographically it refers, roughly, to the hilly region between Florence and Siena, bordered by the Florence–Siena Superstrada del Palio and the A1 from Florence to Arezzo. The part within Siena province is known as *Chianti Storico* or *Chianti Geografico*, once the territories of the Lega del Chianti, a consortium of barons formed in 1385 to protect their interests (and their wine), who adopted a black cockerel as their emblem.

But Chianti is an oenological name as well as a geographical one, and as such first became official in 1716, when Grand Duke Cosimo III defined which parts of Tuscany could call their vintage Chianti, in effect making wine history—it was the first time that a wine had its production area delimited. The Lorraine grand dukes promoted advances in wine-making techniques and the export of Chianti. Yet the Chianti as we know it had yet to be developed, and it was largely the creation of one man—the 'Iron Baron', Bettino Ricasoli, briefly the second prime minister of unified Italy. The baron was very wealthy but not very good-looking, and Luigi Barzini, in *The Italians*, recounts how jealous he became when a young man asked his new bride to dance at a ball in Florence. Ricasoli at once ordered her into their carriage and gave the driver the address of the ancient family seat at Brolio in the Monti del Chianti—an isolated castle that the poor woman rarely left ever after.

To pass the time the baron began to experiment with different vines and processes, eventually hitting upon a pleasing mix of red Sangiovese and Canaiolo grapes, with a touch of white Malvasia, twice fermented in the old Tuscan manner. At the same time the famous dark green flask was invented, the *strapeso*, with its straw covering woven by the local

women. The end product took the Paris Exhibition of 1878 by storm; imitators soon appeared, and in 1924, the boundaries of Chianti Storico were slightly more than doubled to create *Chianti Classico*, drawn by local producers to protect the wine's name, adopting the now familiar black cockerel of the Lega del Chianti as its symbol. In 1967 Chianti Classico, along with Tuscany's six other Chianti vinicultural zones, was given its *denominazione di origine* status, and production soared, but quality and sales declined. To improve the wine, the Chianti Classico Consortium was upscaled to a DOCG rating to guarantee that all wines bearing the black cockerel would be tested and approved by a panel of judges.

But it was tales of Elizabeth Barrett Browning quaffing Chianti and finding her inspiration in its ruby splendour, as well as the sunny rural elegance of the region, that attracted first the English and Dutch, then the Swiss, Americans, French and Germans, especially in the 1960s and 70s, who form one of Italy's densest foreign colonies, wryly nicknamed 'Chianti-shire'. They brought into the region more money than Chianti's mouldering barons and contessas had seen since the Renaissance; real property prices shot to the moon. But the presence of so much money has begun to cast a shadow over the heart of this ancient, enchanting region; snobbery and pretensions threaten to poison the pleasurable plonk of yesteryear; limited edition numbered bottles, offered by some vintners, are a bit too much; designer-label Chianti is just around the corner. The old vines, following the contours of the hills, are being pulled out for specialized vines in geometric straight lines. And as any old-timer will tell you, the modern DOCG Chianti Classico sniffed and gurgled by wine professionals isn't anything like the joyous, spontaneous wine that made Chianti famous in the first place.

Some 800 farms and estates (only a selection of the most historic are listed in the text below) produce wine in the mere 70,000 hectares in the Chianti Classico zone, and one of the chief pleasures in visiting is trying as many labels as possible—with the different mixtures of grapes, different soils, and bottling methods, each should be, or at least strives to be, individual. Nor do the estates limit themselves to Chianti; many produce Vinsanto, a white wine called Bianca della Lega, and many reds, as well as Chianti's other speciality, a delicate *extra-vergine* olive oil. Before setting out, ring in advance to check hours.

Getting Around

The two main north–south routes through Chianti, the old Roman Via Cassia (S2) and the Chiantigiana (S222) rival one another in beauty; an ideal motoring wine tour would take in the east–west S429 between the Badia a Coltibuono and Castellina. Distances aren't great, though the single-lane winding routes make for leisurely travel.

Public transport is fairly easy in Chianti and all by bus, though you may not always find connections between two towns very commodious; from Florence SITA buses will take you to Greve (25km/45min), Gaiole (55km/1½hrs), Castellina in Chianti (44km/1hr), Mercatale, S. Casciano in Val di Pesa (17km/25min)

Tavernelle Val di Pesa (29km/40min), Panzano, Strada, and Radda (42km/1hr); CAP buses run frequently from Florence to Impruneta (14km/20min). From Siena TRA-IN buses go to Castellina (20km/25min), Radda (30km/40min), Tavarnelle (38km/50min) and S. Casciano (49km/1¼hrs), Tavarnuzze and Strada.

Chianti begins 10km south of Florence, but on the way you may want to follow the sign west off S222 just past the autostrada, for **Ponte a Ema** and the prettily sited 14th-century chapel of the Alberti, **Santa Caterina dell'Antella**, with contemporary frescoes on St Catherine's life, one of Spinello Aretino's greatest works (*closed Sun*). Further along, at Grassina, there's a turn-off to **Impruneta**, a large town on a plateau noted for its terracotta tiles (including those on Brunelleschi's dome) and pottery, very much on sale, especially during the enormous **St Luke's Horse and Mule Fair** in October. The fair takes place in the main piazza, in the shadow of Impruneta's pride and joy, the ancient **Collegiata**, built to house a miraculous icon of the Madonna and Child attributed to St Luke, dug up by a team of oxen in the 10th century. Bombed during the last war, restorers took the opportunity to bring the Collegiata back to its Renaissance appearance to match its two beautiful chapels, one housing the icon and the other a piece of the True Cross, both designed by Michelozzo and richly decorated with enamel terracottas by Luca della Robbia. In an adjacent chapel there's a marble relief of the *Finding of the Icon* by the school of Donatello; the bronze crucifix in the nave is attributed to Giambologna. The campanile survives from the 13th century, and the fine portico was built in 1634. Among the many terracotta shops **Atrenova** in Via della Fonte 76, ✆ (055) 2011060, has creative designs and a good selection of gifts.

Machiavelli in Exile

From the S222 south of Florence, a by-road leads west from Tavarnuzze (8km) to **Sant'Andrea in Percussina**, long the country fief of the Machiavelli. Here Niccolò spent his tedious exile, which he described in a letter as whiling away the day in the tavern 'playing at *cricca* and tric-trac, and this gave rise to a thousand arguments and endless exchanges of insults, most of the time there is a fight over a penny . . . and so surrounded by these lice, I blow the cobwebs from my brain and relieve the unkindness of my fate.' In the evening he would retire to work on *The Prince*. His old tavern is still a tavern and his home, the **Albergaccio**, contains a small museum devoted to his life. Near Chiesanuova, to the north, there's the 16th-century **Palazzo al Bosco**, attributed by some to Michelangelo, an interesting villa built atop a 13th-century structure (✆ *(055) 8242212; tours of the cellars, tastings and sales of Chianti and Rosso di San Valentino, and olive oil available*). The stately, theatrical 15th-century **Villa Tattoli** to the west (on the Chiesanuova-Cerbaia road) features two levels of arcades (✆ *(055) 827042; offers tours of the cellars*). Near Cerbaia itself, 5km from San Casciano, **Villa Talente** is the former property of the artists who built Orsanmichele in Florence (✆ *(055) 826388; offers Chianti, white wine and olive oil*).

In this section of Chianti, hotels tend to be small and usually annexed to restaurants, though note that many of the larger wine estates have a few rooms or apartments to let; call ahead to see what's available. One exception is ★★★★★**Villa la Massa Bagno**, Via della Massa 6, Candeli, © 6510101, ✉ 6510109 (*luxury*), a large hotel with a swimmimg pool and 39 rooms all with a bath and air-conditioning. A cheaper option is ★★**Gli Scopeti,** Via Cassia 183, Tavarnuzze, © 2022008, ✉ 2373015 (*moderate*). Bagno a Ripoli's **Centanni**, Via Centanni 7, © 630122 (*moderate*), is an exceptionally pleasant restaurant among olive groves, where you can dine on a delicious array of antipasti, and Renaissance recipes like *brasata dei Medici*, a sweet and sour braised beef dish dating from the 17th century. *Closed Sat lunch and Sun.*

Impruneta has little in the way of hotels, but ★★★**La Vallombrosina**, Via Montebuoni 95, © 2020491 (*moderate, with bath*), will provide a comfortable roof over your head. **I Falciani**, Via Cassia 245, © 2020091 (*inexpensive*), is a rustic place full of locals, where you may dine with the TV for company or not on tasty *crostini ribollita* and in the fall, hunters' roast meat platter. **Antica Trattoria dei Cacciatori**, Via Chiantigiana 22, Località I Falciani, © 2020432 (*moderate*), offers among other sturdy dishes *rognone al ginepro*, kidneys with juniper berries. *Closed Mon.* Machiavelli's ancient tavern in Sant'Andrea in Percussina is now owned by the Conti Serristori Wine Company and called the **Albergaccio di Machiavelli**, © 828471 (*moderate*), serving simple Tuscan meals—in summer, be sure to order the refreshing *panzanella* for starters—and fine wines from the estate; you can also buy bottles to take home. *Closed Mon.*

Along the Via Cassia (S2)

Up-to-date **San Casciano in Val di Pesa**, 17km south of Florence, is the largest and busiest town in Chianti. Long an outpost of Florence, it suffered numerous vicissitudes until its **walls** were begun by the ill-fated Duke of Athens in 1342. Within these, near the gateway, the church of **Santa Maria del Prato** (1335) has retained its trecento interior and trecento art: a fine pulpit by Giovanni Balducci da Pisa, a pupil of Andrea Pisano, a crucifix attributed to Simone Martini, a triptych by Ugolino di Neri, and framed paintings on the pilasters by Giotto's pupil, Taddeo Gaddi. The recently opened **Museum of Sacred Art** (*open 2–7 Sat, 10.30–12, 4–7 Sun*) includes the **Madonna and Child,** considered to be the first work by Ambrogio Lorenzetti. In the vicinity of San Casciano Florentine merchants and noblemen dotted the countryside with villas: the late Renaissance **Fattoria Le Corti**, 2km east on the Mercatale road, owned by the princely Corsini family for the past six centuries (*© (055) 820123; the estate's Chianti is on sale*) and the 17th-century **Poggio Torselli**, just off the S2, approached through a long avenue of cypresses and surrounded by a lovely garden (*© (055) 820214; offers its own Chianti label*).

Mercatale, Bargino and Barberino Val d'Elsa

Mercatale, 5km east of San Casciano, grew up around its *mercato*, or market, protected in the old days by the **Castle of the Florentine Bishops**, now a ruin fit only to protect the odd lizard. A far more muscular castle, just to the east on the road to Passo dei Pecorai, is the **Castello di Greve**, bound by four round towers. The Bardi put it up in the 11th century, before they moved to Florence and founded the greatest pre-Medici bank (© *(055) 821101; it offers tastings and lunches with advance notice, on sale are its own Chianti, Vinsanto, and olive oil*). Other villas worth visiting near Mercatale are: **Villa Caserotta**, former property of the Strozzi, and the fortified **Villa Palagio**, on the Mercatale–Campoli–Montefiridolfi road, adapted from a 14th-century castle. A narrow lane byway, the Mercatale–Panzano road, will bring you to **La Torre a Luciana**, an unspoiled medieval hamlet once belonging to the Pitti family.

The Via Cassia, between San Casciano and Bargino, passes by the ancient **Castle of Bibbione**, once residence of the Buondelmonte family, who owned much of the surrounding territory in the days when they were throwing fat on the Guelph and Ghibbeline fires in Florence. Near **Bargino**, in the same bellicose spirit, is the impressive fortified hamlet of **Montefiridolfi**, just east of the Via Cassia. This road, meanwhile, rolls south through some lovely hills towards **Tavarnelle Val di Pesa**, a town of mostly 19th-century origin, and the medieval **Barberino Val d'Elsa**, with some Etruscan finds in the town hall and a good Romanesque church, the **Pieve di Sant'Appiano**, built in the 10th century. From here the Via Cassia continues to **Poggibonsi** (*see* p.352), with a possible detour to **La Paneretta**, a sturdy 15th-century fort amid the olive groves, with Baroque frescoes inside.

© *(055–)*   *Where to Stay and Eating Out*

Most of the district's lodgings are here, as well as some of Chianti's best restaurants. **La Tenda Rossa**, located to the north in Cerbaia, in Piazza del Monumento 11, © 826132 (*very expensive, but worth it*), is a family-run abode of haute cuisine: pumpkin-filled *tortellini*, or perhaps lettuce crêpes filled with artichoke hearts for starters, followed by chicken breasts with grated *porcini* mushrooms, or duck's breast in balsamic vinegar. The challenge is trying to save room for one of the Red Tent's excellent, innovative desserts, all prepared with the lightest of touches. *Closed Wed and Thurs lunch.* ★★★**L'Antica Posta**, in S. Casciano's Piazza Zannoni 1/3, © 822313, ✉ 822278 (*moderate*), has 10 comfortable rooms, all with bath, as well as a restaurant to rival the Tenda Rossa, but with more Persian rugs and silver decorations; among the offerings are a risotto with artichokes and crayfish, *taglierini* with razor clams and asparagus, breast of pheasant flavoured with thyme, or rabbit in a sauce of creamed mussels; the wine list is superb. Reservations are obligatory (L40–50,000 à la carte, L45,000 for a *menu degustazione*). Fresh, fresh fish is on the menu at **Nello**, Via IV Novembre 64, in S. Casciano, © 820163 (*moderate*), and you can start with something you don't find every day in Tuscany—*pesto alla genovese*; the wines include most Chianti labels. Other places to sleep in the area are all small: **★★Minisoggiorno**, Via Leonardo da Vinci 5, Bardella, © 820732 (*inexpensive*), has simple rooms; **★Bargino**, Via Cassia 122, Bargino, © 8249055 (*inexpensive*), has seven rooms in a garden along the old Roman road.

In Mercatale, **La Biscondola**, Via Grevigiana, © 821381 (*moderate to expensive*), enjoys a fine sunny and protected location where you can linger over traditional dishes like *pappa al pomodoro*, rabbit in mushrooms and white wine (a Chianti speciality) or a superb *bistecca alla fiorentina*; and you can spend the night in the little **★Soggiorno Paradiso**, Piazza V. Veneto 28, © 821327, 🖂 821281 (*inexpensive*). **Il Salotto del Chianti,** Via Sonnino 92, © 8218016 (*moderate*), is beginning to make its mark on the local culinary scene; *ravioli con formaggio, pappardelle alla lepre* and their wild boar are extraordinary. *Closed Wed.* Tavarnelle has one of Chianti's pleasant **Youth Hostels**, on Via Roma 137, © 8077009, with 60 beds. *Open year round.*

Barberino Val d'Elsa has a pleasant, simple hotel, **★★Primavera**, Via della Republicca 27, © and 🖂 8059223. Tasty roasts, *risotto* with *porcini* mushrooms and great Florentine steaks are to be had at **Mari Giovani,** Strada Monestiero 12, San Donato in Poggio, © 8072849 (*moderate*). *Open Thurs, Fri, Sat and Sun.*

Central Chianti: Along the Chiantigiana (S222)

From Florence the scenic Chiantigiana, or S222 passes the Ugolino Golf Course (*see* **Florence**, 'Sports') and offers its first tempting detour at Petigliolo: turn left after 4km for the ivy-covered **Santo Stefano a Tizzano**, a Romanesque church built by the Buondelmonti, not far from an 11th-century castle-villa, the **Castello di Tizzano** (© *(055) 640026; offers Chianti Riserva, Vinsanto Naturale, and prize-winning olive oil*). The same road continues for 2km to **San Polo in Chianti**, the centre of Tuscany's iris industry, celebrated in an **Iris Festival** in May. On a hill from San Polo you can see a lonely building once belonging to the Knights Templar; an equally ancient church, **San Miniato in Robbiana,** was reconsecrated in 1077 by the Bishop of Fiesole, according to a still legible inscription. San Polo's **Antico Toscano**, © (055) 855110, is a wine shop with offerings from all over the region.

Strada, a village 14km from Florence along the Chiantigiana, is believed to have received its odd name from an old Roman road. Just to the south the road towards the Valdarno was protected in the Middle Ages by the **Castello di Mugano**, one of the best-preserved in the region and polished up by a recent restoration. The rolling countryside is the dominant feature along the Chiantigiana until **Vicchiomaggio** with a distinctive castle that once hosted Leonardo da Vinci. This is now the British-run **Fattoria Castello di Vicchiomaggio,** (© *(055) 853911; offers its own label of Chianti, Vinsanto, olive oil and honey*). Nearby **Verrazzano** is a name that New Yorkers will recognize at once thanks to

Giovanni da Verrazzano, not the usual Chianti landlubber but a captain who, in the service of François I of France, discovered New York Harbour in 1524 and Manhattan island as well. He disappeared on his second voyage to Brazil, but surely smiles down from heaven on the enormous bridge named in his honour, so many miles away from Chianti. His birthplace, the **Castello di Verrazzano**, ✆ (055) 854243, offers a variety of wines and olive oils (*tastings with one week's notice*). Just east of the Chiantigiana, 1.5km north of Greve stands the fine **Castello di Uzzano**, built by the Bishop of Florence in the 13th century and since then gradually converted into one of Chianti's most impressive villa estates (*tastings with one day's notice,* ✆ *(055) 854032*).

Greve in Chianti and Environs

The biggest **wine fair** in Chianti occurs every September in the medieval townlet of Greve (pop. 10,800), and as such it is looked upon as the capital of Chianti. Located on the banks of the river Greve, it is celebrated for its charming, arcaded, funnel-shaped **Piazza del Mercatale**, with a statue of Verrazzano in its centre. And that's about all—its castle was burned in 1387, and its Franciscan convent converted to a prison in the last century. However, in the parish church of **Santa Croce** there's a triptych by Lorenzo di Bicci and a painting by the 'Master of Greve'.

Greve is awash in wine. Seek out specialized wine shops like the **Bottega del Chianti Classico**, Via Cesare Battisti 4, ✆ (055) 853631, and the **Enoteca del Chianti Classico**, Piazzetta S. Croce 8, ✆ (055) 853297, or the **Castello di Querceto** just outside of town on the Figline Val d'Arno road, ✆ (055) 8549064, a lovely place offering a wide variety of wines, including Sangiovese aged in wooden *barriques* and olive oil (*tastings with one week's notice*). On the Chiantigiana, near Sant'Eufrosino, **Fontodi**, Via S. Leonino 87, ✆ (055) 852005, also has wine aged in *barriques*, Chianti, Bianco della Lega and olive oil (*tastings with one week's notice*).

In a nearby hamlet, **Cintoia**, east of Chiocchio, there is the little church of **Santa Maria a Cintoia** with a beautiful 15th-century panel attributed to Francesco Granacci.

A kilometre to the west of Greve is the ancient village and castle of **Montefioralle**, where the people of Greve lived in the bad old days. Recently restored, it is an interesting place to poke around in, with its octagonal walls intact, its old tower houses, and two Romanesque churches, **Santo Stefano**, housing early Florentine paintings, and the porticoed **Pieve di San Cresci a Montefioralle**, just outside the walls. A minor road west of Montefioralle passes in a kilometre the ruined castle of **Montefili**, built in the 900s as the eastern outpost of one of Chianti's most powerful religious institutions, the **Badia a Passignano**, a fortified complex of ancient foundation, since converted into a villa. The old abbey church, **San Michele**, can be visited, and contains paintings by Ghirlandaio, Alessandro Allori and Domenico Cresti (better known as Passignano) and a bust of San Giovanni Gualberto, founder of the Vallombrosan Order, who arrived here preaching reform in the mid-11th century. Most of the buildings you see date from the 14th century, with a few remodellings in the 17th and 19th centuries.

Just east of Greve, **Vignamaggio** is the site of a beautiful old villa built by the Gherardini family, the most famous member of whom, Lisa, was born here, and later married Francesco del Giocondo before going on to pose for the world's most famous portrait. In 1992 it was used as the setting for Kenneth Branagh's film version of *Much Ado About Nothing*. **Panzano**, an important agricultural centre 6km south of Greve on the Chiantigiana, played an important role in the Florence–Siena squabbles, but retains only part of its medieval castle. Today it is best known for its embroidery, and visited for the **Pieve di San Leolino**, 1km south, with its pretty 16th-century portico on a 12th-century Romanesque structure; inside there's a triptych by Mariotto di Nardo. Another Romanesque church south of Panzano, **Sant'Eufrosino**, just off S222, enjoys especially fine views. Near Panzano is the **Fattoria Montagliari** (*sells a wide variety of its own wines, grappa, olive oil, cheese, salami, honey, etc*). **Pietrafitta**, 9km further south and 4km from Castellina, is a lovely old hamlet hidden in the woods.

Castellina in Chianti

One of Chianti's most charming hilltop villages, Castellina (pop. 2700) was fortified by Florence as an outpost against Siena, and for centuries its fortunes depended on who was momentarily on top in their bitter, stupid, endless war. Most grievous to the Florentines was its loss to a combined Sienese-Aragonese siege in 1478, though after the fall of Siena itself in 1555, both cities lost interest in Castellina, and today it looks much as it did in the quattrocento: the old circuit of **walls** is almost intact, complete with houses built into and on top of them; the **Rocca**, or fortress, in the centre, its mighty donjon now home of the mayor; and the covered walkway, or **Via delle Volte**, part of the 15th-century defensive works. Less historic but just as worth visiting is the **Bottega del Vino Gallo Nero**, Via della Rocca 10 (*sells a vast assortment of wines and olive oils*). A kilometre from the centre, you can explore the **Ipogeo Etrusco di Montecalvario**, a 6th-century BC Etruscan tomb that has recently been restored. West of Castellina on S429, **Granaio** is synonymous with one of Chianti's most renowned wineries, the **Melini Wine House**, established in 1705 and one of the big innovators in Chianti technology.

There are many splendid old farmhouses and villas around Castellina, nearly all formerly fortifications along Chianti's medieval Maginot line, like the **Villa La Leccia** just south-west of Castellina, and the **Castello di Campalli** near **Fonterutoli**, an ancient hamlet south on the Chiantigiana. In the 13th century Florence and Siena often met here trying to work out peace settlements, none of which endured very long. Peace, however, is the rule at the **Fattoria di Fonterutoli**, in the family since 1435 (✆ *(0577) 740309; produces wine in traditional oaken casks, Chianti, Bianco della Lega, and other wines, honey, products made from lavender, and an extra-vergine that many consider Tuscany's finest*).

Further south, **Quercegrossa**, 10km from Siena, is practically a suburb of that city, and was the birthplace of the great quattrocento sculptor Jacopo della Quercia. A byroad forks northeast for Vagliagli, site of the medieval **Fattoria della Aiola** (✆ *(0577) 322615; with wines, grappa, olive oil, honey and vinegar*).

Fagioli Cotti Nel Fiasco

The traditional way of cooking *fagioli* (white beans) was to put olive oil, herbs, beans and a little water inside an empty Chianti bottle (with the straw wrapping removed) and leave them to cook for several hours beside or above the embers of a charcoal fire. *Aficionados* will tell you it is the best way to cook beans—the bottle's small opening keeps in all the flavours and perfumes. However, Chianti bottles are no longer made of a glass resistant enough, so it is probably best to use a casserole. Cover and cook the beans (if using dried haricot beans, soak them first) in the above way, on a slow heat for several hours. Just before serving add more olive oil and garnish with tuna fish, herrings or anchovies; alternatively you can add more oil, some sage, garlic and chopped tomatoes and reheat the beans until the tomatoes have disintegrated.

Where to Stay

Greve ✆ (055–)

Near the centre there's the pleasant and recently refurbished ★★★**Del Chianti**, Piazza Matteotti 86, ✆ 853763, ✉ 853764 (*moderate*), with comfortable, stylish air-conditioned rooms, and a pool and garden in the back. ★★★**Giovanni da Verrazzano**, Piazza Matteotti 28, ✆ 853189, ✉ 853648 (*moderate*), has 11 elegant rooms in the middle of Greve. Just south, ★★★**Villa le Barone** in Panzano, Via S. Leolino 19, ✆ 852621, ✉ 852277 (*expensive*), is the 16th-century villa of the della Robbia family, who still own it and run it as a lovely, intimate hotel, a great base for visiting the region, or for just lounging around in the pretty garden by the pool; bring the children. Naturally many of the rooms are decorated in della Robbia blue and white. Minimum stay three nights. *Open April–Oct.* A cheaper option is the local youth hostel **Villa San Michele** in Monte S. Michele, ✆ 851034, which has beds for 60 people.

Castellina ✆ (0577–)

★★★★**Tenuta di Ricavo**, 3km north of Castellina, ✆ 740221, ✉ 741014 (*very expensive*), is more than a hotel—it's an entire medieval hamlet of stone houses, wonderfully isolated in the pines and with a large garden and swimming-pool. Many of the rooms are situated in the old houses, ideal for families. *Open April–Oct.* ★★★★**Villa Casalecchi**, set among the trees and vineyards on a slope, ✆ 740240 ✉ 74111 (*very expensive*), is a comfortable old house, with some elegant rooms full of antiques and some not so elegant, but a big swimming-pool and enchanting views over the hills. *Open April–Oct.* Two old farmhouses have recently been combined to create the smart new ★★★**Salivolpi**, just outside Castellina on Via Fiorentina, ✆ and ✉ 740 484 (*moderate*); a garden and pool are added attractions.

San Polo ✆ *(055-)*

In San Polo, or rather out in the open countryside, **Trattoria Merendero** in Via S. Lavagnini 14, ✆ 855019 (*moderate*), offers some tasty un-Tuscan surprises: fried stuffed olives (a speciality of the Marches) and *spaghetti al pesto*, as well as the region's old standbys.

Greve ✆ *(055-)*

In and around Greve there are plenty of choices; one of the most charming is right in the centre: **Giovanni da Verrazzano**, Piazza Matteotti 28, ✆ 853189 (*moderate*), furnished with 19th-century antiques, and with a lovely terrace for summer dining, overlooking the piazza. The main meat dishes are especially good here—*nana in sugo* (duck in wine sauce), turkey with olives, and a greatly varied mixed grill. **Bottega del Moro**, Piazza Trieste 14r, ✆ 853753 (*inexpensive*), right in the heart of Greve, is a simple trattoria where you can eat typical Tuscan dishes. *Closed Wed.* Nearby in Montefioralle, the **Taverna del Guerrino**, Via di Montefioralle 39, ✆ 853106 (*moderate*), is a fine, rustic place surrounded by a panoramic garden, offering good Tuscan home cooking, including Tuscan gazpacho—*panzanella*—stuffed tomatoes, sausage and beans *all'uccelletto* and wines from the local fattoria. **La Cantinetta**, on the Chiantigiana 93, in Spedaluzzo (near Greve), ✆ 8572000 (*moderate*), has good homemade pasta and country specialities like stuffed rabbit, pigeon, stuffed artichokes and grilled meats. In Località di Mezzano (near Greve) try **Borgo Antico** ✆ 851024 (*moderate*), for tasty pasta with red peppers and cream sauce. *Closed Tues.*

Panzano ✆ *(055-)*

To the south in Panzano, **Montagliari**, Via di Montagliari 28, ✆ 852184 (*expensive*), is decorated in the style of an old Tuscan farmhouse, with tables out in the panoramic garden. First courses include ravioli filled with walnuts or *penne* with raw tomatoes and basil; for seconds try the boar *alla cacciatora* or the *pollastro Montagliari al vino bianco* (chicken with white wine and black olives). *Reservations obligatory.*

Castellina ✆ *(0577-)*

Antica Trattoria La Torre, Piazza del Comune 1, ✆ 740236 (*expensive*), is a popular, family-run place, with a cosy atmosphere and tasty dishes like risotto with mushrooms and an exceptional *fagiano alla Torre*, prepared to an ancient Chianti recipe. *Closed Fri.* On the outskirts of town on the Via Fiorentina 35 (the road to San Donato), **Albergaccio di Castellina**, ✆ 741042, serves fresh food attractively presented, and complimentary rolls and a glass of *spumante* with every meal. Excellent value. *Closed Sun.* Slightly cheaper is the **Pietrafitta bar-ristorante**, Località Pietrafitta 41, ✆ 741123 (*moderate*), owned by an Australian lady and run by English and New Zealanders, offering surprisingly good regional and international dishes. *Closed Tues.*

Monti del Chianti: Radda and Gaiole

East of Castellina lies the steeper, more rugged region of the Monti del Chianti. One of the higher hills supports the ancient capital of the Lega del Chianti, **Radda in Chianti** (pop. 1650) where the streets have kept their medieval plan, radiating from the central piazza and its stately **Palazzo Comunale**, encrusted with coats of arms and a 15th-century fresco in the atrium of the Madonna, St John the Baptist and St Christopher. Just outside the town is a pretty porticoed Franciscan church, called the **Monastero**, dating from the 15th century. There are two resolutely medieval villages nearby: **Ama**, with its castle 8km to the south, near the attractive Romanesque church of **San Giusto**; and **Volpaia**, 7km to the north, with another ancient castle and walls, and an unexpected 'Brunelleschian' church, called La Commenda, in a doll-sized piazza. Also near Radda is the **Fattoria Vigna Vecchia** (✆ *(0577) 738090; offers Chianti, grappa, Vinsanto, olive oil and tastings with three days' notice*).

Gaiole, 10km east of Radda, is reached by way of the ancient **Badia a Coltibuono**, one of the gems of Chianti, a singular place set among centuries-old trees and gardens. The abbey is believed to have been founded in 770, but passed over to the Vallombrosan Order in the 12th century. The Romanesque church of **San Lorenzo** dates from 1049, while the monastery was converted into a splendid villa, owned in the 19th century by the Poniatowski, one of Poland's greatest noble families, and now occupied by a wine estate (P. Stucchi Prinetti, ✆ (0577) 749498), and restaurant (*see* p.204).

Gaiole in Chianti (pop. 4780) was an ancient market town and these days is basically a modern one; the **Agricoltori Chianti Geografico**, Via Mulinaccio 10, ✆ (0577) 749489, is the headquarters of a local cooperative (*sells Chianti, Vernaccia di San Gimignano, Vinsanto and olive oil*); the **Enoteca Montagnani**, Via B. Bandinelli 9, *specializes in Chianti Classico*. Beside wine tasting Gaiole has little to offer, but serves as a starting point for visiting the impressive castles in this strategic area between the Arno and Siena. Just to the west are the walls and imposing donjon of the **Castello di Vertine**, a well-preserved slice of the 13th century and one of the most striking sights in all Chianti. To the east of Gaiole stands the ancient fortified village of **Barbischio**, and just 3km south on S408 is the impressive medieval **Castello di Meleto** with its sturdy cylindrical towers still intact. From here the road continues another 4.5km up to the mighty **Castello di Castagnoli**, guarding a fascinating little medieval town in a commanding position.

Most majestic of all is the Iron Baron's celebrated isolated **Castello di Brolio**, some 10km south of Gaiole along S484, high on its own hill with views for miles around (*open daily 9–12 and 3 to sunset*). First mentioned in 1009, when Matilda of Tuscany's father Bonifacio donated it to the monks of the Badia in Florence, it came into the possession of the Ricasoli in 1167. The castle was bombarded for weeks in 1478 by the Aragonese and Sienese, who later had it demolished, so the 'the walls levelled with the earth'. After the war, Florence rebuilt it, and in the mid-19th century Baron Ricasoli converted it into the splendid fortified residence while experimenting on the modern formula for Chianti ; the **Barone Ricasoli Wine House**, ✆ (0577) 749710, *offers its famous wines, olive oil, and* *more*. At Madonna del Brolio, 10km to the south, you can also visit the **Cantine Barone Ricasoli** by phoning ahead, ✆ (0577) 311961. The **Fattoria dei Pagliaresi**, ✆ (0577) 359070, is located near Castelnuovo Berardenga, between S. Gusmé and Pianella (*offers older wines as well as new, and olive oil*). There are riding stables 5km east at the **Fattoria San Giusto**, at Monti, ✆ (0577) 363011. To the south, **Castelnuovo Berardenga** is an agricultural centre with the remains of a 14th-century castle, and from here it's 16km to **Monteaperti**, where Florence almost went down the tubes (to continue south, *see* p.376).

✆ *(0577–)* **Where to Stay**

Radda

★★Villa Miranda (or Minucci) is located in Villa a Radda, ✆ 738021, ✉738668 (*moderate*), a small inn founded in 1842, an old posthouse, though now there's a swimming-pool instead of a stable. There's a good restaurant, featuring good home cooking and a dish called *coniglio ubriaco al Chianti* (drunken rabbit). **★★★★Relais Vignale**, Via Pianigiani 8, ✆ 738300, ✉ 738592 (*very expensive*), has 27 rooms in a charming old house, with fine views over the pool and countryside. *Open April–Oct.* Much simpler are the nine rooms annexed to a very popular restaurant, **★Il Girarrosto**, in the village centre at Via Roma 41 , ✆ 738010 (*inexpensive*).

Gaiole

★★★★Park Hotel Cavarchione on the Vertine road, ✆ 749550 (*expensive*), is an imaginatively renovated farmhouse with only 11 rooms, run by Germans, with lovely views, pool and garden. *Open mid-March–Oct.* **★★★★Castello di Spaltenna**, in Spaltenna, a hill just above Gaiole, ✆ 749483, ✉ 749269 (*expensive to very expensive*), is beautifully located in a proper old fortified monastery with some theatrical medieval touches and delightful, comfortable bedrooms with stunning panoramic views over the valley or courtyard; 21 antique furnished rooms. *Closed mid-Jan–Mar.* The restaurant (*expensive*) is situated in the ancient castle refectory and serves traditional and creative Tuscan dishes. There are three large apartments available in the famous **Castello di Brolio**, Gaiole in Chianti, Siena, ✆ (0566) 747104. *Reserve far in advance.*

✆ *(0577–)* **Eating Out**

In Radda, **Il Vignale**, Via XX Settembre 23, ✆ 738094 (*expensive*), is a good, family-run place belonging to the Fattoria Vignale and featuring refined Tuscan home cooking, very popular locally. *Closed Tues.* If you're in the mood for a roast meat and wine debauch, try **Il Girarrosto** (*moderate*) see 'Where to Stay' above . *Closed Wed.* At **Le Vigne** along the S408, ✆ 738640 (*moderate*), you can eat similar food out on their terrace. *Closed Tues.* **Badia a Coltibuono**, next to the old abbey of the same name between Radda and Gaiole, © 749031 (*expensive*), offers delicious *tortelloni, tagliatelle ai porcini*, meats roasted on a spit, and tempting desserts. An old mill converted into a restaurant, **Il Molino** along the Via Chiantigiana 31, at Le Bagnaie-Monti, near Gaiole, © 747062 (*moderate*), has a menu featuring a minestrone, *ravioloni*, wild boar and rabbit. In Brolio, **Da Gino**, © 747194 (*moderate*), is operated by the castle and serves good, if not wildly imaginative Tuscan cuisine with Castello di Brolio wines, not surprisingly. *Closed Tues.*

The Mugello

Over the years, as their ambitions became less discreet, the Medici concocted a pretty story of how they were descended from knights of Charlemagne. In truth they came down to Florence from the Mugello, the hilly region just to the north—as did Giotto and Fra Angelico. As far back as Boccaccio's time, the Mugello was considered the loveliest region of the Florentine *contada*, and its bluish-green hills are dotted with elegant weekend and summer retreats, rather smarter than the typical stone *fattorie* of the Chianti. The Florentines come here whenever they can, and if you find yourself stewing with them in the traffic gridlocks approaching Piazza della Libertà, know that all you have to do is turn up Via Bologna and in 10 minutes you'll be in a cool, enchanting world immersed in green.

North of Florence altitudes rise appreciably towards the central Appennine spine that divides Tuscany from Emilia-Romagna. Tucked in these hills lies the Mugello basin, a broad valley along the river Sieve and its tributaries, which, in the Miocene era, held a lake. Most of the towns of the Mugello are here, surrounded by a sea of vines; olives cover the slopes, but soon give way to deep forests of pines, chestnuts and oaks, cool and refreshing, dotted with small resorts. And like any fashion-conscious Florentine, the Mugello changes colours with the seasons, and is strikingly beautiful any time of year, a place to return to, again and again.

Deluxe Virgins

Some day, on a trip to one of the fancier Italian food shops, you may pause near the section devoted to condiments and wonder at the beautiful display of bottles of unusually dark whiskies and wines, with corks and posh, elegant labels—why, some is even DOC, though much of it is far more costly than the usual DOC vintages. A closer look reveals these precious bottles are full of nothing but olive oil. Admittedly *olio extra vergine di oliva* from Tuscany and Umbria makes a fine salad dressing—according to those in the know the oil of the Chianti brooks few rivals, Italian or otherwise. Its delicate, fruity fragrance derives from the excellent quality of the ripe olive and the low acidity extracted from the fruit without any refinements. The finest oil, Extra Virgin, must have less than 1 per cent acidity (the best has 0.5 per cent acidity). Other designations are Soprafino Virgin, Fine Virgin, and Virgin (each may have up to 4 per cent acidity) in descending order of quality. And as any Italian will tell you, it's good for you—and it had better be, because Tuscan or

Umbrian chefs put it in nearly every dish, as they have for centuries. The only difference is that now it comes in a fancy package for a fancy price, a victim of the Italian designer label syndrome and (mostly) Tuscan preciosity. Not only does the olive oil have corks, but the trend in some of the smarter restaurants is to offer an olive oil list similar to a wine list—one restaurant in Tuscany even has an oil sommelier! DOC vinegar and sheep cheese are just around the corner.

Getting Around

The Mugello lies to the east of the A1 Autostrada and north of Pontassieve. It has two exits off the A1: at Barberino (28km/20min from Florence) and Roncobilaccio (47km/35min) near the Passo della Futa. The two principal roads north from Florence, the S65 (Via Bologna) to the Medici Villas and Passo della Futa and the S302 to Borgo San Lorenzo (28km/40min), are both pretty drives. North of the river Sieve, though, winding mountain roads slow travelling times down considerably—count on at least two hours from Florence to Firenzuola (51km) and even more to Marradi (64km). Although it's possible to make a loop by train through the Mugello from Florence, passing through Pontassieve, Dicomano, Vicchio, Borgo San Lorenzo (from where another line continues over the Apennines to Faenza, by way of Marradi), San Piero a Sieve, and Vàglia, SITA buses are more scenic and just as infrequent; check timetables before setting out (most pass through the junction at San Piero). Better still, hire a car.

The Original Medici Villa

Following Via Bologna (S65) north, past the gardens of **Pratolino**, one of the last Medici villas (*see* **Florence**, 'Medici Villas', p.173), it's a panoramic and winding 30km to two of the very first. On the way, a slight detour to the east (from Pratolino or Vàglia) ascends to **Monte Senario** (817m), where in 1233 seven wealthy noblemen from Florence founded the mendicant Servite Order, living in the grottoes and building simple cells in the woods, which you can still see. The Servites went on to build Santissima Annunziata in Florence, but their monastery here, rebuilt in the 16th century, is less striking than the remarkable views over the Arno valley and Mugello.

Further north, towards San Piero a Sieve, there's a turn-off to the west on an untarred road for the Medici **Castello di Trebbio**, an ancient family estate remodelled in 1461 by Michelozzo into a fortified villa with a tower. It has a formal Italian garden, which you can visit; the interior is open only on the first Tuesday of each month (*for details, contact the Municipio of S. Piero—see p. 210*).

A bit further up looms the even grander **Villa Cafaggiolo**, the favourite old estate of Cosimo il Vecchio and Lorenzo il Magnifico, who spent as much of the summer in its cool halls as possible. Cosimo had Michelozzo expand and transform this ancient family seat into an imposing castellated villa, its entrance protected by a bulging tower, adorned with an incongruous clock. There's no admittance to Cafaggiolo, though you can walk through the grounds. To the east of the villa, a minor road leads up to the lovely wooded **Bosco ai Frati**, with a simple porticoed church also by Michelozzo; inside there's a fine Crucifix by Donatello, and another attributed to Desiderio da Settignano.

To the Passo della Futa

Just off the autostrada, the largest town on the western rim of the Mugello basin is **Barberino di Mugello**, a market town spread under the **Castello dei Cattani**. Barberino's 15th-century **Palazzo Pretorio**, like many in the region, is emblazoned with coats of arms; nearby stands yet another work by Michelozzo, the open **Loggie Medicee**.

On S65, 5km from Barberino at Colle Barucci, stands one of the grandest estates in the Mugello, the **Villa delle Maschere** ('of the masks'). Continue 14km north for the breathtaking views from the **Passo della Futa** (903m), a pass on the principal Apennine watershed; from here, the whole of the Mugello is spread out below like a relief map. Not surprisingly, in 1944, the Passo della Futa was the Germans' strong point on the Gothic Line—until the allies rendered it useless by capturing Firenzuola to the north. Beyond the pass the road passes under the craggy **Sasso di Castro** (1276m); at La Casetta you can turn off for Firenzuola (*see* below) or hotfoot it over the mountains in time for dinner in Bologna, the culinary capital of Italy.

Scarperia

Standing at the major crossroads of the S503 north and the S551 along the Sieve, **San Piero a Sieve** is a busy little town defended by a mighty Medici citadel, the **Fortezza di San Martino**, designed by Buontalenti in 1571. Its Romanesque parish church, with a façade of 1776, contains a remarkable octagonal baptismal font in polychrome terracotta, by Luca della Robbia. From here's it's 4km (30km from Florence) to **Scarperia**, the most charming little town in the Mugello, built high up on a shelf over the valley. Florence fortified it in 1306, and laid out its simple rectangular plan, with one long main street.

Scarperia's landmark is **Palazzo Pretorio** (1306), so heavily coated with stone and ceramic coats of arms that it resembles a page from a postage stamp album; its atrium and upper halls have 14th- and 15th-century frescoes, the earliest ones by the school of Giotto. The oratory of the **Madonna di Piazza** has an attractive Renaissance front and a cinquecento fresco of the Madonna and Child, attributed to Iacopo del Casentino; another church in Scarperia is dedicated to Our Lady of the Earthquakes with a fresco attributed by some to Filippo Lippi.

From the 16th century, Scarperia had the monopoly on the manufacture of cutlery in Tuscany, and supplied the duchy not only with knives, forks and scissors, but daggers and swords. At the turn of the century there were 46 thriving firms, though machine-made competition has since reduced this to a mere six who make shepherds' knives and other specialized tools—efforts are now being made to revive the old craft. Scarperia is better known these days for the **Autodromo Internazionale del Mugello**, a 5km track built by Florence's Auto Club in 1976, which sounds ghastly but is fairly well hidden in the hills east of town. Four km north of Scarperia you can visit the Mugello's most fascinating historical relic, the parish church of **Sant'Agata a Fagna**, which was constructed at the turn of the millennium and restored after an earthquake in 1919, with an unusual apse and a pulpit from 1175, decorated with white and green marble intarsia designs and animals.

Refreshingly cool even in August, **Firenzuola** is 22km north of Scarperia. A small holiday resort, it was devastated in World War II and rebuilt along the lines of the original street plan, between the Porta di Bologna and the Porta di Firenze. West 4km in **Cornacchiaia** there's a church believed to date back to Carolingian times.

The Mugello has quite a few hotels, most fairly pricey and nearly all located in the countryside, where you'll need a car to reach them. The most comfortable, in the resort of Bivigliano near Monte Senario, is ★★★**Giotto Park Hotel** and the cheaper **Giotto Park Hotel dipendenza**, Via Roma 11, © 406608, @ 406730 (*expensive or moderate for the dipendenza, depending on the season; there are cheaper rooms, some without bath in the annexe*), a small, newish but restful villa, set in a garden with a tennis-court. . In Barberino itself, ★★**Il Cavallo**, Via della Repubblica 7, © 8418144, @ 8418293 (*moderate, less without bath*), is a posthouse dating from the early 19th century. Il Cavallo also has a good restaurant (*moderate*), with fresh seafood specialities including pasta with scampi and a delicious surf and turf (seafood and beef) grill. In S. Piero a Sieve, ★★★**Ebe**, Via Provinciale 1A, © 848019, @ 848567 (*moderate*), has 25 pleasant rooms, attached to a fine restaurant (*also moderate*) that serves delicacies from nearby Emilia-Romagna like *tortellini* with orange filling and other delicious pasta dishes, as well as tender grilled meats. ★**Ebe Dipendenza**, Via di Cafaggio 11 (*inexpensive*), is a cheaper hotel and none of the rooms has a bath. In Scarperia ★★**Il Cantagallo**, Viale Kennedy 17, © 8430442, @ 8430443 (*inexpensive–moderate*), is a tidy little hotel overlooking a shady garden. In the mountains north of Firenzuola, at Pietramala, ★★★**Antica Casa Gualtieri**, Via Nazionale 81, © 813596, @ 813590 (*moderate*), is a charming place to help you beat the heat.

Borgo San Lorenzo and Vícchio

Borgo San Lorenzo (pop. 14,600) on the river Sieve, is the boom town of the Mugello, surrounded by new residential neighbourhoods with gardens full of little chameleons; and indeed they are fond of animals here, as evidenced by the **Statue of Fido** in honour of man's best friend, in Piazza Dante. Otherwise, the main sights are two fine Romanesque churches: **San Lorenzo**, with an unusual hexagonal campanile built in 1263, and 3km north, the parish church of **San Giovanni Maggiore**, where the bell tower is square at the base but octagonal on top; here, too, there is another lovely 12th-century pulpit in marble intarsia. To the north the road divides into S477 to **Palazzuolo sul Senio** and S302 to **Marradi**, both small resorts as well; in Palazzuolo you can visit a small **Ethnographic Museum** in the 14th-century Palazzo dei Capitani (*open July–Aug 3–7.30; Mar–June and Sept–Dec, Sun only 2.30–6.30; closed Jan and Feb*).

Vícchio, east of San Lorenzo, is a sleepy little town that gave birth to the Blessed Fra Angelico (Giovanni da Fiesole, 1387–1455) and was often home away from home for Benvenuto Cellini. The Palazzo Pretorio contains the **Museo Comunale Beato**

Angelico (*by request;* ✆ *8947026*), with detached frescoes, Etruscan finds from nearby Poggio alla Colla, and a 13th-century holy water stoup. Not to be outdone, the nearby and even more minute hamlet of **Vespignano** was the birthplace of Giotto di Bondone (1267–1337). The simple stone cottage where the father of Renaissance painting is said to have first seen the light of day has been carefully restored as the **Casa di Giotto** (*open 3–7 Tues, Thurs, Sat and Sun in summer; in winter 3–7 Sun only*). According to tradition, Cimabue first discovered Giotto near the old (but also restored) bridge over the torrent Enza, where the young shepherd was sketching his sheep on a stone.

The Valdisieve

The lower Sieve valley is mostly industrial: **Dicomano** can boast of an interesting fresco by the school of Piero della Francesca but little else besides the junction for S67, which climbs east into a pretty range of mountains called the Alpi di San Benedetto. San Godenzo, 10km up S67, is the largest village here, site of an 11th-century **Benedictine abbey**; its plain church has a raised presbytery and a polyptych by the school of Giotto. From San Godenzo a road continues up to the birthplace of Andrea del Castagno, now called **Il Castagno d'Andrea** (727m), a small holiday village that translates as 'Andrew's chestnut', or you can continue winding 18km into the mountains to **S. Benedetto in Alpe**, with a 9th-century Benedictine abbey that sheltered Dante (*Inferno*, Canto XVI, 94–105), where horses may be hired to visit the enchanting Valle dell'Arquacheta with its pretty waterfall. In the old town of **Portico di Romagna** 11km further north, the Portinari family, including the beautiful Beatrice, spent their summers— their house still stands in the main street. Deeper into Romagna lie the fascinating medieval town of **Brisighella**, the ceramic city of **Faenza**, and **Ravenna**, not only filled with ravishing Byzantine mosaics from the time of Justinian but also the site of Dante's real tomb.

There is little along the lower Sieve, though **Rufina**, 10km south of Dicomano, is dominated by the 16th-century **Villa Poggio Reale**, of interest to wine lovers for its production of *Chianti Putto* and *Pomino* wines. In Poggio Reale there's a small wine museum (*call ahead,* ✆ *839003*). From **Pontassieve**, a large town at the confluence of the Sieve and the Arno, scenic S70 leads up to the dramatic **Passo della Consuma** (1023m) before descending into the Casentino (*see* p.403).

The Valdarno, Prato and Pistoia

There are two routes between Florence and Pisa, whether you travel by car, bus or train. The route along the Arno, often hemmed in by the hills, has always been historically and economically the least important and carries less traffic; the large cities of Prato, Pistoia and Lucca grew up in an arc north of the Monte Albano hills, where there's more fertile land and room to grow. The first route described, along the Arno, takes in the nearby Florentine towns of Vinci, Castelfiorentino and Certaldo.

Down the Arno to Pisa

Getting Around

If you're driving, persist: the Florentine sprawl finally gives way at Signa and after that the Arno road (S67) becomes even scenic in stretches. LAZZI buses take the main route to Pisa; SITA goes directly from Florence to Castelfiorentino or Certaldo; for Vinci, COPIT. Trains at least once an hour follow the Arno between Florence and Pisa, and at Empoli turn off for Castelfiorentino, Certaldo, Poggibonsi and Siena. Note that San Miniato and Fucecchio share a railway station; local buses commute from there to both centres.

Florence to Empoli

The old Florentine satellite town of **Scandicci** (6km west), once in the business of renting villas to foreigners like Dylan Thomas and D.H. Lawrence (who finished *Lady Chatterley's Lover* here), has since the war found more profit in industry. Most of the towns along the Arno specialize in certain products; in **Lastra a Signa** it's straw goods, sold in many village shops. Lastra retains its 14th-century walls and the **Loggia di Sant'Antonio**, all that survives of the hospital founded by Florence's Silk Guild in 1411; many believe Brunelleschi was the architect, and that the work was a prototype of Florence's Spedale degli Innocenti, which the same guild also funded. Just outside Lastra, the church of **San Martino a Gangalandi** contains a beautiful, semicircular apse with *pietra serena* articulation designed by Alberti. In **Signa**, the next village, the Romanesque church of **San Lorenzo** houses a remarkable 12th-century marble pulpit and trecento frescoes.

After Signa the road and river continue 12km through a gorge before **Montelupo Fiorentino**, celebrated for its terracottas and delicately painted ceramics since the Renaissance. The new **Museo Archeologico e della Ceramica**, Via Baccio Sinaldi 45 (*open 2.30–7, closed Mon; adm*), has examples from nearly every period, and a display on the lower Valdarno's prehistory, while Montelupo's shops would be happy to sell you a more recent ceramic creation. The old **castle** here was built by the Florentines in 1203, during the wars against Pisa; the church **San Giovanni Evangelista** contains a lovely *Madonna and Saints* by Botticelli and his assistants. On the outskirts of Montelupo, you can see Buontalenti's **Villa Ambrosiana** (1587) from the outside, though you'll probably want to avoid being invited in—it's a mental hospital. From Montelupo a road leads in 20km southeast to San Casciano in Val di Pesa in Chianti (*see* p.197).

Empoli

The modern market town of Empoli, 32km from Florence, was witness to one of the turning points in Tuscan history: in 1260, the Ghibellines of Siena, fresh from their great victory over Florence at Monteaperti, held a parliament in Empoli to decide the fate of their archenemy. Everyone was for razing Florence to the ground, once and for all, and waited for the approval of their leader, Farinata degli Uberti. The Uberti were Florentine gangster nobles famous for their hatred of their fellow citizens, but Farinata surprised all

The Valdarno, Prato and Pistoia

Land over 200 metres

10 km
5 miles

N

when he stood up and announced that, even if he had to stand alone, he would defend Florence for as long as he lived. The Sienese let their captain have his way, and lost their chance of ever becoming *numero uno* in Tuscany. The prosperous new Empoli (pop. 45,000) produces green glass and raincoats; little in it recalls the days of Farinata, until you reach the piazza named after him: here is the palace where the parliament convened, across from Empoli's gem of a Romanesque church, the **Collegiata Sant'Andrea**, with its green and white marble geometric façade in the style of Florence's San Miniato. The lower portion dates from 1093; the upper had to wait until the 18th century, but it harmonizes extremely well.

Tourist Information

Piazza Farinata degli Uberti 9, ✆ (0571) 76 115.

The Pinacoteca

Empoli has its share of 13th- and 14th-century Florentine art as well, much of it now in the small but choice **Pinacoteca** in the Collegiata's cloister (*open 9–12, also 4–7 Thurs, Fri and Sat, closed Mon; adm; if no one's there, ask at the Libreria S. Paolo*). The most celebrated work is Masolino's *Pietà* fresco, with its poignant faces; upstairs there's an elegant relief of the *Madonna and Child* by Mino da Fiesole, a marble *Annunciation* group by Bernardo Rossellino, and a painted tabernacle of *St Sebastian* by his brother Antonio. Lorenzo Monaco contributes a long-eyed *Madonna and Saints*; in Lorenzo di Bicci's scene of San Nicola da Tolentino shielding Empoli from a rain of plague arrows is a quattrocento view of the city. There are a rare series of frescoes by Masolino's master, Starnina, two saints by Pontormo, who was born nearby, and the fine *Tabernacle of the Holy Sacrament* by Francesco Botticini and his son Raffaello, with a good predella. The upper Loggia has works by Andrea della Robbia, and the suspended wooden wings of the donkey that is made to fly down on a wire from the church tower on *Corpus Domine* (although a papier-mâché donkey has of late replaced the original one). Empoli's **Santo Stefano** church has another beautiful fresco by Masolino, but it's only open Saturday evenings for mass.

Cerreto Guidi and Vinci

Northwest of Empoli, in the Monte Albano, lies the old hill townlet of **Cerreto Guidi** (COPIT buses from Piazza Vittoria), former property of the Counts of Guidi and taken over by Florence in 1237. It is known these days for its *Chianti Putto*, and for the **Villa Medicea**, rebuilt by Cosimo I, a relatively simple cottage as Medici villas go, but approached by a grandiose double ramp of bricks called the 'Medici bridges', built by Buontalenti. The grand dukes came here often until 1576, when Cosimo I's daughter Isabella was murdered here by her husband Paolo Orsini for her infidelities; if you look carefully you can find the unhappy couple among the scores of Medici portraits that form the villa's chief decoration (*open 9–7 summer, 9–5 winter; 9–2 Sun, closed Mon; adm*). From the terrace there are fine views of the Monte Albano, almost treeless here.

From Cerreto it's 5km to **Vinci**, a tiny town set among hills of olives and vines. It is, of course, most famous as the home of Leonardo, who was born in a humble house in Archiano on 15 April 1452, the illegitimate son of the local notary and a peasant girl. In his honour, the town's landmark Conti Guidi Castle has been converted into the **Museo Leonardiano** (*open daily 9.30–7, 9.30–6 in winter; adm*), packed full of models of inventions he designed in his *Codex Atlanticus* notebooks, most of which this supreme 'Renaissance man' never had the time or attention span to build. The museum has kindly added descriptions in English of the nearly 100 machines, including some inspired by those invented by Brunelleschi to build Florence's cathedral dome: a flying machine, paddle boat, spring-driven mechanical car, an almost perfect modern bicycle, diving gear, a parachute, and a device to walk on water.

Also present are Leonardo's famous tank, machine-gun and helicopter. 'I'll do anything for money', this otherwise gentle fellow once said, surely one of the most startling quotes of the Renaissance. But nothing could be more typical of the age than brilliance combined with utter immorality; while he often neglected his art, Leonardo was always happy to help the bellicose princes who employed him with their military problems. We should probably be thankful that these gadgets never escaped from his notebook. Leonardo was baptized in the font in **Santa Croce**, next door to the museum.

From Vinci it's a 3km walk (or drive) southeast to **Anchiano** (*open 9.30–1 and 3.30–6, 2.30–5 in winter, closed Wed*), where the simple stone house where Leonardo was born has been restored. There are plans to restore the beautiful landscape between Vinci and Archiano to its 16th-century appearance.

San Miniato

Just southwest of Empoli, the river Elsa flows into the Arno near **San Miniato** (pop. 23,000), a refined old hill town that grew up at the crossroads of the Via Francigena (the main pilgrimage route from France to Rome) and the Florence–Pisa road; on a clear day the view takes in everything from Fiesole to the sea. Its defensibility and strategic location made it the Tuscan residence of the Emperors, from Otto IV to Frederick II; Matilda of Tuscany was born here in 1046, and in the 12th century it was an important imperial fortress, protecting the crossroads and levying tolls on travellers and merchandise. Of the citadel, only two towers survive: the present campanile of the cathedral and the taller 'Torrione', in the shady Prato del Duomo that crowns San Miniato, with peculiar chimney-like structures on top. It was from the top of this tower that Frederick II's secretary and court poet Pier della Vigna, falsely accused of treason, leapt to his death, to be discovered by Dante in the forest of suicides (*Inferno* XIII). Also in the Prato del Duomo stands the 12th-century **Palazzo dei Vicari dell'Imperatore** and the **Duomo** itself, with a Romanesque brick façade, incorporating pieces of sculpted marble and

13th-century majolica that catch the light as the sun sets. Most of the art in the interior is Baroque, except for a fine 13th-century holy water stoup, while most of the earlier artworks from the region have been placed in the **Diocesan Museum**, to the left of the cathedral (*open 9–12, 4–7, closed Mon; winter 9–12 and 2.30–5 Sat and Sun; adm*). Among the prizes are the fresco of the *Maestà* by the Sienese 'Maestro degli Ordini', a bust of Christ attributed to Verrocchio, Neri di Bicci's *Madonna con Bambino* and a *Crucifixion* by Filippo Lippi. Since 1968, the Prato del Duomo has been the site of the **National Kite Flying Contest** every first Sunday after Easter.

More art awaits in the Piazza del Popolo's 14th-century church of **San Domenico**— minor works by Masolino, Pisanello, the della Robbias, and Bernardo Rossellino, who carved the fine *tomb of Giovanni Chiellini*, the Florentine founder of San Miniato's Hospital of Poor Pilgrim Priests in the 15th century; the tomb is modelled after Rossellino's famous tomb of Leonardo Bruni in Florence's Santa Croce. Another beautiful church is **San Francesco** with remains of frescoes by a follower of Masolino.

Kite contests aren't the only sideline to San Miniato—there's a visit paid by Napoleon in 1797, not to glory in this old seat of emperors but to visit his relatives in the **Palazzo Bonaparte**. In the surrounding countryside are rich caches of white truffles, hunted fervently in the autumn for the large market on the last Sunday in November; and many of what appear to be plain-looking Romanesque churches around San Miniato are actually tobacco-curing barns from the 1900s.

Castelfiorentino and San Vivaldo

Some 12km south along the Valdelsa from San Miniato, **Castelfiorentino** (pop. 18,000) is another old hill town, though much rebuilt after damage in World War II. Castelfiorentino's church of **Santa Verdiana** dates from the 18th century and houses the local **Pinacoteca** (*at present closed for restoration*), with some excellent trecento paintings, including a lovely Sienese *Madonna* attributed to Duccio da Buoninsegna, another one by Francesco Granacci, and a triptych by Taddeo Gaddi. The **Cappella della Visitazione** (Via Gozzoli 55) is covered with frescoes by the charming Benozzo Gozzoli and his school (*at the time of writing being restored*).

One of the more unusual sights in Tuscany, the **Monastery of San Vivaldo**, lies in the rather empty zone to the southwest of Castelfiorentino, beyond the old village of Montaione. Vivaldo was a hermit from San Gimignano who lived in a hollow chestnut tree and was found dead there in 1301, still in the attitude of prayer. A Franciscan community grew up in his footsteps, and in 1500, when the monastery was being rebuilt, one member, Fra Tommaso da Firenze, had the idea of taking advantage of the monastery's wooded hills to build a 'New Jerusalem' with 34 chapels replicating the sites of Christ's Passion. To make the symbolic journey seem even more real to pilgrims, the 34 chapels combined polychrome terracottas by Giovanni della Robbia and others, set in frescoes—Pope Leo X immediately granted a fat indulgence to anyone who did the whole route. Today only 17 of the chapels survive, in a lovely wooded setting.

Certaldo

Certaldo (pop. 16,000), former seat of Florence's deputy, or Vicarate of the Valdelsa, is synonymous with Giovanni Boccaccio, who spent the last 13 years of his life up in the lovely old town, known as Castello, which could be a set for the *Decameron* itself. Everything here is of good, honest brick, from the pavements to the palazzi, of which the most striking is the 14th-century castellated **Palazzo Pretorio**, studded with the arms of the former Vicars. Inside it has a beautiful courtyard and museum (*open 10–12.30, 4–7.30 summer, 10–12, 3.30–6 winter; adm*) containing Etruscan artefacts, detached frescoes, and in the annexed church and cloister, Gozzoli's *Tabernacle of the Punished*, not one of his more cheerful works. In the old jail the walls still bear the forlorn *graffiti* of past prisoners.

The house traditionally associated with Certaldo's great author, the **Casa di Boccaccio**, Via Boccaccio 18, has been restored and is now the seat of the International Centre of Boccaccio Studies (*open 9–12 and 3–6*). Boccaccio died here in 1375 and lies buried in **Santi Michele ed Iacopo**, under an epitaph he penned himself; a 16th-century monument erected in his honour was destroyed by prudes in 1783. Boccaccio himself in his later years regretted the racy frivolity of his most famous book, wishing he had spent his time on serious Latin works—not a regret too many people have ever shared. From Certaldo a pretty road leads 13km south to **San Gimignano** (*see* p.350).

© (0571–)   ***Where to Stay and Eating Out***

The lower Arno Valley isn't exactly awash in pleasure domes, but neither will you have to sleep in the car or starve. If it's time to eat just as you're leaving or approaching Florence, consider a stop at **Fiore**, Via di Marciola 112, in Santa Maria a Marciola, near Scandicci, © (055) 768678 (*moderate to expensive*), not only for its delicious crêpes and *fritto misto* of meats and greens, but for its lovely garden setting and pine-clad slopes. *Closed Wed.* Further along in Montelupo, **★★★Tonio**, Via 1 Maggio 23, © 541444, ◎ 541436 (*moderate to expensive*), is a pleasant place to relax, with a large garden and nice, cool rooms in the summer. Vinci has the flagrantly touristy **Da Pippo** near the Leonardo museum, Via della Torre 19, © 56100 (*moderate*); the fare is undistinguished, but there's a pretty view from the terrace.

In Empoli, fresh fish dishes are to be had at **Il Galeone**, Via Curtatone e Montanara 67, © 72826 (*moderate*). *Closed Sun.*

In San Miniato, you can sleep near the top of the town at **★★★Miravalle**, Piazza Castello 3, © 418075, ◎ 419681 (*moderate to expensive*), located in Frederick II's 12th-century imperial palace. **Il Canapone**, Piazza Bonaparte 5, © 418121 (*moderate to expensive*), is a simple place where you can try the local truffles on spaghetti, in risotto, or with veal *scaloppine*; in the spring there's rice with asparagus. *Closed Mon.* Certaldo has three small hotels, of which the most interesting are **★★Il Castello**, Via della Rena 6, © and ❀ 668250 (*moderate*); and **★★★Osteria del Vicario**, Via Rivellino 3, © and ❀ 668228 (*rooms moderate, restaurant expensive*), a beautiful 12th-century ex-monastery with a garden surrounded by a Romanesque courtyard. The rooms are simple with terracotta floors and the restaurant serves fresh local food.

Empoli to Pisa

There is no compelling reason to stop in the lower Valdarno unless you're running low on petrol. If you're spending more time here, consider a visit to **Fucecchio** for its panoramic views, or **Montòpoli in Val d'Arno**, a tiny medieval town dating from the 11th century on the south bank. Further down-river lies industrial **Pontedera**, where the Piaggio Company produces most of Italy's motor-scooters. Here you may detour south on S439 to Volterra (*see* p.360), by way of **Ponsacco** and the four-towered **Villa di Camugliano**, built by Alessandro and Cosimo I, an example of far-flung Medici real estate speculation. Between here and Volterra roll the Pisan Hills, some of the quietest, more rural countryside in Tuscany; the main attraction here may be precisely its lack of art and history. Alternatively, from Ponsacco, you can head southwest to tiny **Lari**, with the remains of a Medici fortress, and if your rheumatism is acting up, to **Casciana Terme**, famous for its cures in Roman times, and rebuilt by the Pisans in the 14th century. **Rivalto**, a hamlet 6km south of the spa, has almost perfectly preserved its medieval character.

Vicopisano, north of the Arno, defended the eastern frontier of Pisa from the ambitions of Lucca, and its impressive *castello* was remodelled by Brunelleschi after the Florentine conquest of Pisa; now vineyards surround its mighty walls and towers. Across the bridge, **Cascina** still has most of its medieval walls and Roman grid plan from its days as a military camp. There are three churches worth visiting: **San Casciano**, an unusual 12th-century Romanesque church, with blind arches and some fine sculptural details; Romanesque **San Benedetto a Settimo**, adorned with a 14th-century alabaster altarpiece of Irish origin; and **San Giovanni Evangelista**, built by the Knights of St John, with trecento Sienese frescoes, recently restored after the church was used as a barn for several centuries. Further west lies the Certosa of Pisa (8km) and Pisa itself (14km; *see* p.276).

Where to Stay and Eating Out

You can find a good inland seafood restaurant in Fucecchio: **Le Vedute**, Via Romana-Lucchese 121, © (0571) 297201 (*expensive*), a pleasant country place, where in summer you can linger on the veranda over your favourite denizen of the deep—good meats as well, especially in autumn. *Closed Mon.* Also in Fucecchio is **★★★La Campagnola**, Viale Colombo 144, © (0571) 260786, ❀ 261781 (*moderate*), with 25 air-conditioned rooms. Across the Arno, in little Montòpoli in Val d'Arno, the old town hall has been converted into an inn, **★★★Quattro Gigli**, Piazza Michele 2, © (0571) 466878, ❀ 466879 (*inexpensive* *without bath, moderate with*), with 28 rooms of varying quality. The restaurant (*moderate*), beyond the permanent display of Montòpoli's painted ceramics, features an imaginative menu, based on Tuscan dishes, with plenty of mushrooms, vegetables and salads depending on the season, and an Italian rarity—roast potatoes. The duck and game dishes are excellent. *Closed Sun evening and Mon.* If you feel irresistibly drawn to the solitude of the Pisan hills, there are plenty of rooms in Casciana Terme, and a good restaurant in Perignano, near Ponsacco, **Lido**, Via Livornese 322, *℗* (0587) 616020 (*moderate*), featuring warm seafood antipasti for starters and sea bass. *Closed Mon evening and Tues.*

Prato

Prato is only 18km from Florence but a world away in atmosphere; this is a city that works for its living, where the population has doubled since World War II to 145,000, the third in Tuscany after Florence and Livorno. And a vibrantly, joyously proletarian city it is, fond of Henry Moore and comic books and avant-garde theatre and Heavy Metal bars, full of people wanting you to sign petitions or buy encyclopaedias, who are proud to live in 'the Manchester of Tuscany'. Living in Florence's shadow for the past thousand years has not dampened Prato's spirits as much as one might suppose; as in the days of the famous Merchant of Prato immortalized in Iris Origo's book (*see* **Further Reading**, p.443), this city still makes its living from the manufacture of textiles, and especially the recycling of old wool and rags. And in the Renaissance Prato made enough profit from these rags to hire the greatest artists of the day to embellish its churches and palaces.

History

Prato made its historical debut in the 9th century, under the name of Borgo al Cornio; outside the town was a meadow, or *prato*, site of the market and fortifications, which gradually became so important that the whole town took the name. It was first ruled by the Alberti, one of the region's more ambitious feudal families, who conquered lands from the Maremma to the Mugello. In 1107 Countess Matilda personally led a combined Tuscan army against Prato to humble the Alberti; in 1140 the Pratesi humbled their counts even more by taking away most of their power and running their city as a free *comune*. In 1193, at the height of its power, it even managed to snatch some of Florence's own *contado*. By this time Prato was one of Europe's most important manufacturers of woollens, so wealthy that the University of Paris even had a special college for students from Prato. Florence, however, could not countenance so near and ambitious a rival, and in 1350, on the charges of fomenting rebellion in the Valdelsa, Florence besieged Prato, and an honourable peace was made; the next year Florence cemented its hold over its neighbour by *purchasing* it for 17,500 florins from its nominal overlord, the Angevin Queen of Naples.

Despite the ignominy of being bought, Prato functioned more as Florence's ally than its possession, retaining a certain amount of local autonomy. The late 14th century was the

Prato

to Bologna

VIA BOLOGNA

VIA STROZZI

Piazza
Ciardi

P

Stazione Porta
al Serraglio

Sant'
Agostino

VIA S. FABIANO

Piazza
S. Agostino

VIA CURTATONE

VIA DEL SERRAGLIO

VIA STUFA

VIA DEL SEMINARIO

VIA MAGNOLFI

to Pistoia

VIA LUTI

VIA FILIPPINO

VIA S. VINCENZO

Cap
Bus Terminal

Piazza
Landi

VIA L. MUZZI

Piazza
del Duomo

Museo dell'Opera
del Duomo

M

VIA CAVOUR

Tourist
Office   i

Duomo

VIA DEL TINTOR

CORSO SAVONAROLA

San
Domenico

VIA C. GUASTI

Palazzo
Comunale

V. G. MAZZONI

VIA G. GARIBALDI

P

Galleria
Comunale

VIA BANCHELLI

Piazza
del
Comune

VIA DELLA MISERCORDIA

VIA S. CATERINA

Palazzo
Datini

V. RICASOLI

VIA CAIROLI

Santa Maria
delle Carceri

i

VIA VERDI

Teatro
Metastasio

Piazza
S. Francesco
S. d'Assisi

Piazza
S. Maria delle
Carceri

P

Lazzi
Bus Terminal

San
Francesco

Castello
dell'Imperatore

VIA G. MAZZINI

Piazza
del Collegio

P

VIA S. JACOPO

VIALE PIAVE

VIA S. TRINITA

VIA CARBONAIA

VIA S. CHIARA

VIA DELL' ABBACO

VIA CARRADORI

VIA FRASCATI

VIA   POMERIA

VIA ROMA

N

250 metres
250 yards

day of Francesco di Marco Datini, the Merchant of Prato, one of the richest men in the world and history's first recorded workaholic businessman. Yet although he built his palace in his hometown of Prato, the big profits were in Florence, and Datini spent most of his time there. Under the influence of Savonarola's preaching, Prato joined Florence in rebelling against Medici rule, but was soon to play the unfortunate role of whipping boy, when the Spaniards, at the instigation of the Medici Pope Leo X, besieged and sacked the city with an unheard-of brutality. Since that dark day, Prato's history has followed that of its imperious neighbour.

Getting Around

Prato is easily reached by train from Florence (18km/25mins), Pistoia (17km/25mins) or Bologna (85km/55mins), and has two stations, the **Stazione Centrale**, facing a pretty green square just on the other bank of Prato's river, the Bisenzio; and the **Stazione Porta al Serraglio**, just north of the walls and closer to the centre, on the Florence–Pistoia line. This was one of Italy's first railways, built in 1848 for the Lorraine grand dukes by an Englishman named Ralph Bonfield, who so pleased the grand duke that he was made the Count of St George of Prato. These days, the Prato tourist office is searching for his descendants, to claim the title and supply a likeness of Bonfield so they can erect a proper monument in his honour. All Bonfields take note! **Buses** from Prato depart from the Piazza del Duomo (CAP buses, every half-hour to Florence and Mugello) and Piazza San Francesco (LAZZI buses, to Florence, Pistoia, Montecatini, Lucca, Pisa and Viareggio). Prato has an exit on the autostrada A11 between Florence and Pisa (from Florence get on it at Peretola). Note that the centre is closed to traffic; Piazza Mercatale is a convenient place to park.

Tourist Information

Via L. Muzzi 51, near the Duomo, © (0574) 35 141; Via Cairoli 48/52, © 24 112.

Frederick's Castle

Open 8.30–12.30 and 3–5.30, closed Tues.

Most people, whether arriving by car, bus, or at the Stazione Centrale, approach the walled core of Prato through the Piazza San Marco, embellished with a white puffy sculpture by Henry Moore from 1970. Viale Piave continues to the defiantly Ghibelline swallowtail crenellations of the **Castello dell'Imperatore**. This marks a strange interlude in Prato's past, built in 1237 by Frederick II, Holy Roman Emperor, Swabian and Hohenstaufen heir to the Normans in southern Italy and Sicily. Frederick, unlike his grandfather Frederick Barbarossa, never spent much time in Tuscany, preferring his more civilized dominions in Apulia and Sicily, where he could discuss poetry, philosophy and falconry (in Arabic or Latin) with his court scholars. When he did come, it was in magnificent progress featuring dancing girls, elephants and the Moslem imperial bodyguard. His Tuscan taxpayers were not impressed; neither did they much appreciate Frederick's tolerant, syncretistic approach to religion. The popes excommunicated him twice. He built this castle here because he had to, not so much to defend Prato, but to defend his imperial *podestà* from the Pratesi, and perhaps to impress the locals with its design—its clean lines must have seemed very sharp and modern in the 13th century. There is nothing in it any more, though the city often uses the space for special exhibitions. Usually it's possible to walk up along its walls for a bird's-eye view of Prato.

Next to the castle stands the unfinished black and white marble face of **Santa Maria delle Carceri**, begun in 1485 by Giuliano da Sangallo. Brunelleschian architecture was always a fragile blossom, as is shown clearly by the failure of this sole serious attempt to transplant it outside the walls of Florence. Santa Maria always merits a mention in architectural histories. It was an audacious enterprise; Sangallo, a furiously diligent student of Vitruvius and Alberti, attempted a building based entirely on philosophical principles. Order, simplicity and correct proportion, as in Brunelleschi's churches, were to be manifest, with no frills allowed. Sangallo, the favourite of Lorenzo il Magnifico, proved unfortunately a better theorist than architect. Santa Maria turned out tedious and clumsy, a tombstone for the theoretical architecture that was a fad in the 1400s, more often expressed in paintings than actual buildings. The interior is better than the exterior, a plain Greek cross very much in the Brunelleschian manner with a decorative frieze and tondi of the four Evangelists by Andrea della Robbia. The name of the church—*carceri* means prisons—refers to a miracle, a speaking image of the Virgin painted on a nearby prison wall, that occasioned the building of the church. Behind the church is Prato's celebrated theatre, the **Teatro Metastasio**, one of the most acclaimed and innovative in Italy.

Piazza San Francesco and Datini

From Santa Maria delle Carceri you can see the apse of Prato's huge brick church of **San Francesco**, dating from the end of the 13th century, and embellished in front with white and green marble stripes. Inside, on the left wall is the *Tomb of Gemignano Inghirami*, one of Europe's crack lawyers of the quattrocento, the design attributed to Bernardo Rossellino (1460s); while near the altar is the **tomb slab of Francesco di Marco Datini**

(1330–1410) by Niccolò di Piero Lamberti. Off the elegant Renaissance cloister you'll find the entrance to the **Cappella Migliorati**, beautifully frescoed in 1395 by Niccolò di Pietro Gerini, one of the period's finest draughtsmen; here he depicts the *Lives of Saints Anthony Abbot and Matthew.*

Niccolò also frescoed the **Palazzo Datini** (nearby on Via Rinaldesca), the showplace palace built in the 1390s by the Merchant of Prato. If there were an Accountants' Hall of Fame, Francesco di Marco Datini would surely be in it; he helped invent that dismal science. Nor did he ever let anyone throw anything away, leaving to posterity 150,000 documents, ledgers (all inscribed: 'For God and Profit') and private letters that are stored in the archives in this palace; these formed the basis for Iris Origo's fascinating account of his life and times. Datini left nearly all of his indecent fortune to the Ceppo, a Pratese charity he founded in 1410 and which now has its headquarters on the first floor of this palace; in gratitude the city had the façade frescoed with scenes of his life, unfortunately now much faded.

Galleria Comunale

Open 9.30–12.30 and 3–6.30, closed Tues and Sun pm; adm.

Just north lies Prato's charming civic centre, the **Piazza del Comune**, decorated with a 19th-century **statue of Datini** with bronze reliefs of the merchant's life, and a pretty fountain by Tacca nicknamed 'Il Bacchino', or Little Bacchus (1659). The city's **Palazzo Comunale**, behind the portico, retains only traces of its medieval heritage; drop in to see its **Sala di Consiglio** with its coffered ceiling, two quattrocento frescoes and portraits of the grand dukes. The rugged **Palazzo Pretorio** is nothing but medieval, a relic of the days when Prato governed itself without any help from the Medici; the stair on the façade leads up to the **Galleria Comunale** with a good collection of mostly Florentine art: there's a tabernacle by Filippino Lippi, which he painted for his mother and which was later restored after damage in the war; up in the grand **Salone Udienza** with the fine wood ceiling is Bernardo Daddi's *Story of the Holy Girdle*, a predella telling the tale of Prato's most famous relic, the Virgin Mary's belt. According to tradition she gave it to Doubting Thomas, from whom it was passed down until it became part of the dowry of a woman who married Michele, a knight from Prato during the First Crusade. Michele returned to Prato and hid the precious relic under his mattress; angels lifted him off, and the girdle was given into the care of the cathedral. In the same hall are fine 14th-century works by Giovanni di Milano, Michele di Firenze, Lorenzo Monaco, and a tondo attributed to Luca Signorelli. Filippo Lippi painted the *Madonna del Ceppo* for the Ceppo offices in the Palazzo Datini; it portrays the tycoon himself, with four fellow donors, who contributed less and thus get portrayed as midgets. In an adjoining room, the most curious work is by Battistello, a follower of Caravaggio, whose unique *Noli me tangere* portrays Christ wearing a fedora at a rakish angle, doing a quick dance step to evade the Magdalene's touch.

Cathedral of Santo Stefano

In the centre of Prato rises its cathedral, like a faded beauty who never recovered from the blow of a broken engagement. It was begun with great promise in the 13th century, and added to on and off for the next 200 years, with ever dwindling passion and money.

Its best features are an exotic, almost Moorish campanile, an Andrea della Robbia lunette of the Madonna and St Stephen over the door, a big clock on the half-striped façade that makes you smile when you notice it sitting where the rose window ought to be, and above all, the circular **Pulpit of the Sacred Girdle**, projecting from the corner of the façade. Perhaps no other church in Italy has such a perfectly felicitous ornament, something beautiful and special that the Pratesi look at every day as they walk through the piazza. Michelozzo designed it (1428) and Donatello added the delightful reliefs of dancing children and *putti* (replaced by casts), along the lines of his *cantoria* in Florence's cathedral museum. The Holy Girdle is publicly displayed from here five times a year: Easter Day, 1 May, 15 August, 8 September and Christmas Day.

The Duomo's interior continues the motif of green and white stripes in its Romanesque arcades and ribs of the vaulting. The **Chapel of the Sacred Girdle**, just to the left as you enter, is protected by a screen, and within is covered with frescoes by Agnolo Gaddi on the legend of the Girdle (*see above*), and adorned with a beautiful marble statue of the *Madonna and Child* by Giovanni Pisano. In the left aisle there's a masterful **pulpit** carved by Mino da Fiesole and Antonio Rossellino, with harpies around the base. Bring L500 to illuminate Filippo Lippi's celebrated frescoes in the choir, on the *Lives of Saints John the Baptist and Stephen* (recently restored), the merry monk's first major work (1452–66); while painting these scenes, Lippi fell in love with a brown-eyed novice, Lucrezia Buti, who according to tradition posed for his magnificent *Herod's Banquet*, either as the melancholy Salome herself or as the figure in the long white dress, second from the right; Fra Filippo placed himself among the mourners for St Stephen, third from the right, in a red hat. The less lyrical frescoes in the next chapel (lit along with the choir) are by Uccello and Andrea di Giusto. There's a lovely, almost Art Nouveau candelabra on the high altar by Maso di Bartolomeo (1440s), a close relative to Maso's work in Pistoia cathedral.

The **Museo dell'Opera del Duomo** (*open 9.30–12.30, 3–6.30, 9.30–12.30 Sun, closed Tues; adm*) is located next door in the cloister, one side of which retains its 12th-century geometric marble decorations and rambunctious capitals. The tragic star of the museum is the original pulpit of the Sacred Girdle with Donatello's merrily dancing *putti* made lepers by car exhaust. Lippi's recently restored *Death of San Girolamo* was painted to prove to the bishop that he was the man to fresco the cathedral choir. Other works include his son Filippino's *St Lucy* with her lamp, blissfully ignoring the knife in her throat, and another full-length portrait, of *Fra Jacopone di Todi*, believed to be an early work by Uccello. More dancing *putti* adorn the *Reliquary of the Sacred Girdle* (1446) by Maso di Bartolomeo, which was stolen but recently recovered at the Todi antique fair. Also worth seeing are the saccharine *Guardian Angel* by Carlo Dolci, a sophisticated Madonna with saints by the quattrocento 'Master of the Nativity of Castello', and a strange reliquary that resembles a mushroom.

Walking Through Prato

Most of Prato's old streets are anonymous, self-effacing Tuscan. Some areas suffered bomb damage in the war, notably the great pear-shaped **Piazza del Mercatale** on the banks of the Bisenzio. This was long the working core of the city, surrounded entirely by porticoes and workshops; it was and is the site of Prato's big market and fairs. A few faded, peeling, porticoed buildings remain, overlooking the river that has laundered Prato's principal industry for eight centuries.

If it's Sunday, it's a good day to visit the sturdy brick **San Domenico** on the west side of town, a large Gothic church begun in 1283 and completed by Giovanni Pisano, one side of it lined with arcades. There's not much to see inside, but in the adjacent convent, the painter Fra Bartolomeo's home and Pratese address of Savonarola, there's the **Museum of Mural Painting** (*open 9–12, closed Tues, or © 29 339; adm*), a collection of detached frescoes from surrounding churches, worth a look for the charming quattrocento *graffiti* court scenes from the Palazzo Vaj, a sinopia from the cathedral attributed to Uccello, and Niccolò di Piero Gerini's *Tabernacle of the Ceppo*. Just north of San Domenico, **San Fabiano**, Via del Seminario 30, has an enchanting pre-Romanesque mosaic pavement, depicting mermaids, birds and dragons biting their own tails (*see* 'Pienza', p.380, for some idle speculation about these); north of San Fabiano 15th-century **Sant'Agostino** contains Prato's most ridiculous painting, the *Madonna della Consolazione* (attributed, naturally, to Vasari), who does her consoling by distributing belts from heaven. South of the city walls on Viale della Repubblica 9 (which begins at a bridge over the Bisenzio), one of Prato's textile institutes has a unique collection of fabrics and looms dating back to the 5th century AD in the **Museo del Tessuto** (*ask at the tourist office for information*).

Prato © (0574–) **Where to Stay**

Prato's hotels are mostly of the businessman variety, but can be a good bet in the summer when Florence is packed to the gills. Convenient if you're arriving by train, ★★★**San Marco**, between the Stazione Centrale and the Castello, Piazza San Marco 14, © 21321, 🖃 22378 (*moderate*), is a pleasant place. Over the river and in the hills to the east the relaxing ★★★**Villa Santa Cristina**, Via Poggio Secco 58, © 595951, 🖃 562623 (*expensive*), has a garden, pool and most other comforts. For modernity and air conditioning, try ★★★**Flora**, Via Cairoli 31, near S. Maria dei Carceri, © 33521 🖃 40289 (*moderate to expensive*). ★★**Stella d'Italia** is Prato's old-fashioned once–grand hotel, looking on to the cathedral in Piazza Duomo 8, © 27910, 🖃 40289 (*inexpensive*), with slightly faded rooms. On a quiet square just on the far side of the Stazione Porta al Serraglio, ★★**Toscana**, Piazza Ciardi 3, ✆ 28096, ✆ 25163 (*inexpensive*), is the best of the budget choice; some rooms are air-conditioned.

Prato ✆ (0574–)   ***Eating Out***

One reason for staying in Prato is the restaurants, especially if you like fish, the speciality of **Il Pirana**, Via Valentini 110 (south of Viale Vittorio Veneto, the main street between the central station and Piazza San Marco), ✆ 25746 (*expensive*). The Pirana has an entirely justifiable reputation as one of the best seafood restaurants in inland Tuscany; try the scampi. Opposite the Metastasio theatre, **Osvaldo Baroncelli**, Via Fra Bartolomeo 13, ✆ 23810 (*moderate*), is an unpretentious small establishment with an innovative chef who turns out dishes like tagliatelle with artichokes, veal *scaloppine* with truffles or stuffed celery, duck stuffed with its own kidney as well as more traditional Tuscan favourites. *Closed Sun and Wed evenings*. **Pietro**, Via Balbo 9a, ✆ 23025, is more elegant and serves among other things an exceptionally good *tiramisù*. The **Trattoria Lapo**, Piazza del Mercatale 141, ✆ 23745 (*moderate*), is unspectacular but usually crowded. For good food, especially the desserts, and a select choice of wine, the Pratesi head over to **Gliaccaniti**, Via Fiorentina 1, ✆ 583345 (*moderate*); in the evening they drift over to Piazza Sant'Agostino for tasty sandwiches, chips and beer. Homesick Brits and anglophiles in Prato meet at the **Nelson Pub**, Via M. Nistri, 51.

North of Prato: the Val di Bisenzio

Prato's river begins some 40km up in the Apennines, and along its valley runs S325, a secondary highway towards Bologna. This valley was long the fief of the Alberti counts, whose fortifications dot its steep sides. **Vaiano**, the first town on the main route, has a Romanesque abbey church and green-striped campanile as its landmark; just beyond are the impressive ruins of the Alberti's **Rocca di Cerbaia** (12th century). The highway continues to **Vernio** and **San Quirico**, with another ruined Alberti castle up above. From San Quirico's neighbour to the west, **Cantagallo** ('Cock's crow'), a lovely walking path leads up to the **Piano della Rasa** in little over an hour, a panoramic valley with an alpine refuge open between April and October. Further north on S325, at the small resort of **Montepiano**, the waters destined for the Tyrrhenian and Adriatic split and go their own ways. There is another ancient abbey here, the Vallombrosan **Badia di Santa Maria**, with good 13th- and 14th-century frescoes. From the abbey begins another fine walking path up to **Alpi di Cavarzano** (1008m), and from there, in another hour, up to the highest peak in the region, **Monte La Scoperta** (1278m).

Figline and Montemurlo

The old road between Prato and Pistoia passes near **Figline di Prato**, a medieval village known for its terracotta vases. Figline has a good 14th-century parish church with contemporary mural paintings, including a primitive *Last Supper* and a *St Michael* with a finely detailed background; a small parish museum contains other 'primitives'. **Montemurlo**, on its hill over the plain of Prato, is another medieval town; in 1537 its castle of the Guidi counts was the Alamo for the anti-Medici republican oligarchs of Florence, led by Filippo Strozzi, who were defeated here once and for all by the troops of Cosimo I. The old walled town of Montemurlo is interesting to explore, with an impressive and rather stylish **Rocca** for its crown, approached these days by a Mannerist ramp. The Romanesque church of 'Beheaded John' (**San Giovanni Decollato**) has a pretty campanile and some good art in its Baroqued interior, including a miraculous Byzantine crucifix and a 16th-century painting by Giovanni da Prato illustrating its story.

Pistoia

You know Pistoia (pop. 94,500) is near when the road plunges into a Lilliputian forest of miniature umbrella pines and cypresses, all in tidy rows. These are Italy's most extensive ornamental nurseries, a gentle craft that thrives in the rich soil at the foot of the Apennines. But Pistoia wasn't always content to cultivate its own garden; this is the place, after all, that gave us the word 'pistol'—originally surgical knives made in the city, and later coming to mean daggers and guns. Today it specializes in light rail trains (the Breda works built the cars for the Washington DC metro), mattresses, cymbals and baby trees. Its notorious, dark past lingers only in Florentine histories; modern Pistoiese laugh it off, and if you find the ghosts of its intrigues haunting the often grim, ancient lanes, there are plenty of lovely old churches where you can exorcize them. Although seldom sampled by the moveable feast of tourism, the historic centre of Pistoia is almost perfectly intact, and behind its medieval walls there is some fine art to be seen, part Pisan, part Florentine, reflecting its position between the two great rivals.

History

> *. . . Proud you are, envious, enemies of heaven,*
> *Friends to your own harm and, to your own neighbour,*
> *The simplest charity you find a labour.*

'Invective against the People of Pistoia', a sonnet by Michelangelo

Pistoia's fellow Tuscans have looked askance at her ever since Roman times, when the city was called *Pistoria* and saw the death struggle of the Catiline conspiracy, the famous attempted coup against the Roman Republic in 62 BC, which ended when the legions tracked down the escaped Catiline and his henchmen near Pistoia. Its position on the Via Cassia helped it prosper under the Lombards, who elevated it to a royal city. In 1158 Pistoia became a *comune*, and enough of a threat that Florence and Lucca ganged up against it twice. In the 13th century Pistoia's evil reputation gave it credit for having begun the bitter controversy between Black and White Guelphs that so obsessed Florence; Dante, himself a victim of that feud, never let a chance go by in the *Divina Commedia* to curse and condemn the fateful city. In 1306 Florence exacted revenge by capturing

Pistoia

200 metres
200 yards

N

to Abetone

VIA DALMAZIA

VIALE

PORTA AL BORGO

VIA PADRE I. DESIDERI

VIA DEL MOLINUZZO

Piazza S. Francesco d'Assisi

P

VIA

SANT' ANDREA

Sant' Andrea

Copit Bus Terminal

San Francesco

VIA P. BOZZI

VIA ABBI PAZIENZA

Giardino Pubblico

VIA S. VERGIOLESI

VIALE POLICARPO PETROCCHI

VIA DEI CANCELLIERI

VIA CURTATONE E MONTANARA

CORSO GRAMSCI

Madonna dell' Umilità

VIA G. MAZZINI

VIA DELLA MADONNA

VIA NICCOLO PUCCINI

CORSO GRAMSCI

to Montecatini and Zoo

VIALE MACALLE

VIA ATTO VANNUCCI

VIALE ANTONIO PACINOTTI

Piazza Treviso

VIA ATTO VANNUCCI

Lazzi Bus Terminal

VIALE VITTORIO VE

Stazione

228

VIALE ITALIA

VIA PADRE G. ANTONELLI

VIA DEGLI ARMENI

GIACOMO   MATTEOTTI

S. MARCO

Piazza
del Carmine

Ospedale
del Ceppo

P

Piazza
San Lorenzo

PORTA

VIA

DI

VIA DEL CARMINE   VIA DELLA PAPPE   VIA DEL CEPPO

ARCADIA

VIA DEL ROSSI

VIA DI SAPIENZA   VIA 27   APRILE

Piazza
Ospedale

VIA

VIA DEL BARONI

VIALE   DELL'

Piazza
S. Bartolomeo

BRACCIOLINI

VIA

Palazzo Comunale

Piazza
San Spirito

San Bartolomeo
in Pantano

Palazzo Pretorio   Piazza del
Duomo

RIPA DEL SALE

FILIPPO PACINI

VIA DEGLI ORAFI

Baptistry

VIA DEI FABBRI

Duomo

VIA DEL BOTTACCIO

VIA LAUDESI

Tourist Office/
Palazzo dei Vescovi

VIA ROMA

Piazza
Leone

VIA PALESTRO

VIA CAVOUR

San Giovanni
Fuorcivitas

VIA NEMORETO

VIA DEL CAN BIANCO

P

San Paolo

Piazza
Garibaldi

Capella
del Tau

CORSO S. FEDI   CORSO AMEDOLA

V. FERRUCCI

San
Domenico

PIAZZA   DELLA   RESISTENZA

VIA DI PORTA CARRATICA

P

Parco Pubblico

Fortezza
di Santa Barbara

VIA ATTILIO FROSINI

P

to Prato

Piazza
Leonardo
da Vinci

VIA IV NOVEMBRE

VIA PROV. PRATESE

VIA FIORENTINA

to Florence
and the Autostrada

Pistoia, and as usual adapted its politics to the nature of its conquest: Prato she made an ally, Pisa she held with fortresses, but Pistoia she controlled with factions. The only interlude came between 1315 and 1328, when Lucca's Castruccio Castracani held Pistoia as part of his short-lived empire, though after his fall the Florentines soon returned. The city, preoccupied with its own quarrels, carried on happily ever after, living well off its old speciality, iron-working. It supplied the conspirators of Europe with fine daggers, and later, keeping up with technology, with pistols.

Getting Around

Pistoia lies along the A11, and at the foot of two important routes north over the Apennines, the S64 towards Bologna and S633 to Abetone. From the station, just south of the city walls at the end of Via XX Settembre, there are frequent trains along the main Florence–Lucca line. COPIT buses for Vinci and Empoli (37km/2hrs—a beautiful, twisting road over the Monte Albano), Cutigliano (37km/1hr 45min), Abetone (50km/2½hrs), the zoo, Montecatini (16km/30min), and other destinations in Pistoia's little province depart from Piazza San Francesco. LAZZI buses depart for Florence (35km/1hr), Prato, Lucca (43km/1½hrs), Montecatini, Viareggio and Pisa (65km/2hrs) from Viale Vittorio Veneto, near the train station. Cars are banned from the city centre, but there's plenty of parking around the Fortezza di Santa Barbara in the southeast corner of the walls.

Tourist Information

Piazza del Duomo, in the bishop's palace, ✆ (0573) 21622.

Post Office: Via Roma 5.

Telephones: Corso A. Gramsci 96.

Piazza del Duomo

Pistol-Pistoia no longer packs any heat, but it packs in the heart of its 16th-century diamond-shaped walls one of the finest squares in Italy, a lesson in the subtle medieval aesthetic of urban design, an art lost with the endless theorizing and compulsive regularity of the Renaissance. The arrangement of the buildings around the L-shaped **Piazza del Duomo** seems haphazard at first. The design is meant to be experienced from street level; try walking into the piazza from a few of its surrounding streets, and you'll see how from each approach the monuments reveal themselves in a different order and pattern, like the shaking of a kaleidoscope; the windows of the Palazzo del Comune echo those on the Palazzo del Podestà, and the striped decoration of the baptistry is recalled in the campanile and Duomo. Much of old Pistoia is like this, shaped by centuries of anonymous builders into a work of art, one that appeals not only to the eye but the brain. Once you learn how to see it, you may find the rigid symmetry of Renaissance and Baroque design looking a little wearisome.

The piazza provides the perfect setting for Pistoia's great annual party, the colourful *Giostra dell'Orso*, the 'Joust of the Bear', which takes place on 25 July after a month of concerts, fairs and exhibits. The Joust began in the 14th century, pitting 12 knights against a bear dressed in a checked cloak. The bear has been replaced by two wooden dummies, but the pageantry remains the same.

The **Duomo**, dedicated to San Zeno, dates from the 12th century; the Pisan arcades and stripes of its façade, combined over the geometric patterns of the Florentine Romanesque and polychrome terracotta **lunette** by Andrea della Robbia, strike an uneasy balance between the two architectural traditions. The outsize **Campanile**, originally a watch-tower, tips the balance towards Pisa, with its exotic, almost Moorish candy-striped arches on top added in the 14th century when it was converted to church use—though you can still see the old Ghibelline crenellations on top. Inside the cathedral (*open 7–12 and 4–7*) there is a wealth of art—on the right a **Font** with quaint medieval heads, redesigned by Benedetto da Maiano, the **Tomb of Cino da Pistoia** (1337), one of Dante's best friends, shown lecturing to a class of scholars, and a 13th-century painted crucifix by Coppo di Marcovaldo. The cathedral's most precious treasure is in the **chapel of St James**: a fabulous altar made of nearly a ton of silver, comprising 628 figures, begun in 1287 and added to over the next two centuries; among the Pisan, Sienese and Florentine artists who contributed to this shining *tour de force* was Brunelleschi, who added the two half figures to the left before he decided to devote all his talents to architecture (*the sacristan opens the chapel for L1500*). Some of the oldest art, fine medieval reliefs of the Last Supper and Gethsemane, have been relegated to the dim and ancient crypt. By the altar there's a fine painting by Caravaggio's pupil, Mattia Preti, and Maso di Bartolomeo's lovely bronze candelabra. On the left the **chapel of the Sacrament** contains a bust of a Medici archbishop attributed to Verrocchio, who also added the statues of Faith and Hope to the wooping angels on the **tomb of Cardinal Forteguerri** just left of the main entrance.

The **Museo della Cattedrale** (*open 10, 11.30 and 3.30 Tues, Thurs and Fri for guided tours*) has been arranged in the partly striped, partly brick **Palazzo dei Vescovi** next door, above the tourist information office; it contains an excellent reliquary of 1369, a beautiful quattrocento ivory box with scenes of Jason, and a reliquary of St James by Lorenzo Ghiberti, as well as some lovely early fresco fragments. In the basement there's a small **Archaeological Collection** (*open Friday mornings*) with relics of Roman *Pistoria*.

The octagonal zebra of a **Baptistry** (*open 9–12, 3.30–6.30*), built to a design by Andrea Pisano and finished in 1359, is one of the outstanding Gothic buildings in Tuscany, embellished with fine sculptural details on the outside. The interior has a remarkable conical ceiling of brick and a Gothic pulpit. Nearby is a medieval well, topped by a Florentine *Marzocco*.

Galleria Comunale

Open 9–1 and 3–7, 9–1 Sun, closed Mon; adm.

The Piazza del Duomo's other two palaces are civic in nature. The 14th-century **Palazzo Pretorio** on the west side has a decorated courtyard and old stone bench where the judges once sat and where they condemned malefactors to a unique punishment—they were ennobled. Not that Pistoia wanted to reward them; rather, to become noble meant losing one's rights as a republican citizen. The tower near here is known as the tomb of Catiline, who according to tradition was secretly buried here. On the other side of the piazza stands the elegant **Palazzo Comunale**, begun 1294, and prominently embellished with the usual Medici balls and the more unusual black marble head, believed to be that of a Moorish king captured by a captain from Pistoia on a freebooting expedition to Mallorca. Besides the town council and offices, the palazzo houses the **Galleria Comunale**, an excellent collection of great and odd paintings to suit even the most jaded of palates. Pistoiese patrons were uncommonly fond of 'Sacred Conversations'—group portraits of saints around the Madonna, and there are good ones by Mariotto de Nardo, Beccafumi, Lorenzo di Credi and Pistoia's own Gerino Gerini (1480–1529), a follower of Raphael. From the 15th-century 'Maestro delle Madonne di Marmo' there's a sweetly smiling marble relief of the Madonna and child; then two fancy St Sebastians with flowing curls, who precede the *Madonna della Pergola*, by local painter Bernardino di Antonio Detti (1498–1554), whose flaccid charwoman of a Madonna holds a child with a large housefly on his chubby arm before a crazy quilt of confusing iconography—children playing with dolls, the Judgement of Solomon, a child with a fruit-bowl, a floor littered with flowers, amulets, spoons and rags. On the mezzanine is the document centre of the great 20th century Pistoiese architect Giovanni Michelucci; a comprehensive collection of models and drawings, as well as photos of his buildings and the media reaction to them. An example of his work is the large, angular Sta Maria Novella station in Florence, another is the restaurant set in the Parco Collodi (*see* p. 241).

Plod up another flight of stairs for some screamingly lurid paintings from the 17th–19th centuries, with plenty of historical canvases of murder and mayhem that suggest the local taste for violence lingered at least in art. There are two eerie mythological paintings swathed in Caravaggesque darkness by Cecco Bravo; a 17th-century *Young Woman with a Flower*, bathed in a ghostly light; a sensuous, pouting St Sebastian, disdainfully plucking arrows from his chest; a ridiculous allegory of Medici rule in Pistoia, with *putti* scattering the family's lily symbol like flowers over the city; a Magdalene fondly patting a skull; and two rather nightmarish, imaginary battle scenes by a 17th-century Neapolitan named Francesco Graziani.

Ospedale del Ceppo and Sant'Andrea

Open upon request, © (0573) 367821, ext 13.

In medieval Tuscany, it was the custom to collect alms in a hollowed-out log (or *ceppo*) left in a public place, to be gathered and distributed to the poor at Christmas-time. *Ceppo* became synonymous with the word charity, as in Datini's famous foundation in Prato, and even earlier here in Pistoia, when the **Ospedale del Ceppo** was founded in the 13th century. Still functioning at the same address (walk down Via Filippo Pacini from the Palazzo Comunale), the building was given a fine arcaded porch in the 1500s, in the style of famous Spedale degli Innocenti in Florence. And as in Florence, the della Robbias were called upon to provide the decoration, in this case the usually insipid Giovanni, who with the help of his workshop and other artists, created not only the typical della Robbian tondi, but a unique terracotta frieze that spans the entire loggia in resplendent Renaissance technicolour, with scenes of the acts of mercy and theological virtues. Inside there's a small museum dedicated to Pistoia's old iron industry, especially surgical knives.

A short walk west of the hospital on Via Sant'Andrea is the 12th-century church of **Sant'Andrea** (*open 8–12 and 3–6*), with a Pisan façade and over the door, a charming bas-relief of the *Journey of the Magi*, dated 1166, and a pair of ghastly, leering lions. The real jewel, however, is inside: Giovanni Pisano's hexagonal **pulpit** (1297), exquisitely carved in stirring high relief with scenes of the Nativity, Massacre of the Innocents, Adoration of the Magi, Crucifixion and Last Judgement, with sibyls in the corners and pedestals in the forms of the four Evangelists—one of the masterpieces of Italian Gothic. Sant'Andrea contains three other crucifixions: Giovanni Pisano's wood crucifix in the right aisle, a medieval version over the main altar, portraying Christ crowned and dressed in a kingly robe, and in the right nave, a large, rather mysterious painting of a saint crucified on a tree.

San Francesco and the Madonna dell'Umiltà

Pretty striped churches circle the centre of Pistoia like zebras on a merry-go-round. The two plain ponies in the lot are to the west. The large **San Francesco al Prato** in Piazza San Francesco d'Assisi, plain and Gothic like most Franciscan churches, has some notable 14th-century frescoes, especially in the chapel to the left of the altar, with Sienese scenes portraying the Triumph of St Augustine. On the side of the church there's an ancient olive tree and a memorial to assassinated prime minister Aldo Moro, a stark contrast with the heroic Fascist-era war monument in the piazza itself. South on Corso Gramsci is Pistoia's main theatre, the 1694 **Teatro Manzoni**; further south, on Via della

Madonna, towers Pistoia's experiment in High Renaissance geometry, the octagonal, unstriped **Basilica della Madonna dell'Umilità** begun in 1518 by local architect and pupil of Bramante, Ventura Vitoni, who graced it with an imposing barrel-vaulted vestibule. In the 1560s Giorgio Vasari was called upon to crown Vitoni's fine start; not content to limit his mischief to Florence, he added a dome so heavy that the basilica has been threatening to collapse ever since. More work to shore it up is currently under way.

San Giovanni Fuoricivitas and San Domenico

South of the Piazza del Duomo (Via Roma to Via Cavour) lies the tiny **Piazza San Leone**, the ancient Lombard centre of Pistoia; its stubby tower once belonged to the nastiest Pistoian of them all, a 13th-century noble thug and church robber named Vanni Fucci whom Dante found in one of the lower circles of Hell, entwined in a serpent, cursing and making obscene gestures up at God. Around the corner of Via Cavour, the 12th-century **San Giovanni Fuoricivitas** claims the honour of being the most striped church in all Christendom, its green and white flank an abstract pattern of lozenges and blind arches that out-Pisas anything in Pisa. In the dark, gloomy interior, only four things are lit: the dramatic pulpit (1270) by Fra Gugliemo da Pisa, a pupil of Nicola Pisano, a holy water stoup supported by caryatids by Giovanni Pisano and a white, glazed terracotta group of the *Visitation* by Luca or Andrea della Robbia.

Little Piazza Garibaldi to the south is adorned with a good equestrian statue of Garibaldi, some florid street lamps, and **San Domenico**, begun in the late 13th century. In its spacious, airy interior, there's a splendid Baroque organ from 1617 and two Renaissance tombs: that of Filippo Lazzari, by the Rossellino brothers, portraying the deceased lecturing to his pupils (one of whom can't help yawning), and the other of Lorenzo da Ripafratta, with a fine effigy. In 1497, Benozzo Gozzoli died of the plague in Pistoia and is buried somewhere in the cloister of San Domenico; you can see a fresco he began of the Journey of the Magi nearby. Although the monastery is still in use, you can ring to see the frescoes in the chapter house, among them good Sienese works and a crucifixion with its sinopia, dating back to the mid-13th century. Even more interesting are the frescoes across the street in the little **Cappella del Tau** (so-named after the blue T its priests wore on their vestments)—vividly coloured scenes of Adam and Eve and assorted saints, attributed in part to Masolino. The convent of the chapel has become the Marino Marini centre (*open 9–1, 3–7, 9–12.30 Sun, closed Mon*). The collection traces his career in both paint and sculpture and includes the bronze *Young Girl* which recalls the antique tradition not only in her facial features but also her truncated arms. Next to it, at No. 72, note the coat-of-arms over the pretty window of two dancing bears, recalling the Giostra dell'Orso. There's another good Gothic façade on **San Paolo**, a block to the east, with broader stripes and a statue of St James on the very top, attributed to Orcagna.

There are more old churches in central Pistoia, but only one other worth going out of your way to visit: **San Bartolomeo in Pantano** ('St Bart in the Bog'), on the east side of town, built on marshy land in the 8th century and sinking gently into the ground ever since. It has an attractive, partially completed façade, and inside, a carved marble lectern of 1250 by Guido da Como.

The Zoo, the Medici and some Iron

The newest stripes in Pistoia may well be on the zebras in the **Pistoia Zoo** (*open 9–5 winter, 9–7 summer; adm exp*), 4km northwest of the city in Via Pieve a Celle. Though the Medici always kept big menageries, modern Italians don't usually care for zoos; this is one of the best in the country, even though it's only 20 years old. Polar bears, kangaroos, giant turtles, reptiles, and all the other zoo favourites are in attendance. Southeast 13km off S66 is yet another Medici villa, the **Villa della Magia in Quarrata**, begun in 1318, and in 1536 the meeting place of Charles V and Alessandro de'Medici. Its grand hall has 18th-century frescoes, and according to rumour visitors are allowed in twice a week (*ask at the Pistoia tourist office*). In Pistoia itself you can visit one of the city's wrought-iron 'laboratories', Bartoletti, in Via Sestini 110, ✆ 452318 (*open Mon–Sat*).

Pistoia ✆ (0573–)   *Where to Stay*

Pistoia is used to lodging and feeding business more than pleasure travellers. The one exception is ★★★**Il Convento**, Via S. Quirico 33, ✆ 452651, ✉ 453578 (*moderate*), 5km east of the centre at Pontenuovo; as its name implies, it is a former convent, preserving its exterior if not all of its interior. The setting is quiet with views over Pistoia; there's a pool and one of the city's better restaurants as well. In the city itself, there's the older, comfortable ★★★**Leon Bianco**, Via Panciatichi 2, ✆ 26675, ✉ 26676 (*moderate*), with views over the campanile, or the newer ★★★**Piccolo Ritz**, Via Vannucci 67, ✆ 26775, ✉ 27798 (*moderate*), near the station, with a bit of a garden and a garage. ★★**Appenino**, also near the station in Via XX Settembre 21, ✆ 32243 (*inexpensive to moderate*), has simple but adequate rooms, most with bath. ★★**Firenze**, a skip away from Piazza del Duomo at Via Curtatone e Montanara 42, ✆ 23141, ✉ 21660 (*inexpensive to moderate*), offers clean and quiet rooms. ★★**Il Boschetto** in Loc. Capostrada, Viale Adua 467, ✆ 401336, has seven rooms (*inexpensive*) and a restaurant next door (*moderate*).

Pistoia ✆ (0573–)   *Eating Out*

Pistoia is known, not for its good restaurants, but for its lack of them. In the city itelf there are mostly simple trattorias and pizzas; on Via Bonellina 111, **La Casa Degli Amici**, ✆ 380305 (*inexpensive to moderate*), is a local favourite, serving wonderful fried rabbit with artichoke and duck with orange. **Valle del Vincio**, near the zoo, Via Vignano 1, ✆ 477012 (*moderate*), serves traditional dishes and lots of mushrooms. Perhaps the best restaurant in town, however, is **Leon Rosso**, Via Panciatichi 4, ✆ 29230 (*moderate*), where the food comes from the owner's farm in the mountains; try their *maccheroncini* with pigeon sauce and wild boar steaks. *Closed Sun.* Pistoia's other dining worthies are outside town: **Rafanelli**, at Sant'Agostino, Via Sant'Agostino 47, ✆ 532460 (*moderate to expensive*), where

Tuscan home cooking, *maccheroni* with duck, game dishes and lamb, is served in a pretty country villa setting. *Closed Sun evening, Mon and Aug.* **Locanda degli Elfi**, Via della Chiesa 3, in Loc. San Felice, ✆ 41490 (*moderate to expensive*), is a beautiful 18th-century villa, offering fish and local dishes. *Closed Tues.*

The Mountains of Pistoia

North of Pistoia rises a fairly unspoiled stretch of the central Apennines, luxuriantly forested and endowed with some lovely mountain escape routes, deep green in the summer and ski white in the winter. Main routes include the beautiful Bologna road (S64) known as the 'Porrettana' which follows the Bologna–Pistoia railway through the sparsely settled mountains, and the equally beautiful, parallel S632, less encumbered with traffic. The main mountain resorts up to Abetone are along the S66 and S12, as easily reached from Lucca as from Pistoia.

Tourist Information

San Marcello Pistoiese: Via Marconi 16, ✆ (0573) 630145, ✉ 622120.

Cutigliano: Via Tigri, ✆ (0573) 68029.

Abetone: Piazza Piramidi, ✆ (0573) 60231.

Due north of Pistoia, 10km along a byroad towards Piteccio, is the ancient hamlet of **Castagno**, converted into a unique open-air art gallery. Its lanes are embellished with 20th-century frescoes on the 12 months; modern statues pose in the nooks and crannies; and Castagno's ancient church and oratory dedicated to St Francis, both with interesting frescoes, have recently been restored. A 4km backtrack will take you to the main S66; at Pontepetri (20km) S632 veers north to the formerly popular little mountain resort of **Pracchia**.

Most visitors these days continue along S66 for the newer summer-winter resorts by way of the lovely state forest of Teso, at the fine old villages of **Maresca** and **Gavinana**. The latter is notorious in the annals of Florentine history for the defeat of its army by the imperial forces of Charles V, a battle that cost the lives of both commanders. The Florentine leader, Francesco Ferrucci, was knifed in the back, and is remembered with his own little museum in the main piazza. S66 continues to **San Marcello Pistoiese**, 29km from Pistoia, the 'capital' of the mountains, in a lovely setting, where since 1854 the inhabitants have launched a hot-air balloon every 8 September as a farewell to summer. All year round, however, you can walk over the 220-metre **suspension bridge of Mammiano**, which would perhaps look more at home in the Andes. **Cutigliano**, 7km north, is a growing winter resort with 27km of ski trails and a cable car up to its highest peak, Doganaccia (1175m). In the village the **Palazzo Pretorio** fairly bristles with the coats of arms of its former governors.

Near the northern border of Tuscany, through a lush and ancient forest, lies **Abetone** (1400m), one of the most famous resorts in the central Apennines. Named after a huge fir tree, the town grew up in the late 18th century, when Grand Duke Pietro Leopoldo built the road to the Duchy of Modena, a road specially designed not to pass through the detested Papal States (the modern province of Bologna). Two milestones at Abetone mark the old boundary. The closest major ski resort to Florence, it is highly developed, with 30km of trails, four cable cars and other chair lifts; in the summer its cool altitude, swiming-pools, and other recreational facilities make it almost as popular, especially as a weekend retreat. At other seasons, rain is not exactly unknown.

© (0573–)   *Where To Stay*

In the mountains, many hotels are open only during the ski season and in July and August. A pleasant hotel open all year in San Marcello Pistoiese is ***Il Cacciatore**, Via Marconi 87, © 630533, ✉ 630134 (*moderate*), green and quiet. Cutigliano is a few degrees smarter, with big resort hotels like ***Piandinovello**, Via Sestaione 131, © 673076 (*moderate*), with a swimming-pool and tennis-courts. *Open 20 Dec–20 April and July–Aug.* Near the centre of the village, ***Rondò Priscilla**, Via della Libertà 2, © 68148/9, ✉ 68513 (*moderate*), is a small hotel with a garden and pool. *Open all year.* Up in Abetone there's the elegant ****Palazzaccio** in Piazza Piramidi, © 60067, ✉ 60585 (*moderate*). *Open July–Aug and Dec–April.* On a quieter street, try the ***Regina**, Via Uccelleria 5, © 60007, ✉ 60257 (*moderate*), *July–mid-Sept and Dec–April.* Abetone also has a youth hostel, the **Ostello Renzo Bizzari**, Via Brennero at Cosuma, © 60117 (*inexpensive*), with room for 92 people. *Open Dec–March and July–Aug.* There are quite a few economical holiday villas near the towns and alpine refuges in the surrounding mountains; the Pistoia tourist office has a complete list.

© (0573–)   *Eating Out*

In Cutigliano, **Fagiolino**, Via Carega 1, © 68014 (*moderate*), offers traditional Tuscan mountain cuisine (*risotto ai funghi*, roast kid, raspberry torte) served on a panoramic veranda. In Abetone, **La Capannina**, Via Brennero 256, © 60562 (*moderate*), has a rustic decor and rustic but excellently prepared dishes, with lots of *porcini* mushrooms, ravioli with walnut sauce, trout, pigeon, and wild berries for dessert, all accompanied by a wide selection of wines.

Montecatini Terme

West of Pistoia lies the Valdinievole, the 'Valley of Mists', a land obsessed with water, though mostly of the subterranean, curative variety, available in Italy's most glamorous thermal spa, Montecatini (pop. 21,500). Leonardo da Vinci's first known drawing was of a view towards Montecatini from Lamporecchio, near his hometown of Vinci (*see* p.215), and it is believed that his lifetime fascination with canals and locks and currents and dams and the misty, watery backgrounds of his most famous paintings come from a childhood spent in the Valdinievole. He even designed a fountain for the baths of Montecatini in one of his notebooks, which after 380 years is currently being built of Carrara marble as his monument.

Even in these days of holistic medicine, preventive medicine, herbal cures and pharmaceutical paranoia, it is the despair of the Montecatini tourist board that Anglo-Saxons from both sides of the Atlantic refuse to believe that soaking in or drinking mere water can do anything as beneficial for them as imbibing a pitcher of Chianti. Unlike continental enthusiasts, we defy the wisdom of the ancients—especially the Romans, who spent the plunder accumulated from conquering the world on ever more fabulous baths. But it is sometimes forgotten that taking the waters, no matter how hot, radioactive, or chock full of minerals, is only half the cure; the other is simply to relax, to stroll through gardens, listen to a little music, linger in a café, to indulge in a bit of the old *dolce far niente*. And in Montecatini you can do just that without touching a blessed, unfermented drop, surrounded by Belle Epoque nostalgia from the days when the spa seethed with dukes, politicians, literati and actresses; you may recognize it from Nikita Mikhalhov's film, *Oci Ciornie*, starring Marcello Mastroianni.

Getting Around

Montecatini is easily reached by train from Florence (51km/1½hrs), Pistoia (16km/25mins) and Lucca (27km/45mins). The station, ☏ (0572) 78551, is on Via Toti, as is the LAZZI bus terminal, ☏ (0572) 766914/5), with connections to Pescia (8km), Monsummano (2km), Lamporecchio, Serravalle (6km), Collodi (13km), as well as Florence, Pistoia, Pisa, Livorno, Viareggio, Prato, Carrara and Lucca.

Tourist Information

Via G. Verdi 66, ☏ (0572) 772244, ✉ 70109.

Parco delle Terme

A short stroll up from the station, past Montecatini's trendy boutiques, cafés, cinemas and some of its 200 hotels to Via Verdi, will take you into Montecatini's mineral water Elysium, the immaculately groomed **Parco delle Terme**, where the high temples of the cult dot the shaded lawn. The Lorraine grand dukes, spa soaks like their Habsburg cousins, were behind the initial development of Montecatini's springs, and many of the baths, or *Terme*, are neoclassical pavilions—monumental, classical and floral architecture that lent itself nicely to the later Liberty-style embellishments of the 1920s. You can take in some of these Art Nouveau fancies in Montecatini's Municipio, on Via Verdi opposite the park, or in the most sumptuous and ancient of its nine major bathing establishments, **Tettuccio**. In the 1370s a group of Florentines attempted to extract mineral salts from the spring and built a little roof (or *tettuccio*) over it; and although they failed it was soon discovered that the water had a good effect on rotten livers—one of the first to come here was Francesco

Datini, the Merchant of Prato, in 1401. By the 18th century, Tettuccio was in a state of ruin, and Grand Duke Leopold I had it splendidly rebuilt. His façade remains, while the interior was redone by Montecatini's greatest architect, Ugo Giovanozzi, in the 1920s, embellished with paintings by Italy's Art Nouveau master, Galileo Chini, and ceramic pictures by Cascella in the drinking gallery; there's an elegant café, fountains, a reflecting pool and rotunda, writing hall, music rooms, a little city within a city—all adorned with scenes from an aquatic Golden Age of languid nymphs—the perfect place to sip your morning glass of liver-flushing water.

Other establishments, each with their special virtues, are nearby—the Palladian-style arcade of the **Regina** spring; the **Terme Leopoldine**, another grand ducal establishment, with mud baths housed in a temple-like building dedicated to Aesculapius, the god of health; the half-neo-Renaissance, half-modern **New Excelsior baths**; the pretty Tuscan rustic **Tamerici**, in its lush garden; the **Torretta**, with its phony medieval tower and afternoon concerts in the loggia. Note that the baths are open May–October, except for the Excelsior, which stays open all year. Tickets for a day or subscriptions are available from the central office in Via Verdi 41, © 7781, ✆ 778444 and prices aren't exactly healthy for your wallet: a morning visit to Tettuccio is L19,000 in the high season.

During Digestion

While the water works its way through your system, you can work your way through Montecatini's diversions. The **Art Academy** consists solely of donations from Montecatini's admirers—the piano Verdi used during his annual stays in the Locanda Maggiore, where he composed *Otello*, and art by Salvador Dali, Galileo Chini, Fattori and many others. There's another wooded park, just behind the Parco delle Terme, called **Le Panteraie** (with a swimming-pool), where deer roam freely; you can sip an elegant coffee at the **Gran Caffè Gambrinus**, or perhaps play a round at the beautiful **Montecatini Golf Course**, set among olive groves and cypresses, © (0572) 62218, or a game of tennis at the courts in Via dei Bari, © (0572) 767587/5; or try to win back your hotel bill at the trotting races at the **Ippodromo**. The **Circolo dei Forestieri** (foreigners' club) and the **Kursaal** (with cinema, night-club, games) are popular meeting places. One of the prettiest excursions is to take the funicular up to **Montecatini Alto**, the original old hilltown, with breathtaking views over the Valley of Mists and a charming little piazza with a charming little theatre; nearby you can visit the stalactites in the **Grotta Maona** (*open April–Oct*).

Montecatini Terme © *(0572–)*   **Where to Stay**

Even if you don't care to take the waters, Montecatini's scores of hotels ensure that you can find a room easily. Italy's choicest spa has no fewer than six hotels that claim the title of 'Grand' and a half-dozen others that only decline to for discretion's sake. **Full board** is the rule here. There is a hotel association on Via delle Saline 66, ©70124, which will help you with bookings.

Of the grandest, ★★★★★**Grand Hotel Bellavista**, Viale Fedeli 2, © 78122, ✆ 73352 (*expensive*), offers golf, tennis, indoor pool, luxurious rooms, sauna, health club, and an infinite number of opportunities for self-indulgence. But for genuine Belle Epoque charm, ★★★★★**Grand Hotel & La Pace**, Viale della Torretta 1A, ✆ 75801, ✉ 78451 (*luxurious*), is renowned throughout Europe, with a similarly impressive array of luxuries, and for L80,000 you can eat in their elegant restaurant. *Open April–Oct.* At ★★★★**Grand Hotel Plaza e Locanda Maggiore**, in Piazza del Popolo 7, ✆ 75831, ✉ 767985 (*moderate*), you can check into Verdi's favourite hotel, with a pool and air-conditioned rooms. *Open year round.* One charming choice is ★★★**Belvedere**, next to the Parco delle Terme, Viale Fedeli 10, ✆ 70251, ✉ 70252 (*moderate*), with an indoor pool, tennis and friendly service. *Open April–Oct.* On a quiet side street near the park, ★★★**Corallo**, Viale Cavallotti 116, ✆ 78288, ✉ 79512 (*moderate*), is small but refined, with a pool and garden. *Open all year.* Up in Montecatini Alto, ★**Belsoggiorno**, Viale Cavallotti 131, ✆ 78859 (*inexpensive*), has rooms over-looking a garden .

Montecatini Terme ✆ (0572–) **Eating Out**

Although most guests dine in their hotels in Montecatini, it's worth breaking loose at least once to try the imaginative fare at the **Enoteca da Giovanni**, Via Garibaldi 25, ✆ 71695 (*expensive*), a unique and much honoured place where game dishes—hare, venison, wild duck—turn into impeccably *haute cuisine* in the hands of a genuine master chef. *Closed Mon.* If you're feeling romantic, **Gourmet**, Via Amendola 6, ✆ 771012 (*expensive*), offers fancy dinners by candle-light, with piano music to set the mood. *Closed Tues.* Up in Montecatini Alto, just above the funicular station, **Lido's**, Via Fratelli Guermani 2, ✆ 766378 (*expensive*), has an elegant dining room with panoramic views, where you can ruin your waistline with cannelloni filled with truffles, or rich lasagne, or pheasant cooked with cream, ham and truffles, and sinful desserts. *Closed Mon.* In Viale IV Novembre 99 is **Pierangelo**, ✆ 771552 (*very expensive*), where a husband-and-wife team prepare creative and traditional dishes; sample the rabbit salad and the stuffed *caramelle* in sauce. *Closed Sun and Mon lunch.* When you get tired of the health-giving waters, dip into the vintages at the enoteca at Via Forini 13, or the Antinori 'Degustazione Vini' on Via Verdi 35.

Monsummano and Serravalle

Lovely narrow lanes crisscross the Valdinievole landscape, offering tempting excursions further afield. Five km east of Montecatini is its sister spa, **Monsummano Terme**, offering vapour baths in natural grottoes. The first of these strange caves was discovered by accident in 1849, when the Giusti family moved a boulder and found the entrance to a stalactite cave, the **Grotta Giusti** (*open April–Nov*), 100m deep, with three small lakes fed by hot springs; a second steamy cave, the **Grotta Parlanti** (*open May–Oct; information (0572) 51029*), is used for serious treatments. Monsummano, however, hasn't rested on its vapours, but has transformed itself into one of Italy's biggest shoe-making towns;

like Montecatini it has an old antecedent atop a hill, **Monsummano Alto**, all but abandoned these days, but with a pretty Romanesque church, a romantically ruined castle and splendid views. Another panoramic view may be had from **Montevettolini**, 4km from Monsummano, site of a villa built by Ferdinando I in 1597.

If you prefer your castles more intact, continue east to the old fortress at **Serravalle Pistoiese**, which, as its name translates, 'locks the valley' between the Apennines and Monte Albano. Its old Lombard tower and 14th-century additions saw considerable action in Tuscany's days of inter-urban hooliganism.

Pescia

To the west of Montecatini, there's another attractive old hilltown, **Buggiano Castello**, and for those who imagine that fresco went out of fashion years ago, there's San Michele in nearby **Ponte Buggianese**, freshly frescoed in stark colours by Pietro Annigoni. The colours are even more dazzling in **Pescia** (pop. 20,000), Italy's capital of flowers, a title this little city with a green thumb has snatched from San Remo on the Riviera. Some three million cut flowers are sent off every day in the summer from Pescia's giant market; besides carnations, lilies and gladioli, it is celebrated by gourmets for its tender asparagus and its *fagioli* (white beans).

Pescia has a number of interesting monuments, beginning with a 14th-century church of **San Francesco**, containing a portrait of St Francis with scenes from his life, painted in 1235 by Bonaventura Berlinghieri and considered to be one of the most authentic likenesses of the saint; also be sure to take a look at the Crucifixion by Puccio Capanna in the sacristy. The **Duomo** was rebuilt in the 1600s, but has a fine Romanesque campanile wearing its little cupola like a beanie, and a late terracotta triptych by Luca della Robbia. On the long, narrow Piazza Mazzini stands the imposing **Palazzo del Vicario**, with the usual mishmash of stone escutcheons; in nearby **Sant'Antonio**, built in the 1360s, look up the 'Ugly Saints', a 13th-century wood Deposition from the Cross.

The green, hilly region of prosperous villages north of Pescia in the upper Valdinievole is fondly known as its 'Little Switzerland'. In its cheerful core, some 12km from Pescia, stands one of Italy's most bizarre churches, the 12th-century **Pieve di Castelvecchio**, decorated with frightening stone masks, grinning and grimacing, that would look more at home in *Heart of Darkness*.

Collodi and Pinocchio

Just west of Pescia is the little old town of Collodi, often visited as a child by Florentine writer Carlo Lorenzo (1826–90), whose uncle was a factor at the local castle; Lorenzo was so fond of it that he took its name as his own when he published his *Adventures of Pinocchio*, Italy's greatest contribution to children's literature. In honour of the creator of the naughty wooden puppet, Collodi has built the **Parco di Pinocchio** (*open 8.30–sunset; adm*), with a bronze statue of the puppet by Emilio Greco and a piazza of mosaics with scenes from the book by Venturino Venturi, as well as other figures, all very much in the angular style of the late 1950s and early 60s; there's a lawn maze, a museum dedicated to the book, a playground and other amusements for the kids. Adults, meanwhile, can try to work their way through a much older labyrinth in the magnificent hillside gardens of the **Castello Garzoni** (*gardens open 8–6.30; castle closed for restoration; adm.*), designed in the 17th century by Ottaviano Diodati of Lucca and considered one of the finest late Italian gardens, ornate with fountains and statuary. The castle itself 'of a hundred windows' has a few grand rooms, and the kitchen where young Carlo sat and dreamed up Pinocchio.

© (0572–) **Where to Stay and Eating Out**

In Monsummano, near the vaporous grottoes, the villa of the family of the poet Giuseppe Giusti has been converted into the charming ★★★★**Grotta Giusti**, Via Grotta Giusti 171, © 51165, ◎ 51269 (*moderate to expensive*), with frescoed ceilings and antiques. *Open April–Oct.* Up above Monsummano in Montevettolini, **San Michele**, Piazza Bargellini 80, © 62447 (*inexpensive*), is a café-bar-enoteca-pizzeria-restaurant where the menu tempts with a tasty array of antipasti (smoked Canadian salmon, caviar, *carpaccio* with truffles), followed by spaghetti with lobster, perhaps, and prawns. *Closed Wed.*

Just outside Pescia, the large ★★★**Villa delle Rose**, Via del Castellare 21, © 451301, ◎ 444003 (*moderate*), has a pleasant garden and pool and comfortable, modern rooms. In Pescia you can dine very well at **Cecco**, Via Forti 84, © 477955 (*moderate*), featuring seasonal dishes starring Pescia's famous asparagus, or wild mushrooms or truffles or *zucchini* flowers; among the desserts, there's *torta di Cecco*, prepared according to an ancient recipe. **La Buca**, in Pescia's Piazza Mazzini 4, © 477339, serves traditional Tuscan favourites like *pappa al pomodoro*, *panzanella* and fish grilled over coals (*moderate*).

Set in the grand Parco Collodi, **All'Osteria del Gambero Rosso**, © 429364 (*moderate*), has made a name for its food as well as its attractive surroundings. The building was designed by Giovanni Michelucci, arguably one of Italy's greatest 20th-century architects. You don't have to agree—nor will your nose grow longer if you do—just tuck into the *cannelloni*, *tagliolini* with *porcini* mushrooms and *prosciutto*, and excellent crêpes stuffed with seafood or spinach. *Closed Mon evening and Tues.*

Lucca, the Garfagnana and Lunigiana

> *Nowhere in Lucca*
> *will you see the face of a Philistine.*

Heine, Travels in Lucca

Of all Tuscany's great cities, Lucca (pop. 92,500) is the most cosy, sane and domestic, a tidy gem of a town encased within its famous walls. Yet even these hardly seem formidable, more like garden walls than something that would keep the Florentines at bay. The old ramparts and surrounding areas, once the outworks of the fortifications, are now full of lawns and trees, forming a miniature green belt; on the walls, where the little city's soldiers once patrolled, citizens ride their bicycles and walk their dogs, and often stop to admire the view.

Like paradise, Lucca is entered by way of St Peter's Gate. Once inside you'll find tidy, well-preserved Romanesque churches and medieval towers that destroyed Ruskin's romantic notion that a medieval building had to be half ruined to be beautiful, a revelation that initiated his study of architecture. Nor do Lucca's numerous Liberty-style shop signs show any sign of rust; even the mandatory, peeling ochre paint and green shutters of the houses seem part of some great municipal housekeeping plan. Bicycles have largely replaced cars within the walls. At first glance it seems too bijou, a good burgher's daydream. But after its long and brave history it has certainly earned the right to a little quiet. The annual hordes of Tuscan tourists leave Lucca alone for the most part, though there seems to be a small number of discreet visitors, many of them German and Swedish, who come back every year. They don't spread the word, apparently trying to keep one of Italy's most beautiful cities to themselves.

History

Lucca's rigid grid of streets betrays its Roman origins; it was founded as a colony in 180 BC as *Luca*, and in 56 BC entered the annals of history when Caesar, Pompey and Crassus met here to form the ill-fated First Triumvirate. It was converted to Christianity early on by St Peter's disciple Paulinus, who became first bishop of Lucca. The city did especially well in the Dark Ages; in late Roman times it was the administrative capital of Tuscany, and under the Goths managed to repulse the murderous Lombards; its extensive archives were begun in the 8th century, and many of its churches were founded shortly after. By the 11th and 12th centuries Lucca emerged as one of the leading trading towns of Tuscany, specializing in the production of silk, sold by colonies of merchants in the East and West, who earned enough to make sizeable loans to Mediterranean potentates. A Lucchese school of painting developed, such as it is, and beautiful Romanesque churches were erected, influenced by nearby Pisa. Ghibellines and Guelphs, and then Black and White

Guelphs made nuisances of themselves as they did everywhere else, and Lucca often found itself pressed to maintain its independence from Pisa and Florence.

In 1314, at the height of the city's wealth and power, the Pisans and Ghibellines finally managed to seize Lucca. But Lucca had a trump card up a secret sleeve: a remarkable adventurer named Castruccio Castracani. Castracani, an ambitious noble who for years had lived in exile—part of it in England—heard the bad news and at once set forth to rescue his hometown. Within a year he had chased the Pisans out and seized power for himself, leading Lucca into its most heroic age, capturing most of western Tuscany to form a little Luccan empire, subjugating even big fish like Pisa and Pistoia. After routing the Florentines at Altopascio in 1325, Castracani was planning to snatch Florence too, but died of malaria just before the siege was to begin—another example of Florence's famous good luck. Internal bickering between the powerful families soon put an end to Lucca's glory days, though in 1369 the city managed to convince Emperor Charles IV to grant it independence as a republic, albeit a republic ruled by oligarchs like Paolo Guinigi, the sole big boss between 1400 and 1430.

But Lucca continued somehow to escape being gobbled up by its voracious neighbours, functioning with enough tact and tenacity to survive even after the arrival of the Spaniards—a fact one can attribute not so much to its great walls as to its relative insignificance. Amazingly enough, after the Treaty of Câteau-Cambrésis, Lucca found itself standing together with Venice as the only truly independent states in Italy. And like Venice, the city was an island of relative tolerance and enlightenment during the Counter-Reformation, its garden walls in this case proving stout enough to deflect the viperous Inquisition. In 1805 Lucca's independence ended when Napoleon gave the republic to his sister Elisa Baciocchi, who ruled as its princess; it was given later to Marie Louise, Napoleon's widow, who governed well enough to become Lucca's favourite ruler and earn a statue in the main Piazza Napoleone. Her son sold it to Leopold II of Tuscany in 1847, just in time for it to join the Kingdom of Italy.

Lucca ☏ (0583–)   ***Getting Around***

The railway station is just south of the walls on Piazza Ricasoli, with lots of trains on the Viareggio–Pisa–Florence line, 47013. Buses leave from Piazzale Verdi, just inside the walls on the western end: LAZZI buses to Florence, Pistoia, Pisa, Prato, Abetone, Bagni di Lucca, Montecatini and Viareggio, ☏ 584876, and CLAP (that's right, CLAP) buses to towns in Lucca province, including Collodi, Marlia, and Segromigno, and the Serchio valley, ☏ 587897. Get around Lucca itself like a Lucchese by hiring a bicycle from the tourist office in Piazzale Verdi and from **Barbetti,** Via Anfiteatro 23, ☏ 954444.

Lucca ☏ (0583–)   ***Tourist Information***

Vecchia Porta San Donato, Piazzale Verdi, ☏ 53888, ✉ 442505 and Piazza Guidiccioni 2, ☏ 491205.

Lucca

to Bagni di Lucca

VIALE AGOSTINO MARI

VIALE P. BATONI

P

Piazzale Martiri
della Libertà

PRETE

PASSEGGIATA DELLE MURA URBANE

VIALE GUGLIELMO MARCONI

P

Piazza Maria
del Borgo

VIA MICHELE ROSI

VIA DELLA ZECCA

VIA DEL FOSSO

San
Frediano

VIA D. CAVALLERIZZA

VIA FILLUNGO

VIA SANTA GEMMA GALGANI

Piazza
S. Frediano

VIA BUSDRAGHI

San Francesco

Roman
Amphitheatre

Piazza
S. Pietro
Somaldi

Piazza
S. Francesco

VIA DELLA QUARQUONIA

VIA DELL'ANFITEATRO

Museo Nazionale
Guinigi

VIA ANTONIO MORDINI

Piazza del
Carmine

Torre
Guinigi

VIA SAN NICOLAO

Villa
Bottini
Gardens

VIA SANTA CHIARA

VIA BRUNERO PAOLI

to Florence,
Montecatini Terme

VIA FILLUNGO

i

VIA SANT'ANDREA

VIA DEL FOSSO

Torre delle
Orre

VIA TATTINELLI

VIA DELL'ANGELO CUSTODE

Porta
San Gervasio

VIA ELISA

Piazzale Don
Aldo Mei

VIA SANTA CROCE

Piazza
Bernardini

Piazza
dei Servi

Piazza Santa
Maria Forisportam

Santa
Trinità

VIA SAN NICOLAO

VIA DELLA ROSA

VIA G. PACINI

VIA DEL BATTISTERO

VIA A. VALLISNERI

VIA DEL GIARDINO

BOTANICO

San
Giovanni

Piazza
Antelminelli

Piazza
San Martino

Duomo

VIA D. MOLINETTO

VIA DEL FOSSO

PASSEGGIATA DELLE MURA URBANE

P

GARIBALDI

LE REGINA MARGHERITA

VIALE GIUSEPPE GIUSTI

Piazzale
Ricasoli

Train
Station

N

300 metres
300 yards

247

The Walls

Lucca's lovely bastions evoke images of the walled rose gardens of chivalric romance, enclosing a smaller, more perfect cosmos. They owe their considerable charm to Renaissance advances in military technology. Prompted by the beginning of the Wars of Italy, Lucca began to construct the walls in 1500. The councillors wanted up-to-date fortifications to counter new advances in artillery, and their (unknown) architects gave them the state of the art, a model for the new style of fortification that would soon be transforming the cities of Europe. Being Renaissance Tuscans, the architects also gave them a little more elegance than was strictly necessary. The walls were never severely tested. Today, with the outer ravelins, fosses and salients cleared away (such earthworks usually took up as much space as the city itself), Lucca's walls are just for decoration; under the peace-loving Duchess Marie Louise they were planted with a double row of plane trees to create a splendid elevated garden boulevard that extends around the city for nearly 4km, offering a continuous bird's-eye view over Lucca. They are among the best preserved in Italy—in the Bastion San Paolino, the headquarters of the 'International Institute for the Study of City Walls' (CISCU), © (0583) 46257, will let you tour the interior of the bastion (*open 10–12.30 and 4–6.30 in summer and 3.30–6 in winter*). Of the gates, the most elaborate is the 16th-century **St Peter's Gate**, near the station, its portcullis still intact, with Lucca's proud motto of independence, LIBERTAS, inscribed over the entrance.

St Martin's Cathedral

Through St Peter's Gate, and then to the right, Corso Garibaldi leads to Lucca's cathedral, perhaps the most outstanding work of the Pisan style outside Pisa, begun in the 11th century and completed only in the 15th. Above the singular porch, with three different sized arches, are stacked three levels of colonnades, with pillars arranged like candy sticks, while behind and on the arches are exquisite 12th- and 13th-century reliefs and sculpture—the best work Lucca has to offer. See especially the *Adoration of the Magi* by Nicola Pisano (*under restoration at time of writing*), the column carved with the Tree of Life, with Adam and Eve crouched at the bottom and Christ on top, and a host of fantastical animals and hunting scenes, the months and their occupations, dancing dragons and a man embracing a bear, the circular Labyrinth of Theseus on one of the columns, even *Roland at Roncevalles*, all by unknown masters. Walk round the back, where the splendidly ornate apse and transepts are set off by the green lawn. The **Campanile**, crenellated like a battle tower, dates from 1060 and 1261.

The dark interior offers an excellent introduction to the works of Lucca's one and only great artist, **Matteo Civitali** (1435–1501), who worked as a barber until his mid-30s, when he decided he'd much rather be a sculptor. He deserves to be better known— but may never be since everything he made is still in Lucca. His most famous work is the octagonal **Tempietto** (1484), a marble tabernacle in the middle of the left aisle, containing Lucca's most precious holy relic, the world-weary *Volto Santo* ('Holy Image'), a cedar-wood crucifix said to be a true portrait of Jesus, sculpted by Nicodemus, an eyewitness to the crucifixion. Saved from the iconoclasts, it was set adrift in an empty boat and floated to Luni, where the bishop was instructed by an angel to place it in a cart drawn by two white oxen, and where the oxen should halt, there too should the image remain. They made a lumbering beeline for Lucca, where the *Volto Santo* has remained ever since. Its likeness appeared on the republic's coins, and there was a devoted cult of the image in medieval England; Lucca's merchant colony in London cared for a replica of the *Volto Santo* in old St Thomas's, and according to William of Malmesbury, King William Rufus always swore by it, '*per sanctum vultum de Lucca*'. Long an object of pilgrimage, the image goes out for a night on the town in a candlelight procession each 13 September.

Further up the left aisle a chapel contains Fra Bartolomeo's *Virgin and Child Enthroned*, and in the transept, the remarkable **Tomb of Ilaria del Carretto** (1408), perhaps Jacopo della Quercia's most beautiful work, a tender, tranquil effigy of the young bride of boss Paolo Guinigi, complete with the family dog, waiting for his mistress to awaken. Here, too, is an altar by Giambologna, of *Christ with Saints Peter and Paul*. Civitali carved the cathedral's high altar, and also two expressive tombs in the south transept. A door from the right aisle leads to the sacristy, with a good *Madonna Enthroned with Saints* by Domenico Ghirlandaio; a side altar near here has a typically strange composition from the Venetian Tintoretto, a *Last Supper* with a nursing mother in the foreground and cherubs floating around Christ. In the centre, unfortunately often covered up, is a particularly fine section of the inlaid marble floor; on the entrance wall, a 13th-century sculpture of St Martin has been brought in from the façade. An **Antiques Market** takes place in the cathedral's Piazza di San Martino the third Saturday and Sunday of each month. Next to the cathedral is the newly opened **Museo della Cattedrale** (*open 10–6 daily exc Mon; winter 10–1, 3–6, closed Mon*) holding some of its treasures, including the *ornaments* (the crown and garments) of the *Volto Santo*, tapestries and paintings from Lucca's ancient cathedral, San Giovanni, and della Quercia's *St John the Evangelist*.

Piazza Napoleone and Piazza San Michele

The pious Lucchesi once required 70 churches to minister to their spiritual needs. Fewer are necessary these days, and even fewer stay open during the day, but their fine medieval façades constitute some of Lucca's chief ornaments. One of these, **San Giovanni** with an 1187 portal, has been recently reopened, along with the excavations of constructions dating back to Roman times. San Giovanni lies on the Via del Duomo between Piazza San Martino and the shady twin squares in Lucca's centre, **Piazza del Giglio** and **Piazza Napoleone**, the focus of the Lucchesi evening *passeggiata*. The architectural hodgepodge of a palace on Piazza Napoleone, formerly the seat of the republican council, has been called the **Palazzo Ducale** ever since it was used by Lucca's queen for a day, Elisa Bonaparte Baciocchi. In the 16th century, Ammannati had a go at it, and the courtyard, at least, still preserves signs of his Mannerist handiwork. One of Matteo Civitali's most beautiful works, the tomb of San Romano, is in the rarely opened church of **San Romano**, behind the Palazzo Ducale.

Via Vittorio Veneto leads from Piazza Napoleone into Piazza San Michele, with a church many people mistake for Lucca's cathedral. Built about the same time, and with a similar Pisan façade, it is a building almost as impressive (*covered for restoration*). The full name, **San Michele in Foro**, comes from its location on what was Roman Lucca's forum. The ambitious façade rises high above the level of the roof, to make the building look even grander. Every column in the Pisan arcading is different; some doubled, some twisted like corkscrews, inlaid with mosaic Cosmati work, or carved with monsters. The whole is crowned by a giant statue of the Archangel, and on the corner of the façade is a Madonna by Civitali; the graceful, rectangular campanile is Lucca's tallest and loveliest. Inside, there's a glazed terracotta *Madonna and Child* attributed to Luca della Robbia, a striking 13th-century *crucifixion* over the high altar and a painting of plague saints by Filippino Lippi. Giacomo Puccini began his musical career as a choirboy in San Michele (his father and grandfather had been organists in the cathedral)—he didn't have far to go, as he was born in Via di Poggio 30, just across the street. The house is now a little **Puccini Museum** (*entrance in Corte San Lorenzo 9; open summer 10–1, 3–6; winter 11–1, 3–5, closed Mon*), with manuscripts, letters, mementoes, the overcoat and odds and ends of the great composer, as well as the piano he used to compose *Turandot*.

Pinacoteca Nazionale

The quarter west of San Michele is perfumed by the big state tobacco factory, a fine aroma that hides the fact that it produces Toscanelli cigars, the world's vilest smokes. Via San Paolino (the Roman *decumanus major*) leads shortly to the church of **San Paolino** where little Puccini played the organ to earn some pin-money. It contains two beautiful works: a 13th-century French *Madonna and Child* brought back by Lucchese merchants from Paris, and an anonymous quattrocento Florentine *Coronation of the Virgin*, with Mary hovering over a city of pink towers; she is crowned by God the Father instead of Christ, who usually does the honours.

The **Pinacoteca Nazionale** is housed in the 17th-century Palazzo Mansi, in Via Galli Tassi (*open 9–7, 9–2 Sun, closed Mon; adm*). Most of the art, as well as the rich furnishings in several of the rooms, dates from the 17th century; the few paintings which are interesting, portraits by Pontormo and Bronzino, are found in the Prima Sala after the large hall. In the Salone hangs a dark and damaged Veronese, and a follower of Tintoretto's *Miracle of St Mark Freeing the Slave*, showing, with typical Tintorettian flamboyance, Venice's patron saint dive-bombing from heaven to save the day. There is also a set of neoclassical reliefs from the Palazzo Ducale of the *Triumphs of Duchess Maria Luisa*. The 1600s frescoes are more fun than the paintings, especially the *Judgement of Paris*, which Venus wins by showing a little leg. And one can't help but wonder what Rococo dreams tickled the fancy of the sleeping occupants of the amazing bedroom.

San Frediano and the Amphitheatre

East of San Michele, medieval **Via Fillungo** and its surrounding lanes make up the busy shopping district, a tidy nest of straight and narrow alleys where the contented cheerfulness that distinguishes Lucca from many of its neighbours seems somehow magnified. Along Via Fillungo you can trace the old loggias of 14th-century palaces, now bricked in, and the ancient **Torre delle Ore** (tower of hours) which since 1471 has striven to keep the Lucchesi on time, and perhaps now suggests that it's time for a coffee in Lucca's historic **Caffè di Simo** at Via Fillungo 58. At Via Fillungo's northern end stands the tall church and taller campanile of **San Frediano**, built in the early 1100s, and shimmering with the colours of the large mosaic on its upper façade, showing Christ and the Apostles in an elegant flowing style. The 11th-century bronze Arabian falcon at the top is a copy— the original is so valuable that it is locked away in a safe. The palatial interior houses Tuscany's most remarkable baptismal font, the 12th-century *Fontana lustrale* carved with

reliefs, and behind it, an equally beautiful lunette of the *Annunciation* by Andrea della Robbia. On the left are several chapels, one containing frescoes by A. Aspertini with details of their restoration. In the last chapel on the left are an altarpiece and two tomb slabs by Jacopo della Quercia and his assistants. The bedecked mummy is of St Zita, patroness of maids and ladies-in-waiting; even in England maids traditionally belonged to the Guild of St Zita. The Lucchesi are very fond of her, and on 26 April they bring her incorruptible body out to caress.

Next to San Frediano, on Via Battisti, the **Palazzo Pfanner** (*10–6 April–Oct; adm*) has a pretty 18th-century garden, a fine staircase, a collection of silks made in Lucca, and 17th–19th-century costumes. In the other direction, skirting Via Fillungo, narrow arches lead into something most visitors miss, the **Roman Amphitheatre**. Only outlines of its arches are still traceable in the outer walls, while within the inner ring only the form remains—the marble was probably carted off to build San Michele and the cathedral—but Lucca is a city that changes so gradually and organically that the outline has been perfectly preserved. The foundations of the grandstands now support a perfect ellipse of medieval houses. Duchess Marie Louise cleared out the old buildings in the former arena, and now, where gladiators once slugged it out, there is a wonderfully atmospheric piazza, where the boys play football and the less active sit musing in the sleepy cafés.

The streets in this part of Lucca have scarcely changed in the past 500 years. Along Via Sant'Andrea and narrow Via Guinigi, you'll pass a number of resolutely medieval palaces, including that of the Guinigi family. Their lofty stronghold, the **Torre Guinigi** (*open 9–7.30 April–Sept,10–4.30 Oct–Mar; adm*), stands next to their palace and is one of Lucca's landmarks; like the walls, it has trees sprouting out of its top—the best example of that quaint Italian fancy. One of the most elaborate of medieval family fortresses, the tower has recently been restored; it's worth the stiff climb up for the view over the city and the Apuan Alps.

The East Side

Roman Lucca ended near the Guinigi palace, and when a new church was built in the early 12th century it was outside the gate, hence **Santa Maria Forisportam** ('outside of the gate') in Via Santa Croce, a pretty church in the Pisan style with blind arcades. Inside, it not only looks but smells terribly old, and contains two paintings by the often-esoteric Guercino. Beyond the church is the best-preserved gate of 1260, the **Porta San Gervasio** giving on to the former moat, now a picturesque little canal running along Via del Fosso. Just across the canal from the gate is **Santa Trinità** (*if closed, ask for the key in the convent next door*), home of Civitali's *Madonna della Tosse* (Our Lady of the Cough), a bit too syrupy sweet, but perhaps that helped the cure. Nearby on Via Elisa is the entrance to the **Villa Bottini gardens** (*open 9–1.30*), one of the few green oases inside the city walls.

At the northern end of Via del Fosso stands a 17th-century column dedicated to another Madonna, and to the east, the church of **San Francesco**, a typical 13th-century Franciscan preaching church with the tombs of Castracani and Lucchese composer Luigi Boccherini (d.1805)— he of the famous *minuet*—and some fine detached frescoes of the Florentine school. Beyond San Francesco stands the palatial brick Villa Guinigi, built in 1418 by the big boss Paolo Guinigi in his glory days. Now the **Museo Nazionale Guinigi** (*open 9–7, in summer, closed Mon; adm*), its ground floor houses an interesting collection of Romanesque reliefs, capitals and transennas, some of which are charmingly primitive—St Michael slaying the dragon, Samson killing the lion, a 9th-century transenna with birds and beasts, spirals and daggers. Upstairs, room XI has a lovely *Annunciation* by Civitali. The painting gallery contains intarsia panels from the cathedral, each with scenes of Lucca as seen from town windows, some trecento works by the Lucca school and a charming quattrocento *Madonna and Child* by the 'Maestro della Vita di Maria'. Other rooms contain a miasma of oversize 16th-century canvases, some by Vasari.

Villas around Lucca

In 16th-century Lucca, as elsewhere in Italy, trade began to flounder, and once-plucky, daring merchants, or at least those sufficiently well-upholstered, turned to the more certain joys of real estate, where they could genteelly decline in a little country palace and garden. For the Lucchesi, the favourite area to construct such pleasure domes was in the soft, rolling countryside to the north and northeast of the city. Three of these villas or their grounds are open for visits. In Segromigno, 10km from Lucca in the direction of Pescia, there's the charming, mid-16th-century but often modified **Villa Mansi** (*open 10–12.30 and 2.30–6; in summer 9.30–12, 3–7.30; adm*), embellished with a lovely half-Italian (i.e. geometric) and half-English (i.e. not geometric) garden laid out by the great Sicilian architect Juvarra. Nearby in Camigliano, the even more elaborate **Villa Torrigiani**, also begun in the 16th century (*villa and park open 10–1 and 3–7 March–Oct, closed Tues; in winter ring ahead © (0583) 928008, ☎ 928041; adm exp*), was long celebrated for its fabulous parties and entertainments. Set in a lush park of pools and trees, it is furnished with 16th–18th-century furnishings. Elisa Bonaparte Baciocchi combined a villa and a summer palace to make her country retreat, now called the **Villa Pecci-Blunt ex-Villa Reale** in Marlia. Only the park and the Giardino Orsetti are open, but they are lovely (*guided tours by appointment, © 30108, March–Nov 10, 11, 3, 4, 5 and 6 daily exc Mon, Dec–Feb ring in advance; adm*).

The Lucchese Plain

East and west of Lucca, what was swampland in the Middle Ages has been reclaimed to form a rich agricultural plain. One of its features are its 'courts'—farm hamlets not constructed around a central piazza, but with houses in neat rows. At one time there were 1100 such 'courts' on the plain. Among the highlights of the area is curious **Castello di Nozzano** just to the west, built by Matilda of Tuscany on a hill, its pretty tower now incongruously topped by a large clock. To the east, one of the first villages, **Capannori**, is the head town of several 'courts' and has a couple of interesting Romanesque churches, especially the 13th-century **Pieve San Paolo**, around which a small village incorporated itself, using the campanile for defence. The most imposing monument near Capannori is the 19th-century **Acquedotto del Nottolini**, which is also visible from the autostrada. Just south is the pretty hilltop village of **Castelvecchio**, its tall houses forming an effective circular wall. **Altopàscio**, on the Lucca–Empoli road, was built around an 11th-century hospice run by an obscure chivalric order called the Hospitaller Knights of the Order of Altopàscio, who originally occupied themselves with rescuing travellers from the swamps. Only the campanile of their church remains in the village today. **Montecarlo** gives its name to a very good dry white wine produced in the immediate area.

Lucca and Around © (0583–) **Where to Stay**

Lucca can be less than charm city if you arrive without booking ahead; there simply aren't enough rooms (especially inexpensive ones) to meet demand, and the Lucchesi aren't in any hurry to do anything about it. Outside the city, at Massa Pisana on Via SS del Brennero 1952, © 379737, ☎ 379019, you can bed down in Castruccio Castracani's own palace, built for the great Lucchese warlord in 1321. ★★★★★**Principessa Elisa** (*luxury, depending on season*), often rebuilt since, currently wears the façade of a stately Rococo mansion, surrounded by acres of 18th-century gardens and a pool. Thoroughly modern inside, amenities include air conditioning, TVs and minibars in the rooms. *Open Mar–Nov.* At San Michele in Eschetto, 4km along the road to Pisa, is ★★★★**Villa San Michele**, ✆ 370276, ✉ 370277 (*very expensive*), a beautiful 14th–17th-century villa in the woods and olive groves. Inside the walls, in central Piazza Puccini, you cannot do better than the slightly frayed, green-shuttered and thoroughly delightful ★★★**Universo**, ✆ 493678, ✉ 954854 (*moderate, some rooms nicer than others*); Ruskin and nearly everyone else who followed him to Lucca slept here. ★★★**La Luna**, in a quiet part of the centre at Corte Compagni 12, ✆ 493634, ✉ 490021 (*moderate to expensive*), is a cosy place, with a private garage for your car. ★★**Ilaria**, Via del Fosso 20, ✆ 47558 (*inexpensive*), offers 14 sparkling rooms on Lucca's baby canal.

★★**Villa Casanova**, in Via Casanova, just outside the city at Balbano (city bus 5), ✆ 548429, ✉ 548429 (*moderate*), has simple rooms but a pleasant garden, tennis and a swimming-pool to lounge by. Friendly, well-run ★★**Diana** near the cathedral on Via del Molinetto 11, ✆ 492202, ✉ 47795, has some of the nicest inexpensive rooms in Tuscany, some with bath. ★★**Moderno**, Via V. Civitalli 38, ✆ 55840, ✉ 53830 (*inexpensive*), has a central location. The modern, comfortable and rarely crowded **Youth Hostel** is 2km north of town on Via del Brennero, in Salicchi (bus 6 from the station), ✆ and ✉ 341811. *Open 10 Mar–Nov.*

Lucca and Around ✆ *(0583–)*   ***Eating Out***

Within the walls: **Il Buca di Sant'Antonio**, Via della Cervia 3, ✆ 55881 (*moderate*), has been an inn since 1782, offering old recipes like smoked herring and kid on a spit, and newer dishes like ravioli with ricotta and sage. *Closed Sun eve and Mon.* Opposite the Hotel Universo on Piazza del Giglio, **Il Giglio**, ✆ 494058 (*expensive*), is Lucca's best seafood place—river trout is a speciality as well. *Closed Tues eve and Wed.* For something less expensive, seek out Via Conce, in the northwest corner within the walls, where you can enjoy some surprising dishes at rock-bottom prices at **Da Giulio in Pelleria** (*inexpensive*), popular enough to warrant reservations, with top-quality 'peasant' fare, ✆ 55948. *Closed Sun and Mon.* **Canuleia**, Via Canaleia, ✆ 47470 (*moderate*), is situated near the amphitheatre in a medieval workshop, serving local food with some surprises and usually a choice of vegetarian dishes. *Closed Sat and Sun.*

Outside the town: Lucca does especially well at table if you have the horsepower to reach its immediate surroundings. Duck with truffles, wild boar and grilled seafood are a few of the treats on the extensive menu at **Solferino**, situated 6km west of Lucca in San Macario in Piano on the Viareggio road, ✆ 59118 (*expensive*). This restaurant has been run by the same family for four generations and is famous throughout Tuscany for almost as long. Simple Tuscan country specialities are in evidence, but this is one place where you might want to splurge. *Closed Wed.* Another good choice, north of town in Ponte a Moriano, is **La Mora**, Via Sestodi Moriano 104, © 406402 (*expensive*), located in an old posthouse with four cosy rooms inside and dining under the pergola in summer; according to season, you can choose delicious ravioli with asparagus or truffles, or gourmet roast lamb. **Vipore**, in nearby Pieve Santo Stefano, © 59245 (*expensive*), is located in a 200-year-old farmhouse, with views over the fertile plain of Lucca. First-quality prime ingredients go into fresh pasta and meat dishes. In Montecarlo try a bottle of local wine, an excellent accompaniment to dishes like truffle *crêpes*, at **Forassiepi** at Porta Belvedere, © 22005 (*moderate to expensive*), located in a former oil press; from the terrace you can see as far as Collodi and the Valdinievole.

The Garfagnana and Lunigiana

The rugged northern finger of Tuscany encompasses the region's 'Alps', the tall and jagged **Alpi Apuane**, which like the real Alps wear brilliant white crowns, though not made of snow—that's marble up there, the 'tears of the stars', the purest and whitest in Italy. Historically the land is divided into two mini-regions: along the bank of the Serchio river, between the Apuan Alps and the Apennines is the **Garfagnana**; while the region north of the village of Piazza al Serchio is the **Lunigiana**, former hinterland of the ancient Roman port of Luni.

The Garfagnana and Lunigiana are fairly undiscovered, and threaten to dispel many people's typical image of Tuscany; the mountains are too high, the valleys too narrow, and pine forests are more in evidence than vineyards and olive groves. Yet a spell in this striking mountain scenery can be just the ticket when the thought of another cathedral or picture gallery begins to pall.

The Garfagnana

For many years the chief export of the Garfagnana has been Italians; the green hills and mountains, the narrow valley of the Serchio, between the Apennines and the Apuan Alps, the stone villages perched on slopes that look so picturesque on postcards were simply never generous enough to provide a sufficient livelihood for their inhabitants. The chief staple of the district until recently was flour made from chestnuts, and chestnut groves still cover much of the region.

Getting Around

 CLAP buses from Lucca connect the city to Bagni di Lucca (27km/40min), Barga (37km/1hr), and Castelnuovo di Garfagnana (50km/1½hrs); trains on the scenic Lucca–Aulla line go up the Serchio valley, though beware that the stations for Bagni di Lucca and Barga are quite a distance from their centres and don't always have connecting buses; you'd be better off taking the bus to begin with. If you're driving from the south, the most convenient way into these mountains begins at Lucca; the S12 and S445 routes follow the river Serchio.

Tourist Information

Bagni di Lucca: Viale Umberto I, 139, ✆ (0583) 87946.

Barga: Piazza Angelio, ✆ (0583) 723499.

Castelnuovo di Garfagnana: in the Rocca Loggiato Porta 10, ✆ and ✉ (0583) 644354.

Lucca to Bagni di Lucca

North of Lucca, the first tempting detour off S12 is to one of the many Romanesque churches in the region, **San Giorgio di Brancoli**, near Vinchiana, as notable for its lovely setting as for its 12th-century pulpit. **Diécimo**, across the river, has a name that survives from Roman times—it lies 10 Roman miles (18km) from Lucca. The landmark here is the mighty Romanesque campanile of the 13th-century church of Santa Maria, standing out starkly against the surrounding hills. **Borgo a Mozzano**, 4km upstream, is famous for its beautiful little hog-back bridge, with arches in five different shapes and sizes, dedicated to the Magdalene, or to the Devil, who according to legend built it one dark and stormy night in exchange for the first soul to cross. The clever villagers outwitted him (as they invariably do in such stories) by sending a dog over in the morning. The real builder in this case was the slighty less lethal 11th-century Countess Matilda who, besides the bridge, endowed the villages around Borgo with a set of solid Romanesque parish churches; in Borgo's church there's a wooden *San Bernardino* by Civitali.

To the north, just above the confluence of the Serchio river and the Torrente Lima lie the long and narrow riverside hamlets that make up **Bagni di Lucca**, Lucca's once-grand old spa, first mentioned in the days of Countess Matilda. In the early 1800s, under the patronage of Elisa Bonaparte Baciocchi, it enjoyed a moment in high society's favour—long enough to build one of Europe's first official gambling casinos (1837; roulette was invented here), an Anglican church in an exotic Gothic Alhambra style, and an unusual 1840 suspension bridge (the **Ponte alle Catene**)—before sinking into obscurity. In Bagni's heyday, though, Byron, Browning, Shelley and Heine came to take the sulphur and saline waters, and perspire in a natural vapour bath. Heine was particularly enthusiastic: 'A true and proper sylvan paradise. I have never found a valley more enchanting,' he wrote; even the mountains are 'nobly formed' and not 'bizarre and Gothic like those in Germany'. Little has changed since, and these days Bagni di Lucca is a sleepy but charming little place, with some pretty villas, elegant thermal establishments that spring into action every summer, a miniature pantheon, and a fancy Circolo dei Forestieri, or foreigners' club (now a restaurant) on the river-front.

Up the Lima Valley

From Bagni di Lucca, the S12 leads towards San Marcello Pistoiese and the ski resort of Abetone (*see* p.236), following the lovely valley of the Lima. A byroad beginning at Bagni leads to picturesque, rugged, stone hamlets like **Pieve di Controne** and **Montefegatesi** which only appear on the most detailed maps; from Montefegatesi, an unsealed road continues to the dramatic gorge of **Orrido di Botri** at the foot of the Alpe Tre Potenze (1940m). As the byroad winds back towards S12 at Scesta, it passes **San Cassiano**, site of a fine 13th-century Pisan-style church with a delicately carved façade; in its isolated setting few people ever see it. Other byroads from the S12 lead to tiny hamlets like **Vico Pancellorum** to the north and **Lucchio** to the south.

Lucca, the Garfagnana and Lunigiana

N

Land over 200 metres

20km
10 miles

To Barga and the Cave of the Wind

The Garfagnana proper begins where the Lima flows into the river Serchio at Fornoli. In the 14th century this area was ruled by the kinsmen of Castruccio Castracani; one of their prettiest mountain hamlets is **Tereglio**, along the scenic northeast road to the **Alpe Tre Potenze**, before it meanders on to Abetone. The Castracani had their base up at **Coreglia Antelminelli**, high above the Serchio and the main S445 (turn off at Piano di Coreglia). Coreglia's parish church contains a magnificent 15th-century processional cross, and there's a **Museo della Figurina** (*open summer 8–1 during the week and 10–1, 4–7 weekends; winter 8–1, closed Sun; adm*) devoted to the Garfagnana's traditional manufacture of plaster figures. To the north, the lovely hill town of **Barga** (pop. 11,000) stands above its modern offspring, Fornaci di Barga on the main S445. Barga was astute enough to maintain its independence until 1341, when it decided to link its fortunes with Florence. At the very top of town stands Barga's chief monument, its **Cathedral**, begun in the year 1000 on a terrace, with a panoramic view over the rooftops and of surrounding hills apparently clad in green velvet, and bare mountains scoured with white marble. Built of a blonde stone called *alberese di Barga*, its square façade is discreetly decorated with a shallow pattern, charming reliefs and two leering lions; on the side the campanile is incorporated into the church; over the portal, there's a relief of a feast scene with a king and dwarfs. There's yet another dwarf inside, supporting one of the red marble pillars of the **pulpit** by the idiosyncratic 13th-century Como sculptor, Guido Bigarelli. The other pillars required a pair of lions, one grinning over a conquered dragon, one being both stroked and stabbed by a man. Less mysterious are the naive reliefs around the pulpit itself, startlingly sophisticated versions of familiar scriptural scenes. In the choir note the venerable polychrome wood statue of St Christopher (early 1100s) and a choir screen with more strange medieval carvings, including a mystic mermaid (*see* Pienza, p.380). Around the back, the cathedral's garden has a magnificent Lebanon cedar. Next to the cathedral stands the **Palazzo Pretorio** and 14th-century **Loggetta del Podestà**; if you go down the stairs towards the dungeon you can see Barga's old corn measures—a medieval Bureau of Standards.

The rest of Barga is a photogenic ensemble of archways and little palazzi piled on top of each other, with walls, gates and a ravine planted with kitchen gardens. Things get lively in July and August with the classes and performances of **Opera Barga** in the old Dei Differenti Theatre, founded in 1600. Between Barga and Fornaci di Barga, you can measure the showy success of the city's emigrants who returned to build modern palaces in the suburb of Giardino.

From Barga you can take a 17-km potholing detour to Fornovalasco in the Apuan Alps to see Tuscany's best cave, the **Grotto del Vento**, a long cavern of fat stalactites, bottomless pits and abysses, and subterranean lakes and streams, set in a barren, eerie landscape (*open April–Sept, at other times Sun and holidays only.; guided tours of one or two hours at 10–12 and 2–6; at 10 and 2, 3-hour tours for real cave fiends; adm exp; try to come in the morning when it's less crowded; for information, © (0583) 722024, ☞ 722053*).

Castelnuovo di Garfagnana

Hanging over the Serchio, 11km north of Barga, is the lively little town of **Castelnuovo di Garfagnana**, the region's 'capital', guarded by the **Rocca**, a fine castle decorated in the best 14th-century manner. Its most famous commander was poet Ludovico Ariosto, author of that great Renaissance epic poem of chivalry and fantasy, *Orlando Furioso*. Ariosto, in the employ of the Este Dukes of Ferrara, competently chased bandits and collected tolls here from 1522 to 1525, but didn't enjoy the job. 'I'm not a man to govern other men,' he wrote to his lover in Ferrara. 'I have too much pity, and can't deny the things they require me to deny.'

Castelnuovo makes an excellent base for excursions into its often wild surroundings. To the northeast, past the small resort of **Castiglione di Garfagnana,** a tortuous mountain road continues through 16km of magnificent scenery to the **Foce delle Radici** (the pass into Emilia-Romagna) and **San Pellegrino in Alpe**, with magnificent views and an ancient monastery, and a good little ethnographic museum, the **Museo della Campagna** (*open 9.30–1 and 3–7 July–Sept; at other times © 649072*). West of Castelnuovo a truly scenic road leads over the Apuan Alps to Carrara and the coast, through the desolate valley of the Turrite Secca, its sombre features relieved by the romantic little oasis of **Isola Santa** (13km)—a tiny village in the trees on its own tiny lake, once a hideout for medieval renegades; now it is abandoned, save for a few old folks and the sheep who lives behind the altar of the church.

North of Castelnuovo the road enters Garfagnana Alta, one of the least-known corners of Tuscany, where Donatello and Piero della Francesca seem far away indeed. Just north of Castelnuovo, explorers can take a winding byroad to the unspoiled **Parco Naturale dell'Orecchiella**, with eagles, mouflons, deer and a botanical garden, its mountains criss-crossed by paths; pick up a map at the park's visitor centre in Orecchiella. At Poggio, back on the Serchio, there's a turn-off for **Careggine**, a lofty old hamlet with commanding views, and the artificial **Lago di Vagli**. Creating this lake submerged the medieval village of Fabbriche, of which the top of the campanile may still be seen sticking stubbornly out of the water. Above, there are more stunning views from **Vagli Sopra**, village of old marble quarries and an 18th-century road, deteriorated into a footpath, which leads into the comely Valle di Arnetola. Towering over all is **Monte Pisanino** (1945m), the tallest of the Apuan Alps; the road approaching the summit and the alpine refuge of Donegani, by way of the lakelet of Gramolazzo, begins at **Piazza al Serchio**, where you leave both the Serchio and the Garfagnana behind.

© (0583–)   ***Where to Stay and Eating Out***

There's nothing exceptional in the Garfagnana, but the Italians, at least, firmly believe the further north in Tuscany you go, the better the cooking, graced by the kindly influences of Liguria and Emilia-Romagna; the pasta dishes in the region are especially good. Specialities include *torte di erbe* (vegetable pies), chestnut puddings and *pattona* (chestnut biscuits). Bagni di Lucca has some quiet, modest old hotels like ★★★**Silvania**, at Lugliano, ✆ 805363, ✉ 867754 (*inexpensive*), with very tranquil and nice rooms. Toscanini stayed in the small ★**Roma**, Via Umberto I 110, ✆ and ✉ 87278 (*inexpensive*), with a shady little garden at the back. These two are in the pretty suburb of Villa di Bagni, a couple of kilometres up the river; in the medieval part of Bagni, there's ★★★**Bridge**, Piazza Ponte a Serraglio 5A, ✆ and ✉ 805324 (*inexpensive*). The best places to eat are **Ruota**, 3km at Fornoli, Via Giovanni XXIII 29/A, ✆ 86071 (*moderate*), with good Tuscan cooking, *closed Mon eve and Tues*, and **Da Vinicio**, a block west of Bagni's bridge at Via del Casino, ✆ 87250 (*moderate*), a chaotic and popular pizzeria, also with good roast pigeon and seafood. Slightly smarter in Loc.Ville is **Circolo dei Forestieri**, ✆ 86308 (*moderate*), where you can eat *filetto al pepe verde* and *crêpes ai funghi. Closed Mon.*

Outside Barga, there's a huge 234-room resort hotel ★★★★**Il Ciocco** in Castelvecchio, 6km north at Pascoli, ✆ 7191, ✉ 723197 (*very expensive*); indoor pool, tennis court, air conditioning, in short, the works. ★★★**Villa Libano**, Via del Sasso 6, ✆ 723774, ✉ 723059 (*inexpensive*), is a lovely place in a courtyard, set next to Barga's city park; there's a restaurant with tables out in the garden. Again, the best restaurant is out of town, at Albiano 5km north, **Terrazza**, ✆ 766155 (*inexpensive*), featuring the half-crazy specialities of the Maremma. *Closed Mon.* In Castelnuovo di Garfagnana, dear old ★★**Da Carlino**, Via Garibaldi 15, ✆ 644270, ✉ 62616 (*inexpensive to moderate*), is the traveller's choice. If you take the route over the Apuan Alps, stop for lunch at Isola Santa. **Da Giacco** (*moderate*) is a downright quaint sort of roadside inn, with a dog sleeping by the wood stove and an owner who remembers a little tortuous English from his days in New Jersey. Roast trout, *polenta* with mushrooms, and a terrace overlooking the lake.

The Lunigiana

Even less populous and less visited than the Garfagnana, the Lunigiana, separating Liguria and Emilia-Romagna from the rest of Tuscany, has traditionally been a tough nut for its would-be governors to crack. The Romans of Luni (founded in 180 BC to contain the fearsome Ligurians) found it a wild place; even in the 7th century, missionaries were still bashing revered ancient idols. This rugged territory of chestnut forests is crowded with the castles of would-be rulers and other toll-collecting gangsters. In the early 1900s the Lunigiana was a stronghold of rural anarchism, and in 1944 its partisans made it one of the bigger free zones in the north. Since then life has been fairly tranquil in the Lunigiana; rocky, forested landscapes, ruined castles (many were bombed in the last war), and simple Romanesque churches form the main attractions.

If you're approaching from the north, trains and autostrade from Genoa (A12) and Parma (A15) merge near Aulla. From here there are frequent trains to Massa-Carrara, Viareggio and Pisa, Pontrémoli or Lucca. From Lucca, trains to Aulla take over 2 hrs (85 km) and to Pontrémoli 2½ hrs (108 km) Bus service in the Lunigiana is provided by CAT, with Aulla as the main depot; there are services to Massa and Carrara, and to Bagnone, Filattiera, Fivizzano, Fosdinovo, Licciana Nardi, Pontrémoli and Villafranca.

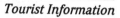

Aulla: Via Gramsci 1, ℗ (0187) 409960, 409627.

Pontrémoli: Piazza del Commune, ℗ (0187) 831180.

Piazza al Serchio to Aulla

Beyond Piazza al Serchio, the first town of consequence along the S445 is fortified **Casola in Lunigiana** (20km); just beyond it a road veers south for the tiny spa of **Equi Terme** in the mountains above. Equi is less visited these days for its waters than for its cave, charmingly called **La Buca del Cane** (Dog's Hole) after its relics of prehistoric man's best friend (*open 9–12 and 2–5, summer 9–12 and 4–7; adm*). Our ancestors also apparently socialized with bears (or ate them), judging by the bones found here. **Fivizzano** to the north (on S63 or by road from Casola) belonged to the Malaspina of Massa until the Medici snatched it and fortified it as a grand ducal outpost. The main square, **Piazza Medicea**, has a grand fountain paid for by Cosimo III, a few Florentine-style palaces, and the 13th-century parish church. There are two interesting Romanesque chapels in the vicinity, **Santa Maria Assunta**, 3km towards Pognana, in a lovely isolated setting, and 12th-century **San Paolo a Vendaso** with carved capitals inside, on S63 towards the Passo di Cerreto. From Ceserano, just south of S445, S446 heads southwest over the mountains to Sarzana, passing by way of **Fosdinovo** (*open daily 10–12, 4–7, 3–7 weekends, in winter 9–12, 3–6; adm*), the Malaspina castle that hosted Dante in 1306, one of the most beautiful and majestic in the Lunigiana. Inside there's an interesting collection of arms and ornaments found in tombs.

Aulla

Aulla grew up at the Lunigiana's hotly contested crossroads, guarding access into the Magra valley. The powerful, four-square 16th-century **Fortezza della Brunella** (*open 9–12 and 2–6, closed Mon; adm*) was built by the Genoese, who bought Aulla in 1543; Napoleon handed it over to his sister Elisa in Lucca. Nearby are the citadels of two other rivals who long fought for the town—the Bishop of Luni's **Caprigliola**, a fortified village still inaccessible to motor traffic (6km southwest on S62) and the Malaspinas' fortified hamlet of **Bibola** and their romantically ruined **Ponzanello**, both due south of Aulla. The Malaspina also fortified the strategic road to the pass, to the northeast at **Licciana Nardi** and especially at **Bastia**, 4km further on.

From Aulla you may want to tuck down into Liguria and the **Italian Riviera** to visit the 'Gulf of the Poets' (or more prosaically, the Gulf of La Spezia), named after Byron, who swam across it, and Shelley, whose last home was in San Terenzo near the old Pisan town of **Lerici**. On the western shore of the Gulf (in Liguria) lies the enchanting old Genoese town of Portovenere, named after the goddess of love herself. The excavations of ancient Luni are near Carrara (*see* p.266).

North of Aulla, **Villafranca in Lunigiana** takes its name from its location on a branch of the Via Francigena, the pilgrimage route from France; it offers the visitor the 16th-century church of **San Francesco** and, in an old mill, an **Ethnographic Museum** (*open winter 9–12 and 3–6, summer 9–12, 4–7, closed Mon; adm*) devoted to rural life in the Lunigiana, especially the chestnut industry. From Villafranca yet another mighty castle beckons up at **Bagnone**, 5km east.

Pontrémoli

Long, low-key, stretched out lazily along the shallow river Magra and the Torrente Verdi, Pontrémoli (pop. 10,200) is chief town of the Lunigiana and the northernmost in Tuscany. It wasn't always so peaceful: in the old days the quarrels between local Guelphs and Ghibellines led Castruccio Castracani to build a fortress in 1322, called *Cacciaguerra* ('Drive-away war') in the town centre to keep the two parties apart until they made peace. Of this noble effort only the **Torre del Campanone** and what is now the campanile of the **Duomo** survive. The Duomo itself has a fine, ballroom interior, unusual for Tuscany. Over the Torrente Verdi, the church of **San Francesco** with a Baroque entrance, contains a lovely polychrome relief of the Madonna and *bambino* attributed to Agostino di Duccio. Between the centre and the station the oval 18th-century church of **Nostra Donna** is a rare example of Tuscan Rococo.

Prehistoric Mysteries

Behind all these baubles, this hidden corner of Italy holds a genuine prehistoric mystery. To learn about it, climb up the narrow medieval lanes above Pontrémoli to the gloomy, 14th-century **Castello del Piagnaro** and its archaeology museum (*open 9–12 and 2–5 Oct–May, summer 9–12 and 4–7, closed Mon; adm*). It holds over a score of large, carved statue-steles of an unknown culture that flourished in the Lunigiana between the 3rd millennium BC and the 2nd century BC. The steles, rather like menhirs with personality, include stylized warriors with daggers or axes, and women with little knobbly breasts. The oldest (3000–2000 BC) have a U for a face and a head hardly distinguishable from the trunk; the middle period (2000–8th century BC) sport anvil heads and eyes; the last group (7th–2nd century BC) are mostly warriors, with a weapon in each hand, just as Virgil described the Gauls who invaded Lazio. They were often discovered near sources of water, and some scholars think they may have symbolized the heavens (the head), the earth (the arms and weapons) and the underworld (the lower third, buried in the ground). Similar statue-steles turn up in southern Corsica and other places around the Mediterranean. Some of the steles had their heads knocked off, a sure sign that the pope's missionaries in the 8th century were doing their job. Curiously, in the nearby hamlet of Vignola, a folk memory survives of the destruction of idols; during the patron saint's festival they make little wooden idols strangely similar to Pontrémoli's statue-steles and burn them to celebrate the triumph over the pagans.

In 1471 the Virgin made an appearance a mile south of Pontrémoli, and to honour the spot the **church of Santissima Annunziata** was built with a lovely marble **Tempietto** by Jacopo Sansovino, a quattrocento fresco of the Annunciation by Luca Cambiaso, an elegant triptych of uncertain hand or date, and some fun *trompe-l'oeil* frescoes by a Baroque painter from Cremona named Natali.

Where to Stay and Eating Out

Pioneers in the Lunigiana will find a comfortable bed (*inexpensive*) and a tasty meal (*moderate*) at Equi Terme's ★**La Posta** in Via Provinciale, ✆ (0585) 97937; delicious antipasti. A good central base in the region, the old-fashioned ★**Alpi Apuane di Malatesta** is in a former posthouse at Pallerone near Aulla, ✆ (0817) 418045, although rooms (*inexpensive*) are only a sideline to the fine restaurant (*moderate*), cosy in the winter with its fireplace. Specialities here include wildfowl excellently prepared—pheasant, duck and pigeon, and for big appetites, kid with polenta. Also in Aulla is the sophisticated and refined **Il Rigoletto**, Quartiere Matteotti 29, ✆ (0187) 409879 (*expensive*) serving unusual and excellent food, such as salmon cooked with fennel and pear strudel with red wine sorbet and liquorice. *Closed Mon.* Up in fortified Bagnone, **I Fondi**, Via della Repubblica 26, ✆ (0187) 429086 (*inexpensive*), offers good, solid country cooking—trout, mushroom dishes, rabbit, stuffed cabbage, venison with polenta—amid Italian rustic elegance. In Fivizzano, **★★Il Giardinetto**, Via Roma 151, ✆ (0585) 92060 (*rooms inexpensive, food moderate*), is a delightful place to sleep and eat overlooking the Piazza Medicea. The rooms are comfortable, and as the name implies, there's a little garden to lounge in. The hot and cold antipasti are especially tempting, as well as the pasta and game dishes, and a flan with spinach and cheese, made from a Renaissance recipe. In Tresana, north of Aulla, **Da Fabio**, Via Matteotti 56, ✆ (0187) 477009 (*inexpensive*), is a popular trattoria in a rustic 17th-century building that people drive out of their way to visit; the specialities are rustic, and the prices are good too. *Closed Fri.*

Pontrémoli is rich in good restaurants, and has two smart hotels, the new **★★★Golf Hotel**, outside town in a pine wood, Via Pineta, ✆ (0187) 831573, @ 831591 (*moderate*), offering 90 very comfortable rooms, all with bath and TV, and the **★★★Hotel Napoleon**, Piazza Italia 2B, ✆ 830544, @ 830544 (*moderate*), with garage and modern rooms. When it's time to eat, there's the age-old **Da Bussé**, Piazza del Duomo 31, ✆ 831371 (*moderate*), featuring Pontrémoli's special pasta *testaroli*, roast meats, stuffed vegetables and other local dishes. *Closed Fri.* **La Romantica**, Piazza SS Annunziata 86, ✆ 830106, offers ravioli with basil and walnuts, artichoke or *porcini crocchette*, and a delicious selection of meat dishes (moderate). Another good bet in the centre, **Da Fernando**, Via San Gimignano, ✆ 830653 (*inexpensive*), is a little bistro in a 17th-century building, where you can dine on *testaroli* with pesto or boar *alla cacciatora. Closed Mon.*

The Tuscan Coast

The Etruscan Riviera, the Tyrrhenian shore, Tuscany by the sea—call it what you will, most of it is flat, straight, dull and endowed with wide sandy beaches that are usually crowded. The sea isn't quite as clean as it might be, and the closer you get to the mouth of the Arno and Livorno, the less savoury it becomes. If you're intent on a spell on the beach, you may well find Tuscany's archipelago of seven islands more congenial—the sea is cleaner and the coast and beaches prettier. But what is harder to escape, unless you go to the smallest islands, is Italian beach culture. Much of the shore is privately owned and you must pay for access to a veritable wall of deck chairs and beach umbrellas, packed as densely as possible; behind this there's inevitably a busy road, where the traffic is mainly vans with loudspeakers and motorcycles; behind the busy road is another wall of hotels, and perhaps a few pine woods.

The most beautiful and fashionable section of the Tuscan coast is the Argentario, around Porto Santo Stefano, but it's also the most expensive. Elba, the largest island, is rugged and beautiful, but very busy as a Euro-holiday beacharama. Other places are an acquired taste: Viareggio, with more character than most and a Puccini opera festival, or Livorno, one of Italy's largest ports, famous for its seafood restaurants. The mellow old city of Pisa, an ancient maritime republic long ago silted up by the Arno, needs no introduction. In Carrara you can learn about marble in the Apuan Alps, in the Maremma you can learn about Italian cowboys and discover the lovely old town of Massa Marittima.

The Riviera della Versilia: Carrara to Viareggio

Getting Around

Transport is very easy along the coast, by train or especially by bus, with three companies—CAT, CLAP and LAZZI competing for your custom. CAT buses link the Marinas of the coast with Massa and Carrara, and the towns of the Lunigiana; CLAP links Forte dei Marmi and Viareggio with Lucca; LAZZI connects the coast with Lucca, Montecatini, Pistoia and Florence. Note that trains to Massa or Carrara leave you exactly between their beaches and their centres, but CAT bus connections to either are frequent. By car you can whip through the dull stretches on the A12, or follow the Via Aurelia (S1), the main Roman route, though both keep their distance from the sea.

Tourist Information

Marina di Carrara: Piazza Menconi 5b, ✆ (0585) 632218.

Marina di Massa: Viale Vespucci 24, ✆ (0585) 240046, 🖷 869015.

Viale S. Leonardo 500, ✆ (0585) 240063.

Pietrasanta: Piazza Duomo, ✆ (0584) 795260.

to Parma

to Genoa

Campo Cecina

Carrara

La Spezia

Marinella
Marina di Carrara
Marina di Massa
Cinquale Capriglia
Forte dei Marmi
Marina di Pietrasanta

Massa

Seravezza   Stazzema

V. Carducci
Pietrasanta
Capezzano

Camaiore

Lido di Camaiore

Viareggio

Torre del Lago

Massarosa

Valle Freddana

Lucca

Lago di Massaciuccoli

A P U A N E

Serchio

to Bologna

Pistoia

Prato

Florence

A11

S436

Gombo
San Piero a Grado
Marina di Pisa

Pisa

Certosa di Pisa

Arno

A12

A1

to Arezzo

Tirrenia

Livorno

Ardenza

I. di Gorgona

Montenero

S206 S1

Castiglioncello
Rosignano
Vada

Cecina

Marina di Cecina

Bolgheri

Castagneto-Carducci

San Vincenzo

Campiglia Marittima

Golfo di Baratti
Populonia

Suvereto

Massa Marittima

Volterra

S68

Poggibonsi

Siena

T U S C A N Y

S439

S1

Porto

I. di Capraia

Piombino

Follonica

Golfo di Follonica

Vetulonia

Braccagni

Roselle

S223

S73

Portoferraio

Isola d'Elba

Porto Azzurro

Punta Ala

Castiglione della Pescaia
Marina di Grosseto

S322

Grosseto

Scansano

Alberese

Magliano in Toscana

to Pitigliano

Manciano

I. Pianosa

Talamone

S74

N

Porto Santo Stefano

Orbetello

Capalbio

Ansedonia

to Rome

Monte Argentario

Port'Ercole

Giglio Castello

Giglio Campese

Giglio Porto

Land over 200 metres

30km
20 miles

I. di Montecristo

I. del Giglio

I. di Giannutri

Carrara

In the centre of the dynamic, up-to-date Carrara (pop. 69,000) there's a garden square called Piazza Gramsci with an unusual fountain, consisting of a large, snow-white sphere of marble that hypnotically revolves, glistening with water, while in the background tower the Apuan Alps, streaked with the white quarries where the sphere was 'liberated'. Carrara means marble; its name is believed to come from 'Kar', the Indo-European word for stone. The Romans were the first to extract it 2000 years ago; they drove wooden wedges soaked in water into the natural cracks in the stone, and when the wedges swelled, the marble would break off, and was rolled away on iron balls and sent to Rome to become Trajan's column or Apollo Belvedere. The same techniques were still being used when Carrara began its brilliant revival in 1502, when Pope Julius II sent Michelangelo to find the marble for his tomb. These mountains are haunted by the memory of the 'divine' sculptor, in his old clothes and smelly goatskin boots, taking his horse into the most inaccessible corners to discover new veins of perfect, white stone. Michelangelo thought of quarrying as an art just as serious as the actual sculptural work; he loved to spend time here with his rock, and he claimed with his usual modesty to have 'introduced the art of quarrying' to Carrara. In some intangible way, marble has also made the Carraresi traditionally a breed apart—although their official past is dominated by the rule of godfatherish noble clans like the Malaspina and Cybo-Malaspina, the undercurrents were always fiercely independent, leaning strongly towards anarchism.

Some of Carrara's marble went into its one outstanding monument, the **Cathedral**, a distinctive Romanesque church begun in the 11th century with marble stripes and an arch of marble animals, and later embellished with an exquisite 14th-century rose window, made of marble lace, and marble art and statues inside, including a huge marble bowl in the baptistry. In the little piazza there's a bulky sculpture called the Giant, but it is really supposed to be *Andrea Doria in the Guise of Neptune* by the Florentine hack Bandinelli. Next to the Piazza Gramsci, on Via Roma 1, is the **Accademia delle Belle Arti**, in a medieval castle converted into a palace in the 16th century by Alberico Cybo-Malaspina, the great Marchese di Massa, whose descendants ruled Massa and Carrara until dying out in 1829, when the little state joined the Duchy of Modena until unification. The Accademia's courtyard contains sculptures from ancient Luni and the *Edicola dei Fantescritti*, a Roman tabernacle found in the Fantescritti quarry, with bas-reliefs of Jove, Hercules and Bacchus, arm in arm like old chums, surrounded by graffiti by Giambologna and other sculptors who visited the quarries.

Marble Quarries and Roman Ruins

Even though Carrara exports half a million tons of different marbles a year, there is little danger of it running out soon; one wonders if they're joking when they gravely mention that there are only a few cubic kilometres of good stone left. Visiting one of the **quarries** surrounding Carrara is an unforgettable sight; usually they extend straight up to the sky, a blinding white scar down the mountain with a narrow access road zigzagging perpendicularly to the top. Signs from the centre of Carrara direct you to the quarries, or *Cave di*

Marmo—**Colonnata** (8km, founded as a colony of Roman slaves), **Fantiscritti** (a Roman quarry still in use) and **Ravaccione** (with fine views over the mountains). Before leaving town stop by the **Museo Civico del Marmo**, on Viale XX Settembre (the main road between Carrara and the train station) (*open 10–8, closed Sun; adm*) which takes you through the wonderful world of marble with remarkable photographs of the marble-workers of a hundred years ago and the surreal world of the quarries; halls of polished slabs introduce the amazing variety of marbles and travertines from the area, and then from around the world; and there's marble art and a room of mod marble to prove it's no fuddy-duddy stone limited to churches and public buildings.

The proximity of the Apuan Alps, only a few kilometres from the sea, gives this stretch of coast a certain majesty. The beach at **Marina di Carrara** is divided in two by the marble port, from which the big blocks are sent all over the world; in July and August the port-resort puts on a big show of marble arts and crafts. Just to the north, on the border of Liguria near Marinella, you can visit the site of Roman **Luni**, a colony built as a bulwark against the fierce Ligurians. The city survived until the Middle Ages; the power-hungry Bishop of Luni survived even longer, until 1929, when the bishopric was combined with that of La Spezia. Excavations have brought to light a sizeable amphitheatre, forum, houses, temples, etc; on the site is the **Museo Nazionale di Luni** (*open 9–12 and 2–5, winter, 9–7 summer, closed Mon; adm*), with an interesting collection of marble statuary, coins, jewellery, portraits, etc., as well as a display of modern archaeological techniques used in excavating the site, which can be toured with a guide. To the east off S446, 20km up in the mountains above Carrara, there is an extraordinary panoramic view over the marble quarries from **Campo Cecina**. The city of Carrara has an alpine refuge here, which can be a base for exploring some of the Apuan Alps' network of trails (the tourist office has a map).

Massa

Massa (pop. 66,200), nearly the same size as Carrara and co-capital of the province, was the principal seat of the Cybo-Malaspina dukes. They were never great builders or patrons, except when it came to their own digs—their polychrome 17th-century **Palazzo Cybo-Malaspina**, on central Piazza degli Aranci, with its orange trees and obelisk, and their **Castello Malaspina** up the hill on Via della Rocca (*closed for restoration at present; otherwise open 9–12 and 4–7, winter 2–5, closed Mon; adm; information © (0585) 44774*), an 11th-century castle with Renaissance additions, including a beautiful, ornate courtyard, loggias, and frescoed rooms. From Massa there are other marble quarries to visit, near **Pasquilio** 11km east, a balcony with views over the Gulf of La Spezia; in the same area, the **Pian della Fioba** has a botanical garden planted with the flora of the Apuan mountains, more stunning views, and another alpine refuge open all year round.

Marina di Massa, on a marsh drained in the last century, is a lively proletarian resort with lots of pine trees; its neighbour, **Cinquale,** is the 'Marina' of the old hill town of Montignoso, is smaller and prettier, and between it and Forte dei Marmi there's a long stretch of free beach. Near Montignoso stand the picturesque ruins of the **Castle of Aghinolfi,** a Lombard outpost built in AD 600 by King Agilufo.

Around Forte dei Marmi

Forte dei Marmi is one of the larger and, for the past decade or so, one of the trendier resorts on the coast. Founded in 1788, when Grand Duke Leopoldo constructed the fortress and seaport to serve the marble quarried from Seravezza, its old loading pier is now used as a promenade. In the 1860s the first holiday villas were built, and today it still has a residential, garden air and a popular white sandy beach. The public stretch is to the north of the town. **Marina di Pietrasanta** is about the same, but has in its **Parco della Versiliana** that last section of the primordial coastal forest, lush with parasol pines, holm oaks and myrtles. This was a favourite haunt of Gabriele D'Annunzio, and in the summer there are concerts, plays and ballets in its small outdoor theatre. **Lido di Camaiore**, the last resort before Viareggio, caters mainly to families, and differs from its neighbours in its elevated garden terrace along the beach front.

Inland from Forte dei Marmi is the important marble town of **Seravezza**, where Michelangelo lived in 1517 during one of his marble pilgrimages, this time to Monte Altissimo, rich in statue stone. Not long afterwards, Duke Cosimo I commissioned Ammannati to build the **Villa Medicea** with its good Mannerist courtyard. The **Cathedral** contains works by Florentine goldsmiths, including a crucifix attributed to one of the Pollaiuolo brothers; 5km away, the beautifully situated **Pieve alla Cappella** has a fine rose window nicknamed the 'Eye of Michelangelo.' Another pretty place to visit in these mountains of quarries and chestnut forests is **Stazzema**, with a Romanesque church and more stunning views. The quarries near Stazzema produce a blue and white streaked marble called 'flowered' that found its way into the Medicis' Princes' Chapel. Among the mountains in the area is the curious Monte Forata (1223m) with a hole near its summit.

Pietrasanta

Pietrasanta, near the coast, is a mellow old town rich in marbly traditions. Its walls date from 1255, though its regular quadrangle of streets suggests a Roman origin. Life centres around the large central Piazza del Duomo, with its Florentine *Marzocco* on a pillar (1514) and the **Duomo di San Martino**, begun in 1256 and restored in 1630 and 1824, with a rose window carved from a single block of marble and more marble inside, as well as a bronze crucifix by Tacca and a 13th-century fresco by the school of Giotto. Its Renaissance campanile looks half finished. It shares the piazza with the **Palazzo Pretorio** and **Sant'Agostino** (14th century) with an attractive minimalist Pisan façade. From here a road leads up to the citadel, or **Rocca Arrighina**, built in the 1300s by Castruccio Castracani and lit up at night; it often hosted emperors on their way to Rome but all they left behind is the view. You can see what contemporary would-be Michelangelos are up to by calling Cosmave, ✆ (0585) 791297, ✉ 790885, who will give information about the work of local artists. Alternatively turn right from the main gate for the central market building, its parking adorned with the world's most erotic market statue, of a woman *en déshabillé* pulling a young bull after her.

The Mountains Beyond Pietrasanta

From Pietrasanta a road heads inland towards **Valdicastello Carducci** (birthplace of the poet Giosuè Carducci) passing by way of the 9th-century **Pieve di Santi Giovanni and Felicità**, the oldest church in the Versilia, with 14th-century frescoes. There are lovely views stretching from La Spezia to Pisa from **Capezzano** and **Capriglia**, on the same road winding further up in the mountains. **Camaiore** (from the Roman *Campus Major*, pop. 31,000) is an industrial town on the road to Lucca, of interest for its Romanesque churches—the **Collegiata, Santi Giovanni e Stefano** (with a stately bell tower and Roman sarcophagus for a font), and the 8th-century **Badia dei Santi Benedettini**, remodelled in the 11th century and adorned with a lovely portal. In Piazza Diaz, the little **Museo d'Arte Sacra** (*open 10–12 Sat only, summer 4–6 Tues and Sat*) contains some lovely Flemish tapestries. A panoramic road from Camaiore leads up to **Monteggiori**, with more fine views. Other destinations around Camaiore include the beautiful **Valle Freddana** and Monte Magno; and **Pieve a Elici**, near Massarosa, with another excellent Romanesque church, 12th-century **San Pantaleone**. From here a minor road continues up through majestic chestnut groves to **Montigiano**, one of the finest balconies in the Apuans.

Where to Stay and Eating Out

Carrara ✆ *(0585–)*

The best hotel is called, naturally, ★★★**Michelangelo**, Corso F. Rosselli 3, ✆ 777161, ✉ 74545 (*moderate*), with modern rooms and parking facilities. There's a youth hostel at Marina di Massa e Carrara, if you're game, called **Ostello Apuano**, Viale delle Pinete 237, ✆ 780034, ✉ 780659, charging L12,000 a head, including breakfast. *Open mid-March–Sept.* If you are planning a camping trip, choose one of many sites along the coast between the marinas of Massa and Carrara. This stretch of beach is also public. There are quite a few good restaurants—if you're lucky you may find a bottle of Candia, the white wine eked from Carrara's mountain terraces. Try **Soldaini**, Via Mazzini 11, ✆ 71928 (*expensive*), which offers simple dishes from other Italian regions, exquisitely prepared. Among the quarries in Colonnata, at **Da Venanzio**, ✆ 73617 (*moderate*)., you can try the local speciality, a delicate bacon, or crêpes, delicious *tortelli*, pigeon in balsamic vinegar or even roast beef. *Closed Thurs.*

Forte dei Marmi ✆ *(0584–)*

Hotels here are more modern than in Viareggio, and the cruel rule of fashion is making prices higher all the time. Try ★★★★**Raffaeli Park**, Via Mazzini 37, ✆ 787294, ✉ 787418 (*expensive to very expensive*) or its less expensive companion, ★★★**Raffaeli Villa Angela**, Via Mazzini 64, ✆ 787472, ✉ 787115 (*expensive*). Both have their stretch of private beach, a pool, tennis court and air-conditioned rooms. Less expensive places go for the same rates as in Viareggio, but there are considerably fewer of these. Dining is a delight at the Versilia's finest restaurant, **Da Lorenzo**, Via Carducci 61, ✆ 84030 (*moderate*), where seafood beautifully and imaginatively prepared is a trump card. Be sure to reserve. *Closed Mon*. Another good seafood restaurant, **La Barca**, Viale Italico 3, ✆ 89323 (*inexpensive*), offers more traditional Italian dishes. *Closed Mon lunch and Tues.*

Lido di Camaiore ✆ (0584–)

Near Camaiore, **Emilio e Bona**, Località Candalla, Via Lombrice, 22, ✆ 989289 (*moderate*), offers excellent food; try their duck breast with herbs or steak with almonds. *Closed Mon*. **Da Mario**, Via Colombo 102, ✆ 66096 (*moderate*), is a large, popular place which serves delicious fish dishes including a warming seafood risotto. *Closed Mon.*

Viareggio

Tourist Information

Viale Carducci 10, ✆ (0584) 962233, 🖂 47336.

Up until the 1820s Viareggio (pop. 59,000), Tuscany's biggest seaside resort, was little more than a fishing village, named after the medieval royal road, the 'Via Regia' that connected Migliarino and Pietrasanta. After the 14th-century battles with Pisa, Genoa and Florence, this little village was the republic of Lucca's sole access to the sea. Fortifications were built—Forte del Motrone (which it lost in 1441) and the Torre del Mare and **Torre Matilde** near the canal (*open on request*), which the Lucchesi managed to hold on to until the 19th century, although it was too marshy to do them much good. It was Lucca's beloved Duchess Maria Luisa who drained the swamps, developed the shipyards and fishing and resort industries, and laid out the neat grid of streets; by the 1860s the first *cabanas* and beach umbrellas had made their debut.

By the turn of the century Viareggio was booming, embellished with playful, intricate, wooden Art Nouveau buildings that lined its celebrated seaside promenade, the Passeggiata Viale Regina Margherita. In 1917 a massive fire destroyed nearly all of this, and when it was rebuilt in the 1920s, its most important buildings were designed by Galileo Chini and the eclectic Alfredo Belluomini. Chini (1873–1956) was one of the founders of Italian Art Nouveau, or the Liberty Style, which first caught the public's fancy in the 1902 Esposizione Internazionale di Arti Decorative in Turin. Chini was especially well known for florid ceramics, but he also designed stage sets for the New York Metropolitan Opera's premières of his friend Puccini's operas: *Turandot, Manon Lescaut* and *Gianni Scicchi*, as well as the throne room of the King of Siam (1911–14). In Viareggio he worked with Belluomini to produce what has become the symbol of Viareggio, the colourful, twin-towered **Gran Caffè Margherita**, in a kind of Liberty-Mannerism; as well as the **Bagna Balena** and what is now the Supercinema, all on the Passeggiata. You can compare their work with the 1900 **Negozio Martini**, the only wooden building to survive the 1917 fire. Chini and Belluomini also designed a number of hotels (*see* below) as well as Puccini's villa on Piazza Puccini, and the buildings at Piazza D'Azeglio 15 and Viale Manin 20.

Even more colourful are the floats used in Viareggio's famous **Carnival**. It was begun in the 1890s but has grown to rival the much older carnivals of Rome and Venice, and in pure frivolity has surpassed them all. In the centre of the action are large, usually very satirical papier-mâché floats; if you can't come on Shrove Tuesday to join the massive parade, you can see them being created in the huge **float hangars** along Viale Marco Polo and they are displayed in the **Hangar Carnivale** (*open 10.30–12, 4.30–7 Tues–Fri*). At the Società Ippica Viareggina, Via Comparini 8, ℰ 391176, you can hire a horse to explore the pine woods just south of Viareggio.

Torre del Lago and Puccini

Tourist Information

Viale Marconi 25, ℰ (0584) 359893.

Puccini spent most of his later years in his villa at **Torre del Lago**, 6km south of Viareggio along Via dei Tigli (buses from Piazza D'Azeglio), a lovely road passing through an extensive pine wood. His villa, now the **Museo Pucciniano** (*open 10–12.30 and 3–5, 4–7 daily in summer, closed Mon; adm*), is on the banks of shallow Lake Massaciuccoli, where he could practise 'my second favourite instrument, my rifle' on passing coots. The villa contains its original furnishings, old photos, the piano on which Puccini composed many of his operas, his rifles and other mementoes. The maestro and his wife and son are buried in the adjacent chapel. In August Torre del Lago holds a popular **opera festival** in its outdoor theatre, presenting famous and obscure works by the great composer; for a schedule and tickets contact the Festival Pucciniano, Piazzale Belvedere Puccini, Torre del Lago, ℰ (0584) 359322.

Most of Lake Massaciuccoli and the marshlands, the *macchia*, and beaches to the south are part of the **Parco Naturale Migliarino San Rossore Massaciuccoli** (*guided tours are arranged from 8am to 2pm, phone in advance, ℰ (050) 525500*) San Rossore is open Sundays and holidays only, 8.30–5.30 winter, till 7.30 summer; to visit on weekdays ℰ (050) 539111). Boats from Torre del Lago explore some of these wetlands, or you can go by car to the tiny village of Massaciuccoli. The wild beaches between Viareggio and Torre del Lago, with their low dunes and scrubby pine forest, are free and undeveloped. The forest of San Rossore, in existence since Roman times, is nowadays threatened by the spray from the polluted sea, which is unfortunately killing the pines.

ℰ (0584–)

Where to Stay

If you're Viareggio bound, why not stay in a Chini-Belluomini confection for the total experience? One of their most extravagant is ★★★★**Grand Hotel Excelsior**, Viale Carducci 88, ℰ 50726, ✉ 50729 (*expensive to very expensive, all rooms with TV*), built in 1923; the original decor of the public rooms is well preserved. *Open 20 May–20 Oct.* Belluomini on his own built the ★★★**Grand Hotel & Royal**, Viale Carducci 44, ℰ 45151, ✉ 31438 (*expensive,* *with an indoor pool and parking*), in a kind of neo-Renaissance eclectic style, with an impressive lobby. Open *April–Oct*. Another ageing queen by both men is ★★★**Liberty**, Lungomare Manin 18, ✆ 46247, 🖃 46249 (*inexpensive to moderate*). *Open April–Oct*. There are scores of other hotels along the beach front, especially less expensive ones in the L35–50,000 range. On the lakeside of Torre del Lago, on Via Puccini, 260 is ★**Albergo Antonio**, ✆ 341053 (*inexpensive*).

✆ *(0584–)*   ***Eating Out***

One might suspect that the hordes of Italians who descend on Viareggio every summer do so mainly to eat; the resort has a disproportionate number of good restaurants. Heading the list, the **L'Oca Bianca** on Via Coppino 409, ✆ 388318, north of the centre, is the place to go for Mediterranean lobster (*aragosta*), all kinds of fish, and elaborately prepared and served gourmet concoctions. Try the *menu degustazione* for L90,000—you could spend considerably more à la carte. *Closed Tues*. **Burrasca**, Via Garibaldi 122, ✆ 31402 (*expensive*), offers a real surprise—Sardinian dishes, not often seen outside the island; not only *mallorredus* (nasty-looking Sard pasta), but great seafood antipasti and stews. *Closed Thurs*. Also very good and creative, and very popular, is **Romano**, Via Mazzini 122, ✆ 31382 (*very expensive*), elegant, with a dining room and interior garden, and delicious seafood *à la Toscana*. *Reserve a table; closed Mon*. **Margherita**, Via Regina Margherita 30, ✆ 962553 (*expensive*), has a sommelier not of wine but olive oil! The seafood is delicious and varied, and there's a good wine list too. *Closed Wed*. For seafood with less pretensions and lower prices, try **Giorgio**, Via IV Novembre, ✆ 44493 (*moderate*), a lively welcoming place decorated with the works of local artists. *Closed Wed*. A good place to go wine tasting is **Il Puntodivino**, Via Mazzini 229, ✆ 31046 (*moderate*); the wines and champagnes come from all over Italy and France, even if the food is local—try the prawns with *prosciutto*, or if you're in a wild mood, anchovies with fennel. *Closed Mon*. The cheap and cheerful **Il Vecchio Casale Poppi** in Via Fossolegname 22, ✆ 960153 (*moderate*), serves seafood and game. *Closed Wed*.

Pisa

Pisa (pop. 104,000) is at once the best-known and the most mysterious of Tuscan cities. Its most celebrated attraction has become, along with the Colosseum, gondolas and spaghetti a symbol for the entire Italian republic; even the least informed recognize the 'Leaning Tower of Pizza' even if they've never heard of Florence or Siena. Tour buses disgorge thousands every day into the Field of Miracles, who spend a couple of hours and leave again for places more tangible, like Florence, Elba or Rome. At night even the Pisani make a mass exodus into the suburbs, as if they sense that the city is too big for them, not physically, but in terms of unfulfilled ambitions, of past greatness nipped in the bud.

Yet go back to about 1100, when according to the chroniclers, precocious Pisa was 'the city of marvels', the 'city of ten thousand towers', with a population of 300,000—or so it seemed to the awed writers of that century, who, at least outside Venice, had never before seen such an enormous, cosmopolitan and exotic city in Christian Europe since the fall of Rome. Pisan merchants made themselves at home all over the Mediterranean, bringing back new ideas and new styles in art in addition to their fat bags of profit; Pisa contributed as much to the rebirth of Western culture as any city. Pisan Romanesque, with its stripes and blind arcades, which had such a wide influence in Tuscany, was inspired by the great Moorish architecture of Andalucía; Nicola Pisano, first of a long line of great sculptors, is as important to the renaissance of sculpture as Giotto is to painting.

Like a Middle Eastern city, Pisa has put all its efforts into one fabulous spiritual monument, while the rest of the city wears a decidedly undemonstrative, almost anonymous face, a little run down. It is a subtle place, a little sad perhaps, but strangely seductive if you give it a chance. After all, one can't create a Field of Miracles in a void.

History

In the Middle Ages, Pisa liked to claim that it began as a Greek city, founded by colonists from Elis. Most historians, however, won't give them credit for anything earlier than 100 BC or so, when a Roman veterans' colony was settled there. Records of what followed are scarce, but Pisa, like Amalfi and Venice, must have had an early start in building a navy and establishing trade connections. By the 11th century, the effort had blossomed into opulence; Pisa built itself a small empire, including Corsica, Sardinia, and for a while the Balearics. Around 1060, work was begun on the great cathedral complex and many other buildings, inaugurating the Pisan Romanesque.

In 1135 Pisa captured and sacked its greatest rival in the western Mediterranean, Amalfi. The First Crusade, when Pisa's archbishop led the entire fleet in support of the Christian knights, turned out to be an economic windfall for the city. Unlike Amalfi, from the start Pisa had adopted a course of combat with the states of the Moslem world, less from religious bigotry than a clear eye on the main chance. When the Pisans weren't battling with the Moslems of Spain and Africa, they were learning from them. A steady exchange of ideas brought much of medieval Arab science, philosophy and architecture into Europe through Pisa's port. Pisa's architecture, the highest development of the Romanesque in Italy, saw its influence spread from Sardinia to Apulia in southern Italy; when Gothic arrived in Italy Pisa was one of the few cities to take it seriously, and the city's accomplishments in that style rank with Siena's. In science, Pisa contributed a great though shadowy figure, that most excellent mathematician Leonardo Fibonacci, who either rediscovered the principle of the Golden Section or learned it from the Arabs, and also introduced Arabic numerals to Europe. Pisa's scholarly traditions over the centuries would be crowned in the 1600s by its most famous son, Galileo Galilei.

Pisa was always a Ghibelline city, the greatest ally of the emperors in Tuscany if only for expediency's sake. When a real threat came, however, it was not from Florence or any of the other Tuscan cities, but from the rising mercantile port of Genoa. After years of

Pisa

constant warfare, the Genoese devastated the Pisan navy at the Battle of Meloria (an islet off Livorno) in 1284. It signalled the end of Pisan supremacy, but all chance of recovery was quashed by an even more implacable enemy: the Arno. Pisa's port was gradually silting up, and when the cost of dredging became greater than the traffic could bear, the city's fate was sealed. The Visconti of Milan seized the economically enfeebled city in 1396, and nine years later Florence snatched it from them. Excepting the period 1494–1505, when the city rebelled and kept the Florentines out despite an almost constant siege of 15 years, Pisa's history was ended. The Medici dukes did the city one big favour, supporting the university and even removing Florence's own university to Pisa. In the last 500 years of Pisa's long, pleasant twilight, this institution has helped the city stay alive and vital, and in touch with the modern world; one of its students was the nuclear physicist Enrico Fermi.

Getting Around

by air

Pisa has Tuscany's international airport, Galileo Galilei, in the suburb of San Giusto, 3km south of the city; ✆ (050) 44325 or 500707 for general information, for British Airways ✆ 501838, for Alitalia ✆ 48025. Most of the big car rental firms are there, ready to equip you with wheels: Hertz ✆ (050) 49187, Avis ✆ 42028, Maggiore ✆ 42574, Budget ✆ 45490, Program ✆ 500296.

by train

The airport is linked to Pisa by train or city bus No. 5, departing from Piazza Stazione, in front of the main station, which lies south of the Arno, ✆ (050) 42291. Many trains (Florence–Pisa or Genoa–Rome lines) also stop at Stazione San Rossore; if you're making Pisa a day trip you may want to get off there, as it's only a few blocks from the cathedral and Leaning Tower—or else bus No. 1 will take you there from the central station.

by bus

All intercity buses depart from near Piazza Vittorio Emanuele II, the big round-about just north of the central station: APT buses for Volterra, Livorno and the coastal resorts (to the left on Via Nino Bixio, © (050) 501038) and LAZZI buses to Florence, Lucca, La Spezia (on Via d'Azeglio, © 42688). Many of these buses also stop at Piazza D. Manin, just outside the walls of the cathedral. The Natural Park Migliarino San Rossore Massaciuccoli (*see* p.273) may be reached by city bus No. 11 from Lungarno Gambacorti. Pisa lends itself well to **bicycles**; you can hire one at Via Nino Bixio, near the station.

Tourist Information

Piazza Duomo, near the Leaning Tower, © (050) 560464. Just outside the central station, there's an accommodation/information office, © 42291.

The Field of Miracles

Almost from the time of its conception, this was the nickname given to medieval Italy's most ambitious building programme. As with Florence's cathedral, too many changes were made over two centuries of work to tell exactly what the original intentions were. But of all the unique things about this complex, the location strikes one first. Whether their reasons had to do with aesthetics or land values—probably a little of both—the Pisans built their cathedral on a broad expanse of green lawn at the northern edge of town, just inside the walls. The cathedral was begun in 1063, the famous Leaning Tower and the baptistry in the middle 1100s, at the height of Pisa's fortunes, and the Campo Santo in 1278. For the museums and monuments on the campo, you can save by getting the joint ticket, for L15,000 .

The Baptistry

Open 9–sunset.

The biggest of its kind in Italy; those of many other cities would fit neatly inside. The original architect, with the felicitous name of Master Diotisalvi ('God save you'), saw the lower half of the building done in the typical stripes-and-arcades Pisan style. A second colonnade was intended to go over the first, but as the Genoese gradually muscled Pisa out of trade routes, funds ran short. In the 1260s, Nicola and Giovanni Pisano, members of that remarkable family of artists who did so much to re-establish sculpture in Italy, redesigned and completed the upper half in a harmonious Gothic crown of gables and pinnacles. The Pisanos also added the dome over Diotisalvi's original prismatic dome, still visible from the inside. Both of these domes were impressive achievements for their time, among the largest attempted in the Middle Ages.

Inside, the austerity of the simple, striped walls and heavy columns of grey Elban granite is broken by two superb works of art. The great **baptismal font** is the work of Guido Bigarelli, the 13th-century Como sculptor who made the crazy pulpit in Barga. There is little figurative sculpture on it, but the 16 exquisite marble panels are finely carved in floral and geometrical patterns of inlaid stones, a northern, almost monochrome variant on the Cosmati work of medieval Rome and Campania. Nicola Pisano's **pulpit** (1260) was one of the first of that family's masterpieces, and established the form for their later pulpits, the columns resting on fierce lions, the relief panels crowded with intricately carved figures in impassioned New Testament episodes, a style that seems to owe much to the reliefs on old Roman triumphal arches and columns. The baptistry is famous for its uncanny acoustics; if you have the place to yourself, try singing a few notes from as near to centre as they will allow you. If there's a crowd the guards will be just waiting for someone to bribe them to do it.

The Cathedral

Open 7.45–1 and 3–sunset, closed to tourists for church services; adm.

One of the first and finest works of the Pisan Romanesque, the cathedral façade, with four levels of colonnades, turned out to be a little more ornate than Buscheto, the architect, had planned back in 1063. These columns, with similar colonnades around the apse and the Gothic frills later added around the unique elliptical dome, are the only showy features on the calm, restrained exterior. On the south transept, the late 12th-century **Porte San Ranieri** has a fine pair of bronze doors by Bonanno, one of the architects of the Leaning Tower. The biblical scenes are enacted among real palms and acacia trees; naturally, the well-travelled Pisans would have known what such things looked like.

On the inside, little of the original art survived a fire in 1595. The roof went, as well as the Cosmati pavement, of which only a few patches still remain. A coffered Baroque ceiling and lots of bad painting were contributed during the reconstruction, but some fine work survives. The great mosaic of Christ Pantocrator in the apse is by Cimabue, and there are portraits of the saints by Andrea del Sarto in the choir and his *Madonna della Grazia* on the right nave. The **pulpit** (*c.* 1300), by Giovanni Pisano, is the acknowledged masterpiece of the family. The men of 1595 used the fire as an opportunity to get rid of this nasty old medieval relic, and the greatest achievement of Pisan sculpture sat disassembled in crates, quite forgotten until this century. Works of genuine inspiration often prove profoundly disturbing to ages of certainty and good taste. Pisano's pulpit is startling, mixing classical and Christian elements with a fluency never seen before his time. St Michael, as a telamon, shares the honour of supporting the pulpit with Hercules and the Fates, while prophets, saints and sibyls look on from their appointed places. The relief panels, jammed with expressive faces, diffuse an electric immediacy equal to the best work of the Renaissance. Notice particularly the *Nativity*, the *Massacre of the Innocents*, the *Flight into Egypt*, and the *Last Judgement.*

The Leaning Tower

The stories claiming the tilt was accidental were most likely pure fabrications, desperate tales woven by the Pisans to account for what, before mass tourism, must have seemed a great civic embarrassment. The argument isn't very convincing. It seems hard to believe that the tower would start to lean when only 10m tall; half the weight would still be in the foundations. The argument then insists that the Pisans doggedly kept building it after the lean commenced. The architects who measured the stones in the last century to get to the bottom of the mystery concluded that the tower's odd state was absolutely intentional from the day it was begun in 1173. Mention this to a Pisan, and he will be as offended as if you had suggested lunacy is a problem in his family.The leaning campanile is hardly the only strange thing in the Field of Miracles. The more time you spend here, the more you will notice: little monster-griffins, dragons and such, peeking out of every corner of the oldest sculptural work, skilfully hidden where you have to look twice to see them, or the big bronze griffin sitting on a column atop the cathedral apse (a copy) and a rhinoceros by the door, Moslem arabesques in the Campo Santo, perfectly classical Corinthian capitals in the cathedral nave and pagan images on the pulpit. The elliptical cathedral dome, in its time the only one in Europe, shows that the Pisans had not only the audacity but the mathematical skills to back it up. You may have noticed that the baptistry too is leaning—about 1.5m, in the opposite direction. And the cathedral façade leans outwards about 40cm, hard to notice but disconcerting if you see it from the right angle. This could hardly be accidental. So much in the Field of Miracles gives evidence of a very sophisticated, strangely modern taste for the outlandish. Perhaps the medieval master masons in charge here simply thought that plain perpendicular buildings were becoming just a little trite.

Whatever, the campanile is a beautiful building and something unique in the world—also a very expensive bit of whimsy, with some 190 marble and granite columns. At the moment, it's also proving expensive to the local and national governments as they try to shore up the tower. Only relatively recently, the tilt has been increasing and in the early 1990s rescue operations began, with counter weights on the foundations and supports under the tower's leaning side, so the Field of Miracles seems more like a building site, with rubble and hard hats, than a sacred place. Work was programmed to finish in 1996 but, in the Italian way, this proved to be optimistic. In September 1995 builders and restorers held their breath as the tower fell a tenth of an inch and work was suspended until it seemed safe. At the time of writing it has been closed indefinitely.

The Campo Santo

Open 9–5 Oct–Mar; 8–8 April–Sept; adm.

If one more marvel in the Campo dei Miracoli is not excessive, there is this remarkable cloister, as unique in its way as the Leaning Tower. Basically, the cemetery is a rectangle of gleaming white marble, unadorned save for the blind arcading around the façade and the beautiful Gothic tabernacle of the enthroned Virgin Mary over the entrance. With its uncluttered, simple lines, the Campo Santo seems more like a work of our own century than the 1300s.

The cemetery began, according to legend, when the battling Archbishop Lanfranchi, who led the Pisan fleet into the Crusades, came back with boatloads of soil from the Holy Land for extra-blessed burials. Over the centuries an exceptional hoard of frescoes and sculpture accumulated here. Much of it went up in flames on a terrible night in July 1944, when an Allied incendiary bomb hit the roof and set it on fire. Many priceless works of art were destroyed and others, including most of the frescoes, damaged beyond hope of ever being perfectly restored. The biggest loss, perhaps, was the set of frescoes by Benozzo Gozzoli— the *Tower of Babylon, Solomon and Sheba, Life of Moses* and the *Grape Harvest* and others; in their original state they must have been as fresh and colourful as his famous frescoes in Florence's Medici Palace. Even better known, and better preserved, are two 14th-century frescoes of the *Triumph of Death* and the *Last Judgement* by an unknown artist (perhaps Buffalmacco, who is described by Boccaccio in the *Decameron*) whose failure to sign the work unfortunately passed him down to posterity as the 'Master of the Triumph of Death'. In this memento of the century of plagues and trouble, Death (in Italian, feminine: *La Morte*) swoops down on frolicking nobles, while in the *Last Judgement* (which has very little heaven, but plenty of hell) the damned are variously cooked, wrapped up in snakes, poked, disembowelled, banged up and chewed on; still, they are some of the best paintings of the trecento, and somehow seem less gruesome and paranoid than similar works of centuries to come (though good enough to have inspired that pop classic, Lizst's *Totentanz*).

For another curiosity, there's the *Theological Cosmography* of Piero di Puccio (*under restoration at time of writing*), a vertiginous diagram of 22 spheres of the planets and stars, angels, archangels, thrones and dominations, cherubim and seraphim, etc; in the centre, the small circle trisected by a T-shape was a common medieval map pattern for the known earth. The three sides represent Asia, Europe and Africa, and the three lines the Mediterranean, the Black Sea and the Nile. Among the sculpture in the Campo Santo, there are sarcophagi and Roman bath tubs, and in the gallery of prewar photographs of the lost frescoes, a famous Hellenistic marble vase with bas-reliefs.

The Museo delle Sinopie and Museo del Duomo

There are two museums surrounding the Campo dei Miracoli: opposite the cathedral, the **Museo delle Sinopie** (*open 9–12.40 and 3–sunset; adm*) contains the pre-painting sketches on plaster of the frescoes lost in the Campo Santo fire. Many of these are works of art in their own right, which, though faint, help give an idea of how the frescoes once looked. The **Museo del Duomo**, near the Leaning Tower in Piazza Arcivescovado (*open 9–sunset; summer 8–7.40; adm exp*), has been newly arranged in the old Chapter House, with descriptions in English available for each room. The first rooms contain the oldest works—beautiful fragments from the cathedral façade and altar; two Islamic works, the very strange, original **Griffin** from the top of the cathedral, believed to have come from

Egypt in the 11th century, and a 12th-century bronze basin with an intricate decoration. Statues by the Pisanos from the baptistry were brought in from the elements too late; worn and bleached, they resemble a convention of mummies. Other sculptures in the next room survived better: Giovanni Pisano's grotesque faces, his gaunt but noble *St John the Baptist* and the lovely *Madonna del Colloquio*, who speaks to her child with her eyes; and in the next room are fine works by Tino di Camaino, including the tomb of San Ranieri and his sculptures from the tomb of Emperor Henry VII, sitting among his court like some exotic oriental potentate. In Room 9 are works by Nino Pisano and in Rooms 11–12, the Cathedral Treasure, Giovanni Pisano's lovely ivory *Madonna and Child* steals the show, curving to the shape of the elephant's tusk; there's an ivory coffer and the cross that led the Pisans on the First Crusade. Upstairs are some extremely big angels used as candlesticks, intarsia and two rare illuminated 12th- and 13th-century scrolls (called exultet rolls), perhaps the original visual aids; the deacon would unroll them from the pulpit as he read so the congregation could follow the story with the pictures. The remaining rooms have some Etruscan and Roman odds and ends (including a good bust of Caesar) and prints and engravings of the original Campo Santo frescoes made in the 19th century. The courtyard has a unique view of the Leaning Tower, which seems to be bending over to spy inside.

North Pisa

With the cathedral on the very edge of town, Pisa has no real centre. Still, the Pisans are very conscious of the division made by the Arno; every year in June the two sides fight it out on the Ponte di Mezzo in the *Gioco del Ponte*, a sort of medieval tug-of-war where the opponents try to push a big decorated cart over each other.

From the Field of Miracles, Via Cardinale Pietro Maffi leads east to the ruins of some **Roman Baths** near the Lucca Gate; two interesting churches in the neighbourhood are **San Zeno**, in a corner of the walls, with some parts as old as the 5th century, and **Santa Caterina**, a Dominican church with a beautiful, typically Pisan façade. Inside there is an *Annunciation* and a sculpted Saltarelli tomb by Nino Pisano, and a large painting from the 1340s of the *Apotheosis of St Thomas Aquinas*, with Plato and Aristotle in attendance and defeated infidel philosopher Averroes below, atributed to Francesco Traini.

One long street near the Campo dei Miracoli begins as Via Carducci, becoming the old, arcaded **Borgo Largo** and **Borgo Stretto**. The twisting alleys of the lively market area are just off to the west, along with the **University**, still one of Italy's most important, and the **Piazza dei Cavalieri**. Duke Cosimo I started what was probably the last crusading order of knights, the Cavalieri di Santo Stefano, in 1562. The crusading urge had ended long before, but the duke found the knights a useful tool for placating the anachronistic fantasies of the Tuscan nobility—most of them newly titled bankers—and for licensing out freebooting expeditions against the Turks. Cosimo had Vasari build the **Palazzo della Carovana** for the order, conveniently demolishing the old Palazzo del Popolo, the symbol of Pisa's lost independence. Vasari gave the palace an outlandishly ornate *graffito* façade; the building now holds a college of the university founded by Napoleon. Next door, **Santo Stefano**, the order's church, is also by Vasari, though the façade was designed by a young

Medici dilettante; inside are some war pennants which the order's pirates captured from the Moslems in North Africa. Also on the piazza, the **Palazzo dell'Orologio** was built around the 'Hunger Tower' (left of the big clock), famous from Dante's story in the *Inferno* of Ugolino della Gherardesca, the Pisan commander who was walled in here with his sons and grandsons after his fickle city began to suspect him of intrigues with the Genoese. A plaque commemorates the occasion. Down Via L. Ghini are the **Botanical gardens**; the institute, in the grounds, has an extraordinary façade entirely covered with shells and mother-of-pearl (*open 8–1, 2–5.30 Mon–Fri, 8–1 Sat, closed Sunday*).

From the piazza, Via Dini and Via S. Francesco lead to the church of **San Francesco**: Gothic, with a plain marble façade, but containing some good paintings—a polyptych over the altar by Tommaso Pisano, frescoes by Taddeo Gaddi, Niccolò di Pietro Gerini (in the Chapter House) and in the sacristy, *Stories of the Virgin* by Taddeo di Bartolo 1397. The unfortunate Count Ugo and sons are buried in a chapel near the altar.

Museo di San Matteo

Open 9–7, 9–1 Sun, closed Mon; adm.

On the Lungarno Medeceo, an old convent which also served as a prison now immures much of the best Pisan art from the Middle Ages and Renaissance. It has works by Giunta Pisano, believed to be the first artist to ever sign his work (early 1200s), and an excellent and well-arranged collection of 1300s paintings by Pisans and other schools gathered from the city's churches; a polyptych by Simone Martini, paintings by Francesco Traini, Taddeo di Bartolo, Agnolo Gaddi, Antonio Veneziano and Turino Vanni; some sculptures by the Pisanos (especially the *Madonna del Latte* by Andrea and Nino); medieval ceramics from the Middle East, brought home by old Pisan sea dogs. In Room 7, after all the trecento works, the Early Renaissance comes as a startling revelation, as it must have been for the people of the 15th century: here is Neri di Bicci's wonderfully festive *Coronation of St Catherine* bright with ribbons, a *Madonna* from the decorative Gentile da Fabriano, a sorrowful *St Paul* by Masaccio, whose features and draperies are softly moulded, an anonymous *Madonna with Angel Musicians*, and a beautifully coloured *Crucifixion* by Gozzoli that looks more like a party than an execution. The last great work is Donatello's gilded bronze reliquary bust of *San Lussorio*, who could pass for Don Quixote. Someday the museum's collection of Mannerists and other later artists will be arranged downstairs.

South of the Arno

After the Campo dei Miracoli, the thing that has most impressed Pisa's visitors is its languidly curving stretch of the Arno, an exercise in Tuscan gravity, the river lined with two mirror-image lines of blank-faced yellow and tan buildings, all the same height, with no remarkable bridges or any of the picturesque quality of Florence. Its uncanny monotony is broken by only one landmark, but it is something special. Near the Solferino Bridge, **Santa Maria della Spina** sits on the bank like a precious Gothic jewel-box. Though one of the few outstanding achievements of Italian Gothic, originally it wasn't Gothic at all. Partially rebuilt in 1323, its new architect—perhaps one of the Pisanos—turned it into an extravaganza of pointed gables and blooming pinnacles. All of the sculptural work is first class, especially the figures of Christ and the Apostles in the 13 niches facing the streets. The chapel takes its name from a thorn of Christ's crown of thorns, a relic brought back from the Crusades.

Only a few blocks west, near the walls where the famous 'Golden Gate'—medieval Pisa's door to the sea—once stood, remains of the old Citadel and Arsenal are still visible across the river. On the southern side, **San Paolo a Ripa del Arno** has an interesting 12th-century façade similar to that of the cathedral. San Paolo stands in a small park, and interestingly it is believed to have been built over the site of Pisa's original cathedral; perhaps building cathedrals in open fields was an old custom. Behind it the unusual and very small 12th-century chapel of **Sant'Agata** has eight sides and an eight-sided prismatic roof like an Ottoman tomb. Just across Ponte Solferino, behind the Palazzo Reale, is the large church of **San Nicola**, with a fine painting of the *Madonna* by Traini, a sculpture of the same by Nino Pisano, and a painting of St Nicholas of Toletino shielding Pisa from the plague. Ask the sacristan to show you the famous spiral stair in the 13th-century campanile.

Down the Arno, the monotony is briefly broken again by the arches of the 17th-century **Logge di Banchi**, the old silk and wool market, at the Ponte di Mezzo and at the head of Pisa's main shopping street, Corso Italia. A bit further down is another octagonal church, **San Sepolcro**, built originally for the Knights Templar by Diotisalvi. **Palazzo Lanfranchi** further down is used for exhibitions. There's a small but shady park in the former Bastion Sangallo.

Shopping and Activities

Pisa is the best place in Tuscany to purchase bizarre and tacky **souvenirs**, and the best selection is crowded around the Campo dei Miracoli. Light-up Leaning Towers in pink and yellow come in all sizes and are an amazingly good buy; some have pen and pencil set attached for the scholar, or grinning plastic kittens for the kids' room, or naked ladies for your favourite uncle. The other specialities are medieval weapons—crossbows, cudgels, maces, whips—and plastic skulls, reptiles and insects. If it is the boutiques you're after head down Via Oberdan and Corso Italia. You can go **riding** at the Cooperativa Agrituristica in Via Tre Colli in Calci, or **swim** in the pool in Via Andrea Pisano, or have a **drink** in Pisa's oldest coffee-house, the Antico Caffè dell'Ussero, at Lungarno Pacinotti 27.

Festivals

In June there's the *Gioco del Ponte* and historic procession (*see* p.282) as well as the historic **regatta and lights festival of San Ranieri**, when the banks of the Arno glimmer with tens of thousands of bulbs. Folklore displays are in order for San Sisto (6 August). Every four years Pisa is the site of the Old Maritime Republics boat race (next 1999), a race between old sea rivals Pisa, Venice, Genoa and Amalfi.

Capital of day–trippers, Pisa isn't known for fine hotels, but there's usually enough room for the relatively few visitors who elect to stay overnight. The best, very close to the Campo dei Miracoli, is ★★★★**Grand Hotel Duomo**, Via S. Maria 94, ✆ 561894, ✆ 560418, a modern though richly appointed luxury hotel with a roof garden and a garage; all the rooms are air-conditioned. Right in the centre of Lungarno Pacinotti, ★★★**Royal Victoria**, ✆ 940111, ✆ 940180, is a tasteful and modern establishment. Its best features are rooms overlooking the Arno and its own garage; parking can be a problem in Pisa (L70,000 without bath, L115,000 with). Many of the middle-range hotels are on the streets around the train station, south of the Arno, like ★★★**Terminus e Plaza**, Via Colombo 45, ✆ and ✆ 500303 (L40–126,000 depending on the plumbing). If you're driving you may want to stay just outside the city on S1 (Via Aurelia) at ★★★**California Park Hotel** in San Giuliano Terme, ✆ 890726, ✆ 890727 (*moderate*), a large hotel with a park and a pool. *Open March–Oct.* The cheaper ★★**Leon Bianco** in Piazza Pozzetto 6, ✆ 543673 (*inexpensive*), has doubles.

Inexpensive places are spread throughout town, and most of them are often full of students; it's always best to call first, or else go up to the Campo dei Miracoli and try ★**Gronchi**, Piazza Arcivesovado 1, ✆ 561823; ★**Helvetia**, Via Don Boschi 31, ✆ 553 084; ★**Di Stefano** at Via Sant'Apollonia 35, ✆ 553559, ✆ 553559 or ★**Albergo Giardino**, in Piazza Manin, just outside the walls, ✆ 563101. All are relatively convivial places within a few blocks of the cathedral. There is a **Youth Hostel** with cooking facilities 1 km from the Campo dei Miracoli on Via Pietrasanta 15, ✆890622 (No. 3 bus). Another option for females is the **Casa delle Giovane** on Via Corridoni 29, ✆ 43061. This has cheap, clean double rooms with bathrooms and serves adequate food. The only drawback is the curfew at 10pm.

In Pisa you will find this difficult on a Sunday night. At other times, walks on the wild side of the Tuscan kitchen seem more common than in other towns—eels and squid, *baccalà*, tripe, wild mushrooms, 'twice-boiled soup' and dishes that waiters cannot satisfactorily explain. Don't be intimidated; there's always more common fare on the menu, and occasionally the more outlandish items turn into surprising treats—especially so at **Ristorante Sergio**, ✆ 580580, a highly regarded temple of Pisan cuisine, in a medieval setting on the Lungarno Pacinotti near the Royal Victoria. The menu changes according to what's available and fresh, and although the quality of the food can vary, the chances are you are in for a truly superb meal. There's a *menu degustazione* for L90,000, where you can sample the best dishes of the day; à la carte may be considerably less. *Closed Sunday.* A less expensive gourmet stronghold in Pisa is the **Ristoro dei Vecchi Macelli**, Via Volturno 49, ℂ 20424 (*expensive*) on the north bank of the Arno, near Ponte Solferino, with highly imaginative dishes based on coastal Tuscan traditions. *Closed Wed and Sun lunch.*

Those eels from Lake Massaciuccoli and other fresh seafood delicacies hold pride of place at **Lo Schiaccianoci** east of the station at Via Vespucci 108, ℂ 21024 (*moderate to expensive*). *Closed Mon.* **Da Bruno**, Via Luigi Bianchi 12, ℂ 560818 (*moderate*), outside the walls a few blocks east of the Campo dei Miracoli, is another place to see how well you like simple Pisan cooking—things like polenta with mushrooms and *baccalà* (dried cod). *Closed Mon eve and Tues.* Pisa is well endowed with unpretentious trattorias, many of them near the centre around the university. On Via San Frediano 16, **Osteria dei Cavalieri**, ℂ 580858 (*moderate*), has good game dishes such as rabbit with thyme. *Closed Saturday lunch and Sunday.* Italian dishes with a sophisticated Greek bias can be had at **Tavern Kostas**, Via del Borghetto 39, ℂ 571467 (*moderate*); try the duck or rabbit. *Closed Mon.* **Da Gino**, Piazza Vittorio Emanuele 19, ℂ 23437, has cheaper prices and simple 'tratt' decor. *Closed Sat eve and Sun.* **La Mescita**, Via Cavalca 2, ℂ 598667 (*moderate*), has varied, good quality food for reasonable prices. *Closed Sun.* If you just want a snack, try the offerings at the **Il Fagiolo**, a tavola calda, Via San Lorenzo 43, east of Piazza dei Cavalieri, ℂ 27336. *Closed Sun.*

Around Pisa

A couple of kilometres up river to the east, stands 'Pisa's second leaning tower', the campanile of the Romanesque **San Michele dei Scalzi. Calci**, under the slopes of Monte Pisano, has a good 11th-century church and an eroded giant of a campanile; 11km from Calci, in a prominent site overlooking the Arno, is the ornate **Certosa di Pisa** (*open 9–4, 9–6 in the summer, closed Mon; adm*), founded in 1366, but completely Baroqued in the 18th century, in a kind of 1920s Spanish-California exhibition style with three fine cloisters. There are lavish pastel frescoes by Florentine Baroque artist Bernardo Poccetti and his school, and a giraffe skeleton, stuffed penguins, Tuscan minerals, wax intestines—all part of the university's **Natural History Collections** (*open all day, closed Mon; adm; for the natural history, by appointment ℂ 937092*), founded by the Medici, housed in the Certosa since 1981.

Towards the coast, 6km from Pisa, is the beautifully isolated basilica of **San Piero a Grado**. According to tradition it was founded in the first century by St Peter himself, and in the Middle Ages was a popular pilgrimage destination. Although first documented in the 8th century, the current buildings are 11th century, embellished with blind arcades and ceramic tondi. Like many early churches and basilicas, it has an apse on either end, though in different sizes; the columns were brought in from a variety of ancient buildings. The altar stone, believed to have been set there by Peter himself, was found in recent excavations that uncovered the remains of several previous churches. Frescoes in the nave by a 14th-century Lucchese, Deodato Orlandi, tell the *Story of St Peter* with effigies of the popes up to the millennium (John XVIII) and a view of heaven.

In 1822, a strange ceremony took place on the wide, sandy beach of **Gombo**, near the mouth of the Arno, described in morbid detail by Edward Trelawny: 'the brains literally seethed, bubbled, and boiled as in a cauldron, for a very long time. Byron could not face this scene, he withdrew to the beach and swam off to the *Bolivar*.' Such was Shelley's fiery end, after he drowned sailing from Livorno. Gombo, and Pisa's other beaches, the **Marina di Pisa** and **Tirrenia** are often plagued by pollution, although Marina di Pisa makes a pretty place to stroll, with its Liberty-style homes and pine forests.

Livorno

> *.. There is plenty of space; it is a fully registered cemetery with an attendant keeper. So, if any of you have the intention of retiring to this very interesting part of Tuscany you will be well taken care of!*

Horace A. Hayward, on the British Cemetery in Livorno

Right from its founding in 1577, the English spent so much time in this city and grew so fond of it, that they decided to rename it. It's time that the bizarre anglicization, Leghorn, be put to sleep. The city that Duke Cosimo founded to replace Pisa's silted-up harbour is named Livorno. It hasn't much in common with the other Tuscan cities—full of sailors and African pedlars, blissfully unafflicted with architecture and art, as picturesque and romantic as Buffalo, New York. Instead of frescoes, Livorno has perhaps the best seafood on the Tyrrhenian coast. Instead of rusticated palazzi and marble temples, it has canals, docks and a very lively citizenry famous for free thinking and tolerance. And instead of winding country lanes, there are big white ferries to carry you off to the Tuscan Islands, Corsica or Sardinia.

History

The site had always been a safe harbour, and in the Middle Ages there was a small fortress to watch over it. It's odd no one thought of making a port here long before Cosimo. The Pisani considered it briefly in the 1300s, when it was becoming clear that Pisa's own port would ultimately fill up with the sands of the Arno. Eventually the fortress fell into the grasp of the Genoese, who sold it to Florence in 1421. Cosimo I, in his attempts to build Tuscany into a modern state, first saw the advantage of having a good port to avoid trading at the mercy of the Spaniards and Genoese. Cosimo expanded the fortress, but it was not until the reign of his successors, Francesco and Ferdinando, that Livorno got off the ground. The first stone was laid on 28 March 1577, and a regular gridiron city soon appeared, designed by Buontalenti, and surrounded by fortresses and canals. Almost from the beginning there was an English connection. Sir

Livorno

Robert Dudley, illegitimate son of the earl of Leicester—Queen Elizabeth's favourite—left England in 1605 after failing to prove his legitimacy in the Star Chamber court. (Perhaps he had other reasons; immediately upon arrival he converted to Catholicism and obtained a papal divorce from the wife he had abandoned back home.) Dudley built warships for the grand dukes, fortified the port of Livorno and drained the coastal swamps, making the region healthy and inhabitable for the first time.

In 1618, Livorno was declared a free port, free not only for trade but for the practice of any faith and for men of whatever nationality. It was a brilliant stroke, designed to fill out the population of this very rough and dangerous new town, and it is to the eternal credit of the Medici dukes, an act of tolerance almost unthinkable in the Catholic Mediterranean of the 1600s. Before long, Livorno was full of persecuted Jews, Greeks, English Catholics, Spanish Moslems and loose ends from around Europe. As the only safe trading port in a sea full of Spaniards, the port acquired thriving communities of English and Dutch merchants. In the 1700s progressive, tolerant Livorno was a substantial city, a breath of fresh air in the decadent Mediterranean and a home away from home for British travellers. Shelley wrote *The Cenci* here, as well as 'To a Skylark'; he bought his fatal sailing boat in Livorno's port.

Livorno declined a little when the same low tariffs and trading advantages became available in other Mediterranean ports. The Austrian dukes, especially Leopold II, helped keep Livorno ahead of its rivals; nevertheless, true to its traditions the city contributed greatly to the mid-century revolutionary movements and the wars of the Risorgimento. After unification it was still a lively place, full of men of many nations; also it began to make its first cultural contributions to the new Italy—the operatic composer Mascagni, the painter Modigliani, and several other artists of the Macchiaioli school. World War II and its bombers hit Livorno harder than anywhere in Tuscany, but the city rebuilt quickly. Long before other ports, Livorno realized the importance of container shipping. As the Mediterranean's first big container port, Livorno today has become the second city of Tuscany, and Italy's second-largest port (after Genoa).

Getting Around

Livorno's train station is on the edge of the city, with plenty of trains to Pisa, Florence and any point along the Tyrrhenian coast. Some trains to

Pisa go on to Lucca–Pistoia–Florence. There are some connections to Volterra, with a change down the coast at Cecina. The station is well over a mile from the city centre; take the No. 1 bus (most other city buses also pass through the centre, though as one old Livornese put it, they make 'vicious circles' before getting there). Buses for all villages in Livorno province (the strip of coast down as far as Follonica) leave from Piazza Grande. LAZZI buses for Florence depart from Scali A. Saffi, on the Fosse Reale, just off Piazza Cavour.

Ferries: Livorno is the main port for ferries to Corsica, with daily departures (NAVARMA line) from late March to early November; it's a 4-hour trip to Bastia, a very pleasant town. NAVARMA has daily ferries as well to Olbia in Sardinia (a nasty town on a wonderful island) from late June until September; there are other departures on the Sardinia Ferries line (prettier boats, higher fares). For the Tuscan Islands, services are handled by TOREMAR: a daily trip to Capraia (once a week, continuing to Elba), and a daily afternoon run to Portoferraio, Elba, from 16 June to 30 September. All ticket offices are in the port area.

Tourist Information

Piazza Cavour 6 (2nd floor), ✆ (0586) 898111, ✉ 896173; in summer a booth in the port, on the Porto Mediceo (0586) 895320 and at Terminal Calata Carara ✆ 210331.

Four Moors, Inigo Jones and the American Market

There isn't a lot to see in Livorno. You may enjoy the place and stay for a day or two, or you may be ready to bolt after five minutes. Though the streets are usually brimming, a combination of the prevailing north Tuscan austerity and an excess of dreary architecture make Livorno a disconcertingly anonymous city. It would have been a perfect setting for a German expressionist film of the 20s; unfortunately, its cinematic possibilities have not yet been exploited. There's nothing disconcerting about the **port**, a busy, fascinating jumble of boats, cranes, docks and canals. Close to the port entrance on Piazza Micheli, the **Fortezza Vecchia** conceals behind its walls the original Pisan fortress and an 11th-century tower built by the famous Countess Matilda. Piazza Micheli, Livorno's front door to the sea, is decorated with Livorno's only great work of art, the **Quattro Mori** by the Carraran sculptor Pietro Tacca (1623). The monument's original design became somewhat mangled, and Tacca's brilliant figures now sit in chains under a silly, earlier statue of Duke Ferdinando I. The four Moors are a symbol of Sardinia, but the original intent of the statue was to commemorate the successes of the great Tuscan pirates, the Order of Santo Stefano, against North African shipping.

From here, the arcaded **Via Grande** leads into the city centre; every original building on this street was destroyed in the bombings of 1944. **Piazza Grande**, the centre of Livorno, features the **Cathedral**, designed on a bad day by Inigo Jones in 1605; the present building is a complete postwar reconstruction. Jones spent some time in Tuscany as a student of Buontalenti, and he took a little bit of Livorno home with him. His plan for Covent Garden (originally arcaded all around and without the market) is a simple copy of this piazza, with St Paul's in place of the cathedral. Via Grande continues on to **Piazza della Repubblica**, contender for the title of the most ghastly square in Italy. There are no trees on it, because the piazza is really a paved-over section of the **Fosso Reale**, the curving canal that surrounded the original city of Livorno. Just off to the north, the sprawling, brick **Fortezza Nuova** stands on an island in the canal, now landscaped as a park and a popular resort of the Livornese on Sundays. Nearby, on Via della Madonna, three adjacent churches (now recycled for other uses) make a fitting memorial of Livorno's career as a truly free city. The first is Greek Orthodox, the second Catholic, and the one next to that Armenian. On the other side of Piazza della Repubblica, Piazza XX Settembre is the site of the Saturday **American Market**, so called from the vast stores of GI surplus on sale here after the war, now still Livorno's street market for clothes and odd items.

Little Venice and the Museo Civico

By now, you may be entirely despairing of finding anything really uplifting in Livorno. But just off Piazza della Repubblica is a neighbourhood unlike anything outside Venice. In fact, they call it 'Nuova Venezia', or 'Piccola Venezia', and for picturesque tranquillity it may outdo its famous precursor. **Little Venice** is a quarter only a few blocks square, laced with quiet canals that flow between the Fortezza Nuova and the port, lined with sun-bleached tenements hung with the week's wash. The pseudo-Baroque **Santa Caterina** church is typical of the ungainly, functional buildings of early Livorno.

Leading east from Piazza della Repubblica, Viale Carducci is Livorno's *grand boulevard*, heading out towards the railway station. On the way it passes the **Cisternone**, a neoclassical palace built for the water works Leopold II constructed in the 1830s, and next to it the **Parterre**, a city park with a sad zoological garden. The other main route out of Livorno's centre starts from Piazza Cavour, and leads down Via Ricasoli towards the southern suburbs. In the Villa Fabbricotti, another park, the **Museo Civico** (*open 10–1, 4–7 Thurs and Sat, closed Mon; adm*), contains a good collection of works by the Macchiaioli, Italy's late 19th-century Impressionists. The museum is on the third floor of the city library, a small collection that includes only one work by Modigliani, but a wealth of paintings that lead up to his art. The painters represented include Ulivi Liegi, Mario Puccini, that rare blossom Lodovico Tommasi and Livorno's own Giovanni Fattori. Together, they make a natural progression

S. Caterina

from the Biedermeier art of the 1860s—stirring scenes of Italian volunteers leaving for the front—to the sweet haziness of the Belle Epoque 1890s.

Along the coast, Viale Italia leads past the **Terrazza Mascagni**, a grandiose overlook on the sea, past the Italian Naval Academy, and then through some neighbourhoods of surprisingly blatant neo-Gothic and Art Nouveau villas of the 1890s, on the way to **Ardenza**, with its seafront park and marina.

The English Cemeteries and Montenero

For a sentimental journey into Livorno's cosmopolitan past, pay a visit to the **English Cemeteries** on Via Pisa and Via Adua, next to the Anglican Church (*ask at Via Adua's Archiconfraternità della Misericordia*). Crotchety old Tobias Smollett, who never stopped crabbing about Italy and never got to leave it, is interred here, along with many members of the British trading community and quite a few Americans. Many of the tombs (dating from 1670) are truly monumental, some with inscriptions from Scripture or Shakespeare; some charmingly original. Many among the British community, including Byron and Shelley, chose to spend their time not in Livorno itself, but up on the suburban hill of **Montenero** to the south. Byron and Shelley spent six weeks in 1822 at Villa delle Rose, a fascinating romantic ruin of a place, open by request of the owner, S. Varvaro di Valentina (at No. 57). A charming, old-fashioned funicular railway takes you to the top, where there has been a sanctuary and pilgrimage site since an apparition of the Virgin Mary in the 1300s. The present church, full of ex votos, is the work of an 18th-century architect named Giovanni del Fantasia; there's also a small museum, an ancient pharmacy and a number of caves, the Grotte del Montenero.

Livorno ℰ (0586–)   ***Where to Stay***

Some of the rooms at ★★★**Gran Duca**, Livorno's most interesting hotel, look out over the Quattro Mori and the busy port; though modern inside, the Gran Duca is built into a surviving section of the walls right on Piazza Micheli 16, ℰ 891024/5/6, ✆ 891153 (*moderate, some rooms with TV*) at the entrance to the harbour area. Another possibility (especially if you have a car) is ★★★**Gennarino**, a converted turn-of-the-century neo-Gothic palace on the shore road, Viale Italia 301, ℰ 803109 (*moderate*). Being a port town, there's an abundance of less expensive hotels. Many, though none especially distinguished, can be found across the wide piazza from the train station. Dozens more crowd the centre around the port and Via Grande. Some of them are screaming dives, though Corso Mazzini, a few blocks south of the Fosso Reale, has some nice ones, especially the old-fashioned ★★**Corsica** at No. 148, ℰ 882280, ✆ 882103 (L65–85,000 depending on the plumbing). Right in the centre, a block off Via Grande at Via dell'Angiolo 23, ℰ 888581, ★**Europa** (*inexpensive*) has clean, remodelled rooms. Another option is ★★**Giardino** near the port in Piazza Mazzini 85, ℰ and ✆ 806330 (*inexpensive*).

The main purpose of a trip to Livorno is to eat seafood. The Livornese have their own ways of preparing it, now much copied throughout Tuscany, and restaurants usually prove easier on your budget than elsewhere. Besides lobster and grilled fish, pasta dishes with seafood figure on all the local menus, as does *the* Livornese dish, *cacciucco*, the famous fish stew that is to Livorno what the Leaning Tower is to Pisa. After a rich meal try a *bomba livornese* instead of a dessert. This is the local answer to Irish coffee and is made with equal quantities of coffee and rum served piping hot.

Try these delicacies at **L'Antico Moro**, on a narrow street near the city market, Via Bertelloni 59, ✆ 884659 (*moderate*). *Closed Wed.* At Viale Carducci 63 towards the train station, **La Barcarola**, ✆ 402367 (*expensive*), is a very big and very noisy place, where *zuppa di pesce, penne* with scampi, and everything else good from the Tyrrhenian is cooked in the good old Livornese style. *Closed Sun and Aug.* At Borgo dei Cappuccini 5, near the mouth of the Fosso Reale, **Osteria del Mare**, ✆ 881027 (*moderate*), is a little place serving grilled fish, lobster and spaghetti *alle vongole*. *Closed Thurs.* Probably the best restaurant in Livorno is **La Chiave**, Scali della Cantine 52, ✆ 888609 (*expensive*); try their *tagliolini* with octopus. *Closed Wed.* Another popular and famous place is **Il Sottomarino**, Via Terrazzini 48 (*moderate*), with a great atmsophere and excellent seafood. *Closed Thurs.* Another popular spot is **Trattoria Galileo**, Via della Campana 22, ✆ 889009 (*inexpensive*), two blocks north of Piazza Repubblica serving some seafood. Some of the best restaurants are to the south in the seaside suburb of Ardenza. **Da Oscar**, Via Franchini 76, ✆ 501258 (*moderate*), has been a favourite for decades; there is a good selection of wines to go with the *linguine* and clams, excellent risottos and grilled *triglie* and *orate*. *Closed Mon.* The wine bar **Cantina Nardi**, Via L. Cambini 6, ✆ 808006 (*moderate*), is a pleasant surprise at lunch time when a few tables are laid and excellent food is to be had. Here you can eat surrounded by hundreds of wine bottles—who would want better company? *Closed Sun.*

Tuscan Islands

The Tuscan Archipelago is a broad arch of islets, stretching from Livorno to Monte Argentario and enclosing Elba, the only large and heavily populated member of the group. Fate has not usually been kind to these islands; after deforestation, Saracen and Turkish pirates, and finally the Italian government, not much is left. Two of the islands are still prison camps, one a nature preserve where no one is allowed to stay overnight. The others will be dealt with later (Elba is most conveniently reached from Piombino, Giglio and Giannutri from Porto Santo Stefano); **Gorgona** and **Capraia** get a daily boat from Livorno—and are in fact administratively part of Livorno.

To see **Gorgona**, 37km from Livorno, you'll either have to get permission from the Ministero di Grazia e Giustizia in Rome (quite difficult) or else punch a *carabiniere*. Gorgona, a hilly, rectangular square mile, was first used as a prison by Pope Gregory the Great. A Carthusian monastery lasted until the new Italian state expropriated the entire island in 1869; in the beginning, it was to be a 'model prison' with workshops and vineyards, but it wasn't long before it deteriorated into just another lock-up. There's nothing to see on Gorgona, except maquis and a handful of olive trees, and you'll have to be content with the view from the boat, which stops daily on the way to Capraia to drop off new cons and supplies. Ambitious plans are afoot to close the prison and turn Gorgona into a wildlife preserve, but so far nothing has been decided.

Capraia

Capraia, 65km from Livorno, is the third largest of the islands, after Elba and Giglio. It measures about 10km by 5km, and has some 400 inhabitants. Like Elba, it is mountainous, but has fewer trees; most of the island is covered with scrubby *macchia*.

In Roman times Capraia seems to have been a private estate, and the ruins of an extensive villa can be seen. In the days of the Empire, the island was occupied by a colony of Christian monks. Such an island was perfect for the Christian ideal of withdrawal and contemplation, but it also prevented the Church authorities from keeping a close watch on the colony, and the monks slipped into unorthodoxy and loose behaviour; an armed mission from Pope Gregory the Great was needed to force them back in line in the late 6th century.

When Saracen pirates began to infest the Tyrrhenian Sea, Capraia, like most of the group, became deserted. The Pisans thought it important enough to repopulate and fortify in the 11th century. Genoa eventually gained control, as she did in Corsica only 32km away. The proximity gave Capraia its one big moment in history; in 1767 the revolutionary forces of the Corsican nationalist leader, Pasquale Paoli, and the weakness of the Genoese, resulted in, of all things, an independent Capraia, which soon learned to support itself by piracy. French occupation put an end to that four years later.

Seven years ago tourist accommodation on Capraia consisted of one hotel and two tiny pensions. Today, by a miracle of 20th-century Eurotourism, these have all grown into three-star hotels, and two more have sprouted to join them. It helps that Capraia is an island, and a pretty one, but its real attraction is its natural setting, its deep-sea diving and marine grottoes. In the last century the northern quarter of the island was put to use as an agricultural penal colony, which is what it still is today. The civilian population is almost entirely concentrated in the port and only town, **Capraia Isola**. The port is actually half a kilometre away from the town, connected by the island's only tarmac road. In the town are the Baroque church and convent of **Sant'Antonio**. Used as a barracks in the last century, it is now crumbling and abandoned. On the outskirts are the ruins of the **Roman villa**, apocryphally the abode of Augustus' profligate daughter Julia, and an 11th-century Pisan chapel dedicated to the **Vergine Assunta**. Overlooking it all is the large and impressive fortress of **San Giorgio**, begun by the Pisans and completed by the Genoese. The well-preserved **watch-tower** at the port was built by the Genoese Bank of St George.

On the eastern side of town there is a beach under the cliffs with an interesting tower, built by the Pisans, and connected to the cliff by a natural bridge. A visiting Californian at the turn of the century was so struck by it that he built a copy of it on a beach near San Diego.

From Capraia Isola a road leads southwest across the island, passing another Pisan church, that of **Santo Stefano**, built on the ruins of a 5th-century church used by the early monks, destroyed by the Saracen pirates. Near Monte Pontica is a cave, the **Grotta di Parino**, a sacred spot used as a place of meditation by the monks. The road ends at a lighthouse on the western coast. Just south of here is a sea cave, the **Grotta della Foca**, where some Mediterranean seals are still reported to live. At the southern tip of the island is another Genoese watch-tower, the **Torre dello Zenobito.**

Livorno's Coast

Livorno's clever tourist office has taken to calling this shore the 'Etruscan Riviera', conjuring up the irresistible idea of Etruscans lounging in beach chairs the way they do on their funerary urns. Beyond Antignano, the shoreline becomes jagged and twisting, dotted with beaches that are usually more than well exploited. **Castiglioncello** is a pretty corner of the coast, but the beaches are narrow and packed with Italians throughout the summer. Nearby **Rosignano** is a similar resort, graced with a gargantuan chemical plant. **Vada** and **Marina di Cecina** are a little better; at least both have stretches of free beach. Marina di Cecina, 36km from Livorno, is a suburb of Tuscany's newest city, **Cecina**, founded only a century ago, now an unkempt town populated by dissipated factory hands and motorcycle-heads. **San Vicenzo** is a booming, awful resort, but it has miles of good beaches on either side, perhaps your best chance on this strip of coast for a little seaside peace and quiet.

Next is the half-moon **Golfo di Baratti**, with more tranquil beaches and some Etruscan tombs from the once mighty town of **Populonia**. Modern Populonia has a small archaeological museum (ask there about visits to the ruins of the Etruscan city and tombs, which include a so-called 'arsenal' where the Etruscans turned Elban iron into armaments, © 34 997). Populonia also has an impressive medieval castle. **Piombino**, at the tip of this stubby peninsula, is Tuscany's Steel City, mercilessly flattened during the war, and mercilessly rebuilt afterwards. The government might close the obsolete steelworks at any time, but Piombino will at least remain the major port for Elba. The towns of interest up in the hills include: **Bolgheri**, near Cecina, centre of a DOC wine area (Bolgheri is a little-known, dry white wine), **Castagneto Carducci**, a pretty town where strawberries are grown, and finally **Suvereto**, a pretty, seldom-visited medieval village with an arcaded Palazzo Comunale and the 12th-century Pisan church of San Giusto.

San Vicenzo © (0565–)   ***Eating Out***

If the vast beaches of San Vicenzo fail to tempt, its seafood restaurants might, most tantalizingly **Gambero Rosso**, Piazza della Vittoria 13, © 701021, with devilishly perfect and delicate crustaceans, pasta, pheasant and pigeon dishes, and fish so fresh and good that it is matched only by an equally thorough wine list. Take the easy way out and order the *menu degustazione* for L90,000; à la carte costs slightly more. *Closed Tues.* If your pockets aren't that deep, the nearby **Il Bucaniere**, Lungomare Marconi 8, Ⓒ 703387 (*expensive*), is under the same management, occupying the beach, cabins, and a bathing establishment from the 50s; delicious seafood and more.

Elba

When the government closed the steelmills on Elba after the war, the national and local governments sought to make up the lost income by promoting tourism on the island. They have been singularly successful; Elba has become one of Europe's holiday playgrounds, and with tourists approaching some 2 million every year, prosperity has returned to its 30,000 inhabitants.

Tourist Elba, however, is no glamour-puss. It is a comfortable place that attracts mainly families. Germans in particular are fond of the island; they have bought up most of the southern coast, and many of them come back every year. There is no single, big, crowded, tourist ghetto, as is true on some other Mediterranean islands, but plenty of quiet, small resorts all around the coast. The lives of the Elbans themselves have adjusted to the cyclical rhythms of tourist migrations. In winter the island seems empty; much of the population stays only to work during the season. Other activities do exist to supplement tourism, such as fishing and mining, but the old iron mines, after thousands of years, have finally given out. The last of them closed in 1984.

In an unspectacular way, Elba is beautiful. Pink and green predominate—pink for the granite outcrops and houses, green because the island is heavily forested. Like its neighbour Corsica, it is a chain of mountains rising out of the sea, the tallest of which are to the west, grouped around Monte Capanne (1018m). For a mineralogist, Elba is a holiday dream—besides iron ore, dozens of common and rare minerals are found there, everything from andalusite to zircon. For most people, however, Elba's greatest attraction is its wealth of beaches and particularly mild climate—it hardly ever rains on Elba. The coastline, all bays and peninsulas, is over 150km in length, and there are beaches everywhere, large and small, sand or pebbles. Even in the crush of August, there's plenty of Elba-room for all, and if you look carefully, you just might find a beach that's not too crowded.

History

Able was I ere I saw Elba

The Napoleonic palindrome

Elba is close enough to the Italian mainland to have been inhabited from the earliest times. When Neanderthal Man was tramping through the neighbourhood about 50,000 years ago, Elba may have still been linked to the peninsula. Later peoples, a seemingly unending parade of them, colonized the island after 3000 BC, drawn by Elba's treasure hoard of metals. In the Copper Age they mined its copper; in the Bronze Age they alloyed the copper into bronze. The copper gave out just in time for the Iron Age, and Elba, conveniently, had vast deposits of this also. Competition was fierce: Etruscans and Greeks fought over the island and established colonies of miners, but neither left any permanent settlements.

For Rome, expanding across the Italian peninsula in the 4th century BC, Elba was an important prize. After its conquest at the end of the century, the Romans founded towns to consolidate their hold; thenceforth, whenever the Roman legions ran their swords through Teutons, Persians, Gauls, Carthaginians, or each other, they usually did it with Elban iron. The mines and forges, then as now, were concentrated on the eastern third of the island; the remainder became a holiday spot for the wealthy, as witnessed by the remains of large villas discovered near Portoferraio.

The fall of Rome brought invasions, disorder, depopulation and pirates to Elba; the Lombards in the 6th century, under the murderous Gummarith, subjugated the island with their usual bloodshed; Saracens and adventurous barons from Italy fought for the scraps. By the 11th century Pisa had assumed complete control, as the island lay across its most important trade route. It held Elba for almost 500 years, constructing fortresses at Luceri and Volterraio and exploiting the mineral resources. At the time the capital was called *Ferraia*, of which the modern capital of Portoferraio was only the port. Not a trace remains of the medieval city, and archaeologists are still trying to discover its site.

From the 13th century on, Genoa contested Pisa's possession of the island. In the 16th century, Duke Cosimo I saw his opportunity and seized it for Florence. He built Portoferraio and the walls around it, but soon had to contend with the growing power of Spain in the western Mediterranean, and after some inconclusive skirmishes, Elba was partitioned between Tuscany and Spain. Spain built the town and fortress of Porto Azzurro as a counter to Portoferraio, an arrangement that lasted throughout the 18th century, despite French efforts to grab the island.

Napoleon on Elba

During the Napoleonic wars, Elba was occupied for a time by the English, and Portoferraio was unsuccessfully besieged for over a year by Napoleon's troops in 1799. Napoleon finally annexed it in 1802, probably with no premonitions that the 1814 Treaty of Fontainebleau would put a temporary end to the First Empire and send him to Elba. After all these centuries, Elba suddenly found itself on the centre stage of world history.

Napoleon himself chose Elba, from the variety of small Mediterranean outposts offered him, for 'the gentleness of its climate and its inhabitants'. Also, perhaps because on clear days he could see his own island of Corsica. No one, however, seems to have consulted the Elbans themselves on the matter, and they can be excused for the cold indifference with which they received their new ruler. On 4 May 1814, he arrived at Portoferraio with some 500 of his most loyal officers and soldiers and a British Commissioner charged with keeping an eye on him. But Napoleon soon won over the hearts of the Elbans by being the best governor they ever had. New systems of law and education were established, the last vestiges of feudalism abolished, and what would today be called economic planning was begun; he reorganized the iron mines and started Elba's modern network of roads.

Not that Napoleon ever really took his stewardship seriously. Remaking nations and institutions was a reflex by then, after doing it all across Europe for 20 years. It was the return to France that occupied his attention. The atmosphere was thick with intrigues and rumours, and secret communications flowed incessantly between Napoleon and his partisans on the Continent. On 20 February 1815, just nine months after his arrival, the Elbans and the embarrassed British watchdog awakened to find the emperor missing. The 'Hundred Days' had begun. Later, after Waterloo, a smaller, gloomier and more distant island would be found to keep Napoleon out of trouble.

Elba was returned to Tuscany, and soon after joined the new Kingdom of Italy. World War II hit Elba hard; Portoferraio and environs were bombed in 1943–4, first by the Allies, and then by the Germans. In 1944, in one of the more disgraceful episodes of the war, Elba was 'liberated' by Free French and African troops, with more murder, pillage and rape than had been seen in the Mediterranean since the days of the pirates.

Getting There and Around

You'll never have to wait long for a ferry to Elba, especially during the summer. Gritty Piombino is the major point of departure. Any train going down the Tyrrhenian coast will take you as far as the station called Campiglia Marittima; from there the FS operates a regular shuttle train to Piombino (don't get off at the central station; the train has a short stop there and continues to the port). Three companies run services to Elba: TOREMAR (head office: Via Calafati 6, Livorno, ✆ (0586) 896113); NAVARMA (head office: Piazzale Premuda 13, Piombino, ✆ (0565) 221212); and Elba Express, ✆ (0562) 220956.

The most frequent passage is the 1-hour Piombino–Cavo–Portoferraio trip, and there are also TOREMAR ferries that go from Piombino to Rio Marina and then to Porto Azzurro (2hrs). Services to Elba can be as frequent as every half-hour in July, down to two or three a day in winter. TOREMAR also has a daily Livorno-Portoferraio run (5hrs) by way of Gorgona and Capraia in the summer. Note that the NAVARMA service is really a part of the ferry trip from Piombino to Bastia, in Corsica. To keep up with demand in the summer, ELBA EXPRESS runs hydrofoils from Piombino to Portoferraio; these only take 25 minutes, but are more expensive.

Elba has an efficient bus service to all corners of the island, and buses depart with some frequency. The hub of the system is Portoferraio, with buses leaving and returning to the terminal by the Grattacielo, facing the harbour. There are a couple of **car hire** agencies on the island: Maggiore, Calata Italia, in Portoferraio, ✆ 915368; or Avis, Via IV Novembre, in Porto Azzurro, ✆ 95,000. Scooters can be hired from Rent Ghiaie, Via Cairoli 26, ✆ 914666.

The office for the island is the Grattacielo, Calata Italia 26, in Portoferraio, just across from the ferry dock, ✆ (0565) 914671; also in Viale Elba, ✆ (0565) 914392. In the summer the Livorno EPT runs a booth in Piombino, just across from the ferry dock, ✆ (0565) 224432.

Portoferraio

Portoferraio, with 11,000 souls, is the capital and only city of Elba. The massive walls built by Duke Cosimo remain, though Portoferraio has spilled out westwards along the bay. Here the ferries dock at the Calata Italia, where the visitor's introduction to Elba is the **Grattacielo** ('skyscraper'), a 10-storey pile of peeling paint built in the 1950s that is one of the most endearingly hideous buildings in the Mediterranean. It is also the most important building for tourists, since it contains the tourist information office, most of the ferryboat offices, and the Portoferraio bus terminal at the back, with connections to all Elba's towns and resorts.

Follow Calata Italia and its various pseudonyms under the walls, next to the old U-shaped harbour. On the far side rises the **Torre del Martello**, from which in the old days a chain was stretched across the harbour in times of danger. The main gate of the city is the **Porta a Mare** at the base of the U, over which can be seen the inscription of Duke Cosimo reminding us with the usual Medicean vanity how he built the whole town 'from the foundations upwards'; the new town had originally been dubbed Cosmopolis.

Directly inside the Porta a Mare is **Piazza Cavour**. Portoferraio is a big natural amphi-theatre; from the piazza the town slopes upwards in all directions towards the walls on the high cliffs. North of the piazza, Via Garibaldi leads up to the main attraction, Napoleon's house, the **Villa dei Mulini** (*open 9–7, Sun 9–1; adm*), yellowing, unloved, unchanged since Napoleon had it built according to his own simple tastes; inside can be seen his furnishings, books and other paraphernalia, including the flag with three golden bees that he bestowed on the Elbans. It's worth the trip just to see the contemporary political cartoons mocking the emperor. The gardens, equally uncared for, offer fine views over the city walls. On either side you can see the two Medici fortresses dominating the highest points in the city: **Forte Falcone** to the west and **Forte Stella** to the east, the former still used by the Italian navy, the latter used as housing.

On the way down Via Garibaldi, you may want to stop at one of the parish churches, the **Misericordia** or the **Holy Sacrament**, both of which have copies of Napoleon's death-mask; on 5 May the Misericordia holds a procession with a replica of Napoleon's coffin to commemorate his death. The **Town Hall**, originally a bakery for Cosimo's troops, was the boyhood home of Victor Hugo, whose father was the French military commander in Elba. There's a Roman altar displayed in the courtyard, and inside, the **Biblioteca Foresiana** (*open 10–12 Mon–Fri, 3–7 Mon, Wed, Fri*) has a collection of books about Elba and a small picture collection. Two blocks west is the **Teatro dei Vigilanti**, built by Napoleon around an abandoned church, while east of Via Garibaldi lies the **Piazza della Repubblica**, the throbbing heart of Portoferraio, with its crowded cafés, 18th-century **Cathedral**, not really a cathedral at all these days, and the nearby market.

Around Portoferraio

Most of Portoferraio's hotels and restaurants are in the modern extension outside the city walls. There's a pebble beach, **Le Ghiaie**, on the north side, and another called **Le Viste** under the walls near Forte Falcone. Two roads lead from the capital, one along the northern coast to the small resorts of **Acquaviva** and **Viticcio**, and to **Capo d'Enfola**, a lovely headland rising sheer out of the sea, barely connected to the rest of the island.

The second road runs south to the junction of **Bivio Boni**, where it branches to the east and west. Nearby there is the thermal spa at **San Giovanni**, and the ruins of a Roman villa at **Le Grotte**, on the south shore of the Gulf of Portoferraio, more interesting for the view than the little that remains. There are beaches here at Ottone, Magazzini and **Bagnaia**, the latter the site of the simple, beautiful 12th-century **church of Santo Stefano**, the best Pisan monument in the archipelago. At **Acquabona** you can shoot some bogeys at one of Elba's two golf courses (nine holes), or continue west from Bivio Boni to the resort at **Biodola Bay** and the **Villa Napoleone di San Martino** (*open 9–7,*

Sun 9–1, closed Sat) which also has a little art gallery including a *Galatea* by Canova. The emperor soon tired of life in Portoferraio and built this house as his country retreat. In later years the husband of his niece (daughter of Jérome) purchased the place and added a pretentious neoclassical façade with big Ns pasted everywhere; it's now another Napoleonic museum.

Eastern Elba

Rio nell'Elba is the old mining centre, though it's not at all what one would expect a mining town to look like—it's as pleasant and pastel as any other Elban town, set in the hills overlooking the eastern coast. Archaeological sites, the scanty remains of mines and Etruscan mining camps dot the neighbourhood. There are many undeveloped beaches on the western side of Rio's peninsula, including Nisporto and Nisportino. The road between Portoferraio and Rio passes the steep hill of **Volterraio**, where you can make the long climb to the 11th-century Pisan castle perched on the summit.

Rio Marina, as its name implies, is the port for Rio nell'Elba. Here, the **Mineralogical Museum** (*open 9–12 and 3–6 April-Oct, 9–12 Sat; rest of the year Sun mornings only, call ahead © 962747*) in the Palazzo Comunale has displays of all the island's unusual rocks and minerals. Rio Marina has a busy harbour, its many small fishing boats under the vigilant eye of an octagonal Pisan watch-tower. The eastern side of this peninsula, like the western side, has some fine beaches where you can sometimes escape the crowds— Ortano, Porticciolo, Barbarossa and many others. On the northern tip stands **Cavo**, an older resort town on a tiny port.

Porto Azzurro and Capoliveri

South of Rio, the road passes through some difficult terrain towards **Porto Azzurro**, built by the Spaniards and now a large holiday town. Until 1947 it was called *Porto Longone*. The fortress, built in 1603 to withstand the Austrians and French, was later converted into a famous Italian calaboose that hosted many political prisoners and criminal celebrities. Besides the town beach, there are several others nearby, including a bizarre one at **Terrenere**, where a yellow-green sulphurous pond festers near the blue sea in a land-scape of pebble beach and ancient mine debris—for those jaded travellers seeking something beyond Elba's mass tourism. During the season, day excursions run from Porto Azzurro to the island of Montecristo.

Just north of Porto Azzurro is the **Sanctuary of Monserrato**, a famous shrine with an icon known as the 'Black Madonna'. The Spanish governor built this here in 1606 because the mountain (Monte Castello) reminded him of the peculiar mountain of Monserrat near Barcelona. Similar Black Madonnas are revered from Portugal to Poland; over the centuries the oxidation of yellow paint has darkened them (just as it threatens Van Gogh's *Sunflowers*). South of Porto Azzurro is another Spanish fortress at **Capo Focardo**, on a large oval-shaped peninsula consisting of Monte Calamita and the rough hill country around it.

On this peninsula is **Capoliveri**, one of the oldest inhabited sites on the island. The town takes its name from the Roman *Caput Liberi*, which may refer either to the worship of

Liber, an Italian equivalent of Dionysus (this has always been a wine-growing area) or to the free men (*liberi*) who lived there. In Roman times Capoliveri was an 'Alsatia', a refuge for any man who could escape to it. It has had a reputation for independence ever since, giving a bad time to the Pisans, the Spanish, and even Napoleon. Today it is a peaceful place, with fine views from its hilltop over the surrounding countryside and sea. Although Capoliveri is very scenic and surrounded by beaches, much of its coast is privately owned. South of Capoliveri, near the coast, is the **Sanctuary of the Madonna delle Grazie**, with a painting of the Madonna and Child by the school of Raphael, miraculously saved from a shipwreck. The coast west of Capoliveri is marked by two lovely broad gulfs, **Golfo Stella** and **Golfo di Lacona**, separated by a steep, narrow tongue of land. Both are developed resort areas, with centres at Lacona and Lido Margidore.

Western Elba

Beyond Biodola, the scenic corniche road west from Portoferraio passes through the adjacent resort towns of **Prócchio** and **Campo all'Aia**; the former is larger and one of the more expensive resorts on Elba. Seven kilometres west is **Marciana Marina**, another popular resort, with a 15th-century Pisan watch-tower, the **Torre Saracena**. This is the port for Marciana, the oldest continuously inhabited town on Elba.

In the 14th and 15th centuries, when life near the coast wasn't safe, Marciana was the 'capital' of the feudal Appiani barons, the most powerful family on the island. Today, high in the mountain forests on the slopes of Monte Capanne, it is a surprisingly beautiful town of narrow streets, stone stairs, archways and belvederes. Sections of the old city wall and gate are still intact, and the old Pisan **fortress** hangs over the town (*not open to visitors*). The palace of the Appiani may be seen on a narrow *vicolo* in the oldest part of town. Marciana's **Archaeology Museum** (*open 9–1 and 4–7, closed Sun and from Oct–Mar*) has a small collection of prehistoric and Roman objects found in the area. In the summer, from Marciana, a cable lift (*runs daily 10–12, 2–6*) climbs to the summit of Elba's highest peak, **Monte Capanne**, with stupendous views over Corsica, the Tuscan archipelago and the mountains of Tuscany itself.

Three churches outside Marciana are of interest: the ruined Pisan **San Lorenzo**, the **Sanctuary of San Cerbone**, who escaped here from the troublesome Lombards (later his body was buried in a miraculous rainstorm, so the Lombards wouldn't see), and the **Sanctuary of the Madonna del Monte**, dating from the 11th century and one of the most important shrines on the island with a Madonna painted on a huge lump of granite. Pagan Elbans may have worshipped on this site as well, as did Napoleon for two weeks, after a fashion, with his Polish mistress, Maria Walewska. Another mountain village, almost a twin of Marciana, is **Póggio**, just to the east. Póggio has a natural spring where the Elbans bottle their local *acqua minerale*—called Napoleone, of course. It's very good, but the Elbans keep it all to themselves.

On the rugged coast to the west and south of Marciana, there are yet more beaches and resorts: **Sant'Andrea, Patresi, Chiessi, Pomonte, Fetovaia** (a lovely stretch, protected by a rocky promontory), **Seccheto** and **Cavoli**. Seccheto has ancient granite quarries from which the stone was cut for the Pantheon in Rome.

Seven kilometres east of Marciana stretches Elba's pocket-sized plain, the **Campo nell'Elba**, extending across the island from Prócchio to Marina di Campo, separating the western mountains from the central range. Elba's small airport is here—it is the only place they could put it. Two old, pretty towns lie on the edge of the plain: **Sant'Ilario in Campo** and **San Piero in Campo**. San Piero's parish church of San Niccolò has interesting frescoes; it was built on the ruins of an ancient temple to Glaucus. Halfway between the two towns are the ruins of the Pisan church of **San Giovanni**, along with a Pisan watch-tower (*covered for restoration at time of writing*). On the coast is **Marina di Campo**, Elba's first and perhaps largest resort, with the largest beach. The watch-tower in the harbour was built by the Medici.

Elba ℂ (0565–)   **Where to Stay**

With more than 150 hotels around the island, Elba has something for everyone. The emphasis is on the not-too-expensive resort, attractive to family holiday-makers. Many hotels stay open all the year round, with substantial off-season discounts. Beware, however, that Elba is a big package-tour destination, and despite its scores of lodgings, you'll need to book ahead to avoid disappointment.

If you want to stay in Portoferraio, an interesting possibility is ★★**L'Ape Elbana**, Salita de' Medici 2, ℂ 914245s (*moderate*). The 'Elban Bee' is the oldest hotel on the island; it entertained Napoleon's guest. For something a little more up to date, ★★★★**Villa Ottone**, at Ottone, ℂ 933042 (*expensive*), is in a 19th-century villa right on the beach, with a shady garden and tennis court, open all year round. Some of the city's hotels are near the beach of Le Ghiaie and the city park; one that is quite pleasant is ★★★**Villa Ombrosa**, Viale de Gasperi, No.3, ℂ 914363 (*moderate*). The resorts begin where Portoferraio's suburbs end. Some areas within a few kilometres offer good value in lovely settings, such as ★★★**Mare**, at Magazzini, ℂ 933069 (*moderate*); and ★★**Tirrena**, also at Magazzini, ℂ 933002 (*inexpensive*). Further out in peaceful Bagnaia, ★★**Clara**, ℂ 961077, ✆ 961191 (*moderate*), is a little hotel.

At Cavo, on the east coast, prices tend to be slightly lower, and as Porto Azzurro tends to be crowded, there are plenty of camp-sites and holiday apartments there. The same is true of most of the beaches on the southeastern peninsula around Capoliveri, although many pleasant hotels are right on the beach like ★★**La Voce del Mare**, at Naregno beach, ℂ 968455 (*moderate*). The best beach on Elba may be at Cavoli, west of Campo nell'Elba; there you'll find ★★**La Conchiglia**, ℂ 987010 (*moderate*), small and air-conditioned. Of the resorts on the west end of the island, there are some smart establishments around Prócchio, more modest hotels at Sant'Andrea and Pomonte, and some which are blissfully out of the way, like ★★**Andreina** at La Cala, west of Marciana Marina, ℂ 908150 (*inexpensive*).

In the long list of restaurants on the island, few really stand out. What does stand out are Elba's DOC wines; both *Elba rosso* and *Elba bianco* can hold their own with any in Tuscany.

To start with, while you're waiting for the ferry at Piombino you might try the **Ristorante Terrazza**, above the bar in the port area, Piazza Premuda, ① 35135 (*moderate*), with delicious *spaghetti alle vongole* and a big picture window with a panoramic view of Piombino's steel mills. One of the most popular places to eat in Portoferraio, right in Piazza della Repubblica 22, is **La Ferrigna**, ① 914129 (*expensive*), offering some extravagant sorts of seafood antipasti, stuffed roast fish, and an Elban version of Livornese *cacciucco*; there are tables on the convivial piazza. *Closed Tues.* The **Scaglieri della Biodola** in Portoferraio, ① 969952 (*expensive*), serves up great antipasti and seconds like lobster stuffed with mussels. *Closed Wed and winter.* In Capoliveri, **Chiasso**, Via Nazario Sauro 20, ① 968709 (*expensive*), offers sole stuffed with shrimp and an Elban favourite that rarely travels to the mainland, *risotto al nero di seppia* (with cuttlefish in its own ink). *Closed Tues.* Again in Portoferraio, a few steps away from the main Piazza, **La Barca**, ① 918036 (*expensive*), is a good honest trattoria on Via D. Guerrazzi, with all sorts of seafood antipasti, crab soup and fishy pastas galore. Friendly service. In Porto Azzurro, among the many seafood restaurants on the beach, is **Tavernetta**, Lungomare Vitaliani 42, ① 95110 (*moderate*), built over the sea for a fine view. *Closed Thurs.* At Póggio, 3km from Marciana, **Publius**, Piazza XX Settembre 13, ① 99208 (*expensive*), is as worth visiting for its lovely views as for its menu, with items you won't find elsewhere on the island: *pappardelle* in boar sauce, *fagioli al fiasco* (Tuscan beans), and game in season—as well as good fish dishes. **Rendezvous** at Marciana, ① 99251 (*expensive*), has a curious dish of baked potato stuffed with fish and seafood.

Pianosa and Montecristo

Two other members of the Tuscan archipelago are included in Livorno province: one you won't want to visit, and the other you usually can't. **Pianosa** is the black sheep of the chain. Its name, taken from the Roman *Planasia*, explains why—it's as flat as a pool table. Like Gorgona, Pianosa's unhappy fate is to serve as a prison island. There are some substantial ruins of a Roman villa, from the days when Pianosa was the playground of Cornelius Agrippa, Emperor Augustus' great general, but to see them you'll need special permission from the prison authorities in Rome.

Likewise, don't count on visiting **Montecristo**, 40km south of Elba. Once the hunting preserve of King Vittorio Emanuele III, the tiny island, no more than the cone of an ancient volcano poking above the sea, has recently been declared a nature reserve. Private boats, and day trips organized from Porto Azzurro on Elba are allowed to dock at Cala Maestra, one of the many coves around the island's coast, but visitors are only allowed to stay on the cove and its beach; the mountain, ruins of a medieval monastery, and the royal villa (now the custodian's house) are strictly out of bounds. In Roman times this was an important religious site, *Mons Jovis*, with a famous temple of Jupiter on the summit; not a trace of it remains. The early Church wasted no time Christianizing the place, renaming it Montecristo. The first monastic community was founded in the 6th century by San Mamiliano (*see* 'Giglio', p.313), who reportedly killed a dragon upon arrival. None of the action of the *Count of Montecristo* is really set here; like most of us, seeing the place on a map is probably as close as Alexandre Dumas ever got.

The Maremma

In a sense, this flat and lonely stretch of coast south of Piombino really belongs to Italy's south. As on the islands, history has been extraordinarily unkind to the Maremma, domain first of the Etruscans, later of the anopheles mosquito. Like so many of the southern coastal regions, the Maremma was a prosperous, happy agricultural region until Roman times. The Romans gave it its name: the 'maritime' zone (recalled in place names like Massa Marittima), gradually mangled over the centuries into Maremma.

Historians sometimes give the Romans too much credit for capable governance; on the contrary, their grasping, bureaucratic state slowly corroded and destroyed the Italian economy. Many centuries of Roman misgovernment—impossible taxes, cheap imported grain and in this case, neglect of the Etruscans' system of drainage canals—doomed the Maremma to a slow death. When the drainage canals failed, much of the land was abandoned and reverted to swamps, breeding the malarial mosquitoes that made the Maremma of the Middle Ages a place of suffering and death, inhabitable only for the *butteri*, tough Maremma cowboys that tended the herds in the abandoned marshy pastures. A considerable body of folklore has grown up around the *butteri*, and the Maremma's proudest moment came in the last century when some of them defeated Buffalo Bill and his travelling Wild West show in a test of cowboy know-how. The first work of reclamation began with the Austrian Grand Dukes. The Italian Kingdom that followed them forgot all about the Maremma, and it was not until after World War II that the task was completed. The Maremma today is back on its feet, a new region and a little rough around the edges, but prosperous once again.

Tourist Information

Follonica: Viale Italia, ✆ (0566) 40177, 🖷 44308.

Follonica and Punta Ala

After Piombino, the coast bends eastwards into a broad arc, the Golfo di Follonica. Since the war, new resort towns have been popping up like toadstools all along the Tuscan coast. One of the biggest and least likeable is **Follonica**, 21km east of Piombino, redeemed partially by the long pine groves that follow its crowded beaches. Forget the beaches; Follonica has other enchantments, notably the **Museum of Iron and Cast Iron**, in an old foundry of the 1830s where Elban iron once was smelted (*open every day but Sun; information ✆ (0566) 43506*). On the promontory that closes the gulf, 14km to the south, **Punta Ala** is a new, entirely synthetic resort, built in the suburban style of the Costa Smeralda. It's an attractive location, with a fine sandy beach and views around the gulf, and it attracts a very well-heeled clientele with unusual (for Tuscany) diversions like golf (at the Golf Hotel, Via del Gualdo) and polo (Polo Club, © 922013).

Castiglione della Pescaia, to the south, is just the opposite, a much less exclusive resort attached to an ancient fishing village. The beach isn't the best around, and the modern resort strip has a blowsy air, but the town itself, up on its hill, full of trees and ivy-covered walls, makes one of the more pleasant detours on this coast. The Spanish left behind a 16th-century castle, the Rocca Aragonese, and the church of San Giovanni has an interesting round tower that could pass for a minaret.

© (0564–)   **Eating Out**

There's an excellent seafood restaurant at **Hotel Miramare**, Via Vittorio Veneto 27 in Castiglione della Pescaia, © 933524 (*expensive*). The dish to try is the *tesoro di Montecristo*, a delicious mixed grill of fish. All the dishes are innovative—like crêpes filled with prawns and baked *spaghetti al cartoccio*.

Grosseto

When Duke Cosimo I gobbled up Grosseto in 1559, along with the rest of the Sienese republic, he resolved to make it into a fortress town, guarding his southern borders against Spain and the pope. Following the manic geometry of the age, Cosimo's architects enclosed Grosseto in a perfect hexagon of walls. But as any good Chinese geomancer (or reader of Doris Lessing's *Shikasta*) could have told the Duke, one can't take such matters lightly. Maybe it was the wrong polygon for the prevailing telluric forces, but Grosseto (pop. 70,000) has certainly been suffering from some strange vibrations. Come to Grosseto, and you will find a city of Art Nouveau buildings and perverse teenagers, a city conducive to hallucinations, its streets alive with swirls of dust and flying plastic bags. Its citizens have a penchant for punk music and American football (the Grosseto 61'ers), also, so they claim, the highest rate of drug addiction in Italy. It is the only city in Italy, outside Calabria, where you cannot buy a decent slice of pizza.

Getting Around

Trains depart regularly for Siena (73km/1½hrs), and on the coastal line for Livorno (134km/2½hrs) or Orbetello (22km) and Rome (187km/3hrs). The RAMA bus station, with connections to Siena and every town in Grosseto province, including Massa Marittima (*see* **Hill Towns West of Siena**, p.369), Arcidosso and Pitigliano (*see* **Southern Tuscany**, pp.392 and 394) is a ramshackle nest of buildings on Via Oberdan, near the post office. Buses are likely to stop anywhere on the surrounding streets; get a few opinions in advance as to where yours might be.

Around La Vasca

Via Carducci leads you from the station towards the fearful hexagon, passing Mussolini's contribution to the city, a circular piazza called **La Vasca** (which can mean the 'tub' or the 'toilet bowl'); here the starring role is played by an exuberant Mussolini **post office**, with heroic statuary in travertine. The main gate is only a block away. Cosimo's walls are perfectly preserved, done in tidy, reddish brick festooned with Medici balls. Much of the old city looks very Spanish; the Art Nouveau pharmacies and shoe shops along the main street, Corso Carducci, contribute to the effect, as does the arcaded Piazza del Duomo, very like a Spanish *Plaza Mayor*. The **Duomo**, built 1190–1250, suffered grievously from over-ambitious restoration in the 1840s; the façade has more the appearance of a Hollywood prop than a genuine cathedral. Around the side, there is an interesting sundial, and in the piazza an allegorical monument to the Maremma's great benefactor, the Lorraine Grand Duke Leopold II; the woman he is raising up represents the suffering Maremma, and the snake he's crushing is Malaria.

Around the corner in Piazza Baccarini, the **Archaeology Museum of the Maremma** (*undergoing restoration*) wants to show you something of life in this region before there ever was a Grosseto. Some parts of the Mediterranean coastline just can't stand still. Thousands of years ago, Grosseto and most of its surrounding plain were under water; by the time of the Etruscans, the sea had receded, leaving a large lake on the plain. Two wealthy Etruscan cities, Vetulonia and Roselle (*see* below), stood on the hills above the lake, and they contributed most of the items here: cinerary urns with scenes from Homer, architectural fragments, and best of all the delicate terracottas, some preserving bits of their original paint. The collection is not a rich one, though well organized and relentlessly didactic. Up on the third floor, the city **Pinacoteca** has been closed for restoration for the last seven years. It houses some good Sienese art, including an amazing *Last Judgement* scene by the 13th-century artist Guido da Siena.

Just north of the museum, **San Francesco** church has an early work of Duccio di Buoninsegna, the crucifix above the high altar, and some good 13th-century frescoes with haunting eyes. From here, you can start a walk around the Medicean walls. After Italian unification, the bastions were landscaped into beautiful semi-tropical gardens; some are still well kept today, while others have decayed into spooky jungles. The liveliest parts of Grosseto are the shopping streets around the Piazza del Mercato; nearby, just outside the walls, the mornings see a large, almost picturesque street market.

Roselle and Vetulonia

In fact, you can learn much more about these two Etruscan towns from the Grosseto museum than from actually visiting the ruins, although this can be fun, and the signs are in English. **Roselle**, 7km north of the city, just off the main road to Siena, is the mother city of Grosseto. It survived Roman rule better than many other Etruscan cities, but writers of the 5th century report it being almost abandoned. Nevertheless, the bishops of Roselle hung on until 1178, when the seat was transferred to Grosseto. Like so many other Etruscan towns, Roselle stands atop a high plateau and is surrounded by over 3km of walls. An ancient Roman road leads up to the complex where there are the foundations of a few buildings, remains of the baths, the imperial forum and the outline of the Roman amphitheatre, a medieval tower, and necropolises all around. To the north of the site are the ruins of a Roman villa (*open 7.30–8.30, 9–5.30 in winter; for guided tours ℗ (0564) 410121 or 496670*) retaining parts of its original mosaic floor paving.

Vetulonia, 17km from Grosseto, out in empty countryside west of the village of Braccagni, lives on in the modern city of Massa Marittima. Like Roselle, it lasted until the Middle Ages, and seems to have been destroyed in a 14th-century revolt against its Pisan overlords. The scanty ruins are more Roman and medieval than Etruscan, but the periphery has some interesting tombs, the massive **Tomba della Pietrera** and the unique tomb called 'Il Diavolino', a long corridor leading under a tumulus, with an arched burial chamber in the middle that had an opening to the sky. The **Archeological Museum** is currently being restored.

Grosetto ℗ (0564–)   **Where to Stay and Eating Out**

If evil chance should find you spending time in Grosseto, at least there are some good restaurants for consolation. Hotels tend to be simple. One exception is the large ★★★★**Bastiani Grand Hotel**, Via Gioberti 64, ℗ 20047, ✆ 29321 (*expensive*). ★**Appennino**, at Viale Mameli 1, ℗ 23009, ✆ 416134 (*inexpensive*), is plain and well kept. ★★★**Leon d'Oro** in Via San Martino 46, ℗ 22128, ✆ 22578 (*moderate*), has double rooms with and without a bath and not a bad restaurant. *Closed Sun.* Generally acclaimed as one of the best restaurants in the Maremma, **Enoteca Ombrone**, Viale Matteotti 71, ℗ 22585 (*expensive*), may be over the top in many respects (they have not only a wine list, but an olive oil list), but they are sincerely devoted to finding the best ingredients and preparing them with artistic balance and judgement; people come here from all over southern Tuscany. Both Maremma cuisine (dishes like *tortelli Maremmani*, filled with ricotta, beetroot and spinach, or the local version of *cacciucco*, or maybe stewed boar) and international dishes. *Closed Sun eve and Mon.* For good, simple pasta and fish dishes, try **La Tana**, Via Aurelia Nord 100, ℗ 455004, or **Italiana** at Via P. Manescalchi 5, ℗ 22452 (*moderate*). **La Buca di San Lorenzo**, Via Manetti 1, ℗ 25142 (*very expensive*), is a restaurant dug into the Medicean walls; a nice setting, good food, but not cheap. Try their *tagliolini* with sea bass eggs. *Closed Mon.*

Grosseto is full of English style pubs which are very popular with the young. The best is **Tredici Gobbi**, Via Mazzini 106, which has large woodpanelled rooms on two floors and a large, welcoming open fire. *Closed Tues.* If you have time to kill at the station, it is worth having a *cappuccino* at **Cafe Marconi** at the right hand corner of the square.

Monti dell'Uccellina: The Maremma Nature Park

The park's visitors' centre is at Alberese, west of the coastal highway, the Via Aurelia/S1). At present, the park is open all year round, although some sections can only be visited by guided tour; it's best to call ahead, © (0564) 407098; also ask about guided tours in English during the summer; adm..

One side effect of the Maremma's long history of abandonment is a relatively unspoiled coastline. In the 1950s and 60s, developers followed the DDT wherever they could, but the Italian government managed to set aside a few of the best parts. The **Monti dell' Uccellina**, a ragged chain of coastal hills south of Grosseto, largely covered with groves of umbrella pines, is a favourite rest stop for migratory birds between Europe and Africa, hence the name. For such a small area, about 5 by 15km, the park has a lot to see: nine old Spanish, Sienese or grand-ducal defence towers, dozens of caves (one of which yielded bones of some of Italy's earliest inhabitants) and the ruins of an 11th-century monastery, **San Rabano**, that retains its campanile and some interesting early medieval stone-carving. Despite the park status, some people are still making a living here, herding cattle, cutting cork oak, and gathering pine nuts for Italy's pastry cooks.

The park's landscapes range from swamps to heather and rosemary-scented *macchia* (mixed Mediterranean scrub) to lovely pine groves, and it includes among its fauna herds of wild horses, deer and boar, along of course with the *uccellini*—herons, eagles and falcons, ospreys and kingfishers, every sort of duck, and even that most overdressed of all waterfowl, the *cavaliere d'Italia.*

Talamone

The Sienese republic never really had a port of its own, a great disadvantage for its foreign trade. Now and again, the Sienese would try to make one out of **Talamone**, a fishing village at the southern tip of the Monti dell'Uccellina. Unfortunately, the little harbour could not be kept clear, a continuing embarrassment for the republic; even Dante dropped a jibe about foolishly 'hoping from Talamone'. Garibaldi had better luck. When he and his 'Thousand' decided to stop here instead of in Sardinia in 1860, they avoided the orders for their arrest that had treacherously been sent by Count Cavour; Garibaldi also found a cache of weapons in nearby Orbetello that came in handy during the conquest of Sicily.

Today the walled village on its rock has become a discreet, laid-back resort with a small marina. Above it, a blank, grey 16th-century Spanish castle sits like some sort of abstract modern sculpture. A new museum devoted to nature in the Monti dell'Uccellina is planned for it.

In the last decade or two, this curiosity of the Tuscan coast has become quite popular. It has a lot going for it: some attractive old towns, a genuine Mediterranean feeling and Mediterranean scenery, a noticeable attraction on the humdrum Tuscan coast. Once, perhaps thousands of years ago, Argentario was an island, the member of the Tuscan archipelago closest to the shore. No one seems able to explain just how it happened, but the Tyrrhenian currents gradually built up two sand bars, connecting the rugged, mountainous island to the mainland. In between, there was a peninsula with the Etruscan, then Roman city of Orbetello; the Romans built a causeway on to Argentario that split the natural lagoon in half. There's a story that sailors gave the Argentario its name in classical times, noticing the flashes of silver from the olive leaves that still cover the mountain slopes.

Most books on Italy that mention the Argentario describe Porto Santo Stefano and Porto Ercole, its two resorts, as 'exclusive', even 'posh'. Not true. The Argentario attracts its share of the high life, but restaurants and hotels are not necessarily more expensive than in other resorts. Neither has the peninsula become an overcrowded beach Babylon like Elba. However, the beaches are not special and Tuscany's art and other attractions are far away. On balance, though, if you're looking for the best place to spend a seaside vacation in Tuscany, the Argentario presents a pretty strong case.

Getting Around

Orbetello is the centre for public transport around the Argentario, with a small bus station facing the northern lagoon, just off Piazza della Repubblica; buses leave regularly for Porto Ercole, Porto S. Stefano, Grosseto, and for the railway station, about 2km east of town, a stop on the Grosseto–Rome coastal line. There are also daily buses to Capalbio and Pitigliano.

Tourist Information

Orbetello: Piazza del Duomo, ✆ (0564) 860447.

Porto Santo Stefano: Corso Umberto 55a, ✆ (0564) 814208.

Porto Ercole: Via Arcidosso (summer only).

Orbetello

Go up to the northern tip of Orbetello's peninsula, near the causeway, and look over the edge of the water; in places, below the modern breakwater, you will see bits of ancient wall in huge irregular blocks. This is all that remains of Etruscan Orbetello, probably the biggest port of the Etruscan coasts. The easily defensible port has given the city at least a minor historical role over the centuries. The Byzantines held out longer here than anywhere else on the Tyrrhenian coast, and after them somehow the city fell into the hands of the Three Fountains Abbey in Rome, who passed it on to the pope—until 1980 the popes were also bishops of Orbetello. After the treaty of Câteau-Cambrésis in 1559, settling political arrangements across Italy, Orbetello found itself the capital of a new state—the Spanish military *Presidio*, ruled by a viceroy directly responsible to the King of Spain.

The Spanish Presidio lasted only until 1707, but it left behind a strong influence in the buildings and the people of this area. Orbetello was something of a resort a century ago, a role now passed on to Porto Ercole and Porto Santo Stefano; its most recent flash of glory came in the 1930s when Mussolini made it Italy's main seaplane base; Fascist hero Italo Balbo began his famous transatlantic flight here in 1933, landing at the opening of the Chicago World's Fair.

Confined on its narrow peninsula, with its palm trees and sun-bleached Spanish walls, Orbetello (pop. 13,500) is a charming town. Buses barely squeeze through the main gate in the land walls, decorated with the arms of the King of Spain. Off to the left, an unusual Spanish arsenal, the **Polveriera de Guzman**, now houses a small archaeological museum. Viale Italia is the main street, running down the centre of the peninsula. Just to the north, the **Cathedral** on Piazza della Repubblica has a beautiful façade with a sculpted portal and rose window from 1376; its interior was rebuilt in the 1600s. At the town hall, across the piazza, you can see the **Frontone di Talamone**, the pediment of an Etruscan temple, reconstructed from fragments found at Talamone; the reliefs portray mythological scenes of the Theban kings.

Orbetello's **lagoons**, on average about a yard deep, are partially used for fish farms, but most of the northern half has been declared a nature preserve, run by the World Wildlife Fund. Like the Monti dell'Uccellina, the area is a breeding ground for marine birds, and also storks and a species of eagle, not to mention the stilt plover, the bee-eater and the lesser hen harrier. When they're nesting, from April to October, the preserve is closed to humans; otherwise there is a visitors' centre and guides to show you around (*on the coast road between Orbetello and Albinia; tours at 10 and 2.30 Thurs and Sun only, adm*).

Porto Ercole and Porto Santo Stefano

Over the causeway from Orbetello on to Monte Argentario, you can go either north or south to begin the *gita panoramica*, the 24km road that makes an (incomplete) circle around the island. To the south, **Porto Ercole** wraps itself around a tiny fishing harbour, guarded on either side by Spanish fortresses. Forte Stella and Forte San Filippo were probably the last word in 16th-century military architecture, with low, sloping walls and pointed bastions draped over the cliffs; they present an ominous, surreal sight today. San Filippo is the most interesting, though you can't visit—it has been converted into holiday condominiums. Above the souvenir shops and seafood restaurants of the harbour, there is a fine old town, entered through a Gothic gate constructed by the Sienese. Little Piazza Santa Barbara is the centre, with the dignified 17th-century palace of the Spanish governor, and a view over the harbour below. Caravaggio was buried in the church of Sant'Erasmo in 1609 after dying in a tavern nearby. Beyond Porto Ercole, the coast road twists and turns under the slopes of Il Telegrafo, Argentario's highest peak (635m). One feature of the *gita panoramica* is the many defence towers, some built by the Sienese, others by the Spaniards.

On the northern side of the Argentario, **Porto Santo Stefano** makes a matching bookend for Porto Ercole. A bit larger and trendier than its sister town, this one also began as a sleepy fishing village, though now the fishing boats are elbowed off to the side of the port by speedboats, big shiny yachts and the Giglio ferries, and the old town has become lost in the agglomeration of hotels and villas on the surrounding hills. There are really two harbours: the first, larger one has the ferries and the fish markets; the yachts—and some real dreadnoughts they are—call at the western harbour, at the other side of a small promontory.

✆ (0564–)   *Where to Stay*

luxury

If you've bushels of money to spend and like swilling gin with yachtsmen and Italian TV stars, try ★★★★**Il Pellicano**. This Relais and Châteaux hotel is located on Cala dei Santi, a cove near Porto Ercole, ✆ 833801, 📠 833418; all imaginable amenities are provided, along with a pool and beach, with possibilities for windsurfing and every other water sport, and tennis—not to mention the presence of a first-class restaurant.

expensive

If you're planning an extended stay in the area, there's a hotel residence hidden away on the western tip of the peninsula. ★★★★**Torre di Calapiccola**, ✆ 825133, 📠 825235, is an apartment complex in a great setting, with a beach and plenty of activities, or equal doses of peace and quiet if that's what you're looking for.

moderate

In between, there is a wider choice at Porto Santo Stefano than at Porto Ercole, where ★★★**Don Pedro** has a nice location on the Via Panoramica, ✆ 833914, 📠 883129, but is some way off from the nearest beach. Porto Santo Stefano's best is ★★★**Filippo II**, ✆ 812640, 📠 814892, with air conditioning, close to the beaches at Poggio Calvella. ★★★**La Caletta** on Via Civinni 10, ✆ 812939, 📠 813698, has pleasant rooms overlooking the sea. A simple hotel in the centre of the action around the harbour is ★★**Alfiero**, Via Cuniberti 12, ✆ 814067.

inexpensive

If you're travelling on a budget and just want to pass through for a look at the Argentario, ★**Piccolo Parigi** on Corso Italia 169, ✆ 867233, is a delightful, very friendly and very Mediterranean establishment in the middle of Orbetello.

✆ (0564–)   *Eating Out*

Orbetello

Here the local favourite is **La Posada**, on the road to Porto Ercole at Terrarossa, ✆ 820180 (*expensive*), with delicate fish dishes (*terrina di salmone*) and robust steaks and grilled meats. *Closed Tues*. Orbetello can claim the absolutely best *pizza a taglio* (by the slice) stand in all Tuscany;

three toques and best wishes for continued success to the **Pizzeria Il Fornetto** on Corso Italia.

Porto Ercole

La Lampara, Lungomare Andrea Doria 67, © 833024 (*expensive*), is an outstanding restaurant right on the port, where the cooking is more or less Neapolitan—so of course there's pizza, too; outside tables, grilled fish. For fancier seafood, like spaghetti with lobster sauce, at fancier prices, try the **Gambero Rosso** next door, © 832650 (*expensive*)—good *zuppa di pesce* on weekends.

Porto Santo Stefano

Some of the places here are almost too swanky to be in such a little resort town: chief offender is the impeccably elegant **Dal Greco** on the yacht harbour, Via del Molo 1, © 814885 (*expensive*). A *terrina di pesce* with vegetables is the star attraction, along with lobster and a wide choice of other dishes. *Closed Tues.* On the other harbour, at Piazzale Facchinetti, **Il Delfino**, © 818394 (*expensive*), has semi-outdoor dining (pleasant, but a little close to traffic), and some more inventive seafood concoctions; they also pride themselves on their homemade desserts and ice cream. *Closed Thurs.* The popular and lively **Orlando** is one of the few genuine places left in town, Via Breschi 3, © 812788 (*moderate*). *Closed Thurs and winter.* Further out about 1.5km east of town at Pozzarello is **La Formica**, © 814205 (*expensive*), with a famous risotto involving caviar and prawns. *Closed Wed.* Also out of town is **La Querciolaie da Clara** in Via Martianese, Località Querciolaie (*expensive*); here you can eat such delicacies as king prawns with beans and pine nuts while sitting on a terrace overlooking the sea. *Closed Wed.*

Giglio and Giannutri

Giglio is the largest of the Tuscan islands after Elba, measuring about 21 by 8km. It is also second in population, with about 1600 souls, almost all of them in the three small villages, Giglio Porto, Giglio Castello and Giglio Campese. Like so many of the Italian islands, Giglio suffered grievously from deforestation and abandonment of the land in the last two centuries. Though much of it is still green and pretty, large sections have become almost barren. A remarkable change in the environmental consciousness of the Giglians seems to have taken place over the last few years; if the big signs posted all over the harbour are any indication, they've gone to the opposite extreme—no camping, no noise, no riding over the wild flowers (and no collecting rocks—they're part of the island too!).

The word *Giglio* means lily, and the lily has become the island's symbol, although it has in fact nothing to do with its name. The Romans called it *Aegilium* or *Gilium*. Under them, Giglio like most of the other Italian islands was a resort for the very wealthy. Pisa, Aragon and various feudal families held the island in the Middle Ages. Duke Cosimo seized it for Tuscany in the 16th century, but did little to protect it against its greatest danger, pirates. Fortunately, the Giglians had the holy right arm of San Mamiliano to protect them. This 6th-century Sicilian bishop, fleeing from the Arian heretics, became a hermit on

Montecristo. When he died, a divine signal alerted fishermen from Elba, Giglio and even Genoa, who arrived at the same time and began to fight over the remains. In the true tradition of Christian brotherhood, they struck a deal and cut Mamiliano in three pieces. Giglio got the arm, which proved its worth by chasing away Turkish pirates in 1799. On other occasions it wasn't so helpful. The redoubtable pirate Barbarossa carried off most of the population in 1534, and his understudy Dragut came back for the rest in 1550.

Getting Around

Porto S. Stefano is the main port for Giglio, a one-hour run twice daily, and more frequently in the summer on the TOREMAR line. The railway station for Porto S. Stefano, along the main Livorno-Rome line, is Orbetello Scalo; buses meet the trains to carry passengers to the port. Giannutri can be reached on a regular basis only in July and August, on a daily boat from Porto S. Stefano. On Giglio, buses run fairly regularly from the ferry dock to Giglio Castello and Giglio Campese.

Tourist Information

In **Giglio Porto** at Via Umberto I 48, ✆ (0564) 809 265 (summer only).

Giglio Porto, the island's metropolis, is a colourful place, with red and green lighthouses to welcome the ferries, and pink and beige houses straggling up the hills. There are two beaches south of the town, at **Cala delle Canelle** and **Cala delle Caldane**, one to the north at **Punta Aranella**, all more or less developed, and in the town itself, the world's smallest beach, tucked behind the houses on the left side of the port. From Giglio Porto a difficult mountain road leads up to **Giglio Castello**, the only secure refuge in pirate days, and until recently the only real town. The fortress itself was begun by the Pisans and completed under the grand dukes. The picturesque town inside, all medieval alleys and overhanging arches, has plenty of gulls and swallows, a few lazy German tourists, and a small Baroque church with an odd tower and the famous arm of San Mamiliano.

From Giglio Castello, a road leads southwards past **Poggio della Pagana**, the island's highest peak (498m), through land largely reforested with pines to Punta del Capel Rosso, at the southern tip, then back along the coast to Giglio Porto. The main road from Giglio Castello continues on to **Giglio Campese**, a growing resort area with an old watch-tower and a large sandy beach.

Giannutri

Giannutri, the southernmost island of the Tuscan archipelago, is a rocky crescent about 5km long, with little water and no fertile ground, and so little history to speak of. The ancient Greeks knew it as *Artemisia*, and the Romans as *Dianium*; perhaps the associations with the moon goddess came from the island's crescent shape. In Roman times it was an estate of the noble Ahenobarbus family, and substantial ruins of a **Roman Villa** (1st century AD) near Cala Maestra are visited by day trippers from Porto Santo Stefano in the summer months. Though Giannutri has no permanent population, there are a tourist village and a few holiday cottages near the well-protected bay, **Cala Spalmatoio**, on the eastern coast.

Giglio Ⓒ (0564–)   ***Where to Stay and Eating Out***

The number of tourists, and of hotels (12) on Giglio seems to have stabilized in the last few years, leaving it not entirely overcrowded even in the summer months. Right in the port there's ★★★**Demo's**, Via Thaon De Revel, Ⓒ 809235, ✆ 809319 (*moderate to expensive*), a little flash in the 60s Miami Beach style, and the smaller, cosier ★★**La Pergola** next door, Ⓒ 809051 (*moderate*). But persevere until you leave the Porto and you can enjoy the more serene ★★★**Arenella**, close to the beach on Via Arenella 5, Ⓒ 809304, ✆ 809443 (*moderate*), with a pretty garden and a good restaurant. And if you really want to get away from it all, your best chance on the entire Tuscan coast is ★★**Pardini's Hermitage**. Located at a quiet cove called Cala degli Alberi, Ⓒ 809034, ✆ 809177 (*moderate to expensive*), this place can only be reached by boat (ask at the Giglio Sub shop on the port, but it's better to book as there are only 11 rooms). They'll keep you busy with sports and nature activities if you want, or you can just enjoy the sea and mountains by yourself. A good, modern beach hotel off in Campese is ★★★**Campese**, Via della Torre 18, Ⓒ 804003 (*moderate*).

Giglio Porto has its share of seafood restaurants around the harbour. **La Margherita**, Ⓒ 809237 (*moderate*), is one of the most popular; good fish and a terrace right on the beach. The real find on the island, however, is up in Giglio Castello: **Da Maria**, on Via Casamatta 3, Ⓒ 806062 (*moderate*); not only good seafood (like stuffed squid or lobster flambé) but game dishes like the house speciality, wild rabbit *alla cacciatora*. *Closed Wed.* **Le Tamerici** at Giglio Castello, Piazza Gloriosa 43, Ⓒ 806266 (*moderate*), has a wide selection of game and seafood, as well as such specialities as scampi with courgettes from Giglio and steamed fish with mayonnaise. Make sure you save some room for their home-made desserts. *Closed Mon and winter.*

Capalbio and the Giardino dei Tarocchi

Back on the coast, 8km south of Orbetello, almost nothing is left of ancient **Ansedonia**, thoroughly destroyed by the Sienese in 1330. There's a long beach, a hotel or two, and some unusual souvenirs of the Etruscans, deep channels laboriously cut out of the solid rock; it is believed their purpose was to keep Cosa's small harbour from silting up. If it's ruins you're after, though, ascend the steep hill above Ansedonia to **Cosa**, a city founded by the Romans in the 3rd century BC, settled with loyal Roman citizens to keep an eye on the restless Etruscan cities nearby—and perhaps planned to help along their economic decline by draining off trade. Cosa never recovered after the Visigoths sacked it in the 5th century, but its recently excavated ruins (*work is still under way, due to reopen in 1994*) are enough to get an idea of what the city was like: a typical Roman rectangular circuit of walls with three gates, a strict grid of paved streets, a 'Capitoline' temple, and cisterns to catch rainwater. Remains of the port in the sea are visible from Ansedonia harbour. There is also a small museum on the site.

Before the coastal highway (S1) passes from Tuscany into Lazio, it runs along the edge of another World Wildlife Fund project, a nature reserve at a narrow lagoon called **Lago di Burano**. Though small, the lagoon shelters the same impressive variety of birds as the Monti dell'Uccellina and the Orbetello lagoons; it is also the summer home of perhaps the only cranes (*fenicotteri*) left on the Italian mainland (*tours at 10am and 2.30 Sun; open Sept–April*).

Capalbio, 6km inland, is one of the loveliest villages in southern Tuscany, a circular, walled hilltop enclave built around a castle of the Aldobrandeschi family. The pretty 12th-century parish church has some bits of 12th-century frescoes inside. A few kilometres to the east, though, almost on the Lazio border, you can stop for a sneak preview of what may some day be one of the best-known sights in Tuscany.

The **Giardino dei Tarocchi**, still under construction (*during construction, the site is open 4–7.30 Sat only, July and Aug; it should be opened in 1996, ☎ 895093 to find out its present state*), is the project of a French artist named Niki de Saint-Phalle. Someone is putting a lot of money into this place; the intention is to create a monumental sculptural work representing each of the 22 major arcana of the Tarot deck, a sort of garden for abstruse meditation. Already at least twelve of them are completed: mad, brilliant works in concrete, brightly coloured ceramics and mirrors that show the strong influence of Antonio Gaudi's architecture in Barcelona. A few are over 12m tall, glittering over the Maremma coast like some interplanetary Luna Park. The artist's symbolism is often obscure, but some works, like the broken *Tower*, are unmistakable.

Over the Border

If you're passing through here on the way to Rome, there are a few attractions in Rome's region of Lazio to distract you along the way. The biggest and richest Etruscan cities were here, not in Tuscany, and consequently the finest painted tombs can be seen along the north Lazio coast at **Tarquinia** and **Cerveteri**. Inland are the remains of the Etruscan town of **Vulci**. In the impressive fortress of Castello dell'Abbadia is an Etruscan museum (*open March, April, Sept 9–6, May–Aug 9–7 and Oct–Feb 9–4; adm*). An Etruscan bridge spans the gorge. Not much has happened on this lonely shore since Etruscan times, but the town of **Tuscania** has two extremely unusual early medieval churches, an introduction to the styles of medieval southern Italy. Head a little further inland and you'll meet a chain of large lakes, including lovely, tranquil **Lake Vico**, and the medieval city of **Viterbo**, once the residence of the popes.

Siena

Draped on its three hills, Siena (pop. 59,000) is the most beautiful city in Tuscany, a flamboyant medieval ensemble of palaces and towers cast in warm, brown, *Siena*-coloured brick. Its soaring skyline is its pride, dominated by the blazing black and white banner of a cathedral and the taut needle of the Torre di Mangia; and yet the Campo, the very centre of Siena, is only four streets away from olive groves and orchards. The contrast is part of the city's charm; densely built-up brick urbanity, and round the corner a fine stretch of long Tuscan farmland that fills the valleys within the city's walls.

Here art went hand in hand with a fierce civic pride to make Siena a world of its own, and historians go so far as to speak of 'Sienese civilization' in summing up the achievements of this unique little city.

Ancient Rivals

 Few rivalries have been more enduring than that between Florence and Siena; to understand Tuscany take a moment to compare the two. Long ago, while Florence was off at university, busily studying her optics and geometry, Lady Siena spent her time dancing and dropping her scarf for knights at the tournament. Florence thought she had the last laugh in 1555, when Duke Cosimo and his black-hearted Spanish pals wiped out the Sienese Republic and put this proud maiden in chains. It's frustrating enough today, though, when Florence looks up in the hills and sees Siena, an unfaded beauty with a faraway smile, sitting in her tower like the Lady of Shalott.

For two towns built by bankers and wool tycoons, they could not have less in common. Siena may not possess a Uffizi or a David, but neither does it have to bear the marble antimacassars and general stuffiness of its sister on the Arno, nor her smog, traffic, tourist hordes and suburban squalor. Florence never goes over the top. Siena loves to, especially in the week around the race of the *Palio*, the wildest party in Tuscany, a worthy successor to the fabulous masques and carnivals, the bullfights and bloody free-for-alls of the Sienese Middle Ages. In fact, Florence has been clicking its tongue at Siena since the time of Dante, who inserted in his *Inferno* a sarcastic reference to a famous club called the *Brigata*—twelve noble Sienese youths who put up 250,000 florins for a year of nightly feasting; every night they had three sumptuously laid tables, one for eating, one for drinking, and the third to throw out the window.

But there's more to Siena than that. This is a city with its own artistic tradition (*see* 'Art and Architecture'); in the 1300s, Sienese painters were giving lessons to the Florentines. Always more decorative, less intellectual than Florence, Siena fell behind in the quattrocento. By then, fortunately, the greatest achievement of Sienese art was already nearing completion—Siena itself.

History

Everywhere in Siena you'll see the familiar Roman symbol of the she-wolf suckling the twins. This is Siena's symbol as well; according to legend, the city was founded by the sons of Remus, Senius and Ascius. One rode a black horse, the other a white, and the simple comunal shield of black and white halves (the *balzana*) has been the other most enduring symbol of Siena over the centuries. It is most likely that somebody was living on these three hills long before this mythological pair. Excavations have found traces of Etruscan and even Celtic habitation. The almost impregnable site, dominating most of southern Tuscany, would always have been of interest. Roman-era *Sena Julia*, refounded by Augustus as a colony for his veterans, never achieved much importance, and we know little about the place until the early 12th century, when the emerging *comune* began keeping written records. In 1125, an increasingly independent Siena elected its first consuls. By 1169, the *comune* wrested political control away from the bishop, and some ten years later Siena developed its own written constitution.

The political development is complex, and with good reason. Twelfth-century Siena was a booming new city; control over its rich countryside, supplying some of the best wool in Italy, helped start an important cloth industry, and a small silver mine, acquired from Volterra in the 1160s, provided seed capital for what was to become one of the leading banking towns of Europe. Like so many other Italian cities, Siena was able early on to force its troublesome rural nobles to live within its walls, where they built scores of tall defence towers, fought pitched battles in the streets and usually kept the city divided into armed camps; in the narrowest part of the city, the *comune* once had to lay out new streets parallel to Via Camollia because of one particularly boisterous nobleman whose palace most Sienese were afraid to pass. Yet Siena was never completely able to bring its titled hoodlums under control. The businessmen made the money, and gradually formed their city into a sophisticated self-governing republic, but the nobles held on to many of their privileges for centuries, giving an anachronistically feudal tinge to Siena's life and art.

Like its brawling neighbours, medieval Siena enjoyed looking for trouble; in the endless wars of the 13th century they never had to look very far. Originally a Guelph town, Siena changed sides early to avoid being in the same camp with arch-rival Florence. Along with Pisa, Siena carried the Ghibelline banner through the Tuscan wars with varying fortunes. Its finest hour came in 1260, when a Florentine herald arrived with the arrogant demand that Siena demolish its walls and deliver up its large population of Ghibelline exiles from Florence. If not, the armies of Florence and the entire Guelph League—some 40,000 men—were waiting outside to raze the city to the ground. Despite the overwhelming odds, the Sienese determined to resist. They threw the keys of the city on the altar of the yet unfinished new cathedral, dedicating Siena to the Virgin Mary (a custom they have repeated ever since when the city is endangered, most recently just before the battle for liberation in 1944). In the morning, they marched out to the **Battle of Monteaperti** and beat the Florentines so badly that they captured their *carroccio*.

After the battle Siena had Florence entirely at her mercy and naturally was anxious to level the city and sow the ground with salt. One of the famous episodes in the *Inferno* relates how the Florentine exiles, who made up a substantial part of the Sienese forces, refused to allow it. Unfortunately for Siena, within a few years Florence and the Tuscan Guelphs had the situation back under control and Siena was never again to come so close to dominating Tuscan affairs. Nevertheless the city would be a constant headache to Florence for the next three centuries. When things were quiet at the front, the Sienese had to settle for bashing each other. The constant stream of anti-Siena propaganda in Dante isn't just Florentine bile; medieval Siena had a thoroughly earned reputation for violence and contentiousness. The impressive forms and rituals of the Sienese Republic were merely a façade concealing endless, pointless struggles between the various factions of the elite. Early on, Siena's merchants and nobles divided themselves into five *monti*, syndicates of self-interest that worked like political parties only without any pretence of principle. At one point, this Tuscan banana republic had 10 constitutions in 27 years, and more often than not its political affairs were settled in the streets. Before the Palio was invented, Siena's favourite civic sport was the *Gioco del Pugno*, a general fist-fight in the Campo with 300 on a side. Sometimes tempers flared, and the boys would bring out the axes and crossbows.

Siena's Golden Age

The historical record leaves us with a glaring paradox. For all its troubles and bad intentions, Siena often managed to run city business with disinterest and intelligence. An intangible factor of civic pride always made the Sienese do the right thing when something important was at hand, like battling with the Florentines or selecting a new artist to work on the cathedral. The Battle of Monteaperti may have proved a disappointment in terms of territorial ambitions, but it inaugurated the most brilliant period of Sienese culture, and saw the transformation of the hilltop fortress town into the beautiful city we see today. In 1287, under pressure from the Guelphs and their Angevin protectors, Siena actually allied itself with Florence and instituted a new form of government: the **'Council of the Nine'**. Excluding nobles from office, as Florence would do six years later, the rule of the Nine was to last until 1355, and it gave Siena a more stable regime than it knew at any other period.

Business was better than ever. The city's bankers came to rival Florence's, with offices in all the trading centres and capitals of Europe. A sustained peace, and increasing cultural contacts with France and Naples, brought new ideas and influences into Siena's art and architecture, just in time to embellish massive new building programmes like the **Cathedral** (begun 1186, but not substantially completed until the 1380s) and the **Palazzo Pubblico** (1295–1310). Beginning with Duccio di Buoninsegna (1260–1319), Sienese artists took the lead in exploring new concepts in painting and sculpture and throughout the 1300s they contributed as much as or more than the Florentines in laying the foundations for the Renaissance. Contemporary records betray an obsessive concern on the part of bankers and merchants for decorating Siena and impressing outsiders. At the height of its fortunes, in the early 14th century, Siena ruled most of southern Tuscany. Its bankers were known in London, in the Baltic and in Constantinople, and its reputation for beauty and culture was matched by few cities in Europe.

The very pinnacle of civic pride and ambition came in 1339, with the fantastical plan to expand the as yet unfinished cathedral into the largest in all Christendom. The walls of that great effort, a nave that would have been longer than St Peter's in Rome, stand today as a monument to the dramatic event that snapped off Siena's career in full bloom. The **Black Death** of 1348 carried off one-third of the population—a mortality not greater than some other Italian cities, perhaps, but the plague hit Siena at a moment when its economy was particularly vulnerable, and started a slow but irreversible decline that was to continue for centuries. Economic troubles led to political instability, and in 1355 a revolt of the nobles, egged on by Emperor Charles IV, who was then in Tuscany, overthrew the Council of the Nine. Then in 1371, seven years before the Ciompi revolt in Florence, the wool-workers staged a genuine revolution. Organized in a sort of trade union, the **Compagnìa del Bruco**, they seized the Palazzo Pubblico and instituted a new government with greater popular representation.

The decades that followed saw Siena devote more and more of its diminishing resources to buying off the marauding mercenary companies that infested much of Italy at this time. By 1399 the city was in such straits that it surrendered its independence to **Giangaleazzo Visconti**, the tyrant of Milan, who was then attempting to surround and conquer Florence. After his death Siena reclaimed its freedom. Political confusion continued throughout the century, with only two periods of relative stability. One came with the pontificate (1458–63) of Pius II, the great Sienese scholar **Aeneas Silvius Piccolomini**, who exerted a dominating influence over his native city while he ruled at Rome. In 1487, a nobleman named **Pandolfo Petrucci** took over the government; as an honest broker, regulating the often murderous ambitions of the *monti*, he and his sons kept control of the republic until 1524.

The Fall of the Republic

Florence was always waiting in the wings to swallow up Siena, and finally had its chance in the 1500s. The real villain of the piece, however, was not Florence but that most imperious Emperor, **Charles V**. After the fall of the Petrucci, the factional struggles resumed immediately, with frequent assassinations and riots, and constitutions changing with the spring fashions. Charles, who had bigger prey in his sights, cared little for the fate of the perverse little republic; he feared, though, that its disorders, religious toleration, and wretched financial condition were a disease that might spread beyond its borders. In 1530, he took advantage of riots in the city to install an imperial garrison. Yet even the emperor's representatives, usually Spaniards, could not keep Siena from sliding further into anarchy and bankruptcy on several occasions, largely thanks to Charles's war taxes. Cultural life was stifled as the Spaniards introduced the Inquisition and the Index. Scholars and artists fled, while poverty and political disruptions made Siena's once proud university cease to function.

In 1550, Charles announced that he was going to build a fortress within the city's walls, and that the Sienese were going to pay for it. Realizing that even the trifling liberty still left to them would soon be extinguished, the Sienese ruling class began intrigues with Charles' great enemy France. A French army, led by a Piccolomini, arrived in July 1552. Inside the walls the people revolted and locked the Spanish garrison up in its own new fortress. The empire was slow to react, but inevitably, in late 1554, a huge force of imperial troops, along with those of Florence, entered Sienese territory. The siege was prosecuted with remarkable brutality by Charles's commander, the **Marquis of Marignano**, who laid waste much of the Sienese countryside (which did not entirely recover until this century), tortured prisoners and even hired agents to start fires inside the walls. After a brave resistance, led by a republican Florentine exile named **Piero Strozzi** and assisted by France, Siena was starved into surrendering in April 1555. Two years later, Charles's son Philip II sold Siena to Duke Cosimo of Florence, and the ancient republic disappeared into the new Grand Duchy of Tuscany.

If nothing else, Siena went out with a flourish. After the capture of the city, some 2000 republican bitter-enders escaped to make a last stand at Montalcino. Declaring 'Where the *Comune* is, there is the City', they established what must be the world's first republican government-in-exile. With control over much of the old Sienese territory, the **'Republic of Siena at Montalcino'** held out against the Medici for another four years.

With its independence lost and its economy irrevocably ruined, Siena withdrew into itself. For centuries there was to be no recovery, little art or scholarship, and no movements towards reform. The Sienese aristocracy, already decayed into a parasitic *rentier* class, made its peace with the Medici dukes early on; in return for their support, the Medici allowed them to keep much of their power and privileges. The once great capital of trade and finance shrunk rapidly into an overbuilt farmers' market, its population dropping from a 14th-century high of 60–80,000 to around a mere 15,000 by the year 1700. This does much to explain why medieval and Renaissance Siena is so well preserved today—for better or worse, nothing at all has happened to change it.

By the 'Age of Enlightenment', with its disparaging of everything medieval, the Sienese seem to have quite forgotten their own history and art, and it is no surprise that the rest of Europe forgot them too. During the first years of the Grand Tour, no self-respecting northern European would think of visiting Siena. Few had probably ever heard of it, and the ones who stopped overnight on the way to Rome were usually dismayed at the 'inelegance' of its medieval buildings and art. It was not until the 1830s that Siena was rediscovered, with the help of literati like the Brownings, who spent several summers here, and that truly Gothic American, Henry James. The Sienese were not far behind in rediscovering it themselves. The old civic pride that had lain dormant for centuries yawned and stretched like Sleeping Beauty and went diligently back to work. Before the century was out, everything that could still be salvaged of the city's ancient glory was refurbished and restored. More than ever fascinated by its own image and eccentricities, and more than ever without any kind of an economic base, Siena was ready for its present career as a cultural attraction, a tourist town.

Getting Around

by car

The fastest route from Florence to Siena (68km) is the unnumbered toll-free Superstrada del Palio (1hr); the most scenic are the Chiantigiana S222 through the heart of Chianti and the Via Cassia (S2), which weave amongst the hills the Superstrada avoids. Both take about two hours. From the south, there are two possible approaches from the A1: S326 by way of Sinalunga (50km) or the more scenic and winding S73 by way of Monte Sansovino (44km).

Cars are forbidden to enter the centre, but there are clearly defined parking areas along all entrances to the city, especially around Piazza San Domenico, the Fortezza and along Viale del Stadio. One of the best places to hire a car is Autonoleggio A.C.I., in Via Vittorio Veneto, © (0577) 49001, ✆ 47003.

by train

Siena's station is located below the city, 1.5km from the centre down Viale G. Mazzini and is linked to the centre by frequent city buses. Siena's main line runs from Empoli (on the Florence–Pisa line) to Chiusi (Florence–Rome line). There are trains roughly every hour, with frequent connections to Florence from Empoli (97km, 1hr), less frequently to Pisa from Empoli (125km, 2hrs) and to Chiusi towards Umbria and Rome (65km to Chiusi, 1hr). There is a secondary line that runs towards Grosseto (70km, 1hr)—six a day, with three that continue on to Orbetello. To save a trip down to the station, all rail information and tickets are available at the SETI travel agency, No. 56 on the Campo.

by bus

Almost every town in southern Tuscany can be reached by bus from **Piazza San Domenico**, the big transport node on the western edge of Siena, with tourist information and hotel information booths. A board is posted with all departure times and the exact location of the stop; the ticket office (with a fancy, computer-operated information dispenser) is in the little building next to San Domenico church. The name of the company serving the whole of Siena province is TRA-IN, © 221 221, causing endless difficulties, according to the local tourist authorities, with English tourists looking for TRA-INs in the train station. Other companies depart for other cities like Florence (SITA, about once every hour, Rome, Perugia, Pisa, etc.), but all leave from San Domenico. Within the walls, there is no public transport, though regular buses to the **train station** and everywhere else in the modern suburbs depart from **Piazza Matteotti** north of the Campo.

Tourist Information

Piazza del Campo 56, © (0577) 280551, ✆ 270676. Via di Città 43, © (0577) 42209.

Post Office: Piazza Matteotti 1. **Telephones**: Via dei Termini 40.

Siena

324

Orientation: *Terzi* and the *Contrade*

The centre of Siena, the site of the Palio and, importantly to the Sienese, the 'farthest point from the world outside', is the famous piazza called simply **Il Campo**. From here, the city unfolds like a three-petalled flower along three ridges. It has been a natural division since medieval times, with the oldest quarter, the **Terzo di Città**, including the cathedral, to the southwest; the **Terzo di San Martino** to the southeast; and the **Terzo di Camollia** to the north.

Siena is tiny, barely over a square mile in size. The density, and especially the hills, make it seem much bigger when you're walking. There are no short cuts across the valleys between the three *terzi*. Although there are no cars in the centre, taxis and ambulances (medieval Siena is full of medieval hospitals) will occasionally try to run you down.

Contrade

The Sienese have taken the *contrade* for granted so long that their history is almost impossible to trace. Basically, the word denotes the 17 neighbourhoods into which Siena is divided. Like the *rioni* of Rome, they were once the original wards of the ancient city—not merely geographical boundaries, but self-governing entities; the ancients with their long racial memories often referred to them as the city's 'tribes'. In Siena, the *contrade* survived and prospered all through classical times and the Middle Ages. More than anything else, they maintained the city's traditions and sense of identity through the dark years after 1552. Incredibly enough, they're still there now, unique in Italy and perhaps all Europe. Once Siena counted over 60 *contrade*. Now there are 17, each with a sort of totem animal for its symbol:

Aquila (eagle), *Onda* (dolphin), *Tartuca* (turtle), *Pantera* (panther), *Selva* (rhinoceros) and *Chiocciola* (snail); all southwest of the Campo in Terzo di Città.

Leocorno (unicorn), *Torre* (elephant), *Nicchio* (mussel shell), *Civetta* (owl) and *Valdimontone* (ram); in Terzo di San Martino southeast of the Campo.

Oca (goose), *Drago* (dragon), *Giraffa* (giraffe), *Lupa* (wolf), *Bruco* (caterpillar) and *Istrice* (porcupine); all in the north in the Terzo di Camollia.

Sienese and Italian law recognize each of these as legally chartered communities; today a *contrada* functions as a combination social and dining club, neighbourhood improvement organization, religious confraternity and mutual assistance fund. Each elects its own officials annually in May. Each has its own chapel, museum and fountain, its own flag and colours, and its own patron saint who pulls all the strings he can in Heaven twice a year to help his beloved district win the Palio.

Sociologists, and not only in Italy, are becoming ever more intrigued with this ancient yet very useful system, with its built-in community solidarity and tacit social control. (Siena has almost no crime and no social problems, except of course for a lack of jobs.) The *contrade* probably function much as they did in Roman or medieval times, but it's surprising just what up-to-date, progressive and adaptable institutions they can be, and they are still changing today. Anyone born in a *contrada* area, for example, is automatically a member; besides their baptism into the Church, they also receive a sort of 'baptism' into the *contrada*. This ritual isn't very old, and it is conducted in the pretty new fountains the *contrade* have constructed all over Siena in recent years as centrepieces for their neighbourhoods.

To learn more about the *contrade*, the best place to go is one of the 17 little *contrada* museums. The tourist office can give you a list of addresses. One of the best is that of the Goose in the Terzo di Camollia. Though the caretakers usually live close by, most of them ask visitors to contact them a day or two in advance. The tourist office also has details on the dates of the annual *contrada* festivals, and the other shows and dinners they are wont to put on; visitors are always very welcome.

The Palio

The thousands of tourists who come twice a year to see the Palio, Siena's famous horse race around the Campo, probably think the Sienese are doing it all just for them. Yet like the *contrade* which contest it, the Palio is an essential part of Sienese culture, something that means as much to the city as it did centuries ago. Here are the plain facts on Italy's best-known annual festival.

The oldest recorded Palio was run in 1283, though no one can say how far the custom goes back. In the Middle Ages, besides horse races there were violent street battles, bloody games of primeval rugby and even bullfights. (Bullfights were also common at Rome and there's an argument to be made that Italy is the place where the Spaniards got the idea, back in the 16th and 17th centuries when Spain's own medieval passion for such things had been almost forgotten.) At present, the course is three times around the periphery of the Campo, though earlier it was run on various routes through the city's main streets.

The *palio* (Latin *pallium*) is an embroidered banner, the prize offered for winning the race. Two races are held each year, on 2 July and 16 August, and the *palio* of

each is decorated with an image of the Virgin Mary; after
political violence the city's greatest passion was
always Mariolatry. The course has room for only
ten horses in each race. Some of the 17 *contrade*
are chosen by lot each race to ensure that everyone
has a fair chance. The horses are also selected by lot,
but the *contrade* are free to select their own jockeys.
Although the race itself only lasts a minute and a
half, there's a good hour or two of pageantry
preceding the event; the famous flag-throwers or
alfieri of each participating *contrada* put on a dazzling
show, while the medieval *carroccio*, drawn by a yoke of
white oxen, is pressed into service to circle the Campo,
bearing the prized *palio* itself.

The Palio is no joke; baskets of money ride on each
race, not to mention the sacred honour of the district.
To obtain divine favour, each *contrada* brings its horse into its chapel on race
morning for a special blessing (and if a little horse manure drops during the ceremony, it's taken as a sign of good luck). The only rule stipulates that you can't
seize the reins of an opponent. There are no rules against bribing opposing
jockeys, making alliances with other *contrade*, or ambushing jockeys before the
race. The course around the Campo has two right angles. Anything can happen;
recent Palii have featured not only jockeys but *horses* flying through the air at the
turns. The Sienese say no one has ever been killed at a Palio. There's no reason to
believe them. They wouldn't believe it themselves; it is an article of faith among
the Sienese that fatalities are prevented by special intervention of the Virgin Mary.
The post-Palio carousing, while not up to medieval standards, is still impressive; in
the winning *contrada* the party might go on for days.

No event in Italy is as infectiously exhilarating as the Palio. There are
two ways to see it, either from the centre of the Campo, which is
packed tight and always very hot, or from an expensive
(L200–300,000) seat in a viewing stand, which you must book well in
advance. Several travel agencies offer special Palio tours (*see* p.7);
otherwise book by April.

Walking in Siena

If you keep your eyes open while walking the back streets of Siena you'll see the city's
entire history laid out for you in signs, symbols and a hundred other clues. You usually
won't have trouble guessing which *contrada* you're in. Little ceramic plaques with the
contrada symbol appear on many buildings and street corners, not to mention flags in the
neighbourhood colours, bumper stickers on the cars and the fountains, each with a
modern sculptural work, usually representing the *contrada*'s animal.

Look for noblemen's coats of arms above the doorways; aristocratic, archaic Siena will show you more of these than almost any Italian city. In many cases they are still the homes of the original families, and often the same device is on a dozen houses on one block, a reminder of how medieval Siena was largely divided into separate compounds, each under the protection (or intimidation) of a noble family. One common symbol is formed from the letters IHS in a radiant sun. Siena's famous 15th-century preacher, San Bernardino, was always pestering the nobles to forget their contentiousness and enormous vanity; he proposed that they replace their heraldic symbols with the monogram of Christ. The limited success his idealism met with can be read on the buildings of Siena today.

They don't take down old signs in Siena. One, dated 1641, informs prostitutes that the Most Serene Prince Matthias (the Florentine governor) forbids them to live on his street (Via di Salicotto). Another, a huge 19th-century marble plaque on the Banchi di Sotto, reminds us that 'In this house, before modern restorations reclaimed it from squalidness, was born Giovanni Caselli, inventor of the pantograph'. A favourite, on Via del Giglio, announces a stroke of the rope and a 16-lire fine for anyone throwing trash in the street, with proceeds to go to the accuser.

The Campo

There is no lovelier square in Tuscany, and none more beloved by its city. The Forum of ancient *Sena Julia* was on this spot, and in the Middle Ages it evolved into its present fan shape, rather like a scallop shell or a classical theatre. The Campo was paved in brick as early as 1340; the nine sections into which the fan is divided are in honour of the Council of the Nine, rulers of the city at the time. Thousands crowd over the bricks here every year to see the Palio, run on the periphery.

For a worthy embellishment to their Campo, the Sienese commissioned for its curved north end the **Fonte Gaia** from Jacopo della Quercia, their greatest sculptor, though what you see now is an uninspired copy of 1868. He worked on it from 1408 to 1419, creating the broad rectangle of marble with reliefs of Adam and Eve and allegorical virtues. It was to be the opening salvo of Siena's Renaissance, an answer to the Baptistry doors of Ghiberti in Florence (for which della Quercia himself had been one of the contestants). Perhaps it was a poor choice of stone, but the years have been incredibly unkind to this fountain; the badly eroded remains of the original can be seen up on the loggia of the Palazzo Pubblico.

No one can spend much time in Siena without noticing its fountains. The Republic always made sure each part of the city had access to good water; medieval Siena created the most elaborate engineering works since ancient Rome to bring the water in. Fonte Gaia, and others such as Fontebranda, are fed by underground aqueducts that stretch for miles across the Tuscan countryside. Charles V, when he visited the city, is reported to have said that Siena is 'even more marvellous underground than it is on the surface'. The original Fonte Gaia was completed in the early 1300s; there's a story that soon after, some citizens dug up a beautiful Greek statue of Venus, signed by Praxiteles himself. The delighted

Sienese carried it in procession through the city and installed it on top of their new fountain. With the devastation of the Black Death, however, the preachers were quick to blame God's wrath on the indecent pagan on the Fonte Gaia. Throughout history, the Sienese have always been ready to be shocked by their own sins; in this case, with their neighbours dropping like flies around them, they proved only too eager to make poor Venus the scapegoat. They chopped her into little bits, and a party of Sienese disguised as peasants smuggled the pieces over the border and buried them in Florentine territory to pass the bad luck on to their enemies.

Palazzo Pubblico

If the Campo is like a Roman theatre, the main attraction on stage since 1310 has been this brick and stone palace, the enduring symbol of the Sienese Republic and still the town hall today. Its façade is the face of Siena's history, with the she-wolf of Senius and Ascanius, Medici balls, the IHS of San Bernardino, and squared Guelph crenellations, all in the shadow of the tremendous **Torre di Mangia** (*open daily 9.30–7.30; winter 10–4; adm*), the graceful, needle-like tower that Henry James called 'Siena's Declaration of Independence'. At 102m, the tower was the second tallest ever raised in medieval Italy (only the campanile in Cremona beats it). At the time, the cathedral tower up on its hill completely dominated Siena's skyline; the Council of the Nine wouldn't accept that the symbol of religious authority or any of the nobility's fortress-skyscrapers should be taller than the symbol of the republic, so its Perugian architects, Muccio and Francesco di Rinaldo, made sure it would be hard to beat.

There was a practical side to it, too. At the top hung the *comune's* great bell, which had to be heard in every corner of the city tolling the hours and announcing the curfew, or calling the citizens to assemble in case of war or emergency. One of the first men to hold the job of bell-ringer gave the tower its name, a fat, sleepy fellow named *Mangiaguadagni* ('eat the profits') or just Mangia for short; there is a statue of him in one of the courtyards. Climb the tower's endless staircase for the definitive view of Siena—on the clearest days you'll also be able to see about half of the medieval republic's territory, a view that is absolutely, positively worth the slight risk of cardiac arrest. At the foot of the tower, the marble **Cappella della Piazza**, with its graceful rounded arches, stands out clearly from the Gothic earnestness of the rest of the building. It was begun in 1352, in thanks for deliverance from the Black Death, but not completed until the mid-15th century.

Most of the Palazzo Pubblico's ground floor is still used for city offices, but the upper floors have been made into the city's museum (*open daily 9.30–1.30, until 7 in summer; Sun 9–1; adm exp*).

Here the main attraction is the series of state rooms done in frescoes, a sampling of the best of Sienese art throughout the centuries. The first, the historical frescoes in the **Sala del Risorgimento,** were done by an artist named A. G. Cassioli only in 1886: the meeting of Vittorio Emanuele II with Garibaldi, his coronation, portraits and epigrams of past patriots, and an 'allegory of Italian Liberty', all in a colourful and photographically precise style. If anything, it is a tribute to Sienese artistic conservatism; finally liberated after 300 years of Florentine rule, they immediately went back to their good old medieval habits.

Next on the same floor is the **Sala di Balia** with frescoes depicting the story of Alessandro VII and some vigorous battle scenes by the Sienese Spinello Aretino (1300s) and the *Sixteen Virtues* by Martino di Bartolomeo. The adjoining **anticamera del**

Piazza del Campo

Concistoro has a lovely *Madonna and Child* by Matteo di Giovanni. In the **Sala del Concistoro**, Gobelin tapestries adorn the walls while the great Sienese Mannerist Beccafumi contributed a ceiling of frescoes in the 1530s celebrating the political virtues of antiquity; that theme is continued in the vestibule to the **Chapel**, with portraits of ancient heroes from Cicero to Judas Maccabeus, all by Taddeo di Bartolo. These portrayals, along with more portraits of the classical gods and goddesses and an interesting view of ancient Rome, show clearly just how widespread was the fascination with antiquity even in the 1300s. Intruding among the classical crew, there's also a king-sized St Christopher covering an entire wall. Before setting out on a journey it was good luck to catch a glimpse of this saint, and in Italy and Spain he is often painted extra large so you won't miss him. In a display case in the hall, some of the oldest treasures of the Sienese Republic are kept: the war helmet of the Captain of the People, and a delicate **golden rose**, a gift to the city from the Sienese Pope, Pius II.

The **Chapel** (*Cappella del Consiglio*) is surrounded by a lovely wrought-iron grille designed by Jacopo della Quercia; when it is open you can see more frescoes by Taddeo di Bartolo, an altarpiece by Il Sodoma, and some exceptional carved wood seats, by Domenico di Nicolò (*c.*1415–28). In the adjacent chamber (the **Sala del Mappamondo**), only the outline is left of Lorenzetti's cosmological fresco, a diagram of the universe including all the celestial and angelic spheres, much like the one in the Campo Santo at Pisa. Above it, there is a very famous fresco by Simone Martini (*c.*1330), showing the redoubtable condottiere **Guidoriccio da Fogliano** on his way to attack the castle of Montemassi, during a revolt against Siena. Also by Martini is an enthroned Virgin, or *Maestà*, that is believed to be his earliest work (1315).

The Allegories of Good and Bad Government

When you enter the **Sala dei Nove** (or Sala della Pace), meeting room of the Council of the Nine, you'll understand at a glance why they ruled Siena so well. Whenever one of the councillors had the temptation to skim some cream off the top, or pass a fat contract over to his brother-in-law the paving contractor, or tighten the screws on the poor by raising the salt tax, he had only to look up at Ambrogio Lorenzetti's great frescoes to really feel like a worm. There are two complementary sets, with scenes of Siena under good government and bad, and allegorical councils of virtues or vices for each. Enthroned Justice rules the good Siena, with such counsellors as Peace, Prudence and Magnanimity; bad Siena groans under the thumb of one nasty piece of work, sneering, fanged Tyranny and his cronies: Pride, Vainglory, Avarice and Wrath among others. The good Siena is a happy place, with buildings in good repair, well-dressed folk who are dancing in the streets, and well-stocked shops where the merchants appear to be making a nice profit. Bad Siena is almost a mirror image, only the effects of the Tyrant's rule are plain to see: urban blight, crime in broad daylight, buildings crumbling and abandoned, and business bad for everybody—a landscape which for many of us modern city dwellers will seem all too familiar.

Lorenzetti finished his work around 1338, probably the most ambitious secular painting ever attempted up to that time. The work has been recently cleaned and restored; fittingly, Good Government has survived more or less intact, while Bad Government has not aged so well and many parts have been lost. In the next room is Guido da Siena's large *Madonna and Child* (mid-1200s), the earliest masterpiece of the Sienese school. If you're not up to climbing the tower, at least take the long, unmarked stairway by Sala Risorgimento that leads up to the **loggia**, with the second-best view over Siena and the disassembled bits and pieces of della Quercia's reliefs from the Fonte Gaia, not particularly impressive in their worn and damaged state.

Around the Campo

Part of the beauty of the Campo lies in the element of surprise; one usually enters from narrow arcades between austere medieval palaces that give no hint of what lies on the other side. Two of Siena's three main streets form a graceful curve around the back of the Campo; where they meet the third, directly behind the Fonte Gaia, is the corner the Sienese call the **Croce del Travaglio** (a mysterious nickname: the 'cross of affliction'). Here, under the eternal scaffolding of bureaucratic restoration, sleeps one of Siena's landmarks, the three-arched **Loggia della Mercanzia**, in a sense Siena's Royal Exchange, the place where the Republic's merchants made their deals and settled their differences before the city's famed commercial tribunal. The Loggia marks the transition from Sienese Gothic to the early Renaissance style—begun in 1417, it was probably influenced by Florence's Loggia dei Lanzi. The five statues of saints around the columns are the work of Antonio Federighi and Vecchietta, the leading Sienese sculptor after della Quercia.

The three streets that meet here lead directly into the three *terzi* of Siena. All three are among the city's most beautiful streets, in particular the gracefully curving **Banchi di Sotto**, main artery of the Terzo di San Martino. Just beyond the Campo, this street passes Siena's most imposing *palazzo privato*, the **Palazzo Piccolomini** (*open daily 9–1, closed Sun*), done in the Florentine style by Rossellino in the 1460s. This palace now houses the old Sienese state archive—not a place you might consider visiting but for the presence of the famous *Tavolette della Biccherna* (the account books of the *Biccherna*, or state treasury). Beginning in the 1200s, the Republic's custom was to commission the best local artists to decorate the covers of the *tavolette* ; the most interesting show such prosaic subjects as medieval citizens coming in to pay their taxes, city employees counting their pay and earnest monks trying to make the figures square—all are Cistercians from San Galgano (*see* p.371), the only people medieval Siena trusted to do the job. Among the other manuscripts and documents you'll find Boccaccio's will.

Terzo di Città and the Cathedral

Southwest from the Croce del Travaglio, Via di Città climbs up to the highest and oldest part of Siena, the natural fortress of the Terzo di Città. Among the palaces it passes is the grandiose **Palazzo Chigi-Saracini**, with a wretched old tree, barely surviving, hanging over the street from its stony courtyard. The palace contains an internationally important music school, the Accademia Musicale Chigiana, and a large collection of Sienese and Florentine art which is open by appointment, ✆ (0577) 46152. Next door is yet another reminder of the Piccolomini, the **Palazzo delle Papesse**. The family, along with the Colonna of Rome and the Correr of Venice, was one of the first to really exploit the fiscal possibilities of the papacy; Aeneas Silvius (Pius II) built this palace, also designed by Rossellino, for his sister, Caterina Piccolomini.

All approaches from Via di Città to Siena's glorious **Cathedral**, spilling over the highest point in the city, are somewhat oblique. Easiest, perhaps, is Via dei Pellegrini, which winds around the back, past the unusual crypt-baptistry tucked underneath (*see* p.338), up the steps to the Piazza del Duomo, and through a portal in a huge, free-standing wall of striped marble arches, a memorial to that incredible ill-starred 1339 rebuilding plan confounded by the plague. The cathedral the Sienese had to settle for may not be a transcendent expression of faith, and it may not be an important landmark in architecture, but it is certainly one of the most delightful, decorative ornaments in Christendom.

Piazza San Giovanni

Via Monna Agnese

Piazza
Jacopo della Quercia

Piazza
del Duomo

1 Pisano's Pulpit
2 Chapel of San Giovanni Battista
3 Tomb of Cardinal Pecci (Donatello)
4 Tomb of Cardinal Petroni (Tino da Camaino)
5 Stained Glass of Duccio
6 High Altar
7 Piccolomini Altar (della Quercia, Michelangelo)
8 Campanile
9 Sacristy
10 Cantorie
11 Choir
12 Piccolomini Library
13 To Cathedral Museum
14 Cathedral Extension
15 Baptistry (lower level)

A Hermes Trismegistus
B Allegory of Virtue
C Wheel of Fortune
D Massacre of the Innocents
E Judith Liberatino Bethulia
F Seven Ages of Man
G Allegories of Faith, Hope and Charity
H Story of Absalom
I Emperor Sigismund on his Throne
J Sacrifice of Elias, Execution of the False Prophets
K Samson and the Philistines
L David the Psalmist
M Sacrifice of Abraham
N Moses Receives the Commandments
O Story of Jephta

333

Begun around 1200, one of the first Gothic cathedrals in central Italy, it started in the good Gothic tradition as a communal effort, not really a project of the Church. There doesn't seem to have been much voluntary labour—even in the Middle Ages Italians were a little too blasé for that—but every citizen with a cart was expected to bring in two loads of marble from the quarries each year, earning him a special indulgence from the bishop. One load must have been white and the other black, for under the influence of Pisa, the Sienese built themselves one thoroughly striped cathedral—stripes darker and bolder than Pisa's or Lucca's. The campanile, with its distinctive fenestration, narrowing in size down six levels, rises over the city like a giant ice-cream parfait. Most of the body of the church was finished by 1270, and 14 years later Giovanni Pisano was called in to create the sculpture for the lavish **façade**, with statues of biblical prophets and pagan philosophers. The upper half was not begun until the 1390s, and the glittering mosaics in the gables are, like Orvieto's, the work of Venetian artists of the late 19th century.

The Cathedral Interior: the Marble Pavement

Open 7.30–5 winter, 7.30–7.30 summer.

This is a treasure-box of a cathedral, perhaps the only church in Italy that could keep a serious visitor busy for an entire day. Upon entering the main portal, the ferociously striped pilasters and the Gothic vaulting, a blue firmament painted with golden stars, inevitably draw the eye upwards. However, the most spectacular feature is at your very feet—the marble pavement, where the peculiar figure smiling up at you is **Hermes Trismegistus**, the legendary Egyptian father of alchemy, depicted in elegant *sgraffito* work of white and coloured marble. In fact, the entire floor of the cathedral is covered with almost 12,000 square metres of virtuoso *sgraffito* in 56 scenes including portraits, mystical allegories and events from the Old Testament. Like the Biccherna covers in the Palazzo Piccolomini, they are a tradition carried on over centuries. Many of Siena's best artists worked on them, beginning in 1369 and continuing into the 1600s; Giorgio Vasari claimed that Duccio di Buoninsegna himself first worked in this medium, though none of the pictures here are his.

Hermes Trismegistus

Hermes Trismegistus is someone rarely seen in art, though a mysterious protagonist in a great undercurrent of Renaissance thought. 'Thrice-great Hermes', mythical author of a series of mystic philosophical dialogues from the 2nd century AD, had a profound influence on Greek and Arabic thought, gradually becoming associated (correctly or not) with the Egyptian god Thoth, inventor of writing and father of a deep mystical tradition that continues to this day. In the 1400s, the Hermetic writings were introduced in the west, largely the work of Greek scholars fleeing the Ottoman conquest of Constantinople and Trebizond. They made quite a splash. Marsilio Ficino, the Florentine Humanist and friend of Cosimo de' Medici, completed the first Latin translation of the Hermetic books in 1471—Cosimo specifically asked him to put off his translations of Plato to get this more important work finished!

To the men of the Renaissance, Hermes was a real person, an Egyptian prophet, who lived in the time of Moses and was perhaps his teacher. They saw, revealed in the Hermetic books, an ancient, natural religion, prefiguring Christianity and complementary to it—and in fact much more fun than Christianity, for the magical elements in it were entirely to the taste of neo-Platonists like Ficino. From a contemporary point of view, the recovery of Hermes Trismegistus was one of the main intellectual events of the century, a century that witnessed a tremendous revival of natural magic, alchemy and astrology.

The memorable Hermes in Siena is surrounded by a bevy of ten Sibyls: those of Cumae and Tivoli (the Italians), Delphi, Libya, the Hellespont, Phrygia and the rest. These ladies, part of a pan-Mediterranean religious tradition even older than Hermes Trismegistus, are far more common in Tuscan religious iconography (as in the Baptistry and Santa Trínita in Florence, or most famously on Michelangelo's Sistine Chapel ceiling), for the belief that they all in some way foretold the birth of Christ.

Even in a building with so many marvels—the Piccolomini Library, Nicola Pisano's pulpit, Duccio's stained glass, works by Donatello, della Quercia, Pinturicchio, Michelangelo, Bernini and many others—this pavement perhaps takes pride of place. The greatest limitation of Sienese art was always the conservatism of its patrons, accustomed to demanding the same old images in the same old styles. Commissions from the Office of Cathedral Works, controlled by the state, were usually more liberal, allowing the artists to create such unique, and in some cases startling images, one of the greatest achievements of Renaissance Siena.

The Hermes on the cathedral pavement, by Giovanni di Stefano, was completed in the 1480s, a decade after Ficino's translation; it shows him together with Moses, holding a book with the inscription 'Take up thy letters and laws, O Egyptians'. On either side, all 10 prophetic *Sibyls* done by various artists at the same time decorate the aisles of the church. Nor are Hermes and the sibyls the only peculiar thing on this floor. Directly behind him begins a series of large scenes, including a Wheel of Fortune, with men hanging on to it for dear life, another wheel of uncertain symbolism, and emblems of Siena and other Tuscan and Latin cities. Oddest of all is a work by Pinturicchio, variously titled the *Allegory of Virtue* or the *Allegory of Fortune*; on a rocky island full of serpents, a party of well-dressed people has just embarked, climbing to the summit where a figure of 'Socrates' accepts a pen from a seated female figure, and another, 'Crates', empties a basket of gold and jewels into the sea. Below, a naked woman with a gonfalon stands with one foot in a boat, and another on land.

Unfortunately, many of the best scenes, under the crossing and transepts, are covered most of the year to save them from wear. You'll need to come between 15 August and 15 September to see the visionary works of Alessandro Franchi—the *Triumph of Elias* and other events in that prophet's life—and Domenico Beccafumi's *Sacrifice of Elias* and the

Execution of the False Prophets of Baal. (Hasn't anyone in Siena ever heard of Plexiglass?) Other works uncovered all year include *The Seven Ages of Man* by Antonio Federighi, *Scenes From the Life of Moses* by Beccafumi, Matteo di Giovanni's *Massacre of the Innocents* (always a favourite subject in Sienese art), and best of all the beautifully drawn *Judith Liberating the City of Bethulia*, a collaboration of Federighi, Matteo di Giovanni and Urbano da Cortona.

Elsewhere in the Cathedral

Perhaps the greatest attraction above floor level is the great Carrara marble **pulpit** done by Nicola Pisano in the 1280s. Pisano started on it directly after finishing the one in Pisa; one of the assistants he brought here to help with the work was the young Arnolfo di Cambio. The typical Pisano conception is held up by allegorical figures of the seven liberal arts—more sibyls, prophets, Christian virtues and saints tucked away in the odd corners, and vigorous, crowded relief panels from the Passion as good as the ones in Pisa. Nearby, in the left transept, the **chapel of San Giovanni Battista** has frescoes by Pinturicchio and a bronze statue of St John the Baptist by Donatello, who also contributed the **Tomb of Giovanni Pecci**, a 1400s Sienese bishop. Another tomb worth a look is that of Cardinal Petroni, an influential early Renaissance design from 1310 by Tino di Camaino.

Some of the **stained glass** in the cathedral is excellent, especially the earliest windows, in the apse, designed by Duccio, and the rose window with its cornucopia. Over the high altar is a bronze **baldachin** by Vecchietta, and in the north aisle, the **Piccolomini Altar** includes four early statues of saints by Michelangelo, and one by Torrigiano, the fellow who broke Michelangelo's nose and ended up in exile, working in Westminster Abbey. There is also a *Madonna* by Jacopo della Quercia. Throughout the cathedral, as everywhere else in Siena, be sure to keep an eye out for details—little things like the tiny, exquisite heads of the popes that decorate the clerestory wall. The Office of Works never settled for anything less than the best, and even such trifles as the holy water fonts, the choir stalls, the iron grilles and the candlesticks are works of genuine artistic merit.

Piccolomini Library

Open daily 10–1 and 2.30–5; 9– 7.30 in summer; adm.

This is the room with the famous frescoes by Pinturicchio maintained as part of the cathedral complex. It was built to hold the library of Aeneas Silvius, the greatest member of Siena's greatest noble family. The entrance is off the left aisle, near the Piccolomini Altar.

Aeneas Silvius Piccolomini, eventually to become Pope Pius II, was the very definition of a Renaissance man. Probably the greatest geographer of his age, his works were studied closely by Columbus. Beyond that, and his activities as a poet, diplomat and historian, founder of Pienza and an important patron of artists and humanist scholars (although scholars are still debating this), he had, of course, a busy clerical-political career, working fitfully to reform the church of Rome and the constitution of his native city. In 1495, 31 years after his death, Cardinal Francesco Piccolomini, a man who would become Pope Pius III, decided his celebrated uncle's life would make a fine subject for a series of frescoes. He gave the job to Pinturicchio, his last major commission; among his assistants was the young, still impressionable Raphael—anyone who knows his *Betrothal of the Virgin* will find these paintings eerily familiar.

The 10 scenes include Aeneas Silvius' attendance at the court of James I in Scotland—a Scotland with a Tuscan fantasy landscape— where he served with an embassy. Later he is shown accepting a poet laureate's crown from his friend Emperor Frederick III, and presiding over the meeting of Frederick and his bride-to-be, Eleanor of Aragon. Another fresco depicts him canonizing St Catherine of Siena. The last, poignant one portrays a view of Ancona, and its cathedral up on Monte Guasco, where Pius II went in 1464, planning a crusade against the Turks. While waiting for the help promised by the European powers, help that never came, he fell ill and died.

Art historians and critics, following the sniping biography of the artist by Vasari, are not always kind to Pinturicchio. As with Gozzoli's frescoes for the Medici Palace in Florence, the consensus seems to be that this is a less challenging sort of art, or perhaps just a very elevated approach to interior decoration. Certainly Pinturicchio seems extremely concerned with the latest styles in court dress and coiffure. However, the incandescent colour, fairy-tale backgrounds and beautifully drawn figures prove irresistible. These are among the brightest and best-preserved of all quattrocento frescoes; the total effect is that of a serenely confident art, concerned above all with beauty for beauty's sake, even when chronicling the life of a pope. Aeneas Silvius' books have all been carted away somewhere but one of his favourite things remains, a marble statue of the Three Graces, a copy of the work by Praxiteles that was much studied by the artists of the 1400s.

Museo Metropolitana

Open daily 12 March –30 Sept 9–7.30; otherwise 9–1.30; adm.

Around the side of the cathedral, off the right transept, Piazza Jacopo della Quercia is the name the Sienese have given to the doomed nave of their 1330s **cathedral extension**. All around the square, the heroic pilasters and arches rise, some incorporated into the walls of later buildings. Beyond the big, blank façade, a little door on the right gives entrance to the **Museo Metropolitana**, built into what would have been one of the cathedral transepts. This is the place to go to inspect the cathedral façade at close range. Most of the statues now on the façade are modern copies, replacing the works of great sculptors like Nicola Pisano, Urbano da Cortona and Jacopo della Quercia. The originals have been moved to the museum for preservation, and you can look the cathedral's marble saints right in the eye (if you care to; many of these remarkable statues, fairly alive with early Renaissance *prontezza* (alertness), seem ready to hop off their pedestals and start declaiming if they suspect for a minute you've been skipping Sunday mass).

Besides these, there are architectural fragments and leftover pinnacles, as well as some bits of the marble pavement that had to be replaced. On the first floor, a collection of Sienese paintings includes Duccio di Buoninsegna's masterpiece, the *Maestà* that hung behind the cathedral's high altar from 1311 until 1505. Painted on both sides, the main composition is a familiar Sienese favourite, the enthroned Virgin flanked by neat rows of adoring saints—expressive faces and fancy clothes with a glittering gold background. Among the other paintings and sculptures are works by Pietro and Ambrogio Lorenzetti, Simone Martini, Beccafumi and Vecchietta.

Among the works on the top floor is the *Madonna dagli Occhi Grossi* ('of the Big Eyes') by an anonymous artist of the 1210s, a landmark in the development of Sienese painting and the original cathedral altarpiece. There's a hoard of golden croziers, reliquaries, and crucifixes from the Cathedral Treasure, including another lovely golden rose from the Vatican—probably a gift from Aeneas Silvius. A stairway from here leads up to the top of the **Facciatone**, the 'big façade' of the unfinished nave, where you can contemplate lost ambitions and enjoy a view over the city.

Baptistry

Open 9–7.30 summer, 10–1, 2.30–5 winter; adm.

Outside the unfinished cathedral nave, a long, steep set of stairs leads down around the back of the church to Piazza San Giovanni. In this lower but prominent setting the Office of Works architects squeezed in a baptistry, perhaps the only one in Italy situated directly under a cathedral apse. Behind its unfinished 1390s Gothic façade, this baptistry contains some of the finest art in Siena. It's hard to see anything in this gloomy cellar, though; bring plenty of coins for the lighting machines. Frescoes by Vecchietta, restored to death in the 19th century, decorate much of the interior. The crown jewel, however, is the **baptismal font**, a king-sized work embellished with some of the finest sculpture of the quattrocento. Of the gilded reliefs around the sides, *Herod's Feast* is by Donatello, and the *Baptism of Christ* and *St John in Prison* by Ghiberti. The first relief, with the *Annunciation of the Baptist's Birth*, is the work of Jacopo della Quercia, who also added the five statues of prophets above. Two of the statues at the corners of the font, the ones representing the virtues Hope and Charity, are also by Donatello.

Across the street from the baptistry, the Renaissance **Palazzo del Magnifico** by Cozzarelli was the family headquarters of the Petrucci, Sienese power-brokers (and perhaps would-be rulers) in the late 15th and early 16th centuries.

Open daily 8.30–7; 8.30–1 Sun; 8.30–1.30 in winter, closed Mon; adm.

Opposite the old cathedral façade, one entire side of the piazza is occupied by the great **Ospedale di Santa Maria della Scala**, believed to have been founded in the 9th century and for centuries one of the largest and finest hospitals in the world. According to legend, the hospital had its beginnings with a pious cobbler named Sorore, who opened a hostel and infirmary for pilgrims on their way to Rome. (Siena was an important stop on medieval Europe's busiest pilgrimage route, the Via Francigiana.) Sorore's mother, it is said, later had a vision here—of babies ascending a ladder into heaven, and being received into the arms of the Virgin Mary—and consequently a foundling hospital was soon added. A meticulous attention to the health of its citizens was always one of the most praiseworthy features of Siena; even in the decadence of the 1700s advances in such things as inoculation were being made here. Today, old Siena is still full of hospitals. Only a part of this huge complex is still in use; the hospital and its chapel preserve some fine frescoes, and there has been some talk of making part of it into a museum.

The ancient quarter of steep narrow streets north of the cathedral is the *contrada* of the *Selva* (forest)—rhinoceros country. In its heart, Piazza della Selva, one of the most charming of the new *contrade* fountains has a bronze statue of the neighbourhood's rhinoceros symbol. Leaving the cathedral in the opposite direction, south down Via del Capitano, will lead you into the haunts of the dolphin and turtle (*Onda* and *Tartuga*). Where the street meets Via di Città, it changes its name to Via San Pietro, passing the 14th-century Palazzo Buonsignori, one of the most harmonious of the city's noble palaces, now restored as the home of the **Pinacoteca Nazionale**.

This is the temple of Sienese art, a representative sampling of this inimitable city's style; many of the works have been recently restored. The collection is arranged roughly chronologically, beginning on the top floor with Guido da Siena and his school in the middle 13th century (Room 2), continuing through an entire room of delicate, melancholy Virgins by Duccio and his followers, reaching a climax with Duccio's luminous though damaged *Madonna dei Francescani* in Room 4. More Madonnas and saints fill room after room, including important works of Siena's greatest 14th-century artists; those of Pietro and Ambrogio Lorenzetti (*Madonna Enthroned* and the *Annunciation*, both in Room 7) and Taddeo di Bartolo (*Triptych*, in Room 11) stand out, with their rosy blooming faces and brilliant colour, a remarkable counterpoint to the relative austerity of contemporary painting in Florence. One element that is clearly evident in many of these paintings is Sienese civic pride; the artists take obvious delight in including the city's skyline and landmarks in the background of their works—even in nativities.

Sienese Renaissance painters are well represented, often betraying the essential conservatism of their art and resisting the new approaches of Florence: Domenico di Bartolo's 1433 *Madonna* in Room 9; Nerocchio and Matteo di Giovanni of the 1470s (Room 14); Sano di Pietro, the leading painter of the 1440s (Rooms 16–17). The first floor displays some of Il Sodoma's most important works, especially the great *Scourging of Christ* in Room 31 (1514); in Room 37 the *Descent into Hell* is one of the finest works by Siena's greatest Mannerist, Beccafumi.

Around the Terzo di Città

Next to the Pinacoteca, the church of **San Pietro alle Scale** contains *The Flight into Egypt*, an altarpiece by Rutilio Manetti, the only significant Sienese painter of the Baroque era, a follower of Caravaggio. **San Giuseppe**, at the end of Via San Pietro, marks Siena's uneasy compromise with the new world of the 1600s. One of the city's first Baroque churches, it was nevertheless built not in Baroque marble or travertine but good Siena brown brick. This is the church of the *Onda* district; the *contrada*'s fountain is in front. Just around the corner, the gloomy bulk of **Sant'Agostino** conceals a happier Rococo interior of the 1740s by Vanvitelli, the Dutchman (born Van Wittel) who was chief architect for the Kings of Naples. Most of the building dates back to the 13th century, however, and there are surviving bits of trecento frescoes and altarpieces all around. In the north aisle, the Piccolomini chapel has a fine painting by Il Sodoma, an *Epiphany*, and a *Massacre of the Innocents* by Matteo di Giovanni (usually shut).

Via Piero Andrea Mattioli leads from here to the city walls and the Porta Tufi, passing along the way a path that leads to Siena's small **Botanical Gardens** (*open 8–5 Mon–Fri, 8–12 Sat; book in advance for the guided tours,* © *298874*). Further west, the *contrada* of the *Chiocciola* (snail) centres on the church of **Santa Maria del Carmine**, a 14th-century church remodelled by Baldassare Peruzzi in 1517; inside is a painting of *St Michael* by Beccafumi and a grimly Caravaggiesque *Last Judgement* by an anonymous 16th-century artist.

Terzo di San Martino

Beginning again at the Croce del Travaglio and the Palazzo Piccolomini (*see* p.332), Banchi di Sotto leads into the populous eastern third of the city, passing the **Loggia del Papa**, a Renaissance ornament given to Siena by Aeneas Silvius Piccolomini in 1462

(*under restoration*). The most intriguing parts of this neighbourhood are found on the hillside behind Piazza del Mercato, old streets on slopes and stairs in the *contrada* of the *Torre*—one of the 'unlucky' *contrade* that hasn't won a Palio in decades. Nevertheless they have a fine fountain with their elephant-and-tower emblem on pretty Piazzetta Franchi. One of the more characteristic streets in this part of town is **Via dell'Oro**, an alley of overhanging medieval houses, much like the ones in the Palazzo Pubblico's frescoes of Good and Bad Government. For something different, **Via Porta Giustizia** will lead you on a country ramble within the city's walls, down the valley that separates Terzo San Martino and Terzo di Città.

Some of the noteworthy churches in this Terzo are: **Santo Spirito** on Via dei Pispini (*closed indefinitely*), with another set of frescoes by Il Sodoma in the first chapel on the right; and **Santa Maria dei Servi**, to the south on Via dei Servi in the *contrada* of *Valdimontone* (ram). Here, in the north transept, is one of the earliest and best Sienese nativities, the altarpiece in the second north chapel by Taddeo di Bartolo. Among the many other good paintings in this church is a Madonna by Coppo di Marcovaldo and the *Madonna del Popolo* by Lippo Memmi. An interesting comparison can be made between two versions of that favourite Sienese subject, the *Massacre of the Innocents* : one from the early trecento by Pietro Lorenzetti, and another from 1491 by Matteo di Giovanni.

Nearby on Via Roma, the *Società Esecutori Pie Disposizioni* keeps an **oratory** and a small but good **collection of Sienese art** (*call ahead, © 284300, open daily 9–12, closed Sun*). This Terzo also has two of the best surviving city gates, the **Porta Romana** at the end of Via Roma, and the elegant **Porta Pispini** on the road to Perugia. Once this gate was embellished with a painting of the Nativity by Sodoma, but only traces of it can be seen today.

Terzo di Camollia

Leading north from the Campo, **Via Banchi di Sopra**, a most aristocratic thoroughfare, lined with the palaces of the medieval Sienese elite, forms the spine of this largest and most populous of the *terzi*. The first important palace is also one of the oldest, that of the Tolomei family, a proud clan of noble bankers who liked to trace their ancestry back to the Greek Ptolemies of Hellenistic-era Egypt. The **Palazzo Tolomei**, begun in 1208, is the very soul of Sienese Gothic; it gave its name to Piazza Tolomei in front, the space used by the Republic for its assembly meetings before the construction of the Palazzo Pubblico. Just a few blocks down Banchi di Sopra, **Palazzo Salimbeni** on Piazza Salimbeni was the compound of the Tolomeis' mortal enemies; their centuries-long vendetta dragged Sienese politics into chaos on more than a few occasions. Together with the two adjacent palaces on the square, the Salimbeni is now the home of the *Monte dei Paschi di Siena*, founded in 1624, a remarkable savings bank with a medieval air about it that has a tremendous influence over everything that happens in southern Tuscany—they also have a good art collection, sometimes open to the public along with special exhibitions. A little further up the street, the plain brick **Oratory of Santa Maria di Nevi** is almost always locked up; if you should chance to see it open, stop in to see the altarpiece, the finest work of the late 1400s painter Matteo di Giovanni.

On the streets to the east of these palaces, in the neighbourhood of the *Giraffa* (giraffe), you'll find one of the last important churches to be built in Siena, the 1594 proto-Baroque **Santa Maria di Provenzano**, at the end of Via del Moro. This particular Virgin Mary, a terracotta image said to have been left by St Catherine (*see* p.343), has had one of the most popular devotional cults in Siena since the 1590s; the annual Palio is in her honour. The quiet streets behind the church, Siena's red-light district in Renaissance times, lead to **San Francesco**, begun in 1326, one of the city's largest churches. It's a sad tale; after a big fire in the 17th century, this great Franciscan barn was used for centuries as a warehouse and barracks. Restorations were begun in the 1880s, and the 'medieval'

brick façade was completed only in 1913. The interior is still one of the most impressive in Siena, a monolithic rectangle with vivid stained glass (especially so in the late afternoon) and good transept chapels in the Florentine manner. A few bits of artwork have survived, including traces of frescoes by both the Lorenzettis in the north transept. To the right is the fine Renaissance cloister.

Next to San Francesco is the equally simple **Oratorio di San Bernardino** (*open 10.30–1.30, 3–5.30; adm*), begun in the late 1400s in honour of Siena's famous preacher and graced with the preacher's heart. Its upper chapel, one of the monuments of the Sienese Renaissance, contains some fine frescoes by Beccafumi, Il Sodoma, and the almost forgotten, High Renaissance master Girolamo del Pacchia, few of whose works survive.

 The areas west of San Francesco, traditionally the solid working-class quarter, make up the *contrada* of *Bruco*, the caterpillar; their fountain is under the steps on Via dei Rossi. Bruco's name recalls the famous Compagnia del Bruco, the trade union that initiated the revolt of 1371 and at least temporarily reformed Siena's faction-ridden government. The workers paid a terrible price for it; while the revolution was under way, some young noble *provocateurs* started a fire that consumed almost the entire *contrada*. Today Bruco is the worst of the 'unlucky' neighbourhoods; it hasn't won a Palio since 1955.

St Catherine, St Dominic and the Goose

 In contrast to poor caterpillar, the equally proletarian *Oca* (goose) seems to have always been the best organized and most successful of the *contrade*. On occasions during the Napoleonic Wars when the Tuscan and city governments were in disarray, the Oca's men temporarily took charge of the entire city. The goose's most famous daughter, Caterina Benincasa, was born here, on Vicolo del Tiratoio, in 1347. She was the last but one of twenty-five children born into the family of a wool dyer. At an early age the visions started. By her teens she had turned her room at home into a cell, and while she never became a nun, she lived like a hermit, a solitary ascetic in her own house, sleeping with a stone for a pillow. After she received the stigmata, like St Francis, her reputation as a holy woman spread across Tuscany; popes and kings corresponded with her, and towns would send for her to settle their disputes. In 1378, Florence was under a papal interdict, and the city asked Catherine to plead its case at the papal court at Avignon. She went, but with an agenda of her own—convincing Pope Gregory XI to move the papacy back to Rome where it belonged. As a woman, and a holy woman to boot, she was able to tell the pope to his face what a corrupt and worldly Church he was running, without ending up dangling from the top of the palace wall.

Talking the pope (a French pope, mind you) into leaving the civilized life in Provence for turbulent, barbaric 14th-century Rome is only one of the miracles with which Catherine was credited. Political expediency probably helped more than divine intervention—much of Italy, including anathemized Florence, was in revolt against the absentee popes. She followed them back, and died in Rome in 1380, at the age of only 33. Canonization came in 1460, and in our own century she has been declared co-patron of Italy (along with St Francis) and one of the Doctors of the Church. She and St Teresa of Avila are the only women to hold this honour; both of them for their inspired devotional writings and practical, incisive letters encouraging church reform.

The *contrada* of the Goose stretches down steeply from Banchi di Sopra to the western city walls. At its centre, on Vicolo di Tiratoio, St Catherine's house is preserved as a shrine; the **Santuario e Casa di Santa Caterina** (*open daily 9–12.30, 3.30–6*) includes the whole of the Benincasa home and the dyer's workshop, each room converted into a chapel, many with frescoes by 15th- and 16th-century Sienese artists. The adjacent oratory is now the Oca's *contrada* chapel (note the goose in the detail of the façade).

Via Santa Caterina, the main street of the Oca, slopes down towards the city walls and **Fontebranda**, a simple pointed-arched fountain of the 13th century. It doesn't seem much now, but medieval and Renaissance travellers always remarked on it, an important part of Siena's advanced system of fountains and aqueducts. **San Domenico** church, on the hill above Fontebranda, similarly fails to impress, at least when you see it close up from the bus depot on Piazza San Domenico. From Fontebranda, however, the bold Gothic lines of the apse and transepts give a great insight into the straightforward, strangely modern character of much Sienese religious architecture. It's a long climb up to the church from here. Inside, the church is as big and empty as San Francesco; among the relatively few works of art is the only portrait of St Catherine, on the west wall, done by her friend, the artist Andrea Vanni. In this church, scene of so many incidents from the saint's life, you can see her head in a golden reliquary, though the real attraction is the wonderfully hysterical set of murals by Il Sodoma in the **Cappella Santa Caterina**, representing the girl in various states of serious exaltation.

The open, relatively modern quarter around San Domenico offers a welcome change from the dark and treeless streets of this brick city, in a shady park called **La Lizza** and the green spaces around the **Fortezza Medicea**. Though the site is the same, this is not the hated fortress Charles V compelled the Sienese to build in 1552; as soon as the Sienese chased the imperial troops out, they razed it to the ground. Cosimo I forced its rebuilding after annexing Siena, but to make the bitter pill easier to swallow he employed a Sienese architect, Baldassare Lanci, and let him create what must be the most elegant and civilized, least threatening fortress in Italy. The Fortezza, a long, low rectangle of Siena brick profusely decorated with Medici balls, seems more like a setting for garden parties or summer opera than anything designed to intimidate a sullen populace. The Sienese weren't completely won over; right after Italian reunification they renamed the central space of the fortress **Piazza della Libertà**. The grounds are now a city park, and the vaults of the munition cellars have become the **Enoteca Nazionale**, the 'Permanent Exhibition of Italian Wines' (*open 12–1 summer, 12–12.30 winter*). Almost every variety of wine Italy produces can be bought here—by the glass or by the bottle; the Enoteca's purpose is to promote Italian wines, and it ships thousands of bottles overseas each year.

East of the fortress, beyond the Lizza and the city stadium, lie the twin centres of modern Siena, **Piazza Gramsci**, terminus for most city bus lines, and **Piazza Matteotti**. Continuing northwards towards the Camollia gate, you pass the little Renaissance church of **Fonte Giusta**, just off Via di Camollia on Vicolo Fontegiusta. Designed in 1482 by Urbano da Cortona, this church contains a fresco by Peruzzi (another sibyl) and a magnificent tabernacle over the main altar; there is also a whalebone, according to local legend left here by Christopher Columbus. The **Porta Camollia**, in the northernmost corner of Siena, underwent the Baroque treatment in the 1600s. Here you will see the famous inscription 'Wider than her gates Siena opens her heart to you'. Old Siena was never that sentimental. The whole thing was added in 1604—undoubtedly under the orders of the Florentine governor—to mark the visit of Grand Duke Francesco I, who wasn't really welcome at all.

Peripheral Attractions

From Porta Camollia, Viale Vittorio Emanuele leads through some of the modern quarters outside the walls. Soon after the Camollia gate it passes a pretty stone column, commemorating the meeting of Emperor Frederick III and his bride-to-be Eleanor of Aragon in 1451—the event captured in one of the Pinturicchio frescoes in the Piccolomini Library. Next looms a great brick defence tower, the **Antiporto**, erected just before the Siege of Siena, and rebuilt in 1675. Further down, the **Palazzo dei Diavoli**, built in 1460, was the headquarters of the Marquis of Marignano during that siege.

There isn't much to see on the outskirts of the city—thanks largely to Marignano, who laid waste lovely and productive lands for miles around. Some 2km east of the city (take Via Simone Martini from the Porta Ovile), in the hills above the railway station, the basilica and monastery of **L'Osservanza** has been carefully restored after serious damage in the last war. Begun in 1422, a foundation of San Bernardino, the monastery retains much of its collection of 13th-and 14th-century Sienese art.

To the west of the city, the road to Massa Marittima passes through the hills of the Montagnola Sienese, an important centre of monasticism in the Middle Ages (*see* San Galgano, p.371). Near the village of Montecchio (6km), the hermitage of **Lecceto**, one of the oldest in Tuscany, has been much changed over the centuries but retains some Renaissance frescoes in the church and a 12th-century cloister; nearby, the hermitage of **San Leonardo al Lago** is mostly in ruins; the 14th-century church survives, with masterly frescoes (*c.* 1360) by Pietro Lorenzetti's star pupil, Lippo Vanni. Just outside the village of Sovicille (13km), there is a Romanesque church of the 12th century, the **Pieve di Ponte alla Spina**. The village of Rosia (17km) has another Romanesque church, and just to the south the Vallombrosan **Abbey of Torri** has much to show from its original foundation in the 1200s; there is a rare three-storey cloister, with three different types of columns.

Siena, with its population of only 60,000, is blissfully short of designer boutiques and such. Even the usual tourist trinkets seem lacking—illuminated plastic models of the cathedral are harder to find every year! Nevertheless, a thorough search of the back streets will turn up plenty of unpretentious artisan workshops—almost all of them so unconcerned with tourism they don't even bother hanging out a sign. Some examples:

Just off Piazza Independenza, at Via Galuzza 5, an artist with a distinctive modern style creates works in stained glass (most of them portable). He also gives informal talks about his art. Via di Città 94 sells interesting ceramic pieces, just down the street from Siena's best bookshop, the Libreria Senese, at No. 62–64. Also along Via di Città at numbers 71–73 is the **Antica Drogheria Manganelli** with one hundred-year-old original wooden shelving jammed full of delicious regional foods and wines. **Pizzichieria**, Via di Città, is an unusual food shop, not only because of the welcome you receive from a stuffed, bespectacled boar. Inside you can buy delicious sandwiches made at your request, as well as local specialities like porcini mushrooms and truffles.

Siena ℂ (0577–)   **Where to Stay**

Many of Siena's finest and most interesting hotels are outside the walls—out in the lovely countryside, or near the city gates, as close to the centre as cars can logically penetrate. What's left, in the centre, is simple but comfortable enough. In the summer, rooms are in short supply and it would be a good idea to book ahead. If you come without a reservation, your first stop should be the **Hotel Information Centre** run by the city's innkeepers, ℂ 288084, ✉ 280290 (*open 9–8 Mon-Sat, 9–7 winter*). It's conveniently located in Piazza San Domenico, the terminus of all intercity bus routes. If you arrive by train, take the city bus up from the station to Piazza Matteotti, and walk a block down Via Curtatone. Even at the worst of times, they should be able to find you something—except during the Palio, of course, when you should make your bookings several months in advance.

If you have a car, a number of hotels outside the walls have a rural Tuscan charm and views of the city that more than make up for the slight inconvenience. About 1km southeast of the city, near the Porta Romana, ★★★★**La Certosa di Maggiano**, ℂ 288180, ✉ 288189 (*luxury*), is one of the most remarkable establishments in Italy. In this restored 14th-century Carthusian monastery, where there are only 18 rooms, the luxuries include a heated pool, air-conditioning that works, a quiet chapel and cloister, a salon for backgammon and chess, tennis courts, an excellent restaurant, and a library that would be an antiquarian's dream.

Of course all this doesn't come cheap. For a second choice, there are sunset views over Siena from ★★★★**Villa Scacciapensieri**, 3km north of the city at Strada Scacciapensieri 10, ✆ 41441, 🖅 270854 (*expensive*). This is a quiet country house divided into 28 spacious rooms; besides the view, it features a pool and a good restaurant with an outdoor terrace.

Many of Siena's two- and three-star hotels cluster around the entrances to the city. Just inside the walls, ★★★**Palazzo Ravizza** and its 30 rooms, ✆ 280462, 🖅 271370 (*moderate to expensive*), occupy an old town house on Pian dei Mantellini, near the Porta Laterina; the restaurant isn't anything special, but the rooms are cosy and there is a pretty terrace. Closer to the centre, there are a number of choices, including the comfortably old-fashioned ★★★**Duomo** south of the Duomo on Via Stalloreggi 38, ✆ 289088, 🖅 43043 (*moderate*); ★★**Centrale**, around the corner at Via Cecco Angolieri 26, ✆ 280379, 🖅 42152 (*inexpensive to moderate*); and ★★**Canon d'Oro**, a well-run establishment and a good bargain, on Via Montanini 28, near the bus station, ✆ 44321, 🖅 280868 (*inexpensive to moderate*). ★★**Piccolo Hotel Il Palio** is a little way from the centre, at Piazza del Sale 19, ✆ 281131 (*inexpensive to moderate*), but it has a friendly, English-speaking proprietress. ★★★**Garden**, Via Custoza 2, ✆ 47056, 🖅 46050 (*moderate*), has a swimmimg pool. Highly recommended in readers' letters is ★★**Il Giardino**, Via Baldassare Peruzzi 35, ✆ 285290, 🖅 221197 (*moderate*), situated near the Porta Pispini, with good views and a swimming pool. Inexpensive places are a little hard to find—especially before term when they're full of university students looking for a permanent place. In Via delle Terme there is ★**La Perla**, ✆ 47144 (*inexpensive*); and the more genteel ★**Tre Donzelle**, ✆ 280358 (*moderate*) is in Via delle Donzelle. The city of Siena runs its own youth hostel, the **Ostello della Gioventù Guidoriccio**, Via Fiorentina 17, ✆ 52212, 🖅 56172 in Lo Stellino, 2km from the city (buses No. 15 from Piazza Gramsci). No cards are required, but in 1995 good modern doubles and dorm rooms with breakfast were going for L19,000 a head; arrive early in July and August.

Siena ✆ (0577–)   ***Eating Out***

Sitting between three of Italy's greatest wine-producing areas, the Chianti, the Brunello of Montalcino and the Vino Nobile of Montepulciano, there is always something distinguished to wash down the simple dishes of the Sienese table. This city's real speciality is sweets, and quite a few visitors to Siena find they have no room for lunch or dinner after repeated visits to the pastry shops for slices of *panforte*, an alarmingly heavy but indecently tasty cake laced with fruits, nuts, orange peel and secret Sienese ingredients, or *panpepato*, similar but with pepper in it. They are all artists—shop windows flaunt gargantuan creations of cakes and crystallized fruit, metres high, and as colourful as a Lorenzetti fresco, set out for all to admire before they are carted off to some wedding party. The **Enoteca** inside the Medici fortress (*see* p.343) is another distraction; sometimes they organize special tastings, concentrating on one particular region of Italy. Siena being a university town, snacks and fast food of all kinds are common; a *cioccina* is Siena's special variation on pizza; *pici* (thick south Tuscan spaghetti) with a sauce prepared from ground fresh pork, *pancetta*, sausages and chicken breasts, added to tomatoes cooked with Brunello wine, is the city's favourite pasta dish.

Siena's Salami

There are hundreds of different types of salami in Tuscany, each made to an age-old, much treasured recipe and tasting far better than some of the ingredients might suggest. Siena has several of its own. *Buristo* is a cooked salami made from the blood and fatty leftovers of sausages and heavily spiced; *finocchiona* is peppered sausage meat seasoned with fennel seeds and stuffed into the sausage skin; *soppressata* is a boiled salami made from a mixture of rind and gristle; the alternative version, *soppressata in cuffia*, is made in the same way and then stuffed into a boned pig's head. The *salsiccioli secchi* are perhaps the most appetising salami of all, made from the leanest cuts of pork or wild boar, enhanced with garlic and black or red pepper.

If you've survived the wine and the pastry shops, you'll appreciate the succulent risottos and pasta dishes at **Osteria Le Logge**, just off the Campo at Via del Porrione 33, © 48013 (*moderate*), with exotic second courses like stuffed guinea-fowl (*faraona*) and a fine wine list. *Closed Sun.* Also near the Campo, **Taverna di Cecco**, Via Cecco Angioleri 19, © 288518 (*moderate*), specializes in pasta dishes, meats and nearly everything else done up with either truffles or *porcini* mushrooms. *Closed Wed.* **Tullio ai Tre Cristi**, © 280608 (*moderate*), has been on Vicolo Provenzano since about 1830; perhaps the most authentic of Sienese restaurants, its menu includes things like *ribollita*, tripe with sausages and roast boar from the Maremma. The *pici* are home-made. There are outside tables in the summer. *Closed Mon.* On Via del Castoro 3, just off the Piazza del Duomo, **Al Marsili**, © 47154 (*expensive*), is another of Siena's best, in a singularly elegant setting—not very traditional, with dishes like *gnocchi* in duck sauce, but it's hard to complain. *Closed Mon.*

inexpensive

Less expensive places—and there are many good ones—are usually found a little further away from the Campo. **Da Marino** on Via Salicotto 137, © 42249, is always busy, offering home cooking. *Closed Sun.* **Trattoria da Dino**, Casato di Sopra 71, © 289036, makes a good *spiedini alle Senese*. *Closed Fri.* The restaurant **La Torre** in Via Salicotto 17, © 287548, is a fun, lively place, popular with students. *Closed Thurs.* **Il Cavallino Bianco** on Via di Città 20, © 44258, serves regional food and pizza, but its main bonus is that it is open until late. *Closed Wed.* Just outside Siena on the road to Gaiole (S408) is **Antica Botteganova**, Strada Chiantigiana 29, © 284230 (*moderate*), offering earthy Sienese cooking, such as veal cooked in Chianti Classico. *Closed Sun.*

Hill Towns West of Siena

In the late Middle Ages, this dramatically diverse, often rugged country-side was a border region, both culturally and politically, its people alternately subject to the strong pull of Florence and Siena. Its towns do not have all that much in common: Poggibonsi is almost all new, while parts of Volterra go back to the Etruscans. San Gimignano presents its famous skyline of medieval skyscrapers, while parts of the Metal Hills show outlandish silhouettes of cooling towers from the ubiquitous geo-thermal power plants. San Gimignano and Volterra are the main attractions, both beautiful cities containing some remarkable works of art. Massa Marittima, often overlooked, has one of the finest cathedrals in Italy. Beyond that there is a doll-sized walled city, bubbling sulphurous pits, alabaster souvenirs, a Roman theatre, lonely moors, and a sword in a stone, not King Arthur's but someone else's.

Colle di Val d'Elsa and Poggibonsi

Getting Around

The main routes between Florence and Siena—the Via Cassia (S2) or the Superstrada del Palio—have exits for Colle di Val d'Elsa (27km/35mins from Siena, 49km/1hr from Florence) and Poggibonsi, 7km further north on S68. Poggibonsi is a major bus junction in south Tuscany, with easy connections to Florence, Siena, San Gimignano, Volterra and Colle di Val d'Elsa (TRA-IN buses if you're coming from Siena, SITA from Florence). Poggibonsi is also on the Empoli–Siena rail line, with a branch or bus beyond to Colle in 15mins.

Colle di Val d'Elsa

Tourist Information

Via Campana 18, ✆ (0577) 912111, ✉ 212270.

Eleven km north of Siena, the S2 passes a genuine curiosity, the tiny forti-fied town of **Monteriggioni**. For much of Siena's history, this was its northernmost bastion, often in the front lines in the wars with Florence after its construction in 1219. Now, a neat circle of walls with 14 towers, it sits like a crown on its roundish hill, with just enough room inside for two oversized piazzas, a few houses and their gardens. Some 3km further towards Colle di Val d'Elsa, there is a turn-off to the left for the 12th-century Abbey of Santi Salvatore and Cirino, better known as the **Abbadia dell'Isola**. The Cistercians began it in 1101 on an 'island' among the marshes, hence the name. Inside this stark Romanesque building is a restored fresco by Taddeo di Bartolo, and a Renaissance altarpiece.

Colle di Val d'Elsa (pop. 16,300), a striking, ancient town up on a steep hill, presents an impressive silhouette if you see it from the right angle—it's long enough but at most only

Hill Towns West of Siena

three blocks wide. Though probably as old as the Etruscans, Colle first became prominent in the 12th century, a safe fortified stronghold that attracted many migrants from the surrounding plains. In later centuries, it was known for the manufacture of wool, paper and ceramics; today Colle is Italy's largest producer of fine glass and crystal. The Collegiani will never allow the world to forget that their town was the birthplace of Arnolfo di Cambio, the great architect who built Florence's Palazzo Vecchio and began its cathedral.

Down on the plain below the citadel, the modern part of the town surrounds the arcaded **Piazza Arnolfo di Cambio**. Via Garibaldi or Via San Sebastiano will take you up to old Colle—but for a proper introduction you'll need to come on the road from Volterra, passing through a grim Renaissance bastion called the **Porta Nuova**, designed by Giuliano da Sangallo, and then across the medieval-Renaissance suburb known as the **Borgo**. Between the Borgo and the old town, called the **Castello**, there is a picturesque narrow bridge and the **Palazzo di Campana** (1539, by Giovanni di Baccio d'Agnolo); the arch in its centre is the elegant gateway to the town.

Via del Castello runs straight up the centre, with narrow medieval alleys on both sides. Here you'll find the cathedral, rebuilt in 1603, a few Renaissance palaces, and some neglected little museums: opposite the cathedral, in the Palazzo Pretorio, a small **Antiquarium** (*open Oct–Mar 3.30–5.30 Tues–Fri and 10–12, 3.30–6.30 weekends and holidays; April–Sept 5–7 Tues–Fri and 10–12, 4–7 weekends and holidays*) with Etruscan objects, and a permanent exhibition on Arnolfo di Cambio; and a small picture collection in the nearby **Museo Civico** (*open Nov–Mar 10–12 and 3.30–6.30, 4–7 summer, closed Mon; adm*). The best of them all is the **Museo d'Arte Sacra** in the old episcopal palace (*telephone tourist information for opening times*), with a few Sienese and Florentine paintings in addition to the frescoes commissioned by some jolly 14th-century bishop—scenes of the hunt, believed to be the work of Taddeo di Bartolo.

Near the end of Via del Castello, the Collegiani claim an old tower-fortress as the **House of Arnolfo di Cambio**. Arnolfo's father, a gentleman and an architect, probably came to Colle di Val d'Elsa from Lombardy sometime in the 1230s, bringing the great tradition of the Lombard master-masons into Tuscany. Arnolfo himself may have received his initiation into the new (for Italy) Gothic style from studying works in nearby Siena or the new Cistercian abbey at San Galgano. He worked for Nicola Pisano on the Siena cathedral pulpit, and for Giovanni Pisano on the Fonte Maggiore in Perugia, and probably moved to Florence in the 1270s.

South of Colle, many of the villages in the hills retain their simple Romanesque churches from the 11th–12th centuries, beginning with the isolated **Badia à Coneo**, a Vallombrosan foundation of the 1120s (5km, on an unsealed lane off the road to Casole). At **Casole d'Elsa** (15km south, local bus), a town that took hard knocks in the last war, there is an interesting **Collegiata** church begun in the 12th century, with Sienese frescoes, two fine late 14th-century sepulchres by Gano da Siena, and terracottas by Giovanni della Robbia. Casole's Sienese **Rocca** held out into the 16th century, long after the rest of the Valdelsa flew the Florentine flag. South from Casole, the road winds through pleasant green countryside leading up to the Colline Metallifere, the 'metal hills', and you can seek out more Romanesque churches in **Mensano** (7km) and **Radicondoli** (15km, the church of San Simone).

Poggibonsi

If you spend enough time in Tuscany, sooner or later you are bound to pass through Poggibonsi (pop. 25,700), a major knot on the S2, S429 and Superstrada del Palio road links from Siena to Florence and Pisa. These days, residents of the pretty tourist towns of central Tuscany are not always above having a laugh at the expense of this homely, hard-working industrial centre. Poor Poggibonsi! Founded only in 1156, the original *Poggiobonizzo* grew rapidly. By 1220, it was probably one of the largest cities in Tuscany, with a population of some 15,000; in that year, Emperor Frederick II declared it a 'Città Imperiale' with special rights and privileges. Poggiobonizzo's Ghibelline politics and its imperial favour, however, were to prove its undoing. In 1270, its neighbours San Gimignano and Colle di Val d'Elsa, along with the Florentines and the troops of Charles of Anjou, besieged and conquered the city, after which they razed it to the ground. Most of its citizens migrated elsewhere, but a number of the poorer ones stayed behind, refounding the town as a modest market village on the plain. Poggibonsi was thoroughly wrecked again during the battles of 1944, but has grown tremendously since to become the biggest town between Florence and Siena.

There isn't much to see: the 14th-century Palazzo Pretorio and the collegiate church on the main street recall at least something of the appearance of prewar Poggibonsi. Nearby, the **Castello della Magione** is an interesting small complex from the 1100s; the Romanesque chapel and outbuildings form a little closed square, a fortified pilgrims' hospice said to have been built by the Templars. Above the town, an unfinished fortress begun by Lorenzo de' Medici covers much of the original city of Poggiobonizzo.

Just 2km south of town near the S2, the austerely Franciscan **basilica of San Lucchese** occupies an attractive site in the hills; inside are some good frescoes, including works by Taddeo Gaddi and Bartolo di Fredi. Not surprisingly, this strategically important corner of Tuscany has plenty of castles scattered about, including the 13th-century **Castello della Rochetta**, once the home of the famous *condottiere* Sir John Hawkwood, and the romantically ruined **Rocca di Staggia** (5km south of Poggibonsi on the S2), built by the Florentines in the 1430s—a counterpart to Sienese Monteriggioni, just a few kilometres down the same road.

© (0577–)   ***Where to Stay***

With the Superstrada del Palio running through these parts, roadside inns and quiet country hotels are not hard to find. A kilometre or so east of Colle di Val d'Elsa, at Località Belvedere near the Siena highway, ★★★**Villa Belvedere**, © 920966, ✆ 924128 (*moderate to expensive*), is a pretty, old villa with a big garden, a restaurant and 15 simple rooms. Up in the town itself, there is ★★★**Arnolfo**, a simple, comfortable place in the Borgo at Via Campana 8, © 922020, ✆ 922324 (*inexpensive to moderate*). In Poggibonsi ★★★**Alcide** in Via Marconi 67a, © 937501, ✆ 981729 (*inexpensive to moderate*) has doubles with air conditioning.

© (0577–)   ***Eating Out***

Heading from Florence to Siena, or from Siena to the west, a good place to stop for lunch is the little castle-village of Monteriggioni, and **Il Pozzo** on Piazza Roma 2, © 304127; they do some of the simpler dishes very well—bean soup and roast meats, but their real forte is fancy desserts (even *crêpes suzettes*). *Closed Sun evening and Mon.* In Colle di Val d'Elsa, the **Arnolfo** hotel (*see* above) has a very popular restaurant (*very expensive*). *Closed Tues.* At Piazza Arnolfo 23, **Antica Trattoria**, © 923747, is a family-run restaurant; try their *gnocchi* with pigeon sauce. *Closed Tues.* For something cheaper, with good home cooking, **Marechiaro**, Via Gracco del Secco, © 922115 (*moderate*), is good value. *Closed Fri.* Out among the olive groves in the nearby hamlet of Mugnano, an old farm called the **Fattoria di Mugnano**, © 959023 (*expensive*), has become a thriving business. The delightful restaurant offers local favourites but also Sicilian cuisine; they'll also sell you some of the wine and olive oil they produce, or arrange horseback riding and tours of the countryside. *Closed Thurs.* If you're spending time in Poggibonsi, the restaurant of the **Alcide** hotel (*see* above; *expensive to very expensive*) is one of the better places for seafood in this land-locked province, featuring dishes with a south Italian slant like Apulian *orecchiette* in a sauce with cuttlefish and several different varieties of maritime risottos. *Closed Wed.*

San Gimignano

In the miniaturist landscape of this corner of Tuscany, San Gimignano, Italy's best-preserved medieval city, is an almost fantastic landmark. From Poggibonsi, or from the Volterra road, its medieval towers, some of them over 50m tall, loom over the surrounding hills. Once, almost every city in central Italy looked like this; more than just defensive strongholds in the incessant family feuds, these towers served as status symbols both for the families and the cities themselves, a visible measure of a town's power and prosperity, even if it also betrayed the bitterness of its internal divisions.

By the 16th century, most of Italy's towers had succumbed to age, decay and particularly to the efforts of the urban *comuni*, which pruned and destroyed these symbols of truculent nobility at every opportunity. For whatever reason, this did not happen in San Gimignano, famous even in the 1300s as the '*città delle belle torri*'. Originally there were at least 70 towers (in a town barely one-eighth of a square mile in size). Now only 15 remain, though enough, along with San Gimignano's beautiful streets, churches and public buildings, to give the impression of having been hermetically sealed in a time capsule from the Middle Ages.

History

According to legend, the town was originally called Castel della Selva. When the Gothic army of Totila passed through in the 550s, the townsfolk for some reason chose to pray to an obscure saint named Gimignano, a martyred bishop of Modena, for their salvation from what appeared to be a guaranteed sacking. Gimignano came through in style, looming down from the clouds in golden armour to scare away the besiegers.

Although it evidently must have been an important and prosperous place, San Gimignano does not cut much of a figure in the medieval chronicles. The city was an independent republic from the early 1100s until 1353, when it came under the rule of Florence. It certainly participated in the Guelph-Ghibelline strife, and in all the other troubles of the period, though today it is probably best remembered as the home town of that excellent poet, Folgore of San Gimignano (*c.* 1250), famous for his lovely sonnets to the months of the year. As in so many other medieval towns, San Gimignano has the air of a false start, a free *comune* that could build a wall and defend itself, yet lacked the will or the money to make itself into a Siena or a Florence. When this city lost the wealth or the fierceness that briefly made it an important player on the Tuscan stage, it crystallized into its medieval form, a perfect preparation for a role as a tourist town. Today San Gimignano has a population of some 7700. On a good day in July or August it may see several times that in day-trippers.

Even during the Renaissance the town seems to have been a resort for the Florentines; Dante, Machiavelli and Savonarola all spent some time here, and artists like Ghirlandaio and Gozzoli were only too happy to come up for a small commission. Don't let the prospect of crowds keep you from coming. San Gimignano handles them gracefully; its fine art, elegant medieval cityscapes and the verdant rolling countryside right outside its gates make this one of the smaller towns of Tuscany most worth visiting.

Getting Around

The railway station is 11km away, an infrequent run on the Empoli–Siena line. Buses to the town *usually* coincide with the trains, but from either Siena or Florence you'll be better off taking the bus, which leaves you right at the Porta San Giovanni, the main entrance to the town. TRA-IN buses from Siena (38km/45 mins—the same bus that goes to Colle di Val d'Elsa) are very frequent, though for most you will need to change in Poggibonsi. Several daily SITA buses arrive from Florence (54km/1hr 15mins) and there are four buses a day to nearby Certaldo.

If you're driving, San Gimignano is 11km west of Poggibonsi, 13km south of Certaldo, or 14km from Colle di Val d'Elsa, each route more scenic than the last. Within the walls San Gimignano is almost always closed to traffic; the main car park is just outside Porta San Giovanni. You'll need to get a pass from the police if you want to take your car to one of the hotels inside.

Admission

If you plan to visit everything it is worthwhile buying the reduced price joint ticket for the four museums, the tower of Palazzo del Popolo and the Capella di Santa Fina.

Tourist Information

Piazza del Duomo 1, ℂ (0577) 940008, ℮ 940903.
Hotel Association, Via S. Giovanni, ℂ and ℮ (0577) 940809.

Piazza del Duomo and the Museo Civico

From the southern gate, Porta San Giovanni, the street of the same name leads towards the town centre, passing on the way the little churches of **San Giovanni**, built by the Knights Templar, and **San Francesco**, with a good Pisan-Romanesque façade, now deconsecrated and converted into a wine shop. Another ancient gate, the Arco dei Bacci, leads into the triangular **Piazza della Cisterna** and the adjacent **Piazza del Duomo**—a superbly beautiful example of asymmetrical, medieval town design, seemingly haphazard but really quite sophisticated. Piazza della Cisterna contains the town's well, whence the name, and some of its towers.

On Piazza del Duomo, two stout Gothic public buildings with Guelph crenellations and lofty towers compete with the Collegiata church for your attention. The **Palazzo del Podestà**, with its vaulted loggia, was begun in the 1230s by Emperor Frederick II at the height of imperial power for his *podestà*. Above it stands the Torre della Rognosa, with a small cupola on top; at 51m it once marked the height limit for private towers—the *podestà* didn't want anyone putting him in the shade. Later, when the *comune* was able to wrest effective self-government from the emperors, it built an even taller tower for the **Palazzo del Popolo** across the piazza (*open Nov–Feb 9.30–1.30, 2.30–4.30, March, Oct 9.30–6, April–Sept 9.30–7.30, closed Mon*); the awesome 54m Torre Grossa was completed about 1300 and the rest of the Palazzo about 20 years later.

Underneath this tower, an archway leads into the charming, thoroughly medieval **Cortile**, or courtyard, with bits of frescoes (one by Il Sodoma) and the painted coats of arms of Florentine governors from after 1353. A stairway leads up to the **Museo Civico** (*open same hours as the tower*), with an excellent collection of art from both Florentine and Sienese masters. One of the oldest works is a remarkable painted crucifix by Coppo di Marcovaldo (*c.*1270) that predates (and some might say surpasses) the similar, more famous crucifixes of Giotto. The museum has two sweet Madonnas by Benozzo Gozzoli, a pair of tondi by Filippino Lippi portraying the Annunciation, and a big, colourful enthroned Virgin of Pinturicchio's that looks like it strayed here from that artist's Piccolomini chapel in Siena. Taddeo di Bartolo contributes a set of paintings with the definitive *Story of San Gimignano*, a saint worthy of having a town named after him judging by these scenes; he is pictured calming the sea, exorcizing a devil who had been inhabiting the daughter of Emperor Jovian, and succumbing to the flesh while saying mass—he has to pee, but when he sneaks out of church a winged devil attacks him; fortunate enough to have a cross on him, Gimignano drives it away without much difficulty.

To the San Gimignanese, the biggest attraction of the museum is the Sala del Consiglio, or **Sala di Dante**, where the poet spoke in 1299 as an ambassador of Florence, seeking to convince the *comune* to join the Guelph League. The frescoes on its walls include more works by Gozzoli, a glittering company of angels and saints in the *Maestà* of the Sienese artist Lippo Memmi, and some trecento scenes of hunting and tournaments. After this, contemplate a climb up the **Torre Grosso** (*see above for opening times; adm*)—several hundred steps, but there's a view over San Gimignano and the surrounding countryside that is worth the effort.

The Collegiata

The name Piazza del Duomo is a little misleading: San Gimignano doesn't have a cathedral any more, but a **Collegiata**, begun in the 12th century and enlarged in the 15th, which would make an impressive seat for any bishop. It turns a blank brick façade towards the world, but the interior is a lavish imitation of Siena cathedral, with its tiger-striped arches and vaults painted with a firmament of golden stars. Its walls, however, outshine the larger cathedral with first-class frescoes of the 14th and 15th centuries, mostly by artists from Siena.

In the north aisle, Bartolo di Fredi painted the Old Testament scenes in the 1360s. Note *Noah with the Animals*, and *The Torments of Job* (also how each scene is accompanied by a neat explanation in simple Italian, a fascinating example of the artists, and the Church, coming to terms with a newly literate public). Some of Bartolo's best work is in the lunettes off the north aisle: a medieval cosmography of the Creation, scenes of Adam naming the animals and a graphic view of the creation of Eve. New Testament pictures by Barna da Siena (about 1380) cover the south wall; his *Crucifixion* is an exceedingly fine work. On the west wall, over the entrance, is a well-punctured *Saint Sebastian* by Gozzoli and a real surprise, the most perverse *Last Judgement* in Italy. It isn't recorded what moved Taddeo di Bartolo, a most serendipitous painter of rosy Sienese Virgins, to this madness. You may think you have seen the damned suffering interesting tortures and indignities before; Italy has plenty of them. This is the first time, however, that delicacy forbids us to describe one. It's a little faded, unfortunately. Nearby stand two wooden figures of an *Annunciation* by Jacopo della Quercia.

The Cappella di Santa Fina

Open April–Sept 9.30–12.30, 3–6, 3–5.30 Oct–March.

A ticket from the Museo Civico will get you into the **chapel of Santa Fina**, off the south aisle, with an introduction to one of the most irritating hagiographies in Christendom. Little Fina was going to the well for water, according to the story, when she accepted an orange from a young swain. Upon returning home, her mother told her how wicked she was to take it, whereupon the poor girl became so mortified over her great sin that she lay down on the kitchen table and prayed for forgiveness without ceasing for the next five years. Finally, St Anthony came down to call her soul up into heaven, and the kitchen table and all the towers of San Gimignano burst into bloom with violets. Domenico Ghirlandaio got the commission to paint all this; he pocketed the money and did a splendid job (1475) in the brightest springtime colours. In the last scene, note San Gimignano's famous towers in the background.

Just to the left of the Collegiata, there is a lovely small courtyard where musicians sometimes play on summer weekends. Here, on the wall of the Baptistry, you will see another fine fresco by Ghirlandaio, an *Annunciation* that has survived reasonably well for being outside for 500 years. The town's two other museums are here: the **Museo Etrusco** with a small collection of local archaeological finds, and the **Museo d'Arte Sacra**, which, besides the usual ecclesiastical clutter, has some good painted wood statues from the late Middle Ages (*both open April–Sept 9.30–8, Oct–March 9.30–12.30, 2.30–5.30*).

Around the Town

From Piazza del Duomo, it's not too difficult a climb up to the **Rocca**, a somewhat ruined fortress of the 1350s that offers one of the best views of this towered town. During the summer it is the site of an outdoor cinema. Down Via di Castello, in the eastern end of town, the **Oratory of San Lorenzo in Ponte**, now unused, has quattrocento Florentine frescoes and an exhibit of finds from a 16th–18th-century pharmacy that once functioned in the nearby Hospital of Santa Fina. The busiest and finest street of San Gimignano, however, leaves Piazza del Duomo towards the north: Via San Matteo, lined with shops and modest Renaissance palaces. It begins by passing the three truncated **Salvucci Towers**, once the fortified compound of one of San Gimignano's most powerful families (the Salvucci were Ghibellines; the towers of their mortal enemies, the Guelph Ardinghelli, are the ones on the west side of Piazza della Cisterna).

The day-trippers do not often venture into the quiet streets on the north side of town, and so usually miss the church of **Sant'Agostino**, famous for a series of frescoes by Gozzoli on the *Life of St Augustine* on the walls behind the high altar. The merriest of all Renaissance painters has a good time with this one; many of the frescoes are faded and damaged, but not the charming panel where the master of grammar comes to drag sullen little Augustine off to school. Another well-preserved scene shows Augustine in Rome, with most of the city's ancient landmarks visible in the background. Gozzoli also contributed the *Saint Sebastian* on the left aisle. There is a haunting altarpiece, done by Piero Pollaiuolo in 1483 with an anticipatory touch of the El Greco to it, and some good trecento Sienese painting in a chapel off to the right. Across the piazza from Sant'Agostino, the little church of **San Pietro** has more Sienese painting of that era. Via Folgore di San Gimignano leads off to the northeastern corner of the town; the church of **San Jacopo** stands under the town wall, another simple but interesting building left by the Templars.

Around much of San Gimignano, the countryside begins right outside the wall. There are plenty of opportunities for pleasant walks or picnics in any direction, and a few landmarks to visit along the way: the **Fonti**, arched medieval well-houses much like Siena's, can be seen just outside the Porta dei Fonti, south of San Jacopo. Further from town, the **Pieve di Cellole** is a pretty 12th-century church in a peaceful setting, 4km west from the Porta San Matteo; its harmonious serenity amid the cypresses inspired Puccini's opera *Suor Angelica*. There are several ruined castles and monasteries within a few miles of the town, and every height offers a different view of San Gimignano's remarkable skyline.

Shopping

There isn't any particular artisan tradition here, but so many tourists visit that enterprising shopowners have assembled a host of interesting things—the town hasn't quite turned into a great trinket bazaar, but it's getting there. Some of the best buys are pretty, inexpensive things in alabaster from nearby Volterra—especially at the little shop at Via San Matteo 85, north of the Piazza del Duomo. Just within Porta San Giovanni is a 13th-century church now converted to a shop for local wine, olive oil and other farm products. Artists' studios and ceramics are everywhere, though nothing really stands out. This is an agricultural area, and its specialities are a formidable white wine called *Vernaccia* (*see* below) and a sweet called *mandorlato*, very much like the *panforte* of Siena. Many vineyards around this area would be glad to sell you a bottle of Vernaccia—there's one at Casale, the **Cantine Baroncini**, ✆ (0577) 940600.

San Gimignano ✆ (0577–)   *Where to Stay*

All the hotels in San Gimignano are in the moderate range, but the vacuum of low-cost accommodation has been filled by a score of San Gimignanese who rent out rooms, usually about L40–50,000 (the family at the Il Pino Restaurant—*see* below—is among these; Via San Matteo 102, doubles without bath; the tourist office can give you a list of the others). An excellent hotel, on the Piazza della Cisterna, is ★★★**Leon Bianco**, ✆ 941294, 📠 942123 (*moderate*), with modern rooms. If it is full, readers have also highly recommended ★★★ **La Cisterna**, ✆ 940328, 📠 942080 (*moderate*), located in the same square. If you would prefer the tranquillity of this very lovely patch of Tuscan countryside, there is ★★★**Le Renaie** north of town at Pancale, about 7km towards Certaldo, ✆ 955044, 📠 955126 (*moderate*). The attractive modern building has a garden, pool and tennis court. The only hotel with less than three stars is ★**La Steccaia** just outside town in Località La Steccaia, ✆ 944758, 📠 944429 (*moderate*).

The cheapest option is the **Youth Hostel**, Via delle Fonti 1, ✆ 941991, costing L16–18,000 for bed and breakfast.

San Gimignano ✆ (0577–)   *Eating Out*

With all the visitors it entertains, it should come as no surprise that San Gimignano is full of good restaurants. One of the most popular, as much for its panoramic views as for the cuisine, is **Le Terrazze** in the Hotel La Cisterna, ✆ 940328 (*moderate*). The *medaglione al vinsanto* is a surprise treat, or else the *osso buco 'alla Toscana'*, following old house specialities like *zuppa sangimignese* and *pappardelle alla lepre* (wide noodles with hare sauce). Altogether it makes a memorable dinner. *Closed Tues evening*. Another possibility, at the opposite end of town at Via San Matteo 102, is **Il Pino**, ✆ 940415 (*moderate*). Here the main attraction is the inviting antipasti; more if you thoroughly indulge in the dishes with truffles that are Il Pino's pride. *Closed Thurs*. **Osteria delle Catene**, Via Mainardi 18, ✆ 941966, has good regional food at a moderate price; try their *ribollita alla sangimignese*. *Closed Wed*.

The adventurous might like to try **Dorando**, on Vicolo del Oro 2, ✆ 941862 (*expensive*), where the chef claims to reconstruct Etruscan cuisine—game hen with juniper berries, and things stranger still. Readers have written to us with high praise of this place. *Closed Mon.* Less extravagantly, **La Stella** is a fine trattoria down the street from Il Pino on Via S. Matteo 75, ℂ 940444 (*inexpensive*): good Tuscan *ribollita* and a succulent *stracotto alla Chianti. Closed Wed.*

Activities

If you want to explore the surrounding countryside on horseback, there are two riding centres nearby. **F.lli Farini**, Loc. Pugiano, ℂ (0577) 953079, is 13km out of town in the direction of Volterra. **C.E.M.**, Sant'Andrea 22, Ulignano, ℂ (0577) 950232, is 5km on the road to Certaldo.

Local Wine

San Gimignano has its own wine—*La Vernaccia di San Gimignano* (makes one think of varnish), a dry, light yellow white, with a pungent bouquet and a slightly bitter aftertaste. It is generally drunk with fish dishes and as an aperitif, but it's also good to try with typical San Gimignano dishes such as liver, tripe, rabbit and *panzanella*. The wine is made only from the hills around San Gimignano and has been around since antiquity. It gets a mention in Dante's *Purgatory*: Pope Martin IV apparently drowned eels in Vernaccia before roasting them over a charcoal fire. It has recently been awarded the D.O.C.G..

Volterra

How you see Volterra may well depend on the cast of the skies when you come. On a good day in spring or summer, the sunshine illuminates elegant streets and piazze full of Volterrans going about their business, and bouncing holiday Germans come to buy alabaster cups and lampshades. A cloudy, windy day may remind you of fate and of the Etruscans, who arrived here some 2700 years ago. Like so many other cities in central Italy, the Etruscans founded Volterra on top of a steep hill with a flat top; from a distance you see only a dark silhouette looming over an eerie, empty landscape. The soil around Volterra (pop. 12,796) is a thin clay, not much good for vines or olives. Few trees grow here. It makes good pasture land—not as barren as it looks, but disconcerting enough among the green woods and well-tended gardens of this part of Tuscany.

History

Etruscan *Velathri*, one of the largest and most powerful cities of the Dodecapolis, grew up in the 9th or 8th century BC from an even earlier settlement of the Villanovan culture; it is undoubtedly one of the oldest cities in Italy. The attraction that has kept this hill continuously occupied for so many centuries is easily explained—sulphur, alum, salt, alabaster, lead and tin, the centre of one of the richest mining regions in Italy. In Etruscan days there was iron, too, and the people of Velathri did a thriving trade with the Greeks and Carthaginians.

Velathri reached the height of its prosperity in the 5th and 4th centuries BC, leaving as testimony three great circuits of walls; the largest is over 8km in length, enclosing an area three times the size of the present city. The Romans captured it sometime in the 3rd century, and Velathri began to decline. Along with most of Etruria, the city chose the populist side in the Social Wars, and was punished with a siege and sacking by Sulla in about 80 BC. Yet Roman *Velaterrae* remained an important town. It was the home of Saint Linus, successor to St Peter and the second pope. Even though many of the mines were giving out, Volterra survived the Dark Ages intact. The Lombards favoured it, and for a time it served as their capital. Medieval Volterra was ruled by its bishops, increasingly finding themselves in conflict with the rising middle class. An independent *comune* was established late in the 12th century, a good Ghibelline town that participated in most of the factional wars of the period, finally coming under the nominal control of Florence in 1361.

The Florentines were content with an annual tribute until the 'affair of the alum' in the 1470s, that wonderfully Italian ruckus that caused Pope Sixtus IV to plot the murder of Lorenzo de' Medici, excommunicate him, and finally declare war on him. Lorenzo had taken over a syndicate to mine here for alum, a key material used in dyeing cloth, on which the popes had a monopoly from their mines at Tolfa. Besides alarming the pope, Lorenzo also caused the Volterrans to revolt when they realized that he wanted to keep production down and prices high without letting any profit trickle down to them (the Medici Bank, not surprisingly, also controlled the sale of the pope's alum). Lorenzo eluded the pope with some difficulty (*see* **Florence**: 'History') and then hired the mercenary captain Federico da Montefeltro—none other than the famous broken-nosed Duke of Urbino, patron of artists and scholars—to subdue the Volterrans. This he did with a brutality quite unbecoming to the 'ideal Renaissance prince'. Lorenzo wept some crocodile tears over Volterra; after extinguishing the city's independence once and for all, he offered it the magnificent sum of 2000 florins in damages.

Fortunately for the Volterrans, the mining business was picking up again. Between 1400 and 1800, many pits that had been abandoned since Roman times were reopened. In particular, Volterra became Europe's centre for the mining and working of **alabaster**, a craft tradition that is still the city's biggest business today.

Getting Around

Volterra lies 81km/2½hrs southwest of Florence by way of Colle di Val d'Elsa and winding S68; 50km/1½hrs west from Siena; and 61km/2hrs southeast of Pisa by way of Cascina and S439. It isn't the easiest town to reach if you don't have a car. The only train service gets as far as Saline di Volterra, 10km southwest of the city. This is an infrequent branch line that goes to Cecina, 30km to the west on the coast south of Livorno. Some trains continue on from Cecina to Pisa. (It wasn't like this in the old days: as late as the 1920s, if old photographs are to be believed, a little steam train used to climb right up to the town.) Buses connect the Saline station with Volterra, but not always when you need them.

All **buses** leave from Piazza Martini della Libertà just inside the walls. You can get information and buy tickets in the tourist office. There are plenty of buses direct to

Pisa and Montecatini Terme, four a day to Florence and Siena (change at Colle di Val d'Elsa for Siena and San Gimignano), three to Livorno and two to Massa Marittima (you usually have to change at Monterotondo).

Tourist Information

Palazzo dei Priori, Via Turazza 2, © (0588) 86150.

A Little Archaeology

Coming from Florence or Siena, the entrance to Volterra will be the eastern gate, the **Porta a Selci**, with a moving tribute to the *partigiani* of Volterra killed in 1944–5. Inside the gate, Via Don Minzoni leads towards the bus terminal at Piazza XX Settembre, passing along the way at No. 15 the **Museo Etrusco Guarnacci** (*open daily 1 March–30 Oct 9–7; rest of the year 9–2 pm; adm exp*), repository for finds from the Velathri necropolises. Over 600 sculpted alabaster, travertine or terracotta cinerary urns make up the core of the collection. The exhibits have been arranged in chronological order, except for the original Guarnacci collection which is grouped by subject matter. These tend to be conventional— an Etruscan family would ask the artist for a scene from Greek mythology, from the Trojan war perhaps, or something like the death of Actaeon, or a daemon conducting the souls of the dead down to the underworld. Perhaps the artist already had one in stock. One rule of Etruscan art is its lack of rules. Expect anything: some of the reclining figures of the dead atop the urns are brilliant portraiture, while others could be the first attempts of a third-grade crafts class. All, holding the little cups or dishes they carry down into Hades, look as serene and happy as only a defunct Etruscan can be.

As always, the Etruscans do their best to make you laugh. One terracotta, the *Urna degli Sposi*, portrays a hilariously caricatured couple who look as if they are about to start arguing over whose turn it is to do the dishes. Another Etruscan joke is the famous *Ombra della Sera* (evening shadow), quite a celebrity around Volterra, a small, carefully detailed bronze of a man with a quizzical expression and spidery, grotesquely elongated arms and legs. Also present are prehistoric finds, Roman mosaics from the baths and artefacts discovered in the theatre, and a collection of Etruscan jewellery.

The museum lies a stone's throw from Piazza XX Settembre, the bus terminal; from here Via Gramsci leads towards the town centre. Climb any of the alleys to the south of the museum, however, and you'll reach Volterra's **Parco Archeologico** just inside the walls (*open 11–5*). There isn't much archaeological about it—some Etruscan foundations and a huge ancient cistern called the *Piscina* (swimming-pool) *Romana*—but the park is a marvel, a lush English garden of manicured lawns and shady groves unlike anything else in Tuscany. Above the park stretches an exceptionally long and elegant castle, the **Fortezza Medicea**, begun in 1343 and completed by Lorenzo de' Medici in 1472. You can't get in; it has been a prison almost from the day it was built, perhaps the fanciest in this nation of fancy calabooses.

Piazza dei Priori

This is a fine little republican piazza, surrounded by plain, erect palazzi that call your attention ever so discreetly to the sober dignity of the *comune*. The **Palazzo dei Priori**, of 1208, is said to be the oldest such building in Tuscany, the model for Florence's Palazzo Vecchio and a score of others. Its tower has been closed to visitors for several years, but if you ever find it reopened, climb up for a view that literally takes in all of Tuscany; on a clear day you'll see Monte Amiata, all the coast from La Spezia to the Argentario, and Corsica and Elba as well. Across the square, the simple **Palazzo Pretorio** is almost as old; next to it, the rakishly leaning **Porcellino Tower** takes its name from the little pig sculpted in relief near the base, just barely visible after almost seven centuries.

The Cathedral and the Etruscan Arch

Just to the right of the Palazzo dei Priori, a bit of green and white striped marble façade peeks out between the palaces. This is the back of the archiepiscopal palace, located around the corner in the **Piazza del Duomo**. Quiet and dowdy, the contrast of this square with well-built Piazza dei Priori is striking, a lasting memory of the defeat of Volterra's medieval bishops by the *comune*. Its octagonal **Baptistry**, begun in 1283, has its marble facing completed only on one side. Within, there is a fine baptismal font sculpted by Andrea Sansovino in the early 1500s, an altar by Mino da Fiesole, and a holy-water dish carved out of an Etruscan boundary stone. Unfortunately, bits of the cornice have been dropping down on the Volterrans lately, and so it is closed while restoration takes place.

The plain **Cathedral** façade has a good marble doorway. This forlorn mongrel of a building was begun in the Pisan Romanesque style in the 1200s, and worked on fitfully for the next two centuries. The campanile went up in 1493, and the interior was entirely redone in the 1580s when the blatant Medici coat of arms was placed over the high altar. Do not pass this old Duomo by; the works of art inside are few in number, but of an exceptionally high quality. Fittingly, as this is Volterra, some of the windows are made of thin-sliced alabaster, a stone that was also used in the intricate, Renaissance **tabernacle** by Mino da Fiesole over the high altar. The chapels on either side have excellent examples of Tuscan woodcarving: a 15th-century one attributed to Francesco di Valdambrino off to the left, the *Madonna dei Chierici*, and to the right, a polychromed *Deposition* with five separate, full-sized figures, among the best of 13th-century Pisan sculpture, shining immaculately after a recent restoration. Another chapel off to the right contains fragments of some unusually good anonymous trecento frescoes of the *Passion of Christ*, very much ahead of their time in composition, in the figures and the folds of the draperies—even Giorgio Vasari might have liked them.

In the left aisle, the **pergamo** (pulpit) is one of the lesser-known works of the Pisanos, less spectacular than the ones in Pisa, Siena and Pistoia, but still showing something of the vividness and electric immediacy seen in the best Pisan sculpture. Guglielmo Pisano did the fine relief of the *Last Supper* (note the faces of the Apostles, and the sly metaphorical monster sneaking under the table). The pulpit's supporting columns rest on two lions, a bull and one unclassifiable beast, all by Bonamico Pisano. In the oratory, off the left aisle near the entrance, behind a 16th-century wooden statue group of the *Adoration of the Magi*, is a small fresco said to be by Benozzo Gozzoli, though perhaps because of its deterioration or early date, it lacks Gozzoli's usual charm.

Just around the corner in the Archiepiscopal Palace, a small **Museo d'Arte Sacra** (*open daily 9–1 pm; in summer also 3–6pm; adm*) has some sculpture and architectural fragments, and a della Robbia terracotta of St Linus, Volterra's patron.

From the Duomo, if you retrace your steps back towards Piazza dei Priori and turn down Via Porta all'Arco, you'll find the quaintest old relic in Volterra, the **Arco Etrusco**. The Etruscans built the columns at least, though the arch above them was rebuilt in Roman times. Set into this arch are three primeval black basalt sculpted heads from the original gate, *c.* 600 BC, believed to represent the Etruscan gods Tinia (Jupiter), Uni (Juno) and Menvra (Minerva). Some of the features of Juno are barely traceable; 2700 years of wind and rain have worn all three into great black knobs—carved out of the voussoirs, they resemble nothing so much as garden slugs.

The Pinacoteca

Open daily 9–7 in summer, 9–2 in winter, closed Mon; adm.

Just off Piazza dei Priori, the intersection of Via Roma and Via Buonparenti is one of the most picturesque corners of Volterra, with venerable stone arches and tower houses such as the 13th-century Casa Buonparenti.

On Via dei Sarti, the elder Antonio da Sangallo's Palazzo Solaini (note the elegant arcaded courtyard) has been restored to hold Volterra's **Pinacoteca**, another small but choice collection. Trecento Sienese painting is well represented, including a glorious altarpiece of the *Madonna and Child* by Taddeo di Bartolo. To complement the remarkable 1300s wood sculptures in the Duomo, the Pinacoteca has two figures portraying the *Annunciation* by a local artist named Francesco di Domenico Valdambrino. Neri di Bicci was a quattrocento Florentine, but his *St Sebastian* here looks entirely Sienese—probably at the request of the customer. Among the works of other Tuscans, there is a big shiny altarpiece by Ghirlandaio, and two by Luca Signorelli (or his workshop): a *Madonna and Saints* and an *Annunciation.* Only tantalizing fragments are left of another altarpiece by Giuliano Bugiardini (1475–1554), a little-known Florentine with a very distinctive style.

For all that, the prize of the collection is the Rosso Fiorentino *Deposition*, dated 1521 and perhaps his greatest work in Italy. Even out here in the boondocks of Volterra, it attracts considerable attention from the art scholars, a seminal work and one of the thresholds from the Renaissance into Mannerism, with all the precision and clarity of the best quattrocento work, yet also possessing an intensity that few works had ever achieved. The Descent from the Cross is a starkly emotional subject; in Rosso's work it is terror and disarray, a greenish Christ and a small, nearly hysterical crowd dramatically illuminated against a darkening deep blue sky. You'll find little that this painting has in common with

Rosso's contemporaries, not even with his fellow madman Pontormo (who did his own, quite different *Deposition* in Florence's Santa Felicità)—but oddly enough it could almost be mistaken for a work of Goya.

San Francesco and the Roman Theatre

On the corner east of the Pinacoteca, the church of **San Michele** has a Pisan Romanesque façade. If you go in the other direction, towards the Porta San Francesco on the western edge of town, you will pass through back streets dusty with alabaster workshops and finally arrive at the church of **San Francesco** on Via San Lino. Here the attraction is off to the right of the altar, the **chapel of the Holy Cross**, completely frescoed in 1410 by a Florentine artist whose name seems to be Cenni di Francesco di Ser Cenni—a rare soul, indeed, with a sophisticated, wonderfully reactionary medieval sense of composition and his own ideas about Christian iconography, done in a bold style that in places almost seems like modern poster art. The *Legend of the Cross* frescoes generally follow those of Gaddi at Santa Croce in Florence (*see* pp.151 and 154), and there are also scenes of *St Francis*, the *Passion*, and the *Massacre of the Innocents*, many with fantasy city backgrounds. Note the *Dream of Constantine* (or of Heraclius), in his tent adorned with the Imperial Eagle; naturally the artist had never seen a Roman eagle, but he painted a very nice medieval German one instead.

Just to the right of San Francesco, a pedestrian passage under the walls takes you out to Viale Francesco Ferrucci, home to a lively outdoor **market** on Saturday mornings. Beneath the walls, ancient Velaterrae's large **Roman theatre** has been excavated (*open 11–5 in summer*). Not much of the *cavea* is intact, but enough marble slabs and columns survived for the archaeologists to reconstruct part of the stage building, an impressive testimony to the importance of the city long ago. Behind the theatre are ruins of **baths** and a large rectangular **palestra**, a yard for exercise and gymnastics.

The Balze

Leaving Volterra from the San Francesco gate, you pass the Borgo San Giusto, with the ruins of the 12th-century Pisan Romanesque church of **Santo Stefano**. The road to Pisa exits through the outer circuit of the **Etruscan walls**; though barely more than foundations, they are traceable for most of their length around the city, and easily visible here.

Some 2km beyond these, decorating the lonely moors are the *balze*, barren eroded gullies that may have begun as Etruscan mining cuts. They have been growing ever since; chronicles from the Middle Ages report them gradually gobbling up farms and churches around the city. No one has yet discovered a way to stop the inexorable growth of these deep clay-walled chasms. In the 1700s the *balze* tried to atone for their appetite, uncovering some of the most important Etruscan necropolises yet discovered, contributing their urns to the Guarnacci Museum. Now even most of these necropolises have disappeared completely. On the edge of one steep cliff you will see the **Badia**, an 11th-century Camaldolensian abbey now half-devoured by the *balze*.

Alabaster and Where to Find It

Archaeological evidence has the Villanovan culture in Tuscany finding creative uses for the *pietra candida*, alias $CaSO_42H_2O$, as early as 800 BC. The Etruscans made good use of this luminous, easily worked mineral in their funeral urns and everyday objects. During the Dark Ages, the locals appear to have forgotten about it, though now and then some artist would turn a chunk into a vase or cup (the Medici, with their insatiable lust for dust magnets, bought quite a few). The craft of carving alabaster revived dramatically in the last two centuries. Volterra today is full of small workshops, and even a few large firms that turn the stone into vases, figurines, ashtrays and everything else that's serviceable or collectable. Many of the alabaster workers are genuine artists, turning out one-of-a-kind pieces at high prices; the city runs a contest each year for the best. Others produce vast numbers of attractive little baubles from L5000 and up.

There are shops selling alabaster in every corner of Volterra; you'll do well to seek them out, and avoid the temptations of the big glossy establishments in the most prominent places. Paolo Sabatini, who has won several prizes in the annual competition, has his shop at Via Porta all'Arco 45, with some of the most original creations in town. Just down the street, there are some unusual alabaster miniatures at No. 26. More of the best can be found on Via di Sotto: simple, elegant vases and lamps at No. 2 and at the shop 'Come una Volta' at No. 6. Via Antonio Gramsci also has many shops; the more interesting ones are at Nos. 20 and 53. The avant-garde is represented by Via Guarnacci 26, with some splashy modern work in coloured alabaster. Beyond these, there's the City Artisans' Cooperative on Piazza dei Priori, and some conservative, well-crafted pieces at Giuseppe Bessi, Via San Lino 52; just next door at No. 46 there is a shop specializing in carved olive wood. For really serious alabaster—say, complete bathrooms, or life-size copies of the Trevi Fountain—try the big shops with big car parks around the outskirts of town.

If Auro Bongini's workshop on Via Don Minzoni 54 is open, it is well worth taking a look. He makes doll's house furniture from local olive wood to the style of the last century. His exhibition work fills the small workshop, but there are also afew individual pieces for sale. If you are interested you can ring in advance to make an appointment, ☎ 88040.

Volterra ☎ (0588–)   ***Where to Stay and Eating Out***

Volterra does not see as many tourists as San Gimignano, but is nevertheless just as expensive—at least, double rooms under L50,000 are almost impossible to find. Students aren't entirely out of luck: there's the hostel, **Ostello della Gioventù** on Via Don Minzoni, ☎ 85577–institutional atmosphere for L12,000 a person. ★★★**Nencini** is a 16th-century villa with lovely views, just north of the city centre on Borgo S. Stefano, ☎ 86386, ✆ 80601 (*moderate; some cheaper without bath*). Within the walls, ★★★★**San Lino**, Via San Lino 26, near Porta San Francesco, ☎ 85250, ✆ 80620 (*moderate*), stands out only for being the only place with parking; simple accommodation. Closer to the centre, ★★★**Etruria** at

Via Matteotti 32, ✆ and ✉ 87377 (*rooms inexpensive to moderate; meals expensive*), has one of Volterra's best restaurants—roast boar and game dishes in season.

Most restaurants in Volterra, for that matter, specialize in roast boar and the like, good medieval cuisine entirely in keeping with the spirit of the place. The menu at **Il Porcellino**, Vicollo delle Prigioni 18, ✆ 86392 (*moderate*), combines seafood and familiar Tuscan favourites with local treats like roast pigeon and boar with olives; a good bargain. *Closed Oct–March.* After a morning in the Etruscan museum, you can regale yourself for about the same price at **La Pace** just inside the gate at Via Don Minzoni 55–61, ✆ 86511; roast boar or lamb, as well as rabbit cooked in Vernaccia; the *spaghetti alla boscaiola* for starters is a good choice. Not too many tourists make it to **Tre Scimmie** (three monkeys) on Via del Mandorlo 3, ✆ 86047 (*moderate*), a small, delightful place where the usual boar and bunny are an even better bargain. Another alternative offering hearty Tuscan fare is **La Tavernetta**, Via Guarnacci 14, ✆ 87630 (*moderate*). One of the restaurants most popular with the Volterrans is outside the town: **A Biscondola**, about 3km away on the S68, ✆ 85197, ✉ 87284 (*moderate*). The country setting is plain enough, but the cooking is superb; lots of ducks—lasagne with duck sauce is the inspired speciality, also duck *alla cacciatora* and game dishes in season. *Closed Mon.* For a quick bite the **Taverna dei Priori**, Via G. Matteotti 19, ✆ 86180 (*inexpensive*), essentially a *tavola calda,* has sandwiches, salads and cooked food.

There is a disco in Volterra called **Tequila's** at Via dei Sarti 37A, which stays open during the winter. It is a lively place, although a little small, and has a wide variety of music from Italian pop classics to the latest house music.

The Val di Cecina and the Metal Hills

In the romantic emptiness of the Volterran hills, there are not many other attractions. For a complete change in scenery, take S68 west along the valley of the river Cecina from Volterra as far as Guardistallo, a lovely, rolling valley with the pines and cypresses in just the right places—a suitable Tuscan background for any Renaissance painting. **Montecatini Val di Cecina**, in the hills just to the north, is a quiet medieval village with a 12th-century castle. Further west, a big wine-producing area extends around **Montescudaio**: Montescudaio (both red and white) is a distinguished though lesser-known dry variety with a DOC label.

The best road from Volterra, the S439, leads south, over the **Colline Metallifere** towards Massa Marittima and the coast. These 'metal hills', along with the iron mines of nearby Elba, did much to finance the gilded existence of the ancient Etruscans. Several of the mines are in operation today, though driving through these hills you may see little but oak forests and olive groves along the way. **Pomarance**, a town that has retained some buildings from the Middle Ages and Renaissance, holds few surprises, but wait until you get to **Larderello**, the self-proclaimed 'World Centre of Geothermal Energy'. This is the northern boundary of volcanic Italy; that extinct volcano, Monte Amiata, and the ancient crater lakes of Umbria and Lazio are not far away. This far north, the only subterranean manifestations are benign little geysers and gurgling pools of sulphurous mud. Larderello is a growing town; huge ugly cooling towers of the type that would signify a nuclear power plant anywhere else are all over the landscape wherever there is a geothermal source worth tapping. Near the centre, there is a strange, post-modernist parish church designed in the 1950s by Michelucci, the architect of Florence's rail station, and also the little **Museo Lardarel**, which may explain something of this overheated little town's career.

After Larderello, and almost as far as Monterotondo, the landscape is downright uncanny. It smells bad too; miniature geysers and steam vents (*soffioni*) whistle and puff away by the roadside, while murky pits bubble up boric salts amidst yellow and grey slag piles. Follow the yellow road signs of the '*itinerario dei soffioni*' to see the best of it. Despite the sulphur and borax, the cooling towers and occasional rusting hulks of old mining equipment, the Metal Hills are really quite winsome, especially south of Larderello (still on S439) around the medieval village of **Castelnuovo di Val di Cecina**, surrounded by chestnut groves and the pass of the *Ala dei Diavoli*, or 'Devils' Wing' at the crest of the hills. **Monterotondo Marittimo**, further south, has more than its share of subsurface curiosities; nearby **Lago Boracifero** is the centre for borax mining in Italy. And in some places the ground is covered with strange webs of steam pipes, ever since the *comune* discovered its unique resource could power almost everything in town for free.

Massa Marittima

This lovely, ruggedly hilly area is part of the coastal district of the Maremma only in name; as early as Roman times it was considered part of the 'maritime' province. And for just as long, Massa Marittima has been making its living from the mines, though today its 10,000 people are not nearly enough to fill the space within the medieval walls. Small as it may be, its brief period of prosperity left it a beautiful little city, with two good reasons for visiting: first, to see the second city of the Sienese Republic, like Siena a lesson in urban refinement in a small place; and second, an enormous, exquisite cathedral that is one of the great medieval monuments of Tuscany.

This mining town appeared as a free *comune*, the *Repubblica Massetana*, about 1225, just at the time it was beginning a dizzying period of prosperity from the discovery of new silver and copper deposits nearby. Unfortunately, this wealth had a fatal attraction for Massa's bigger neighbours. Pisa and Siena fought over the little republic for a century, and it finally fell to the latter in 1337. It wasn't long before the mines gave out, putting Massa into a decline that lasted for centuries. Malaria was a problem from the 1500s, and not until the Lorraine dukes drained the wet places and reopened some of the mines did things start looking up.

Getting Around

Massa is only 22km off the coastal Via Aurelia at Follonica, absolutely worth the diversion if you are passing that way; direct from Siena it's a not particularly captivating 65km/1hr 20mins drive on S73 (passing by San Galgano) and S441. If you are using public transport, there are three or four buses a day from Volterra (change at Monterotondo), five to nearby Follonica, and frequent bus and train connections from there to Grosseto (Massa is in Grosseto province); also two a day to Florence and Siena, and one direct to Grosseto: information and tickets for all of them at the *Agenzia Massa Veterensis* opposite the Duomo. Most buses stop on Via Corridoni, behind and a little downhill from the Duomo.

Tourist Information

Opposite the Duomo; the town museum in the Palazzo del Podestà also functions as an information office, ℂ (0566) 902289. In the summer, there is an office in Via Parenti 22, ℂ (0566) 9027561.

The Duomo

It's quite a sight, rising up incongruously on its stepped pedestal above the little town, its effect greatly heightened by its brilliant setting, above and at an angle to Massa's main square, **Piazza Garibaldi**, a *tour de force* of medieval town design. Massa began its cathedral around 1200, reconstructing a smaller cathedral of the 11th century, and finished it in 1250. Some additions were made later; note the striking contrast between the original Pisan Romanesque building, with its blind arches and lozenges, and later Sienese work like the campanile, added about 1400. Some of the best features of the building are the Gothic windows, capitals and the carvings of animals protecting humans on the façade and the left side.

The interior, under massive columns with delicately carved capitals, each one different from the others, has a few trecento and quattrocento frescoes, including one of St Julian tending the sick near the main entrance. On the left side, there is a luminous *Madonna* by Duccio (1318) and a unique collection of reliefs from the original 11th-century church: staring priests and apostles in a vigorous, cartoon-like style. On the right side hangs the *Nativity of Mary* by the last and most peculiar great Sienese artist, Rutilio Manetti (d. 1639): woebegone ladies and a jellicle cat attend a pug-nosed, thumb-sucking, very unbeatific baby Mary. Nearby is a fine baptismal font with reliefs by Giraldo da Como (c. 1250) and a Renaissance tabernacle added in 1447. A wooden crucifix by Giovanni Pisano hangs over the high altar; behind it, in the impressive Gothic apse, is the *Ark of San Cerbone* with more good early reliefs (1324) of the life of Massa's patron saint.

Up and Down Massa

Next to the cathedral on Piazza Garibaldi, the 1230 **Palazzo del Podestà** now holds Massa's town museums, including a well-organized but not especially interesting **Archaeology Museum** (the Medici dukes carried the best local finds off to Florence long ago), and a small **Pinacoteca** (*open daily exc Mon; April–Oct 10–12.30, 3.30–7 pm; Nov–Mar 10–12.30, 3.30–5 pm; adm*), in which the best work is a *Maestà* by Ambrogio Lorenzetti, aglow with rosy faces, flowers and golden trim, worthy to have hung over the

high altar of the cathedral. Note the angel with the distaff and spindle in the centre—a sure sign that the local wool guild paid for the painting.
The present-day city offices are in the **Palazzo Comunale** across the square, a group of connected tower-houses from the 13th and 14th centuries. Note the inscription above the door of another old building on the piazza: MASSA VETERNENSIS CELEBRIS VETULONIA QUONDAM. Just as Grosseto thinks of itself as the successor to Etruscan Roselle, Massa is the heir to lost Vetulonia, the once-great city of the Dodecapolis whose ruins can be seen on the coast (*see* p. 307).

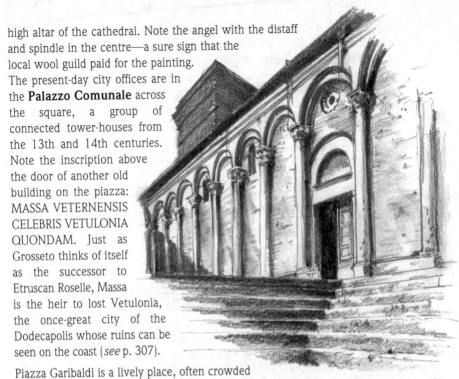

Piazza Garibaldi is a lively place, often crowded with Teutons perching on the steps of the Duomo or swilling beer in the two outdoor café-pizzerias. Via Libertà leads off into the older quarter of town, a tiny, tidy nest of arches and alleys that hasn't changed much over the centuries. Like Siena, Massa is divided into three *terzi*; this is the *terzo* of Civitavecchia. Another street, Via Moncini, climbs up to the **Città Nuova**, a 14th-century suburb behind some unusual Sienese fortifications; the street ends at Piazza Matteotti, with the 1330 **Torre del Candaliere**, or Torre dell'Orologio, connected to the fortifications by a long, slender walkway called the **Sienese Arch**; it's a beautiful ensemble, built more for show than for any military consideration, à la Siena (*open daily exc Mon; April–Oct 10–12.30, 4–8; closed in winter, ring the tourist information office to visit; adm*). Across the piazza, the Palazzo delle Armi has a small **Museum of the Art and History of Mining**. Up Corso Diaz, the main drag of the Città Nuova, the big church of **Sant'Agostino** was completed in 1313; inside are more paintings by Rutilio Manetti.

Finally, no visit to Massa would be complete without a trip to the **Mining Museum** (*open daily exc Mon; guided tours every half-hour; April–Sept 10–12, 3.30–7pm; Oct–Mar 10–12, 3.30–5pm; adm*), behind the Duomo on Via Corridoni. Mining, after all, is what Massa is all about (if you go to the city library and ask them politely, they may show you the city's great treasure, the 1310 *Codice Minerario Massetano*, modern Europe's first code of laws concerning mining rights). The entrance of the museum leads down into nearly a half-mile of old mine tunnels, with exhibits to show how the job was done from medieval days to the present.

Massa seems to be becoming an increasingly popular spot—especially with the Germans and Swiss—and the town's hotel capacity of 38 rooms is often stretched to the limit. Two of the three hotels are just below the town centre on the Via Massetana, both in lovely settings with gardens and views over the countryside (Massa lies on a rather steep hill), and both in modern buildings with simple *trattorie*. In fact, ★★**Duca del Mare**, Via D. Alighieri 1/2, ✆ 902284, ✆ 901905, and ★★**Girafalco** on Via Massentana, ✆ and ✆ 902177 (*inexpensive*), are nearly impossible to tell apart—both have doubles for the same prices. In town, on Via degli Albizzeschi, ★**Cris**, ✆ 903830 (*inexpensive*), is adequate enough for the price. Dining in Massa is uncomplicated; there are cafés in the square in front of the Duomo; otherwise try **Ricca**, Via Colombo, ✆ 201070 (*moderate to expensive*), with excellent fresh fish and grilled meats. Before that, as an appetizer, we recommend *primi piatti* such as *penne* with scampi and *porcini* mushrooms; or try **Taverna del Vecchio Borgo**, Via Butigni 12, ✆ 903950 (*inexpensive*), which is highly recommended, not only for its food but for its extensive list of *grappas*. *Closed Sun eve and Mon.* Nearby in Località Ghirlanda, **Da Bracali**, ✆ 902318 (*moderate*), offers variations on the local regional cooking and some seafood dishes. *Closed Tues.*

San Galgano and the Sword in the Stone

The S73 east from Massa to Siena skirts the southern edge of the Colline Metallifere, through quiet landscapes that in the Middle Ages saw a great flowering of domestic and foreign monasticism. The monks are mostly long gone, but they left behind one of the most unusual, least-visited sights in Tuscany, the ruined Cistercian **Abbey of San Galgano**, some 2km north of the village of Palazzetto. In some of the older paintings in Siena's Pinacoteca, you will notice the oddly Arthurian figure of a man apparently drawing a sword out of a stone. This is San Galgano, and in fact he is putting the sword in.

Galgano Guidotti, born in the nearby village of Chiusdino, was a dissolute young soldier who one day had a vision of St Michael, here on the slopes of Montesiepi, commanding him to change his ways. Thrusting his sword into a rock as a symbol of his new life, Galgano became a holy hermit. For this and a long career of miracles that followed, he was canonized only a few years after his death in 1181.

Almost from the start, the community he founded on Montesiepi was associated with the Cistercian Order, attracting monks from France as well as new members from around Siena. For three centuries, they played an extremely important role in the life of the community, draining swamps, building mills and even starting up a small textile industry. The Republic of Siena came to find them indispensable as architects, administrators—and especially as accountants. Many of the painted *Biccherna* covers in the Siena archives show white-robed Cistercians puzzling over the books or handing out workers' pay. With its immense wealth, and its French architects eager to initiate the backward Italians in the glories of the new Gothic style, the order began its great **Abbey Church** in 1218. The Cistercians were already in a bad way when the abbey was dissolved in 1600; not too long after their departure the roof, the marble façade and the campanile collapsed, leaving the grandest French Gothic building in Tuscany a romantic ruin. Its beautiful travertine columns and pointed arches remain, with the sky for a roof and a green lawn for a floor.

Parts of the monastery survive, now in the care of Olivetan nuns. On a hill above the abbey, St Michael appeared again, just after Galgano's death, to command his followers to build the **Cappella di Montesiepi** over the sword in the stone. The curious round chapel, one of very few in Italy, was begun in 1185. The sword is still there, sticking up from its rock right in the centre of the chapel; as with all the sites associated with St Michael, it is a reminder of a branch of medieval mysticism that while not entirely lost, is hardly well understood. Note the altar, with a cross of the type often seen on buildings of the Knights Templar, and the shallow dome of the ceiling, done in a pattern of 22 concentric white stripes, perhaps a representation of the heavenly spheres of the medieval cosmology (as in the famous fresco in Pisa's Campo Santo). In a chamber off to the side is a series of frescoes by Ambrogio Lorenzetti on the life of the saint.

In the silent land around San Galgano, possible detours include the mildly tortuous routes 8km west to **Chiusdino**, the dense, sleepy medieval village where San Galgano was born, or **Monticiano**, south on S73, just as old, where the Romanesque church of Sant'Agostino has frescoes by the trecento Sienese painter Bartolo di Fredi in its cloister.

Along Route 223

Possibly the least interesting of the roads south from Siena is the one for Grosseto, passing through the prosperous and fertile but nearly empty valley of the River Merse. Once over the border into Grosseto province it becomes even emptier, though there are a few towns which are worth a visit: **Bagni di Petriolo**, an old walled town with thermal springs that will relieve your gout; **Civitella Marittima**, a hill town with the Romanesque church of San Lorenzo al Lanzo, and **Paganico**, a charming village that retains its Sienese walls and gates. Its parish church of San Michele has some well-preserved frescoes by Bartolo di Fredi.

Southern Tuscany

Not counting the coastal Maremma around Grosseto, the old territories of the Sienese Republic make a complete and coherent landscape, rolling hills mostly given over to serious farming and pastureland. It isn't as garden-like as some other parts of Tuscany, though tidy vineyards and avenues of cypresses are not lacking. Hill towns, ready landmarks, poke above the horizon—Montepulciano off to the east, Pienza a bit to the left, while that castle on the left of the road must be Castiglione d'Orcia. At times it seems the whole region is laid out before you, bounded on one side by the hills around Siena, on the other by the cones of Monte Amiata and Radicófani.

In the little tourist offices in these towns, they remark that not too many English or Americans pass through, which is a pity. It's beautiful country, the food and wine are among the best in Tuscany, and there are delightful towns with charming souvenirs from the Renaissance and Middle Ages.

Asciano and Around

S326 from Siena heads east, and its main purpose is to get you out to Cortona (*see* p.419) and then to Umbria. Before it leaves Siena province, the road passes the village of **Monteaperti**, where the Sienese won their famous victory over Florence in 1260, and **Rapolano Terme** (27km), a small spa that retains some of its medieval walls. Besides the hot springs there is a surplus of natural gas in the area, some of it pumped out from wells, and some just leaking out of the ground—don't drop any matches. **Asciano**, 10km south of Rapolano, has walls built by the Sienese in 1351, and a good collection of Sienese art in the **Museo d'Arte Sacra**, next to the Romanesque church of the Collegiata (*open by appointment only, © (0577) 718207*). From Etruscan necropolises in the area, finds have been assembled in the church of San Bernardino, a modest **Museo Archeologico** (*open daily exc Mon 10–12.30; also 4.30–6.30 June–Sept; adm*). In a house at Via del Canto 11, there are some recently discovered Roman mosaics; ask at the pharmacy on Corso Matteotti if you want to arrange a visit.

The countryside around Asciano is dotted with *biancane*, knobbly chalk hills exposed when the soil above erodes away, that often appear in the backgrounds of 14th- and 15th-century Sienese and Florentine paintings. This has always been sheep country, and it suffered much in the changes after World War II, when many of the men went off to look for work in the cities. Today, immigrants from Sardinia make up a sizeable minority of the population, born shepherds who are trying to get the business back on its feet. Old **Sinalunga**, up on its hill, is the next town (22km west), but offers little to detain you; the main square is named after Garibaldi, to commemorate his arrest here in 1867, at the orders of King Vittorio Emanuele, who was afraid his volunteers were about to attack Rome. **Torrita di Siena**, 6km southwest of the junction with the A1 from Florence to Rome, takes its name from the tall towers of its old walls, some of which remain.

Southern Tuscany

Land over 500 metres

20km
10 miles

N

375

South of Siena, lovely S2 makes its way towards Rome, roughly following the routes of the Roman *Via Cassia* and the medieval pilgrims' path to Rome, the *Via Francigena*. Along the way, it passes **Lucignano d'Arbia** (16km), a charming, tiny village with a medieval church, and **Buonconvento** (27km), a gritty industrial town that hides a miniature, walled, medieval town at its centre. The walls, no longer very proper and military, are peppered with windows of the houses that have been built against them. There are two fine gates at either end of the main street, and in the middle the 14th-century parish church with an altarpiece by Matteo di Giovanni; across the street from the church, the **Museo d'Arte Sacra** has a small collection of choice Sienese paintings by the likes of Matteo, Sano di Pietro and Bartolo di Fredi.

East of Buonconvento, the valleys of the Ombrone and the Asso enclose the country of the *crete*. Like the *biancane* and the *balze* of Volterra, these are uncanny monuments to the power of erosion; in the broken, jumbled hills south of Asciano, austere green meadows alternate with ragged gullies and bare white cliffs. At the centre of these *crete*, in the bleakest and most barren part, there is a huge grove of tall, black cypresses around the monastery of **Monte Oliveto Maggiore**, 9km from Buonconvento on S451 (*open daily 9.15–12, 3.15–5.45 summer, 3.15–5 winter*). Some of the great gentlemen of Siena's merchant elite founded Monte Oliveto, including Giovanni Tolomei and Ambrogio Piccolomini, both jaded merchants and sincere Christians who retired here in 1313 to escape the fatal sophistication of the medieval city. Their new Olivetan Order was approved by the pope only six years later.

With such wealthy backers, the monastery became a sort of elite hermitage for central Tuscany. An ambitious building programme carried on throughout the 1400s made it a complete, though little-known monument of quattrocento architecture and art. In its isolated setting, Monte Oliveto is a marvel of Renaissance clarity and rationality, expressed in simple structures and good Siena brick. The beautiful, asymmetrical **gatehouse**, decorated with a della Robbia terracotta, makes a fitting introduction to the complex. Inside, the well-proportioned brick **Abbey Church** (finished in 1417) has an exceptional set of wooden intarsia choir-stalls by the master of the genre, Fra Giovanni da Verona, among the best work of this kind in all Italy.

The monastery's greatest treasure, however, is the **Great Cloister**, embellished with 36 frescoes of scenes from the life of St Benedict (whose original rule Tolomei and the Olivetans were trying to restore). The first nine of these are by Luca Signorelli, with formidable ladies and bulky, white-robed monks in the artist's distinctive balloonish forms and sparing use of colour. All the rest are the work of Il Sodoma (1505–8)—some of his best painting, ethereal scenes of Pre-Raphaelite ladies and mandarin monks, with blue and purple backgrounds of ideal landscapes and cities. If you are of that persuasion, popular enough a century ago, that it was with Raphael and Michelangelo that the Renaissance started to go wrong, you owe a visit here. Il Sodoma, not a Florentine or really even a Sienese (he was from Vercelli in the north), wrote the last word to the mainstream tendency of Florentine painting before the excesses of Mannerism. Mr Sodomite himself appears in the scene '*Come Benedetto risaldò lo capistero che era rotta*' (How Benedict repaired the broken sieve); he's the dissipated fellow on the left with the white gloves. Look carefully—not only did Sodoma paint himself in, but also his pet badgers, of which he was very fond. The badgers and others of Sodoma's many pets appear in various other frescoes as well.

Unlike so many great Tuscan art shrines, Monte Oliveto, isolated here in the Sienese hills, retains something of its original aloof dignity. Although Napoleon himself suppressed the monastery in 1810, a group of talented brothers still works here, specializing in the restoration of old books.

In the *crete* around Monte Oliveto, the village of **San Giovanni d'Asso** (8km southeast) is built around a Sienese fortress; the church of San Pietro in Villore is from the 12th century, with an ambitious, unusual façade. From here a byroad east leads to **Montisi** (7km) and **Trequanda** (12km), two other fine little villages, seldom visited; the latter has a 13th-century castle and another Romanesque church.

⊙ (0577–)   ***Where to Stay and Eating Out***

Accommodation isn't always easy to find in this quiet corner of Tuscany. Often, towns and villages have only one real hotel, or none. Quite a few restaurants have rooms to rent, and there are always a few private homes with rooms to rent that don't advertise. Don't be shy; ask around and you'll find something.

The closest rooms to Monte Oliveto Maggiore are in Buonconvento, the simple **★★Albergo Ristorante Roma**, on the main street of the old town, Via Soccini 14, ⊙ 806021, ✆ 807284 (*inexpensive*). For something really special, reserve far in advance for one of the seven rooms at **★★★★Locanda dell'Amorosa**, 2km south of Sinalunga at Locazione L'Amorosa, ⊙ 679497, ✆ 678216 (*very expensive*). More than an inn, this is a tiny, medieval hamlet, complete with a manor house and frescoed church. There are no particular amenities—but beautiful rooms, in a memorable setting, and a prize-winning restaurant. The menu follows the seasons, but usually includes freshwater fish dishes (Lake Trasimeno isn't far away) such as the *ravioli di pesce*; for the seconds, try stuffed pigeon or the big Florentine steaks. *Closed Mon, Tues lunch and Feb.* A simpler restaurant near Sinalunga Loc. Bettole, Via di Vittorio 12, ⊙ 624192, is **Al Cacciatore** (*moderate*). As the name implies, expect some game dishes—boar with *porcini* mushrooms, little birds on the spit, also grilled fish. **Da Miretta** near Asciano at Loc. La Pievina on the Laurentana road, ⊙ 718368 (*moderate*), is a very friendly, reasonably priced place serving regional dishes and seafood—make sure to save some room for the home-made desserts. *Closed Mon and Tues.* After visiting Monte Oliveto Maggiore, the restaurant in the gatehouse is a nice place to have a snack.

Beautifully situated on a hill inhabited since Etruscan times, swathed in vineyards and olive groves, the walled village of Montalcino (pop. 5400) dominates the serene country-side 14km south of Buonconvento. Its major attraction is liquid—*Brunello di Montalcino*, a dark pungent red that holds a proud place among Italy's finest wines.

Every year at the Palio in Siena, there is a procession of representatives from all the towns that once were part of the Republic. The honour of leading the parade belongs to Montalcino, for its loyalty and for the great service it rendered in 1555 after the fall of Siena (*see* **Siena**, 'History', p.319). During the siege, a band of diehard republicans escaped from Siena to the nearly impregnable fortress of Montalcino, where they and the local populace established the 'Republic of Siena at Montalcino', holding out against the Medici until 1559. Today, Montalcino tries hard to be up to date (signs on the outskirts proclaim it a *'comune* of Europe' and a 'denuclearized zone'); in reality it's a friendly, resolutely sleepy town where people often forget to wind the clocks.

Getting Around

There are regular buses from Siena (41km/1hr), a few involving a change at Buonconvento, near the S2 crossroads for Montalcino. Buses stop at Piazza Cavour at the eastern end of town; tickets and perhaps informa-tion can be obtained at the bar on the piazza. There are no convenient buses to take you to Sant'Antimo.

Tourist Information

A Pro Loco office, open now and then, is on Costa del Municipio near Piazza Cavour, ✆ (0577) 849331.

Within the Walls

Right on Piazza Cavour is one of Montalcino's modest museums: the small **Archaeology Museum**, set in a former hospital pharmacy with detached frescoes by a student of Il Sodoma. Via Mazzini leads west to the Piazza del Popolo, and the attractive **Palazzo Comunale**, begun in the late 13th century, with a slender tower that apes the Torre di Mangia in Siena. Nearby, **Sant'Agostino** is a simple Sienese church, preserving some original frescoes from the 1300s. The **Diocesan and Civic Museum** around the corner (*open daily exc Mon, summer 9.30–1, 3.30–7pm, winter 10–1, 3–5; adm—reduced price combined ticket available for the museum and the Rocca, see below; reopening after renovations in summer 1996*) has a collection of Sienese painting and polychromed wood statues, including some of the earliest successes of Sienese art, an illuminated Bible and painted crucifix, both from the 12th century. Besides some minor works of the 14–15th-century Sienese masters, there is a collection of locally produced majolica from the same period.

Just down Via Ricasoli, at the eastern end of Montalcino, the impressive 14th-century **Rocca** was the centre of the fortifications that kept the Spaniards and Florentines at bay. This citadel means a lot to Italian patriots; it was the last stronghold not only of the Sienese, but symbolically of all the medieval freedoms of the Italian cities, blotted out in the bloody, reactionary 1500s. Near the entrance is a plaque with a little poem from the 'Piedmontese Volunteers of Liberty', extolling Montalcino's bravery in 'refusing the Medici thief'. Now a city park, with views that on a clear day stretch over half the province, the Rocca itself (*open daily exc Mon 9–1 and 2–8, winter 4–6*) contains the last battle standard of the Sienese republic and an **Enoteca** where you can become better acquainted with Montalcino's venerable Brunello and other local wines such as Moscadello and Rosso di Montalcino.

Following the town walls on the north side, you pass through neighbourhoods largely made up of orchards and gardens—Montalcino isn't nearly as busy a place as it was in the 1400s. The **Cathedral**, on Via Spagni, was mostly rebuilt in the 1700s. Follow that street past the Baroque church of the Madonna del Soccorso, and you come to the city park, the 'Balcony of Tuscany', with views over Siena and beyond.

Sant'Antimo

Open daily 10–1.30, 3–6.30; Sat and Sun 9–10.30, 3–6.

A few of the vineyards that produce the famous Brunello di Montalcino are on the road south for Sant'Antimo. Two of them welcome visitors: the Azienda Agricola Greppo, and the Cantine dei Barbi (℃ *848087 and 848277 respectively; ring first if you plan to visit*). **Sant'Antimo** itself, about 10km south of Montalcino, is worth the detour. One of the finest Romanesque churches in Tuscany, it originally formed part of a 9th-century Benedictine monastery founded, according to legend, by Charlemagne himself. The present building, begun in 1118, includes parts of the Carolingian works, including the crypt.

This half-ruined complex could easily serve as the set for *The Name of the Rose*. An important monastic community once flourished here; what buildings remain are now used as barns. The church, though, is exquisite, with its elegant tower and rounded apse. Some of the stone inside, on the capitals and elsewhere, is luminous alabaster from Volterra. The sophistication of the architecture is impressive—in particular the Byzantine-style women's gallery, and the ambulatory behind the apse with its radiating chapels.

℃ *(0577–)*

Where to Stay and Eating Out

There are two hotels in the town centre of Montalcino, ★★**Giardino**, right by the bus stop on Via Cavour 4, ℃ 848257 (*inexpensive without bath*), or ★★★**Il Giglio**, Via Soccorso Saloni 5, ℃ 848167 (*moderate*). ★★★**Al Brunello** in Loc. Bellaria, ℃ 849304, 📠 849430 (*moderate to expensive*), is an attractive place in a garden setting.

Besides wine, Montalcino is known for its honey, which comes into its own in early September at the National Honey Fair. Some of it goes into the desserts served at **Cucina de Edgardo**, Via S. Saloni 9, ✆ 848232 (*expensive*), which has some of the best and most creative *cucina nuova* this side of Siena; be sure to reserve, especially in the summer. **Il Pozzo** in Loc. S. Angelo in Colle, Piazza del Pozzo, ✆ 864015 (*inexpensive*), is worth the detour for a cheap, full-blown traditional meal. *Closed Tues.*

Pienza

Some 50km south of Siena on S2, turning left at San Quirico d'Orcia (*see* p.390), you'll come across a perfect, miniscule core of Renaissance order and urbanity, surrounded by a village of about 2500 souls. Pienza is a delightful place, even if it does get more than its share of tourists. Like Monte Oliveto Maggiore, it is a small dose of the best of the Renaissance, a jewel set among some of the best, most archetypal of Tuscan landscapes.

During a period of political troubles, common enough in Renaissance Siena, the great family of the Piccolomini had chosen to exile itself temporarily in one of its possessions, the village of Corsignano. Aeneas Silvius Piccolomini (*see* p.336) was born there in 1405; later, as Pope Pius II, he became determined to raise his country birthplace into a city. No historian has ever discovered any compelling economic or military reason for a new town here. Architect Bernardo Rossellino designed it, with some help from Pius, the pennies of the faithful paid for it, and Pius named it after himself, Pienza. No one knows if Rossellino merely meant to build the pope a monument, or was consciously creating a model city of Renaissance town planning. Perhaps fortunately, after the first wave of papal patronage Pienza was nearly forgotten. The strict grid of streets that was to extend over the Tuscan hills never materialized, and only the central piazza with a new cathedral and a Piccolomini palace was ever completed—enough, at least, to reveal something of the original intention.

Tourist Information

There is a Pro Loco office on Piazza Pio II, ✆ (0578) 748502, offering occasional guided tours of the town.

Pienza's Piazza Pio II

Piazza Pio II, the heart of Rossellino's design scheme, is a simple, decorous square, displaying the chief buildings of the town without any of the monumental symmetricality of the later Renaissance, seemingly relying on proportion alone to tie the ensemble together. Such a square suggests that despite all its paintings of ideal buildings and streetscapes, the Early Renaissance had little interest in city design. Compared with the sophisticated planning of the Middle Ages, Piazza Pio looks somewhat austere.

Rossellino designed a truly elegant façade for the **Cathedral** (1462), capturing the spirit of the times by omission—there is no hint anywhere on this façade that it belongs to a

Christian building, though the arms of the Piccolomini and the papal keys are prominently carved on the pediment. The interior, though equally elegant, is a surprise: it's done in a squarish, tamed Gothic—as if this bold Renaissance architect were a slightly embarrassed humanist who believed that only Gothic truly suited a church. Rossellino also carved a marble altar and baptismal font in the lower church; in addition, some of the leading Sienese artists contributed altarpieces: Sano di Pietro, Matteo di Giovanni, Vecchietta and Giovanni di Paolo. Nothing in this cathedral has been changed, or even moved, since the day it was completed; Pius' papal bull of 1462 expressly forbade it. See it while it lasts. The cathedral, built on the edge of a slight cliff, has been subsiding almost since it was built. Occasionally sulphurous fumes seep up from the floor. If you walk around the left side of the building, there is a fine outlook over the surrounding countryside, also a glimpse of the fearfully large cracks that have been developing in the apse. No one has yet discovered a way to shore it up, and it could collapse, at least partially, at any time. The cathedral has a small **Museum** in the adjacent Canon's House (*open daily exc Tues 10–1, 3–5pm; adm*) with paintings from the Sienese school.

Next to the cathedral, the columned **well**, a favourite sort of Renaissance urban decoration, is also by Rossellino. So is the **Palazzo Piccolomini**, a rehash of the more famous Palazzo Rucellai in Florence, built by the architect after designs by Alberti. The best part of the design is at the rear, where a fine three-storey loggia overlooks a 'hanging garden' on the edge of the cliff. The interior of the palace and gardens are open to visitors (*open daily exc Mon 10–12.30, 3–6pm, 2–4pm in winter; adm*). Other buildings on the piazza include the **Archbishop's Palace** and the Gothic **Palazzo Comunale**. Behind the Palazzo Piccolomini, the church of **San Francesco** predates the founding of Pienza; there are some 14th–15th-century frescoes inside including one small work attributed to Luca Signorelli.

Few people visit the 11th-century **Pieve** of old Corsignano, 1km west of the town. This unusual church, where Aeneas Silvius was baptized, has some even more peculiar carvings over its entrance. Mermaids, or sirens, turn up with some frequency in Romanesque tympana and capitals, and here are several—one spreading its forked tail to display the entrance to the womb, flanked by others, and a dancer and a musician, with dragons whispering into their ears. Such symbols are steeped in medieval mysticism, not entirely inaccessible to the modern imagination. Some scholars interpret this scene as a cosmic process: the sirens, representing desire, as the intermediary by which nature's energy and inspiration (the dragons) are conducted into the conscious world. It has been claimed that they betray the existence of an ecstatic cult, based on music and dance and descended from the ancient Dionysian rituals.

Shopping

Corso Rossellino leads from the centre of the village to Porta Murello and the bus terminus, passing trendy artisan shops selling ceramics and leatherwork, antique shops and health food stores. Pienza for some reason has dozens of these, offering among other things the very good, locally made honey and preserves. And if Renaissance architecture leaves you cold, you can at least come for the sheep's cheese, maybe Italy's best. Pienza's variety of *cacio* is mild, even delicate in taste; this self-proclaimed 'capital of sheep's cheese' has been making it at least since the time of the Etruscans.

Pienza ✆ (0578–)

Where to Stay and Eating Out

In Pienza, choices are few; the modern, but comfortable ★★★**Corsignano** in Via della Madonnina 9, ✆ 749054 (*moderate*), is the only hotel in town. Although near the bus stop, at Piazza Dante 3, ✆ 748551, the **Ristorante del Falco** (*inexpensive; also serves cheap meals*) has quite a few spartan rooms for rent. *Closed Fri.* Across the piazza at Viale S. Caterina 1/3, **Del Prato**, ✆ 748601, ✉ 748534 (*moderate*), is the best place to stop for a bite—outside tables in the little garden and a huge menu of simple local dishes, featuring home-made *pici* (thick spaghetti), also *crêpes* filled with ricotta cheese and other delights. *Closed Wed.* In the village centre, the **Sperone Nudo** in Via G. Marconi, ✆ 748596/748641, offers wine and *bruschetta*, sandwiches and snacks. *Closed Mon.* Trattoria **Latte di Luna**, Via S. Carlo 2/4, ✆ 748606 (*moderate*), is very popular with the locals and serves good homemade pasta with truffles, and grappa made in the town. *Closed Tues.*

Montepulciano

Another graceful hill town lingers south of Siena, also with a distinguished past and best known for wine—Montepulciano. Montepulciano is larger (pop. 14,500) and livelier than Montalcino, with some fine buildings and works of art. Old Montalcino was a home-from-home for the Sienese, while Montepulciano usually allied itself with Florence. And this town's *Vino Nobile di Montepulciano*, while perhaps not as celebrated as Montalcino's *Brunello*, was being praised by connoisseurs over 200 years ago, and can certainly contend with Italy's best today.

Inhabitants of this town, which began as the Roman *Mons Politianus*, are called *Poliziani*, and that is the name by which its most famous son is known. Angelo Ambrogini, or Poliziano, scholar at the court of Lorenzo de' Medici and tutor to his children, was one of the first Renaissance Greek scholars, also an accomplished poet and critic. Botticelli's mythological paintings may have been inspired by his *Stanze per la Giostra*. Today's Poliziani are a genteel and cultured lot, still capable of poetic extemporization and singing. The town's biggest festival is the *Bruscello*, a partly improvised play on medieval and Renaissance themes in music and verse, acted by the townspeople in the Piazza Grande each August. Montepulciano's other festival requires no poetry but plenty of sweat: the *Bravio delle Botti*, also in August, when teams from the various neighbourhoods race up the steep main street pushing huge barrels.

Montepulciano is 12.5km/20mins east of Pienza on S146, 66km/1½hrs from Siena, and 16km/30mins west of the Chiusi exit on the A1. The rail station (Florence–Rome line) is far out in the countryside, irregularly served by buses to town, and usually only local trains stop; a better possibility is to use the station at Chiusi-Chianciano, which has bus connections up to Chiusi town, to Chianciano Terme, Montepulciano and occasionally Pienza. The bus station in Montepulciano is just outside the Porta al Prato, the main gate into the city. There are several buses a day to Pienza, and to Chianciano Terme–Chiusi–Chiusi Station; one each in the morning and afternoon for Siena (via Pienza and San Quirico), also daily connections to Abbadia San Salvatore, Montalcino, Perugia and Arezzo. There is an LFI bus information booth inside the train station at Chiusi; outside, besides the buses mentioned above, there are infrequent LFI connections to Cortona, Arezzo, Perugia, Orvieto and Città della Pieve.

Tourist Information

There's a very helpful office at Via Ricci 9, just off the Piazza Grande, ✆ (0578) 757442.

Palazzi and Pulcinella

Entering the city through the **Porta al Prato**, the first monument you encounter will be a stone column bearing the *marzocco*, a symbol of Montepulciano's longtime attachment to Florence. Though nominally under Florentine control, the city was allowed a sort of independence up to the days of Cosimo I. The main street, called here Via di Gracciano del Corso, climbs and winds in a circle up to the top of the city (if you follow it all the way, you'll walk twice as far as you need to, and end up thinking Montepulciano is a major metropolis). This stretch of it is lined with noble palaces: the **Palazzo Avignonesi** at No. 91 and the **Palazzo Tarugi** at No. 82 are both the work of the late Renaissance architect Vignola, famous for his Villa Giulia in Rome and the Farnese Palace in Caprarola (Lazio). Further up, at No. 73 the **Palazzo Bucelli** has the most unusual foundation in Italy—made almost entirely of rectangular Etruscan cinerary urns, filled with cement and stacked like bricks, many still retaining their sculpted reliefs. Montepulciano was an Etruscan settlement, though most likely the urns came from nearby Chiusi.

Piazza Michelozzo, where the street begins to ascend, takes its name from the Florentine architect of the **Sant'Agostino** church, with an excellent, restrained Renaissance façade, similar in attitude to the cathedral in Pienza though much more skilfully handled. Michelozzo also contributed the terracotta reliefs over the portal. Across the piazza, note the figure atop the old **Torre del Pulcinella**. To anyone familiar with Naples, the white

Commedia dell'Arte clown banging the hours on the town bell will be an old friend. There's a story that a Neapolitan bishop was once exiled here for some indiscretions with the ladies back home, and when he returned he left this bit of Parthenopean culture as a remembrance, and also to thank the Poliziani for their hospitality.

Continuing along the main street, you pass a dozen or so more palaces, reminders of what an aristocratic city this once was. There is one florid Baroque interior, in the **Gesù Church** by Andrea Pozzo. Further down, the street curves around the medieval **Fortezza**, now partially residential, part of a fascinating quarter of ancient alleys, the oldest part of Montepulciano.

Piazza Grande

In these times, when even the stalwart citizens of the Italian hill towns are becoming a little too spoiled to walk up hills, the old centres of towns sometimes become quiet, out-of-the-way places. So it is in Montepulciano, where the **Piazza Grande** is the highest point in the city. On one side, Michelozzo added a rusticated stone front and tower to the 13th-century **Palazzo Comunale** to create a lesser copy of Florence's Palazzo Vecchio. Opposite, there is a pretty Renaissance well in front of the **Palazzo Contucci**, built by the elder Antonio da Sangallo. On the west side of the piazza, a tremendous pile of bricks, a sort of tenement for pigeons, proclaims the agonizing unfinishability of the **Cathedral**, victim of a doomed rebuilding that began in 1592. Like the toad, believed by medieval scholars to conceal a precious jewel in its brain, this preposterous building hides within its bulk a single transcendent work of art. Atop a marble Renaissance altar adorned with putti stands an *Assumption of the Virgin* by Bartolo di Fredi, quite possibly the greatest of all 14th-century Sienese paintings. Set in glowing, discordant colours—pink, orange, purple and gold, this is a very spiritual Madonna, attended by a court of angel musicians. Don't miss the predella panels beneath; each is a serious, inspired image from the Passion, including one panel of the *Resurrection* that can be compared to Piero della Francesca's more famous version in Sansepolcro.

The **Museo Civico**, holding the **Pinacoteca Crociani** just down Via Ricci (*open 9.30–12, 3–6, closed Mon and Tues*), has a somewhat disappointing collection—some della Robbia terracottas from the dissolved convent that was once downstairs, a *Crucifixion* from the workshop of Filippino Lippi, an *Assumption* by the Sienese Jacopo di Mino, an odd work by Girolamo di Benvenuto—baby Jesus as an *objet d'art*—and even more peculiar, an inexplicable *Allegory of the Immaculate Conception* by one Giovanni Antonio Lappoli (d. 1552). Continue down Via Ricci and you will find the church of **Santa Lucia**, with a small *Madonna* by Luca Signorelli in a chapel off to the right.

Antonio da Sangallo's San Biagio

One of the set pieces of Renaissance architecture was the isolated temple, a chance to create an ideal building in an uncluttered setting, often on the edge of a city. Giuliano da Sangallo's Santa Maria delle Carceri in Prato was the first and worst, followed by Bramante's San Pietro in Montorio in Rome and the Tempio della Consolazione in Todi

(Umbria) by one of his followers. Montepulciano's fine example of this Renaissance genre lies just south of the city (a long walk downhill, and back, if you don't have a car) near the road junction for Chianciano; a stately avenue of cypresses, each over a small marker commemorating a local soldier who died in World War I, leads to the site.

Antonio da Sangallo, long in the shadow of his less talented brother Giuliano, left his masterpiece here. **San Biagio** stands in a small park, a central, Greek-cross church of creamy travertine. As with so many other Renaissance churches, there is more architecture than Christianity in the design, a consciously classical composition, using not the Doric, but an adaptation of the 'Tuscan' order on the ground level, then Ionic on the second and finally Corinthian on the upper storeys of the campanile, gracefully fitted into one of the corners of the Greek cross. The interior, finished in fine marble and other expensive stones, is equally symmetrical and rational and impressive, appealing to an entirely different side of the religious sensibility than do the flowering Gothic churches or the soaring histrionics of the Baroque. Over the handsome altar, a Latin inscription proclaims '*Hinc deus homo et homo deus. Immensum Concepti—Aeternum Genuit*'. The beautiful **Canon's House**, with its double loggia, is also the work of Sangallo.

Vino Nobile and Other Delights

Montepulciano and environs are full of *cantine*, and each of these is full of people ready for long discussions on the virtues of this famous wine. After two years, it carries the bouquet of unknown autumn blooms, a perfume that confounds melancholy; its colour is a mystery of faith. Certain writers are known to be very fond of it.

A wine tour of Montepulciano should begin with the **Cantine Cantucci**, on the Piazza Grande, where they might show you the salon with frescoes by Baroque artist Andrea Pozzo. The **Cantina Gattavecchia**, next to the church of Santa Maria at the southern end of town, has a cantina dating back to the 1500s; and don't neglect the venerable cellar built into the embankment beneath Piazza Grande, next to the Teatro Poliziano.

Vino Nobile isn't the only variety of wine made in these parts. There is a version of Chianti—*Chianti Colli Senesi*, a creditable white *Valdichiana* and a sweet dessert *Vinsanto*. And on those evenings when quantity means more than quality, try any of the mass-produced Montepulciano red sold all over Italy; a more honourable plonk is hard to find.

Besides wine, Montepulciano has some local surprises to offer—**jams, preserves, honey** and other farm specialities have all recently become prominent in this corner of Tuscany, where the ideology of natural food has become just as popular as in the trendiest neighbourhoods of New York. You'll find them in almost any grocer's. Montepulciano has some very good **antique** stores on its back streets, and a sound **crafts** tradition, especially in woodcarving. On Piazza Grande, there is a **School of Mosaics**, with a permanent exhibition and some pretty examples of the craft on sale—even if you're not buying, take a peek at the mosaic fountain in the courtyard.

Around Montepulciano

There are some beautiful villages on the hills around Montepulciano, beginning with **Montefollonico** (8km northwest), a walled town with a frescoed parish church and Palazzo Comunale, both from the 13th century. **Monticchiello**, 7km southwest on a back road leading towards Pienza, hangs languorously on its hillside; here there is another 13th-century church, with an altarpiece by Pietro Lorenzetti.

Montepulciano and Around ✆ (0578–)　　**Where to Stay and Eating Out**

Montepulciano puts out the welcome mat at a few very amiable hotels, especially ★★★**Marzocco**, ✆ 757262, ✆ 757530 (*moderate*), an airy and serendipitous family-run establishment next, of course, to the Marzocco on Via G. Savonarola 18, just inside the main gate . Up near the cathedral, ★★**Duomo**, Via San Donato 14, ✆ and ✆ 757473 (*moderate*), has rooms without a bath . If you can't find a room in town, there are millions of them a few miles south at Chianciano Terme (*see* below) and at a pinch in Sant'Albano, 3km from Montepulciano—seven hotels, all in the inexpensive range, stuck bizarrely in the middle of nowhere; there are more thermal baths nearby.

The best restaurants in Montepulciano are outside town. In the lovely village of Montefollonico, with panoramic views back towards Montepulciano, **La Chiusa** in Via Madonnina, ✆ 669668 (*very expensive*), has been acclaimed as the best restaurant in southern Tuscany, where typical local cuisine is raised to transcendent heights, and there is an exhaustive wine list for those not satisfied with mere Vino Nobile from nearby. Many of the products are grown on the premises, but not the olive oil. La Chiusa is located in an old *frantoio* (olive press), unfortunately closed since a big frost not long ago killed off most of the trees in these parts. You might wish to sample the seven-course *menu degustazione. Closed Tues.* If that's too extravagant, try **Il Pulcino**, 3km down the road to Chianciano, ✆ and ✆ 716905 (*moderate*), specializing in grilled meats and fish. Montepulciano itself has a few restaurants, but none particularly stand out. Why not have a picnic? Stock up on some of the fine local products—honey and preserves, *pecorino* cheese, ham or boar salami and a case of Vino Nobile; the back roads off S146 will eventually take you to an ideal spot.

Chianciano Terme

Tourist Information

Piazza Italia 67, ✆ (0578) 63167.

Chianciano—Fegato Sano

This is the slogan you see everywhere in Chianciano Terme (pop. 7500): on the signs that welcome you to town, on the municipal buildings, even on the garbage trucks. 'Chianciano, for a healthy liver'. And after rotting yours on too much Montepulciano wine, how convenient to have one of Italy's most attractive spas close at hand to flush it out and get it pumping again. The waters here were known to the Etruscans, but only in the last 50 years have they been exploited in a big way. There is an old walled town, Chianciano Vecchio, with a medieval clock tower and a small Museo d'Arte Sacra; at the gate is the bus station and information booth. Beyond it, modern Chianciano stretches out for miles down its one main street, Viale della Libertà, passing hundreds of hotels, lovely gardens with clipped lawns, and bathhouses in a clean, modern style from the 1950s.

Everything is just as pleasant as it could be, and besides repairing your liver, Chianciano has mineral mud packs for your acne, hot aerosol douches and plenty of other medically respected treatments for whatever is wrong with you: they'll lock you in a room full of gas for a collective dry nebulization, throw you in the hydro-gaseous bath and then hand you over to the masseuses (this for patients suffering from trauma), or put you face to face with the sulphurous sonic aerosol spray. They can make hot mineral water go up one of your nostrils and come out the other. 'Ah,' said the Italian in seeming despair: 'The English never come. They simply do not understand the baths . . .'

Chiusi

If anyone, when you were a child, ever read you Macaulay's rouser about Horatio at the Bridge, you will remember the fateful name Lars Porsena of Clusium, leading the Etruscan confederation and their Umbrian allies to attack Rome in the brave days of old. Thanks to Horatio, of course, Rome survived and made a name for itself; you can come here to see what happened to Clusium—or *Camars*, as the Etruscans actually called it. Many of its 9500 citizens live down in the newer districts by the railway station, but the charming hill town up on the site of Lars Porsena's capital is still doing well.

Tourist Information

Pro Loco at Via Porsena 67, ℗ (0578) 227667.

Archaeological Museum

Open daily 9–2, Sun 9–1; adm.

From the brave days of old, Chiusi retains at least an excellent **Archaeological Museum**. As with so many other Etruscan collections, here the main attraction is the large number of cinerary urns, and as usual the Etruscans are able to produce a bewildering variety of styles and themes. Large urns with thoughtful, reclining figures are common, as well as mythological battle scenes with winged gods in attendance. Not all the tombs contained the well-known rectangular urns; some Etruscans chose to be buried in 'canopic' jars, surmounted by a terracotta bust of the deceased. Other sculptures and terracottas include a strange horse-headed serpent and a few alert sphinxes with curving wings. Camars was a wealthy town, and the excavations at its necropolises unearthed a large amount of Greek pottery, some of it very fine work—note the urn with Achilles and Ajax playing at dice, and the Dionysiac scenes with sexy maenads and leering satyrs. Many Etruscan imitation vases are present; it's easy to believe the local talent could have done as well as the Greeks, had they only possessed thinner paintbrushes. To end the collection, there is a glittering hoard of nice barbaric trinkets from some 6th–7th-century Lombard tombs on the Arusa hill just outside town.

Etruscan Tombs and Tunnels

If you're interested in seeing some of the Etruscan tombs (5th–3rd century BC) where these items were discovered, mention it to the museum guards, who arrange guided tours—in fact they'll probably ask you first. These are the only good painted tombs in Tuscany; the best of them, the Tomba della Scimmia, contains paintings of wrestlers and warriors, in addition to the monkey that gives the tomb its name. The Tomba della Pellegrina and the Tomba del Granduca are also interesting, as is the Tomba Bonci Casuccini, in a different necropolis east of town. Ask the guards if there's any way to get into the Etruscan tunnels that honeycomb the ground under Chiusi. The huge Roman cistern, built in the 1st century BC under what is now the cathedral, is usually opened for visitors; the rest of the tunnels, several centuries older, are something of a mystery. Whatever their original purpose, some of them were converted into catacombs by the early Christian communities: the Catacomb of Santa Mustiola and the smaller Catacomb of Santa Caterina.

The Cathedral

Across the street from the museum, Chiusi's Cathedral is the oldest in Tuscany. Only parts of it—the recycled Roman columns in the nave—go back to the original 6th-century building. The cathedral was rebuilt in the 12th century and again in the 19th. Have a look at the mosaics that cover the walls inside. Astounding works they seem at first, an unknown chapter in early Christian art. Then you'll notice they have a touch of Art Nouveau about them—and finally you'll realize they aren't mosaics at all, but skilfully sponged-on squares of paint, a crazy masterpiece of mimicry completed in 1915. The small Cathedral Museum contains Roman fragments and some beautiful 15th-century illuminated choir books.

Around Chiusi: Lakes, Sarteano and the *Crete*

Just northeast of Chiusi, the **Lago di Chiusi** and the **Lago di Montepulciano** are pretty patches of blue on the border between Tuscany and Umbria, the smallest in the chain of lakes that begins with nearby Lago Trasimeno. Lago di Chiusi in particular makes a nice place for a picnic, not too far from the autostrada if you're on your way from Florence to Rome or Orvieto.

Nine km south of Chianciano or Chiusi, **Sarteano** is a smaller resort-spa, attached to a fine old hill town with some Renaissance palaces, a squarish medieval fortress, and the church of **San Martino in Foro**, with an *Annunciation* that is one of the best works of the Sienese Mannerist Beccafumi. Another 6km south of Sarteano, just off the ruggedly scenic S321, lies **Cetona**, a small, untouristed gem of a town, while along the S478 from Sarteano towards Monte Amiata you'll pass one of the loneliest, most barren regions of *crete* en route to the Val d'Orcia (*see* p.390).

© (0578–)   ***Where to Stay and Eating Out***

Chianciano

You may not be ready to entrust yourself to the thermal torture of the spa, but Chianciano can be a very useful place in July or August when hotels are booked solid everywhere else. The Azienda Autonima di Cura on Viale Roma 67 offers help with accommodation. Almost all of Chianciano's hotels were built in the last 30 years—nothing special, but there's a place to stay in every price range.

Chiusi

Most of the hotels are down by the railway station in Chiusi Scalo, unremarkable places like ★★★**Centrale**, Piazza Dante 3, © 20118 (*moderate*), with modern rooms. Chiusi has a famous restaurant; plenty of Italians in the know make the long detour off the Rome–Florence autostrada to **Zaira**, up at Via Arunte 12 in the oldest part of Chiusi, © 20260 (*moderate*). They come for the speculative 'Etruscan cuisine'. Surely the Etruscans, so often portrayed with plates of food on their funerary urns, had some tasty dishes, but every restaurant that tries imaginatively to reconstruct an Etruscan menu comes up with something different. No matter; it's a useful fancy, and with dishes here like the *pasta del lucumone* (with ham and three different cheeses), duck cooked in Vino Nobile, and pheasant *al cartoccio* it's hard to complain. Zaira takes special pride in the wine list; they have one of the largest cellars in Tuscany. It's good value too. *Closed Mon.* **La Casanova** on Strada della Vittoria 10, © 60449 (*expensive*), has good quality, typical food.

If your car can't climb the hill up to Chiusi, take it out to Lago di Chiusi to the north. At Conciarese al Lago, **La Fattoria**, © 21407 (*moderate*), is an old house with views over the lake, specializing in fresh fish from it, and every sort of roast and pasta dish made with *porcini* mushrooms. *Closed Mon.* Down in Sarteano (6km southwest of Chiusi), at Viale Europa 2, © 265 511, **La Giara** (*moderate*) is usually crowded with Sartanese, and with its home-made pasta, roast duck and lamb chops it's no surprise. *Closed Mon.* Even cheaper is **Da Gino**, Via Cabina Lago 42, © 21408. *Closed Wed.*

San Quirico d'Orcia, a humble little agricultural centre where the S146 from Pienza joins the S2, still has some of its medieval walls. The **Collegiata church**, rebuilt in the 12th century over an earlier 8th-century church, is the only reason for a visit; it has an exceptional façade and three portals from the 1200s, sculpted with lions and telamones. There are a couple of points of interest nearby: **Ripa d'Orcia**, a hamlet with a stately castle of its own, 7km south on a white road, and **Bagno Vignoni**, a small, modern spa town just to the south.

Before the modern S2 was built, the old Via Francigena traversed the valley of the Orcia, passing a patch of castles and fortified towns that began in the early Middle Ages. **Castiglione d'Orcia** (9km south of San Quirico) is as medieval-looking a town as you could ask for (though its cobbled piazza and fountain are from the 1600s). There are two parish churches, with Madonnas by three great Sienese artists—Martini and Pietro Lorenzetti in one and Il Vecchietta in the other. The ruined fortress overlooking the town was built by the Aldobrandeschi family, who controlled much of southern Tuscany as late as the 1200s. If you're spending time around Castiglione, get in touch with the Centro Agriturismo 'I Lecci', © 887287. They can arrange horses for tours of the countryside, hunting trips and nature excursions.

Another 15km south of Castiglione, **Vivo d'Orcia** began as a Camaldolensian monastery in 1003; when the monastery withered the village gradually replaced it, leaving only the pretty Romanesque Cappella dell'Ermicciolo in the woods above the town. **Bagni San Filippo**, some 8km east of Vivo, circling back towards the S2, may go into the books as the world's smallest thermal spa—a telephone booth, a few old houses, an outdoor spring with glistening limestone formations, and one small hotel. It takes its name from San Filippo Benizi, a holy hermit of the Middle Ages who hid here when he heard there was a movement to elect him pope.

Radicófani

Some wonderfully rugged countryside lies in the valley of the Orcia, east of this chain of villages, especially along the roads approaching **Radicófani**, a landmark of southern Tuscany, with its surreal, muffin-shaped hill topped by a lofty tower. The ruined fortress around it, originally built by Pope Adrian IV (the Englishman Nicholas Breakspear), served in the 1300s as headquarters for the legendary bandit Ghino di Tacco, solid citizen of Dante's *Inferno* and subject of a story in the *Decameron* (day 10, number 2), about how he imprisoned the Abbot of Cluny in this tower. The elegant loggias on the highway, just outside town, belong to the 17th-century Palazzo La Posta, once the only good hotel between Siena and Rome; most of the famous on the Grand Tour stopped on their way through.

Where to Stay

Bagno Vignoni © *(0577–)*

    Albergo Le Terme in Bagno Vignoni, © 887150, ✉ 887497 (*moderate*), was the summer house of Pope Pio II Piccolomini. It is now a comfortable hotel that overlooks a basin filled with hot spring water. To swim in the hot water go to the pool in the nearby **Hotel Posta Marcucci**, ✆ 887112, 🖷 887119 (*closed for cleaning on Thurs; adm*).

Radicofani ✆ (0578–)

La Palazzina, ✆ 55771, 🖷 53553 (*moderate*), has a pool, and a restaurant that serve delicious homegrown vegetables.

Abbadia San Salvatore and Monte Amiata

A thousand years ago, you might have heard of this town, home of the most important monastic centre in Tuscany and a fair-sized city in its own right. History passed by Abbadia San Salvatore a long time ago; today it makes a modest living as a mountain resort, the gateway to nearby Monte Amiata.

Getting Around

Transport isn't always easy around these towns if you don't have a car. Don't try to get there by train; there's a 'Monte Amiata station' on an infrequent branch line from Siena, but it's really some 40km on the other side of the mountain, near Castiglione d'Orcia. Buses stop on Viale Roma in the centre of Abbadia S. Salvatore (tickets and schedules in the toy store behind the information booth)—a few daily to Siena (79km/2½hrs), Montepulciano –Chiusi (48km/1½hrs) and Arcidosso (25km/1hr). Note that Arcidosso and the other towns on the west slope of Amiata are in Grosseto province; almost all the buses there go on to Grosseto.

Tourist Information

In Abbadia San Salvatore, Via Mentana 97 (2nd floor), ✆ (0578) 778 608 or 779 013; also a little booth (on Via Trieste by the bus stop) for information on Monte Amiata.

Abbadia San Salvatore

Abbadia (pop. 7900) at first glance seems a modern town, but just behind Viale Roma a narrow gateway leads into the grey, quiet streets of the **medieval centre**. It isn't very large, and there are no buildings of particular interest, but it is as complete and unchanged as any medieval quarter in Tuscany. Note the symbols carved into many of the doorways: coats of arms, odd religious symbols (a snake, for example) or signs like a pair of scissors that declare the original owner's profession.

The **Abbey Church** is outside the centre, a few blocks north in Via del Monastero; in the Middle Ages it must have been open countryside. According to legend—there's even a document telling the story, dated the Ides of March, 742—the Lombard King Rachis was on his way to attack Perugia when a vision of the Saviour appeared to him. Rachis not only founded the monastery, but retired to it as a monk. Historians think the whole business a convenient fabrication, but by 1000 the abbey had achieved considerable wealth and influence, ruling over a large piece of territory and waging occasional wars with the Bishop of Chiusi. In 1036, the present church was begun, an excellent Romanesque work that may seem plain to us, but was undoubtedly one of the grandest sights in Tuscany when it was new.

Behind the twin-steepled façade, the church is surprisingly long; the eastern end consists of a raised chancel, leading to a series of arches over the altar and choir; here is a series of quirky frescoes by an early 1700s artist named Nasino, telling the story of King Rachis. The **crypt** of King Rachis, under the chancel, was the original 8th-century church. The proportions and even the shapes of the arches are thoroughly Byzantine, with stone vaulting and oddly carved columns and capitals, no two alike.

South of Abbadia San Salvatore, **Piancastagnaio** is a smaller mountain resort. It has a **castle** of the Aldobrandeschi, with a small museum inside, a 17th-century palace and, as its name implies, lots of chestnut trees.

Abbadia San Salvatore ⓒ *(0577–)*　　　　**Where to Stay and Eating Out**

Abbadia San Salvatore has become a popular place, not just for winter skiing, but also as a cool retreat in the summer. There are a dozen or so hotels in town, including ★★★**Adriana**, a few blocks north of the centre at Via Serdini 76, ⓒ 778116, ✆ 777177 (*moderate*) and the newer ★★**San Marco**, on Via Matteotti 19, ⓒ and ✆ 778089 (*inexpensive*). The San Marco has a *ristorante-rosticceria* with a good menu; just down the street, **Da Aldo** also has an inexpensive menu—but you'd do better to pay a bit more for à la carte—good *pici* and *tortelli* (big south Tuscan zravioli), and roast meats. The menu seems to include beaver: *scottiglia di castoro!*

Monte Amiata

Monte Amiata, 13km west of Abbadia, an extinct volcano a bit over a mile high (1738m), is impressive enough in its setting. With no real competition west of the Apennines, it has become a skiing and hiking centre, a popular resort in both summer and winter. The presence of Europe's second-largest mercury mine (a complex that has been putting dinner on the table for Abbadia San Salvatore since the Middle Ages) does not detract from the natural beauty of the area. The lower slopes, where they are not cultivated, are largely covered in chestnut and beech forests—beautiful mature forests, at the higher altitudes, without so much of the usual Italian prickly underbrush and vipers. They turn colour marvellously in the autumn.

If you take the panoramic route around Amiata, here are some of the towns and villages you'll encounter: **Seggiano**, 20km northwest of Abbadia, where there's an unusual 16th-century church with a square cupola, the Madonna della Carità; pretty **Castel del Piano**, 7km south of Seggiano, with a lower town and upper *borgo*; and **Arcidosso**, another 4km south, the largest town (pop. 4500) on the Grosseto side of Amiata.

Arcidosso has been around for a long time; there's one church outside town, the triple-apsed Santa Maria in Lamula, begun in the 900s and redone in the 12th century. The town is best known, however, for the strange career of David Lazzaretti, a millenarian prophet gunned down by the Carabinieri during a disturbance in 1878. People in this area still talk about Lazzaretti; his movement, combining reformed religion and plain rural socialism (in an age when land reform was Italy's biggest social issue), spread widely in southern Tuscany. Before Lazzaretti's murder, his followers had started a sort of commune on **Monte Labbro**, 10km south. The tower, bits of buildings and remains of the church they built on Monte Labbro still stand, and a small number of the faithful occasionally hold 'Giurisdavidical' services there.

Above Arcidosso, another strong medieval **castle** testifies to the power of the Aldobrandeschi family. **Roccalbegna**, 20km south on S323, has another one, and a small collection of mostly Sienese art in its Oratorio del Crocifisso. The Aldobrandeschi also built at **Santa Fiora**, a pleasant town 7.5km south, with della Robbia terracottas in its three churches.

A large part of Monte Amiata has been made into a nature reserve, accessible only on foot (*open daily exc Mon dawn to sunset, © (0564) 966867*).

Activities

As one of the few good skiing areas close to Rome, Monte Amiata can be a busy place when the snow flies. The pistes begin almost at the very summit (decorated by the obligatory giant crucifix); to reach them there are two chair lifts and 15 ski lifts. The 15 runs (longest 1500m) are connected by paths through the forest. There is also a ski school. For snow news and other information, call the tourist office in Abbadia San Salvatore, © (0578) 778608. With a perfect landscape for it, cross-country skiing and hiking are also very popular here. A whole network of hiking trails have been marked, extending as far as Castiglione d'Orcia.

Where to Stay and Eating Out

© (0577–)

For skiing, there are pleasant new facilities; the ★★★**Rifugio Cantore**, © 789704 (*inexpensive*), stays open all year for summer mountaineering; it is located at 'secondo rifugio 10' along the road from Abbadia; a little further up, at Vette Amiata, there is the cosy ★★★**La Capannina**, © 789713 @ 789777 (*moderate*). The hotel restaurant is probably the best in the area; lots of dishes with mushrooms (including polenta, that northern Italian alternative to pasta that is also popular around here); also stuffed pigeon. *Open 15 Dec–Easter, also June–Sept.*

© (0577–)

If it's mushrooms you're after do not miss a meal at **L'Aiuole** in Loc. Aiole near Arcidosso, © 967300 (*moderate*), where the speciality is porcini mushroom soup; there are other sturdy dishes and excellent local cheeses. *Closed Mon in winter.*

Not many readers, we suspect, will be planning to spend some of their holiday in Saturnia or Pitigliano this year. Only a true connoisseur of regional obscurity would appreciate the inland reaches of Grosseto province, the largest stretch of territory in Italy (north of the Abruzzo) without a single compelling attraction. Once part of the Etruscan heartland, these towns have been poor and usually misgoverned ever since—by Romans, the Aldobrandeschi, the popes and the Tuscan dukes. Some people don't consider the area part of Tuscany at all, and it does seem to have more in common with the Lazio towns just to the south.

Southeast 20km from Santa Fiora, **Castell'Azzara** takes its name from a medieval game of dice (the word similar to our *hazard*); one of the Aldobrandeschi won it in a crap shoot. **Sorano**, a grim, grey town to the south, clings tenaciously to its rock. Bits of it have been sliding down into the surrounding valleys for centuries; after a big landslide the town was declared uninhabitable and largely abandoned, though efforts to restore it have been undertaken. Sorano is dominated by two equally grim castles; the larger is the 15th-century Rocca degli Orsini.

Sovana

Sovana, 10km west, with its population of about 190, is another medieval time capsule, a town almost perfectly preserved in its 13th- or 14th-century appearance. Sovana was an important Etruscan city, and in the 11th century it was thriving as the family headquarters of the Aldobrandeschi. This powerful clan, controlling much of southern Tuscany and northern Lazio, played a role in politics on a European level. The zenith of its influence came with the election to the papacy of one of its members in 1073. Gregory VII (his common name *Hildebrand* betrays the Aldobrandeschis' Teutonic origins) made a great reforming pope, the man who defeated the emperors in the great struggle over investiture, but he also took good care of the family interests.

On Sovana's humble main street, the Via di Mezzo, you can see the 13th-century Palazzo del Pretorio, with only a clock and bifore windows to betray its civic dignity. There is some interesting early Christian and medieval sculpture preserved in the 12th-century church of Santa Maria, and the **Duomo**, just outside the village, has an octagonal dome from the 900s, a crypt 200 years older, and some sculptural work on the façade that may have been recycled from a pagan temple. Just west of town, there is perhaps the best **Etruscan necropolis** in Tuscany (*open dawn–sunset daily*)—no paintings, but many architectural details carved out of the living rock have survived, notably in the temple-like construction called the 'Tomba Ildebranda'.

Pitigliano

Just 8km away is Pitigliano, another ominous-looking place that could be Sorano's twin. Pitigliano makes a memorable sight, its grey houses perched along the edges of the cliffs; underneath are countless holes in the cliff faces that once were Etruscan tombs, now often used as stables or storehouses. Its city walls are built on Etruscan foundations. Piazza della Repubblica, the centre of Pitigliano, has a big fountain and the 14th-century palace of the Orsini, the powerful Roman family that aced the Aldobrandeschi out of many of their holdings in southern Tuscany. There is another picturesque medieval centre, and a 16th-century aqueduct, running across Via Cavour. The alleys around Vicolo Manin, where a ruined synagogue still stands, were once Pitigliano's Jewish ghetto; the centuries-old Jewish community was decimated in 1945.

Saturnia

Little **Saturnia**, 25km west of Sovana, sits all by itself above the Val d'Albegna, one of the most ancient centres in Italy, claiming nothing less than to be the first city ever founded in Italy—by Saturn himself, in fact, during the Golden Age. The present village has the form of a Roman settlement, but fragments of monolithic, pre-Etruscan walls can be seen, and aerial photography has discerned traces of an older city beneath the Roman level. There are hot sulphur springs in the neighbourhood, still in use as they evidently were throughout antiquity; ruins are everywhere. **Manciano**, 12km to the south, has a Sienese fortress and not much else.

To the west on S323, **Magliano in Toscana** was given a fine set of walls by the Sienese. The city, heir to the Etruscan town of Heba, has a Sienese-style Palazzo dei Priori, and the church of San Giovanni Battista, with a Renaissance façade. Its best-known attraction, though, is the **Ulivo della Strega** (the witches' olive), a weirdly gnarled tree well over a thousand years old, said to be the site of ritual dances in pagan days, and still haunted today. The tree is just outside the town's Porta San Giovanni, near the Romanesque **Annunziata** church, with some good Sienese frescoes inside. About 2km southeast, on the road for Marsiliana, are the ruins of the 12th-century abbey of San Bruzio.

© (0564–)   ### Where to Stay and Eating Out

Real pioneers passing through this region will find reasonable food and accommodation throughout—though usually they'll have to look hard to find it. The region produces some good but little-known wines, notably Morellino di Scansano, a severe dry variety with a beautiful deep red colour.

Pitigliano

Just outside Pitigliano, the **★★Corano**, Loc. Corano on the S. Maremmana, © and ✉ 616112 (*inexpensive to moderate*), has 35 modern rooms and a pool. In town, the **★★Guastini** on Piazza Petruccioli 4, © 616065, ✉ 616652 (*rooms inexpensive to moderate*), has a restaurant (*moderate*) which specializes in homemade pasta, Bianco di Pitigliano wine, and 'Etruscan-style' dishes like *biglione d'agnello*, well worth the price.

Sovana

Try the Dark Ages ambience of the Piazza Pretorio and the ★★★**Taverna Etrusca**, ✆ 616183, ✆ (yes, a fax) 614193; roast boar and the other south Tuscan favourites (*moderate*); pleasant, simple rooms upstairs (*inexpensive, though prices double for the high season, July–Sept*). The ★**Scila,** Via del Duomo 5, ✆ 616531, ✆ 614329 (*moderate*), has inexpensive rooms and a nice restaurant where you can eat spinach and ricotta soup out on the terrace. *Closed Tues.*

Saturnia

Saturnia, being a spa of sorts, has a wider choice of restaurants. The best is in the ★★★★**Hotel Terme di Saturnia**, Strada Provinale della Follonato, ✆ 601061, ✆ 601266. It's hard to imagine anyone paying for the very expensive rooms up here, but the moderately priced restaurant repays a visit with fresh seafood, including a good *risotto marinaro*, besides game dishes like quail with olives.

Montemerano

For peace and quiet in the countryside, **Locanda Landomia** at Poderi di Montemerano, ✆ 620062, ✆ 620013 (*moderate*), is a good option. They have 12 pretty bedrooms all with lovely views of the landscape. The hotel's restaurant is over the road where *raviolo* and *aquacotta* (vegetable soup) are very good. In the hamlet of Montermerano (600 inhabitants) you can find the elegant restaurant, **Caino**, Via Canonica 3, ✆ 602817, ✆ 602807 (*very expensive*). The menu varies regularly according to the availability of fresh ingredients and the delicacies arrive on silver platters. *Closed Wed and Thurs lunch.*

Arezzo and its Province

to Rimini

La Verna

S208

Chiusi della Verna

Pieve Santo Stefano

Sestino

Badia Tedalda

Alpe della Luna

to Urbino

S73 bis

Caprese Michelangelo

Alpe di Catenaia

Sansepolcro

VALTIBERINA

Anghiari

Tiber

S3 bis

Monterchi

S73

Città di Castello

Foce di Scopetone

U   M   B   R   I   A

Castiglion Fiorentino

Montecchio

Convento delle Celle

Camucia

Umbertide

Cortona

Terontola

S3 bis

Tiber

Lake Trasimeno

PERUGIA

Between Florence and Umbria lies a lovely region of nature and art, most of which is included in the province of Arezzo. Watered by the newly born Arno and Tiber rivers (at one point they flow within a mere 15km of each other), it occupies a keystone position in Italy, not only geographically but as amazingly fertile ground for 'key' Italians: Masaccio and Cosimo il Vecchio's humanist Greek scholar and magician, Marsilio Ficino, were born in the Arno Valley; Petrarch, Michelangelo, Piero della Francesca, Paolo Uccello, Luca Signorelli, Andrea Sansovino, Vasari, the great satirist Aretino, Guido Monaco (inventor of the musical scale), Pietro da Cortona and the Futurist Gino Severini were born in Arezzo or its province. Because of its strategic location battlefields and castles dot the countryside, yet here too is St Francis's holy mountain of La Verna, where he received the stigmata.

There are two possible routes between Florence and Arezzo: the quick one, following the trains and Autostrada del Sole down the Valdarno, or the scenic route, through the Passo della Consuma or Vallombrosa, taking in the beautifully forested areas of Pratomagno and the Casentino.

The Valdarno: Florence to Arezzo ○

If a Tuscan caveman ever sang 'O give me a home, where the giant mammoth roam', he would have wanted to live in what is now the Arno Valley. In the Pliocene age the valley was a lake, a popular resort of ancient elephants, and farmers are not surprised when their ploughs collide with fossils. The typically Tuscan towns of the Valdarno, however, are hardly fossilized. On the contrary, it is a highly industrialized region: lignite and felt hats are important, but new factories and power-lines seem to be going up all the time. Besides the autostrada, the main valley routes are the old A69, and the beautiful 'Strada dei Sette Ponti', following the old Etruscan road of 'Seven Bridges' from Saltino by Vallombrosa to Castiglion Fibocchi, along what was once the upper shore of the ancient lake, between the Valdarno and the Pratomagno ridge. Along it, here and there, are areas strikingly eroded into pyramids, around Pian di Scò and Castelfranco. By public transport the Valdarno's peripheral attractions are harder to reach; buses from **Arezzo** to **Loro Ciuffenna** and **Castelfranco di Sopra** will take in much of the Strada dei Sette Ponti.

The most scenic route from Florence to the Valdarno follows the A1 down to Incisa (23km), although it's worth turning west at Torre a Cona for **Rignano sull'Arno**, with sculptures by Mino da Fiesole and Bernardino Rossellino in the church of San Clemente, and for **Sanmezzano** (2km across the Arno). A medieval castle here was converted into a Medici villa and in the 19th century purchased by the Ximenes d'Aragona family, who gave it a Spanish-Moorish fantasy face-lift. Down river, at **Incisa Valdarno**, cliffs and hills begin to squeeze the Arno; in the upper old town Petrarch spent his childhood. There's an old bridge off which, the Italians claim, Lucrezia Borgia jumped in 1529, fleeing the Prince of Orange, despite the fact that she had died in childbirth 10 years earlier.

Five kilometres south, **Figline Valdarno** (pop. 15,000) was, in 1439, the birthplace of Ficino, after whom the main piazza is named. The historic centre, especially around the piazza, has preserved much of its character from Ficino's day: the loggia of the old Serristori Hospital, the Palazzo Pretorio, and the **Collegiata di Santa Maria**, containing a beautiful painting of the *Madonna with Child and Angels* by the 14th-century 'Maestro di Figline' and a fresco by the school of Botticelli among its works of art.

San Giovanni Valdarno

Tourist Information

Palazzo d'Arnolfo, Piazza Cavour 1, ✆ (055) 9126320/9126321, ✉ (055) 9120152.

If you're only planning one stop in the Valdarno, San Giovanni (pop. 19,500) is the logical choice: it is one of the most industrial towns but also one of the most interesting. The Florentines fortified it in the 13th century against the warlike Aretini and sent Arnolfo di Cambio, a jack of all trades like most artists of his day, to lay out the streets for defensive purposes, and to design for the centre the handsome arcaded **Palazzo Comunale**; its arches are echoed by the buildings giving on to the piazza, and are covered with a collage of escutcheons left by local Florentine governors. The oft-restored **Basilica di Santa Maria delle Grazie** (1486), with a rich 17th-century interior, has a *Madonna, Child and Four Saints*, long attributed to native son Masaccio (1401–28), a beautiful *Annunciation* by Jacopo del Sellaio, Baroque paintings by Giovanni di San Giovanni (also born here, 1592–1636), and an interesting fresco of a local miracle, in which a grandmother is suddenly able to give milk to her starving grandchild (14th century); earlier frescoes adorn the Gothic church of **San Lorenzo**. Best of all, 2.5km south of San Giovanni at the Renaissance **Convento di Montecarlo**, is an enchanting *Annunciation* by Fra Angelico, in deep, rich colours, seemingly a model for the *Annunciation* in Florence's San Marco, though here Adam and Eve can be seen off to the left, fleeing the Garden of Eden. From the convent the road continues to the Monti del Chianti by way of **Cavriglia**; the hills are scarred with the amphitheatres of open lignite mines. Yet not all the earth is exploited: Cavriglia is also the site of a Nature Park, where modern deer and buffalo roam in the company of other animals from around the world.

The Valdarno also offers a look at former animals, especially the large *elephas meridionalis* in the **Museo Paleontologico** in **Montevarchi** (*open 9–12 and 4–7, Sun 10–12, closed Mon and Sept–June*). Montevarchi is a major marketing centre of the region, famous for its hats and chickens; in its ancient core, you can trace the oval medieval street plan. In the centre of town stands the old **Collegiata di San Lorenzo**, which had a complete face-lift in the 18th century. Within it is an unusual reliquary 'of the holy milk', brought from a cave in the Holy Land where the Holy Family is said to have rested and where a fountain of milky water flows; a small museum holds a quattrocento **Tempietto** covered inside and out with Andrea della Robbia's cherub friezes. In Rendola, 6km south, there's a **riding**

stable, Rendola Riding, ✆ (055) 987045 (*open late Sept–early June*). Across the Arno, **Terranuova Bracciolini** is an old Aretine fortress town, its walls still standing.

Along the Road of Seven Bridges

East of the Arno, the panoramic Strada dei Sette Ponti passes several medieval towns en route to Arezzo. **Reggello** (8km east of Sanmezzano) stands amid its famous olive groves in a beautiful setting; some of its streets retain their medieval arcades, and the 12th-century parish church of **San Pietro a Cascia** has good, early Romanesque columns with carved capitals depicting striking figures on horseback and other lively scenes. **Castelfranco di Sopra**, 12km south, was another Florentine military town laid out by Arnolfo di Cambio, with fine palaces, and to the north at **Pulicciano**, you'll find a landscape eroded into pyramidical forms, or *balze*, more common around Volterra. Oddly named **Loro Ciuffenna** offers some picturesque medieval corners, a Romanesque bridge and tower, and a triptych by Lorenzo di Bicci in **Santa Maria Assunta**. Best of all is the tiny 12th-century parish church of **Grópina** (from the Etruscan *Kropina*), 2km away, an excellent example of rural Romanesque. Although it was referred to in the 8th century, the current church was built in the early 1200s. Dominated by its huge campanile, the façade is simplicity itself, while the three naves and little semicircular apse have never been altered; the columns are carved with primitive tigers, eagles, etc., while the round marble **pulpit** is a bizarre relic of the Dark Ages, carved with archaic figures raising their arms over a marble knot; over them is a kind of totem pole, geometrical and floral decorations, and a sexy siren with a snake whispering sweet nothings in her ear. **Castiglion Fibocchi**, 13km from Arezzo, is another typical town where little has changed, except for the industry on its outskirts.

✆ *(055–)*   ***Where to Stay and Eating Out***

In Figline Valdarno, you can have a comfortable stay in ★★★**Antica Taverna Casagrande**, ✆ 9544851, 🖷 9544322 (*expensive*); 13 rooms and a garden. At the elegant **Vicolo del Contento**, in Castelfranco di Sopra, Loc. Mandri 38, ✆ 9149277/9149906 (*expensive*), the cuisine matches the decor: delicious ravioli filled with crab meat, well-prepared meat and fresh fish, followed, perhaps, by a slice of *pecorino* from Pienza. Fine Chianti and other wines. *Closed Mon evening and Tues.*

At Montevarchi, ★★★**Delta**, Via Diaz 137, ✆ 901213, 🖷 901727 (*moderate*), is the best hotel in town, with a garage, air conditioning and TV in each room. At tiny **Adriano**, in Piazza Masaccio 15, San Giovanni Valdarno, ✆ 9122470 (*moderate*), you can dine on the local stew *stufato alla sangiovannese*, homegrown roast chicken, home-made desserts and wines from all over Tuscany. **Da Giovanni**, Piazza della Libertà 24, ✆ 9122726 (*inexpensive*), serves typical Tuscan fare in a family-run place. *Closed Wed.* In Castelfranco di Sopra, **Il Corvo**, Via Sette Ponti, ✆ 9149011, has excellent fish.

Pratomagno and Vallombrosa

The Strada dei Sette Ponti skirts the west rim of Pratomagno, not a big meadow as its name suggests, but a forested mountain ridge. Its highest peak, Croce di Pratomagno (1592m), is due north of Loro Ciuffenna; winding roads from Loro go through tiny mountain hamlets, while the Loro–Talla route crosses over into the Casentino.

Other roads from the west into the Casentino are much further to the north. The two routes from Florence, both taking in fine, wooded scenery, are S70 over the **Passo della Consuma** (1025m), a favourite Italian rest stop, and the secondary route through **Vallombrosa** ('shady valley'), famous for its abbey founded by San Giovanni Gualberto of Florence, and still the headquarters of his Vallombrosan order. The abbey itself has gone through enlargements and remodellings in the 15th and 17th centuries and is mainly of interest for its splendid position, while **Saltino**, a kilometre away, is a small summer resort surrounded by firs where most people end up, an excellent base for walking or motoring excursions. One of the most beautiful routes is the road up to the Monte Secchieta (1449m), affording views over most of north-central Italy; in the winter the skiing facilities spring into action. For a longer outing, drive or walk along the newly opened **Panoramica del Pratomagno**, which crosses nearly the entire Pratomagno to join the Strada dei Sette Ponti near Castiglion Fibocchi.

The Casentino: North to South

The Casentino's blue mountains, pastoral meadows and velvet valleys have long been Tuscany's spiritual refuge. Since the 18th century, travellers have trickled into the area, attracted initially by its famous monasteries, then charmed by one of the loveliest and most peaceful regions in Tuscany.

The Arno, such a turgid, unmannerly creature in its lower reaches ('the emblem of Despair', Norman Douglas once called it), is a fair, sparkling youth near its source at Monte Falterona (1658m); one of the classic excursions is to take the trail up and spend the night, to witness the sunset over the Tyrrhenian sea and dawn over the Adriatic. **Stia** (pop. 3000), the first town the Arno meets, is pretty and medieval, centred about large porticoed Piazza Tanucci and **Santa Maria Assunta**. The 17th-century façade hides a fine Romanesque interior, with some curious, primitive capitals, a triptych by Lorenzo di Bicci and a Madonna by Andrea della Robbia. Wool—the thick, heavy, brightly coloured *lana del Casentino*—is the main industry; in the old days Stia was the market for the Guidi counts, whose ruined **Castello** at Porciano guarded the narrow Arno valley from the 10th century. Near this (4km north of Stia) is the **Sanctuary of Santa Maria delle Grazie**, a 14th-century church with frescoes, works attributed to Luca della Robbia, and a painting by Lorenzo di Niccolò Gerini. This road continues into the Mugello (*see* p.205), while the S310 from Stia goes around the other side of Monte Falterona towards the **Passo la Calla** and Emilia-Romagna; near the pass the Alpine pasture **Burraia** (15km from Stia) is a good place for a cool summer picnic.

Down the Arno from Stia, **Pratovecchio** was the birthplace of Paolo Uccello in 1397, and chances are he'd still recognize its narrow, porticoed lanes. A couple of kilometres from the centre is the most beautiful Romanesque church of the Casentino, **Piero di Romena**, founded in 1152, which has retained its original lines in spite of several earthquakes and subsequent repairs. Although the façade is plain, the apse has two tiers of blind arcades, pierced by narrow windows. Inside, the well-preserved capitals are decorated with a medieval menagerie of people, animals and monsters. Among the works of art, dating back to the 1200s, is a Madonna by the Maestro di Varlungo. Nearby, the Guidis' **Castello di Romena** was one of the most powerful in the Casentino, with its three sets of walls and 14 towers (now reduced to three), and wide-ranging hilltop views down the Casentino. Dante mentioned it in the *Inferno*, as well as the **Fonte Branda**, the ruins of which are close by.

Dante knew this region well; at the age of 24 he fought with the Guelphs against the Ghibellines of Arezzo and their allies at the Battle of **Campaldino** (1289), a small plain just to the south of Pratovecchio. The victory was of paramount importance for Florence; it made her the leading power in Tuscany, and from there she went on to conquer Pisa and Arezzo. A column commemorating the battle was erected near the crossroads in 1921. At the head of the plain, just off the S70, Countess Matilda's **Castel San Nicolò**, the wee medieval hamlet of **Strada** and its little Romanesque church form a picturesque ensemble in the wooded hills.

Poppi and Camaldoli

Between 1000 and 1440 the Casentino was ruled by the Counts Guidi, who had their headquarters in the compact little bump of a hill town of **Poppi** (pop. 5700), set above a charming landscape of low rolling hills. From miles around you can see the Guidis' stalwart and erect **Castello**, modelled on the Palazzo Vecchio in Florence. The best-preserved medieval castle in the region, it has a magnificent courtyard, emblazoned with coats of arms and stairs that zigzag to and fro with a touch of Piranesi. If you ask the custodian, he'll show you the grand hall with Florentine frescoes of the 1400s, the frescoed chapel, and the commanding views from the tower.

The centre of Poppi is made up of ancient porticoed lanes, winding around a small domed chapel with a train station clock; at the end of Poppi's long, arcaded, main street is the Romanesque church of **San Fedele**, with a 13th-century Madonna and child. Shops selling locally-made copperware line the main street of lower Poppi (or Ponte a Poppi), and there's the little **Zoo Fauna Europea** for the kids.

A beautiful road northeast leads up from Poppi to the ancient hermitage and monastery of **Camaldoli**, founded in 1012 by St Romualdo. Romualdo was a Benedictine monk who longed to found a community of hermits similar to those of the early Christians, and was given this forest by Count Maldolo (hence the name 'Camaldoli'). A conflict, however, arose even during the lifetime of Romualdo, for the piety of the hermits soon attracted pilgrims and visitors who interfered with their solitary meditations. Romualdo's solution was ingenious: to found another community lower down, a monastery with a more relaxed rule, whose sole purpose was to entertain visitors and care for the forest domains that belonged to the order. Perhaps of all monastic orders, the Camaldolese are the most ecologically minded; self-sufficient vegetarians whose rule orders them to plant at least 5000 new trees every year. Little remains of San Romualdo's original foundation, except for portions of the 11th-century cloister, the rich library, and the 16th-century pharmacy, where the monks sell their balsams, herbal remedies and liqueurs. Some 300m further up, a beautiful hour's walk, is the **Eremo**, or Hermitage (only men admitted past the gate), with its 20 cottages in an amphitheatre of pines, each with its own chapel and walled kitchen garden, where the hermits live silent and solitary existences, meeting only on certain feast days and in the church, which was decorated inside by Vasari and has two marble tabernacles by Desiderio da Settignano.

Badia Prataglia, 10km from Camaldoli, is the region's most popular secular retreat, a summer resort spread out among the trees and hills, with beautiful walks along streams and waterfalls leading off in all directions.

Bibbiena and La Verna

Only a few kilometres from Poppi, the modern Casentino's chief town, **Bibbiena**, has been enveloped in sprawl and lacks Poppi's quaint charm, though in its heart it retains its old Tuscan feel. Few buildings stand out—a good Renaissance palace, **Palazzo Dovizi**, and the church of **San Lorenzo**, where there are some excellent polychrome terracottas by Andrea della Robbia. From Bibbiena, S208 crosses east over into a range of hills bravely called the Alpe di Catenaia, which divides the Arno from the Tiber valley, to the famous Franciscan monastery of **La Verna**, high up on a bizarre rocky outcrop, which, according to one of St Francis's visions, had been rent and blasted into its wild shape at the moment of the Crucifixion. The land was given to Francis in 1213 by another pious nobleman, Count Orlando, and the saint at once built some mud huts here for a select group of his followers. He found La Verna a perfect spot for meditation, and came to his holy mountain on six different occasions. During the last, on 14 September 1224, he became the first person ever to receive the stigmata—an event pictured in the frescoes of Assisi and elsewhere—after which he could only walk in extreme pain. The churches, chapels and convent at La Verna are simple and rustic, though the main church, the chapel of Stigmata and St Francis's tiny church of **Santa Maria degli Angeli** are decorated by the most transcendently beautiful blue, green and white terracottas Andrea della Robbia ever made, especially the wonderful *Annunciation* in the nave. You can also visit the **Sasso Spicco**, Francis's favourite retreat under a huge boulder, and **La Penna** (1283m), on a sheer precipice, with romantic views of the Arno and Tiber valleys. The nearby village of Chiusi della Verna is a small resort and there are many summer homes in the area.

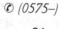

© (0575–)

Where to Stay and Eating Out

Stia

Try **Falterona o Filetto**, Piazza Tanucci 28, © 58631 (*moderate*), which offers *pappardelle* with wild boar. They also have nine cheap rooms in the piazza at No.85, © 58797 (*inexpensive*). **La Roma**, Località Tirasso, © 582226 (*moderate*), pleasantly situated in a forest on the banks of the Arno, is a family-run affair specializing in choice home-produced *charcuterie*. ★★**La Buca**, Via Fiorentina 2, © 58797 (*inexpensive*), has simple, good accommodation, with bathroom; it is a friendly, family-run hotel—if a bit dark.

Poppi

★★**Casentino**, Piazza Repubblica, © 529090, right opposite the castle (*inexpensive*), is a shady little *pensione*—the only one up in the old town. Down in the lower town, Ponte a Poppi, ★★**Campaldino**, Via Roma 95, © 529008, ✆ 529032 (*inexpensive*), is a little inn in business since 1800. There are 10 simple rooms; in the pretty, old-fashioned dining room upstairs (*moderate*) you can dine on tasty local *prosciutto*, ravioli filled with vegetables and *ricotta*, and succulent lamb and chicken, and for dessert, *semifreddi* made *in casa*. A couple of kilometres from the monastery at Camaldoli, ★★★**Il Rustichello**, Via del Corniolo 14, © and ✆ 556046 (*inexpensive*), is a small but modern resort hotel, a great place to bring the kids; attractions include tennis, mini golf and walks in the woods. The hotel's restaurant (*moderate*) is a good place to stop even if you're not staying, featuring great pasta dishes from nearby Emilia-Romagna, grilled meats, and Casentino cheeses.

Arezzo

Strategically located on a hill at the convergence of the valleys of the Valdarno, Casentino and the Valdichiana, ancient Arezzo (pop. 92,000) was one of the richest cities of the Etruscan Dodecapolis. Nor is modern Arezzo a loser in the money game—it has one of the biggest jewellery industries in Europe, with hundreds of small firms stamping out gold chains and rings, and bank vaults full of ingots. Its second most notable industry, one that fills the shops around its main Piazza Grande, is furniture making and marketing antiques; on the first Sunday of each month the entire square becomes an enormous antique curiosity shop.

Arezzo itself is a bit of an antique curiosity shop. It had only a brief, but remarkable, moment in the Renaissance sunshine, though in the Middle Ages it was a typical free *comune*, a Ghibelline rival to Florence and a city of great cultural distinction. Around the year 1000 it was the birthplace of Guido Monaco (or Guido d'Arezzo), inventor of musical notation and the musical scale; in the 13th century it produced Margarito, an important painter in the transition from the Byzantine to the Italian styles. In 1304 Petrarch, the 'first modern man', was born here into a banished Florentine Black Guelph family; his Arezzo contemporary was Spinello Aretino, one of Tuscany's trecento masters. Arezzo was at its most powerful in the early 1300s, when it was ruled by a remarkable series of warrior bishops. One died in the Battle of Campaldino; another, the fierce Guido Tarlati, ruled the city 1312–27. He expanded its territory, built new walls, settled internal bickerings, renewed warfare with Florence and Siena, and was excommunicated. After Bishop Guido

N

Arezzo

200 metres
200 yards

San Domenico

Casa
Vasari

Piazza
S. Domenico

VIA SAN DOMENICO

VIA GIUSEPPE GARIBALDI

VIA DI SAN LORENTINO

VIA 20 SETTEMBRE

Museo d'Arte
Medioevale e Moderna

PIAGGIA DI MURELLO

VIA LEONE LEONI

Santissima
Annunziata

VIA GIUSEPPE GARIBALDI

VIA CAVOUR

VIA SASSOVERDE

VIA MADONNA LAURA

Duomo

VIA RICASOLI / Piazza
del Duomo

Palazzo
del Comune

VIA DEI PILETI

Passeggio
del Prato

VIALE BRUNO BUOZZI

VIA PORTA BUIA

VIA DELLA FIORINA

VIA ANDREA CESALPINO

Petarch's
House

Medici
Fortress

SS. Flora
e Lucilla in Badia

Palazzetto della
Fraternità dei
Laici

Palazzo
del Popolo

Piazza
del Popolo

VIA CAVOUR

CORSO ITALIA

Piazza
Grande

Loggia
Vasari

Santa
Maria
delle Pieve

VIA GUIDO MONACO

San Francesco

VIA FRANCESCO PETRACA

VIA GIUSEPPE GARIBALDI

VIA DEL PRATO

VIA G. MAZZINI

VIA PELLICCERIA

Piazza
G. Monaco

VIA G. OBERDAN

CORSO ITALIA

BORGO DI S.CROCE

VIALE PIERO DELLA FRANCESCA

VIA FRA' GUITTONE

VIA GUIDO MONACO

VIA MADONNA

Piazza
S. Agostino

GIUSEPPE GARIBALDI

VIA D. MINERVA

VIA FONTANELLA

Piazzale
Repubblica

VIA VITTORIO VENETO

VIALE

VIA NICCOLÒ ARETINO

VIA MARGARITONE

VIA FRANCESCO CRISPI

VIA PIETRO ARETINO

VIA RODI

Train
Station

T

MICHELANGELO

Roman Amphitheatre
and Archaeology Museum

VIA ANTONIO GUADAGNOLI

VIA ANTONIO GUADAGNOLI

VIALE LUCA SIGNORELLI

VIALE GIOTTO

VIA TRASIMENO

VIALE MECENATE

to Santa Maria
delle Grazie

Parco
Giotto

407

came the deluge—his brother sold the city for a brief period to Florence, family rivalries exploded, the plague carried away half the population, and to top it all, in 1384 the French troops of Louis d'Anjou sacked the city and brought it to its knees, refusing to move on until Arezzo paid 40,000 florins. Florence came up with the ransom money, and in effect purchased Arezzo's independence. Although henceforth an economic backwater, on the fringe of the Renaissance, it managed to produce two leading personalities: Giorgio Vasari and Pietro Aretino, the uninhibited writer and poet whose celebrated poison pen allowed him to make a fortune by *not* writing about contemporary princes and popes—the most genteel extortionist of all time.

Getting Around

From Florence (75km/1½hrs), Perugia (73km/1½hrs), and Cortona (32km/45mins), the train is the easiest way to reach Arezzo; the station is at the southern end of town, where Via Guido Monaco crosses Viale Piero della Francesca and the old city walls. Buses for Cortona and other towns in Arezzo province, as well as for Siena, leave from the station directly opposite on Viale Piero della Francesca, © (0575) 22663. The little LFI trains from Arezzo to the Casentino are being restored like everything else in Italy, and at the time of writing only go as far as Subbiano, where buses meet the train.

Tourist Information

Piazza Risorgimento 116 (one block north of the station, and one block to the right from Via Guido Monaco), © (0575) 23952. There is another office in Piazza della Repubblica 22, © (0575) 377678. For information on any aspect of Arezzo's gold industry, Sindico Orafi Aretini, © (0575) 300761.

San Francesco

If you arrive by train or bus, Via Guido Monaco leads up to the old centre of Arezzo by way of a stern statue of musical monk Guido, and passes on the left one of Italy's prettiest post offices with an ornate ceiling, before ending in Piazza San Francesco, site of **San Francesco** (*open 8.30–12 and 1.30–7*). This dowdy barn of a Franciscan church contains the star attraction in Arezzo: Piero della Francesca's frescoes on the popular pseudo-classical/Christian subject of the *Legend of the Cross* (*see* **Florence**, 'Santa Croce', p.153), the most riveting cycle of frescoes of the 1400s and the gospel of Renaissance painting, the ideal—other works seem mere commentary. Piero literally wrote the book on the new science of artificial perspective, and yet as strictly as these frescoes obey the dictates of the vanishing point they make no concessions to realism; simplified and drawn with geometrical perfection, Piero's beings are purely spiritual creatures. It is intriguing that Piero and Uccello, the two artists most obsessed with perspective and space, should have created the most transcendent art; few compositions are as haunting as Piero's *Dream of Constantine*, a virtuoso piece of night lighting, colouring, and perspective, the angel swooping down from the upper left-front of the scene—and yet all is uncannily still, the scene of the dream itself like a dream; the soldiers stand guard, woodenly unaware, the sleeping emperor's attendant gazes out with a bored expression. Note too the rather uncanonical *Annunciation* in which Gabriel announces both the birth and death of her son to Mary.

The fact that Piero's frescoes exist at all is nothing short of a miracle. The walls have been damaged by an earthquake, struck by lightning, burned twice, and shot at by Napoleon's troops, who also scratched the eyes of the figures. To keep the church standing after so much abuse, the first restorers injected tons of cement into the walls, which, combined with humidity, nearly ruined the frescoes once and for all. Although the frescoes were cleaned in the 1960s, no attempt was made to protect them from further damage. However, the massive restoration project (due to finish by the end of 1996) will address both problems, and everyone has their fingers crossed that it works.

Piazza Grande

Few *piazze* in Italy have the eclectic charm of Arezzo's **Piazza Grande**, the perfect back-drop for the monthly antiques fair and the *Giostra del Saracino* in early September. On this occasion, the town sports from the four quarters of Arezzo don 13th-century costume to re-enact an event that was first documented in 1593, a celebration of the feats of arms against Saracen pirates who menaced the Tyrrhenian coast, and penetrated inland even as far as Arezzo. Revived in 1932, the festival begins with a parade of costumes and flag-tossing by the *sbandieratori*, and is followed by a test of individual prowess between eight knights, two representing each quarter, who tilt against a wooden figure named 'Buratto, king of the Indies' for the prize of a golden lance.

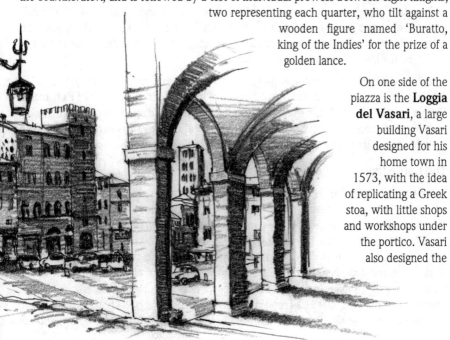

On one side of the piazza is the **Loggia del Vasari**, a large building Vasari designed for his home town in 1573, with the idea of replicating a Greek stoa, with little shops and workshops under the portico. Vasari also designed the clock tower of the **Palazzetto della Fraternità dei Laici**, an old ornate building, half Gothic and half by Renaissance master Bernardo Rossellino. Although it looks like a town hall, the palazzo is really the home of a lay brotherhood founded in the 1200s. Arezzo's old Palazzo del Popolo exists only in ruins, behind Vasari's loggia on Via dei Pileati. Like Pisa's, it was destroyed by the Florentines after they captured the city.

Santa Maria della Pieve

Perhaps most impressive on Piazza Grande is the round, Romanesque arcaded apse of Arezzo's great 12th-century church of **Santa Maria della Pieve**; rather eccentrically it turns its back on the piazza, while directing its unusual Pisan-Lucchese façade towards narrow Via dei Pileati, where it's hard to see well. Few things in Tuscany look as ancient as these four tiers of shallow arcades, rough hewn and eroded like a vertical stone cliff. Each tier of arches is successively narrower, in a unique rustic style with no two columns or capitals alike (*covered for restoration at time of writing*). The campanile 'of a hundred holes' has so many neat rows of double-mullioned windows it resembles a primitive skyscraper, complete with a protruding elevator shaft.

Under the arch of the front portal, note the interesting early medieval *Reliefs of the Twelve Months*: April with her flowers, February with his pruning hook, and the pagan two-headed god Janus for January. The dim interior has an early Romanesque relief of the *Three Magi* on the entrance wall and finely decorated capitals in the nave. Like many early churches, the presbytery is raised above the low crypt, the most ancient part of the church, with primitive capitals—human faces mingling with rams, bulls and dragons. On the left wall there's another primitive relief of the *Nativity* and *Christ's Baptism*, while above in the choir is a beautiful polyptych by Pietro Lorenzetti (1320), which has been recently restored to its glimmering original appearance, featuring the *Madonna and Saints* modelling the latest Tuscan fashions and fabrics.

Below Santa Maria descends Corso Italia, Arezzo's main evening parade, while above, Via dei Pileati continues up into the oldest quarter of the city, passing by way of **Petrarch's House** (*open 10–12, 3–5, closed Sat*), a replacement for the original bombed in the last war; it stands near the picturesque 14th-century **Palazzo del Pretorio**, decked with coats of arms of imperial and Florentine governors.

The Cathedral

Narrow streets from the Piazza Grande lead up to the **Passeggio del Prato**, an English-style park with lawns, trees, a café, and a big white elephant of a Fascist monument to Petrarch. All of Arezzo slopes gradually upwards from the railway station, ending abruptly here; from the cliffs on the edge of the Prato there is a memorable view over the mountains, extending towards Florence and Urbino. Overlooking the park is a half-ruined Medici fortress of the 1500s and at the other end is the back of the **Cathedral**, with a lovely Gothic bell tower—from the 19th century. The cathedral, built in bits and pieces over the centuries (1276–1510), has a nondescript façade but several great works of art in its sombre, dimly lit Gothic naves, not the least of which are its stained-glass windows created by the greatest 16th-century master of the art, the Frenchman Guillaume de Marcillat, seeming almost like illuminated frescoes by a Gozzoli or a Luca Signorelli. The magnificent marble Gothic High Altar is dedicated to San Donato, and there are impressive tombs—the first is of Pope Gregory X (1205–76) with a canopy and 4th-century sarcophagus, holding the mortal dust of the pope who holds the record for taking the longest to be elected; the enclave, in Viterbo, lasted from 1268 to 1271, and only ended when the Viterbans starved the cardinals into deciding. The second, even more impressive, is the 1327 **Tomb of Bishop Guido Tarlati**, a fascinating early predecessor of the heroic sculptural tombs of the Renaissance, perhaps designed by Giotto. The tomb is divided into three sections, with a relief resembling a miniature theatre and a Ghibelline eagle like a party badge on top; below lies the battling bishop's effigy; and below that, 16 fine relief panels that tell the story of his life, his battles and his good works. Near it is Piero della Francesca's fresco of the *Magdalene* holding a crystal pot of ointment. The **Museo del Duomo** (*open 10–12 Thurs, Fri and Sat; ring © 23991 for information*) contains detached frescoes by Spinello Aretino and his son Parri di Spinello, a terracotta *Annunciation* by Bernardo Rossellino, and paintings by 13th-century master Margarito d'Arezzo, Signorelli and Vasari.

Art Museum

Open 9–7; adm.

Diagonally opposite the cathedral stands Arezzo's Ghibelline **Palazzo del Comune** with its distinctive tower; from here Via Ricasoli descends past the birthplace of Guido Monaco (with a plaque of Guido's do-re-mi), to the **Museo d'Arte Medioevale e Moderna**, where you can get to know some local medieval and Renaissance artists not often seen elsewhere. The collection is housed in a medieval palace, remodelled in the Renaissance, perhaps by Bernardo Rossellino, and later used as a customs house. All is arranged chronologically: the attractive courtyard contains medieval columns and capitals, a fine sculpted horse's head and gargoyles, while the two rooms on the ground floor contain sculptural details from the cathedral façade and a fine 10th-century *pluteo* carved with peacocks. Among the works on the first floor are a stylized Byzantine *St Francis* by Margarito d'Arezzo, painted just after the saint's death and an *Enthroned Virgin* by Guido da Siena, studded with chunky, plasticky gems. Next you'll find detached frescoes by Spinello Aretino, the city's greatest trecento artist, and by his son, Parri di Spinello (1387–1453), whose ghostly battle scene, the *Sconfitta di Massenzio*, was discovered in the Badia after the war; the museum also has one of his beautifully dressed Madonnas. Another native of Arezzo, Bartolomeo della Gatta, painted the plague saint Rocco praying to liberate the city from the Black Death. Also on the first floor is a fresco attributed to Signorelli; a huge busy canvas by Vasari of *Esther's Wedding Banquet*; a collection of small Renaissance bronzes, including a bear with a monkey on his head; beautiful ceramics from Urbino, Deruta, Montelupo and a plate by Master Giorgio of Gubbio with his secret red. On the second floor there's a strange painting by Angelo Cacoselli (d. 1652) called the *Maga*, of an enchantress with her animals, a small room of 18th-century Neapolitan *presepi* figurines, and some splashy Mannerist canvases by Vasari, Allori and the great Rosso Fiorentino.

Vasari, Cimabue and more Vasari

Around the corner, on Via 20 Settembre 55, is the **Casa del Giorgio Vasari** (*open 9–7, ring bell*). Vasari was so fond of his own brand of spineless Mannerism that he wasn't about to leave it all for Duke Cosimo, but decorated his own house with the same fluff. Mediocrity attracts mediocrity; besides the frescoes there are several rooms of nondescript paintings, of which three stand out: the most repugnant St Sebastian ever committed to canvas, a terracotta portrait of Galba, one of Rome's ugliest mugs, by Sansovino, and a painting by a follower of Santi di Tito, of Christ and the Apostles dining in a 17th-century greasy spoon.

From Vasari's house, Via San Domenico will take you to the 13th-century church of **San Domenico**, with a simple asymmetrical exterior and a fine stone Gothic chapel (1360s) on the right wall, while the rest of the walls are covered with frescoes that overlap like the funny colour pages mouldering on the bottom of a canary cage. The main altar has a crucifix by Cimabue (*c.* 1265); the chapel to the left contains a fine triptych of the Archangel Michael by the 'Maestro del Vescovado'.

Via Garibaldi from the art museum returns to the centre by way of **Santissima Annunziata**, Arezzo's late response to Brunelleschi, begun by Bartolomeo della Gatta in the 1490s and completed by Antonio da Sangallo; the fourth altar has a painting by Pietro da Cortona and in the choir there's a stained-glass window by Marcillat. Further up, off Via Porta Buia, stands **Santissime Flora e Lucilla in Badia**, a 13th-century church with an unusual interior remodelled by Vasari. He also designed the two-sided altar, with reliefs from the Gospel of St Matthew on the front and St George slaying the dragon on the back. Over the presbytery the impressive cupola is actually a masterful fake by 17th-century *trompe-l'oeil* master Andrea Pozzo. On the entrance wall there's a good fresco of St Lawrence by della Gatta; the fine cloister is by Giuliano da Maiano, a student of Brunelleschi (entrance No. 2, Piazza della Badia).

Roman Amphitheatre and the Archaeology Museum

On the southern edge of Arezzo, near the station on Via Margaritone, the remains of a small **Roman Amphitheatre** have become a quiet city park. A former monastery, built on a curve over the amphitheatre's foundations, has been restored to house the **Museo Archeologico** (*open 9–2, 9–1.30 Sun, closed Mon; adm*). Not much has survived of the thriving Etruscan and Roman city of *Arretium*, but there are some mosaics and sarcophagi, Etruscan urns and Greek vases, examples of the Roman-era red *corallino* vases and an excellent portrait of a rather jaded-looking middle-aged Roman, worked in gold.

Finally, you can take a 15-minute walk from Via Mecenate out through Arezzo's southern suburbs to see a simple but exceptionally pretty Renaissance church, **Santa Maria delle Grazie**, finished in 1444 and given a delicate jewel of a loggia by Benedetto da Maiano, in 1482. On the main altar, in a colourful tabernacle by Andrea della Robbia, is Parri di Spinello's *Madonna della Misericordia* (1430).

No hotels in Arezzo really stand out; unlike some of Tuscany's art cities, the forces of tourism have yet to convert old villas into modern accommodation. What the city does have is clean, comfortable, and up-to-date, but nothing to tempt you into lingering. If you're travelling by car, ★★★**Minerva**, Via Fiorentina 4, ℂ 370390, ✉ 302415 (*moderate*), may be the most convenient; it's a few blocks west of the city walls, but besides pleasant rooms, TV and air conditioning, it can offer you a parking place. It also has an excellent, unpretentious restaurant (*moderate*). In town, most of the rooms are close to the station. You may enjoy contemplating the towers and red rooftops from the roof terrace of the ★★★**Continentale**, a fine, older hotel in Piazza Guido Monaco 7, ℂ 20251, ✉ 350485 (*moderate*). Its competitor, ★★★**Europa**, Via Spinello 43, ℂ 357701, ✉ 357703 (*moderate*), is just across from the station, and is similarly modern and plain, but many of its rooms are air-conditioned. ★★**Truciolini**, Via Pacinotti 6, ℂ 984104, ✉ 984137 (*moderate*), has parking and air conditioning.

Budget hotels are a bit cheaper than their counterparts elsewhere in Tuscany, and there's a youth hostel at Via Francesco Redi 16, ℂ 29047.

Arezzo isn't going to blind you with science in the kitchen (though while you wait for the train you can enjoy Tuscany's best railway cuisine in the station bar). One restaurant that tries hard (it even has a piano bar, which may seem a little incongruous after a day in medieval Arezzo) is **Le Tastevin**, Via de' Cenci 9, ℂ 28304 (*expensive*); *carpaccio*, also good *penne* with pepper sauce; wines from around the world. *Closed Mon*. Tourists favour the **Buca di San Francesco**, opposite Piero's frescoes in Via S. Francesco 1, ℂ 23271 (*expensive*), but don't let that discourage you—the Buca has an honest-to-goodness medieval atmosphere and tasty Tuscan cooking to match, though slightly adapted for the uninitiated. *Closed Mon eve and Tues*. The restaurant in the hotel **Continentale** (*see above; expensive*) serves *zuppa del Tarlati*—chicken soup prepared according to a 12th-century recipe—as well as a tender turkey breast with truffles. *Closed Mon*. For a meal in the country, one of the best restaurants near Arezzo is the **Osteria La Capannaccia**, Loc. Campriano 51/c, ℂ 36759 (*inexpensive to moderate*), where the specialities are those of the Aretine countryside—simple dishes like *minestra di pane*, roast meats and wines from the Colli Aretini—and the price is equally unpretentious. *Closed Sun eve and Mon*. Another fine country place offering traditional dishes, **Al Principe**, Via Giovi 25, ℂ 362046, near the Arno, between Arezzo and Subbiano (*moderate*), still serves eels in a *piccante* tomato sauce, once but no longer fished out of the Arno itself, as well as home-made spaghetti (*pici*), also *minestra di pane*, and good local wines. *Closed Mon*.

The Valtiberina, or upper valley of Old Father Tiber, is a luminous patchwork of pasturelands and pine and beech woodlands, and the birthplace of Michelangelo and Piero della Francesca.

Getting Around

CAT buses from Arezzo serve the area efficiently if not especially frequently. Sansepolcro is the terminus of Umbria's LFI line, which can slowly whisk you down to Città di Castello (16km/25mins), Umbertide, Perugia, Todi and Terni. Buses from Sansepolcro (station just outside the walls) go to Città di Castello, Caprese Michelangelo (26km/45mins), Arezzo (38km/1hr), Florence and Pieve Santo Stefano.

Caprese Michelangelo

Michelangelo's father, a minor noble of Florence, was *podestà* in the tiny town of Caprese (pop. 1850) when his wife gave birth to little Michelangelo. As was the custom in those days, the baby was sent into the countryside to be nursed, in this case by the wife of a mason. 'If my brains are any good at all, it's because I was born in the pure air of your Arezzo countryside,' Michelangelo later told Vasari. 'Just as with my mother's milk I sucked in the hammer and chisels I use for my statues.' Although he only returned once to the Valtiberina, to select sturdy firs to float down the Tiber for the scaffolding in the Sistine Chapel, Caprese does not let any opportunity slip by to remind us of its most famous son, even changing its name to **Caprese Michelangelo**. The artist's purported birthplace, the 14th-century **Casa del Podestà**, has been restored and now houses a museum in his honour, with photographs and reproductions of his works. Caprese's medieval castle contains questionable tributes from modern sculptors. From here it's only a few bumpy kilometres into the Alpe di Catenaia and La Verna (*see* p.405).

Caprese to Sestino

East of Caprese the countryside is the biggest attraction; between **Pieve Santo Stefano** (Roman *Sulpitia*, mostly rebuilt after World War II) and **Badia Tedalda** (a small summer resort) lie the rolling Alpe della Luna, the Mountains of the Moon.

Sestino (from the Roman woodland god Sextius), Tuscany's easternmost *comune* on the border of the Marches, was ruled by the Montefeltro dukes of Urbino until 1516. It has been the agricultural centre for its area since antiquity and preserves many medieval buildings. Near its little Romanesque parish church, the **Antiquarium** will show you the headless 'Venus of Sestino' and other local finds. The church, built in the 8th century, shows the influence of Ravenna, Byzantine capital of the west; its 13th-century altar sits on a Roman boundary stone.

Arezzo to Sansepolcro

Although Michelangelo took fresh air and stone-flavoured milk from his native place, Piero della Francesca carried the light and luminous landscape along the Tuscan-Umbrian frontier with him throughout his career, and left more behind in his native haunts than Michelangelo. From Arezzo, it's a pretty 41km drive to Sansepolcro, especially along S73, which ascends through the Foce di Scopetone (with panoramic views back towards the city) then continues another 17km to the short turn-off for **Monterchi**. Dedicated to Hercules in Roman times, Monterchi is a tiny triangle of a medieval town; while strolling its lanes, don't miss the curious underground passageway around the apse of the parish church, dating back to the Middle Ages but of uncertain purpose. Monterchi is most famous, however, for Piero della Francesca's extraordinary fresco in the little chapel at the cemetery. The *Madonna del Parto* (1445) is perhaps the first (and last?) portrayal of the Virgin in her ninth month, a mystery revealed by twin angels who pull back the flaps of a tent, empty but for Mary, weary and melancholy, one eyelid drooping, one hand on her hip, the other on her swollen belly, almost painful to see—one of the most psychologically penetrating paintings of the quattrocento. It is now housed in a former primary school which is well signposted from all directions. Details of its recent restoration are exhibited with the painting.

Anghiari (pop. 6200), between Monterchi and Sansepolcro, is a fine old town located on a balcony over the Valtiberina. Once a property of Camaldoli and later of the Tarlati family, it was the site of a 1440 victory of the Florentines over the Milanese, a decisive victory in corking up Visconti ambitions over Tuscany and the rest of Italy. Leonardo da Vinci chose it as his subject matter in the Battle of the Frescoes in Florence's Palazzo Vecchio—one of the Renaissance's greatest un-happenings, though the cartoons left behind by the master were often copied and became one of the inspirations of Florentine Mannerism. In Anghiari's Renaissance Palazzo Taglieschi at Via Mameli 16, the **Museo delle Arti e Tradizioni Popolari dell'Alta Valle del Tevere** has exhibits relating to traditional crafts of the Upper Tiber Valley. Just over 1km to the southwest, there's the pretty Romanesque **Pieve di Sovara**, and on the Sansepolcro road, you can still make out the 8th-century Byzantine origins of **Santo Stefano**.

Sansepolcro

Sansepolcro (pop. 15,500) is the largest town of the Valtiberina, famous for its lace, its pasta (the Buitoni spaghetti works are just outside the city), and for Piero della Francesca. The painter was born here sometime between 1410 and 1420, and given his mother's name as his father died before his birth. Although he worked in the Marches, Arezzo and Rome, he spent most of his life in Sansepolcro, painting and writing books on geometry and perspective until he went blind at the age of 60.

Sansepolcro was founded around the year 1000, and like Anghiari belonged to the monks of Camaldoli until the 13th century. The historic centre, with its crew-cut towers, has plenty of character, though a bit dusty and plain after several earthquakes and rebuildings. It is enclosed within well-preserved walls, built by the Tarlati and given a Renaissance face-lift by Giuliano da Sangallo. **Piazza Torre di Berta** is the centre of town, where on the second Sunday of September crossbow-men from Gubbio come to challenge the home archers in the *Palio della Balestra*, an ancient rivalry. Along Via Matteotti are many of the city's surviving 14th–16th-century palaces, most notably the Palazzo delle Laudi and the 14th-century palace housing the **Museo Civico** (*open daily 9–1.30 and 2.30–7. 30, 2.30–6 winter; adm*). Here you can see Piero della Francesca's masterpiece, the *Resurrection*, an intense, almost eerie depiction of the solemnly triumphant Christ stepping out of his tomb surrounded by sleeping soldiers and a sleeping land, more autumnal than springlike. It shares pride of place with two of Piero's early works, the *Misericordia Polyptych*, a gold-background altarpiece dominated by a serene, giant goddess of a Madonna, sheltering under her cloak members of the confraternity (note the black hood on one) who commissioned the picture, and a damaged fresco of San Giuliano. Other works are by his greatest pupil, Luca Signorelli, a *Crucifixion* (with two saints on the back), Pontormo (*Martyrdom of San Quintino*), Santi di Tito, Mannerist Raffaellino del Colle, and the 16th-century Giovanni de' Vecchi, also of Sansepolcro, whose *Presentation of the Virgin* is interesting for its unusual vertical rhythms. You can see a 16th-century scene of Sansepolcro in the *Pilgrimage of the Company of the Crucifix of Loreto*, a relic of the days of the Black Death, as are the wooden panels of Death (one showing a fine strutting skeleton). Downstairs, a room contains sculptural fragments gathered from the town, including a rather mysterious 12th-century frieze of knights from a local palace; upstairs there's a collection of detached frescoes.

Sansepolcro also has a couple of pretty churches: near the museum is the Gothic church of **San Francesco**, with a fine rose window and portal. The **Duomo** on Via Matteotti was built in the 11th century but has been much restored since; among the art inside is a fresco by Bartolomeo della Gatta and a polyptych by Matteo di Giovanni. Another church, **San Lorenzo**, has a *Deposizione* by Rosso Fiorentino.

© (0575–) ***Where to Stay and Eating Out***

Up in the Alpe Faggeto, above Caprese Michelangelo, ★★★**Fonte Galletta**, © 793652, is a pleasant little mountain hotel (*inexpensive*) and restaurant (*moderate*), in a lovely forested landscape. The hotel has simple rooms; the restaurant uses local ingredients—chestnuts, mushrooms, truffles, game, mountain hams—to create tasty dishes. The pasta is excellent, as are the homemade *semifreddi*. **Locanda al Castello di Sorci**, near Anghiari at San Lorenzo, © 789066 (*moderate*), is a country beanery located in a former tobacco barn; the fare is simple and rustic, much of it (the wine and meats) coming from the farm annexe. In Sansepolcro, ★★★**Fiorentino**, Via L. Pacioli 60, © 740350, ✆ 740370, has been the town inn since the 1820s; rooms provide the basics, and there's a garage for your car (L55,000 without bath, L70,000 with). The restaurant (*moderate*), however, is Sansepolcro's best; it's a good place to try Italian onion soup; other local specialities are especially well prepared, and there's a wide assortment of local cheese. *Closed Fri.* Also in Sansepolcro is ★★★★**La Balestra**, Via del Montefeltro 29, © 735151, ✆ 740370 (*moderate*), with modern, comfortable rooms and parking; it also has a good restaurant (*moderate*), with delicious homemade pasta; for seconds try the lamb chops with courgette flowers. The unusual **Paola e Marco Mercati dell'Oroscopo**, Loc.Pieve Vecchia, © 34875 (*expensive*), mixes traditional with more creative cooking, such as flamed king prawns in garlic sauce and a chocolate tart with *zabaglione* and *mascarpone*. *Dinner only, closed Sun.* They also have a small hotel (*inexpensive*) with 12 rooms. A cheaper and more conventional choice is **Da Ventura**, Via Aggiunti 30, © 742560 (*moderate*). *Closed Sat.*

South of Arezzo: the Valdichiana

The flat Valdichiana south of Arezzo is the largest, broadest valley in the Apennines, rimmed by surrounding hills and old towns like a walled garden. The Etruscans, headquartered at Cortona, were the first to drain its marshlands, making it their bread-basket, so rich, it is said, that even after Hannibal's troops pillaged and burned on their way to Lake Trasimeno, there was still more than enough to feed the army and its elephants. By the Middle Ages, however, the valley had reverted to a swamp, forcing the inhabitants back into the hills. And so it stayed, until the beginning of the 19th century, when the Lorraine Grand Dukes initiated a major land reclamation scheme. Now, once again, prosperous farms are the main feature of the Valdichiana. The equally prosperous-looking cattle you may notice are a prized breed called the Chianina, named after the valley, and descendants of the primal herds whose fossils were discovered in the vicinity.

Monte San Savino and Lucignano

But there is more to the Valdichiana than farms and *bistecca alla fiorentina* on the hoof. On both sides of the valley are some of the most beautiful villages in this part of Tuscany. Cortona is the most famous, but there are others, like **Monte San Savino** (21km from Arezzo, on the west side of the valley), the birthplace of Andrea Contucci, better known as Andrea Sansovino (1460–1529), artistic emissary of Lorenzo de'Medici to Portugal and one of the heralds of the High Renaissance; his Florentine pupil Jacopo adopted his surname and went on to become chief sculptor and architect in Venice in its Golden Age. Monte San Savino, spread out on a low hill on the west rim of the Valdichiana, is an attractive town with a *mélange* of medieval and fine Renaissance palaces. Andrea Sansovino left his home town an attractive portal on the church of **San Giovanni**, terracottas (along with others by the della Robbias) in the little church of **Santa Chiara**, and the lovely cloister of **Sant'Agostino** (13th-century, with a small rose window by Guillaume de Marcillat); Antonio da Sangallo the Elder designed the beautiful and harmonious **Loggia dei Mercanti**, with its grey Corinthian capitals (early 1500s, also attributed by ~~~ Sansovino) and the simple, partly rusticated **Palazzo Comunale**, or~ the Del Monte family, whose money paid for most of Monte Sa~ ornaments. Foremost among the medieval monuments, the **Pala~** by the Perugians, while the city walls are the work of the Sienese.

On a cypress-clad hill 2km east, **Santa Maria della Vertighe** was built in the 12th century and restored in the 16th; within it is a 13th-century triptych by Margarito d'Arezzo and, from the next century, works by Lorenzo Monaco. Some 7km to the west there's the pretty hamlet of **Gargonza**, with its mighty tower dominating a tight cluster of houses on a wart of a hill, the whole of which is now a hotel (*see* p.418).

Best of all, perhaps, is cheerful little **Lucignano**, south of Monte San Savino, unique in the annals of Italian hill towns for its street plan—it will literally run you round in circles; Lucignano is laid out in four concentric ellipses, like a kind of maze, with four picturesque little *piazze* in the centre. One piazza is dominated by the Collegiata with a theatrical circular stair, another by the 14th-century **Palazzo Comunale**, now the Museo Civico, containing a good collection of 13th–15th-century Sienese works, a Madonna by Signorelli, and most famously, a 14th-century masterpiece of Aretine goldsmiths, the delicate reliquary *Albero di Lucignano*. There are more good Sienese paintings in the little tiger-striped church of **San Francesco**. Outside the centre there's a 16th-century Medici fortress, and the **Madonna delle Querce**, a Renaissance temple sometimes attributed to Vasari, with a fine Doric interior.

Marciano della Chiana, 6km northeast of Lucignano, is another old fortified village with an impressive main gate, which also does time as clock and bell tower. **Foiano della Chiana**, just to the south, is encompassed by newer buildings, but in its **Collegiata** has a good *Coronation of the Virgin* by Signorelli and a terracotta by Andrea della Robbia. Between Marciano and Foiano, keep an eye open for the curious octagonal church of **Santa Vittoria**, built by Ammanati for Cosimo I.

Castiglion Fiorentino

Across the Valdichiana to the east, **Castiglion Fiorentino** was known as Castiglion Aretino until the Florentines snatched it in 1384. Within its walls it has retained its medieval street plan, with some Renaissance touches—the 16th-century **Logge del Vasari** and the **Palazzo Comunale**. The latter houses yet another small Pinacoteca Civica (*open 10–12.30, 4–6.30, closed Mon*), where the prized pieces are a gilded silver reliquary bust and the *Stigmata of St Francis* by Bartolomeo della Gatta. The old Gothic church of **San Francesco** was frescoed within by 14th-century Florentines, and has a painting by Margarito d'Arezzo (1280). Like many a larger Tuscan town, Castiglion Fiorentino built a little Renaissance geometric temple in an isolated position below the walls, the charming octagonal **Madonna della Consolazione**, untampered with since the 16th century; inside you'll find a fresco called the *Maestà di Geppe*, which is attributed to Signorelli.

Dilapidated castles from the bad old days are all around Castiglion, most impressively at **Montecchio**, 4km south, with its tall honey-coloured tower and walls, a landmark visible 'l over the Valdichiana. For a while in the 1400s it was the stronghold of the *condottiere* 'ohn Hawkwood, he of the famous 'monument' by Uccello in Florence cathedral.

The top place in the Valdichiana, at least for peace and quiet and medieval atmosphere, is ★★★★**Castello dei Gargonza**, an entire walled village near Monte San Savino, just off S73, © 847665 (*very expensive*), with 20 rooms in restored houses, a pool and forests all around; the restaurant, with local specialities, is also very popular. In the very centre of Lucignano, ★★★**Da Totò**, Piazza del Tribunale 6, © 836763, ✆ 836988, is the best (and only) place to sleep (*inexpensive*) and eat (*moderate*); the menu proposes an unusual variety of tastes, in dishes like *pici* in duck sauce, or *pappardelle* with boar, and rabbit with fennel.

Cortona

Seemingly floating high above the Valdichiana plain on terraced slopes covered with olives and vines, Cortona (pop. 27,000) may not be entirely undiscovered, but it is still one of the real jewels among hill towns. Some 600m above sea level, sweeping down a spur of Monte Sant'Egidio, the town's crooked, cobblestone streets climb precipitously to the old fortress—even halfway up, if there's a space between the houses, you can see as far as Lake Trasimeno in Umbria. It produced three celebrated artists: Luca Signorelli; Baroque painter Pietro Berrettini (1596–1669), better known as Pietro da Cortona, master of the rooms in the Pitti Palace; and Futurist-Impressionist-mosaicist Gino Severini (1883–1966), all of whom left works in Cortona.

Cortona's remarkable site brought it notoriety early on; according to popular tradition, the city is nothing less than the 'Mother of Troy and Grandmother of Rome'—founded by Dardanus, who according to legend was fighting against a neighbouring tribe when he lost his helmet (*corythos*) on the hill, thus giving the name *Corito* to the city that soon grew up. Dardanus went on to Asia to found Troy and give his name to the Dardanelles. Like all myths from the mists of time, there is apparently a germ of truth in it, in an important Etruscan-Anatolian connection. The mysterious Etruscans themselves always claimed to have come from Western Anatolia (perhaps around the year 900 BC), and inscriptions very similar to Etruscan have been found on the Greek island of Lemnos, near Troy; artefacts from the Iron Age found in Anatolia and Tuscany suggest cultural affinities. Cortona was an important Etruscan city, one of the Dodecapolis and one of the largest in the north; the ragged, monolithic Etruscan stonework can still be seen in the foundations of its walls. These are over three kilometres in perimeter, but still cover only two-thirds of the area of the original Etruscan fortifications. As a medieval *comune*, Cortona held its own against Perugia, Arezzo and Siena, while internally its Ghibellines and Guelphs battled until the Ghibellines came out on top, and when that fight was settled the ruling family, the Casali, spent the 14th century knocking off each other. The typical Tuscan orgy of self-destruction ended in 1409, when King Ladislas of Naples captured the city and sold it to the Florentines at a good price.

Getting Around

Cortona is just off the main Florence–Arezzo–Rome railway line; the nearest station is Camucia, 5km west; however, if you're coming up from Umbria, the station is Teròntola, 10km south. Both stations have frequent LFI buses up to Cortona. There are also LFI train connections to Arezzo (34km/50mins), Castiglion Fiorentino, Foiano della Chiana, and Castiglione del Lago on Lake Trasimeno (22km/30mins); schedules for both buses and trains, and tickets for the former are posted in the office in Via Nazionale, near the bus terminus and car park in panoramic Piazzale Garibaldi. Bicycles may be hired at Santa Caterina from G. S. Fratta, ✆ (0575) 603009.

Tourist Information

Via Nazionale 42, ✆ (0575) 630 353.

Palazzo Casali—Museo Civico

Open April–Sept 10–1 and 4–7, 9–1 and 3–5 in winter, closed Mon; adm.

The heart of Cortona, the **Piazza della Repubblica**, is a striking asymmetrical square, with lanes leading off in all directions. Dominant here is **Palazzo Comunale**, a 13th-century building with a tower from 1503, its monumental steps a favourite place to dally away the early evening. Just behind it is Cortona's most impressive medieval palace, the 13th-century **Palazzo Casali**, home of the city's former lordlings and now the seat of the Etruscan Academy and the **Museo Civico**. This has a fascinating eclectic collection encompassing 15th-century ivories with court scenes; a good set of Etruscan bronzes; Greek vases, attesting to the city's wealth and trading contacts of long ago; Egyptian mummies and a doll-like Egyptian funeral bark; and Cortona's most famous relic, an Etruscan bronze chandelier with 16 lamps dating back to the 5th century BC, found in a nearby field. Each of the lamps is a squatting male or female figure, while in the inner circle there's a ring of stylized waves and dolphins, and in the centre, an archaic gorgon— the total effect resembles an Aztec calendar stone. There is also a fine collection of paintings, the oldest of which is a Roman portrait of the Muse Polyhymnia. Other works include *Two Saints* by Niccolò di Pietro Gerini, a 12th-century mosaic of the Madonna, a Madonna by Pinturicchio, and another by Signorelli, who portrays her in the company of the patron saints of Cortona, with a nasty-looking devil laying low. Other rooms contain souvenirs of a Knight of Malta from Cortona, ivory chess-sets, old globes, costumes, some out-of-the-ordinary ceramics, Etruscan urns, works by Gino Severini, and a fine Roman alabaster Hecate, the queen of the night. The latest permanent exhibition is the town's pride and joy. Two new rooms on the top floor house the artefacts from and a re-creation of the inside of a nearby Etruscan tomb, excavated in 1991. It is also possible to visit the tomb itself, situated 1km from Cortona on S71 towards Arezzo.

Museo Diocesano

Open April–Sept 9–1 and 3–6.30, Oct–March 9–1 and 3–5, closed Mon; adm.

Behind the civic museum signs point the way back to the **Duomo**, an 11th-century church unimaginatively rebuilt in 1560, probably by Giuliano da Sangallo; inside there's a mosaic by Gino Severini. However, across the piazza in the deconsecrated church of Gesù there's the excellent **Museo Diocesano** with one of Luca Signorelli's finest works—a *Deposition*, with background scenes of the Crucifixion and Resurrection (the latter composition inspired by his master Piero della Francesca) and a beautiful, luminous *Annunciation* by Fra Angelico, in which the angel appears to be gently whispering. Other works include a 14th-century crucifix by Pietro Lorenzetti, a triptych by Il Sassetta, a fine Sienese Madonna by the school of Duccio di Buoninsegna, and a Roman sarcophagus with reliefs of the Battle of Lapiths and Centaurs that was closely studied by Donatello and Brunelleschi. Don't miss the fine coffered wooden ceiling of the church itself. Below the Piazza del Duomo is one of Cortona's most picturesque lanes, the medieval Via Jannelli (or del Gesù); here and around Cortona you'll see *porte del morto* (doors of the dead), more common in medieval Umbria than in Tuscany. Other especially picturesque streets around town are Via Ghibellina, Via Guelfa, and Via Maffei, with its town palaces.

Up and Down Cortona

You'll need your climbing shoes to see the other monuments of Cortona, although **San Francesco** is only a short walk up from Piazza della Repubblica. St Francis's controversial lieutenant Brother Elias was a native of Cortona and founded this little church at an interesting angle in 1245; it still retains its original façade and one side. Both Brother Elias and Luca Signorelli are buried here, and on the left wall is a fine fresco of the *Annunciation*, the last work of Pietro da Cortona. On the high altar is a relic of the Holy Cross brought back from Constantinople by Brother Elias, housed in an ivory reliquary that Byzantine emperor Nicephoras Phocas took with him to battle against the Saracens in the 960s, as described in the Greek inscription on the back. From here Via Berrettini continues up to Piazza Pozzo and Piazza Pescaia and the medieval neighbourhood around **San Nicolò**. This handsome little Romanesque church, built by an anachronistic architect in the 1440s, was the seat of San Bernardino da Siena's Company of St Nicholas, for whom Luca Signorelli painted a magnificent standard of the *Deposition* still hanging in the church.

You can reach the loftiest church of them all, the **Santuario di Santa Margherita**, from San Nicolò or by way of Via S. Margherita and the Via Crucis from Piazzale Garibaldi. The Via Crucis was built in 1947 by the people of Cortona to thank their patron saint Margherita for sparing their city from the war; it is lined with mosaic shrines by Severini. The views become increasingly magnificent, until you reach the pretty 19th-century neo-Romanesque sanctuary. The original church here was built in the 1200s by Santa Margherita, who is buried in a silver urn on the high altar; her fine but empty Gothic sarcophagus on the left wall has been attributed to Giovanni Pisano. To the right of the altar are standards and lanterns captured from the Turks in 18th-century sea battles, donated by a local commander. The overgrown **Medici Fortress** above occupies the site of the old Etruscan acropolis.

As in many Etruscan and Roman towns, Cortona's four gates are oriented to the four points of the compass. The northern **Porta Colonia** has an Etrusco-Roman arch and is near some well-preserved remains of the Etruscan walls; from here it's a 15-minute walk to the late, tall Renaissance church of **Santa Maria Nuova**, one of the more serene works to come out of the Counter-Reformation, designed in a Greek cross and crowned by a dome. Outside the southern gate, at the end of Via Nazionale and beyond Piazzale Garibaldi, the Gothic church of **San Domenico** has just been restored; in its elegant interior there's a grand altarpiece by Lorenzo di Niccolò Gerini, given to the Dominicans by Lorenzo de' Medici; and in the apse there's a *Madonna with Angels* by Signorelli. Nearby is a good stretch of Etruscan wall and the beginning of the pretty Passeggiata Pubblica through Cortona's shady public gardens, **Il Parterre**, with more great views of the Valdichiana. Halfway down the hill, in an isolated position, stands **Santa Maria delle Grazie al Calcinaio** (1485–1513), done in perfect and elegant Renaissance symmetry by Sienese architect Francesco di Giorgio Martini—a simple central plan with an octagonal drum. The stained glass is by Guillaume de Marcillat; the harmonious interior, done in Brunelleschian dark and light accents, is light and airy and pure.

Around Cortona

Not surprisingly, a number of Etruscan tombs have been discovered around and below Cortona. Among the best-preserved is the circular **Tanella di Pitagora**, down near Camucia, named after Pythagoras (from an ancient confusion of Cortona with Croton in Calabria, where the philosopher lived), prettily surrounded by cypress trees, with an unusual vault over its rectangular funeral chamber. Very near the Camucia station is a large tumulus called the **Melone di Camucia**, 200m in perimeter, with two doors of uncertain purpose; in a place called Il Sodo (3km north, from the western Porta Santa Maria) there are two other 'melons', the first of which is especially impressive, with a corridor leading into the five mortuary chambers.

Beyond Santa Maria Nuova the road continues for another 3.5km along the slopes of Monte Sant'Egidio to the **Convento delle Celle**, founded by St Francis in 1211 in a beautiful setting. Little has changed in subsequent years; its simple rustic buildings have preserved their Franciscan spirit better than many others—the humble founder's cell retains the saint's stone bed.

Antiques are big business in Cortona; besides the offerings in the town's shops, the national antique furniture market is held here at the end of August and September. Another speciality is handmade copperware, given its own show and market in April. The 15 August is the time of the *Sagra di Bistecca*—the festival of the beefsteak, with a huge outdoor grilling of the Valdichiana's main product. From June to October Italian language and cultural courses help bring this ancient hill town to life. Just off the mountain road above Torreone, set amongst the chestnut woods at Tornia is a swimming pool called the 'Priest's Hole'. It is far prettier and more tranquil than the public pool at Il Sodo (*give donation*). Horses can be hired from Centro Equitazione Casale, on Via Teverina 134, ✆ (0575) 616088. In July concerts are held in the public gardens, as part of the Umbria Jazz festival. Ask at the tourist office for information.

Cortona ✆ (0575–)

Where to Stay

In Cortona, available lodgings have yet to catch up with demand, especially since the town is the site of both a language school and a University of Georgia art programme. ★★★**San Luca**, Piazza Garibaldi 2, ✆ 630460, ✉ 630105 (*moderate*), is simple but comfortable; many of the rooms enjoy wonderful views. In town ★★★★**San Michele**, Via Guelfa 15, ✆ 604348, ✉ 630147 (*inexpensive without bath, moderate with*), is a comfortable hotel on a medieval street. High up in the old town, ★**Athens**, Via S. Antonio, ✆ 630508, ✉ 604457 (*L43,000 without bath, L50,000 with*)—named after Athens, Georgia, not Greece—is a good budget choice with spacious rooms in an older building. **Ostello San Marco**, Via Maffei 57, ✆ 601392, a 3km walk up from Piazza Garibaldi (*L14,000; inexpensive meals available; IYHA card required*), is one of Italy's more pleasant youth hostels, and a viable option if all is full. *Open March–Oct.*

Cortona ✆ (0575–)

Eating Out

Cortona's restaurants are not fancy, but make a point of using local ingredients—homemade pasta, *salumeria* and beefsteaks from the Valdichiana, mushrooms and truffles in season, and the local white wines, called *Bianchi vergini* (the white virgins). **La Loggetta**, Piazza Pescheria, ✆ 630575 (*expensive*), is a pretty little restaurant where you can try some of these prepared *alla Cortonese. Closed Mon.* **Portole**, Via Umbro Cortonese 39, ✆ 691008 (*moderate*), is a good place for steaks. *Closed Fri.* A ★★★ hotel (*moderate*) is attached. **Tonino**, Piazza Garibaldi, ✆ 603500 (*expensive*), is Cortona's most elegant restaurant, with wonderful hot and cold antipasti, followed by traditional pasta dishes and the Valdichiana's tender beef. *Closed Tues.*

Trattoria Dardano, Via Dardano 24, © 601944 (*moderate*), is a simple restaurant with an elegant vaulted ceiling. It is popular with the locals, and so is often noisy and busy, but the food is good, especially the homemade *pici* with mushroom sauce. *Closed Wed.* **La Grotta**, Piazzetta Baldelli 3, © 630271 (*moderate to expensive*), is a restaurant that the Cortonese would like to keep a secret and is hidden away off the main square. The atmosphere is friendly but intimate. *Closed Tues.* On the edge of town in Frazione Torreone 6 is the aptly named **Miravalle**, © 62 232 (*moderate*), with stunning views over the valley. The food's not bad either; try their home-made *tagliatelle. Closed Mon.*

Acroterion: decorative protrusion on the roof-top of an Etruscan, Greek or Roman temple. At the corners of the roof they are called *antefixes*.

Ambones: twin pulpits (singular: *ambo*), often elaborately decorated.

Ambulatory: an aisle around the apse of a church.

Atrium: entrance court of a Roman house or early church.

Badia: an abbey or abbey church also (*abbazia*).

Baldacchino: baldachin, a columned stone canopy above the altar of a church.

Basilica: a rectangular building, usually divided into three aisles by rows of columns. In Rome this was the common form for law courts and other public buildings, and Roman Christians adapted it for their early churches.

Borgo: from the Saxon *burh* of S. Spirito in Rome: a suburb or village.

Bucchero ware: black, delicately thin Etruscan ceramics, usually incised or painted.

Calvary chapels: a series of outdoor chapels, usually on a hillside, that commemorate the stages of the Passion of Christ.

Campanile: a bell tower.

Campanilismo: local patriotism; the Italians' own word for their historic tendency to be more faithful to their home towns than to the abstract idea of 'Italy'.

Campo santo: a cemetery.

Cardo: transverse street of a Roman *castrum*-shaped city.

Carroccio: a wagon carrying the banners of a medieval city and an altar; it served as the rallying point in battles.

Cartoon: the preliminary sketch for a fresco or tapestry.

Caryatid: supporting pillar or column carved into a standing female form; male versions are called *telamones*.

Castrum: a Roman military camp, always neatly rectangular, with straight streets and gates at the cardinal points. Later the Romans founded or refounded cities in this form, hundreds of which survive today (Lucca, Aosta, Florence, Pavia, Como, Brescia, Ascoli Piceno, Ancona are clear examples).

Cavea: the semicircle of seats in a classical theatre.

Cenacolo: fresco of the Last Supper, often on the wall of a monastery refectory.

Architectural, Artistic and Historical Terms

Chiaroscuro: the arrangement or treatment of light and dark areas in a painting.

Ciborium: a tabernacle; the word is often used for large, free-standing tabernacles, or in the sense of a *baldacchino* (q.v.).

Comune: commune, or commonwealth, referring to the governments of the free cities of the Middle Ages. Today it denotes any local government, from the Comune di Roma down to the smallest village.

Condottiere: the leader of a band of mercenaries in late medieval and Renaissance times.

Confraternity: a religious lay brotherhood, often serving as a neighbourhood mutual-aid and burial society, or following some specific charitable work (Michelangelo, for example, belonged to one that cared for condemned prisoners in Rome).

Contrapposto: the dramatic, but rather unnatural twist in a statue, especially in a Mannerist or Baroque work, derived from Hellenistic and Roman art.

Convento: a convent *or* monastery

Cosmati work: or *Cosmatesque*: referring to a distinctive style of inlaid marble or enamel chips used in architectural decoration (pavements, pulpits, paschal candlesticks, etc.) in medieval Italy. The Cosmati family of Rome were its greatest practitioners.

Crete: in the pasturelands of southern Tuscany, chalky cliffs caused by erosion. Similar phenomena are the *biancane*, small chalk outcrops, and *balze*, deep eroded ravines around Volterra.

Cupola: a dome.

Decumanus: street of a Roman *castrum*-shaped city parallel to the longer axis, the central, main avenue called the Decumanus Major.

Dodecapolis: the federation of the twelve largest and strongest Etruscan city-states (*see* **History**, p.50).

Duomo: cathedral.

Ex voto: an offering (a terracotta figurine, painting, medallion, silver bauble, or whatever) made in thanksgiving to a god or Christian saint; the practice has always been present in Italy.

Forum: the central square of a Roman town, with its most important temples and public buildings. The word means 'outside', as the original Roman Forum was outside the first city walls.

Fresco: wall painting, the most important Italian medium of art since Etruscan times. It isn't easy; first the artist draws the *sinopia* (q.v.) on the wall. This is covered with plaster, but only a little at a time, as the paint must be on the plaster before it dries. Leonardo da Vinci's endless attempts to find clever short-cuts ensured that little of his work would survive.

Ghibellines: one of the two great medieval parties, the supporters of the Holy Roman Emperors.

Gonfalon: the banner of a medieval free city; the *gonfaloniere*, or flag-bearer, was often the most important public official.

Graffito: originally, incised decoration on buildings, walls, etc; only lately has it come to mean casually-scribbled messages in public places.

Greek cross: in the floor plans of churches, a cross with equal arms. The more familiar plan, with one arm extended to form a nave, is called a *Latin Cross*.

Grisaille: painting or fresco in monochrome.

Grotesques: carved or painted faces used in Etruscan and later Roman decoration; Raphael and other artists rediscovered them in the 'grotto' of Nero's Golden House in Rome.

Guelphs (see *Ghibellines*): the other great political faction of medieval Italy, supporters of the Pope.

Intarsia: decorative inlaid wood or marble.

Loggia: an open-sided gallery or arcade.

Lozenge: the diamond shape—along with stripes, one of the trademarks of Pisan architecture.

Lunette: semicircular space on a wall, above a door or under vaulting, either filled by a window or a mural painting.

Martroneum: the elevated women's gallery around the nave of an early church, a custom adopted from the Byzantines in the 6th and 7th centuries.

Narthex: the enclosed porch of a church.

Naumachia: mock naval battles, like those staged in the Colosseum.

Opus Reticulatum: Roman masonry consisting of diamond-shaped blocks.

Palazzo: not just a palace, but any large, important building (though the word comes from the Imperial *palatium* on Rome's Palatine Hill).

Palio: a banner, and the horse race in which city neighbourhoods contend for it in their annual festivals. The most famous is at Siena.

Pantocrator: Christ 'ruler of all', a common subject for apse paintings and mosaics in areas influenced by Byzantine art.

Pietra Dura: rich inlay work using semi-precious stones, perfected in post-Renaissance Florence.

Pieve: a parish church.

Pluteo: screen, usually of marble, between two columns, often highly decorated.

Podestà: in medieval cities, an official sent by the Holy Roman Emperors to take charge; their power, or lack of it, depended on the strength of the *comune*.

Predella: smaller paintings on panels below the main subject of a painted altarpiece.

Presepio: a Christmas crib.

Putti: flocks of plaster cherubs with rosy cheeks and bums that infested much of Italy in the Baroque era.

Quattrocento: the 1400s—the Italian way of referring to centuries (*duecento, trecento, quattrocento, cinquecento*, etc.).

Sbandieratore: flag-thrower in medieval costume at an Italian festival; sometimes called an *alfiere*.

Sinopia: the layout of a fresco (q.v.), etched by the artist on the wall before the plaster is applied. Often these are works of art in their own right.

Stele: a vertical funeral stone.

Stigmata: a miraculous simulation of the bleeding wounds of Christ, appearing in holy men like St Francis in the 12th century, and Padre Pio of Apulia in our own time.

Telamon: see *caryatid*.

Thermae: Roman baths.

Tondo: round relief, painting or terracotta.

Transenna: marble screen separating the altar area from the rest of an early Christian church.

Travertine: hard, light-coloured stone, sometimes flecked or pitted with black, sometimes perfect. The most widely used material in ancient and modern Rome.

Triptych: a painting, especially an altarpiece, in three sections.

Trompe l'œil: art that uses perspective effects to deceive the eye—for example, to create the illusion of depth on a flat surface, or to make columns and arches painted on a wall seem real.

Tympanum: the semicircular space, often bearing a painting or relief, above the portal of a church.

Voussoir: one of the stones of an arch.

The fathers of modern Italian were Dante, Manzoni, and television. Each did their part in creating a national language from an infinity of regional and local dialects; the Florentine Dante, the first 'immortal' to write in the vernacular, did much to put the Tuscan dialect in the foreground of Italian literature. Manzoni's revolutionary novel, *I Promessi Sposi* (The Betrothed), heightened national consciousness by using an everyday language all could understand in the 19th century. Television in the last few decades is performing an even more spectacular linguistic unification; although the majority of Italians still speak a dialect at home, school, and work, their TV idols insist on proper Italian.

Perhaps because they are so busy learning their own beautiful but grammatically complex language, Italians are not especially apt at learning others. English lessons, however, have been the rage for years, and at most hotels and restaurants there will be someone who speaks some English. In small towns and out of the way places, finding an Anglophone may prove more difficult. The words and phrases below should help you out in most situations, but the ideal way to come to Italy is with some Italian under your belt; your visit will be richer, and you're much more likely to make some Italian friends.

Pronunciation

Italian words are pronounced phonetically. Every vowel and consonant (except 'h') is sounded. Consonants are the same as in English, except the *c* which, when followed by an 'e' or 'i', is pronounced like the English 'ch' (*cinque* thus becomes cheenquay). Italian *g* is also soft before 'i' or 'e' as in *gira*, pronounced jee-ra. *H* is never sounded; *z* is pronounced like 'ts'. The consonants *sc* before the vowels 'i' or 'e' become like the English 'sh' as in *sci*, pronounced shee; *ch* is pronouced like a 'k' as in *Chianti*, kee-an-tee; *gn* as 'ny' in English (*bagno*, pronounced ban-yo; while *gli* is pronounced like the middle of the word million (*Castiglione*, pronounced Ca-steely-oh-nay).

Vowel pronunciation is: *a* as in English father; *e* when unstressed is pronounced like 'a' in fate as in *mele*, when stressed can be the same or like the 'e' in pet (*bello*); *i* is like the i in machine; *o* like 'e', has two sounds, 'o' as in hope when unstressed (*tacchino*), and usually 'o' as in rock when stressed (*morte*); *u* is pronounced like the 'u' in June.

The accent usually (but not always!) falls on the penultimate syllable. Also note that in the big northern cities, the informal way of addressing someone as you, *tu*, is widely used; the more formal *lei* or *voi* is commonly used in provincial districts.

Language

Useful Words and Phrases

yes/no/maybe	*sì/ no/ forse*
I don't know	*Non lo so*
I don't understand (Italian)	*Non capisco (italiano)*
Does someone here speak English?	*C'è qualcuno qui che parla inglese?*
Speak slowly	*Parla lentamente*
Could you assist me?	*Potrebbe aiutarmi?*
Help!	*Aiuto!*
Please	*per favore*
Thank you (very much)	*(Molte) grazie*
You're welcome	*Prego*
It doesn't matter	*Non importa*
All right	*Va bene*
Excuse me	*Mi scusi*
Be careful!	*Attenzione!*
Nothing	*Niente*
It is urgent!	*È urgente!*
How are you?	*Come sta?*
Well, and you?	*Bene, e Lei?*
What is your name?	*Come si chiama?*
Hello	*Salve* or *ciao* (both informal)
Good morning	*Buongiorno* (formal hello)
Good afternoon, evening	*Buonasera* (also formal hello)
Good night	*Buona notte*
Goodbye	*ArrivederLa*(formal), *arrivederci, ciao* (informal)
What do you call this in Italian?	*Come si chiama questo in italiano?*
What?	*Che?*
Who?	*Chi?*
Where?	*Dove?*
When?	*Quando?*
Why?	*Perché?*
How?	*Come?*
How much?	*Quanto?*
I am lost	*Mi sono smarrito*
I am hungry	*Ho fame*
I am thirsty	*Ho sete*
I am sorry	*Mi dispiace*
I am tired	*Sono stanco*
I am sleepy	*Ho sonno*
I am ill	*Mi sento male*
Leave me alone	*Lasciami in pace*
good	*buono/ bravo*
bad	*male/ cattivo*
slow	*lento*

fast	*rapido*
big	*grande*
small	*piccolo*
hot	*caldo*
cold	*freddo*
up	*su*
down	*giù*
here	*qui*
there	*lì*

Shopping, Service, Sightseeing

I would like...	*Vorrei...*
Where is/are...	*Dov'è/ Dove sono...*
How much is it?	*Quanto viene questo?/ Quant'è/ Quanto costa questo?*
open	*aperto*
closed	*chiuso*
cheap/expensive	*a buon prezzo/ caro*
bank	*banca*
beach	*spiaggia*
bed	*letto*
church	*chiesa*
entrance	*entrata*
exit	*uscita*
hospital	*ospedale*
money	*soldi*
museum	*museo*
newspaper (foreign)	*giornale (straniero)*
pharmacy	*farmacia*
police station	*commissariato*
policeman	*poliziotto*
post office	*ufficio postale*
sea	*mare*
shop	*negozio*
room	*camera*
telephone	*telefono*
tobacco shop	*tabaccaio*
WC	*toilette/ bagno*
men	*Signori/ Uomini*
women	*Signore/ Donne*

Time

What time is it?	*Che ore sono?*
month	*mese*
week	*settimana*
day	*giorno*

morning	*mattina*
afternoon	*pomeriggio*
evening	*sera*
today	*oggi*
yesterday	*ieri*
tomorrow	*domani*
soon	*fra poco*
later	*dopo/ più tardi*
It is too early	*È troppo presto*
It is too late	*È troppo tardi*

Days

Monday	*lunedì*
Tuesday	*martedì*
Wednesday	*mercoledì*
Thursday	*giovedì*
Friday	*venerdì*
Saturday	*sabato*
Sunday	*domenica*

Numbers

one	*uno/ una*
two	*due*
three	*tre*
four	*quattro*
five	*cinque*
six	*sei*
seven	*sette*
eight	*otto*
nine	*nove*
ten	*dieci*
eleven	*undici*
twelve	*dodici*
thirteen	*tredici*
fourteen	*quattordici*
fifteen	*quindici*
sixteen	*sedici*
seventeen	*diciassette*
eighteen	*diciotto*
nineteen	*diciannove*
twenty	*venti*
twenty-one	*ventuno*
twenty-two	*ventidue*
thirty	*trenta*
thirty-one	*trentuno*
forty	*quaranta*

fifty	cinquanta
sixty	sessanta
seventy	settanta
eighty	ottanta
ninety	novanta
hundred	cento
one hundred and one	cento uno
two hundred	duecento
one thousand	mille
two thousand	duemila
million	milione
a thousand million	miliardo

Transport

airport	aeroporto
bus stop	fermata
bus/coach	autobus/pullman
railway station	stazione ferroviaria
train	treno
platform	binario
port	porto
port station	stazione marittima
ship	nave
automobile	macchina
taxi	tassì
ticket	biglietto
customs	dogana
seat (reserved)	posto (prenotato)

Travel Directions

I want to go to...	Desidero andare a...
How can I get to...?	Come posso andare a...?
Do you stop at...?	Ferma a...?
Where is...?	Dov'è...?
How far is it to...?	Quanto siamo lontani da...?
What is the name of this station?	Come si chiama questa stazione?
When does the next ... leave?	Quando parte il prossimo...?
From where does it leave?	Da dove parte?
How long does the trip take...?	Quanto tempo dura il viaggio?
How much is the fare?	Quant'è il biglietto?
Have a good trip	Buon viaggio!
near	vicino
far	lontano
left	sinistra
right	destra
straight ahead	sempre diritto

forward	*avanti*
backwards	*indietro*
north	*nord*
south	*sud*
east	*est/ oriente*
west	*ovest/ occidente*
round the corner	*dietro l' angolo*
crossroads	*bivio*
street/road	*strada*
square	*piazza*

Driving

car hire	*noleggio macchina*
motorbike/scooter	*motocicletta/ Vespa*
bicycle	*bicicletta*
petrol/diesel	*benzina/ gasolio*
garage	*garage*
This doesn't work	*Questo non funziona*
mechanic	*meccanico*
map/town plan	*carta/ pianta*
Where is the road to...?	*Dov' è la strada per...?*
breakdown	*guasto or panne*
driving licence	*patente di guida*
driver	*guidatore*
speed	*velocità*
danger	*pericolo*
parking	*parcheggio*
no parking	*sosta vietata*
narrow	*stretto*
bridge	*ponte*
toll	*pedaggio*
slow down	*rallentare*

Useful Hotel Vocabulary

I'd like a double room please	*Vorrei una camera doppia, per favore*
I'd like a single room please	*Vorrei una camera singola, per favore*
with bath, without bath	*con bagno, senza bagno*
for two nights	*per due notti*
We are leaving tomorrow morning	*Partiamo domani mattina*
Is there a room with a balcony?	*C' è una camera con balcone?*
There isn't (aren't) any hot water, soap, light, toilet paper, towels, blankets, pillows, coathangers	*Manca/Mancano acqua calda, sapone, luce, carta igienica, asciugamani, coperte, cuscini, grucce*
May I pay by credit card?	*Posso pagare con carta di credito?*
May I see another room please?	*Per favore potrei vedere un' altra camera?*

Yes, that's fine, thank you
Is breakfast included?
How do I get to the town centre?

Sì, va bene, grazie
E' compresa la prima colazione?
Come posso raggiungere il centro città?

Italian Menu Vocabulary

Antipasti

These before-meal treats can include almost anything; among the most common are:

Antipasto misto	mixed antipasto
Bruschetta	garlic toast (sometimes with tomatoes)
Carciofi (sott' olio)	artichokes (in oil)
Crostini	liver pâté on toast
Frutti di mare	seafood
Funghi (trifolati)	mushrooms (with anchovies, garlic, and lemon)
Gamberi ai fagioli	prawns (shrimps) with white beans
Mozzarella (in carrozza)	cow or buffalo cheese (fried with bread in batter)
Olive	olives
Prosciutto (con melone)	raw ham (with melon)
Salami	cured pork
Salsicce	sausages

Minestre (Soups) and Pasta

These dishes are the principal typical first courses (*primi*) served throughout Italy.

Agnolotti	ravioli with meat
Cacciucco	spiced fish soup
Cannelloni	meat and cheese rolled in pasta tubes
Cappelletti	small ravioli, often in broth
Crespelle	crêpes
Fettuccine	long strips of pasta
Frittata	omelette
Gnocchi	potato dumplings
Lasagne	sheets of pasta baked with meat and cheese sauce
Minestra di verdura	thick vegetable soup
Minestrone	soup with meat, vegetables, and pasta
Orecchiette	ear-shaped pasta, often served with turnip greens
Panzerotti	ravioli filled with mozzarella, anchovies, and egg
Pappardelle alla lepre	pasta with hare sauce
Pasta e fagioli	soup with beans, bacon, and tomatoes
Pastina in brodo	tiny pasta in broth

Penne all'arrabbiata	quill-shaped pasta with tomatoes and hot peppers
Polenta	cake or pudding of corn semolina
Risotto (alla Milanese)	Italian rice (with stock, saffron and wine)
Spaghetti all'Amatriciana	with spicy sauce of salt pork, tomatoes, onions, and chili pepper
Spaghetti alla Bolognese	with ground meat, ham, mushrooms,etc
Spaghetti alla carbonara	with bacon, eggs, and black pepper
Spaghetti al pomodoro	with tomato sauce
Spaghetti al sugo/ ragù	with meat sauce
Spaghetti alle vongole	with clam sauce
Stracciatella	broth with eggs and cheese
Tagliatelle	flat egg noodles
Tortellini al pomodoro/ panna/ in brodo	pasta caps filled with meat and cheese, with tomato sauce/with cream/in broth
Vermicelli	very thin spaghetti

Carne (Meat)

Abbacchio	milk-fed lamb
Agnello	lamb
Animelle	sweetbreads
Anatra	duck
Arista	pork loin
Arrosto misto	mixed roast meats
Bistecca alla fiorentina	Florentine beef steak
Bocconcini	veal mixed with ham and cheese and fried
Bollito misto	stew of boiled meats
Braciola	chop
Brasato di manzo	braised beef with vegetables
Bresaola	dried raw meat similar to ham
Capretto	kid
Capriolo	roe-buck
Carne di castrato/ suino	mutton/pork
Carpaccio	thin slices of raw beef served with a piquant sauce
Cassoeula	winter stew with pork and cabbage
Cervello (al burro nero)	brains (in black butter sauce)
Cervo	venison
Cinghiale	boar
Coniglio	rabbit
Cotoletta (alla Milanese/ alla Bolognese)	veal cutlet (fried in breadcrumbs/ with ham and cheese)
Fagiano	pheasant

Faraona (alla creta)	guinea fowl (in earthenware pot)
Fegato alla veneziana	liver (usually of veal) with filling
Lepre (in salmì)	hare (marinated in wine)
Lombo di maiale	pork loin
Lumache	snails
Maiale (al latte)	pork (cooked in milk)
Manzo	beef
Osso buco	braised veal knuckle with herbs
Pancetta	rolled pork
Pernice	partridge
Petto di pollo	boned chicken breast
(alla fiorentina/ bolognese/ sorpresa)	(fried in butter/with ham and cheese/ stuffed and deep fried)
Piccione	pigeon
Pizzaiola	beef steak with tomato and oregano sauce
Pollo	chicken
(alla cacciatora/ alla diavola/ alla Marengo)	(with tomatoes and mushrooms cooked in wine/grilled/fried with tomatoes, garlic and wine)
Polpette	meatballs
Quaglie	quails
Rane	frogs
Rognoni	kidneys
Saltimbocca cooked	veal scallop with prosciutto and sage, in wine and butter
Scaloppine	thin slices of veal sautéed in butter
Spezzatino	pieces of beef or veal, usually stewed
Spiedino	meat on a skewer or stick
Stufato	beef braised in white wine with vegetables
Tacchino	turkey
Trippa	tripe
Uccelletti	small birds on a skewer
Vitello	veal

Pesce (Fish)

Acciughe or Alici	anchovies
Anguilla	eel
Aragosta	lobster
Aringa	herring
Baccalà	dried salt cod
Bonito	small tuna
Branzino	sea bass
Calamari	squid

Cappe sante	scallops
Cefalo	grey mullet
Coda di rospo	angler fish
Cozze	mussels
Datteri di mare	razor (or date) mussels
Dentice	dentex (perch-like fish)
Dorato	gilt head
Fritto misto	mixed fried delicacies, usually fish
Gamberetto	shrimp
Gamberi (di fiume)	prawns (crayfish)
Granchio	crab
Insalata di mare	seafood salad
Lampreda	lamprey
Merluzzo	cod
Nasello	hake
Orata	bream
Ostriche	oysters
Pesce spada	swordfish
Polipi/ polpi	octopus
Pesce azzurro	various types of small fish
Pesce di San Pietro	John Dory
Rombo	turbot
Sarde	sardines
Seppie	cuttlefish
Sgombro	mackerel
Sogliola	sole
Squadro	monkfish
Stoccafisso	wind-dried cod
Tonno	tuna
Triglia	red mullet (rouget)
Trota	trout
Trota salmonata	salmon trout
Vongole	small clams
Zuppa di pesce	mixed fish in sauce or stew

Contorni (Side Dishes, Vegetables)

Asparagi (alla fiorentina)	asparagus (with fried eggs)
Broccoli (calabrese, romana)	broccoli (green, spiral)
Carciofi (alla giudia)	artichokes (deep fried)
Cardi	cardoons, thistles
Carote	carrots
Cavolfiore	cauliflower
Cavolo	cabbage
Ceci	chickpeas
Cetriolo	cucumber

Cipolla	onion
Fagioli	white beans
Fagiolini	French (green) beans
Fave	broad beans
Finocchio	fennel
Funghi (*porcini*)	mushrooms (boletus)
Insalata (*mista, verde*)	salad (mixed, green)
Lattuga	lettuce
Lenticchie	lentils
Melanzane (*al forno*)	aubergine/eggplant (filled and baked)
Patate (*fritte*)	potatoes (fried)
Peperoni	sweet peppers
Peperonata	stewed peppers, onions, etc. similar to ratatouille
Piselli (*al prosciutto*)	peas (with ham)
Pomodoro (*i*)	tomato(es)
Porri	leeks
Radicchio	red chicory
Radice	radish
Rapa	turnip
Sedano	celery
Spinaci	spinach
Verdure	greens
Zucca	pumpkin
Zucchini	courgettes

Formaggio (Cheese)

Bel Paese	a soft white cow's cheese
Cacio/ Caciocavallo	pale yellow, often sharp cheese
Fontina	rich cow's milk cheese
Groviera	mild cheese (gruyère)
Gorgonzola	soft blue cheese
Parmigiano	Parmesan cheese
Pecorino	sharp sheep's cheese
Provolone	sharp, tangy cheese; *dolce* is less strong
Stracchino	soft white cheese

Frutta (Fruit, Nuts)

Albicocche	apricots
Ananas	pineapple
Arance	oranges
Banane	bananas
Cachi	persimmon
Ciliege	cherries
Cocomero	watermelon

Composta di frutta	stewed fruit
Datteri	dates
Fichi	figs
Fragole (*con panna*)	strawberries (with cream)
Frutta di stagione	fruit in season
Lamponi	raspberries
Macedonia di frutta	fruit salad
Mandarino	tangerine
Mandorle	almonds
Melagrana	pomegranate
Mele	apples
Melone	melon
Mirtilli	bilberries
More	blackberries
Nespola	medlar fruit
Nocciole	hazelnuts
Noci	walnuts
Pera	pear
Pesca	peach
Pesca noce	nectarine
Pinoli	pine nuts
Pompelmo	grapefruit
Prugna/ susina	prune/plum
Uva	grapes

Dolci (Desserts)

Amaretti	macaroons
Cannoli	crisp pastry tubes filled with ricotta, cream, chocolate or fruit
Coppa gelato	assorted ice cream
Crema caramella	caramel-topped custard
Crostata	fruit flan
Gelato (*produzione propria*)	ice-cream (homemade)
Granita	flavoured ice, usually lemon or coffee
Monte Bianco	chestnut pudding with whipped cream
Panettone	sponge cake with candied fruit and raisins
Panforte	dense cake of chocolate, almonds, and preserved fruit
Saint Honoré	meringue cake
Semifreddo	refrigerated cake
Sorbetto	sorbet/sherbet
Spumone	a soft ice cream
Tiramisù	layers of sponge fingers and Mascarpone, coffee and chocolate
Torrone	nougat

Torta	cake, tart
Torta millefoglie	layered pastry with custard cream
Zabaglione	whipped eggs and Marsala wine, served hot
Zuppa inglese	trifle

Bevande (Beverages)

Acqua minerale con/ senza gas	mineral water with/without fizz
Aranciata	orange soda
Birra (alla spina)	beer (draught)
Caffè (freddo)	coffee (iced)
Cioccolata (con panna)	chocolate (with cream)
Gassosa	lemon-flavoured soda
Latte	milk
Limonata	lemon soda
Succo di frutta	fruit juice
Tè	tea
Vino (rosso, bianco, rosato)	wine (red, white, rosé)

Cooking Terms, Miscellaneous

Aceto (balsamico)	vinegar (balsamic)
Affumicato	smoked
Aglio	garlic
Alla brace	on embers
Bicchiere	glass
Burro	butter
Cacciagione	game
Conto	bill
Costoletta/ Cotoletta	chop
Coltello	knife
Cucchiaio	spoon
Filetto	fillet
Forchetta	fork
Forno	oven
Fritto	fried
Ghiaccio	ice
Griglia	grill
In bianco	without tomato
Limone	lemon
Magro	lean meat/or pasta without meat
Marmellata	jam
Menta	mint
Miele	honey
Mostarda	candied mustard sauce, eaten with boiled meats

Olio	oil
Pane (*tostato*)	bread (toasted)
Panini	sandwiches
Panna	cream
Pepe	pepper
Peperoncini	hot chili peppers
Piatto	plate
Prezzemolo	parsley
Ripieno	stuffed
Rosmarino	rosemary
Sale	salt
Salmi	wine marinade
Salsa	sauce
Salvia	sage
Senape	mustard
Tartufi	truffles
Tazza	cup
Tavola	table
Tovagliolo	napkin
Tramezzini	finger sandwiches
Umido	cooked in sauce
Uovo	egg
Zucchero	sugar

Carmichael, Montgomery, *In Tuscany* (Burns & Oates, 1910).

Goethe, J.W., *Italian Journey* (Penguin Classics, 1982). An excellent example of a genius turned to mush by Italy; good insights, but big, big mistakes.

Hutton, Edward, *Florence, Assisi* and *Umbria Revisited*, in *Unknown Tuscany*, and *Siena and Southern Tuscany* (Hollis & Carter). Modern travel classics.

McCarthy, Mary, *The Stones of Florence* and *Venice Observed* (Penguin, 1986). Brilliant evocation of Italy's two great art cities, with an understanding that makes many other works on the subject seem sluggish and pedantic; don't visit Florence without it.

Morton, H.V., *A Traveller in Italy* (Methuen & Co., 1964). Among the most readable and delightful accounts of Italy in print. Morton is a sincere scholar and a true gentleman.

Raison, Laura (ed), *Tuscany: An Anthology* (Cadogan, 1983). An excellent selection of the best by Tuscans and Tuscany-watchers.

Spender, Matthew, *Within Tuscany* (Viking, 1992). Poet Stephen Spender's son, on everything from porcupines to Pontormo's bowel moverments.

Williams, Egerton R., *Hill Towns of Italy* (Smith, Elder, 1904). An Englishman goes exploring in Tuscany and Umbria.

Art and Literature

Boccaccio, Giovanni, *The Decameron* (Penguin, 1972). The ever-young classic by one of the fathers of Italian literature. Its irreverent worldliness still provides a salutary antidote to whatever dubious ideas persist in your mental baggage.

Burckhardt, Jacob, *The Civilization of the Renaissance in Italy* (Harper & Row, 1975). The classic on the subject (first published in 1860), the mark against which scholars still level their poison pens of revisionism.

Castiglione, Baldassare, *The Courtier* (Penguin)

Cellini, B., *Autobiography of Benvenuto Cellini* (Penguin, trans. by George Bull). Fun reading about the vicious competition of the Florentine art world by a swashbuckling braggart and world-class liar.

Clark, Kenneth, *Leonardo da Vinci* (Penguin).

Dante, Alighieri, *The Divine Comedy* (plenty of good translations). Few poems have ever had such a mythical significance for a nation. Anyone serious about understanding Tuscany or Italy and their world view will need more than a passing acquaintance with Dante.

Further Reading

Gardner, Edmund G., *The Story of Florence, The Story of Siena;* also Gordon, Lina Duff, *The Story of Assisi* and *The Story of Perugia* and Ross, Janet, *The Story of Pisa* (J.M. Dent, 1900s). All part of the excellent and highly readable Medieval Towns series.

Ghibert/Linscott, *Complete Poems and Selected Letters of Michelangelo* (Princeton Press, 1984).

Hale, J.R., editor, *A Concise Encyclopaedia of the Italian Renaissance* (Thames and Hudson, 1981). An excellent reference guide, with many concise, well-written essays. Also *Florence and the Medici: The Pattern of Control* (1977) which describes just how the Medici did it.

Hibbert, Christopher, *Rise and Fall of the House of Medici* (Penguin, 1965). One of the classics—compulsive reading.

Hook, Judith, *Siena* (Hamish Hamilton, 1979). A little weak on art, but good on everything else.

Leonardo da Vinci, *Notebooks* (Oxford, 1983).

Levey, Michael, *Early Renaissance* (1967) and *High Renaissance* (both Penguin). Old-fashioned accounts of the period, with a breathless reverence for the 1500s—but still full of intriguing interpretations.

Masson, Georgina, *Frederick II of Hohenstaufen* (London, 1957).

Murray, Linda, *The High Renaissance* and *The Late Renaissance and Mannerism* (Thames and Hudson, 1977). Excellent introduction to the period; also Peter and Linda Murray, *The Art of the Renaissance* (1963).

Origo, Iris, *The Merchant of Prato* (Penguin, 1963). Everyday life in 14th-century Tuscany with the father of modern accounting, Francesco di Marco Datini. Also *Images and Shadows; War in the Val d'Orcia*, about a Tuscan childhood and life during the war.

Petrarch, Francesco, *Canzionere and Other Works* (Oxford, 1985). The most famous poems by the 'First Modern Man'.

Procacci, Giuliano, *History of the Italian People* (Penguin, 1973). An in-depth view from the year 1000 to the present—also an introduction to the wit and subtlety of the best Italian scholarship.

Richards, Charles, *The New Italians* (Penguin, 1995). An observant and amusing study of life in Italy during and since the political upheaval and the financial scandels in the early 1990s.

Symonds, John Addington, *A Short History of the Renaissance in Italy* (Smith, Elder, 1893). A condensed version of the authority of a hundred years ago, but still fascinating today.

Vasari, Giorgio, *Lives of the Artists* (Penguin, 1985). Readable, anecdotal accounts of the Renaissance greats by the father of modern art history.

Index

walking 35
Wars of Italy 47
weights and measures 33
wines:
  itinerary of 15–16
  Tuscany 22–3, 192–4, 304, 360, 378, 379, 382, 385

women 42
words and phrases 430–42
World War II 92, 121, 289, 298
youth hostels 38–9

Zenobius, St 103
Zumbo, Gaetano:
  Florence 163